by Max Lerner

AMERICA AS A CIVILIZATION

ACTIONS AND PASSIONS

PUBLIC JOURNAL

THE MIND AND FAITH OF JUSTICE HOLMES

IDEAS FOR THE ICE AGE

IDEAS ARE WEAPONS

IT IS LATER THAN YOU THINK

PHILIPPE HALSMAN

ABOUT THE AUTHOR

MAX LERNER, author, teacher and columnist, received his B.A. at Yale in 1923 and his Ph.D. at the Robert Brookings Graduate School of Economics and Government in 1927. He has taught at Sarah Lawrence College, Harvard University and Williams College. At present he is Professor of American Civilization at Brandeis University and a daily columnist for the New York *Post*. He is married to Edna Albers Lerner, a clinical psychologist, and is the father of six children.

His previous books include *It Is Later Than You Think* (1938; revised edition 1943), *Ideas Are Weapons* (1939), *Ideas for the Ice Age* (1941), *The Mind and Faith of Justice Holmes* (1943), *Public Journal* (1945), *Actions and Passions* (1949), and *America As a Civilization* (1957). He has published editions of Machiavelli's *The Prince* and the *Discourses,* Adam Smith's *The Wealth of Nations, The Portable Veblen,* Aristotle's *Politics* and Jack London's *Iron Heel.*

Mr. Lerner is currently at work on a book of American education—*Toward a Democratic Elite.* He is spending the academic year of 1959-1960 in India as a Professor of American Studies in the Graduate School of International Studies at the University of Delhi, under a Ford Foundation grant.

MAX LERNER

The
Unfinished
Country

A BOOK OF AMERICAN SYMBOLS

Simon and Schuster

NEW YORK · 1959

FOR MY SISTERS

Ida Borish

AND

Sylvia Williams

*who came with me as children
to the unfinished country*

CONTENTS

The
Unfinished
Country

FOREWORD

The View
From a Column

◢

1

THIS BOOK *was written over the span of a decade, day after day as the deadlines threatened. I have read all the articles—almost two thousand of them—that I wrote for the New York* Post *between 1949 and 1959 (on the page opposite the editorial page, left-hand column) in an effort to pick a few hundred that might be salvaged against the Flood to come. The results, woven together in new patterns, are between these covers.*

Ten years are a good chunk of a man's life—ten years of the A-bomb era, the H-bomb era, the Kinsey era, the McCarthy era, the era of the Hiss and Remington and Lattimore trials, the Truman years, the Eisenhower years, the Acheson and Dulles years, the Stalin and Khrushchev years, the suburban era, the era of automation and mass leisure, the Beat Generation era, the Age of Missiles, the Age of Monroe and Ekberg, the time of troubles, the time of Djilas and Pasternak, the time of revision of Marx and Freud and progressive education, the time of the quiz shows and the spectaculars and the hidden persuaders, the time of Call Me Madam *and* My Fair Lady. *So rich, crowded and absurd were these ten years, as I parade them again here, that one wonders how any of us survived them.*

Not by ignoring them. The newspaperman builds an insulated wall of cynicism around his work, pretending usually that it is routine stuff, that it is written in water, and that he can't remember any of it ten minutes after he has filed it, so what the hell? I can't strike the cynical pose. Every piece in this book has been ripped out of its context shrieking, like one of those fabled mandrake roots. Each of them carries for me memories of the whole matrix of event and thought that originally encased it, writing as I did under the white heat of some event or account which had stirred me. The words seem a bit cold now, but I have only to reconstruct the original setting and mood to recapture the hot, stinging moment of urgency—else why, out of the abundance of themes that offered themselves, would I have chosen that particular one to write on?

These are, then, to steal a phrase from Justice Holmes, "little fragments of my fleece." I use "fleece" deliberately because the way of a columnist is personal, and he needs hide as well as nerve. Or, to change the figure, perhaps all he needs is a capacity for self-exposure. A late American novelist, husband at one point of a distinguished and opinionated woman columnist, used to tell his friends that he was a modern St. Simeon Stylites, martyred on a column. There was a period in the history of Christianity when, if a man had no marked gifts of intellect or character, the way to attract attention was to climb to the top of a column and sit there until a cluster of the faithful gathered to treat him as an oracle, if not always as a saint. We manage things somewhat differently with our columnists, but the basic principle remains. It may thus be of interest for one who has held that perilous and exposed position, four times weekly for some fifteen years, to reflect a bit on what the view is like from a column.

2

It always seems an act of arrogance to place within the covers of a book a number of pieces originally written for a daily paper. I can only say, about those that are collected here, that I had pleasure in writing them and think they may still have some retentive hold on life. The test I used in the first place, in picking subjects to write on, was whether they interested me, from which I concluded that they might interest others. The act of arrogance is not so much in collecting them as in the original act of writing them—in the vocation of a columnist, which assumes that one's views on a random assortment of subjects deserve to be read by other and often better men. Once you get over that original hurdle of immodesty and become a columnist, nothing will save you and nothing else matters much.

In American journalism there are exclusively political commentators and general ones. I fall in the latter category. The political writers give us a running commentary on the meaning of what is happening in Moscow, Peiping, London, Paris, Bonn, Cairo, New Delhi and Washington. I have written my share on these themes too, but I do not limit myself to them.

They represent one phase of the total human comedy or human tragedy—important but only one. As a columnist I find other phases equally worth writing about: my joys and troubles, my itch to roam, my views on a novel or a play, my children or grandchildren or dog, a murder or a trial or a Supreme Court decision, my responses to a number of currents in the realm of culture and conduct, manners and morals. This means I am as likely to write about the death of a movie producer or the life and loves of a TV star as about the UN debates, about the arrest of a prostitute as about the visit of a head of state, and that I take apart teen-age behavior or motivational research or a Kinsey Report as readily as the antics of a delinquent Senator. To be a general columnist is to exclude nothing human from one's perspective, and to treat the personal seriously and the serious personally.

In season and out a general columnist is fair game on two counts. Since he exposes his prejudices and frailties constantly, he invites their further exposure by others; and since he makes a show of being omniscient, he invites the reactions which will disprove his competence in any area and prove his fallibility in all. One of the most cherished natural rights of Americans is the constitutional right to make a target out of a columnist. There is a quite understandable rage at yesterday's expert on adolescent psychology who has become today's expert on corporate management and will be tomorrow's expert on Israeli politics or the history of the Papacy. What makes it worse is that some of your critics may themselves have spent an arduous lifetime in one of these fields, and resent the way you invade it for a fleeting moment, sucking the honey from the flowers they have cultivated.

While I respect the sources of this feeling, I cannot go along with it. A general columnist, by his nature, must roam widely and set down his assertions, not just his doubts and torments. Remember that he is not sitting in judgment as an expert who has mastered what there is to know on the subject. He is only a traveler who has made unsuspected discoveries for himself in the realms of gold, and he wants to share them. I have never asked clemency for any errors into which I may have blundered, since those are the risks of the craft. As a student, I take the trouble to be informed on what I write. But equally I ask the reader to remember that these little essays represent not just chores to be done on a daily job, but adventures in commitment. Each time I start exploring a new subject, I plunge into it joyously, for days or weeks, until my family and friends beg for quarter because I talk of nothing else. Yet all the time I remain quite literally an amateur— one who practices some skill for the love of it, and not as a profession. Out of these goings and comings, these perchings and flights, one hopes to master truly only one art—that of the general proposition. In an era of the specialist, I make an appeal for the vocation of the generalist.

3

If the generalist also finds his métier (at least in part) as a journalist, it is not wholly an accident. The academic environment in America today is, except in rare instances, not one to encourage anything but the specialist. In the academic market place the man who has shown interest in a variety of fields is often dismissed as a dilettante. If a phantom could write a Ph.D. thesis on a narrow enough topic, and have it reviewed without too much rancor by the three other men who had previously hollowed their little dugouts and built their little lean-tos in the same corner of the same barren field, then he would pass muster as a scholar and reign over his petty kingdom of a university department.

Unfortunately life itself is not divided into these specialized patches, but comes to us whole and asks to be grasped whole. The need of our time is for the man of letters, much as we find him in eighteenth-century England and France, who roamed widely in every field but brought to each the touch of the amateur and the humanist. It is only the "research-minded" professors who assign journalism to a limbo somewhere between the hell of "popular culture" and the heaven of "high culture." The Continentals don't do it, and the English journals make use of some of the best minds of the universities. That may explain the rather unusual list of journalists in the European tradition: Defoe, Swift, Johnson, Voltaire, Diderot, Marx, Engels, Dostoevski, Sorel, Peguy, Alain, Bagehot, Shaw, Wells, Bertrand Russell, Keynes, Croce, Salvemini, Borgese, Sartre, Camus, Orwell. It is a list hard for Americans to match, although there is an honorable tradition of American writers and thinkers who have held the craft of journalism to be a not ignoble one.

It has its perils too, if what you care about is the creation of permanence amidst change. Not only were events shifting as I wrote, and with them the perspectives on the events: there was also the fact that I have never pretended to be simply a reporter, *a neutral transmission belt for events. As I look back at these pieces they combined three roles I have played in writing them: that of* social historian, *trying to set down what was happening, making wholes out of episodic events within a frame, often with a sense of wonder at their strangeness; that of* social theorist, *trying to construct meanings for the event that went beyond time and place, era and culture, pushing my thought and judgment as far as they would go, while using language concrete enough for the daily reader; and that of the* man of letters, *approaching every theme from the peculiar angle of vision of a writer who gets drunk with words and lives by their "strange necessity."*

I don't mean that I combined these roles well or successfully, but only that my whole past training—literary, academic, journalistic—compelled me to try to combine them. But in all three roles I always had to reckon with my very human impulses and biases. I have been a man of my time, responding to its felt needs, mirroring its hopes and fears, caught in its intellectual battles, breaking lances again and again in its political struggles. I have tried to stay clear of strategic thinking, as I have also tried to avoid wishful thinking, which means that I have tried hard never consciously to allow my embattled fervor or my dream world to distort my thinking. But while I have sought to think cleanly, I cannot answer for whatever tricks my unconscious

*may have played with these words, as it does with the words that every
writer sets down with what integrity he can muster.*

4

*Like every columnist, I am constantly the target of questions about
my habits of work and the conditions under which I write.*

*"How do you think up a new subject every day?" Alas, madam, you
put the question topsy-turvy. The hard thing is not to think up a topic,
but to pick one out of the many that thrust themselves at you each
day, out of the reading of the wire copy and the papers, out of books,
travel, dreams, out of conversation and the ordinary contacts of an
ordinary day. I keep a notebook and a file into which I jot down ideas
for columns as they occur to me. Before I write I look through the
papers, and often some headline event will converge with one of these
ideas. Most often I have to choose between a half dozen or dozen that
have some possibilities. Sometimes I try them out by trying to outline
several, and I choose the one that seems to go the least lamely.*

"How far ahead do you write?" Alas, again, only a few hours.

*"How long do they take?" Anywhere from an hour and a half to a
week and a half, depending on whether I have to do much reading or
can write out of past preparation.*

*"Where do you write them?" Anywhere—at home if I am there, in
Boston when I am teaching at Brandeis University, in a score of foreign
countries, on planes and trains, at terminals, in hotel rooms, or sitting
out on the lawn if I am writing in the summer, at our house at North
Sea, Long Island, or on the beach while the children are swimming. I am
not one of your conditioned writers who can work only under some
routine. I usually write late at night, between midnight and 3 A.M., but
I snatch the time whenever it offers, and I work best under the pressure of a deadline.*

*"Of course, there are some things they won't let you write." I pre-
sume the "they," madam, refers to the publisher and the editor of my
paper. And my answer is: No, there are no restrictions placed on me
except space (a column is about nine hundred words) and time (getting
it in not too long after the deadline). The only changes ever made in
my column are those made necessary by the rules of punctuation, spell-*

ing, grammar and syntax, on which I am notoriously lax. Obviously, if I were to develop delusions, as Nietzsche did, and identify myself with Napoleon or Hitler, with the Sun-God, the anti-Christ, the Dalai Lama or the Grand Mufti of Jerusalem, I might find my audience slipping and my publisher and editor loath to humor my dreams. Thus far I have never tested it, since I am quite content with the complete freedom they give me within the bounds of sanity.

One further word on this subject. I doubt whether I would have had the freedom, in many papers, to discuss Eisenhower and Dulles, advertising, psychoanalysts, the FBI, corporate power, movie censorship, birth control, abortion, sexual offenders, sexual behavior in both its normal and deviant aspects, civil liberties and civil rights, in the way I have done over the past decade in the Post. *The worst disease of our press is the flabby tissue that has grown around the fear of the prickly and the controversial. I can say about the* Post *that, far more than any newspaper today, it has defied the taboos of the time. I am happy to have had a chance to help in that process of taboo smashing.*

5

One other question sometimes gets asked: "Don't you have to simplify too much, in order to write for a mass audience?" Well, I can (if I try) write as obscurely as almost any of my academic fellows, when they seek to impress each other and themselves. But I prefer communicating. I have done my share of writing for the journals of law, economics, political theory, education. I even wrote a thousand-page book, with a fifty-page bibliography. The columns here gathered were written over roughly the same decade in which I was writing my America as a Civilization. *The style of that book and this one are different, because their mood and purpose were different. I wrote more militantly in my columns, because I was fighting some day-to-day battles, with immediate targets. I wrote more concretely, too, because in journalism you start from a concrete event or person, and you pick the symbols you want, like hooks on which to hang the garments of your thought. The task is to see the subject in all its complexity, but to think it through in human, symbolic and dramatic terms until it is sharpened ("simplified") to a cutting edge.*

The relation of columnist to reader is an intensely close and personal one. "You come between my wife and me," a husband has sometimes said. "We read you often in bed at night, and we argue about what you write." I like being read that way. Sometimes a column is read and discussed by a whole group of friends. Over the years my mail has been heavy, with generous letters, indignant letters, eccentric letters, argumentative letters, philosophical letters, and letters giving the reader's experience with life and love and asking for advice. The columnist is seen as companion, commentator, guide, friend, even psychiatrist. He gets often a not quite comprehensible, but always welcome, amount of devotion. His readers use him partly to articulate what they have themselves been thinking, partly as an opinion litmus test: by matching their judgments with his, setting them side by side, they have a way of confirming their own trend of thinking—or condemning his. Some are confident they could do much better, and doubtless they are right.

If I have enjoyed these amenities of writing a column, I should add that there are dangers as well. It is like groping around in a bramble bush: you stick your hand in and your fingers bleed. The perils are many and great: of the distorted, the sentimental, the portentous, the trivial, of the pathetic fallacy, of dogma and vested ideas, of the partisan and the cocksure and the hysterical, of false idolization, circular reasoning, question begging, word thrashing, of thickness of skull and hardness of heart, and of sheer ignorance of what has been thought and written on your theme.

To say I have not fallen into at least some of these would be arrogant. I can only say that I have tried to be aware of them—aware that the tree of life and thought is surrounded by brambles. To risk dangers, even with casualties, is a venal sin. To shut your eyes to the dangers is the mortal one.

A crucial quality of the columnist must be awareness. Like the novelist and the philosopher, he must lay himself open to experience, from every direction and on every dimension. Nothing can replace this awareness. It is the admission price you must pay in order to get your raw material. It is the net you fling wide to see what it will snare. But what you do with whatever you thus snare is another matter. Always you must subject it to tough and critical reasoning, unfooled even by your own private illusions. There is thus a double process of exposure: of yourself to experience, and of the event to your reasoning. In this

*double process you get a chance at once for sensibility and for tough-
mindedness.*

*It will be apparent, from reading this book, that a disproportionate
number of the columns have been chosen from the "timeless" think-
pieces (books, crimes, psychiatry, love, children, plays) and personal
pieces. The reason is clear enough. In many instances a column or
some current and urgent event has lost its original impact. It may at
the time have made sense, but it may be beyond reprinting simply because later events have taken the edge off its sharpness and transformed
its context. In a sense, even when history proves a commentator to
have been right in his judgment, he is buried in the ruins he has himself
made; the confirmation of his judgment makes it sound stale and trivial
to a reader five or ten years later. Every event is a phoenix which gets
burned so that a new one may arise from the ashes.*

*In a number of instances I have managed to save the topical col-
umns, running them together in a sequence, stripping them of some of
the more ephemeral topical allusions. Often I have changed the original
titles of the columns, on the theory that a change of title does not mean
a change of substance; and in some cases I have stretched the title of
one article to cover the whole sequence of related ones. Let me say,
however, that I have not made any excisions in order to appear after the
fact a wiser man than I was in the heat of actual battle. I have tried not
to cheat the reader by omitting my blind spots, just as I have tried not
to bore him by putting in everything. I have stripped a number of
columns of everything except the skeletal idea line, telescoping a half-
dozen pieces sometimes into a longish single one.*

*To ask an author to pick some of his writings and let the rest die
in their yellowed, musty files is like asking a mother to choose which
of her brood of children she will put into a crowded lifeboat when there
is room only for a few. Like the parent, the author feels that he is committing infanticide. Many readers are bound to feel I have not been
astringent enough, that this book need not have grown to its present size.
I can only plead that my two earlier books of collected columns—*Public
Journal *(1945) and* Actions and Passions *(1949)—were slim volumes
because they were picked from only a few years of column writing, but
this one covers a decade. To keep it even within this compass I have
had to make the book primarily one about America and leave out all
but a few of my travel pieces. I console myself with the reflection that*

this has improved rather than harmed the book, by giving it greater unity.

6

This is, in a sense, a book of American symbols. Every commentator on American life is by necessity a cryptographer of the national character and the human spirit. He writes in a kind of cipher. The names in the news—Eisenhower, Stevenson, Oppenheimer, Teller, Charles Wilson, Walter Reuther, Mike Todd, Ezio Pinza, Arthur Godfrey, Whittaker Chambers, Alger Hiss, Khrushchev, Nasser—are abbreviations for a whole pattern of behavior and feeling. Any "event" or "issue," any novel or play or movie, is worth commenting on only because it marks a trembling of the veil which shrouds from us the face of evil and of good, the potentials to which the plastic human material can be stretched, the curious refractions of time and eternity. "Your business as thinkers," Justice Holmes told a class of law students, "is to see the relation between your particular fact and the framework of the universe."

I think I have had my sharpest sense of failure as a columnist whenever a reader has scornfully brushed aside some piece of mine as being on an unworthy or distasteful subject. Why, I am often asked, do I write about these second-rate actresses, these headline-hunting playboys, these baggages with their dreary loves and divorces, these gutter Confidentials, *these gangster kinglets and princelings, these call girls and pimps and lushes, this sickening procession of rapes and kidnapings, of baby-sitter deaths and "model boy" sex killings? Why do I write about a prize fight or a football game that will all too soon be sunk in the obscurity of the past, or about the doings of sexual deviants whose sickness of soul were far better left undisclosed if not undisturbed?*

It is at such questions that I feel defeated, since they show that the questioner has not begun to understand what a column means to me. I have somehow failed to communicate to him my basic perception of the relation between the individual symbol and its social substance, between the scabrous event and the whole world of life's beauty and love's richness that lies slain thereby, between the culture hero and heroine and the dreams they evoke and express, between the fragment of cultural myth I am dissecting and the not impossible life of reason to which it may be a door.

Sometimes the culture heroes I write about—Lincoln, Holmes, Hughes, Darrow, Truman—are symbols of a cultural health. More often I write about the emptiness of the synthetic heroes and heroines, and the tricking of our best impulses by the deployment of the human mind for profit or power. I am unashamed to celebrate whatever in American life seems to me worth celebrating. But I am equally unashamed to explore the seemingly trivial and the morbid if they will afford me a glimpse of reality that would otherwise lie hidden from me. There was a time when psychologists scorned to deal with the abnormal and with the unconscious, because by definition the one was uncharacteristic and the other inaccessible. But who today will deny that the pattern of a culture, like the style of a personality, is best revealed at the points where it suffers a breakdown of functioning, and best explored in the realm of the unconscious? From them one may get a sudden epiphany of the certain miseries and the not impossible grandeurs of life, both for the individual and for the collectivity.

I call the book The Unfinished Country *because it is my deeply felt symbol for an America whose failures of history must be faced, despite our recoil from failure, but whose possibilities still seem to me limitless. My bitterest quarrel in all these columns is with those who seek to shrink America into the narrow compass of their own impoverished spirit, and those who seek to make rigid what should be changing and growing in the American sun.*

I hope I do not imply a turning away from the harsh facts of man's sojourn on this vast continent and this small planet. I do not believe there is a built-in principle in human society which assures the triumph of the angels of light. I see death and life as intertwined facts. I see regularities in nature and society, but the notion of some design that shapes the governance of men seems to me regretfully a subjective addition to the fact of life. I am content to view the cultural landscape of America as a man-created one, even if its physical landscape is a given. On that cultural landscape I see hard-won victories of the human spirit, to surrender which would mean to cease to be human.

I see both American culture and the human personality as largely plastic, but both of them kept within a stern frame of necessity which defines the human tragedy. I see history as the record of how man has painfully learned to live with men over the millennia, in precarious constellations we call "societies"; how he kills and hates, as well as loves and lives and gives life, how he has tasted the joys as well as the burdens of existence and work; and how through the fires of generosity and growth he has managed to survive by transcending what he has thought to be the limits of "human nature."

But the task is never done, the society is never neatly delineated, human nature is never frozen, and "the only fabulous country" of our reality and our dream remains an unfinished country. We have not come to the end of history.

There are many all over the world who hate, envy or fear America. This is not a book for them, for, while there is much in it that is acidly critical of American life goals, cultural values and leadership, the criticism comes out of identification and love, not out of alienation and hate. There are also many Americans who think they love America —think it so fiercely that they are ready to read out of the national community anyone who differs from their estimate of the N.A.M., the American Legion, the FBI, the A.D.A., the Un-American Activities Committee, the C.I.O., the U.A.W., the N.A.A.C.P., the school desegregation decision, Justice Frankfurter, Chief Justice Warren, the Smith Act, the sex act, the Kinsey Report, the Planned Parenthood Federation, Charlie Chaplin, John L. Lewis, cool jazz, Ingrid Bergman and the Reverend Martin Luther King. This book is in part aimed at them, with the adjuration that Cromwell addressed to his Parliament: "In the bowels of Christ, bethink yourselves, that ye may be wrong."

Mostly, however, it is directed toward those who feel part of America and love it, but who are not compelled to regard the object of their love as anything but fallible and mortal. My America is a society open to the pouring in of experience, so that its characteristic philosopher has been Charles Peirce, its indigenous novelists Mark Twain and Theodore Dreiser, its great historians F. J. Turner and Charles Beard, its poets Walt Whitman and Robert Frost, its legal thinkers Holmes and Brandeis, its composer Charles Ives, its physicist Willard Josiah Gibbs, its psychologist William James, its educator John Dewey, its architects Louis Sullivan and Frank Lloyd Wright, its trade-union leaders Samuel Gompers and Sidney Hillman, its political leaders Abe Lincoln and Franklin Roosevelt. Out of their experience these men have formulated plans of action and working visions, which have then been dipped back into

*the pool of experience, to be transcended by the new currents of life
and to serve as the basis for new ideas, actions and passions.*

*There are some who have felt ill at ease in such a sequence of con-
tinuous flux and have wished for a "mandate of heaven" to give sureness to the fallible judgments of the people. But it is not in the style
or genius of America to accept a mandate of heaven as a substitute for
the hard agony of collective creativeness. Always striving, always hungry, never satisfied, the American spirit jibes well with the inner meaning of a world of process and continuity. None of the issues with which
the pieces in this book deal have been or can be settled. But that is
as it should be, in an open universe of tragedy and conflict and free
choice, in an always unfinished country.*

ACKNOWLEDGMENTS

*I must acknowledge several debts. One is to the Publisher of the
New York Post, Mrs. Dorothy Schiff, and to James A. Wechsler and
Paul Sann, its Editor and Executive Editor. Another is to Roslyn
Mass and Alice Lide, who helped put the manuscript into shape, and
to my friend and former student, Martin Peretz, who helped with the
proofs. Finally I owe a debt to the readers of my columns, who have
taken part in what has often been a dialogue between us, and many of
whom sent me suggestions of the columns they wished to see reprinted.*

M. L.

PART I

Fragments of My Fleece

CONTENTS

PREFACE

FOR A TIME, *when I first began writing a column, I was wary of writing about my own life. What troubled me was not any modesty about using the first person singular, or even some overwhelming sense of privacy, but quite simply the question of whether it would interest my readers. It did, and my hesitations vanished.*

My present feeling is that what marks off the columnist from other commentators is a personal axis between him and the reader: he is interested in all phases of the lives and the minds of his readers and speaks to them in the language of their joys, sorrows and puzzlements; the reader in turn is interested in the life and the mind of the columnist and has a curiosity about him as a person, not simply as a name and a face at the head of the column.

I start this section—and the book itself—with two columns about a grief and a joy of mine, one on the death of my father, the other on the birth of my youngest son. It is hard to write publicly about private experiences that shake you deeply. The danger with many personal columns is that you skirt the surface of the emotions lightly and take the easiest course—that of setting up a self-image which is mock-humble, self-depreciatory and an amiable caricature. I have not always avoided this danger. But in the case of these two pieces, and several others on my daughters and my sons, I may have managed to break through the stereotype. These few columns, along with several on death, were the ones that drew the greatest and most moving response from my readers out of all the writing I have done.

I believe there are definite limits that must be placed around this self-revelation. I am no Rousseauist, wallowing in my own sensibilities and presenting my bared wounds for the edification of my readers. The line I should draw is the line between self-portrayal and self-exploitation. Each writer must draw it in his own way, depending on the medium in which he works. A column is different from an autobiography, and that in turn from a novel.

I shall confess also that it is easier to write of myself than of my family. When you write of yourself, you make your own choices about what to say and what to omit, and you take the consequences. When you write of others, no matter how close to you, it is impossible wholly

*to escape using them, and they have to take the consequences without
making the choices. My wife and children have developed skins tough
enough to take the exposure. As for my grandchildren, fortunately they
were too young to protest.*

*Actually it is not so easy to write of oneself as I have implied. "We
hear others with our ears, ourselves with our throats," Malraux once
said, in Man's Fate. One might adapt it and say that we see others
with our eyes open, ourselves with our eyes intently shut in order to
create a darkness in which (as in a fluoroscope room) we can see the
dim outlines of light through the body to which we are tied.*

*There remains to speak of the columns on aging and death. Their
themes are forbidding and even morbid (why are we afraid of the
morbid, when the weakening and ending of existence are facts of
existence?), but I can only say that I didn't feel lugubrious in writing
them. I think the reader will find that these pieces are assertions of life,
and that even when I put on a long face cheerfulness persists in breaking through.*

END AND BEGINNING

1. My Father Moved . . .

January 6, 1958

MY FATHER died on Saturday, as gently and peacefully as he had lived, and he was buried yesterday. At eighty-seven he had lived beyond the Biblical assignment, yet even an old man leaves a gaping hole when he breaks through the skein of life and hurtles into nobeing.

As I stood at his grave, listening to the service that has come down through the centuries, my mind wound back through the corridors of his life. He came of a line of scholars, men of the Book, simple folk who warmed themselves by the lamps of the past and gloried in the exploits and tragedies of their people.

In Russia he had studied at a Yeshiva and traveled from village to village as an itinerant scholar. But Czarist society was stifling. My father and his young wife wanted a chance to earn something, and wanted their children to breathe a freer air and become someone. At thirty-three, in 1903, he came to New York as part of the great migration of the century, and my mother followed in 1907 with her four children. He went through the familiar immigrant odyssey: He was a small peddler, worked in a garment loft, became a Hebrew teacher, turned to farming and failed at it, tried a milk delivery route, became a small grocer. Finally he went back to what he loved—his work as a Hebrew teacher, keeping at it until a few years before his death.

His was one of the millions of American stories that have woven the history of this country. Life was not easy for my father. He had disappointments, frustrations, tragedies. He was never a big success at anything, nor did he make a great noise in the world. But he loved and was loved, and he had joy in his children. Had he stayed behind in Europe he and they would long ago have been ashes at Auschwitz or ciphers in a Soviet ant society.

When I saw him toward the end of his illness, while he could still talk, he asked me to bring him his notebooks. They were a confusion of ledgers, journals, loose sheets, on which over the years he had written his reflections on a variety of themes, covering his life within and the world outside, dealing with the early prophets and the later-day secular figures, with Hitler and Stalin and Nasser, Roosevelt and Truman, Weizmann and Ben-Gurion.

I am, alas, an ignorant man. With all my years of schooling I am unable to read the languages in which my father wrote, as my sons are already able to read mine. I shall save the bundle of pages on which he spent the burden of his hours, driven as he was by a strange necessity to find a garment for what he felt and dreamt. Someday I may repair my ignorance and discover what thoughts they were that coursed through the mind of this patient, reflective man.

His killer—the killer of so many—was cancer. Mercifully, once it struck it did its work fast. In his remaining few days he was unconscious.

I think I was the last person whom he saw and recognized. When he whispered my name, I felt a stab at the fitness of it. Surely it is a good thing for a father, in his final moments of consciousness, to know that his son is near him. The father-son relation is the basic link of continuity in life, carrying the male principle and the tradition of responsibility from one generation to the next. The need for a father is as crucial as the need for a son, and the search of each for the other—through all the days of one's life—exempts no one. Happy the man who finds both.

My father was a gentle and permissive man. When I think of him I think of the great lines of the E. E. Cummings poem:

> *My father moved through dooms of love*
> *Through sames of am through haves of give,*
> *Singing each morning out of each night*
> *My father moved through depths of height . . .*
> *Because my father lived his soul*
> *Love is the whole and more than all.*

Death seems all the more pitiless when it comes to these gentle people. When I last saw my father, just before he died, he seemed so shrunken and wasted that I fear I broke down shamelessly and wept. It was for more than my father that I wept. It was for death which shows up the final helplessness of life, and for the crazy tragic absurdity of the whole human condition.

And then, along with the other mourners, I heard and spoke the thunderous syllables of the great Kaddish, *"Yisgadal V'yiskadash Sh'me Rabbo,"* and I looked at the little huddle of my father's friends of many years who stood around, and the absurdity became a little less absurd. Even the most rational of us must admit that there is a healing power in the ritual words when you face what reason cannot fathom.

I keep thinking of my father's last words to me. I had been sitting by his side while he slept. Then my father moved a bit, and his eyes half opened. I bent close to him, and barely made out his whispered words. "They are calling from Zion," he said.

It is a good belief with which to die.

2. Enter Adam

November 12, 1956

MY WIFE told me that if it was a boy I could have the naming of him, so we have called him Adam. It's a good name, because for every father a new son is like the first man whom God ever created. As he starts his own individual life it is a sudden wonder, like the start of the race itself.

He was born the day before the elections, which made Edna say that he must be a Republican, since he made her lose her vote. He came into the world along with momentous happenings—the bursting of revolt in Central Europe, the clatter of tanks in the Egyptian desert, the thunder of an American electoral landslide. The events surrounding him were so big, and Adam himself is so little, that his first impact on me when I saw him was a bit on the comic side.

Looking at him through the door at Harkness Pavilion, it occurred to me that with so many crashing stage effects, like *Götterdämmerung* or Michelangelo's "First Creation," something more impressive might have been appropriate. When God created the first Adam out of earth and clay and the fire of his touch, he was a full-fledged man, big enough so that the Almighty could fashion woman out of his ribs. Our Adam is tiny. Yet you don't measure wonder by the inch or weigh delight by the ounce. No universe is too cosmic for a newborn baby to encircle with his smile.

How shall I describe Adam? His head is big and shiny and dominant, so that he looks quite literally like an egghead. He has a lot of dark fuzz that passes for hair. His nose is pug and his ears are delicately framed. He looks at you through sleepy eyes with a deep content. He is perfectly formed everywhere, but above all in hands bound to be an artist's—or a safecracker's.

You have the privilege of sounding silly even when you are a veteran father, as I am. Adam is my third son and my sixth child. Yet the miracle of birth is infallibly re-enacted, even for a repeater like myself. By comparison with it, every other wonder dwindles, even the so-called miracles of the Atomic Age.

For here is something that once *was not* and now *is*. Here is something delicately yet sturdily fashioned out of the merest gossamer, the product of the only forces that count in all history—love and the assertion of life. The ultimate victory, wrote Saint-Exupéry, is the victory of the seed.

His grown-up sisters are amused at the thought of him. His brothers, only a decade or so older, already have plans for his education as an athlete. They contemplate making him the first switch-pitcher in baseball, which they think they can do by early conditioning and constant training. Since he follows my two grandchildren, he comes into the world a ready-made uncle, with a nephew and a niece both older than himself. This will provide an infinite topic for jest at family gatherings and at school.

But it is hard right now to think of him as anyone's uncle—as anything but his own contented inner-directed little self, already very much a person, nonconformist from his affirming eyes to his stubborn toes and his warm earthy smell.

If you think I don't enjoy my role, then think again. No one knows where any man gets the pieces that go into his picture of himself, but somewhere I must have taken over the self-image of an Old Testament patriarch. I expect soon to grow a beard and talk in Biblical sentences.

The father-son relation comes close to the center of things. To be the son of a father is to taste the arrogance of life, which can turn into a chastening thing when you grow up and confront reality. To become the father of a son is to taste the humility of life, which turns into a heady thing as you watch the body of the boy shooting up and the senses awakening and a talent and a personality budding.

With all his dreams, a father these days is not unprepared for what lies ahead. He knows that there will be wonderful years when the boy tries on all the garments of his father's personality, copies his walk and talk and gestures, worships him as a hero. He knows that inevitably the years of disenchantment come, when the boy must break away in order to find and assert his own selfhood. And he hopes that those years, in turn, will be followed by the friendship of two men who, after finding themselves, find each other.

The going will be hard for both of us—a bit harder for Adam, perhaps, because he will have a somewhat ancient father while I shall have a very young son. It will be a good thing for me to have to keep up with the world of the young—with the DiMaggios and the Dylan Thomases and the Dizzy Gillespies still to come.

And so enter, Adam, into the only fabulous country where everything is possible and no dreams are excluded. Enter into a world which is shut off from Eden by a flaming sword, where you will endure your own hells and fashion your own Paradise.

But with all the death in it, this world you enter is still committed to life. What better proof could anyone ask than the fact of your coming into it?

JOYS OF A FAMILY MAN

1. On Being a Multiple Father

December 27, 1949

THESE ARE WEEKS when I am a captive of the extended family. When the phone rings, it is not one of my readers who must see me to give me the key of prophecy for the future, but one of a series of young men with whom Connie and Pam (twenty and seventeen respectively) have managed to become embroiled, and I scribble down cryptic messages which I can never decipher even when they are found. Then there is Joany (eleven) who knows (and persists in singing) all the tunes in all the musicals, who hangs breathless over the soap operas on the radio. Nor is this all. Add Mike and Steve (six and three), both dressed to the hilt in cowboy costumes complete from boots and spurs to kerchief and hat and holsters, using their father's head and neck as a target for practice-lassoing.

But don't ever believe me if I tell you I don't enjoy being a five-time father. I do. I must have been bitten by a Latin lesson when we were studying the paterfamilias back in New Haven High. I have suddenly taken to reading the Old Testament, partly (I suspect) because the Old Testament family was a patriarchate, and the impulse to be a patriarch is strong in me.

When I was one-and-twenty my regular line of approach to a likely-looking lass whom I thought to woo was to paint a word picture of going off to the Arizona desert to live in an adobe hut and raise seven sturdy children. Goethe used to say, Be careful of the dreams you dream when young, because in middle age they will come true. Almost all of my dream has—except that an adobe hut would prove even more crowded than a New York apartment.

The traffic problems in the apartment are not negligible. With Connie home from Sarah Lawrence and Pam from Putney, with Joany (who lives in Colorado) visiting for the holidays, and with Mike and Steve being homebodies instead of Dalton schoolboys, things get cluttered.

In his matchless passage in the *Symposium,* where Socrates discusses the nature of love with Diotima, Plato talks of the men "who seek through the production of children what they imagine to be happiness and immortality and an enduring remembrance." No doubt he is right about the motive. But at the moment, with the ironing board in great demand, and French and anthropology books lying about, and two small boys taking almost nonexistent baths to conserve water, the house smells not of immortality but sweetly of mortality.

It was a good Christmas. One doesn't forget the rounded wonder in the eyes of a boy as he comes bursting upstairs on Christmas morning and finds the two-wheeler or the fire truck of which for weeks he scarcely dared dream. This is the idyllic age, the last in growing up when life is brimming fulfillment. Or almost the last—for there is a magic of expectancy at seventeen or twenty when you stand on the threshold of love and life, and everything still seems possible.

The American family, especially in the cities, is too scattered and skeletal. The anthropologists, who study primitive as well as civilized tribal living, have a name for these family types. They talk of the nuclear family (just parents and offspring) and the extended family, like the Chinese family or one on a Midwestern farm, where there is room for sons and daughters, grandparents and cousins and aunts. Even in a New York apartment, I think children grow up best in the extended family, where they have a range of behavior to study and imitate, and a sense of spaciousness, and no unhealthy concentration on any one of them.

2. On Reading the Bible

March 6, 1952

FOR SEVERAL GENERATIONS the Bible has been slipping out of the lives of presumably educated people. There are signs that it is on its way back into favor and grace. I think it is because so many of us, recoiling from the spectacle of the public life, have been thrown back on the private life. And more than any other book, the Bible is the book of the family.

In my own case, the Bible was almost left out of my schooling and childhood. My father, who is something of an Old Testament scholar, could have fed my hunger for the great old stories, but there was the language difficulty: He did not know the Old Testament in English, nor was I willing to learn the necessary Hebrew. Fortunately English literature is saturated with the King James version, and it led me back eventually to the book itself.

But only in the past decade have I really been caught by it. I turn to it to look up some allusion and find myself snared in the often barbaric drama.

I am still ignorant, but one way to learn is to read the Bible with your children, especially the young ones in whom the wonder and the glory of life have not yet worn thin. I was too stupid to do it with my two elder daughters. But Joanna, next in age, tells me from the full rationalism of her thirteen years that the stories "are not true, Daddy." How can I tell her that while she is right as a scientist, they are nevertheless true as all stories are true, as dreams, only these happen to have furnished the collective dreams of a big chunk of mankind? She will someday discover it for herself.

I have better luck with Mike at eight, and Steve at six. In the past few weeks I have been reading to them from the Bible, and also from Joseph Gaer's *Folklore of the Old Testament,* which gives some of the surrounding tales. At this age of the boys, I stick mostly to the heroic tales, a few Psalms, and some of the wonderful poetry of the Prophets and the Revelations. Thus we are rediscovering together the great primitive episodes in the childhood of humanity.

This question of the reading dietary of the growing child, which will feed his hunger for the heroic and stir his moral imagination, has no better answer. Children want the poetic and the wild, and they want improbable folk tales. It is our failure to give it to them that has turned them to TV and the comic books, which have a vein of folk tale violence that feeds them.

There are ways and ways of reading the Bible with children. It can be read, as it has been for generations, as a fountainhead of revealed religious truth. That isn't how I read it, although inevitably a child forms from it a vivid and powerful image of a personal God, and you let it form. The Bible can be read also as the foundation of great style and art. It can be read as great allegory. It can be read as the repository of the moral conscience of the Jewish-Christian tradition. All these ways have meaning for me, but mostly I read it as a transcription of the human heart and fate, and the key to one's own.

However you read it, don't force it. There is a wonderful passage in John Ruskin's *Autobiography,* where he tells of the "long morning's hours of toil" when, as a child, he read the Bible with his mother from Genesis to Revelation, learning a few passages by heart each day, always rigidly disciplined. Even though it worked, it is a dubious method. The test of a great book is whether it leaves a scar. Joseph and Moses, Jesus, Paul, David and Absalom, Job, Solomon, Tamar and Ruth, Esther and Judith and Jael—these leave scars enough by themselves. You don't need to clank the chains.

3. Music in My Head

January 28, 1957

WHEN YOU ARE WEARY, jangled, discouraged, or just unsure of what to do next, have you ever picked up your fiddle and found it a better tranquilizer than Miltown? I have. That is why I praise the art of the musical amateur who may be fitful in applying himself, clumsy in execution, and nightmarish in retrospect, but who getteth the peace that not only passeth understanding but defieth harmony.

Note that I celebrate an ancient instrument called the fiddle instead of the newfangled crazes of pumping the accordion or of strumming a guitar accompaniment to some bawdy folk songs. Did you know that at least a million Americans are playing the accordion under the supervision of some five thousand teachers? Did you know that in New York City alone there are at least 25,000 impassioned guitar players, who are all probably rendering Harry Belafonte or Elvis Presley at this very moment?

I speak feelingly because my son Michael is one of them. I should add that all my children are terrifyingly musical and are instrumental double threats. All of them have sung in choirs, and in addition Connie plays the piano, Joany the flute, Pam and Steve each play both the recorder and the clarinet, and Mike the fiddle as well as the guitar. (Adam alone is too young to play on anything but our emotions, but we expect him to become a drummer.) You can guess how drastically this musical talent violates all heredity laws when I tell you that my singing range is less than an octave, that I can't carry a tune and am almost totally deaf in one ear.

But don't write me off. Despite these handicaps I am a fiddler. I play wherever and whenever I can—confidently, blatantly, and shamelessly, to the dismay of my friends, the disgust of the kinfolk, and the amusement of my family. Much as I like to listen to virtuosos like Menuhin and Stern, I would rather be a crude performer than an accomplished listener. I am a do-it-yourself man. For hours into the night I fiddle while the neighbors burn.

When I was a ten-year-old in New Haven, I lived in a Jewish lower-middle-class neighborhood, where there was no surfeit of money but plenty of love and some aspirations toward culture. It was assumed in all these families that the daughter would inevitably learn to play the piano and the son would take violin lessons. I was the only son, and the ritual of giving me this instruction was like a musical version of the belief in the Messiah. Who knows—I might have become a Heifetz.

Alas, I didn't. My trouble as a violinist was that I got no preparation in ear, taste or sensibility. I came to associate the violin wholly with the two half-hour lessons a week (when the teacher would correct my fingering and despair at my bowing) and the torturing hour of daily practice.

There was a wild moment early in my development as a violinist when my sister got me a job playing at an open-air canvas-covered neighborhood movie house. It must have been around 1915-16 and I was twelve or thirteen but very ambitious. It was in the days of Mary Pickford and Richard Barthelmess, and the movies, while silent, were pretty emotional. The orchestra was a piano and myself as fiddle, and while the piano was incompetent the failure of my own performance was outstanding. I lasted one night and was paid off by a bewildered proprietor whose eyes were eloquently upbraiding.

I didn't play again for at least thirty years. But in my mid-forties something happened. My sister-in-law was moving to a new house, and in the usual cleaning-up mania she found two violins that had come down to her over the years. When my eye lighted on them I said, "Good, this is exactly what I have been waiting for. Now I shall be able to play." Connie looked at me skeptically, as she had learned to be wary of some of my other assertions of competence. Edna said, "All right, we'll take it home. If you can play 'Silent Night' by Christmas, we'll eat the fiddle."

She had to. For me it was a case of challenge-and-response. I started with the carols, then when Mike began to take violin lessons we did duets of his pieces, and then I was invited to play in the Dalton School orchestra on a father-son occasion. It was at a time when Wallingford Riegger had written a special concerto for young people at the school's invitation, and we improvised an orchestra to perform it. Someone told the conductor that I played, so he made me first violin. I had memories of the old movie house experience, got panicky, and fluffed a few times, but the enthusiasm of the occasion muffled my errors and carried me to safety.

I was thinking about this the other day, when I was reading Vincent Sheean's autobiographical reminiscences of his adventures in musical listening—*First and Last Love*. There is a passage toward the end which describes Toscanini's decision to end his career as conductor. Sheean is nothing if not dramatic, and as he describes the rehearsal of April 3, 1954, with its terrifying episode when the maestro was conducting the "Tannhäuser Bacchanale" and there was the wrong entry of brasses, and he cried to the orchestra in Italian, "I am ashamed of you, ashamed," it was almost like the time at Gandhi's death when Sheean's fingers bled with the authentic stigmata of belief.

As I read this my mind went back to times when I have played with others and repeatedly made the wrong entry, but there has never been a Toscanini to terrify me with his perfectionism. My musical autobiography would not be knowledgeable, as Sheean's is. It would be that of a man who plays for fun whenever he can and carries about with him in the intervals either snatches of Vivaldi or of "Eine Kleine Nachtmusik" that run with an inaccurate delight through his head.

4. My Half Acre

July 31, 1952

A PROFESSOR C. B. RAYMOND, of the Vegetable Crop Department at Cornell (so a third-class release from the State College of Agriculture tells me) regards mid-July as "the most critical period of the entire season in the home food garden." He warns of "weeds, . . . Mexican cucumber beetles, bean beetles, Colorado potato beetles, . . . blight of tomatoes." But even in this dire H-hour of our gardening destiny, it seems we can still stake down the future by making asparagus plantings. "It is not too late now," he says, "even if you have to send away to get the asparagus seed."

Alas, it is too late for me, whether for asparagus planting or beetle battling. After what has happened to my little half acre, the professor's words are like acid poured into a raw wound.

I suppose I am one of Long Island's most futile gardeners, but it has not been for want of trying. It all began six or seven years ago, when my wife and I had tired of shopping around for a different vacation house every summer, and she finally found an old farmhouse a hundred miles out on Long Island that we have clung to ever since. I am not one of those who, like Whittaker Chambers and S. J. Perelman, have fled to the country from the bedizened corruptions of the city. I love this unlikely pile of masonry and madness called New York, and sometimes I think I must have been born with asphalt in my blood. But that doesn't keep me from also loving life at North Sea.

That's what the little harbor inlet is called where our house is. In some recent magazine I have seen the neighboring Hamptons described as the Ninevehs "where the rich sun and sin." Our own motives in coming to North Sea were less garish. We wanted some woods for the children to roam and some waves to splash in and a long beach to walk on, and a fireplace for autumn and winter days, and a plot on which to start a garden. A French geographer, Jean Brunhes, once said that "every human enterprise is the mixture of a little bit of humanity, a little bit of soil, and a little bit of water." We found all three.

The garden was a new experience. Here I was, plunging into a strange idiom of life for a city-bred man, molding rows of little mounds to stick the seed into, or standing for hours in the sun while gnats assaulted me, tying tomato plants to tall sticks which never survived a hard rain.

How often and how wistfully have I repeated the lines from George Meredith's "Love in the Valley":

> *Trim little scholars are the flowers of her garden,*
> *Trained to stand in rows, and asking if they please.*

Alas, neither the flowers nor the vegetables of our garden were so docile. Year after year our gardens have been flops.

This year Edna and I determined to succeed. How we worked at it—harrowing the soil, choosing the seeds, pulling up weeds, fighting insects with liquid and dust sprays, getting new lengths of hose to replace the rotted ones. We battled larvae and drought and our own anxieties. We hadn't much skill or knowledge, but we figured that the way to bring up vegetables, like children, was to pour your love into them.

Then the other morning, while I was pretending to be a writer, I heard curdling screams from the boys in the direction of the garden. I ran out to find two cows from the herd in the neighboring pasture just getting through with the corn after having trampled the lettuce and torn up the cucumbers. They had jumped over the old wire fence and found a feast to console them for the parched grass of the pasture.

There was rage in my heart as I measured the devastation. I understood how King Lear felt when his daughters tricked and betrayed him: "I shall do such things—what they are yet I know not, but they shall be the terrors of the earth." All I did was to chase the two intruders back into the pasture, and mourn the death of my half acre.

5. *A Member of the Picnic*

September 6, 1953

I WRITE as a recent convert to the summer picnic. There used to be a time when I recoiled from the thought of a medley of adults in dripping bathing suits squatting on a stretch of desolate sand, surrounded by squirming, squalling children, blinded by smoke from a badly made fire, munching at inedible hamburgers half filled with gritty sand, scorched by the sun and eaten alive by the flies. My surly answer to picnic invitations used to be that there are some things—among them, eating—that ought to be done entirely indoors.

Maybe I am mellowing, but what has chiefly changed me is the discovery of the ritual aspects of the summer picnic. Some men like the ritual of fishing and some even—heaven forbid—that of golf, but I like rituals that the whole family can take part in.

I don't have in mind the elaborate affairs that sometimes masquerade as picnics. I have watched in disgust while impeccably dressed people came down to the beach with sun umbrellas, beach chairs, wicker hampers laden with food, small folding bars, grills, bags of charcoal or neatly cut logs, portable radios, and a library of newspapers and magazines. These are not picnics, they are formal dinner parties held outdoors.

Nor do I go for those sybaritic clambakes I read about, where you have to heat the stones forty-eight hours in advance, and the formula seems to require burying four dozen lobsters wrapped in moss and surrounded by clams and corn.

My own picnic rituals are modest but exacting. There must be an assortment of children of every age. There should be a chance to splash in the water or go crabbing before the picnic starts. Then everyone scatters, scouring the beach for driftwood, and soon they come back with their treasures. There are heretics who hold that you can have a picnic without a fire, which I regard as subversive doctrine. None of your cold food for me, and none of your insipid prepared sandwiches, even on a hot summer day. A picnic is no picnic without wood-gathering, and the Promethean act of firemaking, and hamburgers sizzling on the griddle, and some ears of corn in the ashes, and an old and battered coffeepot blackened with use but still ready to be heated to round out the meal.

Part of a picnic's rituals may be found in its mishaps. No matter how many lists you make before you start, there is always something you forget to remember—the salt, or butter for the corn, or milk for the children, or paper plates or cups, or the cherished asbestos gloves that give me the professional feeling a chef gets from his towering white hat.

Then there is the great enemy—the sand, which gets into everything. A veteran picnicker finally learns how to accept the sand, knowing that it has engulfed numberless civilizations in Africa and Asia and that it cannot be kept out of the corn or watermelon.

What is best about a picnic is to see how everyone, from the smallest to the biggest, finds a function in it. It is good to see a little boy of seven staggering under a load he has himself assumed—a load that measures his eagerness to be a member of the picnic more than it measures his strength. There is an age-group democracy about the whole affair, with each valued as a person in his own right, carrying his own weight rather than dependent on father or mother.

Then as dark begins to fall the air grows chill, and the sweaters and pullovers are hauled out. The fire, which was kept low for cooking, is now piled high to make a blaze. There are stories and songs and rounds, until eyes get heavy with sleep and everything is loaded into the station wagon for the trek home.

I recall a row of such fires stretching for several miles on our ocean beach on Long Island a year ago on Labor Day. I thought of Kipling's threnody on the British Empire: "On dunes and headlands sinks the fire." But the reverse was happening. The kind of American empire I like is that of fires rising on all the dunes and headlands of our continent because families of every kind have been out on summer picnics.

6. Zip

February 1, 1951

I MAY AS WELL confess that things have not been the same in the Lerner household since Zip came into our lives.

It all started with a seven-year-old boy and a too indulgent family friend who knows dogs and boys equally well. A few days before Christmas our friend Jonas Reiner asked Mike, "What would you want best in all the world?" It didn't take Mike long to make the decision. He had been thinking about just this moment for millions of years. "A dog," he said, every nerve concentrated to make his voice very quiet and not too eager. "What kind of a dog?" Jonas asked. Mike spoke now almost in a whisper. "A cocker," he said, "a—a cocker pup."

"I shouldn't be surprised," said Jonas, "if something were to arrive next Wednesday between five and five-thirty." And it did.

That was how Zip happened. Almost promptly at five on Wednesday a car stopped at our house, a bell was rung. White-faced and tense, like an acolyte about to be received into the mystery, Mike for once didn't dare go to the door, fearful that his slightest move might break the impossible spell. And suddenly there in a small packing carton, tan of color, moist of nozzle, gentle of eye, long of ear, short of wisdom for all his two and a half months, was the most complete and satisfying cocker-pup vision that had ever swum into a small boy's ken.

Mike's eyes became big saucers, burning with radiance. He picked up the shivering, yammering little morsel of dog. "It's all right, Zip," he said, and it was all right.

Let me say right off that I have never been one of your dog lovers that keep kennels solvent, make dog food manufacturers millionaires and buy those execrable volumes of dog stories that trivialize every bookstore but keep it going.

Perhaps I owed my bias to Thorstein Veblen, about whom I wrote my thesis when I aspired to scholarship. In his *Theory of the Leisure Class,* Veblen (who must have had some unhappy canine experiences) called the dog "the filthiest of the domestic animals in his person and the nastiest in his habits. For this," he added, "he makes up in a servile, fawning attitude towards his master, and a readiness to inflict discomfort on all else."

I tried once to read this passage to a bedraggled mongrel whom I picked off a New York street and named Perdita until I found I had the wrong Latin gender, but Perdita—bored with Veblen—disappeared into the dogs' underground. In Williamstown we had another mongrel, called Orestes because he was pursued by the Fates in the form of my three hoyden daughters. This got Orestes so neurotic that when we left we had to pay a fraternity to adopt him.

Zip is the first dog we have ever tried to keep in a city apartment. Either you know from experience what this means, or there is no use telling you. Mike has tucked away somewhere in his head the age at which you start housebreaking a pup, but judging from the way people's noses wrinkle up when they walk into the house the date is not yet. My study and workshop happen to be on the same floor as the nursery-cum-kennels, but fortunately I had a dual attack of pneumonia and measles when I was nine months old, and my olfactory sense is quite absent. The defect seems to have endeared me to Zip, who shows it by chewing up any stray morsel of paper wisdom that slips from my typewriter, and by nibbling at the books on my lowest shelves.

What is most exhausting is his vitality at six-thirty in the morning, when I am ready to hate anything that looks spry. After his breakfast his dynamism increases, if that is possible. The great morning ritual is going to school. If some morning you see two small boys and a cocker pup on a leash, racing along Lexington from Ninety-second to Eighty-ninth with a panting, puffing, yellow-faced and disheveled man about a block behind them, you will know that Zip and Mike and Steve are in pursuit of knowledge and that I am lagging in the quest, and am inclining toward Veblen on the dog.

But at night when I look in on the boys, and see Zip curled up next to Mike, half on the blanket and half on the pillow, happy yet ever alert, I throw away all the books. For nothing literary, and least of all a column, can hope to describe the way of a boy with a dog and of a dog with a boy.

May 17, 1953

Of the 22,000,000 dogs in America and the 300,000 in New York, my vote for the dog of distinction goes to Zip. It is he alone who makes me regret that I am not in public life, which deprives Zip of the wider audience he deserves more than less distinguished dogs like Richard Nixon's Checkers. Hence these notes, to repair his obscurity. Perhaps some female dog, reading this in the springtime of the year and under a full moon, will be moved to seek Zip out.

He is a child of nature, very direct in his affections. I told him about

Marital Infidelity, hoping to assuage him for his lack of a life companion, but he will not be consoled. He smells everything and everybody with an embarrassing purposiveness, and climbs up anyone's leg with a zeal that would grace a better cause. When we protest, my son Mike's answer is that Zip can't help it because "it's just little dogs' mating time."

But soon we will be moving to the country again for the summer, and Zip will be 'able to sublimate his love impulses by roaming the woods, swimming the creeks and persecuting the cows. He has sworn eternal war against all birds and beasts, and especially squirrels and rabbits. But once at dusk a reddish-hued fox crept through a fence and along our fields—and Zip, as if warned by some prenatal racial memory, hid in the kitchen.

When he straggles home with the boys at the end of the day, after wading through mud and squirming his way through brushwood, he looks like a disheveled canine Ulysses coming back from the wars. There are brambles sticking to his hindquarters, and his matted hair has to be untangled. He brings home with him all the ticks in the world, and it is Mike's loving job to pry them out one by one and burn them while Zip sits with a massive patience, happy to be free of the blood-swollen parasites.

An amiable friend of ours presented him with a basket to sleep in, but he persists in bedding down on our best living-room chair. Edna finally resorted to one of the fancy "stay-off" sprays and drenched the chair with it. The only result was that she had to shun the chair for weeks, while Zip clung to it more fondly than ever.

His encounters with other dogs are like an idiot's tale, full of barking and bragging and signifying nothing but high spirits. When he is securely on the leash, he has the courage of a lion and strains to break away and attack even the mastiffs as huge as mastodons. But when he is off the leash, knowing he won't be held back, he keeps a respectful distance from any mongrel bigger than himself.

Since he shows equal interest and affection for either dog sex, we have become well acquainted with the veteran members of the Society of Dog Walkers, which I find to be the most numerous society in New York. Its members meet and converse at the lampposts, wire trash baskets, parked cars, and magazine racks. In an impersonal city it is the quickest way to break down the barriers between strangers.

One woman, whose dog kept following Zip, asked me, "Is yours neurotic too? You know, they now have psychoanalysts for dogs." I don't think Zip needs one. To be sure, he bolts his food and is over-possessive about bones, and he howls with anguish when Steve plays discords on the harmonica. But that is because he has the life principle in him.

He has many advantages over people. He doesn't want to gumshoe around Europe. He doesn't ask for new clothes, or go to first nights. He doesn't want to run for Mayor of New York, or worry about his golf score. Most of all, he doesn't accuse people.

I like Zip.

7. Teen-Ager

June 4, 1952

LOOKING AT LIFE through the eyes of a teen-ager makes you accept many things about the Big Media otherwise staggering. For example, Dagmar. I note that a Congressman called Gathings, from Arkansas, is greatly disturbed over what Dagmar reveals on TV, his fears receding only to the degree that Dagmar's neckline moves up. To Joany, and to many teen-agers like her, Dagmar is not an incitement to juvenile delinquency, but quite simply a fact she takes in her stride. Just as she takes the fact of Aldo Ray's voice in the movies, which she describes as that of a cement mixer.

Having a thirteen-year-old in the family is like having a general-admission ticket to the movies, radio and TV. You get to understand that the glittering new arts of our civilization are directed to the teen-agers, and by their suffrage they stand or fall.

Joany is my guide and adviser in the jungle of the jukeboxes. When confronted by a jukebox I feel curiously helpless; one song seems like the others in the deadly array of sentimental titles. But armed with a quarter's worth of my nickels, Joany swoops down on the jukebox, and soon we are all caught up in the abandon of her delight.

Have you suffered through the moanings of something called "Wheel of Fortune," sung by Kay Starr? Did you know what a lethal combination Guy Mitchell and Doris Day are in "A Little Kiss Good Night"? Have you followed the lilt of "A Guy Is a Guy"? Do you know a heavy trifle called "Perfidia," with the lugubrious closing lines, "I now know my love was not for you/And so I'll take it back with a sigh, perfidious one, goodbye"? And have you, oh, have you, heard Johnnie Ray do "Cry" and "Brokenhearted" and "The Little White Cloud That Cried"?

After such pleasures, I tell Joany that they suggest to me nothing so much as the agonies of a sick musk ox or a stricken moose. She regards me with the affectionate disdain that a college sophomore has for a parent who has not heard of the theories of Ortega y Gasset. All of Joany's friends seem to be aficionados, and they discuss the latest nuances of some new Hit Parade item over their sodas.

Joany eats movies, good and bad alike, just as she consumes food (she has picked up some horrendous item that a teen-ager needs ten times as much nourishment as a man of fifty). She has seen *Broken Arrow* five times, and Pier Angeli in *Tomorrow Is Too Late* twice, and is ready for more. She has her outbursts of passionate enthusiasm, and each month there is a new reigning king or queen to whom the family must bow. But she also eats books, and you will find her on a rainy weekend, her flaming red hair drawn back in a knot, sprawling near the fireplace consuming Sinclair Lewis or *All About Eileen* or Frederick Morton's *Asphalt and Desire,* or probably all of them in Faustian succession.

What the teen-agers hunger for is a sense of dedication, and they have a way of reaching out for it, even in the most unlikely places, with the same gusto with which they will raid the icebox.

All the time they are preparing for what lies ahead—trying out clothes (what belt with what school blouse and skirt? which of Dad's frayed shirts with the dungarees?), learning to drive, trying out ideas about politics, watching their older sisters going out on dates. They still torture their teachers and are sometimes quite outrageous hoydens, but they are trembling on the threshold of life, with the fleeting image of the child behind them and the foreshadowing of the woman ahead.

8. I Gave the Bride Away

March 29, 1953

I GAVE THE BRIDE AWAY yesterday—the bride being my daughter Connie.

I loved her and she was surpassingly beautiful. Nevertheless I want to say about weddings that they were contrived by women, to give expression to women's dreams. The girl in her years of being courted is the most cherished object in our whole society, and at her wedding she is on the dizzying heights of her world. That is what makes weddings at once joyous and a little fearsome, as all heights are.

What I am setting down is, of course, a father's-eye view of weddings. The preliminaries of a marriage are not calculated to feed his ego much. Nowadays the young man who has courted your daughter doesn't ask you formally for her hand—a custom fallen into grievous disuse that ought to be restored. They don't give you much warning. Connie and Dick simply announced to the Russells and us that they had decided to get married. I am all for the independence this expresses, but it gives the parents a bad start. The only one who gets a chance to retrieve his ego is the bride's father, who struts down the stairway with a floating dream on his arm and carries his shoulders higher than he ever will again.

I don't know how many American industries would crash if weddings were done away with. After the engagement is announced, you become a target for high-pressure sales campaigns. Your mail suddenly doubles in volume. For days the phone rings, and you become entangled in endless conversations. The man wants to sell you flowers, or furnish you with an umpty-piece band. He will make the most distinctive-looking marriage announcement, engraved with a delicate embossed art on priceless paper. He can contrive just the wedding cake you want, built with intricate skill to tower into the sky. He has a photographer's studio and will do a dozen pictures for a trifle just a little short of your total income tax.

One morning the phone roused me from a deep dream of peace. Still asleep, I reached over, picked it up, and heard someone whom I recall as associated with music. "I come very highly recommended," he said. I said No, we had music. A moment of silence and then, in tones of deep hurt: "But I come very highly recommended." "He comes very highly recommended," I mumbled to my wife as I plunged again into a troubled dream of marching armies of angry caterers, each of whom came very highly recommended.

But all this foolishness is washed into oblivion when the real moment comes. I was moved when Pam and Joany, who were the bridesmaids, walked solemnly ahead of their sister, and when I found myself in the traditional one-two, one-two shuffle with my daughter on my arm and an eternity in every step.

I was most moved when bride and groom finally stood opposite each other, a little pale, giving their answers in tones you had to strain to hear. I am a pushover about these rituals. I don't know just when it came, but suddenly I felt struck by a joy so sharp that it became an intolerable sadness.

Why try to explain it, or defend myself? All I know is that compared with the great phases of the life cycle—from birth to death—very little else counts in life. The anthropologists call them the "rites of passage." The marriage of your first child is not unimportant in these rites. Somewhere between a man's reaching middle age and his oncoming dotage he finds that his relation to his child has suddenly changed. Up to then the child has been a projection of you—an extended vertical line, as it were. Suddenly, with marriage, you find another line that no longer runs out of you but runs parallel to your own, generating a new source of the life force.

I looked at my own mother and father, and saw that this was what they too were feeling.

Maybe I ought to add as a postscript, in all honesty, that I didn't really give the bride away. I brought her up to where her husband-to-be was standing, and then I faded into the ranks of those enclosing them. The bride gave herself away, and so did the groom. There can be no other way, ever, of being married.

9. On Becoming a Grandfather

October 3, 1955

IT HAS HAPPENED for me—the next great stage in the life cycle after seeing your child married. On Saturday I got word from Cambridge saying that my daughter Pamela Schofield had given birth to a lusty boy, and congratulating me on becoming a grandfather.

It is a great event in a man's span of years, this discovery that someone to whom you have helped give life has in turn given life to someone else, and that a new cycle has thus been started. It makes the life-giving miracle of birth not just a single act but a continuing process. Suddenly it hits you that the ancient symbol of runners in a race, passing the torch from one to another, had as its prototype the succession of generations. With your own children you are too deeply absorbed in them to notice the overarching span; it isn't until your children have children that you see yourself part of a process in which the individual counts for little and the continuity is all.

I do not deny some shock in getting the news that I was a grandfather. We are all doltish enough to cherish fantasies of eternal youth. But when you look at yourself in the mirror and say "Grandpa," it begins to sink in that you are no longer a man about town.

I used to think of myself as quite a blade. I recall when I wheeled my first daughter around in a baby carriage, how careful I was to stay away from the main-traveled streets, lest I encounter someone whose image of me would be jarred by the sight of the carriage. Later I careened to the other extreme, became the arduously fanatical father and swelled with pride as the number of my children multiplied. Once started on this trend, I mean to do it with a vengeance, and with each grandchild my sum of pride will mount.

I look with more than equanimity toward the growing brood of the progeny of my progeny. I am starting to read the Old Testament again, and the Books that absorb me most are the ones that contain all the "begats." They were towering men in those days, and they knew that once you have played the young roles to the hilt the one that becomes you best is the patriarch. Nothing of the measly roles in between.

I trust that Timothy, which is what Pam and Joe have named my grandchild, will be only the beginning of my new career as a patriarch. I look forward to one of those wonderful family portraits showing the three generations ranged like steps in an escalator, from the then current infant to myself. Maybe I'll even grow a white beard, like my own grandfather.

I think we Americans miss something by restricting ourselves to the "nuclear" family, of just father, mother and two or three children. The European peasants (and our own early New England and Midwestern farm families) used to hold together the "extended" family, with all the subgenerations and the collateral branches. I also admire the Chinese family system. It would be very satisfying to be addressed by your children and grandchildren in terms of ritual deference, and to receive all the homage with a studied, impassive grace. It would be even better to look forward to the time when you will be worshiped as an ancestor.

I fear I shall have to dress and talk and act my part now—that of one of the elders. Which means no getting mixed up with any Susannas. It means stopping all the foolishness of taking some young thing to the Algonquin for a drink in the falling twilight, or worrying about what Marilyn Monroe reads, or running through the Los Angeles airport with Anita Ekberg in pursuit of a plane. There is a time for all things, saith the Preacher. When a man gets to be a grandfather, it is time to put away foolish things.

When I get my first glimpse of Timothy, I may also glimpse, peering around the corridor of the years ahead, a dream image of *his* child, who will call me Great-Grandfather.

Much of what I have set down here is fantasy and foolishness. But what is not fantasy is the invincible knowledge that not all the powers and principalities of the Czarist and Nazi darkness could snuff our line out—a knowledge that is part of the mingled shock and pleasure of becoming a grandfather.

April 16, 1956

I have just returned from welcoming my first granddaughter, Debra Russell, to form the distaff foundation of what I count upon as a far-stretching dynasty.

Everyone wants to hold and cuddle Debra, and she is a very satisfactory young lady for cuddling, quite ready to be passed from arm to arm of the large kin-family into which she has come. The real religion of America is, of course, baby worship. Grown people, who presumably know the value of time, seem ready to sit for hours making nonsensical cooey and goofy sounds to a little bundle that lies drowsy in a state of magnificent contentment with the milk it has just guzzled.

Of course, all parents and grandparents have the illusion that their particular idol is a thing of beauty, but here it happens to be true. Her weight is just short of eight pounds, her curves are curvy, her hair is dark and copious, her skin is miraculously unwrinkled, her eyes have a lazy seductiveness, her fingers have a clutching tenacity, her nose has just the right snubness, and her ears are perfection itself. She has her faults, I am sure, but at this moment they escape me.

She is part of the spate of babies which is pushing the American population curve up and up. But she is not just a statistic, but a firm little personality trying to find some form and shape in the buzzing confusion around her.

And what an extraordinary equipment this morsel of humanity seems to require. She has a perambulator and an old-fashioned cradle as well. She has little baby sheets galore, not only white sheets and pink sheets but even flowered sheets. She has the most fragile-looking sweaters. The females of my family, jaded with the sight of dirty blue jeans around the house for the last ten years, look forward ardently to a succession of crinolines, organdy dresses and dancing pumps. The feeling we all have with a girl child is that God gives her to us "to dress her and keep her" like the Garden of Eden. This may be a man's world, but the things that move it are female garments.

My two young sons thought she would be a boy and were ready to present her with an outfielder's glove, but now they have shifted and are ready to teach their niece the Lindy Hop. As for me, I am busy with her education. I am sure she will go to Dalton, but after that I try to figure out whether she is the Radcliffe or Brandeis or Sarah Lawrence type. Will she have as lovely a voice as her mother and aunts have? Will she write biting satirical novels about her family? Will her dramatic talents enchant first-nighters on Broadway? Or will she be political and roam around the world as a foreign correspondent before she settles down to start a new round with her own Debra?

I had expected her mother and father to be planners, and on my first visit I brought them as a gift a new *Manual for Parents*. But I was silly. I look at them looking at Debra and I see that manuals and planning and all the rest are superfluous. It is the moment itself that contents them, the magical present moment when they have brought their own child to their own home and can gaze and gaze at her.

I see that what was before a marriage has become a family, and the circle is completed.

10. Confessions of an Inept Man

April 14, 1956

IN THE SPRING a young man's fancy lightly turns to love, but a family man's duties turn heavily toward the household chores that need doing but never get done.

On one side of our back yard the fence collapsed. I tried shoring it up last year and the year before, but I am an unhandy man with a hammer and don't understand the engineering aspects of what makes a fence stand or sag, and now Nemesis is upon me. The same goes for our oil furnace and boiler in the cellar; all the pipes and valves strike me as devilish contraptions put there to entangle me, and I can never remember what to turn on or off when the furnace gets too dry or the boiler too hot. As a result, we live in continual fear of the house blowing up. Once, in the middle of the night, the boiler sprang a leak and flooded the cellar, and I had to call a police emergency car to show me how to turn it off.

As for the state of my study and files, I must report the conviction in my family that if a tornado twisted through them while I was away I wouldn't know on my return that anything had happened. I can neither throw away anything nor find a proper place for it. I am only one degree removed from the pathological hoarding of the Collyer brothers.

Let me confess it: With all the things at which Americans are traditionally handy you will find me all thumbs.

The magazine *Perspectives* recently reprinted a long article of mine on American technology, which was very learned and must have sounded impressive in foreign editions. The secret I didn't reveal to my foreign readers is that while I can write on technology I haven't the foggiest notion of what to do when a TV set starts to shimmy, or how to locate and change a blown fuse.

The climax came last week when my family was away on a ski expedition to Vermont and I stayed home to catch up with my work. One of my bachelor chores was to see that Zip, our cocker spaniel, wasn't allowed to starve. We have one of those gadgets on the wall that is supposed to open a can when you crank it. I gaily tried it on a can of dog food for a half hour, while Zip moaned with tense expectancy and drooled at my feet. Finally I gave up, looked in vain for a hand can opener, found an ice pick, tried to rip open the cover and ripped my finger in the process. Zip's food that night was mixed with blood, sweat and frustration.

Some people are accident-prone. Happily, I am not, but I seem to stir up the evil spirits that slumber in apparently inanimate objects. I must have been the only boy in the history of Hillhouse High School in New Haven who flunked woodwork in the school shop. I shall never forget the look on the face of my teacher when I finished my first bookrack and was ready to take it home. Today when I approach a jammed window sash it won't budge, and then suddenly it slams down and breaks the pane. When I chop wood out in the country I am bound to chop a toe, too. When I try to hang curtains they end up by looking as gnarled and knotted as a Madison Avenue executive's stomach.

The worst instrument of torture for an unmechanical man is a car. When a tire blows out, it is always on a parkway, and when I look in the back of the car I find that the spare is flat and beyond recovery.

And when I call the AAA to rescue me I can never locate my membership card.

I have an intense admiration for all my fellow American males who can follow a blueprint and put anything together, from a toy train to a house and annex. They are the fine flowering of our machine civilization and our Permanent Industrial Revolution, and I feel toward them as Thomas Mann in *Tonio Kroger* felt toward the flaxen-haired youth who seemed to belong to his society, instead of sticking out of it like a nonconformist sick thumb.

Since we have created this machine civilization, I keep asking myself, why should I be so inept at it? In this do-it-yourself era, where everyone can do anything, I seem to be the last of the primitives, the ultimate disproof of the triumph of mechanism.

11. Through Europe with Children

Bergerac, France, July 8, 1957

THIS TIME Edna and I have ventured to bring along our three boys. I suppose it was a thoroughly mad thing to do, but sometimes mad things make some sense. We shall leave Michael and Stephen (thirteen and eleven) for a month in the village of Ciboure, with a Basque fisherman's family, right near the Spanish border, and we hope that the French they learn will be intelligible outside the Basque country. Meanwhile, we shall ourselves see something of Spain.

As for Adam, who will be all of eight months soon, the unanimous family decision was to take him along and see what happens. Since he has no words of any sort, he will have no worries about French or Spanish or Italian, as his elders do. He has a passport of his own, signed by John Foster Dulles, requesting all and sundry to permit Adam Lerner safely and freely to pass and, in case of need, to give all lawful aid and protection to him.

Right now he is in a pension in Paris, being made much of by the Spanish waitress and kitchenmaid and a circle of admirers. In a few days he will fly to Madrid and catch up with us there. We have his canvas bathtub and a makeshift crib and a carton of canned American foods for him packed away, but we are trying to spare him the rigors of road travel.

But for the two older boys, what can surpass a series of days which start with a strange breakfast in a strange hotel in a strange French town, and then the marketing in the shops for lunch stuff, and the packing of the car (it is really a small bus), and the drive all morning along the rolling landscape, through farms where machinery is still

rarer than the yoked teams of oxen, and the sheaves are packed carefully in the fields? At lunchtime we try to find a shady spot, perhaps on
the bank of a river, and spread out the bread and cheese and fruit,
and discuss the vagaries of the language and the erratic behavior
of the car.

Then back to the road, with a changing countryside, and the narrow
streets of villages that have not changed for centuries. And toward
evening the all-important capstone of the day: the study of the
Michelin to decide what town to stay in, the reconnoitering of the
hotels and the available rooms, the unpacking of bags for the night,
the incredible delight of a bath (if the hotel quarters boast of one),
the choice of a restaurant where the food and the price look right.

And then, after the late dinner, the walk together through the
quiet streets, digesting the events of the day. And then the sleep of
two tired but healthy boys.

I think American parents leave too much of the education of their
children to the schools and the teachers, and retain too little for themselves. In the fifteenth and sixteenth centuries in Europe, the scholars
often wrote books on the education of princes. Well, in a democracy
like ours it is our own children who are the princes and who will have
to make the decisions for the state and for themselves.

We have to do a good deal more thinking than we have done—
about the best sequence of reading for our children, about when Kipling should come, and when O. Henry, and when the great myths and
the great religious traditions, and when Keats, and when Shakespeare,
and when Eugene O'Neill. The schools do their best, and some do
very well, but what you learn within and with the family is what is
likely to stick.

The great chance for parents to exercise some guidance is during
vacations. Curiously that is exactly the time when so many parents
pack up their children and send them off to camp. Where the children
have been too closely watched and protected, and need to be on their
own, this makes sense. But a family traveling together, by jalopy or
station wagon or Microbus, whether in the national-park areas of our
own Western states or across Europe or down through Mexico, may be
a better solution.

Enough new things and new situations keep happening so that the
children must learn how to meet them, yet the parents are there to
serve as a bridge of sorts. And neither the parents nor the children are
running away from the hardest thing there is in life, harder even than
a love affair or a marriage—the growing of a family into maturity,
each member learning from the rest yet remaining part of a whole.

I underscore the wholeness because, more than anything else, that
is what is lacking in our fragmented individualist life. Driving through
Europe with children is often a tough assignment, and it has its comic

and irritating and nightmarish episodes, along with its lyrical passages. But whatever happens, happens to all. The problems have to be faced by all, no one can quite stay out of the decisions, the disasters concern all, the triumphs belong to all.

This is what I, for one, got as a member of an immigrant family arriving in New York a half century ago and having to stick together and learn together or perish. If you were the oldest child in one of these families that were jammed into the steerage hulls of crowded ships, what you remember is the responsibility you felt in riding herd on the rest of the kids. If you were the youngest—as I happened to be when our family came over in 1907—you found yourself always tagging along at the tail end of a human rope, moving in bewilderment through one nightmare episode after another. My own transoceanic odyssey, at the age of four, seems to have been one continuous nosebleed; at every crisis, and there were plenty of them, the sanguinary stream spurted out of my nostrils like a New York faucet before the water shortage.

Those that were not destroyed by the experience were tested and strengthened by it. Our children have no chance to get their sense of family cohesion that way. The immigrant frontier in America is as good as over. A family that can face new experiences together and accumulate common memories along foreign highways and byways is a lucky one.

12. End of Summer

September 26, 1958

THE END OF SUMMER has come, and I am back to where I used to be as a boy when the coming of fall meant primarily that school was open again and I could step once more through the portals of wonder and begin a new year of entrancing new experience. The fact that the leaves were turning and that the golden browns of late summer were giving way to barer grays, and that a sharper tang was in the air, did not mean for me that anything was dying, but always that something was being born.

Thus it is still after so many years of school openings. We have moved back into New York from our summer farmhouse at North Sea. The house on Eighty-fourth Street which has been so gloomy and empty all summer is now full of children's voices again. There are neat little heaps of fall clothes being tried on to see whether Steve and Adam have outgrown them over the summer, and there are lists, lists of everything, being checked for all those obscure but sufficient purposes that mothers and housewives know about.

As for myself, the end of summer means that I am back at Brandeis University after my sabbatical year of idleness and wandering. My teaching sword seems a bit rusty as I draw it out and shine it up for the encounters of the classroom. I have, after hours of exploration, dug out of the files those yellowed folders, with strange-looking sheets full of cabalistic writing, which are supposed to recall what I said on past occasions to earlier batches of students. I keep reading them and wondering what I could possibly have meant by these curious scribblings. When I face my new classes I have to do what every despairing teacher is doing right across the country—forget about the funny old notes and start all over again.

My own vacation last summer consisted chiefly of a week in British Columbia with Mike and Steve. The boys were agile and hardy and filled with wonder at the most stunning landscape that the world offers anywhere. They climbed a glacier, darted around the lake on motorboats, wore heavy boots on the rough trails and spent hours listening to a wondrous man called Ernie who had worked in the logging camps and the now abandoned mines. As for me, I trudged up a long trail with them to get at some mountain trout, and felt the ache in my bones for days.

The rest of the summer, except for a few brief excursions by air, I spent out at North Sea with my clan—including all the children and grandchildren—which has had a chance to gather but has since dispersed again. I spent my time sitting in the sun, trying to work on a book while Adam—who had his own ideas—clambered all over me.

Burned by the sun, lolloping across the pasture, a friend of the horse, an intimate of the cows, an admirer of all the birds and of our faithful hound Zip, Adam has had a lyrical summer. He has discovered all the miracles of the world of nature, running barefoot across the grass, adventuring on the prickly stubble of the fields, wading on the beach, bending his head to listen to the sound the wind makes. And through him, I too rediscover the simplest miracles to which I had almost closed my being.

Adam lives on tiptoe, trying to stretch his tiny body so that he will miss nothing. The day doesn't really start until you see him, and he raids your breakfast tray, and then the sun rises on your universe. He mimics everyone and everything. Mostly he is ambitious to be like Zip, and the phase when he insisted on licking up his food off the floor was a somewhat distressing one.

He has two languages, being equally unintelligible in English and Spanish. This troubles no one, least of all himself, except that his mother has some doubts as to whether his development into a poet may not be obstructed by this bilingual beginning. So she has been assiduously reading English poetry to him, so that he will get the rhythms into his bones and his unconscious.

And so the summer is ended. For me there will be things to remember—walking along the ocean beach in the mist and fog in the early September days, Adam chasing sandpipers and gulls alike, and Steve running along the dunes, clad in a serape that a kind friend gave him because of his broken arm, looking like a Mexican or Peruvian lad, and making an exotic silhouette against the sky.

CONFESSIONS OF A WRITER

1. What Shall I Save?

September 10, 1952

OUR HOUSE caught fire yesterday evening—the one at North Sea where we spend summers. Mike and I were in the village, getting some papers and things, and Steve and my wife and her mother were at home. We got back to find the North Sea volunteer fire fighters and their two fire trucks had moved fast and had things under control. Some sparks from the fireplace must have ignited the shingle roof and burned a hole in it big enough for a couple of men to get through.

I have been mulling over one of the oldest questions of human life: What do you try to save out of a catastrophe? Edna says her first thought was for Steve and for her mother—she had to get them both out of danger. She said I would laugh at what her next impulse was: she rescued a record album of the Bach festival under Casals at Prades.

As I remember the Trojan story, Aeneas at the sack of the city carried his aged father Anchises out on his shoulders, but he must have returned to retrieve the notes he had taken during the siege. That is the impulse of any writer. Once my family was secure what I would myself have chosen to save are the typescripts of the books-in-progress that have weighted down my desk for years. Theodor Reik relates that when he asked Freud, in his late years, how he would sum up the crux of life, the old man's answer was *"Liebe und Arbeit."* I don't know of any wisdom to surpass that.

I have no illusions about my stuff being immortal, or about the present draft being indispensable. Even Carlyle, when Mill's housekeeper burned the manuscript of *The French Revolution,* sat down and rewrote it, probably better. And when T. E. Lawrence left the only draft of *The Seven Pillars of Wisdom* on a train, he too started over again. But impulse is not reason, and my impulse would be to save the old sheets.

Do you remember the traditional riddles—if you could save only your mother or your wife, which would it be, et cetera? They were meaningless, because you can't put riddles to love. The question of what you would save out of a disaster is not meant as a test of where your first allegiances lie. It sheds an indirect light, much as dreams do, upon the kind of person you are and the symbols you live by.

For us Americans, in our peaceful lives, it is mostly a question to play with. But there have been other people for whom there was no playfulness in it. I think of the roads of Europe crowded with refugees in the last war, each carrying a few things most cherished. I think of Anne Frank, and how she had to leave even her diary in the heap of rubbish when the Nazis swooped down on her hiding family in Amsterdam. I think of some of the children wandering across the face of Europe, clutching some pitifully shabby doll that was at least a thread tying them to their former security.

What would you try to save, if a not unimaginable disaster sent you wandering across the face of America? Clothes, paintings, books, jewelry, some old letters, stuff to beautify yourself with? It was Thoreau's idea (and he was right) that a man should shed his bric-a-brac and encumbrances, however glistening, and should always be prepared to travel light. In our rich consumers' civilization we spin cocoons around ourselves and get possessed by our possessions.

I have a notion that there is a double pulse beat in what we all strive for. One is to be linked with others, the second is to know who we are. It is the quest for connection and the quest for identity. I think that what you are likely to save comes down to one of the two. If you are alone and bereft, you save whatever symbol ties you to those you loved. If you are with kin and friends, you save whatever reassures you of your own identity, under the blows that seek to crush it.

February 23, 1953

We had to move from the house we have lived in for seven years, and we are camping in an apartment for a few months until we can move into a house we have bought. This means a double moving, and I leave to your imagination the chaos it involves. All uprooting is painful, because it means severing yourself from old memories as well as encrusted habits. "Continuity with the past," Justice Holmes used to say, "is not a duty; it is only a necessity." That is as good an argument against moving as any I have heard—even better than the high cost of furniture vans, and having to eat for days amidst packing cases, and whatever happened to the shirts I bought last fall?

Once we have accomplished our second moving, which will be in June, I intend to stay put. The mortgage may be galling and the furnace bills outrageous, the walls may sag, the smell from the East River may grow more pronounced, and greener pastures may seem to beckon elsewhere, but this time I mean to remain until the trumpet call of Judgment Day.

My two big trials in the past weeks have had to do with my books and papers. I fear I am a man who lives by books, as some men live by their cars and clothes and bank accounts, and some women by their houses and furnishings. I have been a book hoarder ever since I was ten, when I first began my adventures among the secondhand bookstalls in New Haven. In most cases I got my books or kept them because the encounter with each of them had left a scar on me, and each time I open the book the scar aches again, however faintly.

Imagine, then, how it feels to leave most of my books—except for some current ones—sitting in their packing boxes until we have made our final move. I shall feel only half a man until I can liberate them from their enslavement.

But the grueling experience has been that of going through my papers to see what I could consign to the trash heap. There were notes for old lectures, early drafts of books, illegible scribblings on the backs of envelopes about forgotten incidents, enthusiastic projects for novels and stories never written, yellowed pages I had kept from newspapers and magazines, essays from college and graduate school days, notes taken in Germany during the war, letters from friends I had kept for their affection and hate letters I had kept for their spleen.

I must have spent close to a week burrowing through this mountain of random print and writing, but I am glad I did it. A good businessman takes inventory of his stock and material every year or half year. A writer or teacher is likely to let a decade go by while his notes accumulate and his early freshness decays.

As I went through the heap, three things happened to me. First, I found how much of the mountainous mass I could get along without. Second, I got acquainted with myself again. I found myself stirring the embers of earlier phases of my career with a pleasure and a pain that you seldom get unless you are digging up old love letters or writing your autobiography. Third, I had to come to terms with the parts of myself that I had for one reason or another left behind.

The hard questions any writer must ask himself are concerned with the heartbreaking adventure of every honest thinker who has to seize a little segment of the swirling confusion of the cosmos and try to get its inner meaning before it rushes on and breaks into new forms. Some of us, taking our inventory, may find ourselves a little wronger than others in our past judgments. But the only thing that counts is our honesty in confronting ourselves. Whatever the questions the grand and petty inquisitors of our day may put to others, none of them will ever have the courage to put to himself the Medusa question that turns a man to stone.

2. Any Old Time

December 4, 1952

WHEN I first started writing for daily newspapers, almost a decade ago, I was told that a four- or five-a-week column would set a stiff pace. You never know (my mentors said wisely) when you will have a stomach ache or get into a crash or stop for one drink too many or get absorbed with a girl or just forget. So have a few "barrel" pieces ready, they said, the kind the editor marks AOT—Any Old Time— and files away with a sigh of security.

I did it a few times, but it never really worked. Whenever I was one ahead, it would be only a few days before I would get lazy and consume my substance. The rainy-day column would be hauled out and used on the sunniest of days, when I was able-bodied and sound of mind and wind, and could have written something. Then I'd be back where I started.

As a result, I have been a day-to-day, hand-to-mouth wastrel. This has meant some close calls. Often I have found myself in some small Southern or Midwestern town, after a lecture at the college or the local forum, followed by the routine entertainment. Say it's midnight, and the local telegraph office has been closed since sundown, and the only open one is fifty miles away, and you have two hours before deadline for filing and you have left your notes at home, and you haven't an idea in your head. That's when you review your wasted life and wish you had put an AOT away in the editor's safe.

It's even worse abroad. Say you have been to a Paris cellar café and have found a ravishing girl who insists on talking about Sartre to you in a language that requires your concentration, and you take her to an all-night joint that has good scrambled eggs, and you are about to surrender yourself to existentialism—and then you recall the home office, and you leave her to write something for the mail plane. It doesn't contribute to Franco-American friendship.

Some years ago I got a scare. The boys on the desk had a copy of my page printed up, with a big blank space where my column was supposed to be, and in the center of it a tiny notice that the space was reserved for me but my copy had not shown up. For a moment it shook me. But when I discovered the hoax, I grew cynical about all threats.

Yet I should like to say, with modest boastfulness, that in almost ten years—during which I calculate the dismaying total of at least two thousand columns—I can't remember missing a deadline. Maybe it's because I'm such a healthy ox, or maybe there is some Puritan in the marrow of my conscience.

The question remains: Why the compulsion to wait for the last moment? I think the world is divided into two categories of people:

those who arrive at the railroad station an hour and a half ahead of time and wave the train in, and those who dash up the platform and board it on the run, as in spy movies. Nature or nurture put me somehow into the second class.

No doubt this is something neurotic—the fag end of the romantic tradition about living dangerously on margins. Maybe the psychiatrists have a name for the disease—some kind of "deadline compulsion." I'm afraid to ask one of them, lest I be turned over to the American Psychoanalytic Association as Exhibit A. I should then have to admit to them that I'm this way about everything—catching planes, coming upstairs to dinner, walking into a classroom or lecture hall, applying for passports or visas, showing up for radio shows. No doubt, if I ever reach the heavenly gates I'll just manage to get in under the ropes before they close.

Let me say, in my defense, that too much leeway is degenerating to any craftsman. If I start a column with hours to spare, it sprawls over the terrain. Maybe I need a deadline to give me moorings—at one end, anyway. Like the sonnet form, or the rondel, it sets a frame for your work. If you never had to think about a budget you would enjoy spending less than you do. The deadline is my budget—it gives a finality to my waywardness.

P.S.: I had hoped to consign this column for reserve stock, as an AOT. But it never worked out that way until the deadline—which is now.

3. On Having a Book

December 11, 1957

So YOU put the finishing touches to the manuscript, sweep up all the loose drafts and carbons and throw them into the wastebasket, gaze at the vast bulk of the typewritten pages that have filled so many days and nights of your life—and you ship it off to your publisher. You send with it a covering letter saying: "Here it is. I've done my damnedest, and maybe it's good and maybe it isn't, but I've come to the end."

If you think you're through with it at that point, you're crazy. A woman has a baby once, a writer has a book twice—once when he finishes it, and a second time when it gets published to the world. The first is private, and its agonies and joys are private too. The second is utterly, nakedly public. And the process of public parturition is indelicate, indecent and nerve-rackingly exciting.

As you might guess, these are some reflections on the experience of having a book, such as I am going through now. The baby is a thousand-page trifle called *America as a Civilization*. Thus far the book and I seem to be standing up tolerably under the strain.

Please forgive the insufferable coyness of this language. If there is one thing I dislike more than most others it is an author's whimsy in writing about his book in the imagery of obstetrics. The fact is that writing can't be shared, no matter what source you go back to. You have to conceive, if not immaculately, then at least alone.

The public ordeal comes later. And if I may use the birth parallel for the last time, there is a vast difference between the receptions given to a baby and a book. When a baby is brought home from the hospital, all the reviewers gaze at it rapturously, saying "Oh" and "Ah" and "Isn't he a beauty!" Even your lifelong enemies turn hypocrites on this occasion and suspend hostilities to celebrate the little monster. But when a man has a book, it has to meet the steady, unswerving scrutiny of professionals who usually reserve their ecstasies for other occasions and pleasures.

Not that I'm complaining. Actually I'm a bit addled by the generosity of the critics thus far, and at times I have the uneasy sense that they must be talking about other labors than mine. In the case of some of my past books I got used to spotty weather. It's novel to have the skies so delightfully clement.

I recall one friend of mine who, when he finished a book and sent it to the publisher, used to go off on a freighter through the Panama Canal. I had another friend who wasn't so craven as to flee, but who was stonily determined not to read a single review.

I don't resort to such desperate measures of insulating oneself against the world's slings and potshots. In fact, I have always in the past enjoyed reading the reviews, even the hostile, or should I say imperfect, ones. Any man who takes the trouble to wrestle with you, even if he is hell-bent to throw you, is paying homage of a kind. He may be benighted, but he is your brother under the skin; you and he are locked together in a dialogue against apathy of mind and emptiness of spirit.

I might as well add that I even enjoy all the paraphernalia of being published, which most writers profess to hate. I mean the round of literary cocktail parties, TV and radio stints, interviews, speeches, and even book autographing.

Let's own up to it, O brothers of the writing craft: We all love these little amenities because they nourish our ego, but most of us wouldn't be caught dead admitting it. The worst treason of all is to say you like your publisher and don't regard him as a historic fusion of Newgate rogue, Alcatraz confidence man, and poisoner of wells. Well, I hereby commit treason.

And surely I reveal nothing hitherto obscure when I say that there isn't a writer who doesn't haunt the bookstores after his book is pub-

lished, checking on whether they have the book in stock, whether
they are sharp about reordering, and whether they give it the promi-
nence it deserves. The great events in a book's life are the first reviews, the first big ad, and the wonderful moment when you stop in
front of a bookstore window and see the volume standing there like a
shimmering star. After that everything has to be anticlimax.

How did I dare (my friends ask) try something as nightmarish as
the effort to crowd the sweep of American life onto a single canvas?
Well, if I had known what it would involve, I might never have had
the brashness to attempt it. But as the girl said to the judge, explaining her baby, you take one step, then another, and suddenly you
know you have gone too far to turn back.

And when the book is finished, does a writer have a sense of letdown? I don't know about others, but for me there was a sense of release, not letdown. But there was also the feeling of detachment about
the product. What had been for so long part of me was now *not-I*,
something separate, having a being of its own and a destiny of its
own.

Of one thing I am certain. The pain and the fun were in the writing. And I wouldn't exchange them for all the pleasures of Babylon
and all the treasures of the Indies.

GRANDEURS AND MISERIES OF A TRAVELER

1. Farewell, My Lovely

December 31, 1951

I WANT TO WRITE about someone unimportant to almost everyone except me. She was my Lovely, my old car.

She was born in 1937. They tell me a fourteen-year-old car, like a fourteen-year-old dog, is not old but ancient. Maybe so. Yet she comes of fine stock—a LaSalle, which is a branch of the Cadillacs. During the last war my former car got caught in a garage fire, so my mother-in-law lent me hers, and I liked it too much to give it back. Which is how Lovely came into my life.

She would rarely start for anyone else, because she was death on batteries and carried on a cold war with the ignition. But we have a secret language, and when she feels the pressure of my foot she is shaken by a great throbbing and pounding of her heart, and she lunges forward.

She still has the old gearshift, and not one of those newfangled Dynaflows or Hydramatics that take the skill and muscle out of driving. She has a motor like a ten-ton truck, just as powerful under your hand, and just as hard to manage. Thus we drive through the woods behind the house, or over the pasture, or clattering along the countryside, eating up the miles—and also the gas, oil and water.

The care and feeding of lovelies is one of the problems of modern man, and so it has proved with mine. Her radiator is choked with rust, and she leaks like a Washington bureaucrat talking to a friendly newspaperman. I use the garden hose to fill her with water before each trip, and even the shopping distance to the village and back—some ten miles—leaves her panting and spouting steam.

She eats gas as if I owned a wildcat Oklahoma well. As for oil, she is a Moloch and devours it as if I were in the top income bracket. I was studying the figures for the American oil reserves the other day, and I wondered whether the compilers knew about my car.

Her speedometer gave out a long time ago, so I have kept her speed low by guess and by instinct, to stay within the traffic rules. The water gauge once got excited when the radiator was in one of its boiling-over fits, and it shot up to infinity—never to come down again.

She has no radio, because it would interfere with our rapport when we are on trips together. The last time I tried the windshield wipers, they had gone the way of all flesh. Since she has no heater, the ice that gathers on the windows makes her look like Kris Kringle distributing gifts to the Eskimos. She has only one front light, and when I drive her along the misty ocean roads she is like a groping one-eyed Polyphemus. She is an ungadgeted creature, stripped to her essentials in an age of gadgetry.

Yet I feel about her like a war pilot about his old crate, as a mysterious companion who has been with me through the great crises of our life together. There was the time we struggled on the Adirondack roads and blew three tires in a single day. There was the night I had to get out every five miles to calm a boiling radiator, until the garages closed down and I gave up. And there was the time I had to catch a plane, and my Lovely rebelled, and I had to abandon her halfway to LaGuardia and hitch a ride. As for her encounters with the police, they are best kept dark—as with any lady.

All this belongs in the past tense, for my Lovely is no more. A few months ago I lent her to a friend, and a vast dinosaur of a motor carrier swooped down on her from behind. Luckily my friend, who is a great sculptor, is still alive, but my Lovely stands in the pasture back of the house, nestling against the woodshed, all stove in.

As I read about the new car models, with their glistening polish and their bedizened chassis, I feel not a stir of envy. When I go to my reward, I expect to be met at the heavenly gates by my old LaSalle, throbbing and sputtering, but her wounds all healed.

Until then, farewell, my Lovely.

2. The Far Places

May 9, 1954

AT THE RISK of seeming frivolous, I want to confess that each time I have seen the name Dien Bien Phu, it has stirred me with its aesthetic rightness. It seems the exactly right name for one of those exotic far-away places that we associate with the storybooks about the French Foreign Legion, like the Percival Wren standby, *Beau Geste,* that infested the movie houses when I was younger.

I have been reading a good novel with an Indochinese setting, Norman Lewis' *A Single Pilgrim.* He presents the kind of mixture I like of love, politics and adventure in far places.

It seems that Lewis has traveled everywhere—evidently one of those Englishmen who takes a brisk drink with you and apologizes for not staying because tomorrow he must be off for Ceylon or Saudi Arabia. "I am convinced," he tells us, speaking of the Far East, "that these countries are about to enter upon a long period of seclusion and that when they emerge—probably not in our generation—they will be utterly transformed." Hence he travels—"before it is too late."

Those phrases, "not in our generation," "before it is too late," have had a depressing effect on me. "In every fat man," Cyril Connolly has written, "there is a thin man screaming to be let out." Similarly in the most sedentary bookish man, like myself, there is a furious traveler straining to be let out.

I suppose I have crisscrossed the American continent almost as often as Mrs. Roosevelt, and I know Europe a bit. But that kind of travel has become cozy and tame. I look at myself in the mirror, count my years, and remind myself sadly that I have never yet been in Asia or Africa, South America or Australia.

Don't ask me, please, why I haven't. I give myself all kinds of reasons—I had to get a book finished, I had commitments, I hadn't the funds for far travel—but they are all lame reasons. The fact is that the traveler screaming to be let out of his sedentary prison just doesn't scream loud enough—or he screams just for show. He reads names like Dien Bien Phu, muses a bit over a dream—and takes the plane for Syracuse.

There is a good passage toward the close of *A Single Pilgrim* where the middle-aged hero, about to take a rash plunge into Vietminh territory, decides to take the chance, with the reflection that it is exactly when you are middle-aged that you ought to live dangerously. The young still have too much to live for. "Things ought to have been arranged, thought Crane, so that prudence thinned away with the hair and you passed by stages toward total recklessness."

It is a good thought, but I suspect the middle-aged are too lost in creature comforts and too caught up in their schedules to profit from it. The only way they ever get to the far places is by acting on some sudden impulse—the way H. M. Tomlinson tells about his sudden decision to board the cattle boat that took him to *The Sea and the Jungle*. Alas, the capacity to act on impulse gets trained out of you by what we call "responsible living." The civic triumphs over the dream of the exotic.

A decade from now I shall probably be writing a little essay on how I still hope to see Rangoon and New Delhi, Java and Saigon. I think this is probably the real sin against the Holy Ghost—the putting off of longed-for experience, the never getting "to the lighthouse."

A learned colleague of mine at Brandeis, Simon Rawidowicz, tells me a fascinating item about the doctrines of the Pharisees in the days of the Second Commonwealth. It was their idea that God does not regard Himself as knowing everything because He created everything, but that He continues to be a learning God, even studying some of the commentaries on the laws He Himself handed down. This notion of a learning God, ever restless to know, is what burns in the heart of everyone who longs for the far places.

3. West to the Far East

December 31, 1954

I AM a lucky and happy man, if a man who half lives his dreams can be counted both. I am about to take off for a trip to the Far East. By the time you read this I shall have been in Tokyo for several days, on the first leg of an air journey that will take me through the Asian capitals. This is the first round-the-world trip I shall have taken, and the first time I have been in Asia. I have the same greenhorn's suspense before the unknown I had when I went out on my first foreign assignment ten years ago, more limber and more innocent.

I wrote a column last spring called "The Far Places," in which I confessed unashamedly that I was a sucker for distant place names and their glamorous associations. Maybe my publisher, Dorothy Schiff, felt I had better be packed off before my fantasy world got the better of me, or before I got so old that my blood could no longer be stirred at the sound of Samarkand, Moulmein and Sumatra.

My routing reads Tokyo, Formosa, Hong Kong, Singapore, Djokjakarta, Bangkok, Saigon, Rangoon, Calcutta, New Delhi, Bombay, Karachi. I shall see cities and men, and nations newly awakened to the blessings and burdens of liberty, and fabled exotic places and their women, and priests and pagodas, carvings and dancers and temples, dirt and disease, and swarming millions sleeping in the streets.

I know I shall not come back the person I went. I shall be, in Edmond Taylor's phrase, "richer by Asia." A man starts on a long journey taking account (he thinks) of everything. He gets his tickets, renews his passport, scurries from consulate to consulate for numberless visas, gets himself fingerprinted, has sore arms for days from typhus, typhoid, smallpox, cholera and yellow-fever shots. He sends word ahead to every city, asking for interviews. He gathers a folderful of names and addresses of people whom he will probably never see. He sits late into the night with colleagues who have just come back from their Far East beat and gets from them the whole body of lore which knowing newspapermen hand on to each other as the heritage of their craft.

Yet amidst all these preparations what he doesn't reckon with is the risk of being transformed by his inner experience, as Paul was on the road to Damascus.

Let me speak of externals as well. Every man has an image of what he wants to look like when going off on a long journey. But my two young sons, who had an idea of their own, took care of it for me. They outfitted me in the best tradition of the political reporter as viewed in the cloak-and-dagger movies and the TV dramas. This included tweed coat, blue Oxford shirt and baggy slacks, dun-colored shoes, an Army trench coat which I first wore ten years ago in Europe, and finally a crushable gray hat which my sons insisted had to be worn with the front brim pulled down almost to my chin.

Children, like women and savages, have a wonderful sense of the ritual accord of form and function. I think my sons figured that if I could be contrived to look a bit more like Gregory Peck stalking a covey of Communist spies I might manage to slip over from Saigon or Hong Kong into Iron Curtain territory.

Alas for the image, the reality of foreign reporting in our time is wholly different. The forces that shape the future are not discoverable by having interviews with generals and statesmen, or covering the big international conferences, or skulking about with a false passport under an assumed name. The difficulty with political reporting is the same as the difficulty with political analysis—you have to know what you are looking for before you can know where and how to look for it.

4. The Law of Austere Hedonism

Brussels, June 10, 1956

BY THE TIME you read this I shall be in the Belgian Congo, probably at a place called Stanleyville where an intrepid explorer, with a public-relations eye on the history books, uttered the undying words "Mr. Livingston, I presume?" It all happened very fast. I was firmly set for a summer at home at North Sea on Long Island. But one night about ten days ago we were at a dinner party, and Edna was deep in conversation with a redheaded man while I was discussing journalism with a blonde from *Vogue*. The man told Edna he was getting up a small party of newspapermen to fly to the Belgian Congo, and Edna spoke up in a wifely way and said, "Why not my husband?" The man didn't seem to have a ready answer, so he said to come over, and I left the blonde reluctantly and perhaps forever. He turned out to be Stanley Markusen, of Sabena Airlines, and we agreed that I would join the party headed for the Congo.

I have a simple principle for the conduct of life—never to resist an adequate temptation. It has seen me through many moral quandaries. My test is this: Lying on my deathbed and reviewing the sequence of my life decisions, will I be sorry or happy about how I made this one? I call it the Law of Austere Hedonism, because a man on his deathbed is far removed from the trivia of life's duties and inhibitions. The austere part of it comes from setting an exacting standard for the temptation to be adequate. The long perspective of a dying man burns away the petty pleasures and leaves only the truly happy and fulfilling experiences.

So I applied the Law of Austere Hedonism, and I asked myself how I should feel if I had to die without ever having been to the Congo. I moved fast, took only a few days to find my passport, get police proof that I had no criminal record, secure a visa and get booster shots that swelled my arm as well as my immunity.

What does one wear in the Congo? My son said a pith helmet, because only mad dogs and Englishmen et cetera, but I had an image of those *New Yorker* cartoons of explorers in pith helmets who always end up in the cooking pots for a cannibal dinner, and I decided No. How about one of those all-purpose Gable-Hemingway jackets with big pockets, that make you look rugged and devil-may-care like a hunting guide? Yes. And light ankle-high shoes that never show dust? Yes. How about a gun and a camera? Well, I am not Cartier-Bresson nor Robert Ruark. If an elephant charged at me I should be too startled to shoot him with either my Remington or my Rolleiflex, so why pretend? More likely I would note for my diary his proportions and my sensations, and bound off in prayerful flight.

So my family bundled me in my cab to Idlewild, and the boys shouted, "Good trip to the Congo," and the cabbie turned around and remarked, "Some jokers, huh?"

The itch to gad about the world is something I hope never to lose. I don't measure a life by miles flown or driven, but I count it a high passion to be restless for faraway and exotic places. I think I should rather end my years as a man who has written of what he has seen and known within a far-flung frame than as one who has collected riches or power or "done high deeds to pass all men's believing." Until the other night I scarcely expected so soon to be flying down toward the Dark Continent. But once the original shock of novelty and surprise has been absorbed, you come to take it for granted, like a trip to Chicago in the old days of the railroad.

5. My War with French

August 6, 1954

I HAVE DECIDED that in a man's personal war with a foreign language there is no substitute for blood, sweat and tears.

I have tried hard enough. Getting the hang of strange words and syntax is an impulse that has always been in my blood. If you spend

any time as a foreign correspondent, you are bound to become a dab-
bler in languages. Over the past decade I have tried out my German
in war and postwar reporting from Aachen to Berlin, my pitifully
meager Italian from Milan and Trieste to Rome, my even more
meager Spanish in Guatemala, my Yiddish in Israel (to the mild dis-
approbation of the Israelis, who prefer Hebrew), my French from
Paris and Geneva to the Côte d'Azur.

But I have to confess that my command of these tongues is still as
fragmentary as the surviving ruins of the Druid temples. My efforts
to communicate in them have amused my victims as much as their
fluency has bewildered and frustrated me.

The French have a way of describing those who murder their language. Such people, they say, "speak French like a Spanish cow." I
feel like a couple of cows.

There are American travelers who march through France like a
conquering army, talking only English and outraged because the foreigners don't seem to grasp it. There are others who are helpless and
apologetic about it, but make no effort to learn because it seems so
completely out of reach. I fall in a third group—those who try and
try, and fail.

The first time I saw Paris, which was ten years ago, I brought a
schoolbook French to it along with the confident hope that several
months in France would make me sound like Jean Gabin in the
movies. I don't. Each time I have returned it has been with a mounting fury of disgust at myself for being so impermeable to the language
I love.

My adventures with French have been a little like my adventures
with swimming. I can plunge in, and I can splash around a good deal.
But my progress is always stopped by my fear of letting myself go
and floating. "Give yourself to the destructive element," said Conrad,
"and it will bear you up." But the waters look deep and dark, and I
shy away.

The fault doesn't lie with the words, which I understand well
enough. My Cassell's Dictionary is pockmarked with my notations. I
can read a French novel or play, or a book on politics or economics,
and I devour the Paris newspapers. But when it comes to listening to
spoken French, the words all roll into one indistinguishable jumble of
sounds.

The trouble with French, I find, is that while each of the printed
words has an identity of its own, the spoken words all sound alike. If
I could institute a single reform in France, I should like the French to
take breathing exercises and take a breath after each word so that a
simple foreigner could follow them, as he does in a book. The reason
why a young American child in France learns the language better
than his parents is that he starts with the spoken French, not with the

literary, and for him the unit is the molten flow of phrases hot from the impetuous speaker.

My other insurmountable hurdle is trying to put English into French. I have managed to make myself misunderstood in a score of cities and a hundred French villages. My great trial, even worse than the effort to get the simple things I want, is to keep from getting the things I don't want, or, when I ask directions, from going to exactly the places I want to stay away from.

In composing my thoughts in French I fall between two impulses. One is to plunge immediately into the subjunctive mood and then try to extricate myself from the swamps and quicksands I thereby encounter. Nothing can quite match the look of disbelief on the face of a gendarme in Marseilles or Toulon when I have made one of my dives into the subjunctive and am working my way out. The second way is really a kind of cheating; it is to forget tenses, conjugation and sentence structure entirely, and use only the unadorned infinitive. That was the method the G.I.s adopted to fulfill their primitive needs. It works in a rough kind of way, but you can't always be fulfilling the same needs.

6. Never Forget, Dear One

Florence, August 15, 1954

WHO HAS not had the flashing moments of experience when the day-to-day grubbiness is washed clean and Faust's "Ah linger still, thou art so fair" becomes a kind of injunction-to-remember? The sad fact about many of these unforgettable moments is that you do forget them. Against the risk of oblivion I hurry to jot down a few memories of Europe in the summer which even a meathead traveler like myself still retains.

I shall remember driving in the Alpine sunlight in the little Quatre-Chevaux (as the four-horsepower Renaults are called) with the sure irresponsibility of neither knowing nor caring where we would next stop to eat or sleep . . . waking at an inn at Sallanches, in Haute-Savoie, with a looming mountain outside our window . . . typing my columns, usually after breakfast, in a variety of rural settings, my two-finger efforts followed with fascination by a huddle of waiters, small boys and town hangers-on . . . the rehearsal we stumbled upon one morning in the courtyard at Aix-en-Provence, the conductor and orchestra in shirt sleeves and jerseys, the casual but absorbed listeners standing or sitting in the small archway while inside the courtyard the Eden of hundreds of seats was kept from us by the flaming sword of a bedraggled guard.

I shall remember St. Paul de Vence, ringed by the ancient wall which seems put there to keep it from falling off its hill . . . the old hospital at Beaune, with the wizened, ancient women lying in the alcove beds along the sides of the refectory . . . the room at the Pitti Palace in Florence with the "Annunciation" by Leonardo and near it the two Ghirlandaio portraits . . . the cold Apollonian friezes of antiquity, and the busts of the warriors and emperors who have become steel engravings in the books, contrasting with the passionate splendor of the Risorgimento painting.

I shall remember how we took a boat from Hyères to the Ile de Porquerolles and found there the Auberge de l'Arche de Noé, with an atrocious big painting of the animals on Noah's Ark covering the wall behind the bar . . . and the fishermen after work gathering on the village square in front of the inn to play their century-old games of skill . . . and the steep narrow paths of the still primitive island which we climbed until suddenly we came on a view of the cliffs below us, and the cove between the cliffs . . . and scrambling down the sides of the hill to swim in the clear, cold pool and then lie in the sun in blessed discomfort on the jagged rocks.

I shall remember *Macbeth* under the stars in the courtyard at Avignon . . . and the Palais des Papes, with its vast halls whose present bleakness could not quite blot out the earlier sumptuousness of life of men who confused power with holiness . . . the steep narrow streets of Auxerre, suddenly opening on a gem of a cathedral . . . our picnic lunch on a hill overlooking the Rhone, sitting under the only real tree we could find for miles, looking down at a Van Gogh landscape while we had sardines and tomatoes, and French bread and cheese and peaches, and a bottle of red wine. . . .

I shall remember how we tried to get a room for the night at Porto Venere because the harbor and the village were too lovely to pass by, and every inn was filled . . . and how I found Gino, a handsome young Italian of no special occupation, who in turn found us a deaf old lady up interminable flights of stairs who had a spare room to rent for a dollar and a half . . . waking at dawn in the dingy room to look out over the harbor, with the fishermen already beginning to bring back their first catch, and the nets spread to dry on the dock . . . and everywhere in the warm evenings in Italy the people dressed in their best, walking, walking . . . and everywhere the Italian girls, the Italian girls . . .

At Portofino the white boats gleaming in the harbor in the early afternoon, and the yacht with haughty riggings that is everyone's dream . . . the sight of the riches of the paintings at the Uffizi Palace, and of the Cimabue in the first room . . . the little market squares at Vence, and the terrace in front of the Auberge du Lion d'Or where you can sit and look out at the Matisse chapel poised on the hillside . . . and the room from which I am writing this, while the Arno flows below me, spanned by the makeshift bridges whose timbers rattle as the cars drive over them . . .

This I shall remember, and what Rilke said as he died: "Never forget, dear one. Life is magnificent."

7. What Is Europe to Me?

December 30, 1952

THE POWER SOURCES have moved West and East, and Europe has ceased to be one. Its destiny is being shaped by what happens in Washington and New York—and in Moscow and Peiping. Why, then, do we still go, and why does the phrase "a trip to Europe" still evoke a tingle of excitement?

Maybe you will answer that Americans go to Europe because they have money and power and want to show off both of them. In other words, where we once went as provincials we now go as proconsuls.

The truer answer is that in a curious way we are still learning from Europe—even from a Europe in the shadows. There is a pace of living in France or Italy or Greece which is wholly unlike our own too fervid pace. Even the Hollywood and Broadway people whom you are now likely to meet in Paris or Rome don't stay there solely because of the eighteen-month tax rule that lets them save a sizable sum. They stay because there has always been a two-way legend between America and Europe. The legend of America has been that of New World riches and freedom. The legend of Europe has been that of Old World culture and life-understanding.

When I was coming out of college in the early 1920s, a "trip to Europe" didn't move me much. Perhaps it was because I came of an immigrant family, and the greatly moving symbol for us was still America. All the legends still lay westward, and after college I didn't go to the cafés of the Left Bank or the bullfights of Seville but to the Midwest and the Rockies. Later, in the thirties, my generation was too absorbed with the depression and the New Deal, too caught in the struggle between American pathos and greatness, to care much about Europe.

In 1944-45, when I went to Europe as a war correspondent, I had a chance to see England, France and Belgium, Holland and Germany, for the first time. I saw a Europe largely in ruins. I went back in the summer of 1949, adding Italy, Trieste, Yugoslavia and Israel to my geography of memories. Now I return briefly to visit a Europe rising out of the ruins of one war but obsessed with the possible ruins of another.

Sometimes young people ask me what to do about getting into their careers—be it law, medicine, business, journalism or any other. I'm afraid I usually give them corrupting advice. I ask, in effect, why they are in a hurry. Have you, I say to them, sat in St. Mark's Square in Venice? Have you taken the bus by slow stages through the towns between Milan and Rome? Have you sat in the theaters of Paris, not understanding much but strangely happy anyway?

What I mean, I suppose, is that something about Europe thaws out the tenseness of too purposive Americans. They will have a long time ahead to make money or a name—or perhaps only an ulcer or heart leak. Europe may give them some perspective.

Paris, September 25, 1957

Was it Horace Walpole who remarked that to the man of thought life is a comedy, but to the man of feeling it is a tragedy? Actually in the Europe of today the epigram could be reversed: When the European thinks about his situation he is ready to cut his throat, but when he lets himself just swim on life's tide, he finds that life isn't so bad—in fact, to know just how to live sensually and aesthetically is the greatest of arts.

There is a double impulse now in Europe—one, to unite it through the Common Market and other tying devices; the second, to look outside Europe for the sinews of power. I wrote about the Italian dream of oil power in Iran, Libya and Morocco. Well, the Sahara dream of the French—of a stretch of desert dotted with oil deposits, coal, iron, natural gas and even uranium—is a much older one, but it is now on the verge of coming true. Unless I miss my guess the Germans too—especially after Adenauer goes—will be tempted to put their investment surplus into the "underdeveloped" areas and seek political adventures there as well.

That is one reason why I cannot believe that Europe will unify itself. There are technicians and political leaders in Europe—Monnet, Adenauer, René Mayer among them—who are working to create a European community in coal and steel, in trade, in atomic development. When it comes to the test, each country takes its own currency steps, while the British and French are racing to become nuclear powers.

To the economic troubles, and the nuclear politics, and the temptation to get a cut of the resources in Africa, add the ideological splits. At best, even if Western Europe united there would still remain Eastern Europe. And there is a third Europe as well, including Yugoslavia (which is balancing between the two) and Germany (which is split between them).

Is there then a Europe? I fear not. There is mainly a sense of a common economic plight, and a common nuclear danger, and a common resentment at being caught between the Russian and American giants. But these are negative elements. What really unifies Europe is an attitude toward life—what I spoke of above as the impulse to swim on life's tide, and to make an art of the process. Whatever the politicians may say, the traveler in Europe feels it all around him—a way of life, not a structure of power nor an armory of solutions.

Cagnes-sur-Mer, France, August 7, 1957

Beset by frustrations and fatigue, there are moments when the American traveler in Europe asks himself the inevitable question: What is there in Europe that draws me to it? What is Europe to me?

Last night I turned these questions about in my mind as I sat under the arbor of the Auberge de l'Arche de Noé, on the little island of Porquerolles, sipping a beer and watching the French vacationers dance on the village square to an improvised orchestra. I knew that when I came back to my room at one of the other inns a colony of ants could be waiting to attack me, that the bed would be rickety, that the W.C. wouldn't work and would be dirty besides, that the hot chocolate at breakfast would be indifferent or worse, that when we resumed our drive the next day we would get stuck behind some huge gasoline trucks on the *corniche,* and that we would get into a traffic jam at Cannes or Antibes or both.

That is pretty much what has happened. One way or another, it rarely fails. Europe to me is all these irritations. Yet, as in a marriage, the sum is far more.

Europe is the mother of nations, the source of the New World of which we are part. Without Europe's energies we would not today exist as an American nation, although it is true that we have also helped revive her energies in turn. Europe is the memory of past grandeur, recalled in its ruins. Wherever you step is historic soil. Britain, France, Spain, Italy, Holland—all have been the scene of great empires of the past. It sends a shiver of mortality through Americans to reflect on how brief and spindly their own power may turn out to be.

But Europe is also a place where people are close to the primitive things in life—to food, clothes, song, to hours spent at the table, to tired-eyed youngsters toddling after their parents late at night, to country produce piled in the market stalls, to bread carried along the streets by everyone. And despite its ancient grandeur, Europe is a new continent, where people are learning the ways of industry, technology, refrigeration from us, and are like children caught up in the delight of learning.

Europe to me is a wilderness of separate sovereignties. It is borders crowding each other, and customs officials who examine your *carnet.* It is petty bureaucrats who look starved and defeated, and who stamp endless forms for you. It is banks where they give you a number which you hand to an old man sitting in a cage, counting out incredibly worn bills of every nation.

But Europe is also the place where your sense of wonder is constantly renewed. It is mountains ringing you from every direction. It is a turn in the road, and the sudden glory of a town poised on a hillside. It is a forest of masts in the harbors of fishing villages, and an old man mending a net on the dock, and sturdy fishermen chugging out to sea at dawn. It is young men with the look of being trapped in a blind alley. It is young women with a sense of style and a wisdom in their bodies—before they take on the dowdiness of middle age. It is old men and women in black, with volumes of history written on their wrinkled faces. It is children everywhere, old beyond their years, wise before their time.

Europe is where the vaunted doctrines of democracy and progress took a beating. It is dictators ruling where once there were dynastic kings, and parliamentary governments in constant change that have lost the belief of the people. It is Communists who mock the freedoms that never put their hooks securely into the European mind. It is millions of Jews who rotted away in the camps or were burned in the furnaces, while the European conscience was too tired or confused to cry out in agony against the unutterable evil.

But Europe is also a band of international volunteers saving the day at Guadalajara, and an obstinate old man at the ebb tide of British fortunes speaking undying words in the House of Commons, and French resistance fighters retrieving what Pétain and Laval had dirtied, and students dying for an idea in the streets of Budapest.

Europe is Italian warmth and French grace and British gallantry. It is the sun gleaming on a Greek village. It is dingy little churches and museums lit up suddenly by the canvases of a Greek who lived out his life in Toledo. It is Chagall in a town in Provence, still caught up by the Chassidic mysticism of the old Polish *shtetl*. It is Picasso trying to find a fragmented frame of order for his Spanish anarchist passion. It is Chaplin on the Riviera, still torn by the attraction and repulsion of his American memories. It is Mendès, wondering why the French will not let him build a rational technocratic society. It is De Gaulle, waiting for his destiny with a patience possible only in a society where time is so riddled with tragedy that it has become timeless. It is Malraux, writing of art but dreaming of a not impossible European Man.

Europe to me is a civilization fragmented by wars and split by conflicting idea systems. But even its fragments yield a brilliant light. And someday it may be compelled to become a whole again.

8. *Lo, the Poor Sightseer*

Venice, September 15, 1954

I RISE to defend one of the most maligned of creatures—the American tourist in Europe. The tourists are here in droves, as they have been in Paris and Florence and Salzburg. They are not always attractive, and some are naïve and ignorant, while those who huddle together on the guided tours are a fair target of caricature. But if you dismiss the American traveler wandering over Europe as a gull and an idiot, you shut your eyes to one of the revolutionary facts of our time.

I have seen so many sightseers this summer that I am close to being an expert on them—and a sample. I estimate that I have trudged up and down a quarter-million stairs, walked hundreds of miles through museums, churches, cathedrals and galleries, seen thousands of paintings, strained my eyes in the dusk and shaded them in the glare in order to squint at an unending row of depthless masterpieces, driven five thousand kilometers through five countries, admired several million tons of ruined masonry, seen thousands of murals, frescoes and cupolas, leafed through reams of guidebooks, and paid out a small fortune for entrance fees to the galleries and tips to their superannuated curators.

Each day my feet have ached from walking, my neck has been stiff from peering at walls and ceilings, my brain has reeled with painters and their works. When I have gone to bed I have scarce been able to rest tired eyelids upon tired eyes. I have fallen asleep dreaming of Giottos and Carpaccios and have awakened briskly determined to start the whole round over again.

Obviously there are tourists and tourists. After months of acquaintance with them, and elaborate research, I submit the following types:

First, the Herd-Conscious Tourist, who can't go anywhere unless he goes in droves, and who doesn't know anything until the guide has told him. Like all herd men and herd women, this tourist never really learns from his experience. In spite of moving thousands of miles he never budges from home.

Then there is the Boy-Conscious Young Female Tourist, who hopes to find adventure more easily where she is not known. I wish her luck but, alas, the pickings are usually poor.

Then there is the Art-Conscious Tourist who says (with Baudelaire or some other Frenchman), "I have seen everything twice." I have seen these weary tourists sitting around in hotel lobbies, discussing the techniques of some obscure painter with a pretended Oscar Wilde boredom, and I can report it is not an exhilarating experience.

Finally there is the Unconscious Tourist who wanders about, dazed but dutiful, in a world he never made, mainly because a trip to Europe has now become a social necessity in the upper-middle-class groups.

The neck-craning tourist has been kicked around in print by every snob and slob of our time. It was not always thus. In the eighteenth and nineteenth centuries almost all the great European writers and thinkers did the Grand Tour of the monuments and galleries and the intellectual centers of the Continent. Men like Boswell, Gibbon, Goethe, Byron made good literature out of it in their diaries and notebooks. Ruskin and the Brownings, Shelley, George Sand and Wordsworth were all tourists. What's wrong with belonging to such a breed?

Those were the centuries of self-improvement, when Europeans were discovering old and new worlds and were not ashamed to admit their consuming cultural hunger. The tourist is still, at bottom, a self-improver—but who dares admit such a damning fact about himself?

In the earlier centuries travel was difficult, and the great and near-great and not-so-great endured every discomfort in their single-minded passion for sightseeing. Today the tourist can travel with speed and comfort, but he is shamefaced about his passion and has to bootleg it. Even the newspapermen, who pretend that they have come to study the "German problem," may be found wandering around Venice looking not for Nazis or Communists but for narrow canals and faded paintings and buildings that bear the proud scars of centuries.

What I am saying, I suppose, is that the tourist who moves about to see and hear and open himself to all the influences of the places which condense centuries of human greatness is only a man in search of excellence.

If this sounds too strenuous and self-improving, let me add that the only regret I have about my life is that I didn't—somewhere about the age of nineteen—board a cattle boat or a freighter and go off somewhere, anywhere. Just to invite my soul and try my mettle and see what life was like under another sun, in another part of the forest.

9. Each Island May Be Paradise

February 1, 1957

AFTER A DECADE of annual winter exploring of the Caribbean islands I think I have come to know somewhat the island-hopping tourist, especially the American breed of the species. By now I have been to Nassau and Andros of the Bahama group, Haiti, Puerto Rico and Jamaica of the Greater Antilles group, Trinidad and Tobago of the southernmost islands right off the coast of Venezuela. If my luck and money hold out I hope to visit one of the British Windward or Leeward group and one of the French West Indies.

By the time I am eighty I shall have left none of the accessible islands untouched, and if I am no longer solvent I shall write a guidebook and keep going anyway.

Homer (or whoever wrote his epics for him) obviously got the idea for his *Odyssey* from knowing the many islets of the Aegean Sea. Ulysses was simply an island hopper of the Greek variety, and if he were alive today he would be writing about his adventures on an expense account from *Holiday* or the *New Yorker*.

We Americans are lucky because the airplane revolution has brought within our ken the whole mighty treasure of the Caribbean islands. The jump from one island to another, which used to take a day by boat, now takes less than an hour by plane.

There is a streak of Ulysses somewhere in each of us. I feel the same way about the Caribbean islands as I used to feel about playing poker in my salad days: The reason it was exciting was that you picked up each new hand with the tingling expectation of finding a straight flush, or at least three aces. The world was rebuilt afresh with each draw of the cards. Similarly we travel not to get a rest or be entertained but because each island may turn out to be the Paradisial one.

There is a new kind of tourist coming to the West Indies. The typical tourists in the earlier days were usually the elderly retired businessman and his wife or the young honeymooners. Now you will be more likely to see young married couples who have left children and job behind for a few weeks, perhaps because they want some time together to recapture the honeymoon feeling.

They are deeply American. They are restless and Faustian. They have transferred their acquisitive impulse to the West Indies, and they acquire islands as they tend to acquire anything else. They have become island hoppers and island droppers: "When we were at Antigua," "I picked this up on St. Thomas," "There's a little place we found on a hill at Cap Haitien," "We never go to Montego when we're in Jamaica."

It is for them that the island glories are unfurled—the fishing trips, the raft ride down the rapids, the pretend-voodoo performances in Haiti, the night clubs and floor shows on the gaudier islands, the carnivals wherever the temperament of the people calls for them, the Creole beauties where you are lucky enough to find them, the steel bands and limbo dancers and calypso singers.

Mostly you can tell the American tourist by the equipment he carries with him. We are a gadget-minded people, with the handsomest luggage, the best still and movie cameras, containers for everything, lotions galore, and snorkel masks. If there are ever any trips to the moon or to Mars we will bring our equipment with us. I sometimes feel that for the camera enthusiast nothing exists unless he can snap it. Perhaps it is not the experience that counts for him but the recording of the experience.

Here on Tobago, which is a half hour by air from Trinidad, there is nothing to do except lie in the good sun—which is my own definition of Paradise. That Egyptian Pharaoh who got into the history books by being the first to command the worship of a single god had the right idea when he picked out the sun-god Amon for the One God. And Robinson Crusoe had the right idea too; when he picked the latitude and longitude for his fictional island to get lost on, he fixed almost exactly on the location of Tobago.

I have a dream sometimes—the dream of vacations not just for the rich people, as in the past, or for the luckier and more venturesome middle-class people, as now, but vacations for all. Why not? You may say this would be outwelfaring the welfare state, but again why not? Sure, these islands would get more crowded than they are. But there are lots of them, and right now most are nearly empty.

10. Geographics Anonymous

Rome, September 9, 1957

FALL HAS COME, but happily, here in Europe, there is no grim reminder that signals the end of my misspent summer.

I shall go on for a number of weeks doing what I have been doing—driving around, studying the map, struggling with impossible languages over unworkable telephones, tagging behind oil trucks on perilous narrow seacoast roads, scanning magnificent architectural ruins and beautiful living women, collecting guidebooks that I rarely read, to art treasures that never seem to end, spelling out newspaper and magazine stories with the help of dictionaries that never help you on the irregular verbs, staying away from the big-name stuffed shirts and picking up conversations in several broken languages with whoever will take the trouble to talk to me.

The only thing that changes at summer's end is that the crowds thin out, and you can get a room at the first *albergo* or *pensione* that you try, instead of the fifth. Opera and music leave the open arenas and courtyards, which is their summer abode, and go indoors. At the museums you no longer trip over thousands of religious school-girls being shepherded through the life of St. Francis of Assisi.

I suppose I am learning as I go. The itch for self-improvement is incurably American, and in some cases it has been known to last a lifetime. But by the time a man is in his mid-fifties he ought to be old enough to know better than to spend his time at the hopeless task of stocking his mind and testing his taste.

My own drive, I suspect, is somewhat different. I got a glimpse of it the other day, when I spread some maps out and lost myself in a dream journey, much as a drunkard goes into a daydream of a not impossible lost weekend.

I happened to be at Sorrento, in the midst of the Siren land, and I should have been more than content. But I said to myself that I had never been west to Bari, or all the way south to the toe and heel of Italy, and never been to Sicily or Sardinia. How could anyone face the final accounting, and have to confess that he had never been to Sardinia?

There is a whole tribe of us who suffer from this map mania. Some are lucky and can fulfill at least part of their drive, and I count myself among them. Others have to take it out vicariously, via travel books and films, and sometimes their frustrations mount until they go off with a wayward bus or even with the bank's funds.

Nor has anyone ever discovered a cure. In the case of drunks you have at least the solace of being able to join a branch of Alcoholics Anonymous, where you and your fellow sufferers can give one another the needed moral support to break the habit. But I have yet to hear of a Geographics Anonymous, to deal with the poor stiffs who get drunk on maps and can never get over the impulse to board a plane, a train, a boat or a bus, wherever it may go.

The technique would be simple. A little band of former Geographics could join together, and each would recount publicly to the others the agonies he had suffered when he had the map mania—how it had broken his friendships, martyred his family and depleted his funds. If there were a waverer tempted to go to Patagonia or Cambodia, they would rally around him and cheer on his resolve to stay at home and spend his summer at Fire Island.

There are two ways to travel, and I am torn between the two of them. One is to allot your time between the places you love best and skip the rest, no matter what is happening. Thus I can imagine dividing your summer between Paris, Venice and Rome, with Venice taking the lion's share of it.

The other way is to move around fast, and manage to be where things are happening when they are happening. I am speaking of both political and cultural life of Europe. This would mean being at Edinburgh for the music, at Blackpool for the Labor conferences, at Pamplona for the bull running, at Verona for the opera in the Arena, at Venice for the Film Festival, at Berlin for the theater and art festival, at Siena for the Pallio (the medieval horse race), at Tel Aviv for the opening of the new Auditorium.

On this theory my sons were a little disappointed, when we struggled up Mt. Vesuvius, that we had come there during the long quiescent spell between eruptions. Obviously the idea of being on the spot when things happen can be run into the ground.

11. On Being a Memory Collector

April 17, 1958

I'M OFF AGAIN on an unlikely journey of exploration. Again, as on previous journeys, I should like to get to some places I shall be seeing for the first time—if they let me in.

I am heading first for Tunis and perhaps Algeria, then for Egypt, then Cyprus, then Jerusalem, then Budapest, then Warsaw and back to Western Europe.

What I am exploring for is firsthand impressions among peoples who are challenging us and what we believe. They are largely the colonial peoples who have revolted against the rule of the West under the banners of a new nationalism which is rich in slogans but veils the future in obscurity.

I have few illusions about how much I shall learn on a trip on which I cover much distance in little time. But I have always been hungry for far places, and have been content to taste them even when I could not digest them. I am a little like a glutton at a feast, given only a brief hour and avid to try everything before the viands disappear.

I am no longer as young as I was, and we approach a dark hour for the world. Others may be collectors of money or possessions or artifacts. I guess I am just a memory collector. I want to see many places, especially where there is trouble going on, and store up in my mind persons and places and memories before the lights go out.

I am not talking only of the possibility of atomic war. Even without utter destruction, there are regimes and ways of life which live for a brief moment and are replaced.

My sons, for example, have seen the France and Italy of today, and they will be able to compare them with those of later years. But I never saw prewar Europe (my first visit was in 1944)—the Paris of Proust and Jean Jaurès, the Berlin of Walther Rathenau and Thomas Mann, the Russia of the great writers and liberals even under the Czar. I never saw Budapest or Prague in the days before Hitler and before Communism. I never saw China in the days before the Communist Iron Age.

The point is that civilizations are not like pressed flowers under glass, or those lava-encrusted figures from Pompeii that you see in the museum at Naples. They are living—and dying—things, and you must catch them during the moment of life or not at all.

If a regime is continuous, and if there is a great sense of tradition, as with the British and the Italians, then its cities retain successive layers of civilization. Thus there is still some of Elizabethan England in London. And there is nothing strange about looking out from an apartment whose windows open on the Roman Forum, or on the Piazza Navone which still holds Bernini's great fountains, or in driving from the Emperor Hadrian's villa at Tivoli into the Rome of the great churches tolling their bells at midnight to usher in Easter Sunday.

But wherever the Communists come into power—or the new Moslem soldier-commissars—the past is all but wiped out, and what comes in its place has new evils to replace the old ones, and only an iron-gray flatness to replace what once had a kind of beauty of its own.

Change is the law of life; but what distinguishes one type of civilization from another is the principle by which change takes place, and whether it moves with decency or disaster. In every country to which I am now going the big question is not whether changes will take place—they must—but whether they will be attended by chaos or humanity.

In a review of a book of mine, in the *New Yorker,* the reviewer called me a "dynamist" and contrasted me with Ortega y Gasset, whom he called a "humanist." Well, I have been called many things, but "dynamist" is a new one. Evidently it is because I believe in American dynamism—the restless, continuing impulse to make things over in order to make them better, which is one of the roots of the American character.

But I should have thought that humanism and dynamism were interlocked. The very term "humanism" comes from the Renaissance period, when Europeans rediscovered the emphasis of classical civilization on the human personality. After the stagnation of the Middle Ages, this discovery hit them hard. I like to live in a civilization in which I feel peaceful, almost as if nothing were happening—that is, nothing disastrous. But it is a little like Alice's discovery in Wonderland, that you have to run hard in order to stand still. Many good things must happen if we are to have the wonderful feeling that nothing terrible is happening.

It is the stagnant civilizations, without any true dynamism—like the Russia of the Czars, the China of Chiang, the Italy of Victor Emmanuel, the Egypt of Farouk, the Saudi Arabia of Saud and Faisal—which provide a dangerous opportunity for false and violent dynamisms.

The great lesson of today is that if we are to live as humanists and enjoy the achievements of the past, we must act with dynamism to win the future.

12. My First Night in Cairo

Cairo, April 27, 1958

MY FIRST NIGHT in Cairo was not silvered by any moon over the Nile. I spent it, eight whole hours, at the airport, where I was held incommunicado and under the guard of Zacharia Mohieddin's Interior Ministry cops.

I flew from Tunis via Rome, on a plane that got me to Cairo at the unthinkable hour of 3:20 A.M. I passed police inspection, since I had a perfectly valid Egyptian visa. On the police form I said I was a newspaperman, bent on doing some reporting. My passport was stamped and returned to me, and the police form handed to a busy cop who was leafing through a sheaf of them. I went on to the customs, had my bags passed, and was about to hail a taxi for the Semiramis and a bath and bed, when a guard ran up to say the police wanted me again. They took my passport from me, ushered me into a dingy office where three officers sat—a colonel and two captains—and the questioning began.

Who was I? What paper or papers did I represent? Had I been to Egypt before? Why had I come now? Had I ever written a book about Egypt? Was I now going to write one?

I found myself trying to answer rationally, although I knew that neither the questions nor the answers had any meaning. Obviously these cops had found something suspicious about me or my name and would not let me go until someone higher up told them to. All the rest was a dumb show, put on because these new bureaucrats were feeling their power at the expense of this reactionary American imperialist.

Nevertheless I went through the steps of the dance and asked was there anything wrong, and if so, what? I got no responsive answer, only that I must wait until someone from the Information Bureau would come to escort me to my hotel. I asked how long. A half hour, said a mustached captain in blue uniform. Two hours, said the colonel in olive-drab uniform, and since he was obviously in command I took his estimate more seriously.

Another officer in blue came in, a new one. He was very sorry, but these things do happen in the life of a newspaperman, don't they? Evidently they do, I said. Around 5 A.M. a new plane arrived, and all the officers had to do their duty. I was left alone in the dingy room—alone except for an armed guard, a private with a beret.

The officers came back. A big argument started between Captain Blue and Colonel Olive. It was clearly about my case, since my passport was handed from one to the other, files were searched (the Egyptian filing system has to be seen to be believed), and there was much gesturing.

It was now 6 A.M. Colonel Olive said he felt badly that I had to sit on such a hard chair, so how about the lunchroom? I took a notebook, to keep my Cairo log, and headed for some tea. Private Beret went along with me, planted himself at the next table, gun and all, and took up guard, but quickly fell asleep. He was very young and very tired, so I took the guard over from him and made sure I didn't escape.

Sitting there in that bleak, baleful room, I suddenly understood why I cared about the episode as much as I did. I didn't like being —even for a few hours—in the power of petty bureaucrats who held my name and faith against me.

Beret kept waking and falling asleep, fitfully. At eight-thirty I woke him and we went back to the commandant's office. He was still there, red-eyed now as well as sad-faced. I said I wanted to call the American Embassy. He said it was against his orders.

After a few minutes a large young man, in civilian clothes came in. He was from the Information Office, and he had good news. Everything had been arranged, and I could leave soon. It had been a "misunderstanding." About what, I asked. Well, my name had been confused with a very similar name.

There was a lot of phoning. Captain Blue came in, with his flickering thin smile. "You are an important man," he said. "There is much trouble, much argument for you." I thanked him and said I would rather be in my bath than important. It got to be 10, then 11 A.M. I was weary of being important.

I pressed Mr. Civilian. What was happening? Well, he said, you know how it is. He had reached his superiors, and they had ordered my release. But the military people refused to surrender the body until they had orders from *their* superiors, who (it was the Moslem holy period of Ramadan) had not yet shown up at their office. I was caught in a fight between bureaucrats.

At eleven-fifteen that morning I walked out into the sunlight. My first night in Cairo was over.

I got a number of apologies later from officials. Each had a different version of what may have happened. But a newspaper friend had the simplest. "Your name may have been on an old blacklist, which wasn't updated," he said. "Or maybe someone remembered having heard of it once and didn't want to take a chance, and no one else wanted to take it."

It will have to stand at that. I have tasted the fruits of a police state. I might add that while my mood was a bit soured by it, my judgment was not affected. One thing to be said for the new Egypt is that at least it gave me a visa—which is more than I can say for our Middle East allies—Jordan, Iraq and Saudi Arabia.*

---

* When I applied again for a visa to the United Arab Republic in 1959, I was turned down sharply. Evidently Colonel Nasser was no longer willing to admit a critic of his regime, or else no one would take responsibility for what might again develop into a conflict between two departments of the Government.

THIS BODY, THIS FRAIL FRAME

1. Lying in Bed Late

March 15, 1951

AT THE RISK of corrupting the young, I must sing the praises of lying in bed late. The other day, in reading R. F. Harrod's biography of John Maynard Keynes, I came across a nugget which may change the whole course of my life. Keynes was of a frail constitution, and in order to conserve his strength he lay in bed most of the morning, clearing away his work so that he could get up and devote the afternoon and evening hours to conversation, writing, friends.

Keynes was something of a genius, and I figure that his way of organizing his day might work wonders for more earth-creeping mortals. His example thus lends a garment of respectability to the naked fact of my innate indolence.

During the last three days a flu bug has given me a chance to test this Keynesian theory. Having very late in life made the discovery of the joys and the beauties of this mode of living, I hasten to communicate them to you.

I am aware, of course, of the accumulated prejudices against lying in bed late. They come from the long siege of the Puritan conscience, which associated bed with the devil. But I think we have learned since that His Satanic Majesty is as present at your desk as he is under the cozy comforter.

The other root of the prejudice comes from the fact that America used to be a rural society, when you had to get up with the sun and go to bed with him. President Truman, for example, still keeps farmer's hours. His diarists say he is up at six and has cleaned everything off his desk by ten in the morning. It is a terrifying thought. I remember a wise British Fabian, Graham Wallas, who used to tell me to be sure to avoid the pitfalls of the bureaucrat and the businessman who spend the best morning hours answering routine letters. The fresh bloom of those hours, Wallas used to say, should be for the creative tasks. The letters and the chores can wait.

They say there is something decadent about late rising, and that this decadence will lose us our world while Spartanism alone will save it. The fact is that only the military regimes make a fetish of getting up at dawn, and everyone knows that military regimes exist to destroy, not build.

Ralph Waldo Emerson used to relish those extra minutes in bed in the morning, after waking, when he would "digest his dreams." What America needs is statesmen who are, like Lincoln, at least in part dreamers; reflective men who have the leisure to dream and take the time to digest their dreams, instead of dashing off that letter to Senator Zilch.

But the best part of lying in bed late is not these considerations of state, but the sheer lazy pleasure of it. If you are enough of a dictator in the household, and the flu bug bites you, you get your breakfast served on a tray. You scrawl some notes of ideas you got in a late conversation the night before, you get sudden inspirations for books you will never write.

Meanwhile the household is humming around you: the phone ringing, the bells buzzing, the delivery boys delivering, the dog barking madly at every fresh intrusion, the private universes of the children soaring and collapsing and soaring again—and you in the midst of it all, propped up against the pillows, like the quiet spot in the center of a tornado. The best thing about lying in bed late is that you learn to distinguish between first things and trivia, for whatever presses on you has to prove its importance before it makes you move.

But in the end even a flu bug doesn't retain its lethal power forever, and you come back to reality and to the alarm that wakes you at seven to face the grayness of the city streets.

2. The Ills of the Flesh

March 11, 1953

I THINK BACK to the great ones of the past half century: Woodrow Wilson, Lenin, Lloyd George and Clemenceau, then Mussolini, Hitler, Franklin Roosevelt and Stalin. Now they are all dead: Lloyd George and Clemenceau of old age, Wilson and Lenin of cerebral hemorrhage, Mussolini and Hitler of political violence, Roosevelt and Stalin again of cerebral hemorrhage. The death of public figures, like the death of friends, has always moved men to meditate upon the ironies and vagaries of fate, and the ills of the flesh.

Not that I am any more morbid than most. I tend to be a hardened and congenital optimist. According to the famous Sheldon categories, I am a mesomorph (the chesty type—restless, brash and extroverted) rather than an endomorph (short, fat, amiable) or an ectomorph

(the "lean and hungry" look of Cassius, full of conscience and worries). I don't easily fall prey to floating anxiety.

But whoever you are I suppose such floating anxieties do hit
you when you are middle-aged and your friends and associates
start dying off. Then you discover that you are a walking pesthouse,
harboring dozens of actual and potential diseases, a breeding ground
of powerful bacilli, a once cunning contrivance of degenerating
tissue and nerve cells and failing electrical energy.

You become conscious of every organ in your body. You look at
your tongue in the mirror, examine more carefully that eye that
tends to get bloodshot in the morning, study the sedimentation rate
of your blood. You watch your weight daily or twice a day on the
bathroom scales. You start studying diets, having read somewhere
that salt is your enemy and also that fat people get felled by heart
disease. You begin to have pangs of doubt about your chain smoking.
You wonder whether the pain in your chest and your shortness of
breath are real or the products of panic. You discover your kidneys
and colon. You keep a chart of your blood pressure readings, treasure your fluoroscopes and X rays as if they were Modiglianis and
Braques. You follow the progress of cancer research and clip the
articles about new remedies to file away—just in case. Every tiny
ache in your fingers becomes a harbinger of crippling arthritis, and
every cough may usher in t.b. The cabinet over your basin gets
filled with an assemblage of ugly-looking bottles with mysterious
hieroglyphics on them.

In short, you turn into a sickly Narcissus, except that instead of
being in love with the reflection of your youthful image in the stream
you are fascinated by the death's-head you see forming in it.

There is some consolation for us in the new medical research
which is prolonging the average life span. But I have to add that
every medical advance we make turns us increasingly into a nation
of medical worriers. All the "drives" by the associations—heart, cancer, polio, t.b., multiple sclerosis and the rest—manage through advertising methods to make us more conscious of each disease than of
any others. The sum of the drives, no doubt, saves lives. But it turns
too many of us into pulse-watching, liver-studying, heartbeat-count-
ing glooms.

A debate has raged whether hypertension or the stomach ulcer
is America's national disease, characteristic of the pace of our living. I cast my vote for a third disease—namely, the habit of watching
diseases, a habit illustrated by the present piece.

3. Griefs and Joys of a Hobbling Man

January 11, 1954

IT IS almost four weeks since an ankle fiasco left me hobbling about on one leg with the help of barbarous crutches. But the ordeal does not lack its compensations. My wife and children exempt me from household chores and hover over me, fetching and carrying books and papers. When I walk into a classroom or the City Room or onto a lecture platform, there is a whispered comment that a man would do anything for a dramatic entrance. At parties I find that the beautiful women strangely cluster around me, moved by an obscure compassion where otherwise they would wait arrogantly to be approached.

Thus there are joys as well as griefs in my state. My more cynical friends have even suggested there may have been an unconscious wish on my part that led me to slip down the stairs and twist my ankle. I can only answer that a little psychiatry is a dangerous thing.

If it was an unconscious wish, it has also proved an accursed one. With your body immobilized, everything becomes disproportionate. Your vitality narrows to the chair and the four walls of the room in which for a time you languish. Everything focuses on the injured and offending limb, so that you watch its progress back to health as if everything in life depended on the tensile strength of a bit of bone and ligament and a little network of blood vessels.

One result of being half helpless is that you get a new perspective on everyday normality. It takes forever to wash and dress and undress, to go downstairs for meals, to get in and out of a car or a bus or a plane. All the daily routines that I had come to take for granted, because they had become second nature and could be done with hardly any attention paid to them, now loom as feats of planning and contrivance. The trivial grows to such monstrous proportions that it becomes the heroic. It takes this kind of rude jolt to remind you—if you have forgotten—what a beautiful and intricate thing the human body is.

I know that with my slight and temporary disablement, I have no right to talk of things that the permanently disabled know all too well. But I think my half-comic interlude has given me an insight into the tragedies of the crippled, the polio victims, the amputees, the war wounded, for whom their destiny is no joking matter.

I recall an essay on "The Philosophy of Handicap," written in the *Atlantic* about forty years ago by Randolph Bourne, who had a bad hunchback deformity which did not prevent him from becoming a brilliant literary critic and political journalist. Bourne described the successive phases of humiliation, bitterness and acceptance through which a handicapped person passes, and how he learns (as F.D.R. later learned) how to live with his body and transcend it.

The classic case of the human triumph over destiny is that of Franz Rosenzweig, the Jewish philosopher and theologian. Nahum Glatzer has written a moving book about him, *Franz Rosenzweig: His Life and Thought.* In early manhood, Rosenzweig found he was suffering from a form of multiple sclerosis, which paralyzed one part of his body after another, including his powers of speech, until finally he could "talk" only through a specially built typewriter with his wife's help in guessing at his words as he moved his eyes over the keys.

One of Freud's students, Robert Wälder, reports that when he was told about Rosenzweig's heroism in carrying on his life and writing for years under this burden, Freud asked with some surprise, "Was there any alternative?"

Freud must have known that for most people the easy alternative would have been to give up the struggle. Perhaps his remark betokened a defect in sympathy. But I prefer to think that Freud meant something else—that beyond individual weakness or strength, there is a life force that speaks through us and is the inscrutable answer life gives to the inscrutable whims of destiny.

4. On Being Bitten by a (Little) Bear

May 21, 1958

DON'T TELL ME this country is safe—I know better. For six weeks I traveled through North Africa, the Middle East and Europe, and nothing happened to me. When I got back to these United States I was bitten and clawed by a bear.

I am speaking literally, not in any fancy figure of speech. It has nothing to do with the Russians or the cold war. Nor did it happen in the zoo, nor hunting in the north woods. It happened in Boston, Massachusetts, which has been part of civilized America for some generations. It was after a lecture I gave the other night, and I was sitting with a few friends in an apartment, and we were drinking a bit and talking a lot. There we were, sitting and drinking peacefully, and there was the bear, sitting with us. Then suddenly he bit me.

I know what you will ask, so I will answer it before you do. No, I had only one or two drinks. I was sober then, and am sober now.

Since being bitten by the bear I have learned a lot about how people react to a simple statement of fact. I have found that a truth is much harder to get accepted than a fable or a lie—provided that the truth has anything unfamiliar about it.

For example, a taxi driver will ask me how I got my hand in a bandage—a dozen of them have asked me by now—and I say quite matter-of-factly, "I was bitten by a bear." There is always a moment of dead silence, and then the driver stops at the next corner or light, turns around to face me, and says almost menacingly, "Now, you wouldn't be kidding me, Jack, would you?" I feel I owe some explanation, so I start, "Well, there we were having some drinks, and there was the bear—" but I realize I am only making it worse.

Or else the reaction I get is the "Ha, ha, that's a good one" type. "Was it a male bear or a female?" is the way it will go at the other end of the dialogue stick. Or, "That's the first time I've heard it called a bear"—this one usually accompanied by an idiot grin as broad as Bert Lahr's.

I don't know why the American thinks that any unusual happening must somehow be connected with sex, but I can report that he does. I could tell you a lot at this point about the legendry of American marriage, and what the husband tells the wife when he has had a mishap. And I could also tell you about all the possibilities for punning that revolve around the bear.

There is one thing that puzzles me about all the incredulity I have met. I wonder why Americans are so scared of being taken for suckers. We don't mind so much being wrong about something, or being ignorant of something, or not caring a damn about something. But we can't stand the idea of rising to some bait, of being taken in with some line. We will do anything to avoid being a poor fish and flapping in the sun and looking foolish. It is the last indignity. It is positively un-American.

That's why, when you try to say you have been bitten by a bear, you meet the painful silence, the look of quick surprise quickly frozen on the face lest it give one away for a sucker, the knowing leer that replaces it.

In Dorothy Norman's fine exhibit, "The Heroic Encounter," there are many examples of how ancient and primitive artists celebrated the struggle of the hero with lion, bull or dragon. The hero slays the lion and throws the lion's skin symbolically over his shoulder.

Alas, mine was a very unheroic encounter, and instead of my getting some of the bear's skin he got a fair stretch of mine before he was carried struggling off the battlefield to his kitchen cage. I had done nothing to provoke him—in fact, in my passion for peace I tried not even to notice him. That may have been my error. Maybe, like the rest of us, including Arthur Miller's heroes, he felt that some attention had to be paid to this bear. He clawed at my foot suddenly, and when I tried to get him off, he bit into my hand. I confess that I was not pleased and let out a bellow of pain which only made things worse by scaring him.

I'm glad I was not off in Jack London's Yukon country, but close to modern medical help. My hand got stitched, became infected, got unstitched, soaked, dressed. I got a tetanus shot, swallowed a treasury of antibiotics. To be sure, my doctors have confessed themselves handicapped by never having treated a case of bear bite before, but I have the virtuous feeling of contributing to their education, as the bear contributed to mine.

When Jacques Cartier explored the islands around Newfoundland, he reported finding a polar bear "big as a cow and white as a swan." Well, my bear was neither. I don't want to prettify or romanticize him, as if he were Pooh-bear in Milne. I am no St. Francis and I would just as soon never meet him again. He looked innocent, but turned out mean.

He was one of those pet bears, or Mexican honey bears, of whom I am dismayed to learn there are thousands across the country. This is carrying the idea of pets pretty far. Not that I am against the efforts to bridge the gulf between man and the other animals. I like shaggy dogs, even when they don't live up to their stories. And I have read somewhere about the German—or was he a Swiss?—who used to train arithmetical horses who could do difficult problems of calculation and carry on a conversation by pawing the ground with their hoofs.

Maybe this particular animal was a reading bear. I feel chastened when I reflect on his having chosen to bite my writing hand, which I also rely on heavily for my particular brand of typing. Maybe he meant it as a form of literary criticism.

If so, he is doomed to disappointment. The column must go on —as this one shows.

THE AGE OF AGING

1. Fifty

December 18, 1952

IN TWO DAYS I shall be half a century old. After your twenties or thirties a birthday of any kind means a little stab of pain at each milestone on the downhill road from the youthful peaks. For a woman it is the fortieth birthday that hurts most, since it means she must henceforth fight to keep her looks and must watch her children growing away from her. For a man the fateful transition is later—probably at fifty.

That's when you look back at your half century of life and ask what it amounts to. In a culture that values success and achievement so highly, the question "What have I done?" is the most probing and disconcerting one a man can put to himself.

As for myself, I find that "What have I done?" carries with it the burden of too great a pride. It is the kind of effrontery to which the answer of the worms that eat you is final.

I remember one of my contemporaries who was considered a "promising young man" until he was well in his forties. When you reach fifty you have to make up your mind that if you have not already done something about your promise you never will. At the midpoint of your life you still expect things to happen, but not so vast. When the alarm rings and I stir myself, I find that (except for some warning creaks in my bones) I feel as eager as I did at twenty-five. The day ahead may turn up a good phrase, a beautiful face, a sudden welling up of feeling.

Which means that we all run on two clocks. One is the outside clock, which ticks away our decades and brings us ceaselessly to the dry season. The other is the inside clock, where you are your own timekeeper and determine your own chronology, your own internal weather and your own rate of living. Sometimes the inner clock runs itself out long before the outer one, and you see a dead man going through the motions of living.

When I was twenty I had the conviction of fatality, like Keats, and was sure I should be dead before twenty-five. Now that I am fifty I have the illusion that I shall live forever. In my saner moments I know that I am an oldish machine steadily running down. But what makes all of us something other and better than a machine is this curious animal faith in a life that seems to have no believable bounds—a faith you can't back up because it rests on no evidence and is pure illusion, but there it is.

I distrust the heroics of the recent Hemingway character who at fifty in Venice acts like a dying lion. But I still get carried away by a good fight, so that sometimes I don't heed the sound of the ending gong. Looking back at some of my scuffles I agree with Winston Churchill that "nothing in life is so exhilarating as to be shot at without result."

I hope the time never comes when I don't get angry at injustice and laugh at stupidity and make out on the distant shore the dim lights of an emerging maturity for mankind. Anger and laughter and the capacity to see visions still seem to mark off a man from a mannikin.

I shall not pretend that as you grow older you don't grow crotchety. You do. You get harder to live with. Your reflexes slow up. You watch your weight on a daily scale. You wag your head solemnly over the follies of mankind. And you may even start worrying about the morals of the young generation.

But the real sadness of fifty is not that you change so much but that you change so little. It is true, as one of Dostoevski's characters put it, that the last half of your life is lived with the habits contracted in the first half. My only birthday resolution is to change some of my habits every year, even if for the worse.

At fifty you count what life has showered on you: a cluster of children, a wife whose life rhythms are like your own, an itch for writing, friends and places that leave scars on your memory, an unquenchable pleasure even in a world that at any moment may explode into smoke.

2. The Dance of Middle Life

May 4, 1955

SPRING HAS COME in earnest abandon, and the other night I had a fling and danced most of the night. I confess I was helped in my dancing by the fact of having Benny Goodman there with Lionel Hampton and Teddy Wilson—a trio that hasn't been together since the war. The boys did some very fancy business in making music together. As for me, I had an Einsteinian sense that time, space and reality had all merged and vanished.

At what point in the history of the West was it that social dancing

came to be linked with the idea of romantic love? It must have
been somewhere during the old regime in the French court, perhaps
under Louis XIV. But behind these formal dances were the centuries of country dancing, boisterous and with a lot of kissing; and
behind them in turn were the dancing girls in the Hindu temples,
and the ritual dances of religion in every primitive tribe, and the
courtship and fertility dances.

When I was a teen-ager this whole emotional history of the race
flowered in my imagination, and in my daydreams I saw myself
swirling about a dance floor with a creature of unimaginable grace
and beauty who leaned her cheek against mine and surrendered herself to the rhythm of our bodies.

Alas, the reality was that I used to haunt the stag lines at the
Saturday night neighborhood dances in New Haven. On the few occasions when I could get at the pretty girl in the red dress my steps
were clumsy and my conversation lacked the kind of verve that
pretty girls in red dresses seemed to like. She would quickly signal
to some leering Valentino to come to her rescue, and back I headed
for the stag line and, heartbroken, went home.

I finally learned to dance somewhat, mostly at college (my style
is still that of the 1920s, when you took long sliding steps), but the
great turning point came a few years ago when I rediscovered dancing in middle age. Despite the association of youth and the dance,
from Natasha in *War and Peace* to Scott Fitzgerald, dancing is not
for the young alone. Sometimes I think that dancing, like youth, is
wasted on the young.

If you doubt me, then go to any good dance place and watch
the reedy young college girls and the crew-cut boys down for the
weekend. They hardly move their feet, but shuffle along sedately
like weary old people, spending most of their time looking at each
other and talking. For them the dance is mainly a way of exploring
each other's personality.

If you watch the cavorting couples burning up the dance floor,
they are likely to be middle-aged people who have children at high
school and college. Having launched them on life, they are now
ready to relaunch themselves, and they are out on the town, either
renewing their marriage or breaking up someone else's.

I sing the joys of middle life, when we are all rediscovering continents we have hitherto been too inexperienced to explore. The
pleasures and pleasantries of life become more precious as the
evening hours draw near, and we savor each vanishing moment.

Sure, too often we make fools of ourselves. "The middle-age rebellion," says Edmund Bergler, "is the measles of the late forties
and early fifties." And he adds that what afflicts men in middle age
is the rebellion against the "inner torture-machine" which is work-

ing overtime because of the fears of unproductiveness and approaching death.

This is clever, and may even be half true. But I am tired of hearing middle age described as a second childhood. It may also be the start of a deeper and more sustained melody within the great life theme, not the approaching end of the life cycle but the start of an epicycle within it. Doubtless the fear of death does enter, but fear can be healthy if it reminds you that the hour is getting late and there is much of life still to be enjoyed.

The music starts again, you rise from the table and try not to notice that your joints are a bit stiff, and soon you are caught up in the rhythms of body and spirit that we call dancing. Let the young have their rock 'n roll and their jitterbugging. Give me the calmer joys that are expressed in the dance of middle life.

3. Oh, to Be Eighty

May 19, 1952

BERTRAND RUSSELL was eighty yesterday. I watched him on TV as he spoke his birthday message via tape recording. To millions he is a man for whom the advancing years have brought wisdom without blunting the edge of his mind, a man who gives each of us the hope that he need not become a senile old fool when he has reached the age of creaking joints, rheumy eyes and slow reflexes.

The other day I had fresh proof of what a man can be at eighty, from my old friend Alexander Meikeljohn, who came to Brandeis University to speak to the seniors. Like Russell, Meikeljohn almost convinces me that Shaw may have been on the track of something in *Back to Methusaleh*. Vigorous, witty, utterly fearless, Meikeljohn told the students how he had become president of Amherst College forty years ago, when he was himself forty, and how the trustees had ousted him; how he then had created the Experimental College at Wisconsin, only to have it shut down after a few years; how he had gone out to San Francisco and started an adult education school there which again had closed down.

By every standard the world uses, I suppose he would be judged a failure. Yet as he talked to us, buoyant and still irreverent, we knew he was a successful man because he was an exciting one.

In that children's classic for adults, *Gulliver's Travels,* Jonathan Swift tells of the Struldbrugs, unhappy old men and women who could not die, yet were "incapable of friendship and dead to all natural affection." I am worried about that tribe. At sixty-five the average American male has twelve years and eight months to go, and the American female has fourteen and a half years to go. As a nation, we now live to almost eighty. Yet we treat our old people as if they were the most boring of Struldbrugs.

And I fear that the old people think of themselves that way. That classic quip of Justice Holmes when he and Justice Brandeis were quavering down a windy Washington street and saw a pretty girl with skirts whipped high—"Oh, to be seventy again!"—always gets a laugh because it seems so improbable. Which is our verdict on old age.

Americans have little real devotion for their old people. We repeat by rote the injunction to "honor thy father and thy mother," but we make little more of it than the tinsel commercialism of Mother's Day and Father's Day.

Oh, we try to be humane enough. We pay out billions in old-age social-security payments. We put out dozens of manuals on "how to keep your parents happy while living your own life." We have "Conferences on the Aging," in Washington. Henry Churchill has even come up with some special architectural plans for "housing the aged."

We do everything for the old people: we are fond of them, we tolerate them, we take care of them, we speak jokingly of their crotchets and frailties—we do everything but respect them.

The reason we don't give them respect lies in the American habits of thought. We have been taught that success belongs to those with push and youth, and the old people no longer possess either. We think of old age not as the crown of a life but as the wilted butt of a burned-out cigarette, when there is always a fresh one in the pack.

When I get to be ninety and walk along a windy street, I shall sigh, "Oh, to be eighty again!" And I will thank you not to laugh.

4. I Hereby Resolve

January 5, 1959

IT'S A LITTLE LATE in the New Year to be making resolutions. But since this is the time when most of us start breaking our newly made ones, it might be well to nail mine down by making public confession of them. Then I won't be able to crawl out of the hole I've dug for myself.

Of course, the will is everything. There is a passage in William James (it is from his *Psychology*) where he hands out some advice that might apply to New Year resolutions. "Keep the faculty of effort alive in you," he writes, "by a little gratuitous exercise every day. That is, do every day or two something for no other reason than that you would rather not do it, so that when the hour of dire need draws nigh, it may find you not unnerved and untrained to stand the test."

Now for some gratuitous exercise. I hereby resolve:

To refuse that last drink, or at least not to take it without consulting my wife—provided she has refused her first one, and is in any condition to stop me.

To stay away equally and judiciously from redheads, blondes and brunettes.

To start writing these pieces at least by midnight, and thus be in bed by 3 A.M.

To turn night into night and day into day.

To catch planes before the ramp starts getting moved away and the stairs pulled up.

To get something done for a change without needing a deadline to make me do it.

To write a few columns for the barrel, so that I can feel I have an intellectual savings account for those rainy, tempestuous nights.

To lose enough weight to reach the Heavenly City of 160.

To keep my accounts, my notes and my desk so that they don't look like Jackson Pollock paintings.

To stop signing restaurant checks, with the quaint notion that this disposes of the problem of payment.

To consider the word, to study the nature of a simple declarative sentence, and to use fewer adjectives, more nouns, mighty few conjunctions. Above all, to spare the first-person pronoun.

To remember that a hanging preposition is no word for a supposedly literate man to end a sentence with.

To write shorter, simpler and more luminous sentences on longer, darker and more complex thoughts.

To keep all future books, if any, somewhere below six hundred pages, and also below five pounds.

To write lightly of serious things, and seriously of light ones, and to have a less foggy notion about which is which.

To write less about sex, sin and psychology, and more about economics, religion and the UN.

To remember where I left my keys, gloves, glasses, wits and other accouterments of civilization.

To start out for appointments with some prospect of getting there reasonably late.

To learn, after fifty-six years, how to swim, skate, ski, rhumba, rock 'n roll, and understand French when it is spoken.

To master the relatively simple mechanisms of our basement furnace before it blows up the house.

To keep my mind on what my dinner partner is saying, even though my deaf ear makes it impossible for me to figure it out except by the wildest guess.

To get over my pride and buy an ear trumpet.

To learn that water is not the adversary, whether for drinking or washing.

To learn to say No.

To stop frying potato pancakes for myself, on the fond theory that I owe it somehow to my mother to continue her cooking.

To stay away from bores who start their conversation by buttonholing me and saying, "Now the trouble with you, Max, is . . ."

To think well of my detractors, against my better judgment. To forgive my enemies, despite their unforgivable sins.

To be somewhat less cocksure in my opinions, less sweeping in my verdicts, less unrelenting in my judgments, less portentous in my utterances, and less of an exhibitionist in general.

To read the Bible. To read the Bhagavad-Gita, the treatises on Zen and the Scriptures according to Mary Baker Eddy. To read Meister Eckhart, Kierkegaard and Jaspers. To read the book on existentialist psychology, now that *Time* has explained it all.

To stay put in these United States for at least six months, without succumbing to the urge to wander.

To simplify, simplify.

To develop a few inhibitions, repressions and conflicts—and a sense of guilt.

To get over the notion that whatever impulse I have is merely a contribution to expressive living.

On second thought, why?

THE FACES OF DEATH

1. *"Do Not Go Gentle . . ."*

June 29, 1955

A FRIEND OF MINE died the other day; for a while I had a pang of remembrance and a sense of a place empty that once he had filled, but soon I forgot him and so (I suspect) will his other friends and his family. The most dismaying thing about death is not the gap that it leaves but the fact that it can be repaired, like a hole dug on the shore which the waves wash and fill up until soon you can no longer see the depression.

The tides of life are far stronger than the emptiness caused by any individual death of a person who has had his life. The death of a child, or a young person, is different; you rail at its injustice and you carry around with you for years the scar of emptiness. So, too, the death of a young wife or husband can leave an aching void, for as with a child there was a failure of fulfillment. But when you read of the death of some politician, some businessman busy until the day of his death, some community leader, some distinguished lawyer, be certain in your mind that, after the tears are dried, life will flow on for those he leaves, and life will soon flow over their wounds and remembrances.

I think I have a fond family and good friends, but I have few illusions that when death comes for me it will stop life for them. Perhaps the best tribute you can pay someone who dies is to share his belief in life by putting your life ahead of his death.

It is this belief in life that makes it difficult for me to envisage death. I know it will come, but it is the kind of knowledge that is external and doesn't reach to the inner conviction. I want to live forever, partly because I am interested to see what will happen next year, next decade, next century, but mainly because I like living and functioning, and I don't want the light extinguished.

If you say that there is immortality or reincarnation or whatever, I answer that it may be so, but it must be a matter of guess and faith, since we have no evidence. Immortality seems to me a literary figure, as if to say that a man lives on in his children, his books or pictures or music, his business, his deeds, and the memory of what he was.

A doctor friend of mine in Jamaica, Len Jacobs, once told me that in all his experience of watching people die there had been only one person who fought against death. The rest took death acceptingly. I have heard this from other doctors as well.

I have often wondered why this should be. Is it because the coming on of death, creeping through the limbs or striking at the heart, has a toxic or enervating effect on the spirit, paralyzing the will to fight? Or is there a seductiveness about death when once it has come into view, like the seductiveness of sleep when you have eaten and drunk too heavily and want only to stretch out languorously and sink into nothingness?

For most people who have struggled through a hard nerve-racking life, there is no will to fight death exactly because death offers them the longed-for chance never again to have to fight. It offers them surcease from the agony of living—which is what Keats meant when he wrote, "I have been half in love with easeful Death." In this sense death may seem to take on the qualities of a new kind of life that lies invitingly ahead, one of serenity, while the life full of tribulations that is left behind may seem a kind of death.

Anyway I am sure that when Death presents himself I shall not spread a red carpet for him. I know that a mature man must "accept" many things—middle age, old age, disease, life crises, the death of loved ones —but he accepts them in the sense that he integrates them with his life. In the case of death there is no life to integrate it with.

Dylan Thomas, who could pierce many of our hypocrisies of feeling, made mincemeat of the "acceptance" of death:

> *Do not go gentle into the good night,*
> *Rage, rage against the dying of the light.*

I feel that way too. It won't do me any good, but I shall not go gentle. I shall rage.

My friends tell me this is an infantile reaction, and that my frothing at the prospect of leaving the world is much like the squalling of a child at leaving the dark, secure womb of its mother and being propelled into the glaring light of a buzzing, booming world.

Maybe they are right, but I think it is healthy for a child to squall and for an old man to rage. The gentle virtues have their place, but gentility is out of place when confronted by the monstrous fact of nothingness. When the *malach ha'movis* (which is my rough way of writing the Hebrew for the angel of death) flutters his lethal wings over me, I shall make it unfailingly clear that, while he is an expected intruder, he is a most unwelcome one.

2. Mistaken Identity

February 7, 1951

A FEW WEEKS AGO a friend of mine for whom I had great affection died. He had been a commentator on military affairs on the newspaper *PM,* and his name was Max Werner. When anyone dies whom you have been fond of, a little piece of you dies with him. But when it is someone with a name almost like yours, a twinge passes through you as if you had somehow cheated death.

In browsing through a back issue of a weekly the other day, I came upon an obituary note on Max Werner—"not to be confused with Max Lerner," the magazine noted with its anxious precision. I was grateful for the reprieve.

It isn't considered good taste to write about death in any but the grimmest portentous terms. We in America walk all around death as if it were a porcupine or the Medusa head itself. Instead of saying that someone dear to us died, we say he "passed away." We dress up our "funeral parlors," as we call them, to look like banks.

Yet since candor is what a column is for, let us admit that obituary pages have a human appeal. Aside from life itself, death is the greatest mystery in life. For a fleeting moment when we read the account we are touched by that mystery and are taken out of ourselves. It is as if a slight welt were left on our consciousness, but the moment recedes, and the rest of the day smooths the welt out.

My friend who died was not the usual kind of newspaperman, but I thought he was a good one, which means that he usually put things in a sharp and memorable way even when he was wrong.

That was why I was saddened by a little incident the day the papers carried his obit. Several of us were scattered around the press room in a courthouse waiting for one of those Communist trials to start, and the usual pinochle game was in progress. "Did you read about Max Werner dying?" someone asked. The reporter whose hand I was watching (neither of us knew the other) turned around and asked, "You mean the fellow who writes that column for the *Post?*" "No, that's me," I answered with ungrammatical feeling, and everybody was embarrassed, and then everybody laughed.

Thus did we mark the death of one of our fellow craftsmen, and thus did mortality brush past me by a margin so slight that it might have been a printer's error.

In the simpler days a man was likely to die where he had been born and lived and was known. No one mistook him for anyone else. With us there is the question of "who was he?"

When the obscure die, they die obscurely. When the great or near-great die, there is great to-do, and many mourn or pretend to mourn. But between the grandly familiar and the obscure is the shadowy area to which an increasing number belong. Maybe it was someone you heard a few times on the air, or caught a glimpse of on TV. Or an actor who played a minor role in a hit. You confuse one liberal lawyer with another, one second-rate Washington administrator with another, perhaps one columnist with another. Then you fold your paper and run for the bus.

This was a man who never found roots. Born in Russia, he never fitted into a Communist society. As Hitler's power grew, he had to move from one country on the Continent to another. He was a student of politics and society who lived in a world surrounded by arms and turned his knowledge to military analysis. He was a wanderer in an age of exiles.

Most of us spend our lives trying to figure out who we are really. And just as we feel we are getting close to an answer, along comes death and snuffs out answer and question together.

But the final indignity is mistaken identity. Just as I would not, alive, be confused with someone dead, so would I resent being stripped of the dignity and the mystery of dying by being confused with someone still callowly alive.

3. Gorgon's Head

September 17, 1956

OUR BIG FOUR-ENGINE PLANE had almost completed the nonstop flight from New York to New Orleans. Suddenly the plane veered up steeply (or was it down?) and we were yanked almost out of our seats. The whole ship shuddered and rattled. I had the pit-of-the-stomach conviction that this was it. The pilot's voice, with a tremor in it despite the clear desire to keep it steady, soon told us. We had just narrowly missed colliding with another plane in mid-air. It was an Army plane and had come up from under us in the clouds and the darkness.

We looked at each other with dazed but relieved unbelief. Plane collisions may happen in the headlines; they never happen to you. By definition you are the one reading the headlines; you are not in them. This was about as close as I ever want to come to sudden death in the air.

My seat partner showed me a magazine article he was reading about the collective insanity of our motor accidents. It compared American casualties in war with the highway casualties in recent years and found the automobile the more deadly weapon. The point he was making was that, however thin our margin of escape, we were safer in the air with trained and careful pilots than driving along a death road where you meet and pass lethal missiles driven by who knows what wild men.

He was probably right, and, as one who must fly at least two or three days a week, I was tempted to draw what consolation I could from his figures and his logic. But that pit-in-the-stomach feeling lasted for a while.

You can tell a good deal about a culture by the characteristic ways it has of killing its people. We Americans tend to die by the way we propel our bodies through space, and we kill not in hate but in hurry.

I suppose that if we don't kill people in the ways we do, we will kill them in other ways equally foolish and dangerous. Every now and then, in a burst of adrenalin rage, I write a fighting essay against the bloody senselessness of auto racing or the kind of sadistic mauling that we call boxing. You could get yourself into an equal state about mountain climbing or the testing of jets.

The fact is that men will go on doing these things, or others like them. Why? I think it is because, in an age when we no longer have to struggle with nature for survival or for a living, the impulse to danger and adventure must find new forms. That impulse is always in us and I hope it always will be.

There is a story in *Grimm's Fairy Tales* called "Little Hans Goes Out to Learn to Shudder." There is something wrong, the psychologists tell us, if you can't shudder. The healthy organism must always expose itself to danger and the unknown. To realize itself, a personality has to confront the challenges of life and stretch itself to the utmost, seeking forms of danger wherever they occur. The neurotic organism, on the other hand, fears to confront danger; therapy is a way of getting to face the unknown and to probe the darkness and itself. And the fact of thus living dangerously is one of the fascinations of analysis, especially since the therapist is always there to protect you. It is adventure with Daddy around.

When you brush the edges of death you cannot help wondering about how you will die, and asking how you want to die.

Will it be quick and clean, as by a heart attack or a massive cerebral hemorrhage? Will it be by a bullet on some landing beach, or sitting unsuspectingly in a chair talking with friends? Will it be in a hospital bed after a slow, lingering and painful disease that wastes the body and crushes the spirit? Will it be in the air, with the sharpness of a thunder-clap, or on the highway, bleeding your life away? Will it be cowering in some cellar while the earth above shudders from the sound of bombs, or on a barren radiation-soaked plain?

For myself, I think I should like to die in one of two ways, because either of them has a kind of grace and is neither degrading nor absurd. One would be a quick death at home, perhaps with my family around me, or sitting in the sun and working. The other would be a very different kind of death—somewhere in far places, among strange scenes, doing something I have never before done, and thus reaching into the undiscovered country.

November 13, 1952

There are a number of collections of the witty or tragic deathbed remarks of famous people. But there are few records of how more ordinary men, caught by the prospect of death in the midstream of life, have made their reckoning with death and therefore with life.

I have just read an article in a Canadian magazine, *McLean's,* that described the death of a friend of mine called Harry Cassidy. I met him first in 1925, in Washington, where both of us were studying at the Brookings Graduate School. He dropped out of my life, as classmates do, but I heard about him from time to time in the Canadian labor movement and in Liberal Party politics, and as director of the School of Social Work at the University of Toronto.

Most of us tend to say about someone who has died unexpectedly that it is well death came upon him with a swoop. But is it always well? For a man who has lived richly there are many loose ends to be tied together, goodbyes to say, thinking to be done about what may or may not lie ahead.

You may ask, How about the agony of protracted pain that a man happily misses when death strikes suddenly? But who among us might not be willing to risk even such an agony, if through it he could hold on to life for a period and come to terms with death? That is the point of Harry Cassidy's story.

It was just twenty-three days before his death that Harry Cassidy learned he didn't have more than a few weeks to live. The doctors found that cancerous growth was blocking the intestine, so that he could be kept alive only by intravenous feeding. Finally the doctors told the dying man. When he heard he had only a few weeks, he said only, "There's less time left than I thought."

Then began one of the strangest experiences of any hospital sickroom. Cassidy wanted before he died to see all the people with whom he had been working. He arranged a schedule for them, discussed how they would carry on their work, bade each of them farewell. He saw the director who was to succeed him as the head of the school, the faculty members, bureau heads in the government, old friends and neighbors. Letters poured in from many of his distant friends, which his wife read to him so that they could pass their life in review. He saw his three children, ranging from fourteen to twenty-four, and talked over with them what they would do with their lives. He talked about God with several of his theologian friends, and whether there was a life to come.

Finally, when there were no veins left to be punctured for intravenous feeding, and the pain had become unbearable, the doctors took out the tubes, dosed him with morphine and watched him die. Harry Cassidy had been given his wish of putting his life in order before it ended.

Did the procession of visitors and the "family seminars" have something a bit ghoulish in them? Perhaps. But Harry Cassidy was at bottom a man of order, and a man has the right to choose to die as he has lived.

One of Cassidy's theologian friends, A. C. McGiffert, wrote a wise sentence in a letter to him. We are, said McGiffert, "scared to death of death, and we push it out of our thoughts as an unwelcome intruder." I think this is the part of Cassidy's story that moves me most, his refusal to be "scared to death of death." Everything in our culture, a culture of youth and life, makes us walk around death. As a result, most of us who talk about facing life avoid every encounter that may bring us face to face with death.

I suspect the reason is that to face death is to be compelled to examine searchingly what you have made of life. And most of us would rather not look at that Gorgon's head. Bacon said that "men fear death as children fear to walk in the dark," but perhaps he was wrong—perhaps what we welcome most about death is the dark, and it is only when we have to face it in the full light of day and make our reckoning of it that it requires courage.

4. The Immorality of Death

April 19, 1957

I GATHER, from some letters published in *Time,* that the editors must have run into considerable reader protest against their review of Lael Wertenbaker's book about her husband, *Death of a Man* (Random House).

I should like to get into the scrap, partly because the subject and the author were my friends, partly because it raises issues that cut deep— about death and love, about pain and courage, about reticence and integrity.

I met Charles and Lael Wertenbaker in Paris a few months after the liberation, and we lived in fairly close touch at the Hotel Scribe— the press headquarters—for two or three weeks.

Wert had grace of bearing and mind, and a manner whose charm almost concealed the wall of reserve strength that was always there against encroachment. Lael had quickness of mind, and a fiery intensity which made it clear that she was never a halfhearted woman, and that she would fight for her man—as for everything else she believed in—all the way.

There were others in that press camp whose names are more resounding today than Wert's, but there was no one who left on your mind so memorably the imprint of delicacy of thought and feeling, of half-mocking affection, and of the fumbling yet not-to-be-denied search for happiness.

As most people know by now, the book is about Wert's cancer, which was in the intestines but had spread hopelessly to the liver; about how he learned that he had only a few months to live; and about what he and Lael did about it.

The issues the book raises can be simply put, but they have no simple answers. Is a wife right in telling her husband the whole truth about a fatal disease, from start to finish? Is a man right in deciding, when he knows he must die, to put an end to his life before he becomes a burden on others and an object of helplessness and self-pity? Is a wife —or anyone else who loves the man—right in helping him plan his suicide, sustaining him in his resolve, and collaborating with him in carrying it out?

These are the issues. And they will be debated as long as the indignity of pain and the wild injustice of death and the deathlessness of love stay with men and women. I have a hunch this book will survive the shocked reviews and moralizing reactions to it. It may even, in its minor way, become a little classic.

Basically it is a love story, not a death story. If anyone raises doubts about its morality my answer must be that it is a moral book because it is life-affirming and love-affirming—and what better tests of the moral do you have? Lael Wertenbaker wrote what she wrote, as she did what she did, because she believed in her husband's dignity as a person.

That is why, when the doctor and radiologist in the little French town had spotted "the Thing," she told him. That is why, when the operation in New York showed it had spread, she again told him. That was why she respected and followed implicitly his fierce refusal to live to the end, when he felt he would no longer be a man.

And that was why she joined his conspiracy to get dosages of morphine that would do more than allay his pain, and why—when the morphine and everything else had failed to kill him—she brought him his razor, and held him up as the blood from his slashed wrists flowed into the red casseroles on which they rested, and then—when he was dead—bound the wrists with adhesive tape and dressed him in fresh white pajamas, and in the morning woke and told their two children about their father's death.

There will be debate about whether this is the wrong or the right approach to courage. I doubt whether the differential of courage enters into it, since it takes courage to live under intolerable conditions as it does to put an end to them.

Nor am I myself terribly impressed by Wert's unreasoning revulsion from the image of bodily decay. Wert had a pride in his body, which is a good thing to have; but he seemed to forget that our bodies are dying and decaying every day of our lives. The episode on shipboard, coming back to France from New York, when his scar burst open, and when Wert and Lael shut themselves in their cabin for days and she tended him in a makeshift way, rather than bring in the ship's doctor—this episode in itself sums up the unreasoning communion of two people which defies any logic we may bring to bear on it.

The strength of the book lies exactly in this communion. I suppose love is whatever breaks and bridges the terrible pathos of separateness of human beings from each other. It doesn't mean much, however, unless it exists between two people who are uniquely themselves. Wert was very much a person, and he clung to his proud self-image in the teeth of the Adversary, "the Thing." Part of Lael's being a person was to respect what her husband was and be faithful to it. And together they formed a little insulated shell against the destructive nothingness of death, which was a good thing because it was whole of its kind.

Their story goes beyond the rightness or wrongness of what they did. I might differ from them in what I should myself do, differ on the issue of suicide, but that is irrelevant. The point is that they did it out of what they so completely were—singly and together.

The immorality, if any, was not theirs. It was Death's.

5. But Who Calls That Livin'?

May 2, 1951

AMONG THE ZANIER IMPORTS from the Soviet Union is the recent news item from *Pravda* that you live longer under Communism than under capitalism. It seems there is a man in Russia 144 years old, and another 142, and each still strong enough to cast a ballot for the single choiceless slate of Soviet candidates. It seems also that the Soviet professors who used to believe that only the Caucasus area produced centenarians have now been reproved for their error and will be lucky if they live at all, not to speak of living to be a hundred. For the new party doctrine is that all of Russia, not just one region, is favorable to long life; and that "in capitalist countries there are very few examples of such longevity."

I took a hard look at myself in the mirror this morning, and found hundreds of gray hairs infiltrating behind the lines of the black. Here I am, scarcely at the half-century mark, with a still small voice telling me that the second fifty are the hardest, and that my chances of getting to be 144 like Vassily Serge Tishkin or 142 like Makhmud Elvazov are practically nil.

What possibilities this opens for propaganda! Think of the slogans: "Capitalism may give you the Good Life, but Communism gives you the Long Life." "Embrace the Leninist gospel. If you live at all, you will live till your dotage."

On second thought, the Communist logic is a bit leaky. Take our friends Tishkin and Elvazov, 144 and 142. They were 110 and 108 respectively before the Russian Revolution ever began. They passed their centenary mark under the hated regime of the Czar. The real test of Communism will come a hundred years from now, when the current crop of young Gromykos will face the unimaginable touch of time.

I recall a book a few years ago by a Soviet professor, on the prolongation of life. The author died of a bad heart in his fifties, and out of all his dreams of eternity the most that I can remember now is that his name began with B.

Then there is my own heredity. My grandmother, who lived a few miles on the Russian side of the Polish border, died at a hundred, and then only out of fright when the Nazi armies invaded her village. But my father and mother, who live in New Haven, are still alive and vigorous, one of them past eighty and the other close to it, and they are still thriving and happy in this capitalist civilization.* I guess all it proves is that stout and sturdy stock counts more than ideology.

What is it that has made men, all through the centuries, so anxious to expand their life span? Bernard Shaw dealt with the problem in his play *Back to Methuselah* thirty years ago. Shaw started with the idea that the ancients of our day are still but infants compared to what they could become. He believed that we could extend the life span from three score ten to three centuries by an act of intense will. If the turtle could live almost forever, he reasoned, surely man could do it. Just as the giraffe had stretched its neck by nibbling for generations at the juicy tops of trees, so man could stretch his life if he but willed it.

It's a pretty idea, and Shaw dealt with it prettily. But is it practical? What happens if your life stretches on but your functions don't? There was the terrifying novel by Aldous Huxley, *After Many a Summer,* with its picture of the rich man who sought eternal life but found only mummylike putrefaction-and-decay-in-life.

As for myself, I think I'd be willing to chance the decay if I could be sure of the three centuries—or even one. I don't pretend to have altru-

---

* For my father's death, since this was written, see page 7.

istic motives about living long. It isn't that I want to advance humanity, or do good for my great-grandchildren. With me, as with most people, the impulses are three: the desire to go on doing work that I'm crazy about; just ornery curiosity about what the world will be like at the turn of the twenty-first century; and, most of all, the sheer unexplainable tenacity of life—holding on to life the way a mongrel dog holds on to his bone.

But my answer to *Pravda* is a simple one and comes from a song written by a capitalist called George Gershwin: "Methuselah [he wrote] lived nine hundred years. But who calls that livin' when no gal would give in to any man nine hundred years?"

My own question is: Who calls it livin' when you have to think and vote and pray the same party line from here till eternity?

6. Intimations of Mortality

December 1, 1958

I SPENT Thanksgiving weekend in bed at our farmhouse at North Sea, with the winds howling around the house and the storm lashing the windows. Somewhere on my travels I had picked up a bug who decided I was a good host and settled in my throat and chest, so I had an excuse to stay under the bedcovers for a few days.

I had an armful of books with me and a couple of long yellow pads to write on. When the logs ran out Stephen and his house guest went out to the woods back of our house and chopped enough more to fill the woodshed and keep the fire blazing all weekend. I could be sick in comfort, and I could agonize with a sense that all was in order around me.

Whenever I am completely well and full of energy, I am not only indecently euphoric but I even begin to think that immortality may be possible—not just your watered-down, spiritualized immortality of the soul, but an actual physical conquest of death. I feel then as Henri Bergson felt in the vision he expressed in *Creative Evolution:* "The whole of humanity is one immense army galloping beside and before and behind each of us in an overwhelming charge able to beat down every resistance and clear the most formidable obstacles, perhaps even death."

But when my limbs ache and I am racked by a cough and my throat feels like a hot tin roof, with or without a cat on it, and even the effort to pick up a book seems too arduous, then I know that the clay of which I am made will someday prove brittle beyond mending. And then I feel intimations of mortality.

Some of my readers ask me why I write so much about death. Isn't it morbid of me? they ask. I suppose the answer is that life is bounded by death. You cannot know the preciousness of life unless you know and face the finality of death.

Freud put it rather differently. "If you would endure life," he said, "be prepared for death." One can understand, in terms of his own life, the bitter overtones of his stoicism. He suffered for years from cancer of the palate and had numberless painful operations. Then when Nazism came the whole world of Central European culture, on which he had built his life and thought, went toppling.

But there is another reason for coming to terms with the idea of death—not to make life endurable but to face and outface the fears that otherwise plague your joy in life.

When you know that this curious, complex, febrile thing called life can be ended at any moment, by sickness or sudden disaster, and that it is bound to end at some moment by the wearing out of the body's cells and the stopping of the heart's pumpings—only then can you make peace with your own turbulent fears and plunge deeply and irrevocably into the waters of life itself. You cannot live constantly in the shadow of a shadow.

There are, of course, traditional ways for getting around the fact of death. One is to deny it by saying that we are immortal and that life goes on after death. Another is to say that it is this life on earth which is the shadow, and the only reality is what follows. Still another is to say that whatever happens is somehow for the best, because God has willed it.

If any one of these answers, or all of them, satisfy you, then they are adequate answers and I have no quarrel with them or you. But in all candor I find them inadequate. Death remains for me a harsh, brutal, irrational fact which I don't pretend to understand, any more than I understand the fact of life itself. No preachments can palliate the whimsicality and injustice with which death comes, and no philosophy or religion can console us for the wild irrationality of it. All you can do is face it as a fact, along with the fact of life, and accept it with bitter protest as part of the package deal that includes life as well as death.

It would be a mistake to conclude that it is all a matter of intellectual will power, and that once you face the fact of death you get rid of the fear of it. I don't suppose anyone ever does, wholly. Every man must wrestle all his life, in one way or another, with the angel of death.

He is lucky if death doesn't get a partial stranglehold on him, even before the final one. I think of Milton blind and Beethoven deaf. I think of John Mill and William James and Max Weber—all of them great social thinkers, all of them stricken at some point in their lives by an anguished blight of the mind which made them incapable of thinking or feeling or caring, until the pall was lifted and they were like Lazarus returned from the dead.

In fact no one does return, and we have no news from the undiscovered country. This is what gives death its mystery and adds a dimension of danger to all our acts of living, and a dimension of emphasis to all our too transient joys.

But now I am well again, and shall begin once more to dream that death can be conquered.

PART II

"The Only Fabulous
Country"

CONTENTS

PREFACE

WHAT UNITES MANY *of the pieces in this section is less a common theme than a common element of fable and a common mood of wonder at the cultural incredible. "The only fabulous country" is what Thomas Wolfe called America, and while his books are too often celebrations by declamation, he caught in his phrase the exact accent of the legendary that I wanted.*

The quality of legend runs all through the American experience, but while it is best captured in our earlier history in the essays in William Carlos Williams' The American Grain, *there has been almost nothing to match them by historians and commentators of the contemporary America. It is almost as if the rawness, crudeness and vulgarity of the American experience were so overpowering that only the immediate critical reaction is possible, and the imagination is exhausted before it can glimpse the outlines of wonder that make both praise and contempt irrelevant. There is much in the following pages that touches on a quality in American life at once primitive and decadent—the assault on the mind, the public exploitation of the realm of privacy, the inanities of Hollywood, the ghastly fervors and fevers of popular culture.*

I regard some of these grotesqueries, as the reader will note, with a mixture of affectionate despair and a perverse refusal to take them seriously as anything but documentary evidence that human life contains idiocies as well as grandeurs. When you contemplate the zanier aspects of American being—office parties, beauty contests, women's fashions, suburban doldrums, commuter adulteries, Hollywood fisticuffs, matinee idols, ripe females, high jinks in Bohemia, movie stars with mammary gigantism, censorship follies, high-bosomed and thigh-bared book jackets, cloacal magazines, imperial press lords who belong in the pages of Gibbon, TV giveaways, and salvation by tranquilizers—your first impulse is to resign from humanity. Yet I am almost as much struck by a certain wild clownishness in it all as by its quite obvious wasteland dreariness which is the despair of the intellectual critics and makes them raise their high brows at it.

It should be clear that while this section deals mainly with aspects of American popular culture, such as city and suburban living, press, movies, TV, advertising, market research, public relations and the public exploitation of private scandals, I do not view it as a segment of American culture, but as a dimension of the entire culture. To call it the picturesque dimension would shrink the meaning of Wolfe's term "fabulous." It is at once pathetic and comic, aiming at the middle-class genteel yet saturated with bad taste, with a quality not so much primitive as grotesque. It has the stuff of folk strength in it, and also the phoniness of the folksy. It is the product of an American transforming energy which turns the everyday into the legendary, and legends into actuality.

For all its sophistication the American mind retains the essential quality of the savage mind: it is vulnerable, capturable, manipulable. Perhaps there is something about the American continent itself, with its vast, still virgin stretch, which makes this quality appropriate. It has its appealing aspect, as is clear from Walt Whitman's poetry, or the novels of Sinclair Lewis, or the innocent-sophisticate amalgam in Damon Runyon, or the adolescent enthusiasms of the boola-boola spirit in college football. It even has a kind of primitive strength in it, as with the leaves-of-grass simplicities of democratic feeling which make possible the marriages of rich young men with girls from the wrong side of the tracks, or the theological leveling involved in a "three-religion culture." Those who recoil from the mongrelization of American life will find this capturable quality of the American mind unattractive. I find myself drawn to it, even though I recognize the weakness that goes with it—the lack or loss of a standard-setting and code-shaping group who have the power to decide what is or is not acceptable in the best circles. And if I am told that American culture is shot through with bad taste, my only answer is that I wish it were. Really bad taste has a vigor about it which the "good" taste of "nice" people has wholly lost.

I distinguish between what is vulnerable and capturable in the American mind, and what is corruptible and manipulable. In the pieces grouped under the heading Hollywood: The Maddest, Saddest Place, *I have probed into one of the tragic themes of American life: what it is that happens to the potential promise of writers and actors when they get caught in the suction force of the Big Money and the giddy blandishments and bedevilments of being a "celebrity."*

In no civilization in history has the road upward from anonymity to celebrity been so accessible to the sons and daughters of the obscure as it is today in this only fabulous country. But if the road is open, to those who have beauty and sexual charisma and a quick wit and talents of the mind and imagination, it is also more crowded with deadly perils than Bunyan's Pilgrim ever encountered, or Dante on the road to hell. The difference is that Dante had his Virgil to guide him through the dangers, as he visited in sequence the circles of hell and purgatory and heaven. The beautiful and the damned of contemporary America have to make their way alone, with only the doubtful ministrations of talent agents, press agents, public-relations counsel, tax lawyers and psychoanalysts, and often it is hard to distinguish between the guides and the perils themselves. Moreover, the lives and loves of these young people combine hell and heaven and purgatory in a single beribboned package, which is always being delivered by a special messenger under an intense light of publicity, and always being opened with the same public fanfare, and usually—after the succession of gilt and tinsel wrappings have been stripped off—is found to be empty.

I have grouped under the head The Private and the Public *some phases of the publicity syndrome of American life, and its rape of privacy. And I have tried to cut more deeply into it in the series* The Assault on the Mind. *It is in the latter that the least attractive phase of the manipulable mind is revealed. Whether it is called "motivational research" or "persuasion for profit" or "the engineering of consent" or "subliminal persuasion," the common element in all these fancy new slogans is clear enough. It is the conversion of the person as subject into the person as object, the approach to the human being as primarily a target.*

This is the underlying aspect of TV as well—a great complex of arts which has thus far been burked by its own inner principle. The corrupting element in it is the fact that the audience is a faceless monster endowed with untold purchasing power, which must be reached and held by programs at once arresting and uncontroversial, because its purchasing power is sold by the network and the agent to the sponsor at fabulous prices which befit the only fabulous country. TV is a great documentary art, whose potentials for bringing the authentic event to the nation have scarcely been tapped. The Kefauver hearings, the McCarthy hearings, and the Presidential conventions all illustrate this. So also do some of the current developments in educational TV, which may prove the greatest single force in the educational revolution to come.

There remains the group of pieces headed The Carriers of Promise. *If it belongs here, it is because of my belief that only through the creation of a democratic intellectual elite can the true miracle of a democracy be achieved. I argue in these pieces that the educational revolution which began in the early nineteenth century in terms of the mass society must now be completed in terms of a spearhead society. That the idea of a creative intellectual minority is not incompatible with the idea of a democratic society seems to me almost too clear to be argued. Yet, since it is so often misunderstood, and because the theme of educational reconstruction will be with us far into the calculable future, I have kept a disproportionate number of the columns bearing on it.*

AU REVOIR, AMERICA

Paris, July 12, 1954

I HAVE BEEN in Paris for a week now, tasting again the delights of this city of eternal sophistication and eternal youth.

When the plane rose from Idlewild and headed for Gander, I took what will be my last look at New York until October, and I felt rather sentimental about leaving. But as much as I love America and New York, there are a few things which had begun to pall, which is why it is not too hard to say goodbye to them.

Goodbye, first and foremost, to McCarthy and his satellites and their omnipresent faces. Goodbye to Richard Nixon, at once feline and unctuous. Goodbye to the Senator from Formosa. Goodbye to the diehard isolationists and the preventive-war adventurers, the first ridden by blindness and the second by hate.

Goodbye to the current "cases"—Oppenheimer, Bunche, and the rest, as if to turn a man into a "case" were to damn him forever to the purgatory of the doubted. Goodbye to the lost souls of the little Union Square functionaries of the Kremlin, and to the forever scarred souls of the professional paid informers.

Goodbye to some of the manners and morals of the rich that give only a dusty answer to the heart—to the social wife-swapping circles where a little murder serves to break the monotony, to the mail-order heirs who are found dead, and to the oleomargarine heirs who live off women.

Goodbye to alimony hunters on darkest Park Avenue, who marry millionaires gaily and tire of them quickly. Goodbye to the serialized adventures of dime-store heiresses with assorted international playboys, and to ex-Hungarian playgirls who carry on their blow-by-blow courtships publicly.

Goodbye to bathing-beauty contests and vice dolls, to ledge-sitters and bridge-leapers, to singing commercials, comic books and Mickey Spillane. Goodbye to clerical best sellers on how to build your spiritual resources. Goodbye to journalistic muggers and peepholers. Goodbye to primitives of every description. Goodbye to Fulton Lewis, goodbye, goodbye.

Goodbye also to the trivia that stop being amusing; to insurance agents and ringing telephones and the mailman with bills; to littered streets; to the lugubrious duties of putting out the garbage can and walking the dog. Goodbye to the martyrdom of winding your way through a jigsaw puzzle of double-parked cars; to traffic jams on the homeward trek from Long Island in the broiling sun; to state patrol cars that sneak up on you on the open stretch. Goodbye to mortgage payments on the house, and a leaky roof.

Goodbye to double Scotches and aspirin, to arguments about cigarettes and cancer, to the alarm ringing for the Thursday morning plane to Boston. Goodbye to the pitiless patter of the talking pilots who think they are Bob Hope and audition for their captive audience. Goodbye to jokes about Jane Russell and Marilyn Monroe. Goodbye to Nixon's boyish smile, goodbye, goodbye.

Goodbye to the hot news that will soon be forgotten. Goodbye to investigations of tax-exempt foundations, the C.I.A., children's camps, and Father's Day. Goodbye to the ladies' patriotic societies and their heartrending appeals to get us out of the UN. Goodbye to coddlers and coddle-callers (Coddle me, Daddy, eight to the bar).

Goodbye to the new numbers game—the two thousand security risks whom the Republicans boast about scuttling out of Washington, the 130 spies in McCarthy's war plants, the twenty years of Democratic treason, the eighteen months of Republican foolishness, the Nine Old Men, the five-percenters and the two-platoon system. Goodbye to Eisenhower's press conference sentences, goodbye, goodbye.

Instead of goodbye, I mean, of course, au revoir. Despite my passing spell of waspishness, I wouldn't change this fabulous, contradictory country of ours—this crazy, mixed-up, seething, improbable aggregate of goofiness and glory—for anything else in all history.

MY CITY, MY BELOVED

1. Love Poem to New York

January 4, 1954

UNASHAMEDLY this is a love poem to New York. It is on my mind because new trustees have taken over our city, "to dress it and keep it," and my thoughts have gone back to its past. In celebrating the two hundred years of its own growth, Columbia University has chosen to link it with the roughly three hundred years of New York history.

With my son Stephen, I have spent several afternoons of enchantment over the hundreds of pictures in *The Columbia Historical Portrait of New York,* which has been done by John A. Kouwenhoven (Doubleday). It has given a new dimension of time depth to the affection I already bear this crazy, crowded island, noise-deafened, garbage-littered, smog-filled, carrying fiery monsters in its belly, its skies scarred with towers, its body of earth pock-marked with millions of little two-legged or four-wheeled creatures.

The Dutch, 350 years ago, bought the Isle of Manhattes from the Indians for sixty guilders. The uneven terrain had to be leveled, the grass gave way to cobblestones and asphalt. There was a steady movement northward, so that Columbia itself was pushed from Park Place, to Forty-ninth, and again to Morningside Heights, while the stores and hotels and fashionable houses also moved with great hustle and stir. Thus New York is today the sum of all the changing signatures that time has written on it.

Hugging a strip of shore in a corner of a continental expanse, yet somehow equated with America, New York has had to bear an intolerable share of envy and hatred. No one part of America can be the whole, but New York carries within itself more languages, culture, universes than any other spot on the globe.

Envy and hatred use as arguments against New York the looseness of moral standards for which every village Cato has upbraided the "wicked metropolis." You will find in this book many pictures of the elegant bars and hotels, the cheap lodginghouses, the sporting houses and "concert saloons," the beer gardens, the dives. But you will find no evidence that human nature is any different where a few million people are gathered, rather than a few thousand.

You will also find in these pictures the skeletal frame of New York's power. John Kouwenhoven was a good choice to put this book together, because a few years ago he wrote a remarkable little volume, *Made in America,* in which he argued that Americans have developed their own "vernacular" style in all the arts, as against the "academic" styles borrowed from other cultures. Now in this volume he reproduces the proofs that New York developed its own "urban vernacular" styles— the lithographs advertising stores and business ventures, the prints of warehouses and shipyards, iron foundries and wharves, the "pictorial directories" of shops, the whole range of industrial documentary.

New Yorkers have always known the sources of their power, and despite the pretentiousness of "Greek revival" architecture and the Gothic fronts of the great houses, they have not been ashamed of having been born out of commerce and business.

Yet economic power, while it is the frame of New York, is not its core. I say the same about the extremes of wealth and poverty with which every photographer has been fascinated, and the network of bridges and viaducts, skyscrapers and parkways, that show on all the city plans.

The core of New York must be found in the varied ways of life that are led by New Yorkers, who have evolved in their own groups and circles the compassable little universe that keeps them from being crushed by New York's bigness. These are curious creatures who have been drawn to New York by an irresistible suction force, and who cling to its unlikely canyoned streets against all reason and logic, mainly because something in them would die if they lived elsewhere.

I think the spark that keeps them warm is the freedom of mind and spirit on which life in New York is built. It is sometimes a destructive spark, but it is also a liberating one. As long as it remains, New York will remain; when it is extinguished, then all the glory and glitter, the power and pulsation that we call New York will vanish like a dissolving dream.

2. New York in Summer

July 3, 1953

OF THE FOUR SEASONS, summer is the one we treat most unfairly, bellyaching forever about its intolerable heat. I sing of summer in the city—of its many delights along with its frailties and blemishes.

You get up latish and go out for groceries and the papers. The sun strikes you with the first phase of his fierceness, but you don't mind because you are prepared for him and have tasted his utmost indignity. You get to know your neighbors somewhat, because they sit on their stoops in the summer, and the weather gives you the inevitable topic for striking up a conversation. On the subway as you go to your work, everyone is hot and coatless, so whatever fences separated you from them are broken down and all merge in the freemasonry of summer sweat.

At noon in the downtown business office area the summer streets swarm with clerks and businessmen and the secretaries in their scant summer dresses. They act like foals out in the pasture, knowing that there is a stable they must go back to sometime but meanwhile the sun is bright and work is only marginal at best. They nibble at a cold-meat sandwich of some sort and wash it down with soda or Coke or beer. The whole of the city becomes an astounding collaboration for pouring repeated doses of liquid into dehydrated bodies.

But it is in the late afternoon that I like the summer city best. Those who plan to desert it have done so, driving out to the beaches and the country. The streets wear a serene, stripped look as the quiet shadows start to fall. It's good to walk or drive in the city then, or meet someone at a bar before dinner, and then let the evening peel away aimlessly as you might peel some promising fruit you are in no hurry to eat. It is hard to be purposive. Those who remain behind in the summer city feel a little like beachcombers stranded on an island while the more organized members of the party have gone off to their earnest tasks of getting tanned.

This beachcomber aspect is the seamier phase of summer in the city. If aimlessness and rootlessness have any impact, then summer is an unstable time for marriages. Some of us can luckily afford to take our families away all summer and go to the ocean or lake shore or into the country. For us, summer is the blessed time of family reunions. But most men have to stay in their offices or shops, except for a brief vacation, and they are softhearted enough to send their families out of the city heat. So they stay behind, pretending to work, leading a desultory bachelor existence, rejoining their families on weekends when they make the bumper-to-bumper trek Friday night to Sunday night.

If I were writing one of those novels of Georges Simenon, about people at loose ends who run into an overmastering and destructive passion, I think I should give it a setting in New York in the summer. And if I were writing about what it is like to learn the full power of love, in the rapture of body and the meeting of minds and moods and the matching of will and submission, then I should again set it in New York. For there you can be alone together where the impersonality of the crowd gives a sharp accent of uniqueness to the experience of love.

Night in the city in summer is something never to forget. Coolness comes with darkness. People ride the tops of buses, or sit in the park near the river, or listen to the popular concerts, or sit in shirt sleeves before an open window, or wander through the streets coming home from a visit with friends. With the falling of dark the city takes on a mysterious quality that strengthens the feeling of being part of a jungle, but it is a gentler jungle than during the day. The whole pace of living slows down. This is the time when a haze hangs over the future, obscuring hurt and obstacle and heartbreak, and everything seems possible, and the long dreams are dreamt.

When the streets are almost wholly quiet, and only an occasional late radio is heard, two young people walk down the street slowly, staving off the end of the evening as we all stave off the end of summer.

3. New Orleans: The Ghost of Jazz

New Orleans, April 28, 1952

How DID IT HAPPEN that in so many years of wanderings among these United States, I have only now discovered New Orleans? I have known or flirted with many American cities, yet somehow I left this languorous mistress of the Old South long uncourted. I tremble at how I would have tried to give an accounting to my Maker for not having ever looked upon the wharves and the bistros, the old mansions and the new strip joints of this city.

With a city, as with a woman, you can't hope to know much about it in a three- or four-day visit, even if you spend all of every day and most of every night seeking it out. The old New Orleans hands say that either the city will possess you in your first half hour or else you are beyond saving. I didn't have to risk the damnation because it possessed me fast.

You start with the French Quarter, which is the right way to start because that's how the city itself started until it spilled over canal and rampart and esplanade and spread itself beyond its original bounds. To fly in from New York and be plumped down smack in the middle of the Quarter is like stepping out of the map of the United States into a Montmartre under Southern skies.

During the day the narrow streets are silent and respectable as Paris on a Sunday, and you walk lazily past rows of shop windows, most of them antique shops, or you drive through block after block of bewitching old houses, with tall shuttered windows and grilled ironwork and inner courtyards with the old slave quarters adjoining, which make an architect's paradise.

When darkness falls the life of Bourbon Street begins to stir. The musicians who play in the little bands in the dozens of honky-tonks start to assemble, some of them looking a little like church deacons until they start giving on the trombone or the piano. And the young girls with shapely figures and platinum hair, who act as "strippers" in the numberless floor shows, also come to work. Soon Bourbon Street fills up with tourists from Texas and Iowa and New York, and the barkers at each open night club door seek to add to the allurements of the leggy and bosomy pictures inevitably displayed outside.

The big industry of the French Quarter is the tourists, who are drawn to New Orleans by everything they have heard and read of its legend of sin. To be sure, the open houses of prostitution have long since been closed down by a stern-eyed law, and the more blatant gambling houses are shut too. But legends die hard, and this one is still worth millions, for it draws those who want to drink at all-night bars and step out of their careful everyday role for a brief encounter with anonymous adventure in this languid, bedizened setting.

I don't mean this is the only New Orleans. There is the New Orleans also of the beautiful big houses in the garden section of the city, and that of the warehouses and wharves. There is the Negro New Orleans of Basin Street and First Street. But you go to the Vieux Carré first, just as in Paris you go first to the Boulevard St. Germain. I have been lucky in finding, just across the street from my little French hotel, an unforgettable headquarters called the Cafe Lafitte. It is a broken-down little shack of a ginmill, once presumably a warehouse or blacksmith shop, still in sad disrepair. It is run by Tom Caplinger, husky, half bald and profane, who can remember knowing Emma Goldman and Alexander Berkman, and who talks about the Technocracy movement as though it had happened yesterday.

But eventually, as daylight closes in, even Tom gets a bit tired. The night clubs close too, and the couples who have huddled around the bars all evening weave unsteadily down the street to face whatever they are going to face. I sit for a while on my balcony and wait for the sun to come up and bathe with warmth the little houses and peaked roofs and iron grilles of the Quarter.

March 4, 1953

After my first encounter with it last year, what is it that pulls me back to this city of swamps and deltalands and garish night spots? I think that, like most of the rest who come to New Orleans, I am in search of a vanished glory. I came this time armed with learned books on the history of jazz in America like those of Rudi Blesh and Barry Ulanov. Never did a pilgrim seek the shrines of his saints bearing more talismans than I.

And I found what? Not the saints themselves, or even their spirits, but only their bleached bones. You don't see many jazz men around in New Orleans these days but only the ghost of jazz. The streets which once resounded to the glory of Buddy Bolden and Freddie Keppard,

Bunk Johnson and Joseph Oliver, Jelly Roll Morton and Louis Armstrong now resound only to second- and third-rate stuff ground out by journeymen bands, and late at night you are assailed by the klop-klop-klop of the jukeboxes.

Bourbon Street is a narrow and grasping alley held together only by a common obscenity and a common greed, taut as it waits for the sucker, opening its doors by just enough of a crack to let you glimpse the talcumed strip tease and the glitter of the G strings, luring you on by promises that make Haroun-al-Raschid's life that of an ascetic and King Farouk's an aching void. The total effect is that of the arcades of a provincial city, presided over by barkers who depict the sensualities of a Mohammedan Paradise, and sell only the dirtiest dust and ashes.

I don't mean this as complaining. There is a kind of gargoyle fascination about it, and if you know that what you see is ugliness and not beauty who has a kick coming? Certainly not the middle-aged refugees from their Midwestern home towns—the salesmen and doctors, the teachers and housewives—who stumble from door to door in the euphoria of a protracted Mardi Gras, trying to act like King Rex long after the float has been taken apart and the costumes put away. They don't kick, because what they want is noise and blaring and bare flesh and constant talk of sex, and the abiding memory of having stayed up late and "had fun."

You may ask what there was so different from this in the New Orleans of its Dixieland jazz heyday, at the turn of the century and in the first decades of the present one. It is true that most of the great New Orleans players started in the barrel houses and honky-tonks, the cribs and bawdyhouses of Storyville, which the city fathers had marked off for the unimpeded pursuit of the sins of the flesh. Now Storyville is no more, and in its place is a Bourbon Street patrolled by the cops in radio cars. The gaudy directories of the "mansions," that used to sell openly, are no more. But neither are the players. They have been drawn away by the high prizes of radio and television contracts. There was a thick vitality about the old sins that generated gaiety and music. Now there is only a thin commercialism left, out of which no new music is generated.

I did get to hear one of the great old-timers. He plays in a band at the Paddock, and his name is Alphonse Picou. Fifty years ago, when he played "High Society" on his clarinet, he did it with the authenticity that made it useless for anyone ever to find a new and different way. He must be at least seventy-three now, a little man beginning to wither, peering out at the bar crowd over his specs like a benign Negro grandpa, yet still able to keep a clear line amidst the intricate embroideries, with a volume of tone unbelievable after the gap of a half century.

The walls that used to enclose the regional cultures and let them flower have been broken down by radio and jukebox and the big prizes. The line of musical creation has moved away from New Orleans and

St. Louis. The old fellows, like Alphonse Picou, are dying out. In their place come the young intellectuals and critics, a little disdainful of the old hot jazz, talking of "cool" jazz, unaccented and cerebral.

4. The Heart of the City

November 2, 1953

I NOTE that a group of New York's biggest real-estate men had a meeting the other day. They included William Zeckendorf, Roger Stevens and several others whose business is buying, selling and running the towering skyscrapers around which so much of the business life of New York swirls and clusters. It is natural for them to be concerned about the ills that beset New York's growth and the bottlenecks that hem it in. They are worried about traffic, the suburbs and taxes. The traffic is threatening to strangle the city with a tight metallic noose f.o.b. Detroit. The suburbs draw people out of the metropolis yet pour them back every day to work and play; thus they glut the city while draining its capacity to pay its way—which means higher taxes for those who remain to pay the taxes.

It is somewhat curious for the skyscraper kings to be complaining about traffic. Lewis Mumford has pointed out that to build skyscrapers is no solution of the problem of congestion since it results only in more congestion. The big city is caught in the devil's dance of its own bigness: When it tries to use its inner space intensively, jutting into the sky or burrowing into the ground, it only gets more snarled up. When it tries to spread into the surrounding open areas, it creates the sprawling suburbia that poses further problems.

The skyscraper kings are calling for better long-range city planning for further development. Most American cities have grown up helter-skelter, without plan. Their danger is that they will choke, and then— when their circulation is stopped—that they will rot away. Their danger is also that, being without healthy community centers, the lives of the individuals in them will grow jangled and meaningless.

I have just been browsing through a book which has been badly neglected except by the architects. It is *The Heart of the City* and was edited by J. Tyrwhitt, J. L. Sert, and E. N. Rogers for the I.C.M.A.—the International Congress for Modern Architecture.

Architects have long talked of "cores"—the central place, whatever it may be, around which the great cities of history have lived. If you have been to Milan, you will never forget the Piazza del Duomo; if you have been to Venice the Piazza San Marco will stay forever with you; those who have seen the Mexican cities remember the cores around which they are built. But the sad fact is that there are few U.S. cities which have a heart, or core, in the same sense. Least of all New York.

The trouble with many of the American city planning commissions is that they are more obsessed with traffic than they are with what makes a good life in a great city. What will it profit us if we build vertical automatic garages to take the cars off the streets, or vast radial highways to get them out of town, if at the same time there are no places except street corners for our adolescents to hang around? In Italy or Mexico the heart of the city is where you sit and converse or have a drink, pass the time aimlessly, meet friends, do business, flirt, write poetry, carry on heated political arguments. To have such a core is to develop a tempo of life that goes with it.

It will be said that New York is wholly built up, and that it is no longer possible to carve out new centers of community life. I don't agree. Anyone who has wandered around New York has seen block after block of run-down tenements, rickety, rat-infested, where life no longer has any dignity. Using its powers of condemnation, the city can tear these down and with Federal aid put up new housing that will include cores for a meaningful group life. Maybe if we did more of this, we might have less corruption in city government; for corruption flourishes best where people with empty lives are willing to put up with it.

5. The Suburbanite

November 23, 1959

SAY YOU LIVE in Great Neck—or in Scarsdale or Larchmont, Levittown, Forest Hills, Radnor, Parkmerced, Drexeltown, Park Forest, Sherman Oaks or San Mateo. I could make the list stretch infinitely far, since so much of America today has become suburban America, and to so great an extent our way of life is a suburban one.

There are "old" suburbs and "new" ones; there are rich suburbs and middle-class ones; there are planned and unplanned ones; there are suburbs hospitable to Jews and other ethnic minorities and there are those which resent and exclude them. All of them, however, are part of a vast process of the eating up of the open spaces, of the search for roots and elbow room and good schools, of America resettling itself— and in the process finding a new way of life.

How can we best put this way of life? I would call it the major American effort, since the rise of the city, to find a new garment for living which will give the family a sense of space and place, a feeling of belonging and status, a circle of friends, a web of activities—without giving up the advantages that flow from nearness to the city.

Obviously this is only the suburban dream, which is sometimes pretty distant from the reality. You could say the same about life in the city or small town or in the "exurban" community beyond commuting distance. Life in any of these communities is often dust in the mouth because so much of life in America—or anywhere—is. One of the mistakes that writers about suburban life sometimes make is to ascribe to the suburbs the tinsel values of American life goals—the overemphasis on money, success, power, prestige, security and the dream of happiness. The suburb does not have a monopoly on strained and empty existences, on competitiveness, on life as a rat race.

One of the difficulties with generalizing about the suburbs is that, while we have many studies of American small towns and small cities, we have very few of suburbs. There are two recent books on them. One is *Crestwood Heights* by John R. Seeley and two associates (Basic Books), dealing with a Canadian suburb that shares many traits with the American. The other is a book of first importance—*The Organization Man* by William H. Whyte, Jr. (Simon and Schuster), and while it deals with the broader theme of the new type of person who works for and belongs to "the Organization," a third of its four hundred pages are about the new suburbia as seen in Park Forest, near Chicago.

Whyte sees that the suburbs express "organization man at home," with all his contradictory effort to make a set of individualist beliefs jibe with a collective life. He sees many of the ludicrous aspects of what he calls "belongingness" and "togetherness." Yet he also sees the genuine feeling and striving that go into those efforts at overcoming our sense of loneliness.

The suburbs are too new, too raw, too uniform in look, too hurried in construction, too garish in display, too standardized in mode of life to give me much sense of grace or depth of living. But if they are these things it is because they bring to focus the new forces in American life as a whole. The important fact is that suburban living is a genuine response to felt needs. If you dismiss the response, you must dismiss the needs as well.

Most generalizations about suburbs can be countered by opposite ones. Is the suburb conformist? Often it is standardized, but there is a difference between standardization and conformity. Are the suburbs ostentatious? Perhaps. Yet it is well known that the whole movement of American amateurism—the "do-it-yourself" trend, with its rich exploration of individual hobbies and talents—finds its best expression here. Whyte tells us that in Park Forest the real tyranny of opinion leans not toward conspicuous consumption but toward "inconspicuous consumption"—lest you seem too anxious to outdo your neighbor. Are the suburbs sexually loose? I would doubt that any over-all study of sexual behavior would show this. If anything, life is lived at too close quarters to allow for promiscuity. It is the impersonal big city that favors it.

The suburb is the focus of most of the forces that are remaking American life today, especially the life of the family and the character of the personality. Some are healthy, others vicious, but most of them contain potentials in either direction. The suburbanite has a stir of excitement because of the widening of his horizons, the closeness of new friendships, the accessions of experience.

6. Lo, the Poor Commuter

June 18, 1952

THE LONG ISLAND STRIKE is settled, but during its two-day span it showed up the vulnerable position of that new mugwump, half city and half suburban—the commuter.

Morning after morning he runs for his train to the city, and catches it—or it catches him. Evening after evening he dashes through the Long Island waiting room to catch its sister train for the trip out of the city. And suddenly the trains stop and the waiting rooms are empty, and he has to improvise endless and ingenious substitutes. Suddenly he understands by how thin a thread the two halves of his life are held together.

Do you remember that E. B. White essay on New York, where he noted that there are actually three New Yorks—that of the natives, that of the migrants (who flock here from West and Middle West seeking a career), and that of the commuters? The commuter is part of an army which is camped outside the city but makes daily forays into it. His job is in New York, but his family, school, church, garden and TV set are somewhere outside of it, within a radius of from ten to seventy-five miles.

When I was younger and more foolish, we lived in a series of Westchester suburbs, and for several years I used to commute to New York. The alarm rang at 7:50 A.M. I feverishly phoned for a last-minute taxi, and I became one of the legion who crowded into the 8:12 from Tuckahoe every morning and the 5:43 back every evening. Behind it all was the argument that it was "Better for the Children." Alas, they now tell me they preferred the years they later spent in the crowded city.

The commuting train riders are the most solid and solemn body of citizenry in the world. They are the starch in the white collar of America. A few laugh, and some have their daily game of cards. But with their faces buried behind an unbroken row of papers, most of them seem consumed by the passion to know what has happened in the world since the last bulletin they read on their last ride. If America ever falls because of the lack of an informed citizen body, it will not be the fault of the commuters.

Most commuters are as untalkative as native Vermonters. You have your paper, and he has his. I remember a short story about a commuter who used to admire the girl who took the same train as his for twelve years, but never picked her up.

But sometimes I think the commuters make up for this virtuous self-discipline after they have left the train. If you believe all the novels that have been written about the faithlessness of the knights of the New Haven, the New York Central, and the Long Island, you will wonder that New York has not long since become one of the Cities of the Plain. Generally—in the novels—these fellows work for *Time* or *Life* or some advertising agency. All goes well until the hapless fellow has to work late at the office and takes his seductive secretary (who is not a commuter) out for a late snack. The result is he misses the last train home that night and finds himself more and more frequently calling his wife to make his apologies, and staying the night presumably at a hotel.

They tell me that the hotels were jammed the last two nights as never before in New York history. When did destiny ever provide a man with a better ready-made story to phone home? I hate to speculate on the havoc that the railroad strike wrought in the marital happiness of 125,-000 commuter families on Long Island.

Many scholars have thought the commuter won't last much longer, but my guess is he is here to stay. The big city will be around for many generations, unwieldy as it is. But more and more the ordinary young couples are finding that they can build almost self-sufficient communities outside the city, except for coming in to the job. With TV in every commuter's home, even the city bright lights and theaters and night clubs are losing their attraction. The only problem still to be solved is: What happens when the thread breaks between the two halves of a commuter's life?

THE CAPTURABLE AMERICAN

1. Cocktail Friendships

December 29, 1954

THIS IS THE SEASON when good cheer flows at numberless holiday parties, and cocktail party friendships flourish. What country, other than America, has the cocktail party as its core institution for breaking down the fences between people? Unlike the Europeans, we don't have to break down fences of rank and social distinction. The purpose of the ordinary cocktail party is to break down personal inhibitions—and it succeeds.

Let me celebrate first the office party. For 364 days in the year you write and get memos, exchange distant greetings in the corridor, daydream about what you would say if you had a chance. Then comes the 365th day, at the office party. The inhibitions of the 364 days melt away, and in their place comes a great courage.

The secretaries, who have hitherto had only a phone acquaintance, kiss the department heads and maybe even the boss himself. The underlings, who have been gathering grievances against him silently all year long, find heart enough in a succession of double Scotches to tell him off and jab at his most vulnerable vanities. Rivals in the bureaucratic struggle inside the company let down their guard for a terrible lethal moment and tell each other the truth. In the whole vast corporate hierarchy there are numberless egos the next day that have been left mangled and bleeding. The scene is like a Shakespeare stage at the end of the last act, multitudinous with corpses.

But worse than the corpses, at least for some, are the memories. A busy statistician has estimated that 62 per cent of the office husbands in the average corporation call up their wives between six-thirty and seven-thirty to say they'll be home late and not to wait for dinner. Where they end up is something over which the social historian must discreetly draw the curtain. In the buoyant atmosphere of the office party there is a derring-do that cuts across departmental boundaries and makes everyone seem glamorous. But for the next few weeks in the office there is a muted atmosphere of wry and embarrassed remembrance.

I sing next, O Muse, the joys and sorrows of the ordinary social cocktail party. It is less a party than a monster rally and an athletic event. To make your way into the crowd requires a twisting skill like that of a ball carrier beset by tacklers. Once you have been downed it takes almost as great skill to get free and continue your course.

But, ah, what consolations. Every new cocktail party is like a new poker hand. You never know what kind of full house it might be, what queens and kings and aces it might hold. In spite of past disillusionments, the hope of making a strike and finding heaven remains undiminished.

You come into the room and survey the scene. For a moment you feel like the Almighty about to create the world. Everything seems possible, nothing is beyond your powers. There is a new young blonde on the edge of the crowd. You make your way to her. . . .

Alas, there is always a new young blonde, and she is always graceful and lovely and brilliant, and you always hit it off beyond any imagining, and you always write her name down and where she works and where you can reach her—and in the end you never do.

Cocktail party friendships are like summer vacation and shipboard friendships. They bloom quickly and feverishly, and you think you will never be the same again without their fragrance. The drinks break down all the dams and make your tongue and emotions fluent. You make solemn vows and swear eternal fealty. But then come other cocktail parties and other fair apparitions, and the memory of the old ones grows dim.

There is a blessed anonymity in New York for those who seek it. But a New York cocktail party combines the anonymous with a wonderful sense of privacy. Where there are so many people crowding together you can be alone with the new apparition. The din of other voices drowns out everything except hers and yours, but the vitality all around you gives you a courage you may lack in another situation.

The trouble, as a Greek philosopher saw long ago, is that you can never step twice in the same stream. Only a few months later you pick out of your wallet a little card with a name and a phone number on it. You can remember the rush of emotion with which you scribbled them. But you can't remember who it was that inspired the rush of emotion.

You puzzle a bit, relive the whole scene, groping for the missing clue, and feel tempted to call the number just to see. But by that time dusk is falling, and it is time to put on your hat and coat and drop by at a cocktail party.

2. Riots of Love

May 20, 1952

AT HARVARD the riot was about Pogo. At Yale, it was about a couple of ice-cream vendors. At Columbia, it was an effort to storm the Barnard dormitories. The Columbia-Barnard pattern, taken up at Vanderbilt and at the University of Tennessee, is the one that will stick as the other spring college riots sputter across the campuses of the country.

What causes all the hoopla? Those who say it is the biggest campus craze since the boys ate goldfish miss the point. This isn't just fad stuff. Some kind of campus hysteria you get, I suppose, every year in springtime. Take a sack of middle-aged bones like myself, and note that I am by no means immune to the restlessness of these spring days. And if a curious case of inattention hits us oldsters, think of the youngsters. The sap is breaking through every tree and leaf, and it doesn't leave the contemporary American adolescent male—or female—untouched.

But spring madness doesn't wholly explain the massed assault upon the women's dorms, the plight of the cops at Tennessee who had to fire shots over students' heads, the knife-and-broom defense columns that the coeds pretended to resort to, and the daring girls in the dorms who waved their undergarments out the window as a gesture either of defiance or of invitation.

When I was at college, we had our annual high jinks, sweeping across the campus to rip up the fences or swarming out across the streets of New Haven at night in pajama parades. This was for the record, with an eye to leaving the mark of the class on the history of the college, and to show we were not sissies. But there wasn't much sex in it, or has my memory suffered a blackout?

The simple answer is that sex has come into the colleges because women have. In the old days, college boys had to go out on the town for their girls, and the college riots were usually town-and-gown riots. Now there is a Thurberian war of the sexes between the men's and women's dormitories.

If you want to be ironic, you might say that the college boys and girls are carrying out for our time the kind of tournaments of love that the knights and ladies carried out in the Middle Ages. In those days the knight went into combat wearing on his sleeve, as one historian puts it, a "scarf, veil, mantle, bracelet, or ribbon" belonging to his lady. It was for her service that he did battle. The women's emblems have changed, and the symbolism of chivalry has changed. The unicorn and the pomegranate tree, which were symbols of spring generation in the Middle Ages, are strange to us. We live in the Age of Nylon, and instead of the courts of love we have riots that express the vague sexual restlessness of adolescents cooped up in artificial situations.

My own quarrel with the college boys is in letting the phrase "panty

raids" get attached to these demonstrations of robust he-men. Think of
what the Communist propagandists will be able to do with it, once they
have laboriously translated it into seventy-five different languages, and
how they will be able to mock it as a sign of the degeneration of American manhood.

I shudder when I think of eight hundred virile Columbia under-
graduates chanting in unison, "Drop your panties; throw them down."
This obsession with female undergarments can only be the result of excessive daydreaming or obsessive reading of the lingerie and bra ads.
The Princeton battle cry, "We want sex," with its more robust and direct
clamor for the thing itself instead of the symbols of it, seems to argue
that they manage these matters better at Old Nassau.

What strikes me hardest about the outbursts is that they reveal the
lack of college communities. Girls and boys now go to college almost in
equal numbers, but very rarely do you get a campus where they form
a genuine community, working together on terms of equality, playing together with some dignity, wooing and being wooed as human beings and
not as comic-opera figures. It is in the vacuum of a community that
frustration enters and riots begin.

3. Just Because It's June

June 8, 1950

BECAUSE June is bustin' out all over, the boys at City Hall who hand
out the marriage licenses are doing pretty well these days, and also those
who finish the process by pronouncing you man and wife and shaking
your hand and getting a good tip which you give them as a sort of charm
against evil.

Though I don't believe in going goofy just because it's June, I do like
June. Quite unashamedly, dear lady, I find you almost irresistible as you
wear your new summer clothes in the June sunlight, and I don't care
who knows it. In a wonderful short story, "The Girls in Their Light
Summer Dresses," Irwin Shaw once captured the surge of feeling that
any man has as he watches the vernal procession.

Being catholic in my tastes, in life as in literature, I find something to
like in most of them. Maybe they are the hoydenish wild ones who look
as if they would break out of their new clothes and streak down the
street in a coltish run, or the demure ones who float along the avenue
lost in a dream, or the narcissists with their spread of feathers and their
peacock strut as they mince along clack-clack on impossibly high heels
and snatch a lingering look at their cherished image in the wooing shop
windows, or the haughty ones with queenly gait who impale you on the
hostile spears of their glances—but unconvincingly, since it is clear
about all of them that they are conquerors dying to be conquered.

A maiden named Sallie wrote a very un-Junelike letter to me the other day. Sallie is bothered because of the double standard that men impose on women in America. "Many girls," Sallie mourns, "want no change. It is to their advantage to maintain the status quo. They would rather have men open and close doors for them than forego these luxuries and attain freedom." As for Sallie herself, she "resents man's prerogative in almost every respect." She thinks that women cannot "attain complete equality in the political and economic world without equality socially and sexually." "What I propose," she writes, "is quite revolutionary"—namely, that women work and play and live side by side with men, "first as human beings with dignity, secondly as women."

Alas, Sallie, even on the wild improbability that we were both free, I don't think we could make a go of it on your "revolutionary" basis. There have been two strong ideas that have ruled American women. One has been the cult of romantic love—the idea that there is one man and one only for every girl, and one girl and one only for every man, and the two have been destined since the beginning of time, and the love between them may turn out well or badly but it is love as fatality.

The trouble with the cult of romantic love is that it starts well in June, wilts a bit in the July and August of a relationship, and withers in the winter. It makes woman a toy and plaything—which she is not. And it makes man a hero and protector—which is just as hard a role for him.

As a recoil from the cult of romantic love, we have built up the cult of feminism and equal rights. But just as woman is not a toy for a man to play with, or a mirror to flatter him, so she cannot be used as a weapon with which to deflate his blown-up ego.

The trouble with equal rights is not that they are unattainable but that they are irrelevant. What you ask for in a relationship is not equality but poise and counterpoise. What any man wants of a woman, Sallie, is not that she should be first a person and second a woman, but that she should be first, last, and all the time a woman so thoroughly herself that there is never any question about her being a person.

To ask equality of men and women is like asking equality of the land flung out over the earth and the ocean that bears the land on its breast. They are not equal, because each is incommensurable. Each is an element in its own right, and together they comprise everything we know of the span of the world.

4. The Ezio Pinza Trend

December 20, 1949

THERE CAN BE NO QUESTION that ever since *South Pacific* began its run there has been an Ezio Pinza trend in politics. While I was at the show I scribbled some notes on my theater program, and the next morning this is what I deciphered: "Pinza is a Godsend for the middle-aged and elderly men. They come in stooped and defeated, with the world's weight on their shoulders, envious of the youngsters who are supplanting them. They come out straight and assertive, preening themselves like cocks of the walk. Pinza's conquest of Mary Martin has made the male hormone unnecessary for all of us."

Since Mary Martin, in the South Pacific sunshine, tried to wash that man right out of her hair and send him on his way—unsuccessfully— a series of elderly politicians have gone to the altar with young dream brides of their choosing. The success of the Vice-President's mating is now history, and when the *South Pacific* audience stood up and applauded the Veep and his bride it was not only a tribute to them but a recognition that dramatic art doesn't stop with the stage. And now Bill O'Dwyer, a mere stripling of fifty-nine, and Sloan Simpson, thirty-two.

The public atmosphere within which political figures live has changed considerably in our generation. When Woodrow Wilson, after the death of his wife, married Edith Bolling, attractive and a good deal younger, the reaction tended to be strait-laced and waspish. We are more tolerant now. But this is more than tolerance. It reaches to a change in some of the values we place on male and female youth.

For one thing, the traditional overvaluation of male youth is nearing its end. This overvaluation has been due partly to college sports and professional athletics, partly to the hold of the young matinee idols of Hollywood over the bobby-soxers. But if there is one thing clear about Hollywood, it is that the young males are thoroughly uninteresting to movie audiences, as compared to oldsters like Humphrey Bogart and John Garfield. I can say proudly for my age group that the middle-aged man—or let us call him the *mature male*—is at length getting to be appreciated by the girls and is coming into his own.

The other change taking place is that, more and more explicitly, the young and pretty women are coming to be regarded as the prizes. This has always been true of the American tycoons, as Dreiser recognized in his masterly novel trilogy about Frank Cowperwood (Yerkes). The gentlemen who have preferred blondes have been wealthy gentlemen, and the daddies to whom the young and pretty hearts have belonged have not been impecunious.

But you no longer have to be a millionaire to get the prize. It is even better if you are simply the kind of public figure who can create for your young wife a lambent and burnished life at the heart of things, where the fires of activity burn brightest. What the young women want is not wealth, but the sense of life's stir.

In my piece on the Ezio Pinza Trend I pointed out that there is a South Pacific ground swell in the private lives of our political figures, and that the mature male is coming into his own.

The alert National Affairs staff of *Newsweek* magazine, always on the lookout for the personal motives behind cosmic theories, immediately detected a note of aggrandizement in my innocent words. They searched out my own age and described me as the "47-year-old Max Lerner, the Fair Dealing pundit of the New York *Post*." With both my age and my politics thus nakedly exposed, they twisted the knife in the wound: "Preening himself, Prof. Lerner added: 'The mature male is coming into his own.' "

"Preening himself. . ." It rankled, but my foreign relations with the *Newsweek* staff have always been good, and I decided to let the phrase go and not withdraw my consuls, or inquire into the average age and politics of the *Newsweek* columnists.

After the news magazines came the department stores. Your really talented ad writer has a breeziness of style that makes us all seem stuffy. To be in the department store ads is almost as much of an accolade, for a man of my sober scholarly habits, as it is to be quoted in *Vogue* and find your words enveloped by the shimmering costumes of those willowy and unattainable goddesses. My wife, who does my research in the department store ads, the fashion magazines and other important phases of American culture, has come up with an evocative Gimbels ad.

"E. Z. O. O'Veep," says the ad in front of me, "has a mature mind . . . Sweet romance in Shangri-la . . . a rainbow in the Florida sky . . . the air is fraught with romance. Even a stripling of 48 sees stardust at Waikiki. Blame it on the enchanted evening if you will. But Gimbels agrees with the well-known pundit that 'the mature male is coming into his own.' Life may begin at 40, but love can bloom at any age."

I am frankly bored at being called a "pundit," whether by *Time, Life, Newsweek,* or Gimbels' ad writer. My *Oxford English Dictionary* says of "pundit" that it means a "learned Hindu," and then, by transference, "a learned expert or teacher (joc)." The "joc" is what hits me. I looked it up in the *O.E.D.* table of abbreviations, which amplifies it as "jocularly." Unless the news (joc) magazines stop it soon, I fear I shall go through life labeled as a mature male pundit (joc).

There were some letters from women readers that raised issues more serious than these. With all these December-May marriages, the letters say, what shall the middle-aged (shall we say "mature"?) women who happen to be alone do about getting mates? I intend to write a piece on this, but before my dangerous reflections are published I shall get safely away. Now that I have read in the Gimbels ad that a stripling of forty-eight can disport himself on the beach at Waikiki, I have decided to follow the midwinter crowd on its southward trek. In a week or two I shall be sitting by a waterfall at Ochos Rios, in Jamaica, with my portable typewriter, and with my wife, who —besides being beautiful and female—is something of a pundit herself (not joc).

5. The Ripe Female

January 31, 1950

A LADY who signs herself "Aged Fifty" writes to ask why I have "not one kind word for all the middle-aged widows who are doomed to eternal loneliness by the trend toward December-May marriages? While the 'mature' males thump their hormonized chests and dash off in pursuit of young girls, women of their own age group reflect bitterly on their plight. Don't think the wealthy tycoons, politicians, playboys and Hollywood figures are alone in their belief that they can stir young women. It exists in schoolteachers, bookkeepers, policemen and pants pressers as well. Regardless of age, the male ego is colossal."

Another lady writes me: "What, my dear Mr. Lerner, about the older women whom no man will look at? Imagine how we feel to read that men of seventy-seven and seventy-two marry young women: who then can we expect even to look at us. I don't expect you to be interested—no man ever is—in any woman over thirty. The ones above that who can attract and nab a husband are few and far between. I know it is not vital to the Welfare State that we older women are ignored, many who are witty, intelligent, healthy—but it's worth a thought, *n'est-ce pas?*"

Yes it is, decidedly, many of them. If I were a woman, whether spinster, widow or divorcee, I too would feel bitter about the Ezio-Veep trend among contemporary males. I should look longingly at the structure of French society, where middle-aged women feel at ease even with younger men. I should have some tart reflections about a society like ours, where the women are the prizes but only the males make the choices.

Actually, if some foreign student of American culture were to take a hard and objective look at the marriageable qualities of mature males and ripe females in our social structure, what would he find? He would find that the middle-aged woman is likely to be at least as bright, witty and conversational as the middle-aged man. He would find her better read. He would find that she owns more of the nation's property and dividend coupons than the male does. He would find that, lacking the business strains and money tensions of the men, she has a longer life expectancy and will probably live to bury her male contemporary.

The women should take the offensive. Equipped with these undoubted facts about their strengths and strategic advantages, they should aim far beyond their present humdrum lot. Not for them the dismal lonely-hearts club, where disappointed male and disappointed female try to blot out their common desolateness. Not for them the primping and saving, the dreary club and forum meetings, the patient culling of "beauty hints," the waiting—forever waiting—for some elderly male to make up his sovereign mind to throw a look their way. They should carry the war deep into the enemy's territory and send their advance troops to make forays among the young men.

What we need is another *South Pacific*—but one written from the woman's angle. The part of the female Ezio Pinza could be played by Greta Garbo. No doubt we shall find a thirtyish youngster who will do the male Mary Martin role. Precedent? There is Raymond Radiguet's *Devil in the Flesh.* There is Thomas Wolfe's *You Can't Go Home Again,* about the young novelist and the middle-aged woman scene designer. Only this time there must be no insoluble marital tangles, and after traveling the prescribed rocky road the story must end happily with wedding bells.

The fact is that three kinds of marriages ought to be possible and recognized—between the same age groups, between younger girls and older men, and between younger men and older women. We have the first two, but almost none of the third.

The old bogy about how the older woman will look ten years after marriage need not trouble us much in an era when science has created the utmost in clothes and the permanent silhouette. And there are plenty of young men who would somehow feel more secure with an older woman. The trouble is that the big fear in our society is the fear of seeming ridiculous, and they are afraid to swim against the current.

6. The Revolt of the American Father

February 15, 1951

WHILE I WAS in Jamaica, I read the island's newspaper, the *Daily Gleaner,* chiefly for its morbid accounts of trials. I recall a memorable exchange between a witness and an attorney. There was a police extortion case being tried, and one of the witnesses to the alleged extortion, Beryl Downer, said she was a typist and lived in the "boarding-house" involved in the case. Cross-examined, she admitted she had never worked as a typist but was studying it at school.

Q. What do you do for a living?
A. Nothing, sir.
Q. How do you earn money to live?
A. Everybody have somebody to give them money in this world.

I wonder what Beryl had in mind with this bit of wisdom. The island people are a Bible-reading people. Perhaps she recalled the injunction to "consider the lilies of the field, how they grow; they toil not, neither do they spin; yet even Solomon in all his glory was not arrayed like one of these." Was that why she took no thought for the morrow?

For a long time the preachers and philosophers and those lay-preacher philosophers we call psychiatrists have been telling us not to lay up treasures for ourselves which moth and dust can corrupt, but to get to know ourselves, and cultivate our souls, and cease from the corrosive pursuit of money and glory and power. What if we all would take them at their word, slough off the mortal coil of holding down jobs, and become spiritual beachcombers?

Of the many novels written around this theme, I think of Somerset Maugham's *Razor's Edge,* where the young hero Larry Darrell turns down a good job because he wants to seek the secret of life, and then gives up the girl he loves because she won't marry a man without a job. In an earlier and better novel, *The Moon and Sixpence,* Maugham had shown himself equally fascinated with a different kind of obsessiveness—not the passion for saintliness, as with Darrell, but the ruthless belief in his own creative star that caused Gaugin to trample every human relation. In both cases there is the happy assurance that somehow provision will be made and they shall not want.

It is true of most wives, of course, that "everybody have somebody to give them money in this world." Maybe Beryl had the condition of wifehood in mind, and maybe she reasoned that even if you are not a wife to some man, you can be as good as a wife, and get the same shepherding.

I wonder what would happen if there were a quite general revolt of the men. I don't mean a male version of Lysistrata, or the kind of rancorous revolt implied in Thurber's *Battle of the Sexes.* I mean a genial but nonetheless determined refusal any longer to be the staff on which the woman leans her lovely and languorous weight. "I've supported you long enough," I can hear the male saying to his wife and daughters. "Now try your hand at supporting me, so that I can cultivate my soul, and discover the true, delicate outlines of my personality."

Would it wreak havoc? I fervently hope so. It would clarify many murky relationships and bring them down to earth. We would soon know whether we are valued as check writers or husbands, as allowance givers or fathers. We have made the mistake of regarding the sugar daddy as belonging to a special sucker category. Actually he is the whole genus male. My plan would mean the end of the male as sugar daddy.

My wife, to whom I have broached my weighty proposal, answers, Why not? She'll take it on, she says, but with two conditions. First, that I'll help with the children while she is out breadwinning. Agreed. Second, that we'll lower our living standards, long enough to let me get the itch for idleness out of my system.

You're right, Beryl. Everybody have somebody. As for me, my career as a lily of the field is just starting.

June 16, 1958

Every year, in April or May, I get one of those letters on a National Father's Day Committee letterhead, reminding me that the great day falls sometime in June (when, incidentally, retail-store sales are pretty sluggish) and suggesting a column. I shall write of how fathers have endured all through created time, even before Father's Day was in existence, and how they will go on enduring and enduring, even to the last whimper of self-pitying humanity. In the very beginning, remember, was God the Father. And in his play about the posthistoric last men, *Endgame,* Samuel Beckett generously gives Father a garbage can right next to Mother's. It is a triumph of egalitarianism.

There is a lot of fancy talk these days about the sad state of the father, and a current quickie called *The Decline of the American Male* (Random House) has a section on how the American father is getting more and more woman-dominated, in a society of defeminized women and demasculinized men.

I found my college-junior daughter Joany reading it yesterday and asked what she thought. "Terrible," was her brief review. "These people are too self-conscious about it. I don't want to dominate my male. If anything, I want him to dominate me. I'll keep looking until I find someone who can. And as long as there's one woman like me left in America, the case of the American male isn't hopeless."

I said a silent inner "Amen" for all men. I felt wholly uninclined to decline.

Things are actually worse for the father in other cultures. There are primitive tribes which have not figured out the relation of the sexual act to childbirth and paternity. There are others which do know the facts of biological fatherhood, but also have the idea of social fatherhood, so that a boy may call his mother's uncle "Father," instead of his real father. Compared with these tribes, the case of American civilization is not so bad. My children may not do me reverence always as I deserve, but they do recognize my paternity, calling me by a variety of names depending on their age and mood, all the way from an upbraiding "Father!" to a teasing "Pop," an affectionate "Dad," and Adam's delighted repetitive "Daddee-ee."

And there are compensations about being a father. Every father falls in love with his daughter—first as a pretty thing, then as a hoyden, finally as a flowering woman. And every father finds himself re-created in his sons, reliving his own life through their growth and their intellectual adventures and their final sureness which catches fire from his own and in turn feeds his sureness.

It would be a mistake to think of the American father as a loose collection of his various roles. To be sure, he is father, husband, escort, sexual partner, bill payer, game player, car driver, fire lighter, tire changer, handyman, house putterer, bicycle teacher, morals preacher, character builder, tuition provider, drink pourer, roast carver, meal ticket, insurance rack, Rock of Ages who was there before you were born and will provide for you after he is dead.

He may play all these roles and others too, but if he is any good he is not fragmented into them, the way the woman sometimes is. In all his roles he is still the quester, the fertility giver, the male principle. More than a father or husband, he is a man. If he is not male, then he is no one and nothing.

He has been quiet, patient, hard-working, long-enduring. But don't count on it. Don't push him. If you do, he will not strike back (that is not his way with women) but he may just walk out of the house and the bank job, leaving the womenfolk behind, and turn up in Tahiti to daub at canvas and spend his life in the sun.

Human history, if you read it right, is the record of the efforts to tame Father. Next to the striking of fire and the discovery of the wheel, the greatest triumph of what we call civilization was the domestication of the human male.

The job was not done wholly by the women. The male let himself in for it by his own vulnerability. I don't mean his sexual drive, because he could satisfy that more variously by being a roamer instead of a homer. I mean his drive to fatherhood—the curious, intricate satisfaction of having your seed made blood and bone, and seeing your line preserved and extended. That is why the Old Testament is full of so many "begats."

"God Himself dressed Eve's hair (so runs an old Jewish legend) that the first woman might please the first man." If the American male now lets an apron be tied around him, and diaper pins be placed in his roughened hands, what a fall from Eden that will be.

There has been a succession of women's revolutions in American history. But watch out for the revolt of the father, if he should get fed up with feeding others, and get bored with being used, and lay down his tools, and walk off to consult his soul.

7. The Cult of Number One

December 21, 1955

I HAVE BEEN WAYLAID by two tales in the public prints of the past week. One was about a New York travel agent, Peter Rhonheimer, who saved his wife from what reporters like to call a "masked intruder," and was shot three times before the lady hit the visitor on the head with a hammer, making it clear he was unwelcome. The second was about another husband in Texas, Walter Vaughn, who drove 325 miles to kill a philandering man of God who had embroiled Mrs. Vaughn in an adulterous relationship.

What interests me in both cases is the question of how far the heroic male must go in protecting his lady.

The Rhonheimer incident reversed a lamentable trend. I have been gathering notes for several years on stories in which the general pattern was drearily alike: a parked car with a wooing couple in it, some men with guns, a frightened inaction by the male escort, a violated woman. I recall, for example, the case of a young husband who stood by while his bride was raped. And another of a young man who had just become engaged, who let his hands be tied while the attackers took his girl, who waited for them to return, and who then accompanied them to a filling station while they had some drinks.

All of which may explain why I tip my hat to Peter Rhonheimer, who restores my image of what a human being must do when there is a threat to someone entrusted to his care.

One would expect this to be true as a matter of course, if it were not for the current cult of Number One. All through childhood and adolescence it is dinned in upon the American youth that he must take care of himself. Don't get your feet wet, don't fall off the swing, don't climb the tree, don't cross the street alone, don't get lost, be sure to wire us that you have arrived safely. And as an adult he reinforces the lesson of saving the precious skin of Number One.

It is not even a case of heroism or cowardice, because human beings at a moment of crisis don't turn rational choices of action over in their minds. They act in response to the events and influences that have made them what they are. They do what they do because at the fiery moment of trial they can do no other.

I suppose this was true of Walter Vaughn too—the Texas husband who shot the minister and said, "I don't think any man should be sorry for protecting his wife and home." Yet I wonder whether this wasn't carrying the feudal principle of male honor pretty far, in a world of adult responsibility.

Vaughn's act doesn't reverse an American trend; it confirms one. The newspapers and the courts have shown a special tenderness for the husband who kills his wife's lover, and the wife who kills her husband's mistress. A few months ago there was the case of the Washington wife who came home from her job, found her children uncared for because her vacuum-salesman husband had been with his nineteen-year-old mistress, packed a gun in her handbag, marched off with her husband to the apartment where he kept the girl, and shot her dead.

The jury acquitted her "by reason of insanity," which means she was pretty mad when she did it. There have been other cases, too, of tempering the verdict to fit a new Frenchlike conception of the "crime of passion." It is now established that a jury will probably not convict a wife or a husband who shoots the rival for trying to break up the harmony of the family.

I predict that the Texas jury will acquit Vaughn. It will be hard to use "temporary insanity" as a ground, it being a pretty good feat to sustain a fit of impulsive rage for a 325-mile drive. But the jury will manage. The minister in question seems to have been a no-good specimen who disgraced and exploited the cloth. And the wife now says the husband did the right thing.

The fact is, however, that the philandering wife is a grown person who acts with full responsibility—however much she may afterward want to shed it and become again the loving and loyal little woman. Her acts are her own and she must face their consequences. As for the husband, he is not the heroic male protecting his wife from assault. He is more likely only a man so obsessed with Number One—with his grievance and insecurity—that another death must atone for his sense of injured self-esteem. The self-righteous prig who shoots at sight is as bad as the weakling who thinks only of his own skin.

VARIETIES OF AMERICAN MARRIAGE

1. Love Laughs at Barriers

November 20, 1952

THE THING that strikes me first about the marriage of Pearl Bailey and Louis Bellson, which took place yesterday in London, is that the whole episode is enclosed in music. Bellson is a good drummer and Miss Bailey a good singer. Each must have respect for the other as a craftsman, yet they don't vie with each other. Their meeting and wooing, over the course of only a few months, have been part of the atmosphere of the jive they both love.

Going through the list of prominent people who have married across their race lines in recent years, one is struck by how many of them work in and with music.

What are the reasons? I have a couple of guesses, for what they may be worth. One is that hot music and jive are part of the Negro tradition in America, and one of their great contributions to our popular culture. In this atmosphere the Negro is not placed at a disadvantage, as he is where he has been grudgingly admitted as an alien newcomer.

My second guess is that music is an international language that laughs at barriers of race, nation or religion. When the elder Bellson cabled Miss Bailey, "I don't want my son to marry out of his race," and added that he wanted "no grandchildren of another race," Pearl Bailey's answer was the inevitably right one, "There is only one race—that is the human race."

She might have added that there is only one jive. In practice we break the human race up into sharp and jagged fragments, but we can't break up music in this way. Before two human beings can have a marriage which is a good going concern, they must find a way of communicating as human beings. In this case the two people seem to have found a language that cuts across their diverse birth and breeding and background.

I am not arguing that music is an infallible food of love, and that intermarriage will work if it springs from the clarinet, is stirred into flame by the drums and is proclaimed by the trumpet. You can have unhappy marriages in every group, including musicians, and you can have happy ones. The fact that British hepcats danced in the London streets at the Bellson marriage, that Bellson played two bass drums at the same time and that there was "a wild be-bop celebration" is no assurance of happiness to come. But I do feel that where there is a common atmosphere some of the obstacles to intermarriage are overcome.

The fact that the Bellsons were married in London is itself a recognition that mixed racial marriages are easier in Europe. There are thirty American states with "antimiscegenation" statutes. Even worse, there are few groups in America where a Negro-white marriage is socially accepted or where the children who are its product are not put through a punishing ordeal as they go to school and grow up.

We must remember that white-Negro unions are by no means new. They have been a fact ever since the early days of slavery, as the presence of the large number of mulattos testifies. The difference is that up to now these unions have rarely been avowed or legally recognized, and have largely been one of the prizes for the white male under White Supremacy. But today, even away from the South, and even in New York, marriage across the color line is feasible only among the intellectual groups, the writers, artists, professional people, in whose minds the old prejudices are not caked so hard.

Gunnar Myrdal suggests, in his classic *American Dilemma,* that segregation is maintained largely to keep the two races from meeting socially, and thus prevent what most whites still regard as contamination. But segregation is breaking down, and with it the deeper taboos as well. On the question of how far this will go, and whether it will lead to a complete biological amalgamation, Myrdal's guess is that it will for many generations be limited in scope and effect. The present racial mixture among Negroes, he says, will be relatively stable for some time.

The amazing fact is that, in spite of all the obstacles, love and marriage keep crossing the color line more and more. How does this happen? I think it is a sign that as the caste system breaks up in America, under the hammer blows of legal, political and economic drives for equality, people are beginning to see each other not as categories but as human beings. But it is a mistake to think of intermarriage as any kind of "solution" of the Negro problem in America. Marriage should never seek to solve social problems. It should only unite individuals who feel they can make a go of a dangerous but satisfying venture.

June 27, 1955

After my column on the Pearl Bailey-Louis Bellson marriage, I got a batch of protests from readers who were worried about their sons and daughters. Wasn't I (they asked) advocating intermarriage? And wouldn't their sons and daughters, whom they had so carefully raised to be good Jews and marry Jews, or good Catholics and marry Catholics, or good whites and shrink from the thought of marrying a Negro —wouldn't these youngsters now be able to quote me against their parents, thus upsetting the whole structure so painfully reared?

I came in for quite a drubbing. Yet the fact is that I didn't "advocate" either marrying or not marrying outside your religion or race. It isn't heroic for a writer to sit back and advise someone to go out and do something whose dangers are bound to be great.

My intent was only to tell the facts—the fact that intermarriage of every kind is increasing, the fact that it involves difficulties and dangers arising out of group taboos, the fact that marriage always involves difficulty, the fact that a freer choice in marriage is in harmony with the freedom of an open society.

In every marriage there are bound to be clashes of personality between husband and wife. What is likely to happen in intermarriage is that both of them pick the differences of religion or race as pegs on which to hang their various discontents. The immediate issues may be questions of churchgoing or the kind of religious education the children will get. But behind them you will generally find sexual and temperamental conflicts.

In other words, when two people cross racial or religious lines to seek each other out, they don't escape the deep-lying problems that beset every marriage because they beset the human personality. They take on, in addition, the resentments of their families and the prejudices of their neighbors. And in the crises of their lives these resentments and prejudices may break through.

The difficulty of arresting the trend toward intermarriage is illustrated by the case of the Jews. I sympathize with those who say that Jews pay a penalty for intermarriage because the children of such marriages are swallowed up in the larger Christian culture and are lost to the fragile world Jewish community that is trying against odds to maintain its identity. But I doubt seriously whether Jewish survival— and the same goes for the survival of the Catholics or any other minority culture—is most wisely assured by this jealous inbreeding. The real dangers come from elsewhere.

The Jews of Warsaw had little intermarriage and the Jews of Germany had much, yet both groups were wiped out by Nazism. Theodore Herzl was the product of the assimilationist culture of Vienna and Paris, yet he conceived the idea of the rebirth of a Jewish state. In the American Jewish community there are two simultaneous trends —one toward intermarriage, the other toward a greater pride in Jewish identity. There is no contradiction between the two. Self-respect and freedom of choice are part of each other.

I have never tried to minimize the difficulties of intermarriage. Yet more people every year take them on. Why? I think it is because they take marriage seriously as a marriage of true minds and they do not admit impediments to it. From the start there have been fewer obstructions in American society toward freedom of marriage choice than in any other society. The whole point of American life is the belief that if we make our choices freely we have the responsibility for them, and we grow in the process of making them.

This is what gives America its appeal to other peoples. In India, for example, the taboo on intermarriage has for centuries been so rigid that marriage outside your caste or subcaste was unthinkable. In the last decades these rigidities have begun to break up, and the American idea that you marry for love and happiness—and follow them wherever they lead you—has revolutionized Indian thinking. The same thing is happening throughout the Moslem world too, from Turkey to Indonesia.

Our notions of love and happiness, our continued searching for them even at the cost of divorce and the unsettlement of children's lives—these are all part of this drive toward fulfillment. So is intermarriage, whether between Jews and Christians, Catholics and Protestants, Negroes and whites, Orientals and Occidentals. It takes courage and strength and self-knowledge and an open-eyed awareness of all the difficulties. But when these qualities are present, you would have to play God to deny and suppress them.

2. The End of the Affair

December 15, 1949

EVER SINCE Louella Parsons not so demurely broke the story about Ingrid Bergman's baby, the storms of debate have raged among some of my high-minded friends. I don't mean debate about Ingrid. That's an old story, and most of us have sensibly made up our minds that she is going to live her own life anyway. The debate has been about newspapers and their ethics in splashing this extremely private story across the nation.

I can't imagine any greater invasion of privacy than to have a bunch of snoopers not only on your doorstep but in your bedroom and practically in your bed, calculating the month of birth and almost fixing the day and hour of conception. If there is any indignity in our era that is greater than the others, it is this piracy that we practice against the spotlight personalities of our time, peering into every crevice of their private lives, leaving them in the end depersonalized.

The case of Ingrid Bergman is in one sense unusual. The fact seems to be that she, who has acted out the great legends of Hollywood, has herself been bitten with the Tristan and Isolde legend of the fateful cup and the abandonment to the destiny of lovers beyond all hope of either earth or heaven.

My high-minded friends ask what is gained by airing this kind of romance. Doesn't it debase the public taste and lower the public morals? In this debate I fear I cannot count myself on the side of the angels. All of us are fascinated with the human plight as it is revealed in death and violence, in love and hate, in the departures from commonly held standards. When the recording angel puts out the last edition, I suspect it will deal with the same themes.

The question is not whether you will censor out a whole area of human interest. Any censorship is a form of moral imperialism, based on the arrogant notion that you know better than others just what is good for them to read or hear or see. The real question is how you deal with any theme—whether you deal with it pryingly and furtively (which is often true of the bluenoses as well as of the tough boys and loudmouths), or with an effort to see what light it sheds on the human condition in which we are all caught.

April 17, 1952

Ingrid Bergman's letter to her husband is now part of our popular literature, read into the court record in the wrangle over their daughter. It belongs to the "It is hard for me to write this letter" genre. "It was not my intention to fall in love and go to Italy forever," she writes. "After all our plans and dreams, you know that is true. But how can I help it or change it?" And again, "I know how this letter falls like a bomb on our home . . . And now you stand alone in the ruins and I am unable to help you."

Most of us dress up the role in which we prefer to see ourselves. Ingrid Bergman's role was a blend of the compassion which shrank from inflicting hurt and the sense of tragedy-queen doom in having to inflict it.

The most notable phase of the letter is the element of "can't help" in it. It is in the main channel of the romantic tradition of love-out-of-marriage. It is compounded of surrender, inevitability, helplessness. It implies an irrational daimon which works in you beyond your control, and it harks back to the love potion that Tristan and Isolde drank together, doomed thus beyond earthly help or Heavenly punishment.

It is time to challenge this conception of helpless love. We have learned enough about human relations to know that while romantic love blended with sexual desire works powerfully in us, all human conduct is ethical conduct. Which means that, whether wrong or right, it is a matter of deliberate choice between conflicting values. To be sure, the choice is often made in states of high emotional tension, but it is nonetheless a choice and not a surrender.

The case for divorce must run in ethical terms. I am as impatient of those who count any divorce justified as I am of those who dogmatically condemn every divorce. Miss Bergman and Rossellini had the right to strike their own trial balance. Yet I cannot accept her "How can I help it or change it?" as a principle of conduct. Just as the human being is not a cipher in the calculation of a society or a church, so he is not a bit of spindrift battered helplessly by the current of a great emotion. He is a valuing person, and he does what he does, not by fatality but by weighing the consequences of his action for himself and for others.

Many things count in making such a choice. The hurt you inflict should count heavily. For many this factor, along with the disruption of an ordered if unhappy life, and the scar that a divorce usually leaves on children, are decisive against it. For others the overriding value is the need to build a productive life with a partner whose rhythms and concerns are like their own.

This is not just a question of selfishness, although sometimes the catchwords of romantic love do conceal a crass self-indulgence. Erich Fromm has pointed out, in *Man for Himself,* that ethics cannot be based on selflessness, that you cannot live wholly in others. The duty to children is only partly to shelter them from immediate hurt and to give their life continuity. It is also to give them, as a model for living, not a protracted deception but a confronting of life's choices with responsibility and courage.

We cannot sit in judgment on the choices of others. But we can at least recognize that they are real choices, made by grown men and women, and that life is neither a trap set by society nor a love potion to surrender to.

November 8, 1957

The story of the Rossellinis is a sad story for each of them in a different sense—for her because something she cherished has tumbled to pieces, for him because the compulsive automatism of his life and character must now be as clear to him as it is to the world. But along with the compassion we must give it there are some disturbing reflections on the ideal of romantic love as it operates—oh, how differently —with a man and with a woman.

For Ingrid Bergman, from the start, her love for Roberto Rossellini represented a total commitment. Her assailants at the time were bitter about her infidelity and the illegitimacy of her child. What they didn't see was that she had made an absolute of her love for Rossellini and was willing not only to suffer but even to hurt for it.

I quoted in an earlier column from her classic letter to the husband she left: "It was not my intention to fall in love and go to Italy forever. . . . But how can I help it or change it?" I wrote at the time that I couldn't accept the "can't help" as a principle of conduct. Now, eight years and three children later, Ingrid finds herself in turn a victim of Rossellini's "can't helps." He has found an Indian girl whose appeal is greater, and presumably he too is swept by an emotion that he can neither help nor change.

Thus the wheel has come full turn. In that first letter Ingrid spoke of it as falling "like a bomb on our home . . . And now you stand alone in the ruins, and I am unable to help you." Today it is she who stands alone in the ruins, beyond any help. This isn't the kind of punishment that her haters foresaw, but it will do. What the moralists and moralizers never see is how unnecessary it is for society to punish the tragically daring people who cut across its cherished codes. If they don't surprise the world by making a go of it, they usually punish themselves by the logic of action.

This is the danger that a woman runs when, like Ingrid, she falls back on the romantic tradition of fatality in love. If she uses this logic to chuck one man and sink herself in another, she must submit to the same logic when he in turn chucks her for still another. Hence the stilted and hollow tone of the new "separation" letter. Hence the references to the "unforgettable past" and the "reciprocal profound affection" for each other. Hence the little farewell luncheon with a friend. I think that "civilized" is the curious word that is usually applied to such phrases and gestures, which belie the underlying bitterness. But in Ingrid's case, what could she do but accept from her husband a principle of conduct which she had herself once enshrined?

So we come to the end of the affair. "How much alike we are!" Ingrid had once written about her lover. "With the same desire for the same things, for the same kind of work and the same understanding of life." But in the "separation letter" this has become "the differences in viewpoint and interests which divided us." And the "unforgettable past"? It is the one phrase in the letter that rings true, even if it might also carry some irony with it. Can we say about an eight-year episode like this one that it was justified by the memories it leaves? The implication is that history (in the form of memory) makes morals. My own feeling is that memories may help cement a going relationship, but they usually embitter a shattered one.

At least for the woman. The thin but crucial line of difference between Ingrid and Rossellini, from the start, was that her total commitment was permanent, his temporary. I do not mean here to write sweepingly about the difference between women and men. Maybe it was just the difference between Ingrid and Rossellini. She took the plunge recklessly, almost blindly, and has come through it with courage and grace. And he?

He seems to me a man in constant search of a love object who will prop and nourish the infant in himself. There are some men for whom the perfect life with the perfect woman is always just a little distance beyond the horizon. And so they race on. Such people are never happy unless they are constantly falling in love and thus constantly renewing their belief in themselves and their powers. Generally this goes with a fear of declining power. It is like feeling that if you can get a new car or job or hat or love, you will be a new person with a new creativeness. Maybe, of the two, the case of Roberto is the sadder.

3. The Marriage Agony—and After

April 22, 1956

THERE ARE two novels on marriage on the current list of best sellers. One is Irwin Shaw's *Lucy Crown* (Random), the other John O'Hara's *Ten North Frederick* (Random). They are both symptoms of the obsession of contemporary American novelists with the theme of marriage as a kind of hell.

Lucy, in her mid-thirties, and married fifteen years, has a summer vacation affair with a college boy, is discovered by her young son, and finds her life as well as her marriage in ruins. Three lives—hers, her husband's, her son's—are wrecked in the process. Having been too dependent on her husband at the start, she goes to the other extreme and tries the method of complete candor about her later infidelities, with the result that her husband beats her up and then goes off to war to get himself killed. At the end Lucy and her son, at the site of the husband-father's grave, have a dramatic reconciliation scene that resolves little, and look back at the blunders that destroyed a marriage and a family.

If Irwin Shaw has a catastrophic view of marriage, where everything turns on a single fateful episode, John O'Hara prolongs the marriage agony over a lifetime, in fact over several generations, with no single moment the destructive one. If anything, O'Hara's view is even bleaker than Shaw's, for while Shaw implies that the catastrophe need not have happened if the wife had been a bit stronger, the husband a bit wiser and the child a bit less priggish and neurotic, O'Hara seems to be saying that this is how marriage in America is, and that's that. He is a social historian who sets down faithfully, with a monstrous eye for the exact detail, the change in sexual and marital customs in small-town America over the generations. Yet whatever changes, he says, hate and emptiness inside marriage remain the same.

In fact, instead of leveling all their fire at Kinsey, I wonder why the self-appointed defenders of American womanhood have not run O'Hara out of town. If what he sets down is the truth about marriage, then it is a devastating truth.

For what happens in the two major marriages in O'Hara's book, that of Ben and Charlotte Chapin and that of their son Joe Chapin and his wife Edith, is that the women stifle or eat their men.

Edith knew how to ensnare the most prized and glittering young man of Pottsville's good families. When she married him, and the marriage was completed and he had fallen asleep, her triumph was complete. "I own you, at last," she whispered. And the author adds, "it was going to be her life, the owning of this man . . . It was going to be as though she had covered him with a sac and as though he depended on her for breath and nourishment."

And that was how it worked out. If I were to weave a wreath for Joe Chapin, I should say that he was a better than ordinary man who meant well, who was born to wealth and position, who had every resource of American life available to him, who was attractive and mannerly and restrained, but who succeeded only in getting caught in a web of marriage which broke his daughter's heart, left his son feeble and cynical, and squeezed all the vitality out of his own life and left it empty.

It was only at the end that Joe was able to break out of the stifling web, falling in love with Kate, his daughter's New York apartment mate. O'Hara makes it a hopeless love for both and gives it only a brief and shining moment, for Joe was the product of his Pottsville subculture and Kate knew it. When it was over, everything was over for Joe.

It is a sobering thought that while the American sociologists are on the whole hopeful about marriage in America, the novelists are bearish on it. Maybe it is because the happy and fulfilling marriages, or even the tolerable ones, don't make good novel and theater and movie copy. Or maybe the novelists sense more clearly the corruption of a social order from within and its assaults from without.

June 28, 1951

There is a divorce trial in New York that is getting considerable publicity. But then, there is always some divorce trial or other that millions of people are following. In every American town the daily account of who has been two-timing whom and why and with whom is as indispensable as the toothbrush and the ice-cream-soda parlor. It is part of the daily "love nest literature" which is one of the native products of popular American culture.

It should not be confused with the outpourings of gossip columnists. The difference is one of detail and authenticity. The gossip columnist tells you, at most, only that some once bravely launched marriage is on the rocks, and that the husband (or wife) has been seen in the night spots with some old or new flame. But if you want the lowdown, in its monstrous detailed literalness, you must wait until the case hits the divorce pages, complete with affidavits and pictures.

The spectacle of our private lives that we thus offer the world is scarcely an attractive one: the charges and countercharges, the accusations and denials; the series of clandestine meetings, whose record is kept by a lynx-eyed spouse as by a recording devil; the tallying of the adulteries committed, with time, place and person specified, since the law in its majestic objectivity demands coldly detailed evidence here just as it does in murder or accident cases or in civil suits between two hucksters; the little black book, with names and phone numbers; the indiscreet erotic diaries; the bundles of letters which are invariably described in the press as hot enough to be written on asbestos, but often turn out to be only the sentimental moonings of a grateful Park Ave. Bovary; and then the climactic evidence, snared by private detectives and photographers in hotel rooms or in some mountain cabin or some back-street apartment; the door forced open while the camera is held in readiness, the flashlight explosion, the cry of surprise and humiliation, the sheet thrown around the hapless woman to hide her nudity, the faces full of shame and rage and consternation that turn up in the photos and are handed around to the members of a gravely appraising jury. But what can never be offered in evidence, although it unmistakably fills the courtroom, is the stifling hate that has come to two people between whom once there had been at least a strain of love and confidence.

Not all the love nest literature is divorce stuff. There is a second main branch, the suicide stuff. How many times have readers regaled themselves with some real-life tragedy headed "She Finds Sweetheart Is Wed, Turns On Gas," or "She Thought She Knew About Men, Ends Life." With it perhaps is published a photograph which a quick-talking reporter has filched or an enterprising elevator man has sold to the papers, showing the woman in her better days in an almost undraped pose, with the inscription: "To Bill, with all my heart," or "For Harry, forever and ever." Both the picture and the story that goes with it are likely to be a ghoulish kind of cheesecake—the cheesecake of heartbreak.

Let us face it honestly: The reason why we eat up the love nest literature is that there is at least a little of the Peeping Tom in all of us. We like to read about the tribulations and entanglements of others. In the divorce-and-custody cases we get the double pleasure of identifying ourselves with the boudoir episodes and yet feeling superior because we are safely out of the whole business. In the suicide stories millions of readers learn in death what only a few intimates knew in life. For a fleeting moment the veil is lifted. We are allowed to look back at Sodom and Gomorrah without turning into a pillar of salt.

4. Together and Apart

October 10, 1950

OLD-TIMERS like myself must lament that privacy seems to have gone out of marriage, and the press conference has taken its place. It used to be restricted to Presidents, political candidates and visiting dignitaries, but it has now become the instrument of a new kind of power politics. I mean the power politics involving the loves, hates, marriages, separations, flirtations, attachments, divorces, intrigues and adulteries of the "name elite." It contains actors, actresses, crooners, TV heroes, heirs, heiresses, monarchs, princelings and assorted hangers-on. It is true of the Ingrid Bergmans, Rita Hayworths, Prince Alys, King Farouks, Errol Flynns, Bobo Rockefellers, Frank Sinatras, Ava Gardners, Barbara Huttons and Prince Troubetzkoys of our time that their private lives have become public terrain, and on that terrain they attack, parry and counterattack with missiles carefully polished beforehand by press agents and lawyers.

In most of these cases there is an interesting cycle involved. Their careers and fortunes are built on the millions who pay to see them on the screen, or who buy their theatrical or singing or other wares; and in the end it is these same people who are called on to weigh the rights and wrongs of their loves and hates. In the case of Barbara Hutton the fortune that got her into her troubles was built on the purchases of shopgirls and young housewives. But it seems to have led to a life whose dreams of glory are, if anything, emptier and more forlorn than even those of the five-and-dime consumers.

The pathos of Barbara Hutton's life is that all of "Grandfather's money" failed to wrap her in a sheath of assurance, but only served to make her more vulnerable to the buffetings of life. She proved to be Miss Lonelyhearts (I borrow the term from Nathanael West's novel). Each of us throughout his life takes part in some kind of search for meaning. But Barbara Hutton's pursuit of happiness seems to have had a heartbreaking quality of repeated eagerness and repeated emptiness. She represents the dead end of those more spirited but always vulnerable American heiresses in Henry James's novels who went to Europe to be bruised against the older, more cynical, more obdurate tradition.

The trouble with many of us, as Karen Horney points out in *Neurosis and Human Growth,* is that we build an idealized picture of ourselves and seek compulsively to live up to the pseudo self we have thus built. The unappeasable "dream of glory," in which we dress ourselves and others in the colors of an impossible glamour and perfection, drains us of the energies with which we could clothe our workaday but real selves. The deprivations of life are not to the poor alone. It is ironic that the two groups for whom reality is almost completely distorted in our American society are the very poor and the very rich.

September 11, 1952

When some of the professors—like C. C. Zimmerman of Harvard, who has been for years prophesying the doom of the American family and society—point to something like the Rose divorce case as proof that we are going the way of the Roman empire, I remain unconvinced. Our divorce figures are high, and the American family is rattling along a rocky road. But the case of Billy Rose and Eleanor Holm sheds no more than a marginal light on our intricate ways.

What they represent is what you might call the marquee marriage-and-divorce set. There is a small emerging class in America which is neither the old aristocracy nor the industrial rich nor the middle class nor the workers. They are people who have in most cases risen rapidly from the middle or working class, have come to New York or Hollywood or wherever, have had talent or beauty or ready wit as their capital, and have carried on every detail of their private lives by spelling it out in lights on the theater or television marquee. They make good copy, but they are not America.

It is well known that there are three kinds of divorce in America. One is the Reno kind, for the rich. The second is the perjured hotel room scene, which is mainly the middle-class divorce, for those who can't afford Reno or Mexico. The third is desertion, which is the poor man's divorce. Now we must add a fourth type, divorce by public-relations methods and press handouts.

What distinguishes the Rose case from others of its type is that there is some very high-powered talent invested in the battle of public epithets. Louis Nizer, who is Eleanor Holm's lawyer, is not a novice with words. And Billy Rose, who seems to have been masterminding his own strategy, once had a widely syndicated column on the strength of his crackling gag lines. For a while, a month or two ago, Rose was issuing a series of communiqués so intolerably brilliant that they set most opinion against him. It isn't just that "you can't fight a woman," as Rose puts it. The point is rather that Americans don't like gag lines and verbal brilliance when applied to what was once a marriage relation.

The irony of it is that with all the tumult and shouting, each camp has now come out exactly where it would have been in any case, without the battle of the bulletins. And, beyond irony, the pity of it is the terrible erosion that the human sensibility suffers in a process of this kind.

Here are two people who were once together and are now apart. Often this can't be helped, and when it must be it must be. It is always a shock to see someone you knew once in tenderness, and see him with a strange and cold eye. You hope the deadness will fall away and new sensibility will grow and both persons will be deepened by the bruises. But there are also times when you play it all in public, and then the pity of it is that it doesn't deepen but only coarsens.

August 12, 1953

When Bill O'Dwyer married Sloan Simpson in 1949, I noted that it was a case of the elderly braves deserving the fair, and that the pretty young women were coming to be the prizes for middle-aged males who had made good in public life. I have just reread that column, after the news of Sloan Simpson's divorce action. I don't withdraw what I said, but I want to add some sadder words about what happens when these May-and-December marriages fail. A famous public figure or a middle-aged rich man who marries a beautiful young girl has less of a chance to hold her in our society than in the more settled societies of Europe. For in Europe his place is fixed, and she soon finds her own position in the frame set for her—and both stay there. In America, everything moves cruelly fast. A man who yesterday sat on top of a heap of power and success may find himself tomorrow a shabby, discarded figure—and discarded by the girl as well. The chances are that at marriage they didn't know either themselves or each other. They knew only the gifts the other promised to bring when the headlines were hot. When the public fires grow cold and the promised gifts turn to ashes, the vows also grow stale, flat, and unprofitable.

I am no Domestic Relations Court judge. Maybe Sloan's reported testimony, that she knew right away the marriage wouldn't work, is just a technical divorce form or maybe it condenses one of those marriage tragedies that are irremediable. The reason I write of it is that the whole episode lights up the way in which the quest for happiness in our society overrides every other loyalty. The older conception of marriage was that the bonds of the union took first place, over happiness or wretchedness, glory or tragedy. Our present conception is that people must have the right to recognize their marriage failures and move on to something else that will give meaning to their lives by making them expressive. Like it or not, this is what Americans believe.

I don't judge O'Dwyer, any more than I judge Sloan. Of his political shadiness on the New York scene I have written many times. I think he was a weak man, not a vicious one. I see him now not as the former New York Mayor or the former Ambassador to Mexico, but as a man in his sixties who once went for the big prizes—in private life as in public—and had them within his grasp, and is now broken and forsaken. He may well say, with the Psalmist, "Let not the foot of pride come against me . . ."

What breaks most marriages, when they break, is that men and women try to use them opportunistically, or as crutches for their weakness. They repeat in their marriage, with each other, whatever was wrong in their earlier lives alone. Only the strong of heart can be well married, since they do not turn to marriage to supply what no human being can ever get from another—a sure sense of the fortress within himself.

And so O'Dwyer will go on practicing law in Mexico City, and Sloan will keep going to bullfights in Spain and seeking from someone else that sense of life's great stir that beautiful young women want. And our era, meanwhile, will be the poorer because something that seemed a going concern has gone dead, like a clock when the family is away and the house empty.

February 17, 1954

There are few stories I have found as painful to read as the current Roosevelt story. What gets me is the sense of seeing someone trapped —by his own folly, to be sure, but nonetheless trapped and helpless, a man in a noose, with an embittered woman pulling it tighter and tighter.

Before you start writing "Dear Sir—you cur," let me say that I don't find Jimmy Roosevelt's behavior exactly inspiring either. Men in public life have been known to commit adultery. Husbands have even been known to make telltale lists of initials, which are usually difficult to explain away as industriously compiled lists of insurance prospects. But it is surely a new frill in folly—and worse—to write your wife a letter giving names, dates and locations, and thus place in her power not only your own fate and fortune but the destinies of the women who may once have shown you some tenderness.

A passing act of folly, however stupid, seems minor nevertheless compared with a deliberate act which cruelly exploits that folly. As a sideline observer, with no obligations to wear a black robe and be judicious, I must voice my recoil at seeing the lady tightening the noose. I seem to remember a fateful letter burned in the knowledge that photostats of it have been made; photographs taken of the contents of bureau drawers; scraps of paper picked up from a wastebasket, perhaps, and pieced together to present in court.

None of us is a saint, and few lead lives that could profitably be exposed to public X-ray. The perverse and destructive French writer, Céline, once said that if a single government really told the whole truth for twenty-four hours, every government in the world would fall. I suppose the detailed cross section of any man's acts and thoughts for a similar period, in James Joyce fashion, would be equally damning. I do not pretend to know how to rate the gradations of the calendar of sin. But I tremble a bit when I think how the lady must have hated, and for how long, in order to prepare the noose with so cold a calculation.

Even in an age of cynicism about marriage and slackness about honor, when divorce suits are fought out savagely, the vindictiveness displayed here is breathtaking. American society is a curious affair. We have our codes of sexual morality, which many marriages observe in the breach. We have also certain breaking points, at which infidelities become intolerable, and the marriage is shattered. Then in turn we have a set of rules about dissolving the marriage, in which there is always a certain amount of jungle warfare in the struggle for higher or lower alimony and maintenance. Yet even the warfare is supposed to have its limits, and—ironical as it may seem—its code of honor.

"They order these things better in France," as Laurence Sterne used to say. In fact, they order these things better almost anywhere than we do with our system of divorce laws that are designed to protect the defenseless, but often claim other victims. After this particular display of female savagery, I hope we shall hear less about "the natural superiority of women." On my records this lady is not for praising.

5. Death and the Social Set

October 31, 1955

IF A WHITE-COLLAR or working-class housewife had gone to sleep, been awakened (as she thought) by the sound of a prowler, reached for a gun, fired into the darkness of the hall, and shot her husband instead, it would have rated an inside-page story or perhaps a one-edition headline. But when the woman is a member of the younger "social set," and the husband the owner of a famous race horse, and when the killing happens after husband and wife have come back from a party for the Duchess of Windsor (all of which happened to the Woodwards), it is bound to be at least a seven-day sensation.

What I am saying is that even amidst the shifting class lines of our "classless" democracy there is still a "Society" group spelt with a capital *S,* and the people in it seem to be bigger than life for most of the groundlings and middlings—almost as big as if they were movie or TV stars or baseball heroes.

I don't know what complex strands of accident and incident were interwoven to lead to the death of William Woodward, Jr. But it focuses attention on some of the things that are happening to the "social set" that is the darling of the society editors.

I don't suppose anyone has the illusion any longer that these people are happy, or even that their lives are particularly gay. Every time some tragedy among them breaks into the papers, and we get a chance to take the front off their houses and look in, what is revealed is less glamorous than the legends make out.

I am sure this isn't a class matter, and that it would be true as well of almost any family where tragedy rips the façade off the home. Thoreau's phrase still holds, that most men live lives of quiet desperation. But in the case of the social rich the desperation is not so quiet, the parties tend to be drearier as well as swankier, and the gap is stark between what life might offer and what actually comes off.

The things they have are hard, material things—the gowns and jewels, the race horses, the estates, the spending so much time at night clubs and what Cleveland Amory called the *Last Resorts*. I remember seeing a magazine spread about one of their gala Long Island masquerade parties, and it was a sad business. The Woodward case gives us a glimpse that reinforces the sadness. What sort of life is it, to sleep in separate bedrooms, each with a gun handy in case someone breaks in? And what a prospect of happiness is opened when a wife, hearing a noise in the hall, thinks immediately it is a prowler rather than her husband coming perhaps to join her.

In one sense the Woodward marriage was typical of what has all along been happening to "Society" in America but has now increased its pace. I am thinking of the invasion of pretty girls from across the tracks—the "Cinderella matches" which never discover a real Cinderella and rarely are matches, but which signalize that an attractive and energetic girl has made it. Most rich boys are too herd-minded to break away, but more and more often now you will find a shy boy like Woodward reacting against the formal and frozen relations of his home, and marrying a girl from nowhere in Kansas who seems to have the warmth and energy he needs.

The movement in and out of the "social set" is now so fluid that it has become a kind of perpetual motion. The American social scene as Henry James or Edith Wharton knew it no longer exists. We never had a real aristocracy, but what there was of it has got badly blurred around the edges.

It is usually said that what killed American "Society" and its elegant mansions and big formal dances was the Sixteenth Amendment and the income tax. I don't think so. I think what did it was just the opposite—the overflowing abundance of money everywhere, so that no one class was set off by having it.

Look at any of the picture magazines, and see the handsome clothes horses with their brocades and velvets and minks, their Balenciagas and Capuccis, and note that they reach across the continent from New York, Baltimore and Detroit to St. Louis, Denver, San Francisco and Seattle. Where so many are rich, it is hard for the rich-over-time to feel especially distinguished.

They have lost much of their assurance. They are caught between a formality they no longer dare assert and an informality they don't know how to enjoy. The real elite has moved elsewhere, where things are being done, and the old set is left feeling empty.

ENEMIES OF THE GENTEEL TRADITION

1. "Red" Lewis at High Noon

January 11, 1951

"RED" LEWIS of Sauk Center died in a hospital in Rome, without family or friends near him. There is something not only desolating about this but also curiously fitting, for despite his saltiness of language and his drinking and conviviality he was in essence a lonely man who wrote lonely books about a lonely America.

I think it is wrong to assign Sinclair Lewis to any "school." True, he was a realist and satirist, and one of the "Bad Boys"—perhaps one of the Baddest—in a decade when irreverence became the rage. But there are other reasons why his half-dozen good books will live.

Lewis at his best (and what mountainous masses of mush he turned out when he was not) wrote greatly because his theme was the great one of the impoverishment of spirit in America. Remember that his big decade, which saw *Main Street, Babbitt, Arrowsmith* and *Dodsworth* published, was the decade of Harding and Coolidge and the seeming secret of perpetual prosperity.

Although the twenties were dominated by Mencken, his real master was not Mencken but a man Mencken despised—a Norwegian farmer's son who also grew up in the Midwest, Thorstein Veblen. Lewis read the *Theory of the Leisure Class* when he was writing *Main Street*. The two books are united by their hatred of the dead hand of the past, their scorching satire behind a mask of detachment, and their mixture of rebellion and hopelessness. Remember that Carol Kennicott sets out to reform Gopher Prairie or flee it, and ends by staying in it and bringing her idealism down a few pegs.

Lewis rewrote *Main Street* many times, in each of his books. He would take some theme of American life—business, boosterism, science, religion, divorce, fascism, racism—and "work it up," with an impressive mastery of detail. But always there was the same running refrain: the conflict between idealism and complacency, the attack on whatever was smug and phony, the being smothered under the blanket of mediocrity, the yearning to be free by becoming different.

Not much of a social philosophy, you might say. No, it wasn't much, and the philosophy itself was almost always presented badly because Lewis was a literary craftsman and not a social thinker. Primarily he will live because he painted a gallery of unforgettable portraits with a fidelity at once savage and tender. But a gallery which includes Carol Kennicott, George F. Babbitt, Martin Arrowsmith, Max Gottlieb, Elmer Gantry, Sam Dodsworth, Doremus Jessup, Buzz Windrip didn't just happen.

After the twenties he wrote only one book worth reading: *It Can't Happen Here*. His fruitful work ended with *Dodsworth* in 1929, at just about the time of the Great Depression. My hunch is that his career ended then largely because the America he was satirizing and trying to stir up with gadfly stings also ended then. Franklin Roosevelt and the New Deal, among the other things they accomplished, put Sinclair Lewis out of business, much as they made H. L. Mencken a dead letter.

For with the New Deal the gadflys from Veblen to Sinclair Lewis had done their gadfly work and stirred the complacent American giant from his slumber. In fact, Lewis was himself a bit frightened by the destructiveness of the missiles that came to be hurled against his own former targets, and he turned to defending them.

At first we used to believe that he hobnobbed with the Babbitts only in order to caricature them, and embraced them so that he might the better strangle them. Then we found that there had always been something of Babbitt as well as of Dodsworth in him, and that his attack had been part of that struggle with oneself out of which most meaningful art comes.

The later books were largely empty and barren. But those written in the twenties will endure as the record of America's yearning as well as of the dreariness it possessed at high noon.

2. Mencken and the Dragons

October 19, 1950

THE GREAT ONES are passing. In a Baltimore hospital H. L. Mencken lies hopelessly stricken and dying. I wonder whether he knows how many of us will feel the world diminished by his death. I write these few words in homage to a man whose opinions on politics, economics, democracy, music and mankind I rarely ever shared, a man who much of the time has been perversely and pertinaciously wrong. Yet also to a man who has been a gusty, cleansing figure.

I have been reading Edgar Kemler's delightfully wry yet informative life of Mencken—*The Irreverent Mr. Mencken* (Little, Brown). In the twenties the first editor who ever took one of my articles was Mencken (this was true of many other writers, too), and I proudly saw it in print in the *American Mercury*. It was a piece on J. P. Morgan. I still have somewhere Mencken's letter in which, after saying he would take it, he pointed out one or two gaps in it, and asked some questions about detail that showed the solid knowledge and discipline from which he wrote.

Many years later, in Philadelphia in 1948, we first met when we both covered the political conventions. I remember Mencken especially at the Wallace convention. We sat in agony through the first evening. There were endless speeches from the floor on how to heal the woes of every depressed group; there was a harangue on Puerto Rico by Vito Marcantonio; there was a kind of technocratic talk by the grandson of a former and forgotten U. S. President; and there were assorted crackpots.

The more improbable the talks became, the more Mencken seemed to come to life. He had a lusty passion for crackpots of every kind. At some length he held forth to me on the theme that he had fought his fights against censors, bigots and Puritans exactly because he loved crackpots, and if they were shut up or shut out American life would lose much of its wild flavor.

It occurred to me then that Mencken was in his way more of an anthropologist than many of those produced at Columbia, Harvard and California. He saw America as a bizarre mélange of tribal customs, taboos, incantation, High Priests, stuffed shirts and mumbo-jumbo medicine men.

At Henry Wallace's famous "Guru" press conference, a photographer saw us together. Mencken said, "This is our first—and probably last—convention together. Why don't we let him shoot us?"—and we did. I would give a good deal to locate that picture. For it was at that conference that Mencken reaped part of the harvest of his integrity. When Wallace was calling everyone who asked about the "Guru letters" a "stooge of Westbrook Pegler," Mencken got up and put the question. Wallace had to say, "You are certainly no one's stooge, Mr. Mencken." It was a tribute, however grudging, to a half century of the career of a complete individualist who was what he was because he hated all stooges and lackeys, including the unconscious ones.

Seeing Mencken that day, surrounded by Pegler and O'Donnell and some of the dreary Willies who were the mercenaries of wealth and bigotry and power, I got some perspective on him. I saw that although he shared their Roosevelt hatred and even some of their reactionary views, he was of a wholly different breed. They could never get inside his peculiar passion for freedom, because none of them had ever been part of a liberation movement.

That was Mencken's great historic role. He was not just a good philologist and chronicler and a so-so critic. He was part of America's life force at a time when we needed most to get ourselves loose from the Sahara sands of the stuffy, genteel, smug, intolerant. He was a chronic "agin"er with a brash, egregious style—but he was a good deal more. Almost singlehanded he took on the dragons, and he pierced them with his ridicule.

We will miss him, because the Sahara Age has been succeeded by an Ice Age. The bigots and censors, the snoops and yahoos are with us more than ever. But though Mencken is going, we know it is we who are the inheritors of his passion for freedom—we and not the bigots.

3. Old Man Hemingway

September 4, 1952

WITH ALL THE TIRRA-LIRRA about Hemingway's new little novel, *The Old Man and the Sea,* a postscript to the rave reviews hasn't much left to cover. I don't know how good it means you are when *Life* pays you more than two dollars a word for some thirty thousand words, but let's agree Hemingway is at least that good, with his clean economy of construction and his refraining from the pretty-pretty images and his gravely paced rhythms. There are still cramping things about him too: he no more explores the old fisherman in depth than he does his other characters—the boy and the big marlin and the sea. But with all its mannerisms and its narrowness of focus, the story and its fierceness of belief hold you as unrelentingly as another story once about another old seaman, the Ancient Mariner.

But I am not writing a treatise on style and literary genius, and I doubt whether Hemingway meant his story to be taken that seriously. What strikes me most about it is that it had to be in a Cuban or some other foreign setting, because Americans don't feel about old men— whether workers or politicians or corporation presidents—what Hemingway makes you feel about the old Cuban fisherman.

We concentrate on boyhood, we put the accent on youth, and we deal with grown men in the fullness of their powers. But in our fiction, as in real life, we keep pushing them always down the line to their declining years, when we can forget about them. If an old man gets into our novels in a big way, it is usually to show how he wrecks the lives of his children, or as a study in senility.

I know of a rich man, who built up one of our most successful corporations. He is sixty-two, and when his directors heard he had developed a heart tick they got panicky, kicked him upstairs to a do-nothing job, and brought in a forty-four-year-old as president to give the business "fresh blood."

Hemingway has always celebrated courage, and prowess over nature, and the undefeated. What he adds here is that he celebrates these qualities in a ragged old fisherman, who is too old to eat much or sleep much, whose hands are growing too old to pull at a line with a big one on it. In his youth he had great strength, but it has passed, and now all he has is the cunning of long experience and the distilled wisdom of hundreds of tussles with the fish and the sea. That, and the fierce love of doing what no one had done before.

Try to imagine the same story—the same boat with a single man in it, the same big marlin fighting to the end, the same long helpless pull out to sea, the same sharks eating away the fish's body, the same skeleton at the end—but imagine it with a vigorous young man in the place of the old one. It would still be a good fishing story, but it would no longer say much about whatever it is in man that will remain un-beaten when the seas open up and the heavens fall.

Since every story is in part autobiography, I suppose this one is Hemingway's answer to something that bothers him. Not just an an-swer to the critics who panned that last one about the young Italian countess and the dying bull of a soldier. A writer never answers his critics, he answers what troubles him in himself. When you have written books about a farewell to arms and about a sun also rising, and can't write them any more, you toss on your hard bed and churn in your anguish and dream about the big ones that even an old writer— especially a cunning and experienced old writer—can still land. And each of us, reading the dream, finds something stirring in him that has nothing to do with the cruel and inevitable cycle of the generations.

HOLLYWOOD: THE MADDEST, SADDEST PLACE

1. The Empire of Stratagem

Los Angeles, November 29, 1951

ALMOST EVERYTHING that has been said about Los Angeles is true, but not of great moment. It's true that it is a loose collection of suburbs without any center, and a sprawling aggregate of flashy-looking "homes" which are rarely in any true sense a home to anyone. It's true that its populations grow like cancerous cells. It's true that this Southern California area is the dream world of the automobile manufacturer, with an average of one car for every two persons. It's true that there are hardly any sidewalks in one luxury suburb after another, because nobody walks; and the public transportation system is almost nonexistent, because every family has a car, some have two or more.

Some of the other things said about this collection of suburbs are true too—about the houses built around swimming pools, and the big salaries, and the obsession with taxes, and the toadying of successful producers, directors, screenwriters, agents. There is a goodly percentage of beautiful women, and there are a number of men who boast of their easy progress with them but seem nevertheless to keep the call girl business thriving. And there is constant, compulsive talk of the separations and divorces, the lives and loves and sleeping habits of your friends.

The movie industry is not nearly so important in the whole economic picture of Los Angeles and Southern California as is often believed. The real wealth comes from the oil fortunes and the light industries and real estate and merchandising. Where Hollywood has played an important role has been in giving prestige and glamour to the whole area, and—along with the climate—acting as a magnet to draw population.

Most of all, it has invested the whole surrounding area with the witchery of what can only be called "Hollywood values." Everything in the values is inflated, yet the existence of this hothouse growth at the center gives a feverish blush to the whole way of living that surrounds it. In that sense Hollywood is neither a place nor an industry, but a certain form of American life at fever pitch.

The most obvious aspect of this form of life is that it is a glittering society of prestige and consumption. It is not money alone that makes men throw their talent and energies into this rat race called Hollywood. Mainly it is the compulsive wish to be on top and be a success, to have everyone point you out at the studio commissary, to be known as the top director or the highest paid writer or the actor most in demand. Hollywood is proof that the real incentives that move men to frenzied efforts are in the competitive urge itself, and prestige, and the chance at conspicuous consumption.

What this whole Los Angeles area lacks is any mark of being a community. People here always talk of home as Iowa or Chicago or New York or wherever they came from. Those who have been here even ten or fifteen years still feel and act like transients. Every week the landscape changes, new buildings go up, new suburbs mushroom out. Nothing today is as it was yesterday. You have few links with others, no roots in the past, no great tradition into which you fit. The boom spirit and some of the violence and something of the ethics of the mining camp have carried over into the Los Angeles of today. It is the maddest, saddest place I have seen, and its story—if it is ever well written—would be the maddest, saddest story.

April 19, 1950

The wheel has come full turn, and we seem to be back in the Age of the Snoop, very similar to the days when H. L. Mencken broke his doughty lances against the bluenoses, the Puritans and the Prohibition agents. The current on-the-spot sleuthing by a Senate subcommittee agent, Judge Stephen S. Jackson, into the morals of Hollywood would be funny if it didn't have its pathetic side as well.

The pathetic element lies in the desperate search for some devil on the part of a good many earnest and well-intentioned people. They have a sense of being beset by surrounding diabolical forces, which plague them and account for all the ills of the world. If only they could pin down some particular devil—Communism, the Russians, the spies, Owen Lattimore, Ingrid Bergman, Dean Acheson, the city mobsters and racketeers, the Hollywood sinners—then they would feel that life is not so elusive, and they would have at least something specific to wrestle with.

If Mencken were younger, or if we had another Mencken without some of his blindness but with all his lusty capacity for puncturing the absurd, what a theme he would have in the snoopers of Hollywood. The Senate investigators as the Grand Inquisitors of our national conscience, burrowing into the bedrooms and peeping behind the transoms of our movie idols to keep tally of the number of their embraces and establish their legitimacy—that is one for the history books, like the pictures of those college boys of the nineteen-twenties swallowing goldfish. The day will come when the investigators will look back at this episode sheepishly and wish the picture could be expunged from the record.

It would be naïve to think that bluenose snooping, Anthony Comstockism and Mrs. Grundyism just happen to happen. There was a great Radical Scare in the early nineteen-twenties that went along with the book banning and morals hunting. We have the same alliance today. After every big war, in every transition period when the established standards seem to be crumbling, the hunt starts. It is always a double hunt: for dangerous ideas and loose morals.

When a king dies, and before another king has come in, there is sometimes a period which the historians call an interregnum. What we have today is a kind of moral interregnum in American Life. The small-town morality and the old-time religion are crumbling. Newer standards, which are bound to come, have not yet emerged. One king is dead, but it is not even clear what will be the nature of the new king, out of what material the emerging moral codes will be woven.

Hollywood is like the rest of America, only a little lusher, a little more frantic. The trinity that Americans pay homage to might be described as alcohol, sex and the belief in luck. Strong drink, sexual adventure, the excitement of gambling stakes—these are part of the larger pattern of our lives. Taboos against them don't seem to work.

Hollywood has always been a convenient whipping boy because the glamour of the movie scenes has invested the movie capital in our minds with a haremlike sensuality. A psychiatrist might say that the snoopers are so obsessed with Hollywood because they would secretly like to be in on the Babylonian revels.

Hollywood, October 24, 1954

Each time I come here for a visit my sense of wonder at the Hollywood mind grows rather than lessens.

A visiting journalist I know, here on an assignment, had a lunch date with a big studio executive he had never met. When he arrived on the lot it was clear he had a slight cold. Before he knew it he had been whisked through the whole series of medical services that the executives and stars get—X rays, cardiograph, blood count, penicillin inhalations, a studio car to take him back to his hotel, and a doctor to pay him two visits while he was in bed. My friend feels grateful, of course, but he is also bewildered at being the recipient of all this manna from a public-relations heaven. He says there is no place in the world where they do things quite as they do in Hollywood. He indulges in understatement.

Who that has ever worked in Hollywood has not experienced the runaround, the doublecross, the cynical lie? Who has not seen a man rise with lightning speed to the peak of power and prestige, accompanied by a brigade of flunkies who lick his boots as he stands on the height? Who has not seen the same man, when he has slipped and fallen, left abandoned as an unclean thing?

I was discussing some policy with one of the Hollywood people, and I asked him how he felt about it as a matter of principle. "Principle!" he almost shouted out. "I left that behind me thirty-two years ago when I came here." His bleak ravaged face showed it.

That may be why there are more analysts to the square yard in the Los Angeles area than anywhere in the whole world, including Vienna once and New York now. An analyst who sets up shop here doesn't wait long for business. In a half year he has every hour dated and the earliest time he can give a new patient is four months ahead.

Many commentators have tried to explain the sources of what I shall call the Hollywood syndrome. I don't pretend to have any more of a clue than others have. But just as a suggestion, perhaps what happens is that in an empire of stratagem the whole personality comes to be concentrated on manipulating the universe—perhaps more so in Hollywood than anywhere else except in the TV world of Madison Avenue and Rockefeller Plaza. (If TV had a city to itself, I think it would out-Hollywood Hollywood.) And where stratagems become the daily currency of life, then the great stratagems which the age has to use for sheer survival—the ego defenses—no longer can operate.

They become absorbed and lose themselves in the rest of the stratagems. Since the hapless chronic strategist usually sees through the devices he uses on others and that others use on him, he comes finally to see through the devices he practices on himself. The tricker can no longer be tricked by himself and no longer see himself as a noble and creative figure. Hence he comes to lose his respect for himself. The loss of self-respect—that is to say, the loss of a sense of identity—becomes the great Hollywood syndrome.

I have only one other clue to the high rate of neuroses in Hollywood. The people who drift to it are bitten by the success bug and the glamour virus. By the nature of their jobs in show business they have something of the media madness in them—that is to say, they come to life only when they become (in Harold Nicolson's phrase) "public faces." This is the mask they wear. Without it they cannot live.

Yet neither can they live with it. For they have to confront the gap within themselves between pretension and actuality, between the public mask and the private reality. They make life—through the dream world of the screen—more bearable for millions. But in the end they have to live with themselves, which is the hardest thing in the world to do, even for men who have not eroded their personality by cynicism. Hence they have to pay out big sums to the analysts, whose chief job is to get them to know who they are, and to stop hating the image they confront.

Obviously this isn't the whole Hollywood picture. There is creativeness here, too, and honesty, and hard work, and fair dealing, and genuine love between men and women who learn how to insulate themselves against the corrosions around them, and who can look their private faces in the face. But they are a corporal's guard. The rest are legion.

2. *Charlie*

April 11, 1950

I WENT TO SEE Charlie last night in *City Lights.* In the star-studded firmament of Hollywood, where the Oscars come and go, the continuing radiance of Charlie's appeal—despite the changes and chances of the twenty years since the picture was made, and despite the organized hate campaigns—is the only true miracle.

Why does Charlie last so well? The audience at the Globe had little of the gooey reverence we accord to a "classic." It was an evening of belly laughs. They were not smart-aleck laughs at the verbal gags thought up by some sweating script-writer, but laughs at comic situations. Charlie brings us quickly into a universe of his making, so completely the product of his magic that we shed all our responsibilities and become primitive laughers.

This may be, partly, sadistic pleasure at Charlie's humiliations. But it is also the joy at seeing our familiar universe turned topsy-turvy. Like all great laughter, it is the expression of delight at the incongruous.

Charlie is not arty, in the fake sense of the term. Our laughter is vulgar and basic because his antics are vulgar and basic. When the millionaire whom he has dissuaded from suicide drunkenly pours bottle after bottle of liquor into Charlie's capacious pants while Charlie sedulously keeps his little glass from spilling a drop, we laugh even at the ancient corn.

When Charlie at a gay party swallows a whistle and hiccoughs like a canary, or when he has his boxing gloves on in the fighters' dressing room and finds that he can't perform the human function of getting a drink out of the water cooler, or when he becomes a street cleaner and sees his best efforts marred by a passing elephant, it isn't exactly dainty but it is human.

Among the Italian peasants, in China, in the interior stretches of Africa, among the gauchos of South America, Charlie has been known and loved for decades. He is the eternal proletarian, shuffling down the echoing bleak streets with his flat feet and his ragged pants. There is no one, however much an outcast, who does not feel almost like an insider compared with this pathetic little man, a misfit in every job, always the outsider with his nose pressed against the shop windows of life.

Charlie is the embodiment of all the eagerness for life that was ever felt. He savors the liquor the millionaire gives him, rubs some of it on his chest, pours some for good measure into his pocket. He trusts his fellow men, woos them with a dainty effusiveness which makes us slightly embarrassed. But the embarrassment is due not to any distortion of values on Charlie's part, but on ours. As he watches the apache dance and hastens to rescue the damsel from the low-life brute who is beating her, is he being quixotic? Yes, but in laughing at Charlie we are really laughing at ourselves for having lost our innocence.

Being a great mime, Charlie is also a great dancer. As he teeters over the water's edge his teetering is a dance; even when he shakes the water out of his legs, having just emerged from his ducking, he makes a perfect design. In his eagerness for life, he grabs a woman on the dance floor at the night club and pirouettes frantically with her before her escort can come to the rescue. In the climactic prize fight scene—after which you will never again see one of those heroic boxing pictures without laughing—he turns the whole bewildering scene into a ballet.

But, like Nijinsky, Charlie's dancing is mixed with tragedy. "The writer," Flaubert once said, "amuses the public with his agonies." Charlie's medium is not comedy but tragicomedy. His affections remain unchanged, but it is the world that is fickle. Especially the possessors of the earth, like the millionaire schizophrenic who alternates between hugging Charlie when drunk and turning him out stonily when sober.

The closing scene, in which Charlie is recognized by the blind girl healed of her blindness, might have been intolerable bathos. But it is Charlie's triumph that he keeps joy, shame and apprehension in a balanced tension and makes it a triumph.

3. The Shadow on the Screen

December 26, 1950

SINCE I DON'T SELL, hawk or peddle anything that requires a license I had thought (in my doe-eyed innocence about life) that my ways would never cross the ways of New York's License Commissioner. I was wrong. For I had reckoned without the all-seeing eye and the omniscient conscience of Edward T. McCaffrey, who hands out, suspends and revokes licenses. He has decided that he is the one to decide what movie I can and can't see. And he says that along with eight million other New Yorkers I can't see a picture called *The Miracle*.

Why not? Because, says McCaffrey, he doesn't like the picture himself and he is sure other New Yorkers won't. "Personally and officially," he says—splitting himself neatly in two, and then dexterously joining the two halves in one—he finds it "blasphemous."

He hasn't asked me, and he hasn't asked you. So far as the record goes, he hasn't acted under any official orders or at the unofficial request of any religious authorities. Although he "finds the film to be a blasphemous affront to a great many of our fellow citizens," he is careful to say that there have been no protests against it.

How then does he know we feel as he does and want him to protect us by closing down any theater that may dare show the film? Not from the U. S. Customs, for they let it through. Not from the State Board of Censors, for they passed it. Not from the National Board of Review, for they gave it a high rating.

No, McCaffrey guards the gate that all these others have left unguarded. I doubt moreover that he would claim experience in thought transference. It is simply that he knows because he knows because he knows. And in the plenitude of his knowledge he must establish himself as the Big Brother for the unknowing, who cannot question his judgment because—like Orwell's Big Brother in the nightmare totalitarianism of 1984—he is their eye and brain and conscience.

But not mine, thank you. I'll make up my own mind about what is religious and what blasphemous, and I will fight for the right of other New Yorkers to do the same.

As it happens, I have already been corrupted by the picture. I just missed seeing it in Italy. It was in the summer of 1949, and I had just flown in to Rome from Belgrade. The first person I met was Anna Magnani, who was leaving for Venice where Joseph Burstyn had entered the picture in the Film Competition. I was invited to go along and I felt tempted, but I had a date with my wife in Rome, and Venice was too far to go to see a movie.

I finally saw it in New York, along with a jewel of a picture about French peasant land hunger called *Jofroi,* and a lyrical if slightly sentimental one from Maupassant called *A Day in the Country. The Miracle* isn't even the best of the three, because its turbulence is not always contained, but there is no question of the power of its impact.

It is an impact hard to define. Rossellini has adapted one of the stories from the Italian peasant folklore, about an idiot woman tending her flock on the mountain, who is taken by a handsome bearded hiker whom she confuses with St. Joseph. The townspeople mock her pregnancy, first pretending to do homage to her as a holy person, and then pelting her with garbage. She is cast out to have her child alone, wanders about without help in the agony of her labor pains, and dies as she gives birth to her child just outside the doors of the church that is locked for the night.

Is this blasphemy? Only if you stretch the story into an effort to travesty the original one of Mary and Joseph and Jesus. If this were the intent, it is hard to believe that the picture would have been so well received in Italy itself, whose people have a great religious tradition.

I am against arbitrary censorship, whether it be of *The Miracle* or *Oliver Twist* or *Birth of a Nation.* The menacing shadow on the screen is that of a License Commissioner who does not know the history or the meaning of religious freedom, which demands that state power be never invoked to fortify one group's view of religion as against others.

The real blasphemy is that of a little man who seems for the moment to have blundered into assuming godlike powers of decision for the rest of us.

May 28, 1952

When I think of the Supreme Court's opinion in the case of *The Miracle,* I can't help thinking of it in human terms first: of a gallant, uphill fight by a diminutive fellow called Joseph Burstyn. As the distributor of the picture, he faced pickets and riots, the ban by a License Commissioner, the revoking of his license by the State Board of Regents, the wrath of important church and censorship forces, and successive defeats in the two highest New York courts. He fought his case up to the U. S. Supreme Court—and won.

At the heart of most seemingly impersonal historic episodes there is some kind of personal story of a man who held fast when the walls and the roof seemed to be caving in on him.

Although the court was unanimous in reversing the ban of the Regents, the reasoning differed. Justice Clark, speaking for the majority, wrote a straightforward and unadorned opinion that not only vindicated the right of anyone to see this picture but affirmed broadly the principle of the freedom of the movies. Justice Reed concurred in eight dry and brief lines, seeing nothing complex or difficult about the whole problem. Justice Frankfurter, speaking also for Justices Jackson and Burton, concurred in a learned separate opinion of thirty-four pages, resting on the vagueness of the term "sacrilege," refusing to declare any general proposition about freedom of the movies. It was a bad day in court for the whole clan of censors, including officials, clergy and self-appointed lay vigilantes.

The Clark decision has finally saved the Supreme Court's honor and overruled a decision (standing since 1915) which held that the press is a noble art affecting the freedom of men's minds, but the movies are only a crass money-grubbing business unrelated to freedom. That opinion was written by Justice McKenna, years before the movies began to talk, in the days when they were still housed in nickelodeons. Now the court has caught up with the movement of history. The court is now ready to say that the guarantees of the First and Fourteenth amendments apply to freedom of the movies as they do to freedom of speech and the press. The opinion industries are now gathered under the same roof of freedom.

On the concrete issue of the censoring of religious themes, Justices Clark and Frankfurter are not far apart, even though the latter seems to think it was not necessary to overrule the 1915 case. Both point to the vagueness of the term "sacrilegious." Frankfurter has written a fascinating essay on the history of the term, tracing it through all ages and every dictionary. In the narrow meaning of the defiling of church property, he shows, it does not apply to *The Miracle,* and in the broader meaning of the control of blasphemous views it involves the shackling of men's minds by bigots. Justice Clark, more innocent of semantics, contents himself with saying that with so vague a term as "sacrilege," the field is left open to control "by the most vocal and powerful orthodoxies." It is not the business of government, he says, to protect any religion from views distasteful to it.

This victory over the censors does not solve the problem of censorship. The network of state and local censorship boards around the country will still bay when the Legion of Decency barks, still tend to give in, as the New York Regents gave in cravenly, when the pressure of pressure groups becomes hot. The censors outside the industry will step more warily for a time. But the real censorship takes place inside the industry, at the hands of the Production Code Administration. It is this group that cripples and mutilates American pictures, leaving the force of ideas and the daring of conception to the foreign ones. Or rather, it is the timid men of Hollywood who allow the mutilation to happen to them.

June 1, 1955

When the Supreme Court in 1952 first declared that the movies were not just an industry but also an art, and as such came under the guarantees of free expression in the First and Fourteenth amendments, this marked a great transition for Hollywood. But more was involved in it than just arming it against censorship. It is one thing to have the freedom to say something. It is quite another to have something to say. If the movies are an art, they must have something to say—in the form of art—expressing both the vision of the writers and directors and producers and actors and the ferment of thinking and striving in the American culture itself.

My count against Hollywood today is not in Legion of Decency terms, that it is immoral, but that so much of its product is banal. The discussion of the morality of the pictures diverts us from the real problem, which is that of their creativeness.

This is true of the new Howard Hughes picture, *Son of Sinbad,* released here yesterday. The review of it in *Variety* says dryly that "left to its own devices" the picture "would find its natural level" in the market and that "it is no better and no worse than most of the almost countless such films" of the "sex-and-sand variety." Only the fuss that the Legion of Decency has made over it is likely to make it a box office success.

Obviously you can't judge Hollywood by such pictures. Just as obviously it is the Production Code which, by setting up impossible taboos, makes it difficult to produce mature pictures dealing maturely with real problems for mature people. The Legion of Decency, in its attack on the administration of the code, is trying hard to frighten the Code Administrator into applying it rigorously and mechanically. This can only mean that it will be all the harder to produce mature pictures, dealing with meaningful social problems of our day.

One of the answers that the Hollywood spokesmen have given to the Legion of Decency charges is that Hollywood, for the most part, produces pictures providing good "family entertainment." I don't know just what that much-abused term actually means, unless it means pictures like *A Man Called Peter*. I don't object to them when they are good. But to set a standard of family innocuousness for the products of what ought to be America's greatest national art form seems to me the depth of fatuousness.

Actually Hollywood is at its best when it breaks new ground and attempts controversial themes. Even in terms of box office pictures, *Blackboard Jungle* and *From Here to Eternity* and *Waterfront* are better bets than most of the saccharine products or even the Biblical extravaganzas and the sex-and-sand stuff. And in terms of the craft of movie making they are what gives Hollywood its reason for being.

Hollywood wants a place in the sun in world movie production. Unlike TV, American movies are intended for a world market, leaving an image in the minds of young Frenchmen, Italians, Indonesians. When foreign movie audiences see American movies, they may remember explicitly only the story and how the actors looked and what they said. But there is a different kind of residue left in their minds long after these memories have vanished.

Part of that residue is the imprint of American culture types—the gunman, the playboy, the lovely heiress, the earnest young doctor, the pretty secretary, the resourceful corporation executive, the tough and virile prize fighter or newspaperman or waterfront worker. These culture types are wrapped up in the stars who happen to be high in the Hollywood firmament, until it is hard to distinguish between the type and the star, but they leave the imprint of their image together.

If our movies are first-rate in craftsmanship, these culture types will remain in peoples' minds all over the world, wrapped in an emotional envelope of affection and good will. If they are shoddy, the envelope will be one of resentment and contempt. This is why the prime question about Hollywood is not whether its moral code is severe enough but whether in its art it expresses the ferment and energy of American life.

December 23, 1956

Cardinal Spellman's ill-considered attack on *Baby Doll* may have helped it to get audiences, but it has distorted the perspective in which the picture is best seen. I find the question of whether it is "immoral" a futile one. If it is immoral to portray on the screen a tangled skein of fear, insecurity, sex, revenge, compassion, frustration and love, then call *Baby Doll* immoral—but then you had better shut up shop in Hollywood and leave the movies to the Italians and Japanese to produce. True, it is no picture to which I would delight in bringing my children; a child would miss much of the characterization and the tangle of emotions, and would be baffled and disturbed by the curious forms taken by the sexual dalliance. But the only question worth asking about *Baby Doll*—or any other picture—is whether someone responsible for it has caught a glimpse through the slits that an artist knows how to make in the human mask and seen something beyond it that is worth conveying.

I don't mean that the picture has a moral or a message. To look for one is the other facet of searching for immorality in it. What it has is people: characters drawn by a writer who shows here again that he can make people whom we don't easily forget. And it has satiric edge. I don't know where else you will find this kind of portrayal of how the Southern tradition of gentility ("the Chivalry," as it used to be called) has come to a tattered and degenerate end. Maybe that's what Pegler means when he suggests that Kazan has never really changed his mind about Communism—meaning, I suppose, that to cut into the Southern social structure and personality patterns with the knife's edge of satire is to be Communist.

It isn't a gentle thing to say, but Tennessee Williams says it: that one can find the last embodiment of the tradition in the form of a frightened, inept, insecure man, deep in debt, worrying about impotence, boasting about being related to every good family in the county; and in a blond girl-wife who has never gone beyond short division, who has never allowed her husband to consummate the marriage, and for whom he has bought as a curious kind of dollhouse a big mansion in the emptiness of whose rooms the unfulfillment of love and marriage takes on an added dimension of meaning.

Into this frame Williams brings an "outsider"—a Sicilian from Corpus Christi (how obsessed he has been recently with his theme of Sicilian primitivism and passion intruded into the hypocrisies of our own society). And into it Kazan, whose virtuosity as a director continues to explode in every direction, brings his wonderful feeling for local faces and scenes—the cotton farmers, the local enforcement officials, the Negro workers and retainers.

It is Kazan, also, who is responsible for the sheer visual delight of the major sequences in the picture: the camera moving about the dilapidated house; the burning of the syndicate cotton gin; the macabre game of love, half childish romping, half sexual pursuit, that the Sicilian and the girl play on the long afternoon; the kitchen scene in which the passions come to an explosion; and the final wild scene outside the house with the husband shooting into the darkness at the shadow of his own inner terror.

It is true that the fight against the attempted censorship of *Baby Doll* is a crucial fight for freedom. But I am not content to fight only for freedom from censorship, important as it is. I feel better when the freedom is being used for something.

That is the nub of the matter. The American movies are probably the greatest of the popular arts that our culture has produced. It is the art of Chaplin and Garbo and Disney, and of writers and directors who have done something different from what the Elizabethans or Victorians did. We can keep this tradition alive or we can let it be snuffed out—cooped up, as if we were children, in a baby dollhouse where we are given the right pap to eat and the right instruction for what to see and think.

Hollywood, February 20, 1957

I came here to find out what has happened to the Hollywood mood in the afterwash of *Baby Doll*. I can report the big brass in the large studios to be in a state of near-panic and hysteria about it. Almost without exception, they hate it, recoil from it and wish that it had never been born or made. Geoffrey Sherlock, who administers the Film Code, and who "passed" the Kazan film and incurred the thunderbolts of the Legion and Cardinal Spellman, has been admonished by the studio brass never, never, but never, to let it happen again.

What terrifies the brass is not the aesthetic quality of *Baby Doll* but the fear that the controversy about it is bound to hurt "the industry."

Why then did the Johnston office pass it? The reason is that it came after two other pictures that had made Code history and had left the censors with red faces. Both were Otto Preminger pictures—one *The Moon Is Blue* and the other *The Man with the Golden Arm*. The Johnston office was much too timid in refusing to pass the first, a mild little comedy in which there were a few lines of dialogue about going or not going to bed, and it made a fool of itself. As for the Algren story about a narcotics addict, that clearly came under the senseless Code taboo against the whole theme of addiction, but audiences saw it all over the country in spite of the ban—and were stirred by it.

Thus, by suffering two defeats, Preminger won two victories for the greater freedom of movie making. My guess is that when Kazan submitted *Baby Doll*, the censors, twice burned, were loath to make fools of themselves again, so with a new show of courage they let it pass. Someday the historians of the movies will salute them for having made their stand even while their knees were knocking together.

Thus two pictures that the censors banned made history, as well as a third that they passed. All three times the censors got the brickbats, twice when they deserved them and once when they didn't. I would rather wash dishes in a restaurant on Skid Row than play the silly game of cat-and-mouse as a censor with the smart directors and writers who spend their waking hours figuring out how to get by the Johnston office and still deal with the great themes of sex and morals that are supposed to be kept from the young and old adolescents on whom Hollywood lives.

February 25, 1957

"We're a manufacturing business, like any other." How many times one hears that sentence in conversations with Hollywood producers and distributors. But at least there is a note of honesty in such a sentence, which stands out from much of the hypocrisy about Hollywood "freedom."

Continually you hear the Hollywood censors and their mogul bosses say that the Code isn't censorship; it is free and voluntary self-regulation. Maybe so, but once you have bound yourself to the Johnston office, you must accept its changes and prohibitions. In fact, most of the time you anticipate them. You have bound yourself with your own thongs. Every now and then an independent may break away, take his risk without the seal, rig up his own marketing machinery and buck the Legion of Decency. Of such is the kingdom of the rebels, who by their orneriness save the souls of the self-damned.

The main difference between the American system of censorship and that of other countries is in the stage at which control is exerted over the picture. Since America is the great producing center for movies, and has sensitive religious and pressure groups, we exert our controls at the point of the production of the picture. Other countries bring in the control at the point of exhibition.

From a manufacturing standpoint the trouble with the European system is a double one. It brings the government into the picture; also, if you wait until you get a rating for exhibiting your picture, and children are barred from seeing it, you suffer the loss of the family trade. Incidentally, the only two countries that show signs of following the American system are Germany and Japan—our two great former enemies. You can say it is because both have learned the bitter lesson about government controls. Or you can say that these are the two great imitative countries.

There is one big difference between the European and American viewpoints. The European censors are mainly concerned with the question of the effect of movies on the children. The American Code officials are concerned with church pressure groups. The American Code was originally written mainly by Catholic Church clerics and laymen, and its administrator was a Catholic, Joe Breen. The present administrator, Geoffrey Sherlock, is an Episcopalian who was trained under Breen, while two of his staff members formerly studied to be Jesuits.

Even more striking is the composition of the reviewing groups of voluntary organizations outside the movie industry, who rate and accept or condemn the pictures after they have been censored, passed and released. The Catholic group, the Legion of Decency, is headed by Msgr. Little and Father Hayes, but the reviewing panels are composed of women. The panels of the Protestant and Jewish reviewing groups, far less vocal and powerful than the Catholic, are also staffed by women.

Thus there is a succession of ramparts that a picture maker must overleap. First, he censors himself, from his experiences with the Code and the studio heads and the outside groups. Second, he must reckon with the Code people. Third, his picture is rated or perhaps even condemned by the regiment of reviewing women. Fourth, in some states there are state censor boards that also get their licks in. Fifth, there is always the danger of a boycott, especially by the Legion of Decency or perhaps by Jewish organizations, even after the picture has passed the other obstacles.

These are the Hollywood taboos. How good pictures somehow manage to get made, with these taboos, is one of those miracles beyond definition. A good picture represents the triumph of the creative spirit over idiot obstacles.

Sometimes a Hollywood intellectual will tell you that codes are good for the creative artist, because they represent a challenge to him. If that is so, then the best pictures should be coming from the countries where church or state are most powerful, which isn't so. The only ingenuity the Hollywood code develops is ingenuity in evading the code, like a tax lawyer's ingenuity in evading the income tax. Such trickiness is different from creativeness.

The Code bears no relation to life as it is lived in these United States. It places taboos on sex, even in marriage; on kissing that has some intensity; on the themes of drug addiction, homosexuality and (not wholly) on prostitution. Where there has been illicit love of any sort, there must be punishment or death.

The toll levied on the pictures has been a heavy one, by making many of them phony in their values. Yet Hollywood still gives us better products than TV, which is dominated by timid sponsors. The movies are still a great popular art, not because of the Code but despite it.

4. Oscar—A Cool Million

March 29, 1957

ONCE AT SALZBURG, while lecturing on American civilization, I tried to describe "Oscar" to a class made up of graduates from European

universities. It was hard. I said that he isn't a man, because he was not
born of woman and would go on living beyond the human age span;
that he isn't an institution, because he is still too lively; that he isn't
just a statuette or a trophy, because those come a dime a dozen,
whether for golf, for making the best sales record, or for living a long
time. The best I could do was to describe him as a composite of a
victorious military campaign, an election to the French Academy, a
Dior fashion show and Narcissus gazing in the pool at his own image.
This was, I suspect, making it too complex. But how make Oscar simple? The military campaign is there, as witness the elaborate battle plans
drawn up by every studio before the voting. The French Academy is
there, as witness the desperate importance attached to a figurine, as
to a bit of ribbon. The fashion show is there, as witness the faithfulness
with which the choices express the prevailing modes and tastes of the
Hollywood and American worlds during the year. Finally Narcissus
is there, as witness the loving self-admiration with which Hollywood
stares at its own reflection in the mirror every year.

I should have added that there is a measure of hokum, too, in the
recipe, because man cannot live by the authentic alone—he needs a
dash of hokum thrown in.

As this nonexpert gets the story, the Motion Picture Academy was
formed to raise the craft standards in an industry where most of the
talk is of business. It worked, as is testified not only by the size of the
TV audience, but even more by the prestige the award has achieved.
These members of the Academy who cast their votes—the writers,
directors, producers, designers, actors and technicians who make the
movies—are all pros. Yet nothing in Hollywood can keep out the
element of huckstering, which comes with the deed to the movie lot
and persists to the slab in the cemetery. How can you keep the hucksters out when the major Oscars must each be worth, in the immortal
phrase of Nathanael West, "a cool million"?

No wonder the studios and their public-relations men work overtime and spend handsome sums in the trade papers to tout the artistic
distinction of their products. A picture produced on a shoestring, as
Marty was in 1955, may have more money spent on the Oscar campaign than on the original production.

But while the movie people (like the rest of us) don't work *without*
money, few if any do it for the money alone, but for a crazy wonderful
drive to have their bit of flame recognized. And since the movie people
are people who can't be sure they exist until the audience and their
fellow craftsmen have told them so, the Oscars have a meaning beyond
all dreaming and scheming.

I lunched once with a Hollywood actress, one of those blondes
whose mammary glands have become a national institution, who told
me that there was nothing she wouldn't do—but nothing—if it could

help her on the road to an Oscar. I believed her, because there was a terrifying intensity with which she said it, and the terror in Oscar goes further than the hokum in it.

There are also tragedy and triumph in it—heartache and pain and sheer exultation. I call to witness the case of Ingrid Bergman. She has been, for years, the Scarlet Woman of Hollywood, who dared fall in love with her director, leave her husband and daughter and have a child before her marriage with the man she loved. It wasn't so long ago that clubwomen, churchmen and all the moralists and moralizers of our society were calling for her to be burned at the stake, much like the Joan whom she had dared portray.

It is a rich triumph that she now reaps, when she is honored as a great artist in the same country which lashed out at her as a fallen woman. It is also a belated honor, for she was as good an actress a few years ago—when no studio head would have the courage to make a picture in Hollywood with her—as she is now. But, belated or not, Oscar proves he has a conscience somewhere under his gleaming patina, and the award must be taken not only as redeeming the over-timid but as rebuking the fanatics who periodically terrorize opinion in our country.

5. Mike, Liz and the Gods

March 24, 1958

THE JAUNTY SHOWMANSHIP of Mike Todd's life was equaled by the tragic showmanship which furnished the setting for his death. And death came to him on the crest of the wave. He had married one of the world's beauties. He had made a remarkable movie and was getting ready to make another. He and his wife had toured the world's capitals to the ovations of gaping crowds. He was rich; he flew about in his private plane; there was to be a testimonial dinner for him at the Waldorf, graced by the Governor and the dignitaries of the popular arts.

He was full of plans and schemes. He was riding high. Everything was breaking for him. Then suddenly the charred fragments of his plane in the Zuni Mountains, and a grief-stricken widow at Beverly Hills.

The ancients, who did not live in our kind of power-drenched, money-saturated society, had the idea that the jealous gods punished a too successful man for his overwhelming ambition. This was what the Greeks called *hubris,* the sin of pride. They felt that total power and happiness belonged to the gods alone, and man must not infringe upon it. Behind it was the idea that it was sacrilegious for a man to lay too clamorous a siege to the good things of life.

Mike Todd was not an ancient Greek, but a very modern American. He lived not in Thebes, but in Chicago, New York and Hollywood. In America, where money and power are the fabric of our lives, and everyone is expected to make an effort at amassing them, we don't entertain the notion of the gods being jealous of the man who has everything. In fact, he has become the symbol of our ideal goal.

We have replaced not only the ancient gods, but God Himself, with the new divinities of money, power, prestige and success. Many Americans envied Todd while he was alive. When his life was suddenly snuffed out, it was the kind of tragedy that evokes in us only a nameless awe at the suddenness with which fortune can shift.

Here was a boy born Avram Hirsch Goldbogen, of an impoverished immigrant rabbi's brood of eight children, who grew up on the streets of a big city and learned to hunt down a fast and sharp buck. Here was a man who changed his name to one that fitted the American scene better, who made and lost a couple of small fortunes that a man with less gambling impulse would have put away safely, who went bankrupt owing more than a million, made a comeback to money and fame, and to cap his glittering prizes won the most glittering of all— a famous young movie star of surpassing beauty.

In an era of bigness, requiring big investments for success, there are not many areas of enterprise left where a man can start from scratch—except the talent professions, which are the last Klondike of our time. Todd's talent was that of the showman who aims big, takes risks, talks fast, assesses shrewdly the tastes and demands of his audience, and uses his imagination.

Although he grew up on the pavements and had the smell of asphalt in his blood, Mike Todd's type can be traced back to the boasting, outrageous frontier characters depicted by Mark Twain. He combined the resourceful tenacity of the Jewish immigrant family (he had in large quantity what the Jews call *chutzpa*—sheer nerve) with the vaulting imagination of the open frontier and the highly developed contemporary arts of publicity and salesmanship. When he threw a party, he had it in Madison Square Garden and let TV record it. He figured that if one great star can make a picture a success, why wouldn't a score of stars make a superpicture a supersuccess? He worshiped speed and bigness as the ultimate values. Everything was to be big, everything fast. The sky was the limit—as in the end it turned out with a tragic literalness to be.

The curious reader who may want to trace this theme back a bit will find some things worth noting in Irving Wallace's recent book, *The Square Pegs* (Knopf), a collection of essays on Americans who dared to be themselves. Todd built his picture around Jules Verne's novel, *Around the World in Eighty Days,* but Verne in turn modeled his novel on a trip taken by a fabulous American named George Francis

Train, whose career Wallace describes in a chapter called "The Man Who Was Phileas Fogg."

As you read about Train, you are struck by how much Todd and he had in common. There was the obsession with speed, there was the plenitude of nerve, there was the globe-girdling self-image, there was the extravagance about everything, especially modes of transportation. There was the knack of making business agreements as both men traveled about. There was the ability to make and lose a fortune and make it again. There was the irresistible gift for persuading money and credit out of practically anyone. There was the jaunty self-confidence, the feeling for bigness, the flair for publicity.

What I am suggesting is not only that Todd was drawn by his own nature to the character of the man who was the original model of the Verne story, but also that he existed in the American experience long before he was born. He will be followed after his death by others cut to the same pattern. He had to the full the highly charged Faustian hunger for life. He illustrated what Justice Holmes used to say—that the purpose of life is more life. He was a characteristic part of the dream of infinite energy and infinite possibility in American life. When he died it was as if a dynamo had stopped—except that we cannot hear the noise of its silence because of the din of the other dynamos.

Somewhere on a city pavement there is a hungry boy, charged with the same energy that Mike had, equipped with the same wild sense of life, dreaming of the same success. He will achieve it. That is Mike Todd's best memorial.

February 20, 1959

The great Hollywood drama is approaching its resolution. Mike met Liz and Eddie met Debbie, each couple married and both couples were an ideal foursome; Mike departed this world, and Eddie departed from Debbie to solace Liz; now Eddie and Debbie are lawfully parted; and soon Eddie and Liz will be lawfully wedded.

Hurrah for the headlines, hurrah for the alimony and property settlement, hurrah for the lawyers' fees, hurrah for the hurry-up-please-it's-time judge, hurrah for Debbie's demure answers to rehearsed questions, hurrah for love retrieved and love vindicated and for the bliss ahead.

I am not shaking a moral finger at this familiar press trinity—Debbie, Eddie and Liz. All three are very young still, and pretty immature, and not too badly off. If they want to conduct their emotional and sexual education in public, who is there to say them nay? Nor is their case the typical kind on which moralists are likely to deliver a homily about the sinfulness of divorce. In this American civilization of ours divorce, like any other commodity, is easier for the rich than for the poor and easiest of all for the males of the moneyed elite who practice a kind of polygamy-in-sequence and for their gold-digging young wives who make a good thing of brief marriages and big alimonies.

But this description doesn't apply to the Eddie-Debbie-Liz dance on the hot tin roof of divorce. All three have good earning power and expectation. Debbie didn't really need the money nor want the divorce, Eddie is no sugar daddy getting a jaded thrill out of a new bride-to-be, and Liz is no doll-faced upstart from the other side of the tracks.

No, the story is about love. Eddie seems so much in love that he is willing to leave his two kids and pay a whopping million or so to get his freedom to remarry. As for Liz, it is probably ungenerous and overliterary to go back to Petronius' story of the grieving widow of Ephesus who did not wait too long to find life and love good again. Liz seems one of those women who is meant for fulfillment. Usually, whether in Hollywood or New York, it is the American male who marries a succession of wives. But this time it is Liz who is going to marry her fourth husband.

The divorce proceedings were fast and smooth and synthetic— almost Mohammedan in the ease with which the mate was shed. In the brief colloquy between the wronged lady and the judge, the stress was (appropriately for Hollywood) on the publicity stirred up by Eddie's wanderings after strange goddesses, and the resulting distress of the wronged lady. It was oh so civilized, and oh so phony, which means that it was good legal ritual.

Yet the elemental facts of life remain. Strip away the civilized veneer, and the blood and bitterness gush up. Of the triangle it was Liz who got her man—the beauteous Liz, the Liz of a score of love-goddess roles in glamorous films, the Liz in whose private life everything has seemed golden and everything has dissolved in ashes.

There is a terrible sadness about these publicized private Hollywood lives. The jungle remains. The friend turns, in the stilted language of the courtroom, into the "other woman." The wronged wife puts on a smile as she poses for the photographers, but when you add up her take you find that she has driven a pretty cold-blooded bargain to punish the two who have dared to plunge into a reshuffling love.

Many will doubtless identify with the woman who, despite the money she got, lost out in the jungle struggle, and who must take her alimony back to a loveless home. But I suspect that most of us identify with Liz and Eddie, because our deepest impulses strain toward beauty and love. I can't guess how much appeal Eddie still has for whatever women may read this column. But I will wager that there are few male readers who, in the secrecy of their own hearts, don't daydream of what it might be like to be the love object of Queen Liz. Such is the power of the movie image, and such in a humdrum world the strong undercurrent of the romantic dream.

But having said this, I can't help but be uncharitable and compare this triangle with the great romantic love stories of the past out of which come the romantic pictures-in-our-mind.

For some reason, while thinking about Eddie and Debbie and Liz, I turned to a savagely brilliant book, Robert E. Fitch's *The Decline of Sex* (Harcourt, Brace), which lashes out at the way love is described in our recent novels and the way it is lived in our lives. Fitch turns for contrast to *Romeo and Juliet* and to *Tristan and Isolde,* and notes that, after the strong and tender passions of those lovers, in our own time "love" and "duty" have become four-letter words.

He scores a point. For love, as we sometimes practice it, can be reduced to the dullest litanies of sex, without the tenderness and suffering and courage that give the sexual relation its excitement and meaning. What I wish for Liz and Eddie, who have suffered and shown some courage, is that the prize they have bought so dearly should not turn out to be just dull.

WORDS AND MUSIC

1. Call Me Madam, Softly

October 16, 1950

I WENT to *Call Me Madam* with the hope of seeing a rollicking political satire in the great Kaufman-Gershwin tradition. I saw instead a
genial entertainment contrived with skill to make the Princess Theatre the Hostess to the Mostes' of the Customers. It didn't ever get far
under the skin.

Nevertheless, it's worth seeing. The great footlights are a kind of
ritual, the way an Army-Notre Dame game is. Put a Hayward-Ber-
lin-Lindsay-Crouse-Abbott-Robbins team together, give it a Perle
Mesta theme, add Ethel Merman, and you have something. There are
good dances, songs, lines and spoofing. But for political satire you
draw a blank.

I keep thinking back to the political satire in *Of Thee I Sing.* Why
couldn't that have happened to *Madam?*

It could have. The show starts with some ragging of what is a
heaven-sent natural for satire—the Washington Cocktail Party line.
For a while hope wells up, and you think perhaps they will have
the daring to put on a musical parallel to Bob Allen's biting book,
The Truman Merry-Go-Round, and show how small-town minds
make big-time politics, and how full of frails and frailties the City of
the Gods is. But the strain peters out, and for the rest of the butter-
and-milk evening nobody gets skinned.

Starting with the Perle Mesta story, the authors had to choose between two ways of playing it. One was to go backward from the swear-
ing-in scene, show the whole Washington hothouse out of which it
sprang like an incredible flower, and end with the superb scene of
Perle's distraught and breathless entrance into the Embassy at
Lichtenberg reciting her canned friendly-relations piece and waving a
Rand-McNally map of Europe. The other was to show how the small-
town rich middle-aged American girl Made Good in Europe and in
Love.

They chose the second and easier way. Instead of the conquest of
Washington by the small-town Cocktail Party line, we get the con-

quest of Europe by American energy and friendliness. The Washington story could have been satire. The Lichtenberg story unrolls as an amiable homily proving that Love Conquers All, Money Is Not Enough, and Democracy and Point Four Can Win Europe.

That's what made one of Perle Mesta's friends remark to me that the show was so-so but "Perle came off well"—that is, without any satirical treatment. That was the trouble. Except for some jibes at Margaret Truman's singing, everybody came off well—Democrats and Republicans, Senate and House, Acheson, Truman, and especially "They Like Ike" Eisenhower.

So did the now hardening Ezio Pinza tradition of using young love only as a dreamily idyllic backdrop in a musical, while the foreground story (with which the audience makes its real identification) is one of middle-aged gallantly romantic love.

I hope I'm not too naïve about how easy the Washington story would have been. I know our era doesn't make a good climate for political satire. Under the Russian propaganda attack we have grown sensitive to any ragging from inside our own ranks.

But our fears are mostly liars. Despite McCarran and his cohorts, Americans still have a sense of fun. The play's one sharply satiric line about our jitters—Madam Minister telling "Harry" over the phone, "I'm so happy that I ought to be investigated"—drew a yell of delight from the audience.

American playgoers can stand strong meat. Ethel Merman's hold on us all comes not from her looks or voice or acting, but from her raucous energy and the special quality of toughness she brings to every part. It is the sheer life force she embodies—and Perle Mesta embodies it too. A people with that much life force can afford to laugh at itself, its incredible capital, its lonely men and women huddling for warmth at parties, even its own pretenses.

I'm waiting for another *Of Thee I Sing,* and I don't mean sweetly or softly.

2. Guys, Dolls and Runyon

January 3, 1951

SOME OF MY FRIENDS would no more dream of missing a theater first night than a trueborn Englishman would miss a royal wedding or coronation. I do not count myself among them, being only a middling theatergoer. But once I am inside a theater I catch the footlight fever, and I have found few Broadway seasons that have not offered at least two or three things to remember.

Of the current crop Christopher Fry's nonburning *Lady* had such

word richness that I didn't miss what failed to go with it; and Clifford
Odets' *Country Girl* was a curiously warm and moving portrait of a
lady of another kind; and the Housman *King Lear* with Louis Calhern
presented that wild account of heartbreak with a strength that with-
stood its shattering grandeur.

Why then, after such presents, do I write about a sentimental
whipped-up trifle called *Guys and Dolls,* which for all its endearing
charms will scarcely prove enduring literature? I think it is because
there is something in the Runyonesque mood of this "musical fable
of Broadway" that fills the theater with a genial warmth and—no less
than the playwrights I have named above—presents a world that is all
of one piece.

What Damon Runyon amounts to, I suppose, is a minor classic of
urban American folklore. You feel about Nathan Detroit and Miss
Adelaide, about Harry the Horse and "Nicely Nicely" Johnson, much
as you might about the fables out of *Uncle Remus* or those out of
Marc Connolly's *Green Pastures.* We have simply shifted from the
Southern Negro heaven to the Broadway gangster heaven, but we
retain the same delightful fairy tale unreality.

I should have read Runyon long ago, partly because of Broun and
Lyons and Winchell, partly because my London friends regard him
as America's authentic author and their guide to the American underworld, and my Paris friends have learned their peculiar brand of
English from Runyon and the movies.

But, always a laggard about literary cults and currents, I didn't get
religion until I saw Runyon's short story "Idyll of Miss Sarah Brown"
on the stage, with its plot about the gambler and the Salvation Army
lass, along with the wonderful spun-up counterplot about Nathan
Detroit and his floating crap game and the night club girl who can't
get him to the marriage vows. After that I haunted bookstores and
drugstores and rounded up every reprint volume of Runyon, from a
quarter to $2.95. And almost every night since then, for weeks, I have
read myself to sleep with one of his treacle tales.

What the play takes from Runyon is partly a plot and some random
characters, partly the tension and rhythm of his hothouse Lindy prose,
partly the bad-glad-mad mood of his impossible world with just the
degree of sugary sweetening he used to give it himself. But mainly
what it has caught is Runyon's capacity to simplify our world and
make it come out right by inverting it.

People get hopelessly tangled up in the Runyon stories, but he always has an elaborate, ingenious plot that unties all the knots he has
laboriously tied. And there is an epic simplicity about his heroes and
heroines, as there was about Homer's. When a guy is rich he is a
zillionaire; when he is in love his doom and gloom are deeper than
that of Shakespeare's star-crossed lovers; when a doll is beautiful she

is a Helen of Troy in a night club; when she is shapely she is a walking goddess and distills the shapeliness of all lovelies; when she is a virago her strength makes Samson seem frail. It is bigger than life, and all very satisfying.

But its chief charm is that everything is made to stand on its head. The tough guys and racketeers have hearts of gold and rescue the child or hag in distress. The Neanderthal walking down a dark street rocking a crying baby has just cracked a safe with dynamite. The cops give you a break. To be sure, every now and then you peer with Runyon into the recesses of darkness, as with the shapely night club hostess who turns out to be a Biblical Jael and revenges her gangster husband's death by drowning his three assassins in the Atlantic City surf. But for the rest all is serene.

In short, things are sweeter than they seem. Our world will not be pulverized by a bomb. A sewer is for a colorful dance at a floating crap game, not the coming home of subterranean America. We can have guns and butter too. All men are brothers.

That's why Runyon has become my private pipe dream.

3. Shaw, with Sex Added

March 15, 1957

A FEW DAYS AGO, almost a year late, I finally managed to see *My Fair Lady*. Using shamelessly the coincidence of my name with that of Alan Lerner, I battered my way to the box office and became part of the American theater elite.

It was like seeing a timeless classic. The audience knew every song beforehand and many of the lines as well. They knew that Rex Harrison has no voice but could recite the songs as if he were singing them, and that he had the deceptive effortlessness of an accomplished ham, that Julie Andrews was made in heaven for the part of Eliza, that Stanley Holloway is a flawless Alfred Doolittle, that Alan Lerner and Fritz Loewe have miraculously turned a Shavian sermon into a triumphant musical, and that Moss Hart has pulled all the effects together with his sure touch.

In the American adaptation, Shaw's play has been transformed not just by omission and invention but by the fact that the Georgian England of Shaw has been all but replaced by the Eisenhower America of forty-five years later. Most of Shaw's lines are there, but their spirit has been absorbed in the delightful atmosphere of songs and fun.

Shaw was himself sexually neutral, and his play was meant to celebrate the sexlessness of Henry Higgins. But *My Fair Lady,* which is played to an audience for whom sex has become the most obsessive

thing in life, had to bring sex back. Shaw made fun of romantic endings. But an American musical audience could not have tolerated
Shaw's ending (Eliza marries Freddy after the play, and they set up a
little grocery shop in a spirit of proletarian honesty), and so Eliza
comes back to Wimpole Street to bring Higgins his slippers every
night.

Shaw's Eliza smarts under the indifference of Higgins, thus coming
alive as a human being; but the Eliza of Lerner and Loewe is not
only a spirited hoyden but also a dreamy girl who conjures up visions
of what would be "loverly" and—after a rough session with vowels
and aspirates—sings "I Could Have Danced All Night" with a moody
tenderness.

Don't get me wrong. This musical is a thing of beauty and delight
for young and old alike. My son Mike was entranced by it, as both his
parents were. And Stephen—seeing his first real play at eleven—
clutched my sleeve before the end of the first act and hoped the hour
wasn't late, because he couldn't bear to have the play end.

The elements that compose the delight are clear enough. There is
the amusing boldness of the idea of turning a flower girl into a lady—
the great theme, not of the Cinderella story, but of the Galatea myth,
which is far deeper because it cuts to man's sexual urge to fashion the
woman he loves or dominates. There is the element of craftsman's
triumph at the heady moment when Eliza succeeds with "The Rain in
Spain"—the only time in the theater's history, surely, when an
audience hangs suspended on the turning of a diphthong. There is
the element of suspense: Will she or won't she pass muster under the
cold eye of the world at the Ambassador's Ball? There is the theme of
the assertive woman, Eliza, in the stormy scene where she passionately revolts against being used as a mechanism. And finally there is
the never failing American theme: girl loves boy, girl leaves boy, girl
returns to boy.

Every age and culture sets limits to what its playwrights are allowed
to do and supposed to do. Shaw delighted his England—and delights
us still—with his paradoxes and perversities, his way of transvaluing
values by standing them on their heads. *Pygmalion* as a play would
still be a success on Broadway, as it was in its revivals ten and thirty
years ago. But it would not be the historic hit that *Fair Lady* became
—not just because delightful lyrics and music were added, but because Shaw got a dose of his own medicine and was stood on his head.
As Americans we would not be content with less.

But I was most impressed by the sea change that takes place in
Henry Higgins as he crosses the Atlantic. Shaw makes him a pretty unpleasant fellow—sure of himself, crotchety, consistently rude, a quite
unordinary man. But the musical, especially in its second act, is com-

pelled to turn him into a troubled, smitten fellow who cannot rest until he gets Eliza back.

The American writers find it hard to resolve the problem of the relation between Higgins and Eliza except by giving Higgins the very commonplace sexual yearning ("I'm an Ordinary Man") that Shaw deliberately denied him. Shaw said in his postscript that Higgins had a mother fixation, hence his sexlessness; and he defended him on the grounds that "a person of genius" (surely he was thinking of himself, not just of Higgins) may "achieve by sheer intellectual analysis . . . a disengagement of his affection, his sense of duty and his idealism from his specifically sexual impulses."

A very interesting thought, but scarcely a theme on which to hang a Broadway hit. Nor one that any red-blooded, romantic American male could understand, or that any American woman could identify herself with as she dreams of impaling her love object on the golden spike of marriage.

THE PRIVATE AND THE PUBLIC

1. The Death World of Mickey Spillane

December 13, 1951

IF WE EVER DROP any books over the Iron Curtain countries as an example of our way of life, I hope we don't use Mickey Spillane's mysteries as ammunition. I have read his five Mike Hammer stories, in the Signet Books editions, and I feel as if I had been on a prolonged spree in a series of bawdyhouse booths built inside an abattoir.

The publishers say that ten million copies of these five books have now been printed in less than three years. A fact, I submit, which sums up our sick cravings and the ruthless pandering to them better than any other I know.

I happen to be a devoted, if erratic and rule-breaking, reader of mysteries. And I feel a trifle sad that the great tradition which started with Poe and Conan Doyle should now have everything washed out of it except violence, death and stalking the prey.

The Spillane formula is compounded of equal parts of sex, sadism and surprise. With his cop friend Pat serving as straight man and foil, the brutal and handsome detective hero, Mike Hammer, tracks the killer of someone dear to him with a consuming hate far beyond the call of duty. Before he is through, every book is strewn with more corpses than a Shakespearean stage, not counting the sluggings, beatings and mayhems that are a travesty of Hammett and Chandler.

Alternating with these rounds of violence and death are rounds of lechery at which Mike is also a champ. When the hero is not cutting open faces with the butts of revolvers or spilling brains over the floor, he is seducing and being seduced in boudoirs with the undulant regularity of Spengler's laws of history.

But I must not omit the "socko" Spillane endings. It is unethical to tell them, but it would be useless to analyze Spillane without pointing out that the climactic shock is always an emotional shock, since Mike Hammer must always in the end kill someone with whom he has become deeply involved through sex or trust, so that when he kills he kills part of himself. In one ending, which I hope will never be paralleled in any book ever to be written in any language, there is a solution in terms of transvestitism, one of the most nauseating scenes ever written.

In a hurried slip the other day, for which I now want to make amends, I bracketed Erle Stanley Gardner with Spillane. I must have been recalling the stacks of both of them at newsstands and drugstores across the country. Gardner's hero, Perry Mason, is primarily a lawyer who depends on his wits, and not his brawn or his sex appeal. Both write clumsily, but Mason has no sadism in him and depends rather on courtroom fireworks that I find curiously satisfying. Where Mason and Hammer are closest is in their Girl Friday secretaries, but even here Hammer's Velda is a strip-tease Varga version of Mason's Della.

Spillane's books are really prolonged literary lynchings, strip teases and rapes. The detective hero always plays God, which is why he never delivers the killer over to the law. He is his own law (note the titles: *I, the Jury, My Gun Is Quick, Vengeance Is Mine*).

To justify the acts of this two-fisted sadist, there is always some phony reason why he must purify the world of the killer himself. In *The Big Kill,* it is because of the symbol of a little orphan baby who must be saved for good citizenship. In *One Lonely Night,* it is that the nation must be made *"Roten-rein,"* purified of every Red rat, which may account for the scene where he machine-guns a whole Communist cell. The principle seems to be not that they are wrong and contemptible —which they are—but that they are a breed of submen.

You can see why the books are read. They are daydream books for the frustrated and sick. This may be how a man living an inadequate life wants to take a woman—to the accompaniment of violence and prowess, along with soft lights and snaky shimmering gowns. And this may be how some starved women want to be taken, with their eternally sheer nightgowns and their mesmeric nudity, laying themselves bare to a hero-killer Nemesis.

Maybe so, but if it is so then we would be better off with the frankly smutty books where sex is sex, instead of this picture of the American male who does not feel sexually virile unless he is the sadistic killer who sets scores even.

2. I Remember, I Remember

October 9, 1951

PEOPLE IN GOVERNMENT have to live dangerously. Not only are they targets of unending Congressional quiz shows, with everything in their past raked up from their campus sins to their Aunt Tilly. They now run the added mortal danger of turning up as a headline item in the juicy published diary of the man they sat next to at the stuffy Waldorf dinner, with whom they exchanged too candid remarks between the sparse cocktails and the abundant speeches.

Not that the diary habit is new, even among politicians, who as a class are too busy to read, let alone write. Diplomatic historians would be out of jobs if they didn't dig up who had said what to whom, thus leading to which delicate crisis in the world's chancelleries. But the quotes are hardly ever dug up until all the actors have long been dead, and have been pulled off the stage like kings stuck through the midriff in an Elizabethan tragedy.

Today we don't tarry that long. We don't even wait for the hard book covers to be slapped on the stuff: We hasten to serialize the hotter passages in the papers. The funeral meats have scarcely been cleared away by the diarist's mourners, before the fires are lit to roast the survivors alive.

Everything has become fiercely public in our time. What the diarist wrote is furnished up to damn a rival or impale a victim. The stuff goes directly from the leather notebooks to the composing room, and from there to the investigating session. What makes it deadlier than an autobiography is that it was set down at the time, rather than recalled at a later and wiser date. O that mine enemy had not kept a diary!

We must face the fact that a man in public life can no longer claim even the shred of a private one. To be an officeholder whose colleagues have a sense of their place in history is dangerous—almost as much as to be the financial intimate of a goon who keeps a little black book, or the lover of a Hollywood star with a literary turn and a passion for keeping count.

There are some men who record only their financial transactions in diaries, and others who limit themselves to their amatory ones, recording initials, phone numbers and cryptic symbols. The financier, the lover and the politician are still the three greatest risk takers of our time. I can't say I like the Senator or Cabinet officer who, after every confidential conversation with the great and near-great, runs to his diary like a blushing, titillated schoolgirl after her first high-school prom.

If you are in public life, keep away from diaries. Since a politician has studied lethal weapons of all kinds, he can scarcely plead about this one that he didn't know it was loaded.

I have myself never been better than a fitful diary keeper. When I was very young, I entered in a little red book all my dreams and resolutions. In adolescence I recorded my fears and failures. In early manhood some of my triumphs began to creep into the entries. Now I find that long weeks go by without a single item. I turn to my diary only when I am unusually baffled by the meanings and choices of life. I use it as a way of probing for the heart of darkness.

The true function of a diary is to record not so much what you did and where you went and what someone said, but what you thought and felt in the crisis moments of your life. To use your diary as a mode of revenge by a dead man on the living is an act that may create a paradise for historians, but only a hell for those who must go on with the world's work. When you talk to someone, friend or enemy, in confidence he has the right to assume that you will not betray the trust that the words imply.

The communication between two human beings is in itself the social tissue of life. When it is betrayed, for however noble motives, life itself is invaded and betrayed. This is one of the forms that the desensitizing of man is taking.

May 23, 1954

I have been browsing in the second volume of Harold Ickes' lethal political diary, *The Inside Struggle* (Simon and Schuster), and like everyone who likes escape literature I find it delightful. I call it escape literature for the obvious reason that Ickes has brought vividly back to mind the world of the New Deal days when political leaders vied with each other in their liberalism, and when a truculent reformer like the Old Curmudgeon could wield political power. In the darkness of our own era, this New Deal period seems like something invented in the wild imagination of Ickes—a gleaming never-never land into which we escape as into a historical romance.

I do not mean, of course, to question the accuracy of detail in Ickes' diary. His errors were never unintentional. They were errors of judgment and perspective rather than of fidelity of transcription.

I had a chance to test this fidelity by a passage in which I play a minor part. The diary notation is on May 15, 1938. It tells of my paying a visit to President Roosevelt several days earlier with Felix Frankfurter, who was still at Harvard and not yet on the Supreme Court. And it recounts the circumstantial story I gave the President about Phil La Follette's newly founded National Progressive Party.

Ickes goes on from there to tell of his own conversation with the President about La Follette, and how this led to a discussion of candidates to run in Roosevelt's place for the Presidency in 1940.

Now let me confess that when I first read the Ickes passage about President Roosevelt and myself my first impulse was to rub my eyes in disbelief.

I remembered that I had made a trip to Madison to see La Follette, had interviewed him at length, and had done a pretty severe report in the *Nation*. But, while I also recalled seeing Roosevelt a number of times, I couldn't recall this particular visit or the talk about the La Follettes. It seemed to me an invention with some probability in it, but still an invention.

Let me put it this way. Suppose an investigating committee had me

on the stand in Washington, and were trying to track down all my nefarious New Deal activities. Suppose the Grand Inquisitor of the committee had said, "Did you visit President Roosevelt with Felix Frankfurter in May 1938, and did you tell him the new La Follette party
had fascist elements in it?" I would have had to say, "No, I didn't."

I would have been quite honest, but I would also have been wrong.
The fact is that Ickes is roughly accurate, and that the visit and the
conversation did take place.

I have, let it be said, one of the leakiest memories in contemporary
America. You can't always explain it by the Freudian principle of suppressing—and therefore forgetting—what is unpleasant to remember.
I always found Roosevelt a delight to talk to, and the same holds for
Justice Frankfurter. I think I was right in 1938 about the La Follette
movement, so it is not a sense of guilt that would lead me to drop it
from my mind. The simple fact is that my mind is as full of holes as a
sieve.

Once I started to think back, however, the scene began to reconstruct itself for me. I recalled details not in the Ickes account. In fact,
I recalled so much that I had to start asking myself whether I was not
starting to build up a vivid historical tableau in which a minimum of
remembered facts was surrounded and embellished by a mass of invented fiction. Right now I am in a state of floundering, finding it hard
to distinguish between what actually happened and what might have
happened—or, at least, should fittingly have happened even if it didn't.

I shall not now belabor the point by applying it to the perhaps fallible memories of Paul Crouch or Louis Budenz or some of the other
professional confession craftsmen. I only say that I should hate to have
either my own or another's career depend on whether I could pinpoint
the details of what happened and what was said on that "early morning" (as Ickes wrote it down) of Thursday, May 12, almost exactly
sixteen years ago.

God help anyone else who has far more assurance than I can muster.

I suppose I shall some day, for my sins, write that inevitable I-re-
member-I-remember autobiography. I shall then have to decide
whether to fill it with badly remembered detail (with the help perhaps
of a few scraps of diary and some letters that have survived successive
movings), or whether to do it as a work of art and write my life as
it should have been lived. The extreme of the first—or diary—method
is to be found in the Ickes volumes. At the other end of the spectrum
I note that Ben Hecht is publishing an autobiography in which—as he
assures the reader—he has not consulted a single diary entry or note.

Of the two, the Ickes method may be better material for historians,
but the Hecht method is more aesthetically satisfying. Toward the end

of his fifties, surely a man has earned the right to take over a fraction of God's function and reshape his past closer to his heart's desire.

3. The "Confidential" Neurosis

September 7, 1956

THE SHOT may have been by accident or intention, but Richard Weldy's shot—like Mrs. Woodward's shot in an earlier case—was heard around the world. I am not an insider but an outsider in these circles, and I don't claim to know the confidential details in the shooting and wounding of the publisher of *Confidential*. But even with all the gaps in our knowledge of the case, it lights up the lives and morals of a whole segment of our society and may bear discussing.

The story starts with John Wayne, who was the subject of the *Confidential* piece that set off all the fireworks. Wayne belongs, as do all the others whose lives and loves adorn the pages of Harrison's sheet, to the new American elite of movie and TV stars. These people are the celebrities. They are not a born or inherited aristocracy but the product of our own popular culture. Young and old, male and female, talented and inept created we them—by our hunger for heroes and heroines.

Once thus created they are fearfully vulnerable. Most of them are young people from one social level who have been suddenly catapulted into fame and success and have become celebrities before they have quite jelled as persons. They become names and faces and voices to millions, and after a while—with a gnawing emptiness inside them—they grow dependent on the adulation they inspire and the publicity on which they flourish. But in many cases their direction is confused, their morals are hazy and promiscuous, and their indiscretions flower like a whole grove of green bay trees.

That is where the predatory animals come in. It isn't too hard to dig up dirt—phony or authentic—about these celebrities. And there is a huge audience ready to pay for an "inside" on the dirt.

When I use the term "confidential neurosis" to describe this new thing that has taken place in our society, I mean that it is a collective madness—or silliness—in which the celebrities, the predatory magazines and their audience all take a hand.

Watching newsstands casually and fitfully, I should guess that a large proportion of the four-million-plus readership of *Confidential* is made up of teen-agers, young housewives and fan magazine addicts. What they look for in it and get out of it is anyone's guess. Mine is that they are looking for reassurance that their idols are human, with human lusts and human frailties. Even in Shakespeare's age those who liked to read about the death of kings also wanted to read about the corruption of queens. Our kings and queens are of a different sort, and our hunger for the inside story may be even greater.

The confidential neurosis is the inside story gone mad. I am not against the sexual theme in journalism. And one thing that can be said for Harrison and his magazine is that they don't try to give sex a mawkish sugar coating, as some of the housewives' magazines do, and the Sunday supplements. But the constant scabrous disclosure to the public of the one phase of a man's or a woman's life that ought to remain private is one of the sickening aspects of American life today.

Then comes the Harrison shooting, and there is an audible sigh of satisfaction from millions for whom he, too—like the celebrities on whom he preys—has become a symbol. The story of Weldy and his former wife and Wayne was no different from many others of the *Confidential* genus—a tangled tale of a celebrity receiving burnt offerings of women, and of a husband who presumably offered his own wife, later to become the celebrity's. Nobody came off heroically in it, least of all Weldy—but then, no one comes off heroically in any of these tales. Their purpose is to deflate the celebrities and drag the heroes through mud, to the delight of the four million hero worshipers who want to see a famous face defaced.

The only difference is that instead of suffering in silence or going to court with a libel suit Weldy brooded, quarreled and resorted to the dubiously direct action of happening to turn up in the exact jungle spot where his quarry and dear friend were, and of happening to drop a gun that happened to go off.

Maybe it's all a publicity stunt, but it seems a farfetched one, with Harrison getting shot, spending the night in the forest, and having his own moral frailties exposed for his wife to read and comment on. I go for the theory that it all happened to happen, and that it was a kind of poetic justice visited on a man who will never get any closer to either poetry or justice. The hunter has fallen into his own toils, the preyer has become the prey.

It is too much to hope, as with the highly moral short stories, that the villain who gets a dose of his own medicine gets converted to virtue and goes back to the slower but less antisocial amassing of revenue through garment manufacturing. In Hollywood, perhaps, the sufferers from *Confidential* panic may get less panicky. But I hold to the view that Harrison's pay load will go on producing, because celebrities will go on being human and therefore vulnerable, and the hungry psyches of the four million will go on being hungry.

The irony of it is that the celebrities who are created by publicity should be the ones to become its victims. They can't breathe without it, they watch the papers and magazines every day for it—and then suddenly it turns to pestilence. The name of the magazine is itself a travesty of the publicity neurosis. It is hard to whisper "confidential" inside stuff to four million.

It is some kind of commentary on our upside-down values that our confidences are screeched with a klaxon shrillness, that the morals of our celebrities keep the scavengers busy, and that the scandal about the chief scavenger will only serve to sell millions more of his magazine and prove that it pays off well to live dangerously.

October 5, 1956

Don't ask me how it happened, but I found myself Wednesday night in a fracas on Steve Allen's TV show, trying to figure out what possible reason anyone could dream up for the "scandal" magazines. I suppose it was because I once wrote a piece that I called "The 'Confidential' Neurosis," in which I paid my respects to that highly circulated sheet on general principles, and this TV melee gave me a chance to think out loud about a question that seems to be troubling many Americans—perhaps even more millions than those who read the monthly bulletins of sin and perversion.

The question can be put quite simply: What are the limits, if any, for what a publication can say about the private life of a "celebrity"? Publisher Harrison and Editor Breen of *Confidential* seemed so bemused by the money they were making from all those newsstand sales that their answer was sweeping. For them the sky—or the mud—was the limit. As Breen put it, when I asked where he would stop in the prying: "When the photographer runs out of film."

My co-warrior in the brawl, John Crosby, gaily ventured the opinion (which I share) that the literature spilling out of those printing presses is dismally dull stuff. But it was no night for ventures into literary criticism. The *Confidential* warriors were confident of playing a heroic and virtuous role in exposing the dark places in the lives of assorted characters whose names are generally in lights. They could think of no one who ought to be immune.

When does a newspaper or magazine have the right to tell the story behind the story, and when does it become scabrous and destructive to do so? My own answer is: You can tell it when it has a real bearing on what the man is doing or what he professes to be.

If a politician pretends to be honest, and you have evidence that his itching fingers keep slipping into the public till, then the story behind the story makes sense. Sometimes we even call it crusading journalism. The same applies to a moralist or preacher who pretends to be holier than thou, or a banker who is transferring funds from his customers' accounts to the bookies.

It is no one's business if the politician or the banker has some human frailties on the side, nor is it anyone's business if a movie star is no better than a tramp. At least it is not the public's business, so long as the banker or politician or movie star does his job. Their moral behavior is their own affair, on their own conscience.

The area of privacy is a dwindling one in our time. It gets battered and invaded from every side. The people who are most worried about the secrecy of our "national secrets" and see Bolshevik agents everywhere are often the very people who take pleasure in reading the stuff that leaves no privacy to anyone.

I don't mean to say that the press or magazines can never discuss private lives. They often do, as Harrison argued earnestly, trying hard to see the whole newspaper profession implicated in the guilt of the scandal magazines. But he fails to draw the important distinction. A responsible newspaper deals with a private life when it gets entangled with the law. At that point it enters the public domain, distasteful as it may be to record what is revealed.

A TV program always ends before you have had a chance to say the one thing you most want to say. Mr. Harrison had mentioned my column about him, thereby implying that I, too, was in the business. What I started to say, only to be cut off by the end of the show, was that I didn't write about either the public or the private life of Mr. Harrison until he got shot, down in the Dominican Republic. This very public encounter with the law made his private encounters legitimate copy.

This may seem wearisome and self-evident reasoning, and perhaps the gutter magazines, even with all their millions of readers, are not worth the expenditure of concern about them. Yet I have a hunch they are, not only because of the grief of the victims, but even more because of what they do to the readers.

Think of the picture of life that a habitual reader of *Confidential* gets—a limitless wasteland of adultery, prostitution, sexual perversion and betrayal, all of them associated with figures with whom the youngsters make some sort of identification. If he were to read nothing but a steady fare of these sheets it would never occur to a young American that privacy has any value, or even that it exists.

This is not a question of censorship. When the Post Office tries to precensor even a bad magazine, its action is the cause of all haters of censorship. The real censorship should be done by the people themselves, by growing up enough to give these sheets the intelligent neglect they deserve.

MISERIES AND GRANDEURS OF THE PRESS

1. Hearst the Unloved

August 15, 1951

HEARST LIVED A LONG LIFE and a tumultuous one, intertwined with many of the shaping events of the century. Yet going through all the obits and the plaudits, leafing through the cluttered biographies, what a curiously empty life it was—empty of the simple and honest values that make the life of even the obscurest American rich by comparison.

When a public figure dies, no matter how questionable his deeds have been, there is a tradition for drawing a decent mantle of silence over the naked and ugly places in the life portrait. It is like refraining from the truth at a funeral. I might have followed this, except that his newspapers and his stooges in politics have made it impossible. Their fulsome praise has been heaped not only on the man but on his principles and methods, as if they were using his death to throw down the gage of battle to any who might disagree. Well, I disagree.

For one, I disagree with the Mayor of New York, who laid it on thicker than even a political sycophant had to. "Great American and distinguished journalist . . . American ideals and principles . . . militant crusader for freedom and justice."

I am unaware of anything in his career that merits such words. Grant him the qualities he had: he was able and shrewd; he had an eye for men of talent and knew how to win them over to enterprises they would otherwise have disdained; he had consuming ambition and ate his heart out in his longing for high political office; he was unsteady in political purpose, and in the wide swing of his arc from the left to the extreme right he tried out almost every political position on the spectrum. But always he was hungry for power, ruthless in his methods of getting it, and tenacious in holding on to it.

It is hard to think of a single area in which he added to the quality of American life at home, or the esteem in which we are held abroad. He contributed little that was original to American journalism—even the mass journalism which he made his province—and what he did contribute debased it. He tried to make politics a personal plaything, from the time of the Spanish-American war until his vendetta against Franklin Roosevelt and his crush on General Mac-Arthur.

He helped nominate and elect Roosevelt in 1932, then turned against him bitterly because Roosevelt dared map out a New Deal for all the people, instead of subsidies for privileged industrial groups.

He treated people always as means, never as ends in themselves. He did not seem aware of the lives involved in "Mr. Hearst's War" (as the Spanish-American *opéra bouffe* was called); it was enough that they fed his sense of power and helped the circulation of his papers. He called his principles "Americanism," which was his right; but he insisted that every opponent was a Communist, or involved in a Communist conspiracy—including President Roosevelt.

He could take even a healthy cause, like opposition to Communist principles, and exploit it so irresponsibly and cynically as to dishearten those who genuinely despised Communist values. He dressed even the sound causes in their most unattractive garb. And let it not be forgotten that while he was anti-Communist, he was not anti-totalitarian. He visited and praised Hitler's Germany at the height of the Nazi terrorism, he fawned over Franco, and he was allied with all the forces which might someday bring a native fascism to America.

By a stretch of generosity, one can say that Hearst expressed some of the violent energies of American life in one of its most violent phases. But there are sweet and strong and compassionate things in American life as well as the violent, and these are not reflected in Hearst's career.

That is why the figure that stands out in the backward stretch of the decades is the lonely figure so well portrayed in *Citizen Kane*. For all his power and money, and the weight he could throw around, and the men he could cow, and his castles filled with works of art, here surely was one of the most loveless and unloved figures in our history. In that lies the pity of it.

August 16, 1951

There was a man who died the other day. He was, it seems, "a colossus." He was born with a silver-mine spoon in his mouth, but "he was branded as a renegade to his station in life, a traitor to entrenched greed and selfishness." He campaigned "for sounder education and better schools, on behalf of children, men who had served their country, even animals." He "fought monopolies, the trusts . . . supported labor unions, direct election of U. S. Senators,

women's suffrage, municipal ownership of essential public works"—
so much so that he was called "a socialist, a populist." He "frustrated Wall Street venality." He will "go into the story of our country as a great outstanding liberal."

Who was this man? Was he George W. Norris or "Fighting Bob" La Follette? Was he Louis D. Brandeis? Was he Lincoln Steffens or Heywood Broun? Was he Franklin Roosevelt?

He was William Randolph Hearst, and the quotes I have given come straight out of a full-page editorial eulogy of "the Chief" in that haven of all liberal causes, that champion of the insulted and the injured—the *Journal-American*.

It is a reeling, staggering experience to see these efforts to pretty up the Hearst image, repainting the colors of reaction with pink and even red hues. One is reminded of Orwell's *1984,* where words have ceased to have their own meaning, where "war is peace, tyranny is freedom"—and, no doubt, the blackest reaction is "outstanding liberalism."

Let's examine it a bit. When was Hearst called a traitor to his class? It must have been somewhere in William Howard Taft's time. But some of the things that even Taft's son, Bob Taft, has been urging—like a measure of public housing—have seemed "Communist" to the Hearst press.

When was Hearst against "entrenched greed and selfishness"? Deponent sayeth not. But the Hearst papers have lined up solidly with every aggregate of greed and selfishness to fight the New Deal and Fair Deal. There is scarcely a lobby on Capitol Hill—including the meat packers and the real-estate boys—whose efforts to swell living costs have not had Hearst support.

Let's take another look. On "sounder education" and fighting "on behalf of children": The fact is that the nation's schoolteachers have regarded Hearst as their enemy for at least a generation; and that every movement to limit the teacher's freedom has had Hearst support, and none of the efforts to unionize teachers or lift their income.

As for "municipal ownership," that too belongs in Hearst's Paleozoic Age. In the past generation he has fought the efforts to control the public utilities, fought the TVA and the movement for river basin development which would give ordinary persons cheaper power.

Finally, as for labor: I don't see his papers joining with the C.I.O. and the A.F.L. to support the efforts of New York City cops for decent wages and hours through a union.

In other words, Hearst's radical period was forty or fifty years ago. The movers and shakers who have been running his corporate empire evidently believe that nothing is as valuable as a long-dead-and-buried radicalism—unless it be a dead and still unburied corpse whom you can dress up as a radical.

I hope this highly publicized hypocrisy will soon have an end. If the image of Hearst as "outstanding liberal" is so precious to the Hearst chiefs of staff, they might try some liberalism in action for a change. Until they do, Hearst's great monument will be the fact that his newspapers have debased the taste of three generations of Americans, and that wherever he entered a community which had a good newspaper and poured in his money and his methods, the standards fell.

I wrote yesterday how lonely and unloved a man Hearst was. His eulogists might at least pay him the tribute of not stripping him of the one thing which was his own—an unslaked thirst for power, which he pursued without regard for principle. He was an imperialist and a thunderer, and he had a contempt for the readers whom he spent his life manipulating.

2. Editor on the Firing Line

May 1, 1953

IT WOULD HAVE BEEN FUN to sit in on the Wechsler-McCarthy encounter as a reporter. Knowing Jimmy Wechsler as I have for over fifteen years, I should guess that even so redoubtable an inquisitor as Joe McCarthy didn't find him easy prey. It would be good to see them in a free and equal TV debate, where one of them didn't combine the powers of accuser, Senatorial bully and judge, and where the other didn't have to keep one hand tied behind his back by not having the right to ask questions in turn.

This piece isn't in any sense a defense of a man who doesn't need any defense. Nor does he need a second in his corner of the ring. But this may be the time to stand up and vouch for a few random things I happen to know. To wit: that Jimmy can sharpen a phrase until it is a harpoon driven into the blubber; that he has a sustained purpose which isn't molded in butter; that he has a backbone which isn't carved out of a banana.

While I'm bearing witness let me add how proud I am of this fighting newspaper. Too many papers are behaving like tame mice bewildered in the McCarthy maze. This one doesn't. It's too bad Heywood Broun died when he had written only one column for the New York *Post.* I think he would enjoy writing for it today.

The real story is not about Wechsler and the *Post,* but about all newspapermen and newspapers. McCarthy doesn't dare admit that he called Wechsler before his subcommittee as a newspaper editor. That would be too open an invasion of press freedom. The device he resorts to is grilling Wechsler as the author of a biography of John L.

Lewis, which is presumably to be found in some of the U.S. Information Service libraries abroad. Since newspapermen have a fondness for writing books, this spreads a wide net.

For the time being, the net won't be spread for any newspapermen except those who have been openly and strongly critical of McCarthy. His power has doubled and tripled since President Eisenhower came to office and no one was left in the Administration to challenge and check him. This has meant that the only real opposition has come from a minority of the press.

The intent is clear. The American newspapers form more than an industry. They form part of the structure of political power. In a democracy, power cannot be achieved except through the pathway of people's minds and opinions. In the past the great American newspapers have been conscious of their role and have been proud of their craft. A handful of American newspapers have continued that tradition, even in the face of the compulsive power drive of McCarthy. The *Post* has been one of them.

The disconcerting thing about such papers and about their editors and publishers is that they dare to face the powers of reaction. They even talk back. McCarthy knows that his path to power isn't safe until he has blasted these obstructions away.

If he can do that, then nothing will stand between him and his real targets—the minds of the people. He has chosen an almost sure-fire weapon to confuse their minds in his role as an anti-Communist crusader. Obviously the American people are against Communism, as the *Post* is and every decent person is, but many people have no clear notion of what they are against.

Some weeks back the Madison, Wisconsin, *Capitol-Times* asked a number of people, "What is a Communist?" Ninety-seven out of 241 people interviewed said they didn't know and wouldn't be quoted. Of the ones who did answer, one said, "I really don't know what a Communist is. I think they should throw them out of the White House." Another said, "I guess it would be an undesirable person." Still another, "Well, they are always sneaking around. I think they ought to do something about that." And my final quote: "I don't know what they are but they are no good to us and we have too many of them in this country."

This confusion is what McCarthy feeds on, and in turn he feeds the confusion. Newspapers ought to be not only entertainment media but instruments of adult education. They cannot live up to their great tradition unless they fulfill this function, but they cannot fulfill it unless they stand together against any engine of the government, whatever it be, that tries to ride them down.

That's why their eyes should be now on the editor who is out in front on the firing line.

November 13, 1953

One of the happier results of the McCarthy rampage is that it has led James Wechsler, the editor of the *Post,* to write a full-length political autobiography, *The Age of Suspicion* (Random House). Published today, it will delight neither McCarthy nor the Communists nor the ventriloquist dummies of both.

Wechsler, at thirty-seven, may seem young to be giving us his political testament. Yet we are living in an age when a man, no matter how clean his record and conscience, may be called before grand or petty inquisitors and become a nationally discussed "case." In Wechsler's instance the encounter with McCarthy turned out to be one of the most dramatic clashes of personality and views in the history of Congressional hearings. When the transcript was released —at Wechsler's insistence—the nation discovered that for once the Grand Inquisitor had met better than his match. Every person who felt the excitement of reading the transcript will find in the present book the richly detailed content of a life, a mind and an era which give the episode its meaning.

More than the story of a man, this is the story of a whole generation—the one that was born around the time of the First World War, learned its cynicism during the booming twenties, came of age during the depression, was vulnerable to Communist lies and seductions, regained its hope and idealism through Roosevelt's New Deal, walked through the valley of the shadow of Nazism and war, rose to meet the challenge of Kremlin ruthlessness, and fought hard to keep its political and moral bearings at home in the Kafkalike nightmare of the Age of the Snoop.

While the book itself is modest in mood and ironic in style, never taking itself oversolemnly, its theme is in the grand one of the life history of this generation. At every phase its meaning reaches beyond the personal to the generic. It had to be written, because so much of the American experience is distilled in it.

It is part of the ordeal of our time that the intellectual, the journalist, the political leader, who might at another time have lived out their lives in their specific work, must now retrace the full arc of their careers, render an accounting to their era, come to terms with themselves. The number of ex-Communists who have done this has given its characteristic stamp to the political writing of our generation.

In a sense Wechsler's book belongs in this category. The one peg on which McCarthy was able to hang his hate was the fact that Wechsler had once joined the Young Communist League. Wechsler recounts the moving story of how he blundered into it, how he left when he was disillusioned, and the battles he has fought since then against the self-chosen rulers of the Kremlin and the pathetic bureaucrats of Union Square.

Yet there are two basic traits that distinguish this book from the usual literature of ex-Communist confession.

One is its quality of normality, in a literature which is so often full of self-pity, obsessiveness and delusions of grandeur. Unlike Budenz, Elizabeth Bentley and Chambers—and even Koestler, who should not be equated with them—Wechsler was not mutilated by his Communist experience. Perhaps it was because the experience came early in his life, when he was barely out of his teens, or perhaps because it was so brief; perhaps even it was because Wechsler has a chronic survival power. In any event the fact is that he went through his Communist phase as one goes through intellectual and moral growing pains—and outgrew it.

Hence the note of normality. Wechsler saw through the Communist delusion several years before the Nazi-Soviet Pact, long before some of the most ardent current hunters for dangerous thoughts. He took the measure of its narrow dogmatism; he felt stifled by its intellectual provincialism; he was disgusted by its moral cruelty and treachery. Every ex-Communist has to live with the scars of his past, yet here was one man who did not let the experience embitter him or distort his view of life.

The second distinguishing trait of the book is its note of affirmation. Wechsler is not content with being ex-Communist, just as he is not content with despising McCarthy and crew. To have meaning a life must be lived not only against something but for something.

Even when he was first drawn into Communism at college, it was partly out of a generous contempt for the smug and complacent and an eagerness to set things aright that seemed awry, partly out of the excitement of fighting for something. His college letters to his brother are the fumbling, somewhat grandiose letters that every teen-ager writes whose heart has not turned prematurely to sawdust. As he looks back at his college generation, he indicts the teachers who did nothing to capture the sense of heroism most young people have, and the public leaders who were mediocre and left an easy vacuum for the Communists.

I have known Wechsler when he was subeditor, reporter, labor editor, Washington Bureau manager, editor. What gave him the edge on others each time was that while he always mastered the techniques of his craft with a fierce pride in it, he turned all the resources of his craft to the service of a fighting creed.

I have not always agreed with him nor he with me. I would myself write a different kind of political testament because I have had a different life and different fortunes of war. But I am proud that the generation which is treading on the heels of my own generation has found someone to speak up for it—sins, scars, tenacity and all. How lucky that the editor whom McCarthy chose to be his first sacrificial lamb turned out to be an animal of a very different stripe, with quickness of wit, resourcefulness and, above all, courage.

3. The Times: A History and a Cause

September 22, 1951

EVERY GREAT ENTERPRISE is great because it has become a little piece of ourselves. We come to take it for granted as part of the enduring order into which we were born and in which our descendants will die.

We get a jolt therefore at being reminded that the New York *Times,* which always seemed to have come with the lease and be part of the climate, actually has a history and smells of mortality. It is a little like telling an Englishman about the teething and the growing pains of Stonehenge.

Meyer Berger has written the history of the *Times* (*The Story of The New York Times 1852-1951,* Simon and Schuster) as well as anyone could have done, considering that the job of an official history is bound to carry a strait jacket with it. You have to mention Everybody who is Anybody, yet make the Big Somebodies emerge in their full stature. You have to tell about their nephews and their cousins and their aunts.

But I am happy that a good working newspaperman made the job as unstuffy as it could be. Anyone could have told about the four big names in the history of the *Times*—Raymond, Jones, Ochs and Sulzberger. Anyone could have given the barefoot-boy-to-tycoon, Horatio Alger story of Adolph Ochs, who put the *Times* together out of sheer grit and work and some shoestring options; and his granitelike code of personal integrity and civic virtue, carved like the statue of a Roman senator.

But few could have done this and still written a newspaperman's history of a newspaper—that is to say, a running account of how it got its news and the kind of news it went after, the soldiers and field commanders who took part in the battles, their crises, their grandeurs and miseries and, above all, their scoops.

Berger recounts the big newspaper stories with loving detail, like the beads of a rosary, or—if I dare use the figure in connection with the good gray *Times*—like a string of pearls around the throat of a beautiful woman.

Aside from Ochs, who was an original and liked to rule his domain with a paternalistic hand, the two most interesting figures in the book are those of George Jones, who broke the corrupt Tweed Ring in New York; and Carl Van Anda, the great managing editor who extended the meaning of news by including in it Peary and Einstein, Lindbergh and Tutankhamen—whatever man could find out about his universe and himself through science and exploration, archaeology and technology.

The *Times* today is more than a great newspaper. It is an inseparable part of the pattern of our American culture. It is hard to face the morning without it, wherever you are on the face of the globe; and a Sunday without the Sunday *Times* strewn over the living room—book section, magazine, Review of the Week and all—is not a middle-class American Sunday.

It still has its mild stuffiness and pruderies, sure; it has in its history done its share of news slanting: Berger discreetly fails to mention a *New Republic* supplement by a couple of fellows called Merz and Lippmann on how the *Times* once treated the Russian news.

Jones was offered five million dollars to lay off his crusade against the Tweed Ring; it would be hard to think of anyone making the offer now, partly because everyone knows the *Times* is as unbribable as the U.S. Treasury, but also because it no longer goes off on crusades.

Yet, when you have said this, just compare the history of the *Times* with that of the Hearst papers or the McCormick Axis papers, and you will know that the American newspaper landscape has its glories as well as its slums.

January 6, 1956

As one who used to write editorials, in my distant youth, I have become inured to their spell, and I can take them or leave them. But the editorial page of the New York *Times* for January 5, 1956, is bound to be remembered as marking a turning point in the struggle of our decade over civil liberties. For that page on that day, speaking of the Eastland Committee public hearings on the press and discarding the musty caution and stuffiness of many editorial columns, rose to a pitch of courage and eloquence which should set many newspaper hearts pounding to its beat.

The *Times,* like the *Post,* sees the menace of linking some long-distant Communist associations of a copy editor and the paper's treatment of the news. It has named names—Senator Eastland, Senator Jenner, Committee Counsel Sourwine—and accuses them of gunning for the *Times* because it has opposed many of the things for which they stand. And it warns them that long after they are forgotten—

they and McCarthyism and school segregation and faceless accusers—
the paper "will be speaking for the men who make it, and only for
the men who make it."

I can only add a Bravo and an Amen.

Happily I have never been called before a Congressional committee. I have no tortured "remembrance of things past" to contribute to the archives of the Eastland-Jenner sleuths. I cannot recall
in what subversive cells and cellars was brewed the deadly Bolshevik
broth which every Congressional patriot must expose, even if it is
little and he is late.

If I were called I would not invoke any of the amendments,
whether the First, Fourth, Fifth, Ninth, or Tenth. I should have nothing to hide, not even my disgust for the sound of the bugles and the
sniffing of the beagles and the whole foolish Congressional boondog-
gle.

But I want to go on record on one score: The whole of the current sleuthing into the operations and attitudes of newspapermen
seems to me to be none of the business of Congress. It makes little
sense to me, either Constitutional or common.

I turn first to the Constitutional issue. There is only one passage
in the *Times* editorial from which I dissent—when it says that "any
agency of Congress can make any investigation of the press," and
when it insists only that Congress must have good motives and no
"ulterior purpose."

Surely this gives away far more ground to the inquisitors than
there is any need, reason, or precedent for giving them. It forgets the
whole history of the struggle for press freedom in England and America, which has been largely the struggle for freedom from governmental pressures and oppression, whether direct or indirect.

I agree with the *Times* that a newspaper or newspapermen are not
"sacrosanct." They have no immunity if they have committed a crime,
or sold themselves to an enemy of our nation, or engaged in treasonable or seditious acts. But when Congress investigates the press it has
an enormous burden of proof on its shoulders—to show that it is on
the track of such acts. It is no business of Congress to show some
"penetration" in the past, or get some poor devil fired because he
stands on an amendment. When a committee does this it acts beyond
the bounds of its function and it places in jeopardy for a trivial purpose the precious principle of a free press.

It will be said that Congress has broad investigative powers around
which it is hard to set precise bounds. I answer that it is even harder
to see a Congressional power to investigate in areas—and the press is
one—where its power to legislate is very narrow.

If you say that Communist penetration must be exposed by any
means, I answer that we must all deal with this evil. But for Congress

to go cruising about in the dangerous waters of press freedom is to place a great tradition in hazard in order to come up with a puny and doubtful catch.

Precedent for my view? We have precedent enough in the first effort that Congress made in this field—the Alien and Sedition Acts, more than 150 years ago. Those acts were aimed at muzzling the press. Editors fought the acts, and martyrs were made. Having repudiated these acts, shall we now say that Congress would have been on sound ground if it had tried to achieve the same ends by the pressures of investigation rather than the threat of penalties?

Sure, Congress does have an investigative function—the function of a watchdog. But the press also has the function of a watchdog, and one of its objects of surveillance is Congress itself. That is exactly why the freedom of the press must be jealously guarded—because it is often the only strong opposition to those who assert political power or racist supremacy.

Watchdog for watchdog, I will pick the New York *Times* and the New York *Post* any day as against Eastland, Jenner, Sourwine and Co. I add that these papers don't have the gall to wrap themselves in the flag while they incite open insurrection against the Constitution and the Supreme Court, as Senator Eastland does.

I add one sour note: Heaven protect us from well-meaning friends as well as from self-interested enemies. I speak of the suggestion by Senator Hennings that the newspaper executives be called by the committee to show "that the end product, the newspaper itself, has not been influenced" by the Communist campaign of penetration.

No, dear Senator Hennings, and No again. It is not your business or the business of your colleagues on any committee to sit in judgment on any newspaper "end product," for any purpose whatsoever, evil or good. Senators, stay away from our door. There are men working inside, and their "end product" is the concern only of the men who make the paper, and its readers.

4. City without Papers

January 9, 1959

AFTER A COUPLE OF WEEKS back in harness, since the end of the strike, this columnist confesses that life has again begun to stir in his spavined old bones. In fact, I can even manage to look back at the whole experience without blanching, and try to assess some of its meaning for our city and our culture.

There is a remarkable short story by E. M. Forster called "The Machine Stops," which tells of the moment far in the future when the semianimate creatures who have lived only by the machine revolt against it and stumble out of their cubicles to crawl along the road which will once more make them human.

"There came a day," writes Forster, "when over the whole world the beds, when summoned by their tired owners, failed to appear. It may seem a ludicrous matter, but from it we may date the collapse of humanity." It was also like the moment in the Russian Revolution when the Czar's troops failed to fire at the revolutionists, and Trotsky noted this moment as a crucial one.

Surely a future historian may glimpse some such turning point in our own history when the newspaper readers of New York summoned their papers—and they failed to appear.

Everything went topsy-turvy. People coming out of work gathered around their newsstands only to find the stands bare except for the sinister sign, "All papers on strike." The subway riders, no longer able to read the papers, had dismally to look at each other. The commuters on the train fared worse: for the first time in years they had to face themselves.

But it was the people with success to sell who fared worst. I am speaking of the book publishers and play producers. Two weeks before Christmas is exactly the time when a new "best seller" and a new "smash hit" are made. Think of how frustrating it was to have a book or play hot on your hands, with no way of getting it to the consumer. Even the proverbial "rave reviews" had been typed up by reviewers who were themselves pretty frustrated at having to hide their superlatives under a barrel.

Pity the poor stores too, who had Christmas commodities from armbands and bedsheets to zany hats and zebras, and money to pay for spreading the glad tidings through the advertising pages, and no takers for the money.

Even radio and TV, which tried to repair the gap, were in the end helpless. There was a heavy immigration of Broadway stars into the late shows, to plug their plays: and there was a stepping-up of the newscasts. The *Times* people even made an effort to present their layout to the imagination of the radio audience, who were asked to visualize page 17, column 3 of a nonexistent paper. It only served to make the lack more sharply felt.

What it showed was the way in which the press, for good or ill, has become part of the circulatory system of our society and culture. Despite the decay of reading in a TV and picture magazine culture, we have not wholly ceased to be a nation of readers.

If the press were only a means of scanning the headlines, then radio and TV could easily take its place. But the fact is that they don't. The reasons seem clear enough. The newspapers give us stuff in print that we can take along and read at our own timing and our own pace, as much or as little of it as we wish. The print it gives us, moreover, is not just newsprint, it is also service print.

This service aspect of the newspaper's function may overshadow the others, and it foreshadows the era of leisure which we are entering.

We are playgoers, book readers, liquor drinkers, restaurant patrons, stock investors, gift givers, vacationers. We have to find remedies for our ills, comforters for our psychic chills, and commentaries on our various brands of pills. We have to exchange ideas, attitudes and tastes with each other and try out the newest form of each for fit. We have to think about how to bring up our children, and where to send them to college, and even how many of them to have.

The complex lives we lead today demand some means of shaping and servicing the state of our tastes, manners and morals, just as much as the state of the Union. Before the strike we were in danger of forgetting how big a role is still played here by daily and periodical print.

What we must again calculate is the extent to which papers have become part of our whole structure of habit. And habit, remember, gets its effects by becoming part of our nervous system itself. In this sense it is a conservative force. I go back to the classic description of it in William James: "Habit is the enormous flywheel of society, its most precious conservative agent. It alone is what keeps us all within the bonds of ordinance, and saves the children of fortune from the envious uprising of the poor."

There are some people who have argued, in the past, that Americans suffer from a habit fatigue in the matter of newsprint, and that they would be delighted to have the burden of daily reading lifted from them. Sometimes (they have said) a man takes a big risk, in wooing, by daring the woman to get along without him. The danger is that she may take the suggestion, and find that life without him is not the darkness and dust of spirit she had feared. She may even welcome the release.

I think, however, that the experience of going without papers for so long showed how wrong this view was. The role of the press in our culture does not depend simply on a habit assumed without thought and breakable without notice.

It is linked with the very fabric of life in an open society, where so many judgments and opinions and decisions depend on knowing what's going on and who's doing what. If newspaper publishers and the working newspapermen and women ever had any doubts about their craft, they can take consolation in the fact that a city without papers wore every aspect of being a stricken city.

FERVORS AND FOIBLES OF TV

1. The $64,000 Bonanza

August 29, 1955

I WENT TO A REHEARSAL of *The $64,000 Question* last Tuesday night. I found the narrow corridors backstage crowded with newspapermen, press photographers, studio and agency executives, people from "the trade," magazine writers getting color for their coming stories about the show. I watched a run-through, with studio employees acting as stand-ins for the contestants, and with the emcee, the ad spielers, the cameramen and the orchestra all trying to perfect the flow and the timing of the show. There was the smell of success all over the place—a smell so dense and unmistakable that you could cut into it and take a slice of it home with you.

The basic approach consists of four elements—money, information, suspense and documentary characters. Note not only the elements present in this formula but also those absent from it. There is no sex in it, no violence in it. Instead there is a different kind of tension—that of seeing how people you have come to like are going to make out. There is no highly paid talent, no professional gagsters, no comics, no Hollywood stars. Instead of the big stars there is the Big Money—and the sight and sound and feel of the documentary.

August 30, 1955

Louis G. Cowan, the show's creator, is the product of Chicago—the city of dramatic paradoxes and violent contrasts. A boy growing up there would be exposed to some curiously varied people and symbols: to the cynical showmanship of the Chicago *Tribune* and the highly intellectual showmanship of Robert Hutchins, to the idea of the 100 Great Books and to the folk songs and folk wisdom of Carl Sandburg, to the "Black Metropolis" of Chicago's South Side, to the stockyards and the "Back of the Yard" movement, to Ed Lahey of the Chicago *Daily News* and to Bishop Sheil.

A man is the sum of all the signatures that his life and time have written on him. By the time Cowan came to New York, in the early

1940s, he had served a useful apprenticeship to the earthiness of Chicago.

In this frame of Cowan's apprenticeship take the case of Gloria Lockerman, the twelve-year-old Negro girl who will be a spelling star on the show tonight. Remember that the core of the appeal of *The $64,000 Question* is what the psychologists call "empathy"—not tolerance for someone to whom you feel superior, not sympathy for the unfortunate, but empathy, the identification of the viewer and listener with the person whose face and fortunes he is watching. You will then see how far-reaching can be the impact of Gloria Lockerman on both Southern and Northern opinion about desegregation and the Negro's struggle for civil rights. If she were an adult, she would not have nearly the impact that she has as a child, spelling out words that would puzzle other children of her age, and thereby dramatizing the fact that Negro children have as much claim and right to decent educational opportunities as anyone else.

September 4, 1955

The question will naturally occur, Where does the money come from? What is it that makes the giveaway show possible on so grand a scale? My answer is that in the mass media bigness generates bigness. You can put it in the form of an equation as follows: Big Money equals Big Audience equals Big Market equals Big Advertising equals Big Money. And thus you are back where you started.

Or, translating the equation into more explicit terms, if you start with a TV program that offers staggering prizes you will quite naturally get a big audience for it. If you have the audience—in this case one that approaches fifty million people—then you offer a big market of potential customers to your advertising sponsor. If this market is given to him, he will be willing to pay heavily for the privilege of underwriting the program. Thus you have the funds for offering the big prizes to the contestants and starting a share-the-wealth movement. Thus the wheel has come full circle, and the snake has his tail in his mouth.

What this amounts to is that the mass media like TV, as constituted at present under our system of financing, are rooted in advertising sponsorship on a big scale. It is true of our whole system of radio and TV that it is not based on selling the program to the audience. Instead, what happens is that you sell the potential audience to the advertiser. The more appealing the show the bigger the audience. The bigger the audience the more lipsticks it buys and the higher the sales chart zooms. The dizzier the sales the more is available for advertising costs, and therefore the dizzier the possibilities of spectaculars, quiz giveaways, and star galaxies. This sheds some light on the cultural level of TV in our current year of grace.

As you can see, this is a self-generating process and it could easily become an unending one. Some of the current crop of magazine articles about the $64,000 bonanza have been asking how far you can carry the bonanza idea.

If my equation above is sound, the magnitude of the bonanza program is limited only by the amount of money the American buying public will spend on the commodities it rushes out to buy after having listened to the commercials.

If I were Cowan I should feel that I had let loose a flood that couldn't stop, like the Sorcerer's Apprentice. And I would ask myself, "Where will it all end?"

One of the problems these shows encounter is to convince the people that the money is genuine, the questions are not "fixed," and that nothing is phony. I have received letters from readers who insist that there must be a concealed trap door somewhere. Evidently they feel as if they are in the land of magic, where things are done with mirrors and with sleight of hand. It is to reassure them that *The $64,000 Question* has brought in all the gadgets, including the bank guards and the bank vice-president and the sealed envelopes and the IBM machine and the isolation booth.

Yet the idea of abundance, and of the access of everyone to that abundance, has pervaded the American scene during most of our history. David Potter, at Yale, has done a brilliant book called *People of Plenty* (University of Chicago) in which he reinterprets the American national character in terms of the pervasive effect of the idea of abundance. Clyde Kluckhohn, the Harvard anthropologist, has written me in a letter that "the idea that everybody could have or become everything is the single most distinctive feature of American civilization. I know of no other major society that has so committed itself in idea and in action to the notion that education, material standards of living, the arts, and other things were available to all and attainable by all. This is a more characteristically American invention than the assembly line."

This is the framework within which the new trend in TV takes on meaning. It is a translation, into terms of TV techniques, of the swaggering American idea that if you work hard there isn't anything out of your reach. It is Huey Long's "Every man a king" put into TV language, but altered to say that even ordinary people can become high-bracket taxpayers—at least for one year. It is bound to wreak havoc with the scale of our values.

The trend in all the big-audience media is toward magnificence and magnitudes. This is true of the giveaways and of the spectaculars on TV. It is true of the musicals and extravaganzas in the movies; everything gets bigger there, even the screens. It is true of the production costs on Broadway, and the prices being paid for Hollywood rights to plays.

I don't think that the solution is to lament all this and wring our hands over it. A show can be healthy in its impact even when its scale is supercolossal—and I have written enough about *The $64,000 Question* to indicate my belief that its over-all impact is a healthy one. A show can also be sleazy, trivial and vulgar. We have to learn to stop thinking in terms of quantity and to think about the integrity and artistic quality of our popular culture, and its impact on the minds of the people, regardless of whether its audience rating is colossal or quite modest.

Right now the age seems to belong to magnitude and frenzy, and the quiet voices find it hard to get heard.

2. The Day the Money Stopped

August 31, 1958

DID YOU EVER SEE a dream fading? One of the newest and giddiest American dreams—that of making a quiz show killing by coming up magically with the impossible answers to unlikely questions—seems to be vanishing even more quickly than it came.

The killers of the dream are a part-time butler, actor and bartender called Edward Hilgemeier, Jr., and a graduate student at N.Y.U. called Herbert Stempel. Their victims are two shows called *Dotto* and *Twenty-one,* and the murder weapons are affidavits meant to prove that each show was rigged. The press has pounced on a juicy story, and after a week of competitive headlines and "exclusive" revelations the ordinary TV viewer is now convinced that there is no health or truth even in the shows on which no suspicion has been cast.

What a curious, quickly shifting lot of people the TV audience has proved to be! First it swallows, obsessively and uncritically, every TV quiz show, including some pretty moronic ones as well as the brain twisters. Then just as uncritically and obsessively it rejects all of them.

It isn't too hard to guess at the medley of feelings that the TV viewer now has about the quiz show. Start with the anger of those who feel duped and cheated: There is nothing that an American dislikes more than to be taken for a sucker, and all the more because so often he is. Add to that the stunned feeling of having the ground cut from under their feet: Can it be (they ask themselves) that the whole structure of abstruse questions and brilliantly precise answers was rotten from the start? And again the envy ("All that money in just a half hour!"), which now has a chance to disguise itself as head-shaking virtue. To cap it off, add the never wholly abandoned dislike of intellectuals and their brains: "Well, it's good to know that they weren't so smart after all."

Thus the dream ends, as most dreams do, in bitterness. It is futile to tell people that someone like Charles Van Doren is incapable of dishonesty, and that the rottenness in the quiz shows was marginal. From now on the only contestants to be trusted will be J. Edgar Hoover, Cardinal Spellman, Bishop Pike and Bernard Baruch, and they will have to appear under the auspices of Merrill, Lynch, Pierce, Fenner & Beane and contribute their winnings to the Damon Runyon Fund.

If a few contestants and officials on several of the quiz shows were dishonest, I hope we won't forget that their audience deserved what it got. This is especially true of the merchandise giveaways, which millions of people watched in the apparent belief that in this never-never land called America it is possible to get something for nothing. It is the recurrent dream of every sanguine period of world history, from the Elizabethan Age of Ben Jonson's *Alchemist* to the contemporary era of freeloading, freebooting, free sports cars and refrigerators and speedboats.

It didn't seem to occur to many people that the big purveyors of this merchandise, who were acting like rich uncles just back from Alaska or the gold fields of Kimberley, might have some ideas of their own about how best to build up and maintain the suspense they needed in order to sell their products. Nor did it occur to them that in the big-money giveaways the producer was under a terrible strain of having to deliver an audience to the sponsor, and under the terrible temptation of building up TV personalities by every means in order to hold the audience.

Loose ethics were one side of the picture. The other side was the greed and gullibility of the people themselves.

The day the money stopped the dream collapsed. It had a short-lived career. But I hope the historian of our period will note what was really wrong with the era of the big giveaway. It was not just the questionable morality. Even more it was the meaninglessness of the questions and answers. They advanced no cause, sustained no life, grappled with no problems. They were based on the same principle on which the mechanical brain was constructed—the principle of the feedback. The contestant fed information into his brain and then brought it out again at the proper moment. In fact, even the most perfect quiz show contestant would in the end have to bow to a mechanical brain.

There are a few things about the ending of the dream that make me sad. Think of all the foreign critics of American life who will now be deprived of one of their most telling gibes against our culture. Think of all the proud parents and other relatives of the winning contestants, who used to gain stature among the neighbors and will now have to live out their lives obscurely. But most of all, think of the thousands of hopefuls, all over the country, who have been boning away at encyclopedias, history books, treatises on the art of boxing or old coins or Chinese calligraphy, or the family trees of American Vice-Presidents. The swift current of events has carried away their hopes of riches and glory, and left them stranded with accumulated information they will never use.

THE ASSAULT ON THE MIND

June 24, 1957

WE LIVE IN AN AGE of manipulation which is learning startling new ways of attacking the currents and patterns of the brain, disarranging them and rearranging them.

Consider first the methods that work through the chemical modification of the brain. A grave-faced doctor jabs a needle with some stimulant into the arm of a deeply disturbed patient or administers insulin to him or runs a current of electricity through his brain. The silent grow talkative, the apathetic become excited and relive buried emotional experiences. Something happens in the brain of the patient. The point of toleration is reached and passed. He may go into convulsions. The old patterns break down and new patterns of behavior and personality emerge.

These drugs operate by heightening the emotional excitement of the patient. There now are others to calm him. We are moving into the age of the tranquilizers. A doctor who finds a patient too anxious or excitable may give him reserpine or chlorpromazine or meprobamate or one of the other tranquilizers flooding the market, and the hyperexcitable calm down.

No one knows exactly how it happens, or even what happens, or what the long-range results may be. All they know is that chemical rearrangements in the brain produce new emotional patterns. Frightening? Only in the sense that we are working in the dark and that the human brain is turning out to be more subject to modification by chemicals or otherwise than we had ever suspected.

We have long known that with help from a psychiatrist, a man can recondition his mental and emotional life. The psychiatrist may see him over the course of years, week after week and even day after day. The patient finds himself dredging up forgotten memories from unsuspected crannies of his consciousness. It is painful and he tries to resist, but in the end he ties himself to his guide and achieves a transference to him, putting his emotional burdens on the other's shoulders. The old landmarks are swept away, but in time new ones emerge and things start to rearrange themselves in a new and livable pattern.

This relationship may take place through the fever of group infection as well. But in such cases it is sustained tension and emotional shock that count.

An evàngelist preaching damnation and salvation to an audience works it up to a fever pitch of tension and one after another its members are swept by waves of cleansing and clarifying emotion and come forward to testify that they have seen the light. The leaders and followers of a religious snake cult may handle the snakes with the assurance that divine grace protects them, until a frenzy seizes them and they go into a trance or convulsions. A group at a voodoo ritual will chant and dance through the night until they reach an ecstasy and a peace that pass understanding, or the group infections may take a more sinister political form.

The Chinese Communists used emotional shock and disruption for mass conversions to the new order to make a new China overnight. So effective were the methods used that thousands killed themselves in despair. The sense of guilt artificially implanted in them was so strong that they felt unworthy to accept the Communist salvation, leaving the more resilient millions to dance for joy at their liberation from bondage.

In a more persistent way, the Chinese used the same process to "brainwash" resisting American POWs into becoming defectors and "co-operating" with the new regime. These were also the methods of the Russian commissars to break down political prisoners and get them to confess to acts they had never committed.

But the story is not always about foreigners and totalitarians. The methods can come closer to home. The chief of detectives in a police station "works over" a murder or rape suspect, keeping at him mercilessly until the pressure becomes intolerable and he confesses, adopting the acts and attitudes that have been hammered into him, and a sense of relief and release descends on him. Or to take a long jump, a consumer may be bombarded continually by an advertising campaign on TV, until he becomes conditioned to respond in the terms suggested. He not only buys the product in the package but also feels the symptoms and remembers the jingle he has heard. He incorporates the suggestions from his environment into the reflexes of his brain. And what is true of advertising and salesmanship in commodities may also be true of the same methods in politics.

I have set down all too briefly these instances, which may seem far removed from each other but are tied together by a unifying thread. They deal with induced conformity, with changes in the brain chemicals or the conditioned thought patterns, with the manipulation of the mind so as to make it reproduce expected behavior. Count what follows as an essay in criticism of induced thinking, packaged cure and patterned salvation.

June 25, 1957

Whatever else may be uncertain, one thing is certain about our era —that we are searching for peace of mind. But how get it? The roads are diverse and controversial. In the past the principal road has been through religion, and the current vogue of Billy Graham shows that the evangelist still can reach masses of people with the sense of salvation. After religion came psychoanalysis. Freud and his followers dismissed religion as an "illusion." The reality for them lay in the exploration of the depths of the self, stripping away layer after layer that obscured the hidden obstructions to self-expression, and removing them. In this way many have found it possible to fight fear, allay anxiety and function in everyday life.

But now a new path is being cleared, that of packaged peace of mind through tranquilizer drugs. Three or four years ago they were almost unheard of. Now the books and magazines are full of them, and the comedians have tied their gags to them. In the cases where neither religion's conversion techniques nor psychiatric treatment have yielded results, the tranquilizers seem to be having some effect.

Francis Bello, writing in *Fortune,* estimates that twenty million Americans have taken tranquilizers to some extent, and the sales estimates for 1957 are $175,000,000. The drug firms have fallen upon a bonanza, and they are working it for all it is worth. In an advertising and promotion campaign for such brand names as Thorazine, Equanol, Atarax, Serpasil and Miltown, they promise relief for everything from infantile colic to senile anxiety and for most emotional complaints in between the two.

The dramatic suddenness with which the new drugs came up (they came on the market in 1954) and the eagerness with which the mental hospitals have adopted them have made them a salesman's dream. The competitive drive for profits has operated here, as everywhere.

Judged by the experience of the doctors who have prescribed the drugs to their patients, they have proved effective. The anxious grow less so, the highly excitable calm down, the quarrelsome or apprehensive become more serene. In mental hospitals they have lightened the burdens of treating psychotic patients, who become more amenable to cleanliness and hospital routine, and some get well enough to go home.

But some researchers have begun to issue warnings. What they amount to is that we don't have much notion of how the tranquilizers operate in the jungle of the brain, that we don't know how they get the effects they do and not even what their effects are—indirect and long-range as well as immediate. It is a case of stumbling about in the dark, moving by routes unseen to goals unknown.

The drugs may well be both blessing and danger. Neither rules out the other. To an overworked doctor in a mental hospital, or to a psychotic and his family, they may be a blessing because they bring the patient at least within the reach of treatment. Even here one notes that the drugs may further depress the depressed, or cover up symptoms whose roots need to be discovered. But to the student of society the spectacle of forty million people taking tranquilizers is not one to induce tranquillity.

Even the picture of tens of thousands of Americans getting psychiatric help is a less depressing one. The point about psychiatry is that you can't be helped unless you also help yourself. At least there are strainings and strivings; you have to grapple with the Furies within yourself before you can achieve the self-knowledge that leads you out of darkness. In the best sense, this is true of religion as well. I am not speaking of the work of the evangelists, which is half ritual voodoo and half the product of buildup and organization. I am thinking of the religion of Kierkegaard or Buber or Niebuhr, where there are no gilded promises and no packaged fulfillments, and where you must wrestle with God and yourself before you can overcome the desolating feeling of being alone.

What is dangerous about the tranquilizers is that whatever peace of mind they bring is a packaged peace of mind. Where you buy a pill and buy peace with it, you get conditioned to cheap solutions instead of deep ones. This is the road to packaged conformity. Those who are today lulled into a sense of tranquillity through buying something they will swallow, which will produce changes in their central or autonomic nervous systems, may tomorrow buy and swallow a packaged social nostrum. In both cases they will feel that it is unnecessary to strive and fight to slay the dragons by will and courage.

Thus, whether or not the tranquilizers tranquilize, I regard them as part of the contemporary assault on the mind. They place within the reach of manipulators the possibility of severing the central from the autonomic nervous system, the forepart of the human brain from the primitive back part of it. The forepart, which contains the mechanisms of human choice and will and of social intelligence, is (as Bello puts it) the part on which mankind has relied for its first million years and will have to rely for its next million.

June 26, 1957

Inevitably, any discussion of the assault on the mind must reckon with MR, the abbreviation for "motivational research." In one sense it is as old as advertising itself, which has always tried to search out whatever is vulnerable in the consumer and capture or seduce him there. What is new about it is only that it uses more sophisticated methods of getting at the hidden springs of the human mind that make men and women respond or not respond to a product or brand.

These springs are certainly not rational and not even conscious; they are irrational and unconscious. They reach to the sources of fear, anxiety, guilt, envy, insecurity, hunger for power and status, frustrations and aggressions which Freudianism and other psychologies have uncovered. MR applies what we have learned about these to the arts of selling. It is not a lovely animal that is uncovered when you study the American buyer and seller from this vantage point.

Vance Packard, who has become the unadmiring chronicler of MR and its devices, tells in his new book, *The Hidden Persuaders* (McKay), of the hidden needs of the American consumer on which the advertisers and corporate sales managers play.

Take for example the hunger for emotional security which makes you buy a freezer. "There's always food in the house," so you feel safer on your frozen island of security. Or take the soap advertisers, who are told by the MR experts that they must build up the role of the housekeeper when selling soap and detergents by giving the woman a reassurance of her worth. To go on with the dreary litany of hidden psychic needs, take the MR expert who discovered that you can draw men into an auto salesroom by putting a sleek convertible in the window, even though they end up buying a four-door sedan. (You daydream about your symbolic mistress; you marry the girl next door.) Or take the men's magazines and women's magazines that are sold as symbols for masculine and feminine reassurance. Take the sickening sexual narcissism of women admiring the long sleek lines of the models in the lingerie ads, hungrily satisfying their self-image.

Take the marketers of cake mix who found their sales dropping when they advertised that the housewife only had to add tap water, but found them zooming again when she was told to add fresh eggs and milk. (We don't like to have our creative role erased.) Take the genius who discovered that you can increase sales by increasing the price, as with the rivalry of the automobile manufacturers to build a "prestige car" with the highest price tag, or the concoction advertised as "the costliest perfume in the world." Take the TV sales campaigns that use children as a way of bludgeoning the parents into buying ("the psychoseduction of children," as Packard calls it).

Finally take the shrewd MR man who persuaded an insurance company that the way to sell life insurance was not to sell family security but to sell immortality, to make the man himself dominate the ad, reassuring him that he would continue even after death to control his family's destiny. It was the same MR man who served as doctor for the ailing prune industry by dropping the word "prune," with its semantics of constipation and dried-up spinsters, and renaming it the "California Joy Fruit," with appropriate symbols of beautiful girls in the sunshine.

All this is, of course, a new kind of mumbo jumbo on the part of witch doctors who have rediscovered some ancient secrets in new forms and packages. The instances I have given, out of Packard's book, are not in themselves of great moment. I can't get into a lather of indignation because the "depth boys" (as they are now called) are catching up with Freud's depth psychology and Jung's theory of images and symbols and applying them to the making of money. I can't even get worked up at the unlovely picture of ourselves as suckers. If that's the way we are, then we had better not shrink from confronting this mirror image of ourselves.

What does strike me somewhat hard is the picture of an economy that gets panicky when it can't unload its products fast enough and must continually create psychological obsolescence ("every hat you own just went out of style"). I am not enchanted with the total emphasis, within our culture, on the manipulation of hidden motives, and the constant deployment of our vulnerabilities for the purposes of profit. What also strikes me hard is the picture of a social system that directs the undoubted talents of such brilliant MR experts as Ernest Dichter, Louis Cheskin, Burleigh Gardner, James Vicary and Pierre Martineau into channels such as these.

Dr. Dichter, to take the most publicized of the MR men, was once a lay analyst in Vienna and now is psychoanalyzing not sick minds but ailing sales charts. I have been reading the issues of his ingenious publication, *Motivation,* which sells for $100 a year. He and his staff come up with interesting insights on how to get at the vulnerable points of the customer. But when Dichter, appearing on the *Conversation* radio program, spoke of himself as an educator who also helps to keep going an economic system that might otherwise collapse, I found it an ironic commentary on both our education and our economy.

Here are insights that were developed in order to heal men being applied to making them readier targets for sales campaigns. The original intention of Freud and Jung was to help men understand themselves and thus strive for self-mastery in the struggle with the Adversary in all of us. Yet in MR, as in the case of the tranquilizers I discussed yesterday, the consumer is always passive. He is dissected, acted upon, bought and sold. He is a commodity to be trafficked in.

The human being as a commodity is the disease of our age.

June 26, 1957

There is a growing fear that the techniques of motivational research could be transferred from the manipulation of consumers to the manipulation of voters. In what sense is this true? Obviously the corporation managers don't care a hoot what the consumer thinks, so long as he buys what they are selling. But the customer's frame of mind is nevertheless crucial, since the MR men are counting on him to respond to their psychological triggers as they pull them. Their art lies in knowing roughly where the consumer is vulnerable, and therefore what combination of guilt, fear, pride, insecurity, power hunger and status anxiety will lead him to embrace the packaged peace of mind they want to sell him.

Here is where the political enters. The why of consumer buying is linked with the how of selling. And the how involves the manipulation of the suggestible buyer, by conditioning him to respond in calculable ways to definite symbols. At this point it doesn't make much difference whether the product sold is tooth paste or a political program, lingerie or ideology, a low-slung big long car or a father symbol as President.

The satire on TV in *A Face in the Crowd* is savage, but what historian of TV's inanities would dare say that it is also unjustified? Of all the arts of popular culture, TV is the art of the home. The movie star has glamour and sexual appeal, but the "great man" of TV enters the home every week or every day, and his acceptance is all the more powerful because it is familiar, and therefore unguarded. Schulberg and Kazan make this point well by making their hero, Dusty Rhodes, a homespun Arthur Godfrey with a knack for folk humor and a way with a guitar. But he has in him also a strong streak of the political adventurer that makes him a counterfeit Huey Long. Rhodes sells the pills of his TV sponsor by insinuating that they are aphrodisiac, although in truth the best that can be said of them is that they won't do any harm. But the same kind of personal magic that enables him to sell a fake in the form of harmless pills also enables him to sell a political fake that is not so harmless—a reactionary movement with fascist overtones even to the point of hinting at a potential political strong-arm squad.

We live by symbols that are short cuts to reality, and the new symbol that abbreviates and sums up our fears about the manipulation of the mind is "Madison Avenue." Just a half century ago "Wall Street" was the slogan that stood for the Money Trust. "Madison Avenue" is a convenient slogan because it is the point where three important social facts of today meet and cross. One is TV as a powerful big-audience medium. The second is the advertising agency, acting for the sponsors. The third is the public-relations firm which is ready with equal skill to sell a commercial product or a political personality, using the same techniques of motivational research and symbol manipulation for both.

There is a term just coming into use which best expresses our mood of apprehension about this, although its creator meant it differently. It is the "engineering of consent," used by Edward L. Bernays as the title of a book on how to get public acceptance of projects that need to be made persuasive, but shrewdly picked up by Robert Bendiner in a brilliant *Reporter* article on the 1956 Republican campaign and the synthetic buildup it used. What makes it a natural as a clinical description of what is happening to us is its deadpan combination of "consent" (presumably the free-will decision of free-wheeling citizens in a democracy) and "engineering" (with all its overtones of buildup and manipulation).

One thinks of Nixon in the 1952 campaign, with his TV speech stressing his home and dog, and then one thinks of his engineered transformation in 1956, like Paul struck with a dazzling light on the road to Damascus but careful to have Batten, Barton, Durstine and Osborne along. One thinks of how General Eisenhower's heart attack and his ileitis operation were converted into proof that he would be a better physical risk as President. A psychologist, J. A. M. Meerloo, has called thought control "the rape of the mind," but I fear that the phrase misses the point. It is not rape but seduction. The mind is made suggestible and, whether in a dictatorship or a democracy, is conditioned to accept the advances. As Byron put it once, the lady, "saying she would ne'er consent, consented."

The great indictment of the MR men is that by conditioning the American buying public to respond to the triggers playing upon their anxieties, their fears and their hunger to belong, they reinforce those impulses. Thus they make the buyers, who are also buyers of political candidates and programs, more vulnerable to what might become an Orwellian nightmare.

June 28, 1957

A long time ago Aristotle spoke of man as a "political animal." He meant it with the emphasis on the adjective, but the trend of psychological research recently has been to emphasize the noun.

One of the things that have happened, especially since the purges by the Communist Chinese regime, has been the rediscovery of Ivan Pavlov, the Russian psychologist whose experiments on the conditioned reflex in animals opened the new Age of the Brainwashers. Pavlov is not as well known to Americans as he is to the Russians, who have made him into a heroic figure of Soviet science, despite the fact that he was a figure out of prerevolutionary Russia who courageously expressed his disapproval of the Communist regime.

For a good account of Pavlov's work and its meaning for modern political conversion and indoctrination, read the first few chapters of William Sargant's *Battle for the Mind* (Doubleday), on which I have drawn freely in this series. Pavlov's famous experiments were those involving a dog, a light (or a gong or metronome), and some food. Each time the dog was offered food the light flashed and his saliva flowed. Then the light was flashed on without any food, but the dog's saliva still flowed. This was the famous "conditioned reflex" experiment; the dog was conditioned finally to respond not to the reality of food but to the symbol. It seems pretty well established that Lenin prevailed on Pavlov to submit a memorandum on how to make the leap from dogs to humans. The Soviet leaders gave this opponent of their regime special treatment because his research pointed the way in which human nature could be reconditioned and a "new Soviet man" could emerge.

Edward Hunter in his *Brainwashing* (Farrar, Strauss) tells of a Soviet film he saw in which the dog experiments are performed on a young man. The history of the Russian purge trials suggests that the Soviet commissars somewhere along the way had learned the lesson of Pavlov's experiments. But one problem had bothered Pavlov: How do you wipe out past conditioned experience so that there will be a clean slate on which to write the new conditionings? Sargant tells the story of how Pavlov found the answer accidentally. It was at the time of the Leningrad flood of 1924, when the dogs in Pavlov's laboratory were trapped by floodwater and swam around in terror until they were rescued. He noted that with one group of dogs all their previously implanted responses were wiped out, as if the brain had been washed clean by the experience of terror. When he later allowed only a trickle of water to come under the laboratory door, this group of dogs showed the same behavior they had shown during the flood. Pavlov concluded that every mind has its breaking point if you find the right stress to apply.

The Chinese probably applied some of these principles in trying to get political conversions among the American POWs in the Korean War. But it is a mistake to assume that they followed the same methods of the assault on the mind in the mass conversions of their own people after the Chinese Revolution.

There is a recent *New Republic* article of first importance on "Brainwashing in Perspective" by Dr. Robert J. Lifton of the Harvard Medical School. Lifton doubts whether the Pavlov theories had much influence on the Chinese leaders in planning the mass conversion of Chinese intellectuals. The problem was to get the young intellectuals to reject and denounce their families and their whole past in a culture which was steeped in tradition and held the father in reverence. The young Chinese writer or student was caught in a sharp conflict between his family loyalties and the pressures of the new regime and new era, and became so confused as to lose his sense of his own identity.

Perhaps this very confusion, similar to that of someone in our own culture who is in the midst of an analysis, helped to clear the paths in the brain for the new conditionings. Lifton's article describes the crucial method used in what the Chinese call "thought reform" or "ideological remolding." It is that of the "study group" of six to ten people which becomes a kind of psychoanalytic group therapy. There are self-criticisms and confessions of erroneous thinking; there is the constant pressure from other students and writers and from the whole environment.

In fact, the chief method the Communists use is the control of the social milieu in which the intellectuals find themselves. Where the whole human environment is of a piece you end by becoming almost undistinguishable from it. You do not know what is your own personality and what is the culture. There is no hiding place for the personality, nor a corner where it can develop in its own way, free from the molding pressures all around it. Under these pressures some flee, some break down, many get converted and most learn slowly and reluctantly to adapt themselves.

We in America don't have to fear cultural commissars nor any system of governmental brainwashing or thought control. But the pressures from the culture are stronger than most of us like to admit, and the brainwashers imposing the cultural patterns on us for their own purpose and profits keep pretty busy. Maybe it is the MR "depth man," maybe the TV "great man," maybe the Congressional "Grand Inquisitor," maybe the public-relations firm building up the "indispensable man" in a Presidential campaign. Maybe it is the juggernaut at a political convention crushing a dissenter who has dared question the wisdom of running an anointed candidate along with the indispensable one.

The way out is not by flight or breakdown, and certainly not by tranquilizer pills. Nor is it by withdrawal into the cocoon of one's private life, letting the brainwashers and thought controllers do their worst on others.

It is by knowing who you are, facing the cultural idols and your own fears and anxieties, and fighting for the things you believe in. Foremost among them is the human personality in its precious uniqueness.

THE CARRIERS OF PROMISE

1. School, Teacher and Promise

December 8, 1952

ONE OF THE MYTHS I dislike most is the myth that children dread going to school. It is one of those easy, silly stereotypes invented by fathers to prove what slugger and mucker he-men their small sons are, thereby in turn magnifying their own virility. There are, of course, a number of kids who can't stand the pace, or others whose family life is so demoralized that they must seek their security in souped-up delinquency outside school. But most school kids—whatever they may say to show their toughness—like school pretty well and look forward to opening day.

Maybe I'm prejudiced because of my memories of my own school days. Because of ill health I couldn't start school until I was eight. I remember with what envy I sat at the table at home in the evening with my brother and sisters while they prepared their lessons and I felt shut out of their Eden. Then I would wait for them to come home and talk of their schoolmates and teachers. Even now I can't enter a schoolhouse without recalling with a sharp pang my sense of triumph when I finally reached the coveted Eldorado and was admitted to school.

For an immigrant family, as ours was, school is the great transmission belt of American life and thought under good conditions. It not only unlocks the treasures of American history and literature but offers a place where you have a roughly equal chance to grow and to be accepted by your teachers and your peers.

I know there are many things wrong with American schools today. The school plant is getting run down, and the classrooms are crowded. The costs of buildings and equipment are zooming sky-high, and so is enrollment. Teachers are still paid wretchedly, many of them have left for other jobs, and those who stay are not always the best of the crop. There are too many young girl teachers whose minds are on marriage and too many tired old schoolmarms who have long ago given up hoping for it.

Earl Conrad, in *The Public School Scandal,* points out that of thirty-three million children in elementary schools, three million will eventually end up in mental institutions, and other millions in prisons. He piles up horror upon horror with an abandon which others have reserved for books about Devil's Island. "The parent needs to know," he writes, "that the school situation is living hell for hundreds of thousands of children, quite possibly for his child; that he is sending his child into this hell; and that he and other parents must pitch in, like the devil, to straighten out hell."

The trouble with this bleak indictment is that it makes you wonder how American society has managed to survive and grow strong with its citizenry brought up in such hells. You wonder why such a system has not long ago produced a nation of criminals, psychopaths and degenerates.

Dr. David Abraham, in his book *Who Are the Guilty?*, makes a plea for schools and teachers who will concentrate on helping the child to achieve an emotional balance, get a sense of belonging, learn his own identity and his place in the group. This is the kind of job that private schools are now doing better than public schools. For it takes good teachers and devoted ones, and a lot of money we are unwilling to pay and the kind of social intelligence which we have not been showing.

December 2, 1955

Those who corralled a couple of thousand men and women at the White House Conference on Education hoped they would be nice, tame critters. But they kicked down the fences. President Eisenhower had told them that education is "primarily a local responsibility" and had warned them against Federal aid and its dangers. Yet they came out overwhelmingly for Federal subsidies to school construction, and at least half of them seemed to want Federal aid for everyday school operations. This was worse than treason. It was ornery common sense that recognized the false whiskers on the argument about "Federal control" of our children.

There were some foreign observers at the conference, including a monk from Cambodia. It made my thoughts go back fondly to the huddle of earnest young men with shaven heads and saffron robes I have seen on the streets of Pnom-Penh. I wonder what this monk made of this fabulous country of ours, where with most of the wealth of the world at our disposal we neglect our schools, overcrowd our children in them and underpay our teachers. With the baby boom, our school population has grown faster than ever in our history. Yet in addition to pupils the one thing we have plenty of is shortages—of buildings, of classrooms, of teachers, of salaries and prestige and dignity for them. Despite all our vaunted belief in education, this shows a basic hypocrisy on our part. How can we, making a cult of education, put it so far down on the list of what we spend our big money for?

The basic trouble is that the local financing of schools, which is our old tradition, puts a heavy burden on the owners of dwelling houses and factories from which the local taxes come. This is especially serious in rural areas and also in the suburbs which have not yet developed many industrial plants. Actually education is as much a national problem as the draft is. Like the draft, it is best administered when it is locally administered. But this does not mean that it must be paid for only locally and that any Federal financing would corrupt it.

If I have a basic quarrel with the White House Conference, it is because I think it focused wrongly upon buildings and plant rather than upon the teacher himself. The problems of how to get new buildings and larger classroom space and more money for salaries, how to meet the resistance of the local property owner who objects to a new school bond issue, are real enough. But beyond them the abiding problem is the teacher himself, and how to get good ones and keep them creative.

Which is to say that I would always start and end with the teacher. If you have good and talented and devoted teachers, and if you pay them well and value them so that their lives have dignity and they themselves have self-respect and the respect of their fellows, you have something to build on. The teacher is the center. You build the buildings around him. It is to him that you entrust your children. It is he that lights a spark in them and keeps it alive—or doesn't.

If you can, somehow, get teachers who don't take teaching as just another chore, you won't have to worry about Federal control of education. A teacher worth his salt won't allow himself to be controlled, whether by the Federal government or anyone else.

August 25, 1958

Finally a Federal education bill has gone through Congress, mangled, mutilated and bloody, but a bill nevertheless. We have the Russians to thank for the fact that we got it at all. When the Russians achieved their H-bomb, the first response of Americans was anxiety about whether our scientists were fully loyal, and their remedial action was a hunt for dangerous thoughts, as shown in the witless hounding of Oppenheimer. It was a primitive gesture of tribal jealousy. But when Russian scientists (whose politics the commissars had sense enough not to question) launched their sputniks, the same Americans began to ask why *we* didn't have more of such scientists.

The new response was an anxiety not about loyalty but about schools and teachers. The new remedial action was a hunt not for dangerous thoughts but for any kind of thoughts at all. Suddenly the egghead came into his inheritance, especially if he was a scientist.

For a time there was talk of spending several billions a year for five or ten years on a program of Federal scholarships, on new school construction, on picking promising young people wherever and whoever they might be, spotting and cherishing their promise, and subsidizing their education as the precious possession of the nation. As with so many other enthusiastic beginnings, this one suffered compromise, diminution, dilution, retreat and almost defeat. The school construction aspects of the bill were thrown out, and so was the scholarship program, and it was replaced by a loan program.

The student will be able to get a loan of up to $1,000 a year, which he will repay with interest. If, however, he becomes a science teacher, he will be able to cancel half of his loan, writing off 10 per cent for each of the first five years he teaches.

The new education bill is a halfhearted effort to throw Federal support behind the movement for science education, with special emphasis on luring youngsters into becoming science teachers.

Unfortunately this is only a small part of what should have been a total educational effort. There are many young people whose talent does not lie in science, but who nevertheless need scholarship aid which neither the states nor some of the universities now give. They may have in them the stuff of great promise in writing or thinking or painting, in the professions or politics. They may have the potential for becoming diplomats or social scientists. What happens to them?

It is important to hold a carrot in front of those who will someday become science teachers, and lure them into a profession that badly needs them. It is more important to find the carriers of promise, whatever they may wish to become, and nourish them for what they are.

What caused us to fall behind the Russians was that they take the intellectual life more seriously than we do. It is a curious fact that the new education bill, exactly because it is first and foremost an education bill for national defense, underscores the very anti-intellectualism which landed us in our present plight.

2. Your Business as Thinkers

October 24, 1955

THE OLD GUIDEPOSTS are gone, in education, and there are no new ones to take their place. John Dewey is dead, and much of his educational philosophy is gone with him. The whole branch of psychology that used to be called the "psychology of learning" is interesting enough, just as the art of teaching is fascinating, especially for the practitioner. But learning and teaching must have a goal.

I write as someone who has been a teacher for over twenty years and believes the teacher's art and calling to be high ones. Sometimes you get a born teacher, with a touch of flame, and he will teach well under any system. But most teachers would be better if they had a clear idea of what they were aiming at.

What do we want? I, for one, want to see my own children and my students become free-feeling, free-wheeling persons who will care about the excellent and reject the shoddy, who will use their minds with discrimination, who will (when the time comes) make their moral decisions with courage and strength. I want them to be persons who will have a core of identity within themselves that keeps them from veering to conform with every wind, and who—when the empty dangerous years come along, as they are bound to—will have resources enough within themselves to endure whatever comes, whether it be wealth or poverty, triumph or failure, happiness or tragedy.

A big order? Yes, it is. What I am saying is that education must aim toward the whole life. To stop short at only one phase of life—whether it be the "intellectual" life, or technical skills, or "life adjustment," or preparation for success—is like aiming only halfway when you are jumping a ditch.

We used to talk of the Three R's—Readin', Writin', 'Rithmetic—as the goal of education. I put my own formulation in terms of the "Three Knows."

First, know your needed skill, whatever it may be. Certain skills all of us need—how to read, to communicate, to reason. We must know them well and not fuzzily. Other skills depend on your particular trade, art, business or profession. Those, too, you must know with precision—and, if you are lucky, you will also know them with love. A doctor who knows medicine but hates it, a businessman who knows how to run his business but hates it are like a musician who hates music.

Second, know your world. There are some who believe that an educated man must know the traditional but not the contemporary world. They are as wrong as those who think you can get an education out of today's newspapers and magazines without knowing the great classics of thought.

I come now to the third: Know yourself. There are some who will say that this is not education but psychology, personality development, character development, and that it belongs in the home, the church, on the psychoanalyst's couch—anywhere except in education. But I hold my ground. The failure of education does not lie in failing to keep up with mounting demands on skills or on the knowledge of history and the present. It lies in failing to keep up with the mounting strains on the individual's emotional life, and the tumults that rage inside the hearts of our children.

October 24, 1955

I turn now to the problem of graduate study. American greatness will be lost unless a saving remnant of the young college graduates devote themselves to the life of ideas, and not just the pursuit of power, success, money, prestige and security which are the current gods.

I suspect that graduate study and research in American universities have come to the end of a phase. They started in the last quarter of the nineteenth century, when American scholars went to the German and English universities and brought back with them the ideal of specialized graduate training. In medicine and law, in literature and languages, in history and in the physical sciences and business administration, we have turned out young men and women who are brilliant specialized technicians.

But the specialists can solve no problems except their own technical ones. They develop their own jargon and gobbledegook, they talk largely to each other and they shut themselves up in their private little universe. They do not nourish human life. They have never prevented the rise of a tyranny. Even in the country where they first flourished—Germany itself—they did not prevent the coming of the concentration camps and the crematoria.

As I have talked with graduate students in a number of American universities, each of them seems to be grubbing about devotedly in his own little corner of the forest. But he is isolated there, which is the same as being lost. Many of them, with the generous energies of youth, may want to explore what others are doing—only to find that they are in another part of the forest. And most of the signs say "No Trespassing."

It is on this score that I hope we have come to the end of a phase. Much of the great research work of the university scholars is now largely done in the service of the corporations and of the government armed forces. In either event, it cannot be said to do much to nourish the life of the mind. But the young men of talent who have kept themselves independent of these entanglements may now be able to explore the frontiers of knowledge, to get together with the others in the forest and help each other in a unified effort to chart it.

I think this is what Justice Holmes had in mind a half century ago, when he told a group of students, "Your business as thinkers is to see the relation between your particular fact and the framework of the universe." It is still good advice, all the better because many universities —and especially the graduate schools—have discouraged their students from following it.

3. The Intelligence Race and the Democratic Elite

December 1, 1957

DESPITE the frantic American effort to overcome the Russian arms lead, I question whether it is crucial for us to achieve a supremacy in the ultimate weapons of death. What we should constantly strive for is not supremacy but the kind of adequacy which will deter our enemies from venturing a war and committing the supreme folly.

At this moment we are using every effort to harness science to the invention of new weapons, and technology to their production. This is a welcome change since the days when scientists were regarded as dangerous eggheads, miracle-working zombies or potential Russian spies. But if we value science and the scientists only for what they can accomplish in the weapons race, rather than for what they can do to extend the frontiers of the human condition, it means putting a precious talent to the uses of death and not of life.

There is another race whose reach and importance go beyond those of both weapons and science. It is the intelligence race. The heart of the intelligence race lies not in turning America into a nation of engineers and technicians, nor in building bigger and better rockets to the moon. It lies in helping to educate a generation of value-creating leaders who will direct our enormous resources and energies into building a great nation.

December 2, 1957

If we are to win the intelligence race, not only against the Russians but against time and catastrophe, we shall have to cherish our talent and push its schooling to the limit.

I am tired of hearing only about what the costs will be. I am sick of the hard-shell troglodytes who know the cost of everything and the value of nothing. I propose that we set an admission price for everyone who wants to complain about how we are lagging behind the Russians in our defense capacity. The admission he should have to pay is to give all-out support to the full schooling of the undoubted talent we have—not just in engineering and science, but in society and thought and art as well.

That the talent is there, who can doubt? For the past thirty-five years we have been dolts enough to raise racist immigration barriers against the Italians, Slavs, Jews, Asians and others who don't conform to some idiot notion of Anglo-Saxon and Nordic purity. Luckily the damage to that purity had already been done by the 1920s, when the laws were first passed, and luckily also the Nazi and Communist persecutions of the "lesser breeds without the law" made us lower the barriers just long enough to bring in our Einsteins and Fermis.

The harvest of the generations, in the sons and daughters of all the immigrants since Plymouth Rock, and of all the slaves since the first shipload from West Africa, is ours. We have the talent, and we should be grateful that it is mongrelized enough to produce the mutations we call "genius." What we need to learn is how to help each American youngster to develop and use fully whatever talent he has. We must also find the really rare top talent, under whatever skin and name, in whatever brainpan it may be contained, and give it the special training that extraordinary ability needs.

The first of these needs is the Jacksonian concept of the American educational task. The second is the Jeffersonian concept. It is futile to say they are in conflict. They need not be, if we have the wisdom to assign to each the function it can perform in building our nation, and if we have the collective will to push both.

We need, first of all, a permanent and continuing educational inventory. This means that at every educational level and in every community of the country we should know what each young American is capable of and suited for, in what direction his talents and energies seem to be moving.

He may have a knack for tinkering with machines or juggling figures, or he may put words together deftly, or he may have the abstract ability needed in the difficult reaches of thought. He may have hands that can be taught skills, or a feel for design, or he may be a young man with a horn or a paintbrush or a sculptor's mallet. He may be a good organizer, or capable of the persuasiveness that sways men to buy products, or the incandescence that makes ideas contagious and faiths believable.

We have scarcely touched the surface of the methods available to us for discovering these skills and directions. Once discovered, all we need is school buildings and laboratories to house them (they don't have to be elaborate productions), teachers devoted to the vocation of teaching, and the willingness to spend money for both. Money is the cheapest thing in all this vast country of ours. It is cheaper than our human resources, cheaper than talent, cheaper than will and belief.

All the outcry against Federal scholarships is the claptrap of local and state school administrators who have vested interests in the narrowness of their own jobs and outlook. I don't mean that we should scrap the local school boards and school principals and the rest; they are useful in a talent inventory because they know more about the particular youngsters than anyone in Washington can know. But the energy to sweep away obstacles in schooling must come from the nation as a whole, and the funds must come from every source—local, state, Federal, and from the foundations too.

The crux of the problem is that every child must be helped in every way to go as fast and as far as his potential will carry him—through the universities and graduate schools and professional schools, if he has the brains and stamina to see him through. The money must be the nation's worry, not his.

But the second phase—the Jeffersonian one—is even more important. Jefferson dreamt of a democratic elite—a kind of aristocracy of talent, drawn broadly from every possible group yet trained especially for leadership. I am talking now of getting quality at the top. I am talking not of the task of mass education, but of the relatively few who can give direction and values to the rest—who can become the lonely thinkers and writers and artists, who have the will to sustain them in the darkness of thought and the courage to lead a nation in crisis.

4. Four Fallacies of Our Schools

February 24, 1958

I DON'T LIKE new sacred cows any more than I like old sacred cows. So here are some protests against four fallacies—some old, some new—which seem to be thriving in our postsputnik educational climate.

The first is the fallacy about "academic" and "nonacademic" subjects for school courses. Suddenly our thinkers have made a great discovery, namely that some high schools and colleges are teaching a number of damn-fool courses, such as cosmetics and coed cooking and the physics of home lighting. The result is a big outcry to scrap these and get back to mathematics and chemistry and history and the other subjects that are "academically valid."

I will join anyone in attacking whatever is mediocre, slack and easy in our educational system. But some of the sleaziest and most mediocre teaching I have seen has been in the conventional "academic" courses, and some of the most exciting has been in the "new" courses which explore the frontiers of psychology, anthropology, philosophy and aesthetics. Sure, let's get rid of the monstrosities meant to give students some easy academic credits. But I suspect anyone who tries to draw a line between subject matters, calling some acceptable and others taboo.

The kind of thinking which does this is old, weary and conventional thinking. And when you try to apply it to teaching, you will get old, weary and conventional teaching—which is a far greater menace to education than courses about the human personality.

This bears on the second fallacy—the belief that there is some sacred principle of democracy or equality in education which requires us to treat all students as if they were exactly alike. The fact is, of course, that students (like all human beings) are terribly unlike. Some are quick, some slow; some are bright, some dull; some have a potential that stretches further than you can glimpse, some have the most limited potential.

I am all for treating the dull or disturbed students differently from the extraordinary ones. I don't mean with less attention, but with a different kind. I don't think we should scrap (or suspend) students because they offer difficulties; that is to abdicate the task of teaching. But let us have different classes for the slow ones (white or Negro, poor or rich, whoever they may be), and for the pretty good but average ones, and for the really gifted ones. With the last we can push very hard and try for the difficult art of training leaders.

The third fallacy has to do with the sacred cow of localism in the financing and control of schooling. Provincial thinking dies hard in America, and the brand that dies hardest is the one which thinks that local idiocies are necessarily less idiotic than Federal or centralized idiocies.

The cult of localism has led many to oppose any move toward Federal financing of the needed expansion of scholarships, fellowships, new buildings and laboratories, new courses and research, added teachers and better pay for teachers. I can only say that those who are unwilling to talk realistically about how to pay for better education ought to stop talking about how poor our present education is. And we who know how poor it is had better accept the only real source from which the added money can come—the general treasury, located in the Federal government.

But there is another sacred cow in the pastures of localism. I mean the idea that only the pillars of town or village society can decide what and how the students shall be taught. Apply this to any professional subject like law or medicine or psychiatry or defense, and you see how full of holes it is. But presumably in the precollege years the local boards of education (including some members who never send their children to the public school system, but to private or parochial schools) must be counted the only experts. I say that we ought to turn the question of setting up educational standards and curricula over to the teachers themselves, acting on a national level through their associations. And we ought to give them the power to carry through somehow.

The fourth fallacy is the currently fashionable notion that the Russians have found the key to the good educational society, and that we ought to follow suit. Oh, no one says it quite so explicity. Yet all the people who are pointing out the Russian successes with engineers and scientists, and prodding us to beat them by their own methods, really base their thinking on this assumption.

The Russians have the capacity to gather all the current research and apply it systematically to their technology. But they are the last conceivable model for us to follow in education itself, which should lead to the stretching of the mind, not its hardening, and to the fulfillment of the personality, not its mutilation. The Russians train; they do not dare educate.

5. Russian and American Education

March 31, 1958

WHAT IS THE TRUTH about the current debate on the relative merits of European and American education? Who is superior, in what ways, and for what reasons?

In general the Europeans (especially the French, the Germans and the Scandinavians) work their students harder than we do, apply more discipline, give the students less scope to question and talk back, and push them harder in the secondary school.

Some of this we can certainly profit from, especially the harder and more sustained work. During the past few years I had two semesters of teaching a group of picked European university graduates at the Salzburg Seminar, in Austria. I was impressed by their earnestness, their work habits, their command of languages, their knowledge of literature. But in almost every instance they had been starved for a chance to debate with their teachers and dispute their facts and logic; they embraced eagerly the American method of open free-for-all classroom discussion. They welcomed also the range and spread of the American social studies and the behaviorial sciences, like psychology, psychiatry, anthropology and sociology. Most of it was new to them.

The case of the Russians is a special one. They have largely borrowed the European Continental system, but with a crucial difference. While the Europeans have been content to educate their elite, separating the rest off at a relatively early age to learn agriculture or trades and vocations, the Communists from the start undertook the major task of making an illiterate nation literate, and the second major task of creating an intellectual elite geared to the purpose of the party and the state.

They have largely succeeded in both their aims. It was scarcely a question of choice for them. They had to succeed. They had to build the technology of an industrial culture, so they had to teach their people how to read instructions, how to work machines, how to mend them when they broke; and they had to teach their intellectuals how to pick up the latest scientific advances everywhere in the world and make advances of their own. In forty years, the space of only two generations, they have transformed their people, made them industrially literate, indoctrinated them with a faith in the Russian Motherland as linked with the eternal rightness of the Communist Party.

The Americans have also had two major educational tasks. One was the task of mass democratic education. We had to take the children of immigrants from every part of the world and help them to become part of a working democracy. We had not only to make them literate, but to teach them some of the meanings of freedom.

But our second task has lagged. I mean the deliberate creation of an intellectual elite by picking the best and most gifted of our youngsters and pushing them as far and as fast as they can go.

One thing holding us back is that the nation doesn't take this task seriously enough to pay for it. The Russians support the able students with billions of government funds. Many Americans, however, leave the burden of scholarship and fellowship subsidies on families that can't afford them or else on private philanthropy that has not kept pace with the need.

Another thing holding us back is that we have not learned how best to release the motivations of our students. The Russians have an easy way, since for most of their young people the only road upward is that of state-directed and state-subsidized schooling. Our youngsters go off in many directions, on many roads. Often we have a hard time getting at them to find where their talents lie and release their energies.

In mass education we have done as well as the Russians—and better, since we have not had to resort to indoctrinating "party line truth." In building an intellectual elite we must now move ahead, boldly and swiftly. We can do it better than the Europeans because we can do it on a larger scale, with better facilities, and without the sense of having come to a dead end. And we can do it in our own way better than the Russians because we are educating for freedom and don't have to fear any ideas the young may pick up.

The Russians boast that they are out to change human nature itself and create "Communist man." We are not aiming to put any particular brand on our heifers. We want our young people to grow up into men and women who can use their judgment, make decisions, lead productive lives, act decently and be creative in whatever work they choose.

January 28, 1959

After the passage of the Second Reform Act, which gave the vote to most of the British workers, someone remarked, "Now we must educate our masters." In our present era of the race against Communist world mastery, or even world and cultural annihilation, we can use the same remark with a different twist: "Now we must educate our leaders."

The change is a crucial one for our educational future. For 140 years we have followed a policy of educating the people by free, compulsory and universal education. But while the ultimate power must still rest in the people, the immediate leadership—in the top and intermediate ranks—cannot be trusted to spring spontaneously from them or from those whom they choose in those lotteries we call elections.

Leaders cannot be chosen; they must first be shaped and educated. The time when Americans could assume in a haphazard way that leadership could emerge out of universal education and the ballot box or the big-income bracket—that time is past. In every area, whether political, international, economic, scientific or artistic, the men who count will be not the many but the few. They are, in short, an elite—but one based wholly on merit and on their ability to perform their tasks of leadership and creativeness.

Up to now our school system of universal education has been geared to educating our masters, the people, spreading our effort thin over the many. We cannot abandon that task, but we must now add to it an even more important task: to educate our leaders, the few, deliberately and intensively.

It took a Russian breakthrough to give us the shock of this recognition. Curiously, the man who has emerged for the moment as a spokesman for this new view is not himself an educator or a social thinker, but a man of arms and action—Admiral Hyman G. Rickover. In speeches across the nation, timed and attuned to the new popular mood, he flayed the public schools and the progressive educators with whips and scorpions. He has now rewritten and published these speeches in book form—*Education and Freedom* (Dutton).

There is a good deal of repetition in them, as in the clackety-clack of a tense woman. There is an obsession with a single theme, like a stuck phonograph needle. Yet the book is worth reading as an armory of facts and arguments for those who feel that America must overhaul its schools. Most of the educators won't like it and will attack it not only for the real weaknesses it possesses but for fancied ones it does not.

I find three related main themes in the book. The first is the plea for a heavily scientific emphasis in our education, to keep pace with the Russians and beat them in the weapons race. Here I differ strongly with Rickover. The important race is the intelligence race, not only against the Russians but against chaos.

The second theme I agree with wholly: to give to talent every chance, to ability full scope, to merit the highest rewards.

The third theme is the emphasis on the mastery of subjects and techniques, the almost exclusive cult of the disciplined intellect, the scorn for courses dealing with life experience or with the nature and modes of personality. Here I think he is wrongheaded. The concentration on intellect and will alone can, as the Nazi and Communist experience has shown, be dangerous.

This sheds some light on one curious aspect of the book. Its title is *Education and Freedom*. There is plenty of discussion of education, yet no real theory of it. There is a definition of freedom (men must be ends, not means), yet the few bits of discussion of freedom do not form any part of the essence of the book.

If Rickover were clearer about education *for* freedom, he would be much more savage than he is about the Russian educational system. In an interesting appendix, added as an afterthought, he does make it clear that it is only the Russian educational *means* that we must largely take over and use for our own *ends*. But this is to be superficial about the relation of means and ends. You cannot tear a system of means out of a context of ends. You cannot tear a school system out of the context of the total social and value system.

The Russians do not educate their elite; they train them, as one trains technicians. It is a combination of a party elite plus a number of indispensable nonparty scientists and technicians who are given special incentives and rewards. This is in keeping with the state's use of education purely as a state tool, rather than as all the modes by which a personality grows and is meaningfully stretched. Whether Rickover is aware of it or not, he tends to fall into this way of seeing education—as a tool for the purposes of the state, rather than as a way of growth for the personality, sometimes even counter to the purposes of the state or of the majority.

Thus the new education cannot afford to concentrate on the training of the intellect alone and make fun of the study of the human heart and personality. The elite we want must be a democratic elite— chosen for their promise and ability from all the people, lowly as well as rich and powerful. But it must also be an elite of intelligence, sensitivity, creativeness and a feel for the human connection.

September 22, 1958

Nikita Khrushchev has just made a decision in the intelligence race which may strengthen Russia industrially in the next decade but which is bound to weaken it intellectually in the long pull.

The gist of the new directive is to put Russian youngsters to work after their seven-year elementary schooling, just about the time when ours would be entering high school. They would go to farm or factory, or to some form of on-the-job training. If they want to continue their academic education, they must do it after work hours, by correspondence or in night school. If they want additional training it must be related to the jobs they continue to hold. This will apply to all Soviet youth except the few extremely talented ones in the arts or sciences, who are too valuable to be put to work.

If my own country tried to follow this direction in education I should fight it to the death as a kind of technology obsession gone wild. It can only deepen the Russian trend toward what William Benton has called a "technocratic Sparta"—and it may visit upon Russia the doom of intellectual sterility that befell the Spartans.

Khrushchev tells his people that work has fallen into disrepute among them, and he wants to overcome the "separation from life" that has afflicted education. He is right (as John Dewey was) in his belief that education should not be cut off from the life experience. But since when has it become true that only farm and factory work represents the realities of life, to the exclusion of thought and reflection, play, travel, creativeness? Or that only the useful is life-giving, and not the intellectual, imaginative and emotional? I fear that Khrushchev is on the road to becoming a technological Babbitt who excludes everything as foolishness except the intensely practical.

But there is more than practicalism, or pragmatism, in the Russian view; there is also a strong anti-intellectualism. We in America have been bemoaning (and rightly) the anti-intellectual climate in America, and some have been contrasting it with the Russian intellectual climate, where scientists and technicians are made the lords of the manor and given every honor. But note the Russian trend. Khrushchev regards it as "intolerable" that students are coming out of the elementary and high schools "unfit for anything except more study."

The test of an intellectual climate in any country is the value placed on what education can do in the search for the new and the true and in making the searcher more interesting to himself and to others, and more able to get meaning out of life and put meaning into it. The aim of education is not to "fit" you for anything but to provide the encounters that stretch you meaningfully.

Khrushchev wants young people who will "create values for socialism." That would be fine, if he meant it in the broadest sense. But I fear that the only values he is interested in are the utilitarian values— more crops, more steel, more A-bombs. There is a difference that he fails to see between creating values and producing objects.

His whole discourse is, of course, phrased in terms of a devotion to the proletariat. Too many youngsters from intellectual and middle-class families, he says, are going to college, and not enough youngsters from working-class families. Note that he does not say that they don't belong there by reason of ability, but that they come from the wrong social classes. This is the old Communist formula of discrimination against the classes that might prove to be dangerous.

Why has Khrushchev, after a period of wooing intellectuals, decided to return to this old class standard and to the cult of the useful and practical?

The reason that suggests itself readily is that the Soviet industrial system eats young people who will be "medium-grade" technicians, and (especially in the light of the heavy losses of population in the war) can't get enough of them. But I think there is a deeper and unrevealed reason. When you get a young population hell-bent for learning, you have one that may be getting ideas into its head. Khrushchev and his colleagues find it safe enough to turn out a nation of technicians, but dangerous to let youngsters explore the social and human sciences.

It is a vote of no confidence in Russian youth, in sentencing them to a life of work-without-ideas.

November 16, 1958

In order to achieve their new Seven-Year Economic Plan, the Russian planners must increase their working force. Hence they are reorganizing the educational industry to fit in with the new industrial "control figures."

This is a backward step in education. The formerly publicized "ten-year schools" in the cities are now abandoned. The seven-year school, presumably stretched to eight, will apply to all except a very select few who will go on with their studies. Those eight years for all will be a combined academic and vocational program. After that almost everyone will go to work, with further technical training obtainable only outside of working hours.

Since they have a dismal total control of every aspect of life, the Russian planners can juggle the educational industry exactly like the food or chemical industries, or the production of fertilizers.

But is education only an industry, and thus most meaningfully part of an economic plan? If it is, then the Russians are right to treat the students as just so much raw material for the development of man-power and of technical and scientific schools. The whole school system becomes thereby a vast factory for turning out a number of technical man-hours. And obviously the student with aesthetic or abstract intellectual tastes, or a turn for psychology or the humanities, becomes only a misfit for the assembly line, like a cross-grained worker who will not submit to the discipline of the machine.

The final giveaway on the motives of the planners will be found in the section on the function of the social scientist in the total plan. He too, like the research chemist or physicist or mathematician, is assigned certain tasks. His main task is to be the "criticism of revisionism" and of "modern bourgeois imperialism." And you can be dead certain that not only are the themes assigned to him, but the theories as well—and the answers.

I wonder whether it will take the Russians until 1965 to get a glimmer of what they are doing to their young people. They may produce machine tenders and machine builders this way, and propagandists who will grow old flaying the heresies of Yugoslavs and Poles. But is this the way to produce a planner, a prophet or a poet? Is it the way to produce Nobel Prize winners, whether in physics or literature? Is it, finally, the way to produce another Lenin?

Lest we start crowing with condescension, however, we might look at the assumptions behind our own educational system. The State Universities Association has just ended a Washington meeting with an attack on the idiot drift toward ever higher tuition fees in our higher education. They point out that this betrays the American educational tradition of equal opportunity for all, that in Russia higher education (at least, what there has been of it up to now) has been free, and that the American student already pays more for his education than students in any other country.

To which I say Amen, and again Amen. I have heard college administrators defending the increased tuition on the economically valid ground that the costs of educating a student are going up all the time, and that even the increased fees don't keep pace with the rate of increased cost. This is, I say, a valid argument if you assume that the student is an agent in an industrial transaction, buying something for his own use which he must pay for because he is going to turn it to a profit for himself.

But what a dismal assumption this is. The young people going through our colleges and universities are neither consumers buying a commodity nor producers getting ready to sell one—themselves. They are potential managers, leaders, artists, thinkers, value creators. You cannot apply to them a calculus of increasing cost of production, nor a theory of marginal utility, nor a plan for production and marketing.

Education is the sinew of individual creativeness and national vigor. If we are going to continue to run education as an industry, moaning always over the deficits and appealing for voluntary gifts, but also steadily pricing the bright but impoverished student out of the market, we shall find that the Russians can beat us at the game of using young people for industrial raw material.

Education is not an industry. It is a discipline, an encounter and a commitment.

6. New Ideas for Our Schools

January 26, 1959

THERE IS FERMENT in American education today, some of it healthy, some of it frenetic, but ferment there is. There is a new earnestness about the talented student and what to do with him. The Office of Education has just announced the launching of a National Talent Inventory, which means that an effort will now be made in the high schools to see just what talent we have, with the best measurement devices we can find. Later, periodically, a new inventory will be made of the same groups, to see what has happened to them.

The teachers have joined the Great Debate too. They are concerned not only about their salaries, but also about their standing in the community, about methods for training future teachers, and most of all about how effective their work is. State and local groups of teachers are no longer making their annual meetings narrow craft affairs; they know that there is a national crisis of confidence, and they are willing to listen to new ideas as never before. I have talked to scores of these groups in the past year, and I know their response.

The debate centers on the crucial question of how best to locate the talented youngsters and how to reorganize the curriculum to deal with them. Most of our attention now is being focused on the high school, which probably represents the whopping failure of our public school system. But the university and the elementary school are also coming in for attention. Much of the talk and writing is gimmick stuff: We are being told that we can fix things up by putting in this or that gimmick, adding courses here, subtracting them there, requiring this, dropping that.

No one has yet emerged who can translate this surface stuff into a genuine theory of education, with breadth and depth, as John Dewey did for his own generation a half century ago. But at least Dewey is being revisited, reread and revalued, attacked and defended. And one can see the beginnings of a new emphasis, which Dewey would not have rejected, yet which belongs characteristically to our own time, not his. I mean the emphasis on what the Gardiner Report called "the pursuit of excellence" and what I should myself call the carriers of promise.

I want to be clear about my position on the issue of talent and promise. There are three groups of students to consider: the highly talented; the average or below-average students, who lack either ability or the right motivation; and the underprivileged students, who may or may not have talent but are largely cut off from discovering whether they do.

We must fight the educational war on all three fronts. We must give the underprivileged students—the Negroes who are kept out of good schools, the impoverished students who can't pay their way up the rungs of the ladder—a chance to develop. This means doing away with inequalities of schooling and giving everyone equal access to schooling. We must give the talented students a chance to go as fast as they can. We must find, for the average unmotivated student, ways of releasing his motivations; and even for the untalented students I reject the notion that they need only some vocational skills—they, too, need training of the intellect and the personality, as far as they can take it.

Thus abide my three key terms, to suit this three-front war: *access, promise* (or talent), and *intellect* (rather than vocation). And the greatest of these is promise.

I guess what I am saying is that we have come to the end of one phase of American educational history. I mean the end of the great educational revolution that made schooling free, universal and compulsory, but spent its energy when that was done.

This ideal of universal education is not adequate for the American educational needs of today. Our task today is to build a new democratic educational elite, basing our educational rewards not on the accident of birth or wealth, or the color of a youngster's skin, or religion, but on merit alone.

An English writer, Michael Young, has made fun of this idea in a recent book published in London called *The Rise of the Meritocracy*. I am quite willing to accept the term "meritocracy" for a political and social system in which talent and intelligence replace blood and race and wealth.

January 29, 1959

The high school has been a success in the sense that it has brought together under one roof a larger percentage of the youth than is today being given a secondary-school education anywhere in the world. We have moved rapidly: in 1910 only 55 per cent of our youth were enrolled in the eleventh and twelfth grades; today it is 70 per cent. But our high schools are a failure in the quality of the educational job they are doing. That is why James B. Conant, on returning from his embassy post in Germany, took on the job of studying them. His report, *The American High School Today* (McGraw-Hill), is brief, compact, economical in language, factual in content, restrained in tone, concrete in its recommendations, rooted in a philosophy of democratic education. It is our decade's most important single study of our school system in action. It ranks with the John Gardiner report on *The Pursuit of Excellence*. Together they may start a new era of educational action in America.

I am glad to pay it this tribute, but I have some criticisms about where Conant still falls short of what is needed. He presents in a beguiling fashion the more attractive elements of our system—our belief in equal educational opportunity, our striving toward equal status for all levels of intelligence and occupation. He even defends the chaotic and inefficient system of local controls of education. His defense is that the system works. But that is question-begging nonsense. If it were true the Conant report would not have been necessary and would not have been undertaken. Conant addresses the report to local school boards, superintendents and high-school principals on the theory that they can reform themselves with the help of volunteer citizens' groups in each community. Maybe and maybe not. His only admonition is that school boards must leave the execution of programs to the superintendents and the teachers. It is good advice, but Conant offers nothing to nail it down. His major recommendation is the abolition of the smaller high schools. The danger is that even if it is carried through it will be valueless unless the other recommendations are also carried through.

The rest of the report tries to deal with the triple educational task of the high school. The three problems are these: First, how can you get a good "general education" for all? Second, how can you deal with the need for providing "market skills" for those whose aims and talents are not primarily academic although they may often be quite able? Third, how can you deal with the needs of the "academically talented" and the "highly gifted"?

Conant believes strongly that all three can and should be done under the same roof of the "comprehensive high school." He would even merge the separate vocational schools with it. This is not a smug view. I should call it a radically conservative one, as is all of Conant's thinking. He has thought it through mainly on the ground of maintaining a democratic mixture of all classes and conditions of American youth, even where he recommends radical changes in curriculum. He wants to maintain the "home room" as a base for the democratic mixture.

It might work, with the innovations. I also like his call for tightening up on the "general education," for individualizing the student program, for doing away with across-the-board student ranking (it makes the students pick the "gut" courses). I like especially his proposal for "ability grouping" in all required courses and most electives. He does not favor a general "track" system, but one where students will be divided into three ability groups in each subject, so that your son may find himself in the top group in English, the middle group in social studies and languages and the bottom group in mathematics and he can be shifted as he improves or falls in each.

This ability grouping will be a great reform in the school of the future if we can achieve it. I should like to see it in the elementary school as well, starting at the age of seven or eight. Along with it should go a talent inventory, on which we have now made a start.

Most important of all is what we do for the needs of the carriers of promise. Conant proposes for the "academically talented" (the top 15 per cent) a heavier program in both math and science on the one hand and a four-year course in a foreign language on the other (I agree that a two-year course such as we give now is almost worthless). For the "highly gifted" (the top 3 per cent), he proposes a special counselor to act as tutor in guiding their work and the taking of advanced placement exams for college, which means doing some freshman college work in the twelfth grade.

This has been long needed and will do much good. I should myself, however, go further in combining the two top groups into an honors division in each high school with a special counseling and teaching staff. Conant relies on an eighteen-course load during the four years to give them the right course spread. My own view is that it is not the number of courses that counts for the talented but the depth and reach of their work. The other 85 per cent could then be divided into the three ability groups.

I am disappointed about other lacks. I wish he had given as much stress to work in the human sciences as he does to work in math, physics and languages. Our future will depend as much on social invention as on scientific. I also wish he had given thought to the work of national groups for setting standards of achievement by which to measure each locality and on which to award special Federal aid for the talented.

7. John Dewey Revisited

January 27, 1959

JOHN DEWEY has been getting a bad press recently. Everything from your child's temper tantrum at school, or a teacher's violent experiences with his class hooligans, all the way to America's lag in the satellite and missile race, has been laid at his doorstep. Someone has remarked that if Dewey were alive, there is not a locality in the nation in which he could be elected to the school board. If a scholar writes an article in his defense in some magazine, a bold editor will play it up as if it were hot news—which it is.

There are a few lances I might break in his defense. Yet I come neither to praise nor to bury this intellectual Caesar, who for a half century has overshadowed our educational world. I want merely to revisit him, see what is still usable in him and what had better be discarded, and how we can build something which will do for our age what his educational theory did for his.

I am convinced that the clichés of the struggle between "progressive" and "essentialist" education have very little to offer us today. The recent books and articles about the failure of our schools have scored all the familiar points against progressive education: the classroom as a kind of anarchy-plus-a-schoolmarm; the abdication of the teacher; the denial of all organization and authority; the cult of the child; the obsession with individual attention; the refusal to see any subject matter as more important than any other subject matter—hence the choice of silly snap courses under the elective system; the failure to turn out a generation that can read, write, spell, master a language, or do any mathematics.

The indictment has been built up to the point of nausea. Whether or not it is true of the American schools, it is certainly unfair to Dewey himself. I am glad to be able to say so in this year which marks the centenary of Dewey's birth. If you want a full analysis of Dewey's whole philosophy, with a chapter on his educational ideas, you will find it in a recently published book, *John Dewey in Perspective,* by George R. Geiger (Oxford).

Geiger presents a spirited and intelligent defense, whose basic point is that Dewey was himself no Deweyite, just as Marx said that he was no Marxist and Freud that he was no Freudian. The disciples always run away with the master and that happened also with Dewey's ideas, which were stretched into the dogma of "progressive education."

The basic ones are still worth holding on to: that education is growth, and stretching all your capacities; that the human material is plastic and that human nature is no immutable iron cage in which we are caught but something that is always in process of being formed; that education is not just for childhood, but should be carried on all through a lifetime; that children are people, not objects; that the school must be oriented toward the child, his interests and needs, and not to a fixed curriculum; that you must always touch base by going back to life experience and away from the books; that you learn through doing, in the sense that you discover yourself by trying yourself out; that all life is experimental and all teaching should be; that the individual's potentials are limitless, and that education is simply all the ways by which we try to tap them.

Clearly the man who could see these things sixty years ago was an extraordinary man who saw a good deal.

But he was a man of his own time, not ours, and many of his intellectual garments have worn thin. He lived and wrote under Darwin's influence, which we have now digested—and we want something more than the idea of evolution, of life as a continuing process. We have learned a good deal in the social sciences, especially in psychology and psychiatry.

We have a hunch now, for example, that a teacher is not simply a kindly onlooker but a shaper; that a child doesn't just grow on his own but needs a frame of organization to give him security enough to grow on, and a sense of limits within which he can make his choices with increasing sureness. We know pretty well now that you can't get far by starting with a child's "interests," because he doesn't know what his interests are until he has been exposed to the wisdom of the past, the doubts and insights of the present and the enthusiasms of his teachers.

We also know that there is a drive in each of us, child or adult—a drive toward achieving a self-image in which we can take some satisfaction. The problem of releasing the motivation of a youngster—of making him into someone who wants deeply to learn and grow—is the problem of finding some area in which he has a sense of mastering something worth while, compassable stage by compassable stage. In achieving this mastery he must learn both to compete with others in his group and to work alone during heartbreaking and heroic hours.

This isn't anti-Dewey, but neither is it Dewey. It is simply off on another line of inquiry. So also is the idea of an educational elite which would, I fear, have puzzled someone with Dewey's notions of "education in a democracy and democracy in education." His formula was neat, but it left the crucial problems unanswered. We must educate in a democracy, but not let the level of education sink to the norm set by the slack, the indolent and the unmotivated. We must have democracy in education, yet recognize the teacher as a shaper of personalities, as a searcher for the creative minority which will provide the intellectual and moral leadership without which a democracy perishes.

PART III

Culture and the Conduct of Life

CONTENTS

PREFACE

THE PIECES *gathered together in this section deal with themes that caused more controversy than any other single group I have dealt with, and that steadily evoked the most heated response. In my earlier history as a columnist it was usually the pieces on labor, the New Deal and foreign policy that set the geese flying—in those days political and economic controversy still had the power to stir. But in the past decade it was my pieces in a quite different area that proved most prickly: when I treated of morals, sexual behavior, crime, punishment, the waywardness of adolescents, prostitution, abortion, the role and fate of women, and in general the conduct of life in America.*

The protests came not only from those who disagreed with my views on the topics I wrote about, but even more from those who felt I ought not to write about them at all. They might be discussed by preachers, judges, doctors, psychiatrists and professional scientific students in their scientific journals, but for me or anyone else writing in a daily family newspaper they were out of bounds. Letters poured in from fearful parents who were worried about the effect of my articles on their teen-agers, or who felt that they had to hide the paper from their children of more tender years. They poured in from single-minded and simple-minded liberals who felt I was betraying the cause of liberal political militancy by devoting so much attention to nonpolitical themes. They were moved by a mixture of influences from the Puritan tradition and from the Marxist notion that sex and morals, like religion, were the opiates of the masses, and that any serious discussion of them in the press might weaken class militancy by serving as a safety valve for tensions that might have led to political action. I might add that there was also the usual quota of crank letters and hate letters from people who found in these pieces of mine the final proof that I was a Communist—for was it not the Communist aim to weaken and finally topple the American way of life by undermining the fabric of social morality and natural law?

I had to call, as never before, on my natural perversity and orneriness to keep me impervious to these shafts from various directions. I was lucky in writing for a newspaper whose publisher and editor were as committed as I to the idea that a newspaper should deal with the concerns that come home most directly to the hearts and hearths of men. Time after time they took the offensive in this area, as they were to do also on issues like McCarthyism, and a large number of the pieces reprinted in this section were published originally as parts of a "series." It was an innovation in the history of the big metropolitan press to give front-page headlines to sequences of articles on such themes as the Kinsey Report on American women, morals on the campus, sexual offenders, the tragedy of the homosexuals, the pursuit of happiness, new light on love, and the private lives of teen-agers. The headline titles were dramatic and sometimes flamboyant—a natural enough fact for headlines in a competitive newspaper situation. But the material in the articles themselves, as the reader will note, was as carefully weighed, as scrupulously tracked down in the professional and technical literature, and as honestly and soberly set down as I knew how. I was happy to have had a training in the social sciences which I could now use in the service of human beings, many of whom were harried from without and tortured within. Years earlier I had read James Harvey Robinson's little book The Humanizing of Knowledge, *and I saw my newspaper pieces as part of that process. The fact that the intellectual climate of America was beginning to shift from the public to the private made it easier for me to reach my readers with these columns than it would otherwise have been.*

This was, for me at any rate, a whole new world of inquiry and discussion that was opening up. There had been a period in English history where some of the same issues had been fought out—from Francis Place and John Stuart Mill to Havelock Ellis and Marie Stopes. There had been, in the 1840s and 1850s, a similar liberating struggle among American writers on love, sex, equal rights for women, contraception, criminology. There was a flare-up of interest in the 1920s as well, but it never got fully under way. In the past decade, however, many of us have felt the surge of a great liberating movement of human thought on the mind and the conduct of life, of which the two key figures were Sigmund Freud and Alfred Kinsey. My pieces on Freud will be found in Part V, because they seem to belong better with the other material in "The Underground River." *But the major force of Freud's influence had already made itself felt by the time I came to the* Post. *The new and dominating figure was Kinsey.*

I have called him the great Guilt Killer, and that was his role. He was the explorer of the last remaining unexplored continent. He carried on an unremitting war both with the moralizers, whom he saw as too repressive of human instincts, and with the psychoanalysts, philosophers and poets whose subtleties he regarded as overfancy and too little scientific. His obsessive aim was to release the heavy burdens of guilt which crushed the chances of fulfillment. In that sense he was a modern Rousseauist, who believed that sexually (if not politically) men are

*born free, yet they are everywhere in chains. His belief in a Noble
Sexual Savage seemed to me both primitivist and naïve, and in my later
writings on him I came to see this increasingly. He reacted oversensi-
tively to my criticism, and our earlier friendship was marred before he
died. Yet I valued and still value his liberating role in the history of
American psychic energies and life goals.*

*A columnist owes his readers some explanation of the sources of his
thought, especially on sensitive themes, and of how he came to write
on what he did and as he did. I had been struggling toward a conception of my column as a dialogue between the reader and myself on
themes which came home most closely to both of us. I had found fulfillment in my own personal and family life, in my work and play and
contemplation. I was writing my book* America as a Civilization *and
also giving a course at Brandeis University on "The Conduct of Life."
All these streams of thought and activity converged to make me rethink
in mid-twentieth-century terms the meaning of Jefferson's and Madison's eighteenth-century concept of the "pursuit of happiness."*

*A number of themes emerged in my writing which I had not hitherto
explored—the meaning of love and loneliness, the problem of limits
and freedom in the growing-up process, the going concern of the family,
the burdens of freedom, the liberation from guilt and self-pity, the
acceptance of man's fate. What I read in the psychiatrists served to
sharpen and confirm what I was thinking, and I was lucky to be writing
in the midst of what I regard as a renaissance of American social theory
in our day.*

*There were, of course, problems; I touched on some of them earlier
in this preface when I spoke of the protests I received. There were
problems of tabooed vocabulary, especially in a series (not here reprinted because it was too detailed and technical) on the Kinsey Report
on American women. There were forbidden subjects, such as homosexuality and abortion (see* The Tortured Problem *and* The Tragic
Taboos*). There were curious experiences, such as when—in pursuit
of the story of the State Department scandals—I interviewed Senator
Wherry and Lieutenant Blick of the Washington Vice Squad, or when
in doing my articles on the "gay" I received a sheaf of letters from men
suggesting their readiness to co-operate with me in "field work" on the
subject. On the other hand, there were the responses that really counted
with me, on every side, from people who welcomed the chance to read
in their papers an honest and candid exploration of conduct and morals.*

*In the process of writing these pieces, I came to some conclusions
that I want to set down summarily but tentatively: that the deepest
drives of men and women get short-circuited with the drives and goals
of their culture; that sin and respectability are still (as they were with
the Colonel's Lady and Judy O'Grady) sisters under the skin; that
sex and love often get mixed up with security and commercialism; that*

one of the laws of life is the twisting of healthy emotions until they become unhealthy ones, as in homosexuality, and that it is all too easy to make cheap judgments and offer cheap solutions for these tortured men.

I hope I have learned in the process to have respect for tough facts and groping people, for the bewildering world of the adolescent, for the honesty of most young people, for the idealism that gets shattered under the stress of fear (see "The Man on the Roof"*). I learned to fear the violent adults even more than the delinquent kids whom they were trying to tame, and to recognize the killer in the mob that calls for the blood of the young killers. I learned the ways of anger at the sheer pathos of the avoidable—at the tragedy of the "dark Satanic mills" of abortion, at those who would force unwanted children upon unready parents; at the men who sit in judgment on the dope addicts, even more than at the addicts themselves, and at those who relieve their own sense of guilt by pushing prostitutes around.*

Most of all, I hope I have learned that we ought to replace the idea of guilt *and* blame *with the search for* responsibility; *and that the responsibility rests on the interaction of the victim, the culture, and the whole human situation.*

THE PURSUIT OF HAPPINESS

1. The Need for Love

October 29, 1951

WHEN THOMAS JEFFERSON, listing the "unalienable Rights" of men in the Declaration of Independence, counted "the Pursuit of Happiness" among them, the age he lived in was pretty certain of the nature of that happiness but anxious that men should have the freedom to pursue it. In our own society we have the freedom, but we are not certain of what it is we want to pursue.

We can do little about our society and the current world chaos unless we rethink the conduct of our life in terms of the deep life processes. Each of us must ask himself, What are your life goals? What is it in your life that is most important to you? Is it love, or sex? Is it good times and "fun"? Is it a happy marriage and a pattern of children, family and home? Is it diversity of experience as an end in itself? Is it money and power? Is it a big name, and the ambition of cutting a figure in life? Is it God and religion, and doing good for other people? Is it success? Is it your work, and the sense of a productive life?

"I want to be loved" is in our culture a theme even more powerful than "I want to love." For love, in the receiving and the giving, has become one of the great preoccupations of our time. It holds among our life goals a place it never had in the Middle Ages, when the reigning purpose was the linkage to church and community and one's station in life. The modern society, while stressing the individual's own life, has torn him from his former moorings and left him isolated and desolate unless he feels he is loved and thereby has become linked with someone.

A psychologist would say it is insecurity that makes the Hollywood stars drive so hard for fame, and it is their failure—for whatever reason—to find a satisfying bond with a particular person which makes them eager to become the "imago" of all people. The happy people are unlikely to be great performers; it is the unhappy ones—a Danny Kaye perhaps, a Judy Garland—who in their aloneness strike a chord each member of the audience responds to, or (perhaps better) who respond to the chord of love the audience strikes. The wife of a writer

I know, shrewdly assessing her husband, told me, "He doesn't feel happy unless he has met a half-dozen people on the subway who recognize him and tell him how much they love him."

The American overvaluing of love, in this sense, starts early. The child is asked constantly, from infancy on, whether he loves his parents; he is assured in turn that he is loved; he learns that love is something to be given or withheld, and he comes to use the symbol of love as a whip he can crack over his parents, they in turn using it as reward or punishment. Thus he comes to test the success of his relations with the outside world as he grows up, and his whole sense of life effectiveness, by whether he is loved and therefore accepted.

Thus there are many who have made a life goal out of love not because they have in any sense chosen it themselves but because their upbringing and their whole culture have chosen it for them. What is worst about them is that they pursue love not out of a desire for love's bounty but out of a panicky fear of deprivation. When you have come to value love not for itself but as a test of popularity or success or sexual potency or the fatality of your appeal, or as proof that you are not unwanted and a failure, the proofs have to be repeated in response to an ever increasing urgency. What you have then is not a capacity for love, or even a need for it, but a need for the proofs of love—which is quite a different matter. We are more concerned in love about getting than about giving, as if we could pile love up and hoard it. Or as if it were always, as in a business deal, a question of who comes out ahead in the bargain or competition for love.

Again we borrow the prevailing attitudes from our business society, where we are so fearful of being duped. How many a man has shied away from any but the most transitory love relationship because he is afraid of being made the fall guy and fearful that love is a racket contrived by women for a cushioned existence at the man's expense. But, whether man or woman, it is hard to escape the infection of money values carried over unconsciously into our feelings about love: the conviction somehow that love, like every other transaction in life, has to pay off.

If love is your life goal, it will be wise to follow the injunction in Emerson's poem, "Give all to love." If it is for you the main end of life it doesn't have to be reckoned up in a profit-and-loss column, nor does it have to pay off, nor need it be a weapon in the lethal battle of the sexes that haunts some of Thurber's cartoons. This doesn't mean flinging your own personality away, or fastening yourself upon that of someone else.

Love is not restricted to the need for being wanted in childhood, nor to the romantic dream of the adolescent, nor yet to the powerful thrust of the sexual drive. It may envelop all these phases. But in its fullest sense it is adult- rather than child-centered, open-eyed rather than romantic, containing the sexual desire and pleasure yet not confined to them—the mature love of mature persons who find their relationship not crippling but fulfilling.

Love in this sense is the hardest achievement of modern life, but the goal is worth the pain. For in the end the only real growth possible in the world must come from love.

January 30, 1956

There is a new book about love whose great merit is that it fits the American mood of today so well. It is *Love or Perish* by Smiley Blanton, M.D. (Simon and Schuster). I give a brief excerpt that sets the key: "To say that one will perish without love does not mean that everyone without adequate love dies. Many do. . . . But most of the time, lack of love makes people depressed, anxious and without zest for life. They remain lonely and unhappy, without friends or work they care for, their life a barren treadmill, stripped of all creative action and joy."

In other words, the American interest in love today has shifted from what it used to be. We used to link it with marriage, or with some romantic seizure ("falling in love"), or with some fever of the restless spirit ("Love is bustin' out all over"). But now we link love with mental health.

I wonder how much meaning this kind of book would have for an English or a French audience. The French write books about love, but they tend to be in the tradition of Ovid—graceful, somewhat playful and cynical, sometimes philosophic and sometimes mainly on the art of love. As for the British, Geoffrey Gorer recently did a survey in which he found far less interest in the idea of "falling in love" than we Americans show.

More than any people in history we Americans seem to have developed this craving to love and be loved, taking both of them with the desperate seriousness with which we take most of our life problems. To "pour love" into a child—as the exaggerated phrase goes—is good for the child's security and the parents' expressiveness. But it is even better for the child to see that the parents are capable of adult love for each other; it gives him something to grow into.

With all the emphasis on the need for love, I can discern a new culture type emerging in America. The ideal image of the male is getting to be that of a man capable of making his woman—or women —happy and fulfilled, while remaining undominated by her. The ideal image of the woman is that of a warm, responsive creature who makes her man happy and keeps his love, and brings up his children, and develops herself at the same time.

The trouble is that these ideal culture types conflict with our moral codes and our sexual education, just as they come to grief under the

sway of possessive parents and false cultural goals and hollow standards all around us.

This is the phase of the problem that few psychiatrists, with all their
guidebooks for happiness, seem to be facing. The question is not always
whether you love and are loved. It is often a question of whether you
respect the work you are doing, and whether you find some meaningful
connection between your whole working or business day and that irrational yearning to be joined with something other than yourself
which the Greeks called *eros*.

What I am saying, I suppose, is that man's real need is not so much
for love as for meaning, and that love is the most important form of
meaning.

2. The Lonely People

October 31, 1951; June 18 1957

AN ENGLISH WRITER, Geoffrey Gorer, in his witty book *The American
People,* has said that Americans keep their doors unlocked because
they are eager to have their loneliness broken. One of the life goals
of Americans is human warmth and communication. Anyone who has
observed American marriage knows that, even in the early years of marriage, young couples find they get along better when they are "out on
a party" with other young couples. For the adolescents "dating" and
"having fun" are crucial, just as the older people—unmarried or widowed or divorced—sometimes turn to the "lonely-hearts clubs" that
dot the landscapes of the big American cities.

Many observers have noted what they call the "alienation" of the
individual, torn away from his old roots in the family, the land, the face-
to-face community, work or business or a sense of creativeness.

It is these uprooted people who are likely to worry about "what people will say," whether they "make a good impression." One of the
searching plays of recent years about American life was Arthur Miller's
Death of a Salesman, the tragedy of a man of generous impulses who
is caught by the alienating forces of modern life, so that his prime
drive—for himself and for his sons—is the hollow drive of being "well
liked."

Along with our urge to privacy there is also in most of us an urge
to confide. Before you are married you always have a best friend with
whom you can share your private triumphs and tribulations. After
marriage it becomes a form of disloyalty to your husband or your wife.
But you are none the less pent up and the need to confide is there.
What you want is someone impersonal and professional, preferably
someone "scientific." Hence the role of the psychoanalyst, who would

serve a purpose as listening post and confessional box even if he never opened his mouth. Hence also the easy success of the phone impostors who, in a half-dozen big cities across the continent, pretended to be working for the Kinsey survey and got a number of women to answer intimate questions about their sex life. And, with all the secrecy and the skill of the authentic Kinsey staff interviewers in winning the confidence of those they interview, I should guess that the whole Kinsey survey would have been impossible had there not been in most of us this almost irrepressible urge to confide.

"In my ten years of social work in this country," writes a social worker with a European background, "I have learned one thing: The American male or female is about the loneliest individual in the world. He is ready to pour out his most intimate history easily and gladly, provided it can be done in a 'platonic' way—which means that the other person is not involved. No nation has taken to psychoanalysis as we have done, and only the eternal loneliness of the individual has made the creation of social casework possible. People will not share their feelings with friends or family. They are afraid of pain and mental anguish. The person who is close to us can hurt us, but this is not true in the deepest sense of the analyst, social worker or Kinsey poller."

This is acutely put. My correspondent strikes even closer when she adds: "We seek to avoid pain but the harvest is being alone. I have seen it among people in the middle thirties who go into analytic treatment as the one acceptable way of talking about themselves. I have a feeling that from our constant response, 'Thank you, just fine,' the road leads to the psychotherapist. Somewhere along the road are the social workers." And—one may add—also the priest, the pastor and the rabbi.

There are two kinds of loneliness in our time. One is the loneliness of those without ties or companionship—the millions who recoil from evenings spent alone and want someone to talk to. The other is the basic loneliness of all of us, even the busiest and most social. It is the hunger for human connection which not even marriage or business, life in the big cities or the Army, "dates" and "parties" and careers can satisfy.

In fact, the crowdedness of our lives has built a wall between persons, a wall that can be broken down only if each faces first the loneliness of his own being. This is one of the themes of Erich Fromm's books, especially *Man for Himself*—that only when you have come to accept yourself and build a productive life can you establish the kind of communication with others which breaks down the wall of loneliness.

This is why some of the most productive men have been those who, at some time, have passed through periods of deep self-questioning and even of utter desolation. This was true of John Stuart Mill, as the readers of his autobiography will recall. It was true of William James, who spent a number of years, both at Cambridge and in Germany, wrestling with a sense of guilt and inadequacy.

No one can count himself as being on the path to his life goals unless at some point he has faced himself, wrestled with the Adversary within him and come out alive.

May 4, 1956

Which of us has not wondered what the female celebrity—the beauty queen, the movie star, the café society rage—does when the shouting dies down and the lights expire? She doesn't call for madder music and for stronger wine. She settles down before the mirror and takes her mask off, and wonders whom she can rely on to act as her escort when she puts it back on tomorrow. I knew a young man of no particular ancestry, wealth, talents or accomplishments who was constantly seen with desirable women. He made it a point to be always available, always thoughtful, always gallant, and to make no demands. He had reached to the hidden truth about the loneliness of the glamorous.

To be lonely is the original curse, preceding the original sin. My reading of the myth of Adam and Eve is that they ate the fruit of evil because each was incomplete without the other. We are lonely until something happens to us whereby our image of the ideal other person meets the ideal image of self that we carry with us. When the two converge the sense of being alone subsides—at least for the moment.

For many people this convergence never takes place. I have talked with men and women who live such solitary lives that even our ordinary illusions of lives full of meaningless action are denied to them. They feel better in the morning, when they can at least look forward to the companionship of the shop or office. They feel dreariest at the end of work, when they must turn toward a room or apartment in which they will be forever alone.

There is a news story today about the woman in New Orleans whose lover was about to leave her to return to his wife. She ran her car over him, back and forth, until he was mangled. She seems to have been the religious sort, and she called herself an avenging angel. But I suspect she couldn't bear to be left lonely.

To be lonely in America is worse than being lonely almost anywhere else in the world, because our gods are success and happiness and we make a cult of experience. And also because we are constantly surrounded by the silken symbols of sensual living, and driven by the fear of missing what life should offer.

3. Children and Parents

January 31, 1956

THE CHILD PANIC in America is pretty well over. By "child panic" I mean the terrible anxiety that American parents showed about bringing up their children, from 1920 to the 1950s. During those decades the parents shifted from one "school" and fad of child rearing to another, and from one "authority" on child psychology to another. But always they made a cult of the child and worshiped at the shrine of a Little God who could never do wrong. If anything wrong happened we all assumed it was the fault of the parents, who did not "understand" their children or did not love them enough or did not sacrifice enough for them.

Healthy changes are taking place in this attitude. The cult of the child is giving way to a new perspective which sees both parents and children as being worthy of attention, each from the other. The child as the Noble Little Innocent (the "good child in the bad society" is the way one child expert used to put it) is no longer a tenable conception. "Parents on the Run," as Marguerite and Willard Beecher put it in the title of their new book (Julian Press), are no longer on the run.

We ask ourselves now, What was it all about? Most writers on the subject seem to believe it was the fault of the psychologists and the psychiatrists—of Stanley Hall and John B. Watson, of Freud and his disciples, who told the parents that the destiny of their children the rest of their lives would be decided by what happened to them in the nursery and in their earliest years, and who thereby saddled them with guilt and drenched them with anxieties.

The parents were ready to be ridden with guilt about bringing up their children because they were already emotionally insecure and were filled with guilt about themselves and their position in the society they lived in. The children gave them the most convenient channel for their anxieties, and the child experts were the most convenient reed on which to lean.

I think the deeper source of the child panic was the fact that by the 1920s millions of American parents had moved into the middle and upper classes from the classes below. Many of them were the second generation, some were the third, of immigrant stock. They had come to some income, position, responsibility. They wanted to make sure that their children would keep moving upward, would fulfill all the dreams they had themselves not fulfilled.

We are now in a phase of recoil against this overemphasis. And, as with most recoils, I am afraid we are overdoing it again. "Fifty Thousand Years of Evolution Can't Be Wrong" is the title of the closing chapter of the Beecher book, and the parting bolt of advice is that "Old Dame Nature is on the side of survival"—that "she didn't intend the human being to worry himself to death." This is the right emphasis, but it needs to be balanced by saying that indifference can be used as badly as anxiety. The best way to put it, I think, is that the parents must regain their sense of their own identity without losing any of their love and concern for their children.

There is, for example, the principle of *consistency*. Recent studies of psychically healthy children show that they come from very diverse backgrounds of class and ethnic group and region and family, and have been brought up under different degrees of freedom and discipline. But the important fact they have in common is that of consistency. They came to know what to expect, so that they could drop it from their minds, instead of always being tense under the changing and arbitrary ways of their parents.

There is, second, the principle of *effective love*. I wrote recently about the need of the human personality to be able to give love and receive it. Where we have been wrong in the past forty years was in believing that to let the child have his own way in everything was to give him a sign of our love. It was not a sign of our love, but of our weakness. The child cannot feel you love him if you give in to him so completely that you seem indifferent to what he does or doesn't do. When you set some limits for him, it is also a sign that you care, and therefore of love.

This is a third principle—that of a *sense of limits*. I am not talking of the father-tyranny of the old family, nor of a child's day that is riddled with rules for every trivial occasion. A child must be brought up to become a mature person, which means he must learn how to deal with freedom. He must understand the nature of the limits staked out for him, and the reason for them.

4. Happy and Unhappy Marriage

November 1, 1951

WHEN the European male gibes at the American as a clumsy and blundering lover, or when foreign observers write off the American woman as both frustrated and frigid, they may be hitting at American civilization because of their envy of our power and success. Yet some of what they say is true. The crop of postwar novels by soldiers stationed in France, Italy and Germany bore witness to the sexual memories American soldiers carried home—memories of women who had surrendered themselves to love and were more committed to it than their American sisters. Perhaps if the American occupation army had been made up primarily of women, they might have come back with equally glowing reports. Both by nature and by art, American women are becoming increasingly attractive without being either fulfilling or fulfilled.

This is the more a paradox because America has come to stress sex more blatantly than any civilization since the Roman Empire. The movies with box office appeal are often those with a display of shapely legs; the covers of many of the twenty-five-cent books show an array of almost bare female bosoms which make a book display rack at any drugstore the center not only of literary but of sexual attraction. The cult of female breasts will be noted by future historians as one of the striking facts about American civilization in mid-twentieth century. The sexual emphasis which we don't dare put into words cries out from the female figures in the ads. The Big Circulation magazines become sensuous experiences with their array of stocking, bra and girdle ads. The comedians on radio and television find it impossible to get along without broadly sexual jokes—some of them heavily homosexual.

We have become a sensual civilization. The American—male or female, adolescent or young or middle-aged—finds himself a lonely animal in the midst of a jungle of sexual stimulation.

We treat sex always with a snicker and a leer, by indirection. We surround our young people with verbal and visual stimulants toward a sexual experience on which we frown and which we still punish in antiquated legal codes. Our taboos are still strong, while the sensual surface of our life still mocks them. As a result Americans find themselves often having to get drunk in order to find a sexual expressiveness; and then become drunk again to forget their failure to find emotional fulfillment.

For those who pursue happiness thus, it becomes mainly a mode of despair and a bleak substitute for the real thing. It is a mistake to regard sex as a goal in itself, as a form of reassuring oneself, or again as a weapon with which to subdue another personality. The problem is to balance the violence of the instinctual life with the fullness of love and emotional meaning, and through them to restore that freshness of the instinctual life which has in so many cases been lost.

The "sexual revolution" has brought a spate of sex-and-marriage manuals. This kind of literature is not new. You will find it among the Romans and the French. In the great Hindu civilization of early India one of the four aims of life was Kama, the embodiment of sexual pleasure and love. *The Philosophies of India,* by the late Heinrich Zimmer (Pantheon), says of the Hindu handbooks of the art of love that they were intended for "a society of frozen emotions," where marriages of convenience were always arranged by parents and where some instructions were needed for love life in marriage.

In American marriage the "marriage of convenience" is the marginal exception and the "love marriage" the norm. Montaigne's essays and diary notes about love and marriage show that he was talking of two wholly different realms. The French separate them, approaching the first with ardor, the second with a canny rationalism. The Americans fuse them. We test a love affair by whether it ends in marriage and expect every marriage to be a love match. The same forces which make us an open society, with few hindrances (except for color) to marriages that cross class, income and religious boundary lines, lead us also to put a big emotional investment into marriage. We expect it to give our nights sexual pleasure and fill our days with romance, to build a frame for our life, to provide us with a home and children, and to add whatever is useful and decorative to the core of emotional excitement.

Even by these exacting standards, the reasonably happy marriage does exist. In spite of widespread disillusionment, one must assert that American marriage is not wholly a flop. Marriage at its best gives sexual experience a sanction; it envelops the instinctual life in a casing of love, enhancing both; it adds a feeling for the children who are the products of the sexual union, and for the home which becomes the anchor of the family.

The happy marriage exists, but it is much rarer than the marriages that don't work. Whether you think of marriage (in religious terms) as a sacrament, or (in psychological jargon) as the adjustment and fulfillment of two personalities, the number of failures is dismaying. The American social landscape is dotted with what Tolstoy once called "the tragedies of the bedroom." The "sexual revolution" has made our sexual experience freer, the "kitchen revolution" has made a woman's day less burdensome, our consumer's civilization has made husband and wife more glittering creatures. Yet none of them have made marriage happier.

Some of the fault rests with the intrusion of alien motives. We try to use marriage as a means to other ends. For many girls it is a way of achieving economic security; for many parents it is a way of seeing their children settled in life. For men and women alike, being married becomes proof that they are not failures—even though the marriage itself turns out badly. The crucial fact is not to be among the uncalled and the unchosen. For men especially, marriage may be simply a convenient channeling for their sexual hungers, or an antidote to loneliness, or a way of showing their economic prowess through a decorative home or an equally decorative wife.

The result is the tensions and heartbreak—and often the sheer boredom—of many marriages. Sometimes the path of their failure is marked with forlorn and bedraggled adulteries; sometimes the frustrations are kept bottled up without so desperate an outlet, and the home becomes the arena of a protracted cold war.

Both husband and wife make too heavy demands on marriage. You can't ask marriage to console you for life's defeats, or remedy your inadequacies of personality, or iron out the scars left by childhood. Nor can you expect to use it as a weapon for subduing another personality and giving you power and domination over others which life outside has denied you. Yet when marriage fails to do this, we call it a failure.

From another angle Americans do not ask enough of marriage. Having once resigned themselves to the loss of their original "glory dream," they come to regard marriage in routine terms. There is a comic-strip caricature with which the critics of each sex have approached the marriage role of the other. Yet it is true—perhaps not quite as true of women as of men—that they have given up in their efforts to make a creative thing of marriage and home.

You must know, as I know, a number of husbands and wives who talk of their "homes," by which they mean the house or apartment on which they have lavished the greater part of their income, furnishing and decorating it. But their children leave it as often as possible for "dates" outside and as soon as possible for good. The wives leave it for shopping, theater, bridge. The husbands leave it for business, golf, sports events, or those frequent evenings which they prefer to spend with "the boys" at the club or lodge. The American home is no longer built around any important functions which it fulfills. In most cases it is no longer the center of work, or the carrier of traditions, or the place in which ideas are discussed and conversation can be heard.

We have allowed secondary things to clutter up the marriage relation. Marriage cannot be a way to security, nor a lazy path to sex, nor an excuse for house furnishing, nor a way of asserting your power or finding a refuge from life. If you try to find "happiness" thus, it will elude you, as happiness always eludes those who pursue it too anxiously.

Marriage is a difficult relation between two persons who have similar sexual attitudes and life rhythms, and a respect for each other's differences. It asks mainly a feeling of creativeness about the life they can lead and the family group they can build together. It asks also a measure of what Bernard Shaw used to call the life force. If they have that, they will communicate some of that life force to their home and children.

5. A Girl Is Not a Woman

September 10, 1958

HER NAME USED TO BE Kitty Foyle, and we called her absurdly a white-collar girl, and she had complications with a man from the

Main Line. Now her name is Caroline Bender—or Gregg Adams, or April Morrison—and we call her a career girl, and she has complications with a number of men inside and outside Radio City, where she works.

We are indebted to Rona Jaffe for pinning down this species in the form of a quintet of career girls who work in a paperback-and-pulp publishing firm in her novel, *The Best of Everything* (Simon and Schuster). In its Grand Hotelish sort of way it makes good reading about a cluster of people who are as recognizable as the office buildings that serve as background for the dust jacket.

I suspect that we shall soon have a flood of novels about and by career girls, much as *The Hucksters* fatefully spawned a succession of novels about Madison Avenue. Miss Jaffe must get the credit for having sensed that there is a minor literary genre here, worth cultivating.

I wonder whether any novelist will ever catch the New York career girl in her full meaning. Dreiser worked too massively and was better with a Sister Carrie or a Jenny Gerhardt. Fitzgerald might have done it, for he could catch surfaces and winged dreams without bruising them, but he cared about power and glamour, and these marginal people would not have been big enough game for him.

They come to New York because the loosening of American local roots and class lines lets them leave their home towns, and the metropolis draws them to it. The dazzle of the big city gives them a sense of the life force powerfully at work here, and its anonymity offers them freedom and release. They don't make much money at the jobs they get—secretaries, receptionists, flunkies on magazines and in publishing houses, fashion or editorial researchers, Girl Fridays for TV shows or advertising agencies, part-time models, hopeful candidates for bit parts on TV or Broadway.

They have to crowd together into apartments they can't afford, or use their flair for redoing a loft or walk-up flat with a few gimcracks and pictures and travel posters. They diet almost as much for economy as for looks, and save their appetites until they get taken out to dinner. But they know how to dress, and their budget for clothes is as carefully calculated as the count down of a missile at Cape Canaveral. Their gods are keeping busy and a sense of being alive, and their shining goal is not a career but marriage.

Some time ago Simone de Beauvoir, in *The Second Sex,* tried to write off all American movie actresses as the American version of the Greek hetairai, or courtesans. The big-city career girl uses her body as well as her head, but she does it not to further her career but to end it.

Remember, she is a career girl, not a career woman. She uses New York for that new and characteristic pause between college and marriage which marks the lives of the bright and attractive girls of this generation. She turns her back on both the marriage-only tradition and the career-only tradition. She wants to get married before it is too late, but meanwhile she wants to spread her wings a bit and see if she can fly on her own. Thus the few years as career girl are a constant balancing of adventure and emotional commitment.

Usually her college education has given her a scattering of knowledge she can't use, and few skills she can. But somewhere she has picked up the things that distinguish her from other female populations: a briskness of look and walk, a quickness of word, a willingness of heart and a passionate readiness for experience.

Miss Jaffe sees these facets of her girls. What she emphasizes too stridently is that their jobs are not genuinely *work* for them, in the meaning that work has for men, but only places where they wait for the men who will become their husbands.

While they wait, they are not immobile. There is a lot of rushing into bed and out of bed—so much so that one wonders how the books and the magazines ever get to press, or the boss's letters ever get typed up and sent out. Any employer reading these pages will make a mental note to check up on what the girls in his office do after lunch, and with whom.

But I find it wearying to be told again and again that these bed adventures are transient things (except for the unforgettable girl who scavenges the wastebaskets and garbage of her former lover, with a passion for researching her replacement in his bed and apartment). The author hits you over the head repeatedly to make sure you understand that all the heartbreak is for a worthy cause, that April has found the clean young American she can be happy with, that Mary Agnes has fulfilled her life in a baby, that Barbara will not yield to the man she loves except to find a second father for her child, and that Caroline herself would rather "die inside" than go to Dallas with the married man she loves.

In a flash of insight Caroline sees that it is not only her lover who loves his conventional life more than he does her, but that she too wants this life above all.

The author has, indeed, the "best of everything"—the best of the world of tormented passion so long as it leads to the ordered world of the altar.

6. Eros: Expression and Repression

February 3, 1956

I HAVE DISCUSSED some phases of the life cycle of the American, including love, loneliness, marriage, divorce, parents and children. I come now to the central theme of sexual expressiveness and repression which underlies all the rest, and which was the theme of Kinsey.

We are in a transition in our evaluation of the Kinsey studies. I feel strongly that there is decreasing point in pursuing further the old themes of controversy—the debate about Kinsey's statistical methods and techniques of interviewing, and whether he has taken too biological a view of sexual behavior, and whether he is too hostile to the psychiatrists. A symposium on the Kinsey volumes—*Sexual Behavior in American Society,* edited by Jerome Himelhoch and Sylvia Fava (Norton)—contains some of the classic essays on these subjects, including the report made to the American Statistical Association, the raking criticism by Dr. Lawrence Kubie, an essay by Erich Fromm, material from the religious viewpoint by Seward Hiltner, and some interesting studies on the impact of Kinsey on college students' attitudes and behavior.

Assuming that the Kinsey methods can in time be improved and that his figures are not too far out of the way, what are we to conclude about sexual expression and repression in our culture as a whole?

Certainly the American culture is a sexually repressive one, if we compare it with those of the French, Italians, Norwegians, Swedes, Latin Americans, Caribbeans, Japanese, and some of the primitive groups whom our anthropologists have been studying.

We still live under the sway of historic taboos, which are embodied in religious, legal and moral codes. It is true that many people, perhaps most people, have learned ways of evading these codes, and that our operative morality is very different from what it is supposed to be. But in a sense this makes things worse, since it sharpens the conflicts within the individual between the conduct he furtively embraces and the conduct he has been brought up to think right.

The result is a heavy burden of anxiety and guilt that accompanies the conflicts. It takes a harsh toll from us, as evidenced by the figures on mental diseases, and the crippled and distorted psychic lives that so many Americans seem to live.

But, you will say, is American culture really a repressive one, when you consider how much stress we put on sexual themes at every point? Our culture is laden with sensual and sexual imagery. How reconcile this with a repressive, "antisexual" culture? Surely, you will say, our culture seems oversexed rather than repressive.

But it would be misleading to regard these as evidences of a sexually expressive culture. They are rather the natural consequences of a repressive one. When you block up the channels for the healthy and candid expression of sexual drives, they break out into indirect channels. What you get is the leg-and-bosom cult in pictorial form, and the leering jokes of the comedians, the Peeping-Tom imagery, the Mickey Spillane sexual sadism, and the snideness and furtiveness that coat everything with a layer of sexiness. You get sex by innuendo and in-direction—the kind that serves the purposes neither of the instinctual life nor of the moral life, but makes a travesty of both.

It is also in many instances a partial and mutilated kind of sexual expression. I am thinking of the more and more expertly organized system of call girls that you encounter in various American cities, either as an independent profession or as part of the expense account racket and as an appendage to our system of business favors and entertainment. I am thinking also of the men who divide their libido unequally between the wife they "respect" and cannot associate with sexual pleasure, and the "lower" type of girl with whom they have sexual pleasure but cannot "respect"—thereby managing to miss any kind of genuine love in both instances.

I shall go further and say that in one sense the Kinsey studies themselves, with their focus upon the quantitative measurement of sexual experience, are a sign of how we have isolated the physical experience of the sexual act from everything else. I am not blaming Kinsey for trying to measure only what is in itself measurable. But it is characteristic of our culture that we should have been the first to develop this approach.

March 1, 1951

If you are feeling high and mighty in your role as king of the universe and master of Creation, you might read a book called *Patterns of Sexual Behavior,* by two Yale professors, Clellan Ford and Frank Beach. It will be a chastening experience.

For you will find the sexual patterns of Americans placed in a cold and somewhat shattering perspective: first by comparing them to 190 other human societies, from the Abelam in New Guinea to the Yu-kagher in northeast Siberia and the Zuni in New Mexico; second, by comparing them with the sexual patterns of other primates (ape and monkey) and the lower mammals—armadillo and sloth, whale, bat, rabbit and hare, rodents, elephant, pig, camel, deer and ox, tapir and rhinoceros, cat, dog, weasel and bear, mole and shrew.

The two crucial methods of the book are thus the cross-cultural ap-proach and the cross-species approach. Ford is an anthropologist, Beach an animal psychologist. Although it uses some figures and charts, the book shows the weakness of the cross-cultural method in that the items of sexual behavior from each primitive society lose much of their meaning when they are torn out of the rich cultural con-text.

Yet the book does stretch your perspective. You get a jolt when you read about the mating practices of other animals that are strik-ingly like our own. You get another jolt when you read of the staying power of the Marquesan male, from among the human societies, or of the mink from among the animals. You get a different kind of jolt when you find that on the question of premarital relations or the acceptance of homosexual practices, many of the "permissive" human societies have codes very different from the "restrictive" American society.

If we ask in despair, "Are we then men or mammals?" the answer is: We are both. We share with other mammals a basic physiological structure and the irrepressible force of sexual desire, just as we share with other human societies such universal cultural practices as the ban against incest.

But we are also men, in the sense that we broke away from the other mammals some 75 million years ago, and from the other primates some 30 million years ago. In that time men have become learning animals and social animals. The most original chapters show, for example, that while the sex behavior of the lower mammals is strongly dependent on hormone flow and periods of female ovulation, and that of the primates less so, the human animal is least dependent. Instead men and women respond to their far more highly developed cerebral cortex, the product of the millions of years of biological history. Thus, if men are animals, they are in this sense the least animal of all the animal kingdom.

But if the cerebral cortex really gives us some intelligence, let us use it (the authors plead) in shattering our provincialism. There is more than a hint that our restrictive society produces unnecessary sex tensions and frustrations. And the notion that we can repress the sexual drives that keep cropping out in most of the other societies may be a sign not of wisdom but of cultural blindness.

February 5, 1956

Is it possible to free people in Western culture of the repressive elements which weigh heavily on the individual, with a massive burden of anxiety, conflict and guilt, from early childhood to death? Can we envision a better world, in which the instinctual life has been liberated, flowing freely into the channels of life's fulfillment, allowing us to become capable of truly loving and receiving love, of play, of work in the creative sense, of seeing and fashioning beauty?

I have just been reading a book that raises some of these themes, luckily just when I was fumbling with them on my own. It is *Eros and Civilization*, by Herbert Marcuse (Beacon), and its subtitle is "A Philosophical Inquiry into Freud."

Readers of Freud will remember one of his great later books, *Civilization and Its Discontents*, in which he develops the social theory which is implicit in his system of psychoanalysis. Marcuse has written partly an answer to it, partly a book that accepts the basic ideas but goes beyond Freud to a vision of a society he thought impossible.

He accepts Freud's instinct theory, including the basic role of the sexual drive (the libido), and he accepts the theory of the "genetic" influences on personality development—the crucial role of what happens in infancy and childhood in shaping and distorting the whole personality. He accepts Freud's idea that the individual during these early phases retraces the history of the stages of the human species, with all its conflicts and its dark repressions.

Where he departs from Freud is in Freud's belief that the system of cultural repression of the instincts cannot be avoided. Freud believed that there could not be any civilization without repression, that the workings of the pure libidinal drive would be too anarchic, and that the "reality principle" had to temper and partly replace the "pleasure principle." Marcuse thinks that Freud abdicated too easily on this point and that he gave away more than was necessary to the forces of a repressive civilization. He admits that men had to move away from the free play of the libido and emphasize work and production and mastery over nature in order to build a civilization at all. But now that it has been built, the repressions no longer are needed to fulfill their function. They have taken on a being of their own and ride the human personality like a nightmare.

It is hard not to have sympathy with this view. I confess that I do not have as dark a picture as Marcuse has of our present civilization, which may be because he reached his maturity under the shadow of Hitler at Berlin and Freiburg while I reached mine under F.D.R. here. Yet there is a great measure of truth in his stress on the alienation of modern man from his fellows and from the roots of creativeness, and the heavy load of guilt that he bears.

The two crucial negative symbols for Marcuse are the "performance principle," by which he means our stress on productivity and economic power and the economic virtues, and the "reality principle" —Freud's expression for the whole social universe of rules and taboos and repressions with which the individual must come to terms. They find their stamping ground in the "superego," which harbors so much repression that Marcuse sees it as a graveyard of what might have been life fulfillment.

In place of this he sees the possibility of a culture in which there will be the "free gratification of individuals," but within a framework of order that comes from within rather than from without; a culture in which the "aesthetic dimension" will be the métier in which the individual lives, rather than the work and worry involved in the performance principle; and a culture, finally, in which our present harsh and tortured sexuality will turn into the Eros principle—the embracing acceptance of the sensual universe and the principle of love and life.

The vision is a moving one, but how will it happen? Here, alas, is where Marcuse is weakest, exactly because it is unexplored territory in social thinking. There has been plenty of speculation about how mankind might approach an economic and political utopia, and while most of it has been wrong and much of it tragically wrong, at least the paths of thought have been traversed and retraversed. But the utopia of love and play and sexual freedom? It has seemed so impossible that most thinkers have been frightened off.

The best Marcuse can do is to say that obviously he doesn't believe that such a society will rest on instinct alone, since instinct is beyond good and evil, while every culture must embody the distinction between them. But he does feel that there may be a built-in principle of restraint, indirection and delay within the sexual drive as it manifests itself in human beings, and on this he builds his faith.

This is a slim reed on which to build the edifice of a utopia. But it may help us to give our thinking imaginative scope. Dream? Yes. Folly? I don't think so. For the real folly of our time is the cynicism and tiredness that have made us forget how to dream and act out our dreams.

7. Success and Money as Goals

November 5, 1951

SEVERAL GENERATIONS AGO William James pointed out that Americans had made a cult of the "Bitch-Goddess, Success," and since his time the worship has grown more rather than less fervid. There has never been a civilization in which the "success system" has played so important a role and the fear of failure has been so devastating. In early American history it might have been said that the primary life goals were godliness and work. Today there abideth money and power and success. And the greatest of these is success.

Is there anything wrong with this? Only if the values by which we judge success are false, and the race is too frantic, and the effort to keep up with the success goal makes wrecks of us.

The success ideal can be taken on two levels. On one it means simply that we try to be effective in whatever goal we set. Most Americans want whatever they do to hit the mark. In that meaning, success—to "make a go" of anything you are doing—makes sense, provided it doesn't eat up your life. But the effort to beat out others has made us forget why it was we started in the first place. "Are you a success?" is the question thrown at us from the day we first come home from nursery school, until our friends discuss whether we had a fine funeral.

For the businessman it has come to mean whether he is making a lot of money and every enterprise turns to gold at his touch; for the writer, whether he can turn out best sellers; for the playwright, whether he has a hit; for the politician, whether he wins the election; for the actor, whether he gets the rave reviews; for the football player, whether he has broken away for the touchdown; for the girl at the dance, whether she shows her popularity by having the stag line constantly cut in on her.

Not only does the American feel he must be a success: he also feels left out unless he associates with what is a success. He is eager to be on the "inside," and to know who and what are the latest sensational successes.

The worst disaster is to fail. The social worker, the teacher, the minister, the psychiatrist—all whose job it is to counsel men and women—know how many of them have been harried all their lives by the phantom of failure.

Even failure is overlooked, however, if it is used as a springboard for a "comeback"—that is, for a success made all the more spectacular by the improbable starting point and the overwhelming odds. There was Ben Hogan, who won a series of golf tournaments after an almost fatal auto smash. There was Gloria Swanson, the old-time movie star who made a comeback in a picture about an old-time movie star who didn't. All these are the American equivalents of Lazarus who came back from the dead.

Much of the success cult is the creation of parents and teachers. We are concerned with our children, Margaret Mead says in *Male and Female* (William Morrow), as "little bundles of high achievement," to be trained for success in life. "Life is a race that both boys and girls must run clear-eyed, sweet-breathed, well-bathed, with their multiplication tables in their heads, and feet that come down accurately on the mark." The rest of their lives they are judged by the same adult standards: What grades do they get in school? How are they getting on compared with the other children, compared with their brothers and sisters? Are they popular? Do they make the clubs and fraternities? Are they on the athletic teams, or the Student Council, or chosen as Campus Queen? Do they marry the prettiest girls, or the boys with a future?

This imposes a strain that only the strong can bear. "Hitch your wagon to a star," we are told. But stars are far away, and some wagons get stuck in the mud and never get free. There are not enough prizes to go round for all of us. I don't think the answer is resignation, or seeking peace of mind in artful ways. We have all realistically to understand our limits, but within those limits the challenge is to live productive lives. The best thing about the success system is its constant spur to striving. Our society would dry up if that striving were abandoned. But it is better for the person if it is a striving for an attainable goal, not one off in the wild blue yonder; and a goal which is not set by measuring yourself against the standards of others.

November 6, 1951

Americans are not the only people with the fixed idea that money brings happiness, but they are the only people with enough money to have given the idea a trial run. At Concord, a man called Thoreau wrote in his *Journal* more than a century ago, "Money is not required to buy one necessity of the soul."

But preaching sermons against money is a futile act in a money civilization. We say, "You can't take it with you." We say, "Money isn't everything." We say, "Money doesn't bring happiness." But a Hoff cartoon in the *New Yorker,* showing a wife and husband at a kitchen table in a seedy flat, has the wife saying bitterly to her philosophical mate, "And how do you know money doesn't bring happiness, may I ask?" He could have had a comeback only if he had been sitting on top of a heap of Du Pont preferred.

The appeal of money lies in the apparent ease with which it fills the obvious lacks of a moneyless life. It lies in the things that money can buy—drink and food, clothes, cars, dwellings, paintings, jewels, "service," subservience, sex and the awe of the community. In the things that money can buy it is the great leveler. It gives a common measurement for diverse talents and pursuits. It brings the educated to the level of the ignorant, and the beautiful and graceful within the reach of the dull and clumsy. It is the great common denominator, transforming all other values into standard values.

Yet with all this, the fact remains that people really seek money for the things that money cannot buy. Even power, which money can often buy and which is strongly linked with it in a money civilization, is not enough to still the unquiet spirit.

That is why you will find the offices of the psychiatrists filled with the moneyed people and their wives and daughters. To be sure, the unmoneyed also have their neuroses. Poverty is no road to fulfillment. But the poor have one advantage in this respect over the rich: They can always blame their unhappiness on their lack of money. The rich have even this prop knocked out from under them.

In fact, the psychiatrists have pointed out that the pursuit of money is in itself a source of neurotic conflict. Karen Horney in her *Neurotic Personality of Our Time* has traced much of our psychic difficulty to the clash between the idealism of our religious and ethical tradition and the competitive ruthlessness that a money civilization forces on most of its members. One of the reasons for the single-minded pursuit of money is that we feel the need to throw our energies into one direction in order to flee the uncertainties that surround us. As someone has put it, in commenting on R. H. Tawney's phrase "the sickness of an acquisitive society," the real point to be made is the acquisitiveness of a sick society.

This is, to some extent, the thesis of an interesting recent book by Dr. Edmund Bergler, *Money and Emotional Conflicts* (Doubleday), which gives us a gallery of the various character types of people who misuse money for unconscious ends: the success hunter, the gambler, the gold digger or playboy-gigolo, the miser, the impostor, the embezzler, the dependee, the bargain hunter, the easy-money sucker. One need not agree wholly with Bergler's thesis that they have in common an unconscious yearning for punishment. He has given us instances enough to show the desert wastes of the human spirit in which money seems to offer the mirage prospect for slaking our unquenchable thirst.

In a recent profile of a man called "the Hatcheck King," who has outdistanced most others in the single-minded pursuit of the dollar, Lillian Ross quotes him as saying reflectively, "A guy runs and jumps for the dollars. All I know is I got nothing else to do. . . . I don't sleep good at night, and all day long I'm chasing the almighty buck, when I really got no use for the buck in the first place."

8. Identity and the Productive Life

November 7, 1951

WHILE I HAVE USED the phrase "pursuit of happiness," I trust you will not be misled into thinking that happiness is something to be found or surprised, or caught up with by a forced march, or that will yield to a prolonged siege or a commando raid with the help of money and a psychiatrist. Or that there is an easy formula for it, like conversion or self-indulgence, marriage or divorce, or a course of breathing exercises to relax you.

Happiness is hard because life is hard, and happiness is the working out of a way of living with meaning.

Most of us know some happy people. In the instances I know, it is always someone who has developed an inner core of strength which holds him moored against the buffetings of life but does not isolate him from it. "I know where I'm going," is the way the song puts it, "and I know who's going with me."

Nothing can possibly be a substitute for this quiet inner sureness. In the end it is basically the assurance of identity. Before you can say, "I know where I'm going," you must first ask, "Who am I?" It is not an easy question. It was at the heart of the injunction of Socrates to "know thyself," at the start of the climactic period of Greek philosophy. We still have to face it today in America.

It is especially hard to ask "Who am I?" in our American culture because the flux and scurrying and struggle of an open society are bewildering. The values placed on success and on proving himself outwardly mean that the individual tends to lose track of his inner self.

The quest for identity is nothing more nor less than the effort to find a niche and a position in life that you recognize as yours. It is to place yourself in some meaningful relation, whether to nature and the soil, or to the universe and God, or to family and children, or to community, or to work of hand or brain or imagination.

The problem is not to lose your identity in what we used to call "something bigger," but to find it by finding a relationship that goes beyond yourself because it is deeply rooted within yourself. This does not mean that we must sit forever like minor-league Buddhas contemplating our innards. In a paper at a geriatrics congress, Dr. Martin Gumpert said that what gives men long life is not the stagnant calm of the lotus eaters, but an active career in which they have the sense of functioning and the satisfaction of achievement. A long life, to be sure, does not always mean a happy one; but if to live is to function, then to function well is the basis of a good life.

A productive person is a mature one; he does not try to use love as a crutch, or sex as an opiate, or marriage as a weapon for power over another person, nor does he live by success and the Law of the Fast Buck. He is not ridden by failure, since he has refused to set an impossible glory dream for himself. Nor is he ridden by fear, since he has learned to face a world of reality without either bluster or recoil.

But it is not enough to depict him in negatives, as if all that were needed was to build a Chinese wall around your nerve ends and within that to function like a globule of satisfied desire. The productive person has found himself because he is committed to something. Aware of his own limits, he nevertheless takes a quiet joy in what he can do—in relation to a life partner with whom he shares basic values, and children who give him the sense of extension into life, and a natural universe of which he feels an organic part, and work which is not just money chasing or an arid "job" but expresses a deep part of his being.

No man can avoid scars, because all life is tragic. But a productive one is deepened, not shattered, by the tragedies it encounters.*

* For further discussion of the theme of identity, see (Part V) the section on "Time and Identity," pages 674-686.

ASPECTS OF CRIME AND PUNISHMENT

1. Jury in the Dark

December 20, 1954

FOR MORE than three days we have been sweating out the ordeal of a murder jury verdict, in the case of Dr. Sam Sheppard. The murder trial has become one of the great rituals of American culture, much like the World Series, the Presidential campaign, the TV comedian, the Fourth of July and Christmas. Which is to say that it is a collective experience shared by every class, with a symbolic meaning for the culture that goes beyond the particular murder episode or the fate of the particular defendant.

There is a certain kind of intellectual purist who is condescending toward these murder trials and who is pained at the coverage the newspapers are giving them. I don't pay much notice to him and to his curious notions of the human experience. Sure, your taste can get morbid until you finally read about nothing else and are left hungry despite the steady murder diet now available in the press. But the great murder trial is one that throws its spell far beyond these cult groups and gets everyone involved in its intricacies. The Sheppard case has been such a trial. Its chief quality has been the bafflement it leaves on every mind that cares about evidence, motive and personality.

I have heard any number of theories of what happened and why, but I have heard none which seemed better than a shaky guess. Some have been ingenious, including the theory that Sam Sheppard killed his wife without knowing he had done it, in a genuine blackout. When I have asked where then he got the story of the bushy-haired intruder with whom he grappled, the answer has been that the whole encounter with the intruder was part of his imaginings in the blackout. However extreme, this theory has at least the merit of not leaning—as does the "unfaithful husband" theory—on the rickety motive of his killing her in order to marry a girl whom he could have without marriage. Nor does it leave all the unanswered questions of the defense theory about a burglar who came from nowhere, vanished into nowhere, and left no traces.

Had I been on the jury, I should have voted the Scottish verdict

"Not proven," which has a shade of meaning lacking in the closest American verdict, "Not guilty." But regardless of how the jury votes in the end, the nature of our involvement as an audience in the case sheds some light on our human nature.

We follow these murder cases much as a circus audience follows the juggler or the trapeze performer—will he, won't he? There is the fascination of watching a man's gamble against failure and disaster, even against death—especially against death. But the difference between the vigil we have gone through waiting for the jury verdict and the vigil at, let us say, a mine disaster is that in the murder case every person becomes a chooser. He casts his ballot, even though uncounted. He has all the luxury of sitting in judgment with none of its responsibilities.

In the process of waiting and passing judgment, we tend to identify ourselves with either the defendant or the D.A. Every ritual involves this act of identification. In the case of a murder trial you identify with either the hunter or the quarry.

I doubt whether most people in the Sheppard case identified with the hunter. To be sure, the impulse for vicarious revenge is very strong in all of us, and there must be millions of people who felt that a man immoral in his sexual conduct must also have been capable of killing his wife. But I think the real emotional sources from which identification comes go much deeper.

We live in an age of both guilt and anxiety. As the details of a family life are pitilessly revealed in the course of a murder trial, who is there who doesn't wonder how his own life would look when subjected to the same exposure? And who is there who can say that he has never felt a murderous impulse or been guilty of harboring murderous thoughts?

Thus whenever there is a genuine bafflement in the evidence—except in barbaric cases below the threshold of human sufferance—our identification is with the quarry. I think this has been true in the Sheppard case. The psychiatrist may have some shrewd questions about a man who is depicted as having always contained his emotions, never expressed rage. He may wonder whether it is not exactly such a man who might, when he reached his breaking point, commit exactly this kind of crime.

But most of us are not psychiatrists. We share the human condition and are baffled with it. As we go through the vigil of waiting for the verdict, we have a suspicion that the man waiting alone in his cell might be any one of us.

December 22, 1954

I would give a good deal to know what went on behind the locked doors of the Sheppard jury. Since the defense is making an appeal, the otherwise inevitable leaks about the successive votes and the issues around which arguments swirled will be severely dammed up. Yet even if there were the regular leaks we wouldn't really learn much. It is only in something like Raymond Postgate's classic of mystery fiction, *Verdict of Twelve,* that we get the story of what goes on at the jury table and inside the jurors' minds. In real life we have a curious paradox that must be bitter to many men who feel they are in prison unjustly. The paradox is that the trial of a case is carried on in complete publicity, but the deliberations that lead to the fateful verdict of the jury are shrouded in secrecy.

I'm a bit of a romancer myself, and I can spin some fantasies about what went on among the Twelve. Was there a dominant member who kept them going for over four days, feeding their sense of importance, until they came up with the verdict he had always wanted? Were there perhaps two members who staged a tug of war and finally reached a compromise? Or did the jury, after having sat in the courtroom over nine weeks, develop a kind of bond that they found themselves unwilling to break, much as war correspondents who have drunk and written and campaigned together find it difficult to go home from the wars?

"Hard cases make bad law," said Justice Holmes, talking of the judge's end of the case. They also often make bad jury verdicts. "The longer the trial lasts," wrote Dean Leon Green, "the larger the scanning crowds, the more intensely counsel draw the lines of conflict, the more solemn the judge, the harder it becomes for the jury to restrain their reason from somersault."

Remember that the members of a jury are laymen who have not been trained in close reasoning. Their strength lies in just the opposite fact—that they are human beings and tend therefore to humanize the application of legal rules, especially in criminal cases.

But in a big murder case like the Sheppard case, the jury may get so self-conscious that it tries to become a panel of experts instead of remaining merely human. The expert business is just where a jury is weak. That is why a verdict reached after a few hours is likely to be better than one reached after four and a half days. For the jurors, trying to weigh every bit of evidence like experts, pass beyond the immediate human reactions where their real strength lies.

The nature of the Sheppard case was such that, even after you had added up each item of evidence, accepted some, discarded others, you were still left with only a wild guess in the dark. The guess was no better after four days than after four hours. A series of unexplained items do not add up to a conviction of murder beyond a reasonable doubt.

If the second-degree murder conclusion means anything it means the jury believed that Sheppard killed his wife and intended to, but had not premeditated the killing. This requires a subtle judgment based on a reading of character and personality and the whole inner mind of the defendant. The trouble with making such a judgment is that little of the evidence dealt with the inner psychic life of Sheppard or shed much light on it. Even a panel of trained psychiatrists would have been hard put to reach a judgment on this score, without longer study of Sheppard and more information.

Logically the verdict should have been either first-degree or acquittal. Either he did or he didn't. One suspects that the second-degree verdict measured not so much the jury's judgment of premeditation but its own inner reasonable doubts about whether the young doctor had really killed his wife.

I have lingering doubts, too. However damning the individual items of evidence, the case remains a mystery. A mystery is too mysterious to furnish ground for a conviction. The rule that a man be held innocent unless he is damned by evidence beyond a reasonable doubt is still a good rule. And the more I think of it the more I incline to the view that the jury proceedings—like the court's—should be a matter of record, available to the judges on appeal.

2. The Spoor of the Bomber

December 28, 1956

IT'S AS MUCH as your life is worth to get into a phone booth at Grand Central, perhaps only to call your wife; or to leave a suitcase with a ticking clock inside a locker at Penn Station; or to try to get into a theater carrying a longish wrapped package that might be a bar of lead—or again might only be your son's recorder, newly fixed at the music store; or even to go to the public library to read a book. There are cops and sleuths watching you in every public place.

I caught a cop's eye on me yesterday in the Times Square subway station as I was coming home from a date with the dentist. I must have had my usual ungenteel look, or maybe I hugged my frayed dispatch case too tightly; had he stopped me and opened it, he would have been convinced of my guilt, since it contained several pages scrawled with notes about bombers and psychopaths, with a lot of my usual doodles that could easily pass for pictures of clock mechanisms or plans of Grand Central.

As for going into a jeweler's shop to buy a cheap watch these days— don't do it. Ever since the *Journal-American* enrolled all the city's jewelers in a private Central Intelligence Agency, and had each of them describing every customer who inquired about inexpensive watch springs, I would advise you not to ask for any timepiece worth less than

$500. From now on only the rich will be able to afford to keep track of the time.

I don't mean to belittle the danger of having a sick mind somewhere among us, obsessed with the idea of planting crude devices filled with explosive gunpowder in public places. But I suggest that the degree of public semihysteria over it may be almost equally worthy of a psychiatrist's attention.

The attempt to track down any psychotic through newspaper publicity—which is what the police are now trying to do—has the drawback of bringing out the same psychotic symptoms among scores of eccentrics and paranoids. Where once there was one bomber sending notes about his explosive intentions, there may now be twenty. Every public chase produces pursuers who want to be in on the hunt, but also quarries who want to be hunted. All kinds of fakes, frauds and hysterics are having a field day trying to identify themselves with their comrade in harm. And the public is getting one of the great thrills —the combined sense of brooding danger which titillates lives otherwise pretty dreary, and the exciting tensions of a man hunt.

In the 1820s the English language picked up the word "spoor," to mean the tracks left by a wild animal. We are engaged now in a collective detective quest to track down the spoor of the "Mad Bomber." In addition to the usual police methods and rewards, and the help of seven or more million amateur detectives, there is now the added factor of the psychiatrist.

As I understand it, some of the psychiatrists are now trying to do what the paleontologists have tried to do for centuries—namely, to reconstruct an extinct beast from the evidence of a fossil remnant of his big toe. In this case the effort is directed toward the profile, not of an extinct beast, but of one very much alive and prowling in the New York jungle, but still unseen. Some psychiatric "experts" who have for years testified as to the insanity of accused men on trial are now drawn by the press into testifying about the personality traits of someone whom neither they nor the rest of us have ever knowingly seen.

The only thing certain about the "Mad Bomber," in my view, is that he is enamored of his publicity—very much like some other people, including columnists and psychiatric "experts."

Not that I disbelieve in responsible psychiatry as an aid in criminal detection. In the right hands it can be useful. But it can also be foolish, and wonderful bait for amateurs like myself. It doesn't take any psychological training to guess that whoever the Bomber may be he is a man suffering from a sense of his own insignificance, bruised in his self-esteem by some encounter with his family or the world, and determined to find an equalizer that will make him feel important.

One might guess that for him this equalizer comes from feeling that the vaunted world, which gathers in theaters and railroad stations, is really at his mercy; that at will he can kill people—or at least frighten them into the fear that they will be killed. Through this power to instill terror into others he brings them down to his own level.

Whether he suffers from sexual inadequacies, as several psychiatrists have guessed, is something I leave to them. But what interests me more is that this psychic profile would include very many faces in the crowd that is now looking for its quarry. Maybe our zeal to track him down comes less from our fear than from the fact that this fantasy of punishing an unappreciative world is in most of us, and we recognize him as a brother. Maybe his own zeal in pushing his luck so hard comes from his desire to be caught, and thus be united with his potential victims.

The difference between us and him is that he comes closer to acting out his destructive fantasies, and we virtuously keep them in check. Anyway, we have far bigger bombs to play with than the miserable stick of lead found in Grand Central. We have uranium, hydrogen and cobalt.

3. How Guard Our Children?

December 23, 1949

FROM CALIFORNIA this past week come reports of several particularly brutal crimes. One, from Los Angeles, is the sex murder of a six-year-old girl; the other is the rape-slaying of a seventeen-month baby. Both crimes are horrible beyond the power of expression.

Before we know how to guard our children we must know more about these sex crimes, and their roots in the minds and life histories of twisted men, and their relation to the kind of lives we live as a people.

There is scarcely a sizable community in the country that does not have its annual crop of crimes of this sort. They strike most often in cities, in slum areas, in the low-income groups, among the working classes, among the dispossessed and disinherited. What makes them even more unbearable is that always they strike the innocent and helpless. In fact, the innocence of children is one of the ingredients of their doom, and their helplessness makes bold men out of cowards.

There was a mass meeting in Los Angeles, and a petition was drawn up with thousands of signatures. It was proposed that anyone arrested for a sex crime involving children should be jailed without bail, and that anyone convicted should be jailed for life.

But I like better the equally drastic, but more sensible, proposal of Dr. Winifred Overholser, that habitual sex criminals be held for life, not in jail but in mental institutions. The men who do these things are sick men in the deepest sense. To jail them for life will only make different kinds of sexual perverts out of them, and it will brutalize us in the process.

The psychiatrists have already learned something—but still have much to learn—about the blockages and the arrested emotional growth that lead to these cases. But part of the causes must be sought in the jungle of our life. Within the rules of fair play we hold everything, in our economic jungle, to be fair prey. Should it be so much of a surprise to us if, in the moral jungle, some twisted minds should discard the rules of fair play but hang on to the principle of everything being fair prey?

But even deeper is the fact that the lives we live breed irresponsibles. For many who have moral strength it is a good life. But there are others on the margin who are left with no land they are attached to, no jobs they take pride in, no craft or skill to make them feel useful, no part in the community. They are the landless, prideless, rootless. They are part of the undercutting of the sense of society. So they reach out for what is weaker and more helpless than they, and suddenly everything blacks out and another horrible crime hits the headlines.

March 30, 1950

New York may be the first state in the union to break through some of the layers of social stupidity that have frozen our treatment of major sex offenders as with an idiot ice crust.

Governor Dewey, who is famous for catching public opinion on the wing, knows how badly the rat-tat-tat of daily sex crimes has bruised our nerve ends. Hence his astuteness in getting the Abrahamsen psychiatric study made, and pushing through the new Halpern Act based on it.

Dr. David Abrahamsen and his staff, who prepared the report, have done a workmanlike job. For twenty months they carried on an intensive study of 102 sex criminals. The men they chose to study, their ages ranging from twenty to seventy-two, had been convicted of rape with violence, sodomy (chiefly homosexual), incest with their underage daughters, carnal abuse of minors. The 102 case studies, the heart of the report, are fascinating and shattering reading. They show that two of the things our society knows well are how to produce sex offenders and how not to treat them.

The sex criminal comes out of broken families, alcoholism, desertion, illegitimacy, overcrowding, squalor, neglect, poverty, brutality. The parents are likely to be domineering and tyrannical or else possessive. A child's heart can be destroyed effectively either way. Most of the children were whipped, beaten, kicked, or worked almost to death, generally by drunken fathers, until the father image became one of overwhelming hatred. A few were dressed and worried over like toys, forced into the mold of the parental dream, and were left wholly insecure, with no personality of their own.

From childhood on, the sex offender is likely to be a lonely, sullen, inadequate person, carrying his resentments around in his burning heart. He has no sense of belonging anywhere or to anyone. He is incapable of any close relationship. He is narcissistic, turned in on himself, aimless, without goals to strive for.

Many sex offenders have never grown up in their attitude toward sex. Every boy in a home needs a man to admire and imitate—a man from whom he can learn how a man should act and feel. In many of the Abrahamsen cases the father was dead, or had deserted, or was so brutalized as to be an object of hatred, or so weak as to be an object of contempt.

The result is that this child grown into a man knows how to function only on an infantile level. He is full of sexual fears and doubts, expects rejection, is certain of failure. Hence he turns to molesting children, with whom he cannot fail; or else to the violent rape of adults (often much older women), where he can storm his insecurities by force. Thus too he gets his revenge against the symbols of authority that have battered his spirit.

This is the portrait of our failure. The problem is a dual one. One part of the task is to create the economic and social conditions of a healthy home life and teach parents the elementary things about the fragile emotional structure inside a child. This is a program of prevention. The other task is a program of cure.

The Abrahamsen report asks us not to turn sex criminals out of prison at the end of a set term. It asks for an indeterminate sentence, with continual psychiatric re-examination to decide when a man is ready to cope with society. But this means that they must be studied and treated by psychiatrists, not cooped up in Sing Sing. And they ought to be treated in mental hospitals, not in prisons. Actually this applies to all criminals. But there is a chance that on an issue as burning as that of sex offenders, we may be able to get the camel's nose under the tent.

September 17, 1952

Every reporter knows the priceless chapter in *The Autobiography of Lincoln Steffens* called "I Make a Crime Wave." There was good-natured rivalry between Steffens, who was a crime reporter on the *Post*, and his friend Jacob Riis, who was a crime reporter on the *Sun*. Steffens used to pretend to take naps in the police basement where the detectives played poker, and he overheard a luscious robbery story, which he printed. Riis, needled because of the Steffens beat by his Simon Legree of a city editor, came up with some crime stories he

snitched from the pigeonhole where precinct crime reports were care-
lessly kept. Each tried to outdo the other. That was the "crime wave."
The city seethed with indignation at the mounting crimes. Actually
there were no more crimes than before, but they were being tracked
down and reported.

I thought of Steffens when I read about the hundreds of police
prowl cars on the streets looking for rapists. You can't help wondering what it is, however, that suddenly makes a number of males in a
big city go berserk. I think one part of the answer is the Steffens kind
—that once a few sex offenses hit the headlines, more get reported
that might have remained unreported. The other part is the power of
suggestion and suggestibility.

Tolstoy tells a touching little story of his boyhood: His older brother
instructed him, under terrible threats, to stand behind a tree, close his
eyes tight, and try *not* to think of a white bear; and the harder he tried
not to the more insistently he did. Apply this to the men with the rape
impulse in them. Everywhere they read and hear of the deeds of the
rapists. Their unstable personalities make them especially vulnerable
to the power of suggestion. The harder these men try *not* to think about
their own possible victims, the more obsessed they become with the
fateful inner picture. The result is crime, bred of crime.

I am sure of at least one fact: These are deeply, fatefully sick men.
You may hunt them down with your hundreds of detectives and your
thousands of cops, but even more surely they are their own stalkers,
hunting themselves down. They are at war with themselves, caught
in a terrible compulsion to do the one thing whose image fills their
waking and sleeping hours.

Some of the recent case studies of sex criminals, and their confessions, give us a few clues to the twisted logic of their passions. What
an obsession it can be to see someone unprotected and alluring; to
feel deprived, despised; to brood on the prized image; to roam the
streets or subways; to let the imagination prepare the scene; to find
yourself enacting it, caught in the nightmare that seems to wipe out
the boundaries between what was dreamt and what is happening.

These are monstrous acts, brutal enough when the victims are grown
women, most brutal of all with teen-agers or even young children. We
have in the past used almost every weapon against them, including big
roundups of suspects, constant vigilance, publicity, long imprisonment
terms. The one weapon we have not used enough is a cold study of
the symptoms of these twisted minds and the sources of their disease.

There has been a fierce fight recently between the crime students
who say we must seek the sources in our society itself—in poverty,
slums, alcoholism, in the milieu that surrounds these men—and those
who say we must seek it in their personalities. It is an almost meaningless quarrel. My own tendency is to say that these are psychopathic

personalities, ruled by hysteria and compulsions, ridden with guilt and self-hate, feeling inferior, rejected by parents, brooding in bitterness; and that sex violence has attached itself in a fetish fashion to these cross currents of emotion.

But I would add that when you try to track down any of these drives in the individual's life history you are confronted by the facts of our social life—by life as it is lived by obscure people in our big cities.

4. Wild Beasts and Barbarians

December 9, 1956

WHAT WAS REMARKABLE about the La Marca case was that it was so unremarkable. The kidnaping and murder were brutal—as so many are. The man who committed them was a tortured creature who evoked little fellow feeling from either jury or public. The trial followed a now classic pattern in such trials. There was no doubt of guilt, but the whole trial turned on the question of insanity. There was the inevitable psychiatric expert for the defense who swore in the classic pattern that La Marca, at the time he kidnaped the baby, "did not know it was wrong." There was also the inevitable psychiatric expert for the prosecution who testified that at the time La Marca "knew the nature and quality of his act and knew the difference between right and wrong."

There was the usual defense plea for charity for a defendant who was "a poor slob" (as the defense attorney put it), and the usual D.A.'s impassioned demand for justice which would punish a ruthless killer for his barbaric act. There was the usual judge's charge to the jury on the legal meaning of sanity and insanity (McNaghten's Rule). There was the terrible ordeal of the jurors—laymen who had to decide whether he had been sane or insane.

With all due respect to judge, jury, D.A., defense lawyer and psychiatric experts, I want to say that this is a helluva way to run a railroad—a blundering, wasteful way to dispose of the crucial question of what was happening inside La Marca's head when he kidnaped and then killed the baby.

That is, I assume, the question we want to get at. The problem is not whether we should be tender or tough with La Marca. What we need is a less stupid way of reaching a decision on insanity than is presented by the classic trial pattern I have described.

Consider how it operates. There was an interesting episode in the La Marca case, when the D.A., Frank Gulotta, was cross-examining the defense psychiatric expert, a Dr. Thomas S. Cusack. At the time of the crime, the doctor said, La Marca was so harassed by the pressure of debt and the anxieties and confusions of his life that the "compelling force of fear" clouded his reason, making him temporarily insane. Gulotta then put Dr. Cusack through some stiff questioning about his qualifications and career as a psychiatric expert, charging that he had "made a specialty" of such testimony in murder cases since the Ruth Snyder case.

It has been suggested that someone outside the jury decide the question of sanity, and in New Hampshire it is treated as a question of fact which is settled by the psychiatrists of the state. But this doesn't meet the problem, since under our system—for good or ill—a man has a constitutional right to be tried by a jury of his peers.

A juror's lot in such a murder case is not a happy one. A reader who served on such a jury writes me that the jurors are puzzled by the conflicting expert testimony, that they sit around afterward and argue for hours, but that they usually decide to vote guilty. They figure that if they acquit him it ends the case, but if they convict him and deny the plea of insanity there will always be the chance for him to get a commutation of sentence. So they convict.

The point is that the jurors need help—all the help they can get —to give them some assurance that they are doing the right thing. They don't get it from the present system of "expert" psychiatric evidence in the adversary proceedings of trial-and-battle, or even from the judge's instructions.

Dr. Gregory Zilboorg has presented their viewpoint persuasively in the final chapter of his book of lectures on psychiatry and law, *The Psychology of the Criminal Act and Punishment.* He proposes that in every such trial there be a panel of qualified psychiatrists who can be drawn on, all passed upon within their own profession. This would be much like the present system of jury panel, and they could be challenged by both sides. Once chosen—say three of them—they would testify neither for the state nor for the defense, but simply as men trying to get at and describe the mental processes of the defendant. They would be cross-examined by either or both sides. They might agree or disagree in their findings. But the jury would have at its disposal the best light available on what had happened in the defendant's mind.

It would be the jury who would decide, but they would not make their decision in darkness and ignorance.

April 22, 1957

When Thomas J. Higgins was asked by the police why he had killed two women and attacked a number of others, his answer was: "Attacking these girls was an outlet for myself." Each generation has its pet area whose technical jargon it takes over into common speech. Ours is psychiatry. Murder confessions now come equipped with phrases picked up out of the popular manuals on psychology.

We can call for Higgins' blood, send him to the chair, be rid of him—and be no wiser after his death about the roots of criminal sexual violence than we were before. Or we can try to study him and see what there was in his life history which led to his compulsive, destructive act.

This must be the next stage of our effort as a community. The first stage was the deadly negligence and ignorance on the part of everyone—girls, parents, police, citizens—that made the crimes possible. The second stage was the hunt for the criminal. The third stage must be not the call for vengeance, but a serious study of what kind of man this is who must wreak himself on a succession of helpless women and try to get release through terror.

Several years ago I wrote a series of columns on the sexual offender. They didn't make me even an amateur expert, but they taught me some of the things not to brush aside in studying these cases.

Note first that Higgins attacked a succession of women—at least nine in the same neighborhood, by his own count and account. This should not have surprised us, since we know from the studies that sexual offenders are compulsive. Outwardly it may seem that they act out of whim, but their action is repetitive and compulsive rather than impulsive. They may be seeking, or trying to flee, the clue to some real crime or guilt that burdens them, of which their overt repeated crimes are only the symbol.

Or take the reports that Higgins was considered in his neighborhood a "likable fellow" who worked hard, was pleasantly interested in whatever was happening and "never disturbed anybody." His fiancée, who probably thought she knew him, swears by him. But neither should this surprise us. Often it is the "model boy" who, as it turns out, kills the baby-sitter or the baby or both. This is the fallacy of believing we can know anything about a person by observing his outer shell. When Higgins says that the attacks gave him an "outlet" for himself, he is saying that periodically tensions built up in him and the pressure for release became uncontrollable. The very fact that he was pleasant and quiet in his outer shell meant that he was unconsciously trying to hold the tensions in check and failing.

Perhaps the most striking bit is the report that Higgins did not carry out the act of rape in any of the nine instances. He talks of "necking" and "mushing," but always there was something that prevented the completion of the act and presumably made him go berserk.

Again the evidence of the studies suggests that the problem of sexual offenders may be a good deal deeper. In many cases of sexual brutality and murder the sexual act is never committed; the violence serves as a substitute for it. The very fact of the repeated sadistic hammerings of the two murder victims may be a sign that Higgins found frustration rather than an "outlet," and that in each case the woman was the symbol of his frustration. The anger may have been directed at her not because she was its target but because she was the occasion for the release of rage at himself.

If it is true that Higgins had brain surgery in the Army to relieve pressures, there should be a psychological history there that will shed further light on a case which we had better not dispose of as if we were avenging angels.

June 16, 1957

"I've never killed anyone," Clarence Darrow used to say, "but I frequently get satisfaction from reading the obituary pages." He was no different from the rest of us, only a bit more honest. There is a double satisfaction in hunting down a murderer: You share vicariously in the death done by his hand, and also in his death done by society. When people demand the punishment of a brutal murderer, as is happening now in the Higgins case, the craving for revenge is even stronger than the desire for justice.

The only important question about Higgins is about his whole psychological profile—including his emotional drives as well as his intellect—both at the time of the crime and now. If he is to be examined and studied, why not make it a total study? The answer, I suppose, is that a total study might cheat the community of its revenge. That is why every D.A. feels that an insanity defense is a trap, and that he must prove at the trial that the murderer knew right from wrong. The D.A. becomes not the conscience of the community but the instrument of its revenge.

There are other ways of handling such matters. In New Hampshire the question of whether the defendant is sane or insane is treated as a question of fact, to be decided by the State Hospital for Mental Diseases. In Massachusetts there is (even better) the Briggs Law, passed in 1921, which says there must be a psychiatric examination in every major criminal case, and usually they have proved pretty good. At the latest reports New Hampshire has not tottered and fallen, and Massachusetts is not a shambles of rapists and murderers. What is there so special about New York that gives it the privilege of falling behind these other jurisdictions?

District Attorney Silver, when asked about the record of epilepsy in Higgins' life history, answered that "there is no relationship between epilepsy and insanity." This off-the-cuff judgment might be right or wrong, but how would Silver know? I am no worse an amateur than he, but I find in Fenichel's standard psychoanalytic text a summary of the research on epilepsy, concluding that it is organically rooted, but that "the appearance of the syndrome" may "be dependent on mental factors and in some cases even aroused by mental factors."

The point is that this is the kind of question that ought to be discussed by doctors and psychiatrists, called as expert witnesses for the court and not for either the state or the defense. Their findings are among the things to be submitted to a jury for its verdict.

How did we ever get into our present impasse on legal insanity? Back in 1843 Daniel McNaghten, obsessed with the idea that Sir Robert Peel was plotting against him, killed his secretary by mistake. He was clearly a psychotic, and the jury's verdict was "Not guilty on the ground of insanity." It was in the tense years of the English Chartists, and the English ruling class got jittery over the verdict in the case of a would-be political assassin. So the House of Lords pressed the fifteen judges of England for a formula. They got it: that it was for the jury to decide "whether the accused had a sufficient degree of reason to know he was doing an act that was wrong."

Ever since then the McNaghten Rule has kept its dead hand on the living realities of the mind, the personality and society. Even at that time there was better thinking available. Five years earlier a great American doctor, Isaac Ray, had seen that a man might "know right from wrong" yet be so sick in his whole psychological state as to be irresponsible—mastered by his drives, rather than the master of them.

But Ray was passed by—until 1954, when the three judges of the D. C. Court of Appeals had to deal with the case of a war veteran called Monte Durham, who was in and out of mental hospitals repeatedly and was a car thief, a housebreaker, a passer of bad checks. Speaking through Judge David Bazelon, the Court of Appeals held that the McNaghten Rule could no longer apply. Instead of the rigid right-wrong test, it held "that an accused is not criminally responsible if his unlawful act was the product of mental disease or mental defect." It is not an easy rule to apply, and it puts a burden on psychiatrists and jury, but that is where the burden belongs.

Our American states have made progress recently. They have better mental hospitals, they spend more per capita on them, they have more attendants, they use tranquilizers and other fancy drugs, they get the patients discharged faster. But in one respect all but two of the states remain stick-in-the-muds: they refuse to take the vaunted discoveries in psychiatry and apply them to the law of criminal insanity.

"Wild beasts" is what we call the insane murderers. And, lest we lose the chance to hunt them down, we remain barbarians. Some benighted tribes believe that when you devour your enemy you become that enemy. "You are whom you eat," is the way Reik puts it. There may be more truth in it than we suspect.

ALL THE PARTY GIRLS

1. The Party Girl and Fun Morality

September 16, 1952

THE NEWEST HEADLINER in New York's prostitution scandals seems to be a twenty-year-old girl who sold her services to men. Coming after the Jelke case, this poses again the whole prostitution problem, and not only in New York.

We are a sensual society. The child growing up in America finds himself in a jungle of sights and symbols that portray the seductiveness of sex. Parents who want to keep their adolescent children from the impact of sexual incitement had better put blinders on them, stuff their ears and shut them up in their rooms without a TV set. Even the most sedate newspapers carry a volume of bra, girdle and nylon stocking ads that denude the Canadian forests. Every quarter book shows females in tempting poses. I don't say that the prevalence of prostitution in America is the result of what I have described above. It is part of the total pattern, however, and it is time we gave up being hypocrites about it.

When the elderly fur salesman witness spoke of getting "familiar" with the girl, having an "affair" with her, and having a "party" with her, Justices Breslin and Byrne told him he was old enough to stop using the roundabout phrases. The language a people uses is a mirror of its taboos, and we have developed many evasive phrases about prostitution. One of them which is getting popular is "party girl." Trying to find when it first came into use, I looked it up in the big new two-volume *Dictionary of Americanisms,* edited by Mitford Mathews, but it wasn't there. Neither was "call girl," incidentally.

But even if the phrases have not yet been accepted by the word experts, the practice has been pretty much adopted by our society. Prostitution is an old profession, but there have been some important trends in it in the past decade, especially since the big money started flowing at the beginning of World War II. Kinsey noted that brothels and streetwalkers are no longer as important to American males as they used to be—except in the armed services. Instead of the brothels, there are two important new developments. One is the increased sexual freedom of nonprofessionals, including many teenagers who give themselves without charge. The other is the high-priced call girl services which broke into the headlines in Hollywood in 1949 and have periodically been disclosed in New York. It includes also the kind that has been discussed in the stories of the so-called "Jelke ring," where "models" and "bit actresses" are available to those with money enough to pay for dinner, theater, night spot and the night.

In a recent paper an acute student of American culture, Martha Wolfenstein, spoke of the "fun morality" that is gaining sway in America. You feel you are being cheated in life unless you can always "have fun." This is as true of middle-aged businessmen as of young college boys and girls. Someone on a three- or four-day visit to New York is loath to go back to Iowa or Ohio without being able to report to his cronies that he "had fun." He may even want to be seen with a stunning-looking girl and get the glow of youth again. And he may want to tell his friends at the club about it and give them some phone numbers. To add what is well known, there are some trades where you would be regarded as fuddy-duddy if you didn't provide "fun" for the out-of-town customers and then charge it to business expenses.

February 9, 1953

Not the least bizarre phase of the bizarre Jelke case is the characteristically American fact that we use the law courts as the vehicle for our public debates on morality. We have no state church and no official censors. Hence, as a people, we try to legislate morality and enforce it by the public prosecutor. We are all now engaged in watching one of these judicial combats. Aside from the nausea it produces, it has the great merit of allowing us to feel highly moral and virtuous at the same time that we are vastly entertained by the public display of the vices of others.

But it isn't all entertainment. Don't underestimate the importance of the public debate that the case has set off. It is in large part through such debates that American moral codes get shaped.

What is the nature of the debate? It isn't the black-and-white question of sexual morality. Everyone will agree that prostitution is wrong, that call girls are immoral, that the men who patronize them are breaking the moral code and that the men who live off them are contemptible. But equally everyone ought to agree that prostitution is a social fact, that call girls and party girls seem to thrive, that many men patronize them, that some who don't do so are constrained less by deep moral scruples than by a lack of opportunity, cash or courage.

One problem is where the government is to step in. If I understand the logic of the D.A.'s office, there isn't much point in punishing the girls, as long as they "co-operate"; and to punish the customers would spread a reign of anxiety and terror among the possessors of the Manhattan earth. The way to break up the traffic without spreading havoc is to get at the traffic managers.

This is more than just strategy. I think it expresses a kind of operative moral code of the community. Americans have a weakness for forgiving their erring daughters, on the theory that a girl who "goes wrong" has always been steered wrong by a man. They even have a weakness for overlooking the predatory mission of a man on the prowl, perhaps on the theory that the sexual drive which makes him restless is human, all too human. What we cannot forgive is the callous exploiting of girls, not for sex, not for love or "fun," but to make money out of them.

That is why the *Daily Worker* articles on the Jelke case are so hilariously wrong. They ascribe it all to "capitalism," and they see capitalism as "the conspiracy against the right of chastity among all but the wives of the rich." Actually the point at which the capitalist profit motive becomes most clearly involved is exactly the point at which our morality gets fighting mad.

2. The Girl with the Front-Row Seat

November 14, 1956

THERE HAS BEEN a series of arrests in Philadelphia of people accused of being involved in a sordid "vice ring" exploiting a number of girls, most of them teen-agers. The broad outlines of the picture are familiar stuff, but with a few new twists and adornments. Mostly they were girls of sixteen to nineteen coming from working-class homes, and there were a few night club and burlesque stripper veterans. As the D.A. sketches it out, there was a model agency which was used as a front for enticing unwary girls, and a photographer's studio where they got involved in nude poses.

There seems to have been a traffic in obscene photos and movies, and "orgies" at "reefer parties" in midtown "dens" and on a suburban "estate" with a swimming pool. There was also (one gathers) outright prostitution, with the charge of "unnatural acts."

After the first arrests the girls talked, the "ringleader" too seems to have "co-operated," and the inevitable "little black book" yielded its inevitable quota of names. The arrested men seem to come mainly from the "media" world of TV and radio and its hangers-on.

But there are several things that cry out to be said about the whole malodorous business. One has to do with the way such matters are handled. Surely there must be a better way than the method of releasing daily arrests and indictments as they are made, with the pictures of the men and the names of some of the girls, and with spicy references to "orgies," "wild parties" and "unnatural acts." For almost six weeks there has been a barrage of news stories of accusations and arrests. It is fearful to think of the scars this will leave not only on the men who are accused but also on the girls who are the accusers —and on the families of both.

Is there a better way? I think there is. In all "vice" cases, especially the collective ones where a "ring" is involved and where teen-agers form the essence of the case, the D.A. and the courts should have the power and duty to handle the whole matter quietly, turning it over to a youth authority or to a panel of experts to advise them on the disposition of the cases. At the end they could agree on a carefully worded public release.

There have been blindness and pain enough, and harm enough done even before the arrests, without dragging so many people publicly through so much mud. I suppose every prosecutor sees himself as a kind of avenging sword of the public conscience, chosen to harry sinners and malefactors, and to save the "sin girls" from their destroyers and themselves. But how tragically destructive a process it becomes is shown in the Philadelphia cases.

I am talking now of the impact the cases have already had on people not involved in them. With so many new names released every few days, a kind of metastasis of rumors spread over the city—malicious rumors about "prominent business and social figures" (as the D.A. put it), which had to be flatly denied. It wasn't long before the blackmailers started moving in like vultures where carrion had been provided them. The newspapers reported that at least six businessmen had received phone threats linking them with the "orgies," and in some cases their wives were told that the family name would be blasted unless the husband paid.

But the saddest part of the story has to do with its central victims —the girls. The fact that they could be attracted by the shoddy thrills and seductions offered to them is a measure of how empty their lives must be. As for the men, the way we handle such cases leaves out the fact that these are confused and sick men, and that their trials and convictions will be no substitute for therapy.

Some reader may ask why the law steps at all into the area of sexual relations, which ought to be private. My own answer is that as a general proposition sex is a private matter, so long as it is kept between two individuals. But where it becomes organized exploitation, and where our children are corrupted for the profit and pleasure of twisted or ruthless men, then society must step in.

What a folly it is to apply to these delicate cases the blunderbuss of a legal system that may destroy as much as it saves.

November 28, 1956

I want to add a few footnotes to my comment on the Philadelphia cases. Among the letters I received on it, one was from an irate Philadelphia housewife and mother. "I think the girls are worse than the men," she writes. "If they had one experience, why did they continue? They must have liked that kind of life. . . . If I was on the jury these girls would be put away until they are twenty-one. I would give the men life at hard labor."

The other was a moving letter from a sister of one of the girls involved. She speaks of the vice probe as "making the ruin of a family such as mine. . . . Our phone was tied up with foul, miserable, ignorant human beings who would not let us alone. . . . We also have received anonymous mail that would make your hair stand on end. . . . After this vice probe has died down I expect my sister to return home. I feel certain she has profited from her mistake and, believe me, she has paid *more* than her share for it." It is signed: "Just a teen-age sister."

Alas, I cannot share either the teen-ager's confidence that the wretched experience of publicity will make her sister mend her ways or the elder lady's conviction that a good hard stretch in jail is the cure for the men and the girls alike, the users and the used in the sordid business of prostitution. The idea of vengeance and the reliance on turning a new leaf are both short of the mark, since they ignore the deeply twisted impulses of both the exploiters and the exploited.

In order to attack the whole problem with some hope of effectiveness, we must first be clear about what is wrong with our present attack, as shown by the Philadelphia story. I list three major things that are wrong.

One is the attempt to make a Roman holiday of publicity about the wretched stories of some wretched men and mixed-up girls. I don't mean, and I never meant, that the D.A. should bottle up the cases or that the press should censor the news about them. But I do mean that daily publicity handouts over a period of weeks don't help the problem itself, nor do the spicy garnishments of a basically miserable story.

The second thing wrong is the archaic level of most laws on the subject. The gap between the present condition of the statutes and the known facts about the ordinary life of ordinary men and women is so great as to be scandalous. I say this with some anger because I don't like cant and hypocrisy. I don't like it in international politics, where it may cause a war or the betrayal of a people; and I like it just as little in matters of law and morality, where it so often messes up lives.

The third thing that is wrong is the gap between the world of criminal law and the world of psychiatry. I was glad to read that Judge Reimel ordered the chief defendant held for psychiatric examination. There is a long literature on American prostitution, since the famous novel by

Reginald Wright Kauffman, *The House of Bondage,* back in 1910. But conditions have changed since then.

The news stories I read about the Philadelphia trials reported that the girls "giggled through most of the testimony" of the chief defendant. One girl testified that she had been promised "a front-row seat at the broadcast (of a disc jockey) any time I wanted it."

Both these quotes ring true to me. For many of the girls the question of sexual relations is a kind of game on a corrupted playground, and they giggle about it afterward. How far this is from the great themes of fateful love that dominate the literature of the centuries of Western history. So many of our youngsters act like automatons, as if they had been cut away from the sources of feeling.

We live in a new era of communication, when the phone has replaced the old "house of bondage." We also live in the era of the Big Media, when the *Hit Parade* and a ticket to a broadcast may have more glamour for a teen-ager than can be offset by all our moralizing and our publicized trials. The girl who gets the front-row seat is worth some study—by all of us.

3. The Dirty Game of Entrapment

April 8, 1953

THERE ARE class lines in fun and sin, just as there are elsewhere in our society. The expense account boys have the pick of the professional crop, and the fellows who know their way around seem to find a ready crop of free amateurs. But it is the outcast women, catering to the sex-hungry men with only a few dollars to spend, who are still an abiding problem for a society that likes to keep up the forms.

Chief Magistrate Murtagh has sent a letter to the Mayor in an effort to change New York's way of dealing with these women. The part that makes me cheer loudest is his attack on the degrading job the Vice Squad has to do in first trapping a prostitute in a cheap hotel room and then arresting her. This decoy operation reminds me of what I learned a few years ago in Washington, studying how homosexuals in the government service were tracked down.

Magistrate Murtagh wants the prostitutes to be kept moving on their beat and arrested for vagrancy when they "loiter." He has changed the Women's Court to the "Court for Vagrant Women." He wants more money for probation officers and psychiatric help, to rehabilitate the women. Some of his proposed changes make sense. What is heartbreaking is that the same fight has been fought almost every year for the past twenty years, since the Seabury Report and the Anna Kross Report, yet our methods remain in their archaic form.

Anyone who has been through the literature on prostitution knows the weary repeated refrain that "human nature can't be changed," and that the problem of prostitution is in the end insoluble. I don't look for final solutions here. But surely we have the right to expect some basic decency on the part of law officials.

No matter how you look at it, the dirty game of entrapment remains exactly what it is—a dirty game. If you are dealing with a dangerous enemy, you have the right to use "agents provocateurs" to trap his spies and allies. But these pathetic women are enemies of no one but themselves. They are the products of what happens when a personality is broken and crumbles in a commercial culture, and has nothing left to sell except the body.

I suppose everyone in a measure sells himself. Our modern age deals with what the psychiatrist Erich Fromm has called the "marketing orientation." Some people sell themselves fragment by fragment over the years, until there is nothing left to them—but we accept them because they sell themselves respectably. The common prostitute sells herself in a blatantly degrading way.

She will continue, in some form, to do this as long as the desert wastes in our sexual life supply her with customers. But meanwhile we can at least stop the degrading mockery of trapping a victim who is as easy as a caged bird with broken wings.

February 22, 1956

I am tired of the headlines about "vice dolls" and "V girls" and their "madams," and I am even tireder of a law enforcement concept which pays the taxpayers' money for an elaborate posse of detectives to track down a girl who has gone to a hotel room with a man not her husband. I am talking, of course, of the latest flare-up of the antivice crusade dedicated to keeping New York City moral by hunting down someone quaintly called a "floating madam" and a girl for whom she procured a $100 date. Now we can all rest safely in our legitimate beds, with the assurance that a mighty blow has been struck on the side of the angels.

It took a lot of persistence to catch the girl. Mrs. Cook's telephone was tapped by a group of detectives in a special vice squad, at a time when the city is terribly short on police personnel. They listened in for nine days while various Als, Sals, Joes and Edwards exchanged subversive thoughts with the lady of the house. Then they heard of a date at a swank hotel across the street. A couple of other detectives then took over, laid siege to the hotel, stormed the room, discovered the guilty pair, hauled off the sobbing girl and the madam—and let the man go on condition that he bear gallant witness against the women.

The sequel was publicity, pictures, and even one of the girl with her head hidden in the bedclothes of the luxurious bed. And then the trials, and Mrs. Cook's bravado, and the girl's bewildered and pitiful attempts to shield herself. How great a victory it was for decency and clean-mindedness.

All kinds of questions come up in my mind. Technically, no one can blame the Police Commissioner for enforcing statutes and ordinances that are on the books, and for giving periodic assurance to the prurient and censorious that the Vice Squad is on guard and all's right with New York. But I wonder why the rest of us don't do our duty too, which is to speak out at the folly and the pity of it.

What do we really think we are accomplishing when we send down a little army of detectives to track down two women who may be no better than they should be, but who hardly deserve so high a priority as public enemies? What do we gain, as a community, by all the prying and wire tapping and keyhole-listening? The effort to use prisons and the power of the state in order to make imperfect people sexually virtuous is something that has been tried for centuries and has never worked—and never will.

I don't like commercialized vice. I don't like the commercializing of any human emotion, but when you take a human drive that ought to be connected with love, and when you reduce it to a time schedule and a pay scale, it isn't pretty—nor is it satisfying to anyone concerned.

That is part of the pity of it all. That—and the girl herself. We don't know much yet about her all-too-shabby life history. Let us assume she is honest when she says she was a beginner at the game. It is conceivable that a sensible organization of our society would have led us to deal with the girl quietly, and keep the newspaper pictures from blasting her life forever and scattering it in little pieces over the countryside. But if we did that, what would be the point of a vice squad, and what would we use as a substitute for the periodic vice crackdowns, as a way of titillating our prurient emotions, and making Peeping Toms out of all of us?

If we have to make mistakes, let us make them on the side of over-protecting privacy. If we have to protect people, let us protect the young, the minors, those that can be seduced and exploited. We can leave adults alone to make their mistakes.

You have to make your choice about what you will stress in a culture. If you stress generosity, love, kindliness, compassion, fullness of living, you will get one kind of society. If you stress peeping, repression, intolerance, the policing of morals, you will get a different kind. I prefer the first. And I wish someone like Mencken were still alive and writing, to blast with his anger and laughter our efforts to police the morals of grown-up noncriminal men and women.

4. *The Women on the Streets*

November 17, 1957

THERE IS a legend that Mrs. Patrick Campbell once said about the London prostitutes, "I don't care what they do as long as they don't do it in the streets and frighten the horses." Put in extreme form, this pretty much represents how the members of the Wolfenden Committee approached the problem of overhauling the law on prostitution.

For years London has offered to shocked or titillated spectators one of the most blatant tableaus of female street importuning, on Bond Street and Park Lane, in Mayfair, in Piccadilly Circus, on Sherwood and Great Windmill streets. "It has been suggested to us," says the committee (which never breaks into an overstatement), "that in this respect some of the streets of London are without parallel in the capital cities of other civilized countries." What the committee proposes, in order to remove the affront of the whores to respectability, is to increase the present fines for first and second offenses and impose a three-month sentence for later ones.

Actually the best minds the British have been able to gather admit themselves defeated on how to deal with the trollops. They know as little as the Elizabethans did, or the British at the time of John Gay's *Beggar's Opera*. They know that you can't keep women from selling themselves sexually, nor men from buying a bit of sexual release. What they are concerned about is the appearance, not the reality. This is a kind of hypocrisy, but it is one that is embedded in English law, which does not act against prostitution itself but makes soliciting illegal.

Actually it is hard to see what else the committee members could have done about the streetwalkers, unless they had been willing to face more frankly than they did the possibility of licensed brothels. They do discuss it, but only to sweep it aside as alien to the temper of the times, which is more and more "abolitionist" about state-inspected and state-controlled brothels. The French, the Belgians, the Germans, the Spanish and the Japanese have abolished brothels. The old argument in their favor, that they cut down venereal disease because the prostitutes can be inspected, no longer counts for much, since the recent antibiotics have largely removed the nightmare fear of syphilis.

Yet while controlled brothels no longer are a solution, their abolition has not helped in any way to cut down on prostitution itself. Recently *Le Monde* carried a series of articles on the prostitutes of Paris. The writer, Jacqueline Piatier, did a study of just what the 1946 French law abolishing the *maisons tolerées* had achieved and concluded that it was little or nothing. The number of Paris prostitutes in 1946 was 6,500; today there may be between 7,000 and 8,000. The difference is that once they were registered, now they are more clandestine. The *rues chaudes*—"hot streets"—are today much what they were in 1945.

The Wolfenden Committee members are at least honest about what they cannot do. Having decided to harry the girls off the streets, if possible, they refuse to hound them in the flats that they rent to accommodate their customers. "As long as society tolerates the prostitute," says the committee, "it must permit her to carry on her business somewhere." Since she cannot do it on the streets, and since the law prohibits brothels, her only recourse is to "her own individual premises."

This, then, is what modern "morality" seems to be accomplishing. It is substituting the clandestine "flat" for the more colorful brothel. It is substituting the impersonal telephone for the direct encounter on the street. It is substituting the businesswoman for the soliciting girl. It's a triumph of something or other, but I don't know just what.

5. *The Happy Saleswoman*

March 1, 1957

LIFE in these United States continues to be fantastic. The cause of my euphoria today may be found in a batch of stories from both coasts, which show how love makes the world of people's capitalism go round.

William Graham Sumner, who was a defender of private property when he wasn't being an anthropologist, blurted out in a moment of truth a revealing sentence in his book *Folkways*. We organize our explanations of society around property, he said, whereas in most societies the deep drives are those of the sexual life. I would change his sentence in only one respect—namely, that in America today property and sex are not opposing drives. They are happily linked as elective affinities in one of the memorable partnerships of history. It is the genius of the American way of life that in pursuit of his business career a man may find a lovely thrown in as a bonus, while a woman of joy, in bestowing her pleasure-giving talents, may be aiding the whole intricate system of business enterprise.

If you think I am being unduly lyrical, consider the case of Nella Bogart. She is the happiest saleswoman I have ever read about, and my great regret is that I couldn't get to hear her recital of her inspired efforts to keep the sales of General Electric Supply Company moving. It was on an enchanted evening when she was helping to "entertain" two customer prospects for a new line of Hotpoints.

Listen to her own words: "I tried to help as much as I could. I came to a point where I took a writing pad, and I divided it into lines, and he [the salesman] told me the names of the articles with numbers . . . and I wrote them down at the beginning of the column and filled in the amounts. The orders, they kept increasing, kept increasing. Make this two carloads, make this one carload, they would call. I don't remember the amount, I was just happy. I was doing something. I was very proud. My old saleswoman ego was flattered."

But the end is not yet. When the customers, after the entertainment, reneged on part of the order, Nella also—like the heroic women in Aristophanes—denied them any further installment of love. When the orders were restored her love was once more released. Has any corporation ever had a more dedicated partisan?

You would think that the N.A.M. would choose Nella Bogart to make the opening speech at its next Waldorf convention, or at the very least that a foundation would bestow some prize on her for fortifying the tradition of business freedom. But the injustice is that she is being prosecuted instead for violating the Mann Act. The ecstatic words I have quoted were uttered in a Federal courtroom in New York. The defense that Nella's lawyer has been building up is that she did what she did for the corporation, in order to keep the wheels of industry moving.

Sure she is selling her charms—and also, I don't doubt, selling her girls who were so busily employed answering the calls that came in over the two trunk lines of the answering service. But she was doing it as a working auxiliary of corporations, helping them at convention after convention. At a time when the business boom is threatening to become a faint whimper, we do ill to discourage such zeal in stimulating demand on the part of middlemen. From all the accounts thus far narrated in the courtroom, Nella embodied in her own way the corporate spirit of our age. She was the Organization Woman.

While Nella is being tried in a courtroom in New York a Senatorial committee in Washington is revealing the story of what went on in Portland, out on the Pacific Coast. The business corporation is not alone in allying itself with sex. The union does it, too. A madam from Seattle, Mrs. Ann Thompson, told the McClellan committee how she had negotiated with two henchmen of a West Coast Teamster boss—Frank J. Brewster—to open brothels in Portland under the powerful protection of the union. The proposition fell through, but only because of a disagreement about the division of the take.

This again bears out some of the most cherished theories of the upbeat students of American society, who tell us that the old slogans of conflict between capital and labor simply don't apply in America. Here are the two great institutions of modern American economic life—the corporation and the trade-union—both making an investment in female reinforcements. Thus the class struggle is dissolved in the tenderness of women.

But I must confess to a certain disappointment with labor's role in this story, as compared with that of business. The corporations enlist the services of the girls and madams to give their stockholders bigger dividends and keep the stock quotations on the board from slumping. The individual sales manager may get certain perquisites for himself out of it, but his main concern is to keep that sales chart in the front office moving upward. But this Teamster outfit on the coast didn't have in mind the welfare or happiness of the workers, and didn't try to extend any further benefits to its members. It was purely a private operation, for private shakedown and profit. Trade-unionism will never get anywhere in America by tactics that fall short of the farsightedness of the sales managers who have made the corporate call girl part of business organization.

If anyone says I am basing all this on too little evidence, I can only say that I speak as one who has had to travel across the continent from city to city for twenty years and in every hotel has encountered the convention revelers and their companions. But I didn't understand until now how many of the Nella Bogarts I saw were devoted outposts of the corporate spirit.

6. The Oldest Persuaders

January 21, 1959

I NARROWLY ESCAPED having a cop in my living room to ask me what I know about call girls. I got a call from CBS asking if I would tape some scholarly remarks for an Ed Murrow radio documentary, *The Business of Sex.* Unfortunately I was busy and couldn't make it. I'm sorry I didn't. As it turned out, the show wowed the listeners and scared the daylights out of the police, and everyone connected with the show whose name was known has had a visit from First Deputy Police Commissioner James R. Kennedy, who heads the cadre of our police tracking down vice.

He would have asked me how I had come to know what I know about call girls. I would have been reduced to saying that my knowledge is not of the field trip type, but strictly literary and theoretical. He would have insisted on knowing who taught me literature and theory, and I would chivalrously have become a martyr to protect my sources, and gone to jail for ten days.

My wife, my six children and my four grandchildren would have accompanied me to my cell, and at the end of my term they would all have gathered to bring me home in triumph. I would have gone down in history as the man who went to jail either to break up a call girl ring or else to protect the call girls—I am not clear which.

But I must stop dreaming.

My feeling was that the show did what it was meant to do—get away from nice-nellyisms and police platitudes, and tell the facts about the relation between business enterprise, out-of-town buyers and the use of call girls. I suppose the police were put on the spot and had to react as they did. But it looks pretty silly when the Police Commissioner and the First Deputy Commissioner and the Vice Squad all run to the producers of a radio show to see what names they can pick up. God help our fair city when the only sources of information the police have about an immoral activity comes from sitting in their living rooms and turning on their radios.

Actually I think the police can find better things to do than ferret out call girls, which they admit is pretty hard. In fact, they can find better things to do than arrest those thousands of streetwalkers they arrest every year. The business of sex flourishes because there are men willing to pay for it and women willing to be complaisant for a price. The harm it does is not that of "scandal" and "vice," but the psychic harm to both when something that ought to be connected with love and delight gets bought and paid for, with guilt and shame and hate as the attendant emotions.

I hope that narrator Murrow and producer Gitlin will plan a follow-up show, on a theme that was not explored nearly enough in this one. Not on the "business of sex" but on the psychic drives that bring these girls into the business. I am speaking of the job that has to be done through the big media—that of probing into the life and mind of the call girl herself. Such a show would be a real "exposé," for it wouldn't just put the cops on the spot. It would put our culture on the spot.

Fortunately we have some beginnings. About a year ago a book was published which was a pioneer exploration—*The Call Girl: A Social and Psychoanalytic Study,* by Dr. Harold Greenwald (Ballantine). I recall a meeting held by the Association for Applied Psychoanalysis, just before publication, at which Dr. Greenwald reported on the twenty call girls whom he had interviewed and studied, and some whom he had treated in analysis. A number of experts got up to comment on the paper, including some brilliantly perceptive remarks by Dr. Nathan Ackerman.

The life history of a call girl is usually the life history of a psychic drive that has turned sex away from love toward destructive purposes. The call girl is likely to have been rejected by one or both parents and feels "unwanted, unloved, and unworthy of being wanted or loved." She comes very early to see sex as a commodity she can barter for emotional warmth. But she also comes to see it as something she can use in "collecting damages" from the male for what life and sex have done to her. Call girls' lives are drab, empty and tormented.

They strike up Lesbian relationships often; in many cases they turn for emotional warmth to a pimp; often also they turn to narcotics. They come to feel isolated and worthless.

While it is true that they get pretty good money and are the aristocrats of prostitution, it is a mistake to think that economic factors bring them into it. The world of money and minks is merely the frame within which they operate: what drives them is a complex of psychic factors. Their disturbance is not even a sexual one primarily; sex is only the way they express their crippled and distorted attitude toward life.

The call girl is, in these respects, no exception to the whole history of prostitution. She is simply the prostitute in an economy of abundance, where the aristocracy is an expense account aristocracy, and where you can deduct sex from your taxes as a business expense. Men use many forms of sales persuasion in this economy of ours—some are hidden persuaders and some not so hidden. But the oldest persuaders in history are the women who sell dreams to men when the truth is that they have no dreams themselves, only the nightmares of loveless lives.

January 23, 1959

Maybe it is a bad conscience on the part of some of the papers in being scooped on a story that should have been theirs which makes them attack Edward R. Murrow so violently. Murrow has raised a morals case—the morals of American society, which links sex with profit. I mean, of course, not only the profits of those who sell it, but the profits of those who buy it to influence their own business customers. If the facts are roughly as reported in the broadcast, then they say something we ought to face about the reach of the business spirit into sex or perhaps the reach of the sex drive into business enterprise.

As it happens, the day the Murrow story broke saw also the publication of a delightful book which gives a historic dimension to the episode. It is *A History of Sexual Customs,* by Richard Lewinsohn (Harper), which carries its learning lightly and spans the whole historic distance from Eve in the Garden to Kinsey, our "surplus women" and "the divorce mills of Nevada" with a dry wit and a delightful economy of style.

There are sections in the book about temple prostitutes in ancient times, the hetairae in Greece such as those with whom Pericles and Epicurus spent many years, the adventures of the Roman emperors, the "virtuous adultery" of the medieval knights, the moral atmosphere in the Rome of the Church and the great artists, the morals of Napoleon, the linkage of sex with European diplomacy and the

German Imperial Court, and the eroticism which was given expression by the two world wars.

You can read such episodes lightly to pass some idle hours or you can read them in order to get a perspective about human society and how it has grappled with the problem of morals through the ages. If the New York police heads and the busybody editorial writers want to do something useful with their time, they might buy a book and find that no one is maligning Americans by saying that they have not resolved or transcended the lusts of the flesh.

If I understand the excited critics, they mean that it is all right to say that Americans as individuals do these things, but it is dangerous and unpatriotic to say that American business firms and corporations have any hand in it. To ascribe to the majestic impersonal corporation any of the frailties of the human race is a kind of *lèse-majesté*.

I must confess I am not bothered that way. Read the history of morals and you will find that in every nation and era there are dramatic cases of the relation between sex and power in the society. You can start with King Solomon and Sheba, or with King David and Bathsheba, or with Antony and Cleopatra, or with Lord Nelson and Lady Hamilton, and you can end with the latest weekend party in Moscow, Peking, Bangkok, Vienna, Rome, London or New York. As it happens, business is simply our particular form of power, the sale of products and the pursuit of profit form our particular religion, and the corporate expense account is one of our most interesting rituals.

THE WORLD OF ALFRED KINSEY

1. Portrait of a Storm Center

August 18, 1953

MY FIRST and overwhelming impression when I met Alfred Kinsey was that he was interested in almost everything and knew an enormous amount about many things, and that what he knew he knew with mastery and precision. Our first evening together in New York ranged over the subjects of American law, early Hebrew religious rituals and ethics, American college teaching methods, the practitioners and psychoanalysis, Latin poetry. I stayed away from the topic of gall wasps, on which he is the world's greatest authority, and from birds and their habitat, and the history of music, because I knew that on all three his learning was as vast as my own ignorance. On every topic we touched, he had concrete out-of-the-way information, and sharp and definite opinions.

From the first he refused to pull any punches. When the conversation touched on people we both knew and on their professional work, he could be at once just in his appraisal and cutting when he criticized. He has a gift for disposing of someone with a phrase, which has not made him always popular among his fellow workers in the same field.

Several months ago I was one of a group of newspaper and magazine writers who flew out to Kinsey's headquarters, at the University of Indiana, to read the proofs of his new book on the American woman and discuss it with him. We found a man who was in the great tradition of science, opening the last area of human behavior to be studied inductively and statistically. He was also, in a sense, a briefing officer, in charge of a project that for years had operated under a curtain of military secrecy. He was a professor conducting a seminar in sex research, with ourselves as somewhat bewildered and quizzical students. He talked of the old trinity of love, marriage and morals, except that he came right out with terms that were coldly scientific but that no woman's magazine had ever used—and no family newspaper either. Beyond all these roles, however, he was himself—friendly yet always with an edge of reserve, direct yet canny, with strength of character and purpose. He was a Midwestern university professor whose work had burst through the university walls, a man of learning packed away over years of dedicated work, yet also a man of simple habits and rugged honesty.

When we first met, I said he seemed a Midwesterner to me. He laughed and said, "You wouldn't be good at placing birds in their habitat. I was born in Hoboken, New Jersey, went to high school in South Orange, to college at Bowdoin, and to graduate school at Harvard." This gave me the clue I wanted. Kinsey carries over that sturdy combination of Eastern origins and Midwestern experience that has given American history some of its best figures.

When you see him at Bloomington, you see that he belongs in the Indiana that produced Theodore Dreiser and Charles Beard. I was wandering around on the edges of the campus one day, when I heard a honking and looked up to see Kinsey in shirt sleeves, driving a battered-looking car. He took me for a tour all over the university town, showing me with great pride the new dormitories, the laboratories, and especially the low-rent housing project for young faculty and graduate-student families. Despite his world fame Kinsey remains a professor, and he knows the history of his university as well as he does the life history of the gall wasp or the American human female.

His project is part of that history. Sixteen years ago, in 1937, when Kinsey was forty-three, an age when most men are well into their life work, he stumbled on his. A new and able president had been chosen for the University of Indiana, Herman Wells. Students and faculty alike had a feeling new things might be done. One of the new things was a student request for a good course on sex and the family. A faculty committee was chosen to work on it, and Kinsey, as the professor of biology, was its chairman. He had found in his classes that when the students asked questions about sexual behavior, there simply was no body of concrete factual and statistical material to which he could go for a scientific answer. Out of the committee grew Kinsey's project, financed at first out of his own salary, then out of foundation funds. The university relieved him from his teaching load to do his research.

I have come across a handful of dedicated men in my time, and always I find in them an unmistakable sureness that gives them at once simplicity and authority. Kinsey belongs with that small group. He has mapped out work on the project of studying sexual behavior which will carry him through the end of his life and is training others to take it up from there. He is playing for big stakes. He has driven himself hard on this book about women—much harder than any man has any business to drive himself. The men and women who work with him have caught his contagion. Kinsey is one of the lucky ones who has found something to do with his life.

2. Report on the American Female

August 25, 1953

HERE ARE a few conclusions that thoughtful people may draw from the Kinsey Report on the American female.

1. Kinsey is, in effect, telling American women not to feel inferior about their sexual drives. His work may undercut a good many of the excesses of the psychoanalysts who speak of the trauma of being a woman and the envy that many women are supposed to feel for the male sexual organs. Kinsey's emphasis is that the sexual equipment of the woman corresponds in every respect to that of the man, and that there is no need for envy. Similarly he is skeptical of those who emphasize the special quality of the "vaginal orgasm" of women. He cites the experience of some eight hundred gynecologists who made tests of women's sensitivity in that area and found it not very great.

Thus one thing that women can learn from the new Kinsey report is not to set impossible standards for themselves, to accept themselves, their bodies and their mode of response—and relax.

2. To the American men Kinsey seems to be saying, "Don't feel too superior and condescending." I suspect he is asking them not to make the mistake of assuming that women's sexual responses are the same as men's. Thus, men tend to be impatient with their young wives in the first year or two of marriage, which are the difficult years sexually because so many girls have to make the transition from saying No to saying Yes. Men also make the mistake of assuming that women respond to the same psychological stimuli that men do. Many men may be surprised to read in Kinsey that continuing, rhythmic sexual wooing is more effective in evoking a climax than discontinuous and more varied stimulation.

3. As for the parents of growing daughters, Kinsey may well be asking them to remember that they themselves took part in a "sexual revolution" in the 1920s, which accounts partly for the greater freedom with which their own daughters are behaving; that the revolution has been maintained and is continuing; and that it is making women more expressive and less frigid in their sexual lives.

4. In this continuing revolution, the great changes taking place are a new acceptance of techniques, positions, frequencies, sources of sexual response and sexual attitudes, which the pre-1900 generation found distasteful.

5. A discerning woman may conclude that Kinsey is telling her not to let people instill feelings of guilt in her. If she is worried about her rate and frequency of response, she will find that there are many who exceed her and many others who fall short of her own levels of response. Again the injunction is to relax.

6. This applies also on the distribution of a woman's sex activities

among various forms of outlets. One finds Kinsey saying quite explicitly that there is no evidence of physical harm in masturbation. However, guilt feelings about the activity lead to mental distress. One finds him saying that there is a "homosexual-heterosexual balance" in women as there is in men, and that many persons pass through a phase of being drawn to the same sex, although this is true for fewer women than men. As for petting and coitus—the heterosexual forms of relation—they too are practiced in widely varying degrees, so any individual woman can find her own place in the total spectrum. Thus, Kinsey is skeptical of the scientific value of "nymphomania" as a concept; he believes that in many cases it is the reflection of male legendry about a woman, although there are compulsive patterns of sexual behavior as there are of every other form of behavior.

7. One of the implications of the Kinsey findings is that for many women continuity of sex relations is important. They may start before marriage, as the men do, and some of them may also continue with a variety of sexual partners after the marriage. For most women, as for most men, an effective marriage is the goal; Kinsey makes it quite explicit that there is no human society in which marriage has been replaced and its functions fulfilled in any other way. But while marriage is the goal—and 85 per cent of all women's coitus is marital —many women find it easier to adjust to marriage by experiences before it that provide some familiarity with sexual response; these experiences become for them a way of opening a path of sexual response within themselves and orienting themselves to the whole sociosexual world of men and women, and to marriage as well.

8. There is always a danger of the means becoming the goal. This is true of sexual behavior as of every other kind. The mature person will learn from the Kinsey study that premarital and extramarital relations should not become a norm for the individual simply because other individuals engage in them. Where the sense of guilt enters strongly, they can induce psychological havoc. On the other hand, there is strong evidence that even in the case of religiously devout women, once they have entered into such a relation their frequency is as high as that of the other women.

9. Men can also learn a good deal from the facts in Kinsey about the respective sexual-life-history curves of men and women. A mature man will accept the fact that the whole curve of the woman's history is lower than his in its frequency and sex drive, but that she will in time draw much closer to his, and *maintain* a plateau in the later years while he is aging sexually. Knowing this, he will be more patient in the early years of marriage, not letting his own interests lag or be diverted, not letting himself grow embittered.

10. By token of this same sexual life history, men may learn not to reject older women, whether in marriage or in other sexual rela-

tions. Kinsey does not pass judgment on the fact that American girls are getting married at an ever earlier age. But it should be clear that this often means a more prolonged period of sexual fumbling in marriage than would happen if both persons came to it with more knowledge of human beings and of sexual behavior.

11. Married people can, however, get one consolation from the Kinsey material. With the continuity of women's sexual response deep into the fifties, the middle and later years of marriage can become more satisfying and serene than they are usually pictured. The problem here shifts from the woman to the man. But even with his failing powers, the two can work out solutions which will make the middle years quietly joyful ones.

Throughout the Kinsey volume the spirit is that of a recognition of the changing patterns of life, the ways in which the great life forces —sex among them—break the tidy fences inside which we try to confine them, and our need for creative understanding of each other. Read in this spirit, the new Kinsey study should prove good medicine for us, although very strong medicine for most. One of its immediate consequences should be the sweeping away of many of the repressive state and local laws. Kinsey has dramatized this by saying that, if all our laws of sex were enforced, 85 per cent of the women and 95 per cent of the men would be subject to jail terms or prison sentences. Sexual techniques which are widely practiced by sensitive men and women, and especially among the educated groups in each new generation, are called "perversions." The heavy shadow of the early Judaeo-Christian codes still hangs over our legal system, even though our social organization and our knowledge of science are wholly different. "Somehow," writes Kinsey sharply, "in an age which calls itself scientific and Christian, we should be able to discover more intelligent ways of protecting social interests without doing such irreparable damage to so many individuals and to the total social organization to which they belong."

3. The Kinsey Revolution

June 12, 1953

WE ARE in America in the full swing of a revolution in sexual attitude and acceptance. It has swept across the country like a tornado, and Kinsey's own importance is that he is at the center of the tornado. He could not have created it, although he and his work have done much to give it shape. It is sweeping him with it, along with the rest.

The tiny first printing of the male volume showed that Kinsey himself was taken wholly by surprise and had not understood what changes had already occurred in popular attitudes about the place of sexual relations in love and personality and happiness. It is true that Kinsey's volumes will do much to underline this acceptance, but it is also true that they would not have been so dramatically received if an important change in attitudes had not prepared us for them.

The first Kinsey book was a "sleeper." The second one seems to have been oversold. Nevertheless, the commentary volumes have begun to appear. The first two books I have read deal with the relation between Kinsey and religion. One by Seward Hiltner is *Sex Ethics and the Kinsey Reports*. The other is *Sex and Religion Today,* edited by Simon Doniger.

In his two volumes Kinsey underscored his belief that our sexual codes and taboos are an inheritance from what he calls the "Judaeo-Christian" tradition. He has learned passages and footnotes on the Talmudic Laws, on the early Christian church fathers, on later Catholic and Protestant doctrine. In the library of the Institute for Sex Research, at Bloomington, Indiana, I saw some of the rare books Kinsey has collected on the religious treatment of sex. It is clear from Kinsey's writings that the conflict between the drives of the human body and the needs of the human personality, on the one hand, and what the codes demand, on the other, is at the center of his approach. He puts much of the responsibility for this conflict, and its resulting frustrations and unhappiness, on the archaic character of the religious codes.

It is striking, therefore, that these two books on the Kinsey material, both from religious sources, should be so basically sympathetic. Both authors have been active in the pastoral counseling movement in the Protestant churches which has tried to bring the resources of modern psychiatry to help the mental health of church members. The Protestant churches are thus developing something close to the function of the confessional. In doing so they are searching earnestly for light not only from psychiatry but from sex studies like Kinsey's.

Kinsey found in his female volume that the "devout" members of all three of the great religious faiths show a much lower rate of sexual activity than the undevout ones who are less active in their churches and synagogues. The differences are less striking in the case of men, where the most important factor seems to be economic and educational levels. He also found—for both sexes—that for the undevout groups the lowest sexual activity was among Jews, the highest among the Catholics.

He seems to think that in the case of the Orthodox Jews the relatively low rate of sexual activity is due to "the pervading asceticism of Hebrew philosophy." I have talked with several Jewish scholars who challenge this, and I have had a number of letters to the same effect. They point out that Christian theology de-emphasizes the sexual relation far more than Jewish, and that celibacy and asceticism are largely alien to Judaism, which, as Dr. Joseph Klausner puts it, "has never demanded of man that which is beyond human nature—complete monastic withdrawal from society."

It seems plausible that the rigorous Jewish taboos on sexual behavior in early times represented a recoil from the loose sexual habits of some of the neighboring peoples. Kinsey is on sound ground in underscoring the rigor of the early codes, but not in ascribing it to the spirit of Jewish history. But there is little question that the combined weight of the Jewish and Christian traditions has left a heavy impact on our sexual behavior.

Some of the essays in the symposium will surprise those who think that pastors are stuffy men who, in William Blake's phrase, are "binding with briars our joys and desires." For example, Reuel L. Howe, a professor at the Virginia Theological Seminary, calls for "a positive theology of sex relations." Gotthard Booth, at Columbia University, points out that much of our sexual tension today derives from the violence and anxieties of our time, rather than from the attraction of the sexual partner or an inner vigor. We ought to recognize that these anxieties often frustrate sexual expression, just as they make the sexual relation violent and empty of satisfaction.

What I welcome most in these books is the departure from the idea, found in some phases of religious history, that sex—except for reproduction—is sin. In place of that, we get the remark that the sex relation can be "a means of grace." In the context of respect and love, it can do much to heal the unquiet spirit and serve as one channel for expressing the total personality.

June 6, 1954

In the brief period since the appearance of Kinsey's volume on American women, the great debate on it has moved from the churchmen and the moralists to the psychiatrists. As if to underline how far apart the "experts" can be when dealing with the same body of facts, two books have recently been published taking opposite positions on the Kinsey report. One is on *Kinsey's Myth of Female Sexuality,* by Dr. Edmund Bergler and Dr. William S. Kroger (Grune and Stratton), a full-scale attack on Kinsey's data, interviewing techniques, premises, statistics and conclusions. The other is *Sex Life of the American Woman and the Kinsey Report,* a symposium by twelve experts, edited by Albert Ellis (Greenberg). The two authors of the first book do not find a single valid item in Kinsey and seem unwilling to admit that he could even blunder into a truth. As for the second book, its authors overwhelmingly find Kinsey on the side of the angels.

While I regard Kinsey's work as opening new paths, I think it should be subjected to rigorous criticism. Unfortunately the attack by

Drs. Bergler and Kroger is like a saturation-bombing raid which is intended to leave no enemy installation standing—or recognizable. The authors have little talent for subtlety and none for understatement. They feel Kinsey is evil, ignorant, dishonest. They pronounce his work leaky with fallacies and dangerous to science, morals, mental health and the Republic. A more restrained criticism would have been more effective. Yet the book will be valuable to serious students if they will read it with a heavy sprinkling of salt. It contains the most comprehensive and high-powered anti-Kinsey armory of ammunition thus far put together.

Here are the main points in the Bergler and Kroger indictment:

1. That Kinsey had a poor sample of American women, used faulty interviewing techniques and misused statistical techniques.

2. That Kinsey is ignorant of the unconscious in human beings and is hostile to psychiatry, which seeks to uncover it.

3. That Kinsey sees human beings as animals—"machinelike figures who discharge sex without the element of tender love"; thus he fails to see sex as "the expression of the total personality."

4. That when Kinsey finds certain forms of sexual behavior to be fairly widespread, he takes it to mean that they are therefore "normal." This applies to homosexuality, Lesbianism, "petting," premarital and extramarital coitus, premature ejaculation in the male, the absence of vaginal orgasm in the female.

5. Hence, that Kinsey "misinterprets perversions," fails to recognize neurotic and "counterfeit" sex, and thus gives "implied permission to overlook sexual and emotional disturbances in both sexes."

6. That Kinsey fails to recognize the stabilizing factors in marriage, other than the sexual.

In the opening essay with which Albert Ellis sets his book's keynote, he deals with a number of the familiar attacks on Kinsey's methods. In sections headed "Kinsey, Corrupter of Youth?", "Kinsey, Statistical Skulduggerist?", "Kinsey, Unpsychological Interviewer?", "Kinsey, Assassin of Sexual 'Normality'?", "Kinsey, Saboteur of the Female Orgasm?" and "Kinsey, Unscientific Moralist?", Ellis dismisses the standard objections in too cavalier a fashion, but he does give the essence of the Kinsey defense. The student who is seeking a balanced judgment will do well to examine both the attack and the defense point by point.

The important war, from the start, has been the war between Kinsey and the psychiatrists. He has contended that they are too bound by their Freudian beliefs, that they base their conclusions on a minute number of cases, and that they do not have the large body of concrete material from all walks of life from which every science must draw its generalizations. Their quarrel with Kinsey, in turn, is that he concentrates only on what can be measured statistically, is too concerned with sexual "outlets," accepts the answers of his informants without digging below the surface to find out what motivates them, and that he ignores the whole area of the unconscious.

Let us start with the charge that Kinsey fails to place the sexual act itself in its total emotional setting, including the affirmation of love and tenderness, and the negative elements of fear and anxiety, frustration and aggression. "For Kinsey," say Bergler and Kroger, "orgasm is king," since he seems uninterested in what accompanies the sexual act itself, and in the continuity and permanence of the partnership. One type of answer, which Ellis and several of the contributors to the symposium give, is that it is one thing to study measurable sexual behavior and attitudes, and quite another thing to study the accompanying sentiments and emotions; and that Kinsey set out to do only the first and cannot be blamed for not doing what he did not set out to do.

Yet this does not quite dispose of the problem. Kinsey shows, on repeated occasions, that he is thinking in terms of a satisfying sexual life. This is true of the chapter in which, in effect, he defends premarital petting as a way of exploring personality and adapting to a number of people, thus laying the base for achieving a more effective marriage; it is also expressed in the discussion of marital coitus where he says that the real cement of a marriage is the will to make it work.

The fact is that in his effort to redress the lack of emphasis on biological factors in the study of human sex behavior, Kinsey has understandably swung the balance in the other direction. The history of all human knowledge is the record of this kind of seesawing from underemphasis to overemphasis. It was true of Freud, who was widely accused of overemphasizing sex when his first books were published. No great movement of thought can move toward its goal without overdramatizing what had previously been almost ignored.

Given Kinsey's training as a biologist, it is easy to see that he would regard the human being as part of a natural universe, having to reckon with basically the same sexual drives as will be found among what he calls the "infra-human mammals." At the beginning of each chapter in the report on the female, Kinsey reviews the literature of experimental work in animal psychology and the findings of the naturalists. This is not a new method. Ford and Beach used the same approach in their *Patterns of Sexual Behavior,* comparing the behavior of animals with that of human beings, both in American and in primitive cultures. None of these writers believes that man is only an animal, or that his animal behavior sums him up as a human being. It is rather that they regard him as having the biological base of his sexual drives in the natural universe.

If Kinsey has one foot planted in this world of nature, he has his other foot in the social universe, emphasizing the taboos which society imposes on the human being. In the spirit of Rousseau, Kinsey seems to believe that if we could remove the antiquated Judaeo-Christian legal and moral codes, we could unshackle man and restore him to his natural—and therefore his normal and healthy—state. He feels that it is the social repressions that wreak havoc in the individual's sex life and therefore in his mental functioning.

This is the "reformer" element in Kinsey. It does not conflict with his serious purpose as a scientist. In fact, he would not be so earnest a scientist if he did not believe that human beings can be set free emotionally and enabled to lead lives less laden with guilt, fear and frustration.

Kinsey's reforming impulse expresses itself in two ways: first, in an effort to change sex laws and legal attitudes and make them more humane and closer to the facts of human nature; second, to let people know what are the facts of actual sexual behavior in Americans and thus, by reassuring them, to get them to accept themselves and their own behavior. Thus his purpose is the same as that of the psychiatrists. It is the methods that differ.

Kinsey's basic weakness is that he always associates the "natural" with the healthy, and the "social" and "moral" with the repressive. This is to give a wholly negative weight to the whole laborious construction that we call the social system, which has been built up over the course of centuries, taking the form of family and community life, of art and literature, as well as law and the state, and the church and its moral codes. This intricate web of society forms a framework within which men and women not only inhibit their biological impulses but also give them dimensions of emotional and aesthetic meaning that will scarcely be found among the "infra-human mammals." It may well be that the taboos and inhibitions overshadow the emotional meaning of sex. Thus the psychic price the individual pays for the social framework becomes too heavy to be borne, with a resulting toll on mental health. The first-rate psychiatrists have understood the weight of the social taboos, and the conflict that develops between them and the individual's biological drives and emotional needs. Yet they have also understood that not only the biological drives but also the emotional needs are part of human nature and that both of them require fulfillment.

This may shed some light on the question of what is sexually "normal." The curious fact is that Kinsey, who was deeply concerned to show the psychic devastation wrought by the social taboos, didn't follow up his insight when he had gathered his material. He found, particularly in the upper-level groups, evidences of inhibition which had resulted in homosexuality, premature ejaculation, impotence, sterility; he found the widest possible range of sexual frequency. Yet instead of seeing this as evidence of the psychic toll levied by the conflict between the sexual drives and the social taboos, he allowed his naturalistic emphasis to triumph and refused to regard any of these as posing problems for the individual or for society. For him the statistical frequency determined what was "normal." The only behavior which he flatly rejected was that of the sexual criminal, who exploits and hurts the helpless.

This again illustrates the basic conflict between Kinsey and the psychiatrist, which lies in Kinsey's refusal to recognize neurotic sexual behavior. Or, to put it differently, he regards the neurotic situation as wholly the result of social conditioning, and therefore as having no reality for a student of human drives. He does not regard Lesbianism in the female or homosexuality in the male as either in themselves neuroses (which is the view of Freud, and of psychoanalysts like Edmond Bergler), or as part of a broader neurotic pattern in the personality (which was the view of Harry Stack Sullivan and is followed now by his school of "interpersonal relations"). Similarly he is unimpressed by the emphasis of psychiatrists on "compulsive" sexual behavior, whether in the male Casanova or in the female "nymphomaniac."

July 8, 1954

In the Ellis symposium there are two thoughtful chapters on unsanctioned sex before and during marriage—one by Philip Wylie on "Virginity and Pre-marital Sexual Relations," the second by Robert Lindner on "Adultery—Kinds and Consequences." Wylie welcomes the intent of "the massive and organized viewing done in Bloomington." He underscores the belief that sexual techniques are something to be learned—"a fantastic symphony of voluntary and involuntary muscle-skills" which are "neurologically complex" and "psychologically demanding," but around which our American society insists upon throwing difficulties before marriage. Because "half the women and more than half the men ignore that particular stricture of our society and get in some experience of quite a few sorts before marriage," Wylie guesses that "their bold violation of all religious precepts and thousands of legal statutes may well explain why we Americans are not any daffier than we are."

Yet Wylie finds in Kinsey a certain naïveté of belief that he has only to reveal the facts about American sexual life, and changes will take place—the American people will behave more rationally, will throw off the accumulated moral hypocrisies and taboos of centuries, and will break the hold of their archaic sex laws. Wylie is more skeptical, believing that there is a complex and deeply encrusted religious sense in American society which will resist every effort, like Kinsey's, to strip the taboos away.

Lindner's essay deals with the extramarital sexual behavior of American women. He takes a sharply different view from that of Drs. Bergler and Kroger, who base their whole approach to adulterous relations on the premise that they are forms of "counterfeit sex" and "psychic masochism," and that all extramarital affairs are a form of the "search for the forbidden." Lindner starts with the proposition that there is a basic conflict within monogamous marriage—a conflict between cultural norms and psychic drives. "On biological grounds, at least, any attempt to contain a sexual instinct within a monogamist channel [writes Lindner] is not only absurd but impossible . . . The destiny of every man and every woman is to be torn between the imperative of fidelity and the pressure of human bio-psychic nature."

Lindner notes that Kinsey pays little attention to this conflict, since it is not within his realm but that of the psychiatrist and the clinician. In giving his own classification of the "adulterous personality" ("adventitious," "sporadic," "chronic") he makes the point that these may include both neurotic and integrated personalities. Thus the woman who enters into extramarital partnerships, whether fleeting or continuing, may be doing so out of neurotic compulsions, or, as a relatively mature person, out of deliberate choice. Lindner adds a necessary commentary to Kinsey's chapter on extramarital relations which cuts deeper than the reasons for adultery which Kinsey's women subjects reported and which may often have been rationalizations.

He accepts the Kinsey figures as strengthening the view that there is "an equal adulterous inclination in both sexes" and sees it as revealing "the emergence of a new marriage pattern." What this new pattern amounts to is that there is more "dissembling" in fact in marriage while the basic attitudes which underlie extramarital sex have remained unchanged. Lindner takes this as an instance of increased social hypocrisy and individual conflict, and presumably also of increased guilt. But this is not a necessary interpretation of Kinsey's material. The sociologists know that there is a lag between changing behavior and the more slowly changing moral codes.

Thus there emerge new operative codes which do not jibe with the formal codes. Eventually the gap between them is narrowed, but in the meantime many people manage to live, with greater or lesser degrees of success and conflict, in both worlds.

July 9, 1954

I turn now to the issues raised on the validity of Kinsey's figures and his interviewing techniques. The first problem has to do with Kinsey's statistical sample and his techniques of interviewing. Drs. Bergler and Kroger are convinced that the people who volunteered to "tell all" to Kinsey are "therefore automatically suspect" because "there must have been hidden reasons for the compliance." They strongly hint that many homosexuals became Kinsey volunteers and recruited their homosexual friends as volunteers, in order to over-weight the Kinsey figures, diminish their own sense of guilt and spread the idea that homosexuality is "normal."

I cite this as the kind of conjectural and unprovable surmise which can only leave the reader baffled. Kinsey's treatment of the figures on Lesbians (and on male homosexuals in the first volume) are subject to debate; but if you start by assuming a conspiracy of homosexuals and Lesbians in order deliberately to corrupt Kinsey's figures, you end up in a never-never land where anything becomes possible.

For another extreme example of how far an anti-Kinsey bias can lead his critics, take the question of Kinsey's use of "organized groups" as a statistical corrective for his sampling. That is to say, since Kinsey recognized that a number of his volunteers might be untypical and might skew his figures in one direction or another, he tried wherever possible to get whole groups to volunteer—college classes, church and club groups, theater casts, even prison groups. Kinsey reports that 15 per cent of his sample are drawn from such "100 per cent groups" and that "a considerable proportion" of the rest is drawn from individuals comprising 50 to 90 per cent of a total group. To which Drs. Bergler and Kroger retort that the answers given by the organized groups are also unreliable; that a few people may take the initiative, and the rest will "follow the leader" but will actually resent being drawn in and will express their resentment by "not telling the investigator the truth."

Thus the authors want the investigator to use the method of thoroughgoing psychoanalytical scrutiny—of hours and hours on the psychoanalyst's couch, allowing for a sifting of hidden motives and a laying bare of feelings of conflict, hostility and guilt. The ideal method would be, of course, to subject a group as large as Kinsey's sample of men and women—some ten thousand in all—to weeks or months of interviews-in-depth. But it is an unrealizable researcher's dream.

Meanwhile we must be constantly aware of possible distortions in the Kinsey figures because of what the psychiatrists call "screen memories." With the best of intentions, the women in Kinsey's sample had to make loose guesses about their sexual life histories, largely on the basis of whatever memories had survived the screening process of their total life experience over the years. In an essay entitled "The Kinsey Interview Experience" in the Ellis symposium, Jo Caro, a psychiatric social worker, tells of her own experience in being inter-viewed by Dr. Kinsey. She testifies to the way in which he put her completely at her ease, helped her over "slightly embarrassing material," won her "trust and co-operation." But she tends to slide over the real problem, which is how reliable her screen memories were. She does note, as Kinsey does, that "both sexes tend to be more reliable in reporting what behavior they have experienced than in stating how often their experiences have occurred."

In other words, the subject of the interview will be willing to tell whether she has had premarital or extramarital coital relations, or homosexual ones, or even incestuous ones; she will also respond honestly when asked about the sexual techniques she has used with her partner or partners, even though there may be severe moral taboos against some of them. But if she is asked how often she petted in her high-school days, or the frequency of her marital or extramarital relations and of her own responses, her answers are likely to be approximations of widely varying value.

Kinsey has recently tried to get a statistical check on this kind of inaccuracy also by having a number of his subjects keep sexual diaries and by repeating the interview after the lapse of several years. But both methods can at best check only on the accuracy of the more recent experiences. They can do little to overcome the unconscious resistances which often distort the memories of sexual experience in childhood and adolescence, or with early partners where there was a sense of failure and shame, or at intensely emotional periods in the life history when fantasy and reality were hopelessly intermingled.

This kind of criticism was made with respect to the Kinsey volume on males by two psychoanalysts of great discernment, Lawrence S. Kubie and Robert P. Knight. It could undoubtedly be repeated for the female volume. To say, as Bergler and Kroger do, that this is due to Kinsey's "ignorance about the unconscious," is both unfair and irrelevant. No matter how much he might know about the workings of the unconscious, it would still be difficult to deal with the problem of screen memories through anything short of the intensive, long-drawn-out interviews which are possible for only a few.

July 11, 1954

Ellis points out that a number of recent independent studies, using different techniques, have on the whole corroborated Kinsey's findings. His listing of these studies is impressive, but the trouble is that most of them deal with college students or college graduates, the area where the Kinsey figures are probably strongest; and they neglect the grade school level, the rural groups and the deeply religious groups, which are the areas which Kinsey has also tended to neglect and where his studies' figures are weakest. Moreover, most of the studies are attitude studies, using questionnaire techniques which are less thorough than Kinsey's, whereas what we now need are more thorough ones which can get at the hidden motivations and resistances.

Ellis' reply is that Kinsey cannot study all phases of sexual behavior, and that he frankly concentrated on the "taxonomic"—that is, on classifying his subjects in terms of their overt sexual behavior. This is true enough; but what has been put in question is whether the accounts and memories of this overt behavior are reliable.

This brings us to the crucial problem of sexual "normality." What Bergler and Kroger charge is that Kinsey has confused statistical frequencies with normality. They call this the "application of an approved and reasonable political principle—majority rule—to the problem of disease." Obviously, their use of the term "disease" shows how different are their premises about sexual behavior from Kinsey's premises. The same observation must apply to the familiar remark that because the common cold is statistically so common, it is not thereby an expression of normal health.

Kinsey does not regard sexual behavior as a problem of either health or disease. Wholly convinced that the greatest sexual burden is the burden of social repressions and inherited legal-moral codes, Kinsey tries to use statistical frequencies as the only safe reality which will show the basic facts of human nature. If, as a doctor, he were studying the diseases that weaken people or make them die, he would certainly refuse to equate the coronary diseases or the blood pressure diseases with normal health. But he does not regard sexual experience as a disease which either weakens you or makes you die. The true disease he finds to be the blanket of anxiety, fear and guilt which societies have tended to spread around the varieties of the sexual act.

That is why Dr. Abraham Kardiner wittily observes that for Kinsey "morality is something extraterritorial." He adds that a good deal would be clarified if the word "normal" were abandoned and if instead the word "modal" were used. "Normal" carries ethical implications, and in ethics the individual can neither make his decisions in a wholly isolated way nor judge wholly by the statistics of others. "Modal" is a purely statistical term, and it doesn't get tangled up with either the concept of morality or the concept of health.

But once we have made this point it becomes a bit wearisome to labor it. Kinsey has a certain naïveté as a social thinker, especially in his assumption of a kind of "state of nature" in which the individual can live without inhibitions or repressions. But the statistical material that Kinsey has given us about the American woman need not be applied within his suggested frame of social and moral values; it can be used within other frames as well.

Homosexuality, for example, is not "normal," nor is it "healthy": in its compulsive form, it is a neurotic disease, whose cure is still in doubt. Nor are extramarital coital relations "normal," although they may for many women represent a less intolerable way of life than a loveless and perhaps sexless marriage in an emotionally bleak setting.

It will take many decades before we have assimilated the figures on sexual behavior which Kinsey—and others to follow him—will have quarried for us, and before we can fit them into our social codes and personal conduct. I do not see that Kinsey needs to be considered a moral guide just because he has had the daring to conceive a massive study of behavior, and the will to carry it out.

What we can say is that Kinsey's figures have removed the stigma of the *abnormal*—the sinful and the pathological—from a number of sexual relationships and modes of behavior and have thereby given the American woman a new base on which to build a psychologically healthy and productive life. She will still want to restrain herself from certain modes of behavior, and remain a moral person in the sense of a person making choices which are congruous with her personality and character and which are not harmful in her family and group relations. But she is now less likely to suffer the tortures of conflict and guilt than before.

4. The Guilt Killer

August 27, 1956

ALFRED KINSEY IS DEAD. The many bigots who hated him and his work will light little fires of rejoicing in their hearts. The rest of us will feel deep sorrow and the conviction that America has suffered an irretrievable loss.

It would amuse Kinsey, wherever he may be in the heaven of scientists, to know that I first heard of his death when Polly Adler called me early in the morning to tell me the news. He was a deeply human being who did not consider it his business as a scientist to judge other human beings, and there was an earthly quality of simplicity about him which drew all manner of people to him and disarmed them. The moralizers and preachers will scarcely miss him, but he will be mourned all through the nation by plain people who came to know him—not only by writers and scientists, legal reformers and sociologists, but also by prostitutes and madams, homosexuals and Lesbians, prison inmates, and ordinary people of every sort whose case histories he took and whose confidence he won.

The America that Kinsey studied was half Puritan and half Babylonian. The sensuality of Babylon was in part a recoil from the Puritanism of the past; repression breeds strange products. The Puritans were shocked and angry at Kinsey for daring to invade a domain that had hitherto been the monopoly of morality and religion, while the Babylonians made fun of him for taking seriously something that was in their vocabulary of "fun." Some of the literary people and the psychoanalysts resented him because his statistical approach to sex could not possibly do justice to the dimensions of depth that escape measurement.

As for Kinsey himself, he resented most of this criticism because he thought it was far off base. He felt that the poets, the philosophers, the moralizers, the religionists, the psychologists and the novelists had been given their chance at the study of sexual behavior for centuries and it was time for the scientists to take over. This belief gave Kinsey a sense of sureness about the importance of his work that sometimes seemed arrogant. If so, it was the arrogance of a sensitive man who had been through the ordeal by fire, and the arrogance of the scientist who had opened up the last frontier that had been closed to observation and study.

He had dread of being considered a reformer, even though it was true that in a brief span of time he had succeeded in bringing about a revolution in thinking about sex offenders and their treatment. He thought of reformers as he thought of moralists—that they were both meddlers in a realm that belonged to the private life of private individuals. It is an ironic fact that this man should have been attacked as an invader of privacy when actually his work strengthened the right of every person to his own decisions in the area of his life that is most his own affair.

History will, I think, see him as a liberator, much as Freud was a liberator. Both men did much to break down the taboos surrounding the life of sex and emotions. They were very different men and did very different work, and Freud was easily the greater intellect and the greater figure in the history of science and the scientific imagination. Kinsey used the quantitative method, with its limitations. Yet because this man lived and worked there will be millions of people whose lives will be less stunted emotionally and more expressive.

I don't mean that Kinsey's work changed the sexual behavior of America. Sexual patterns are too ingrained and tough to be changed overnight by books and writers. But, whatever their behavior, Americans have a diminished sense of guilt about it because they now know something about their fellows and about the wide range of human behavior.

This is what Kinsey will mean for future generations as well. He will take his place in the select ranks of the Guilt Killers. Whatever doubts and criticism we may have about the detailed methods of his work and about its underlying premises, no one will ever be able to strip him of that role in the history of the science of human life.

He leaves behind a number of colleagues who have worked with him for years and know his approach and have caught something of his fervor. It will be impossible to find anyone to replace him, but from the start he foresaw that his work would continue for decades, and he trained a research team that would last beyond his own life.

Kinsey and his friends knew the risks he was running in recent years. When I was at Bloomington with a group of other newspaper and magazine writers, we heard about his having had a heart attack. Kinsey knew that he had to slow down if he was to live. Yet he kept pushing himself hard, because his work had become his life. Last summer he made a tour of European universities and research centers. Wherever he went he was greeted by scientists who recognized him as a pioneer in the study of sexual behavior. Despite the ignorant men and the bigots, Kinsey's work is a fact that will outlast them.

THE TORTURED PROBLEM

1. The Making of Homosexuals

July 11, 1950; January 20, 1954

HOMOSEXUALITY has been called the "hidden disease." The question-begging word here is "disease," but there can be little doubt that most things which concern homosexuality are "hidden," that much of the scientific inquiry about it has run into the sand. The prime unsettled question is that of the origin of homosexuality. To put it differently, how are homosexuals made? Or are they, in fact, not made—but born?

There are still some scientists who place stress on biological factors and the bodily constitution, or else on a strong hereditary predisposition. But most agree that it is a matter of what happens to the boy during his period of growth and development, that the important factors are those of his relation to his parents and the emotional structure of the family. Most psychiatrists do not believe that a man who is an exclusive homosexual can be "cured." Thus the paradox: Homosexuals are made, not born; yet once made, they cannot be unmade.

The course of what happens to the boy in his growth is still unclear. Dr. William C. Menninger, formerly head of the Army neuropsychiatric setup, points out in his book *Psychiatry in a Troubled World* (1948) that a child goes through a series of stages of sexual development. At first he is interested only in himself, like an infant Narcissus gazing at his shadow in the pool. Then he begins to transfer his love to others—to parent, to older brother or sister. The first stage in this new interest is generally a "homosexual" stage, in the sense that the boy or girl gets hero-worshiping "crushes" on someone of the same sex. This is a perfectly normal development, and it may or may not be accompanied by overt sexual play and exploration; in many cases it is. This is roughly the age period of eight to fifteen, and it is the time when (as Menninger puts it) "the Boy Scouts, the Girl Scouts, the Girl Reserves, the Hi-Y, and the Campfire Girls thrive because of this normal interest in persons of the same sex."

The next stage is the shift of affection to the opposite sex. Some of the emotional interest in the same sex is never lost, even by the most normal of normal individuals, as witness the sewing circle, the fishing change is generally made. The psychoanalysts stress the role in this process of what they call the "Oedipus relation"—the love of a boy for his mother and of a girl for her father, the corresponding jealous hostility of a boy for his father and of a girl for her mother.

During this time the youngsters are developing the attachments to the opposite sex that lead to the choice of sexual mates. This relation, the Freudians say, will not be a satisfactory one unless the young people have "worked through" their conflicts about their parents and resolved them. The doctors who don't belong to the Freudian schools don't put as much emphasis on the "family romance," but they too agree that the homosexual impulse is a phase through which the individual passes until, in most cases, he finds a sexual mate.

But there is a sizable group of men who remain or become in one way or another "sexually deviated." Some of them never outgrow the stage of early adolescence. They may never develop an emotional attachment to women. Some may find their emotional expression in close friendships with other men, but without overt sexual relations. Others may marry and even raise families, but still find themselves— consciously or unconsciously—strongly drawn to men. Still others may quietly establish a relationship with men. A small number may find themselves compulsively drawn to homosexual practice.

Given the normal life growth of the individual, the scientists tend to see the habitual overt and compulsive homosexuals as cases of "arrested psychological development," like a record that has got stuck somewhere. What makes a person get stuck is something they disagree about. The psychoanalysts (see Otto Fenichel, *The Psychoanalytic Theory of Neuroses*) stress the family relation—the overpossessiveness of some parents, the coldness and hostility of others. Some psychiatrists stress social factors—overcrowding, alcoholism and neglect in the family. Still others stress the moral climate of the time, because it is too lax in some ways, too repressive in others.

Dr. Lawrence Kubie has suggested a good working classification, as follows: First, there is the *exploratory* homosexual. Perhaps the largest number fall into this group. It includes those who have tried homosexual relations out of a vague urge abetted by curiosity and have largely outgrown it, yet it may linger on even after heterosexual relations have been established.

Second, there is the *facultative* homosexual. This includes the men who have a faculty for homosexual relations which may exist along with a heterosexual and even a married life. For these men homosexual relations are optional. Some start as habitual homosexuals but make their more normal adjustment later in life, and thus they become heterosexuals with a homosexual potential. Others may start with every idea that they are like other men, but as they grow older the "aging factor"

may bring out their repressed homosexuality. The facultative homosexual may accept the fact and pattern his life around it as a matter
of habit; or he may work out a sort of double life, involving both men
and women; or he may remain in turmoil about it.

Finally there is the *compulsive* homosexual. He may find satisfaction
in private and never get mixed up with the police and the courts; or he
may haunt public places, cafés, parks, toilets, and end up in trouble
and violence. It is here that the criminal element enters, and it is here
that the homosexual becomes a problem that society must meet and
solve.

One of the puzzling problems is the role that the parents and the
home play in this process.

The most popular theory is that the mother is the most important
character in the play, and that her relation to her son is the shaping
one. Where she is a possessive mother, devouring her son, overpro-
tecting him, using him as a substitute for the emotional failures of her
own life, she may tie him to herself forever by a silken cord. But
deviates also often come from families where the mother neglected or
ignored the boy, or where the dominant parent was a brutal father.

This raises the question of the father's role. It is usually believed
that fertile soil for homosexual growth is that of a family where the
father is dead or absent, or where he is a Milquetoast who quails
before a dominant wife. But there are also cases where the father is
himself the domineering male and it is the mother who does the
quailing. Thus, either overprotection or neglect of the child, pamper-
ing or brutality, a domineering mother or an overrigid father may
provide the impetus toward homosexuality.

Obviously, where the range of possibility is so wide we still have
much to learn in narrowing it down. All we can say with some confidence is that—if you make the Freudian assumption of the "family
romance" or the Oedipus situation—there is a strong chance that an
unhealthy parent-son relation will block the usual development of
the boy beyond this stage and freeze him in it, so to speak. Or if
you prefer not to talk in these Freudian terms, you may say that the
boy fails to find a healthy and normal sexual model on which unconsciously to pattern himself if the emotional structure of the family
is badly askew.

But this raises in turn the question of why homosexuality gives our
society so much concern. One answer is that it is "abnormal," a form
of "unnatural" sex relation. Yet this view has been sharply challenged.
One of the reasons for the continuing debate about the Kinsey Report
is that Kinsey maintains a moral detachment and treats homosexual
"outlets" as he does others. This is the view of what may be called
the school of naturalistic morals, which sees men in biological terms as
part of a natural universe among other animals.

One way of avoiding the whole normal-abnormal problem is to speak of sexual "deviants." But if you ask what the "deviants" deviate from, the answer is some implied "normal" behavior—otherwise "deviant" would have little meaning. Thus, one has not gained much in the switch of terms. But if you say that the "deviant" departs from some social norm which is not a moral absolute, the term becomes once more a useful one.

There is finally the still unsettled question whether homosexuality is a "disease." Freud gave a powerful impetus to the tendency to see homosexuals as mentally sick people, whose neurosis may have originated in the period of infantile sexuality and may have become fixed in puberty and adolescence as part of the Oedipus relation.

2. The Senator and the Purge

Washington. July 17, 1950

IN A LONG INTERVIEW, Senator Kenneth Wherry (R-Nebr.) talked to me about his crusade to harry every last "pervert" from the Federal government services. Senator Wherry, who used to practice law in Nebraska and who also (along with his brothers) ran an undertaking establishment, has the distinction of having beaten the great Republican liberal, George W. Norris. Now in his second term, he has been a power in the Senate as Republican whip and now as floor leader. A man with a hearty manner in the traditional fashion of American politics, a bit pouchy, with glasses and graying hair, he looks like any small-town lawyer or businessman. Sometimes his answers to my questions became harangues so violent as to make me think he would explode, until I saw that they left him unshaken and friendly as ever. Despite years of hard work and political tension, life seems to have left no writing of any kind on his face. It is the face of a man for whom there are no social complexities, no psychological subtleties, few private tragedies.

I asked Senator Wherry whether the problem of homosexuals in the government was primarily a moral or a security issue. He answered that it was both, but security was uppermost in his mind. I asked whether he made a connection between homosexuals and Communists. "You can't hardly separate homosexuals from subversives," the Senator told me. "Mind you, I don't say every homosexual is a subversive, and I don't say every subversive is a homosexual. But a man of low morality is a menace in the government, whatever he is, and they are all tied up together."

"You don't mean to say, Senator," I asked, "that there are no homosexuals who might be Democrats or even Republicans?"

"I don't say that by any means," he answered. "But this whole thing is tied together."

I asked whether he would be content to get the homosexuals out of the "sensitive posts," leaving alone those that have nothing to do with military security. There might be "associations," he said, between men in the sensitive and the minor posts. "There should be no people of that type working in any position in the government."

I asked whether the Senator knew the Kinsey findings about the extent of homosexuality in the male population. He had heard of them. "In the light of these figures, Senator," I asked him, "are you aware of the task which the purge of all homosexuals from government jobs opens up?"

"Take this straight," he answered, pounding his desk for emphasis. "I don't agree with the figures. I've read them all, but I don't agree with them. But regardless of the figures, I'll take the full responsibility for cleaning all of them out of the government."

I asked on what he based his view that homosexuals represent an unusual security risk. I cited a group of American psychiatrists who hold that a heterosexual with promiscuous morals may also be a security risk, that some men might be reckless gamblers or confirmed alcoholics and get themselves entangled or blackmailed.

The Senator's answer was firm: "You can stretch the security risk further if you want to," he said, "but right now I want to start with the homosexuals. When we get through with them, then we'll see what comes next."

This brought me to the question of definitions. "You must have a clear idea, Senator," I said, "of what a homosexual is. It is a problem that has been troubling the psychiatrists and statisticians. Can you tell me what your idea is?"

"Quite simple," answered the Senator. "A homosexual is a diseased man, an abnormal man."

I persisted. "Do you mean one who has made a habit of homosexuality? Would you include someone who, perhaps in his teens, had some homosexual relations and has never had them since? Would you include those who are capable of both kinds of relation, some who may even be raising families?"

"You can handle it without requiring a definition," the Senator answered. "I'm convinced in my own mind that any homosexual is a bad risk."

"But how about those who get pushed out of their jobs when they are only in minor posts, when no security risk is involved, and when they are forced to resign for something they may have done years ago?"

"They resign voluntarily, don't they?" asked the Senator. "That's an admission of their guilt. That's all I need. My feeling is that there will be very few people hurt."

I cited a case in the State Department of a man who had once served in an American embassy and had allowed himself as a young man to be used by the ambassador. He is now in his forties, and his case is troubling the security officials.

"It might have happened," answered Senator Wherry, "but I'm not going to define what a homosexual is. I say not many will be hurt. The Army and Navy have used their rule of thumb on this. The military has done a good job."

"But not a complete job," I pointed out, "if we follow the Kinsey figures. They show that thirty per cent of the men between twenty and twenty-four—the age group most represented in the armed services—have had some homosexual experience. Would you have all of them purged?"

"I repeat," answered Senator Wherry, "we should weed out all of them—wherever they are on the government payroll."

"Would you apply this to Congress also, Senator?" I asked, pointing out that Congressmen are often in possession of top-secret material. I mentioned the article in the Washington *News* that day, applying the Kinsey percentages to the Senate and the House, and estimating twenty-one members of Congress who are "wholly homosexual" and 192 who are "bad risks." "Let us assume hypothetically that the figures are roughly accurate. What would you do about them?"

The Senator waved a depreciatory hand at the *News* story on the Kinsey data. "Once again," he answered, "I don't accept the figures. But anyway, the case of Congress is different. A Congressman is re-elected every two years, a Senator every six years. They have to face the people in grueling contests. If there is anything about their private lives that ought to be known, it comes out. The electorate is the one who elects their Congressmen and Senators."

"Does that mean," I asked, "that when you speak of getting rid of all homosexuals in government pay, you would exempt Congress from your demand?"

"It is the people who have exempted them," he answered. "If they want to elect a Congressman or a Senator who is a homosexual, let them. That's their business. And if Congress wants to investigate itself, that's its own affair."

I raised a question about the encroachments on privacy. "Get this straight," answered Senator Wherry, "no one believes in freedom of speech more than I do. I don't like anyone snooping around. But I don't like Kinsey snooping around either."

I asked him what he meant by Kinsey's snooping around. He said, "That's how he got the figures, isn't it?" I said that the Kinsey interviews were voluntary and asked whether he had ever had a chance to study Kinsey's book or his methods.

"Well," he answered, "all I know is that Kinsey has never contacted me. Has he contacted you?"

I said I'd had a friendly talk with Dr. Kinsey, and I offered to get the Senator in touch with him.

"But look, Lerner," Senator Wherry continued, breaking the cobwebs of our discussion, "we're both Americans, aren't we? I say, let's get these fellows out of the government."

"We have to know what fellows we're talking about, Senator," I answered. "That's just what is bothering many of us. What homosexuals are bad risks? How do you treat the others? Can they be helped? Would you, Senator, bring doctors and psychiatrists into the picture and make them part of the machinery for dealing with this problem?"

"No," he answered, "I don't think doctors are needed. We can handle this by rule of thumb."

3. Lieutenant Blick of the Vice Squad

Washington, July 18, 1950

IN AN AGE of experts Lieutenant Roy E. Blick, of the District of Columbia Police Department, rates as a very important man in Washington. He is head of the Vice Squad, one of whose tasks is to deal with homosexuals. "Go see Blick," I was repeatedly told as I tried to track down the security story about homosexuals. "He has the facts and figures." So I did.

Lieutenant Blick is a tough cop. When I came into his office he was in the midst of a phone conversation about homosexuals which would have been wonderful detail for a documentary except that no one would dare put it on the screen. Burly, graying, and just ungrammatical enough to match a Hollywood pattern for police lieutenants, Blick has been on the Vice Squad nineteen years, and he has a pride in his job. He has four detectives on his squad who do nothing but check on homosexuals.

He seemed worried about our interview. He didn't like being caught, he said, "between the Democrats and the Republicans." He was referring to his star-witness testimony before the Hill-Wherry subcommittee, in which he had given his classic estimate of five thousand homosexuals in Washington.

"I had no idea," Lieutenant Blick told me, "that I was getting into a political football." When I asked what made him think the homosexual inquiry was just politics, he said darkly, "Something I heard this morning," but wouldn't elaborate.

The committee summons to him had come as a surprise. I asked how it could have been, since Senator Wherry had talked privately with him before he had sprung him dramatically on the committee.

"Yes, the Senator came down here," he admitted, "and talked about these cases with me. But I didn't know what the committee wanted me for. I came there without a note. The figures I gave them were guesses, my own guesses, not official figures."

"We would all like to know," I said, "on what basis you reached your guesses."

Blick seemed to grow more restless at this point. He squirmed and twisted, thrust his hands up in a helpless gesture.

"We have these police records," he finally said. "You take the list. Well, every one of these fellows has friends. You multiply the list by a certain percentage—say three per cent or four per cent."

"Do you mean," I asked, "that your police list is only three or four per cent of the total, and you multiply it by twenty-five or thirty?"

A faltering "Yes."

"If your final estimate was five thousand, does that mean your police list was less than two hundred?"

"No," he answered doubtfully. Then he added, "I mean five per cent."

"You mean then that you multiplied your list by twenty?"

Again a "Yes," then a "No." Finally, "I multiply my list by five."

"You mean you started with a list of one thousand and multiplied by five to get five thousand?"

Blick shifted his gaze around the room. Again the upward thrust of the hands, as if to say "How did a good cop ever get into this sort of situation?" But he didn't answer my question.

I made a fresh start. "You have a list of the men you arrested?" He did.

"You also have a larger list, including men you never arrested?" After hesitation—yes, he had a larger list as well.

"Did the fellows you arrested give the names of others?"

"Yes," he answered, this time with eagerness, "every one of these fellows has five or six friends. Take Smith. We bring him in. We say to him, 'Who are your friends?' He says, 'I have none.' I say, 'Oh, come on, Smith. We know you fellows go around in gangs. We know you go to rug parties. Who are your friends?' Then he tells us—Jones, Robinson."

"So you put Jones and Robinson down on your list?" I asked.

"Yes, we put them down."

"And that's how you compiled your list?" Yes, it was.

"But you said a while ago that you took the count of the men you arrested, and multiplied by five."

"Yes, I did."

"Well, which do you do? Multiply by five, or add all the friends you find out about?"

"I do both."

"How much of each?"

Blick finally broke into a smile of relief. "Well, it's sixty-forty. Sixty per cent of it I put the friends down on the list, and forty per cent of it I multiply by five."

This adventure in higher mathematics had exhausted both of us. I thought back grimly to the reverent way Senators and security officers used Blick's estimate of five thousand homosexuals in Washington, with 3,750 in the government, and I reflected that this was how a statistic got to be born.

"Do you think five thousand are too many?" Blick asked me.

I thought of the Kinsey figures. "If you mean just any kind of homosexual, and use it loosely," I answered, "I suspect you are conservative."

He clutched eagerly at my answer. "That's what I keep saying," he went on, "I'm conservative in my figures. I'm conservative about everything, Mr. Lerner."

I asked how he got his figure for the number of homosexuals working for the government.

"Oh," he said, "I took the five thousand for Washington. And I figured that three out of four of them worked for the government."

We spent a long time talking about what types he counted as homosexuals for the purpose of his figures, but the problem of definition proved even more exhausting to both of us than that of statistics. Lieutenant Blick was a cop, not a logician or a mathematician. I knew we would be on stronger ground when we got to his police methods with the homosexuals.

He was helpful there. He described in detail the process by which the men were picked up and booked. Sometimes the four squad members and Blick himself were not enough for a big raid, and then extra police were detailed. This happened, for example, one night in late September of 1947, when the cops descended on Lafayette Park—just opposite the White House—and arrested sixty-five men. Usually, however, things are quieter than that in Lieutenant Blick's domain.

The four detectives go around in pairs, to protect each other. They frequent Washington's restaurants, night clubs, public toilets. Blick read me a handful of their reports. They didn't make savory literature. One of the detectives, without committing himself, lets a suspect talk on until he has made a specific proposal. He takes him to the squad car, where the other one is waiting, and they make the arrest. After he has been questioned at the precinct the arrested man is charged with disorderly conduct and is booked. He pays $25 as a sort of bond to insure his appearance. He always forfeits the $25, never does show up.

I could not detect that the Senators—or, for that matter, Lieutenant Blick—were in any way shocked by the hearsay aspect of the list he had compiled. For Lieutenant Blick's importance in Washington is not only that he has become one of its statisticians, but even more that he is the Great Proscriber. In the days of Marius and Sulla, of schoolboy fame in Roman history, the prominent people in the senatorial and popular parties trembled when they found their names proscribed on a list, for it meant death. Lieutenant Blick's is the most important homosexual list distributed among the government agencies. The hearsay aspect is that the names which appear on it are not only those of the Smiths who have been arrested by Blick's vice squad, but also those of the Joneses and Robinsons whom Smith under questioning had mentioned.

Blick was strongly of the opinion that these men are bad security risks because of their fear of exposure. He put it most sharply when questioned by Senators Wherry and Ferguson:

"I would say that anything I would want from an individual who was a pervert, I could get . . . I could get it quicker by the approach of exposing him than I could by offering him money."

Lieutenant Blick glows at Senator Wherry's recommendation that the District Vice Squad be strengthened with a greater appropriation. He also wishes he had a Lesbian squad.

4. The Ordeal of the Gay

January 22, 1954

IF THE LAWS on "sodomy" and on "crimes against nature" were strictly enforced, millions of people would be in jail—including many married people who engage in heterosexual relations other than the single coital relation which the law recognizes. Fortunately the police and the court authorities enforce the laws on sexual "perversions" only fitfully.

The famous Kinsey estimate that 37 per cent of the American males have at least one homosexual experience at some time in their lives after puberty shows how vague a meaning the term "homosexual" can have. In most cases the experience occurred only once and never established a pattern. I add here the case of the "repressed" homosexual, whose impulses may be strong but do not emerge openly except when they can escape their watchful censor—as, for example, when they get drunk.

More important than the casual or sporadic homosexual are those for whom homosexual behavior forms a regular pattern, whether optional or exclusive. The Kinsey estimate is that during a three-year period of their lives 13 per cent of the American males have a sexual record which is more strongly homosexual than heterosexual, but are capable of both. These have sometimes been called "facultative" homosexuals, and some students have called them "bisexual," although the latter term no longer has the standing it did when Freud first wrote about it. It will be clear on reflection that the essential dividing line between homosexuals and heterosexuals turns on the question of the kind of behavior in which the individual finds himself most expressive. He may be capable of both, yet the true homosexual will strongly prefer sexual acts with his own sex.

The Kinsey estimate is that 8 per cent of American males have been exclusively homosexual during at least a three-year period, and that 4 per cent have been exclusively homosexual in their entire life history. It is these 4 per cent who form the bedrock of the homosexual male population. They may be called "compulsive" homosexuals in the sense that neither guilt nor community hostility nor legal penalties nor therapy is likely to change their pattern. They may be relatively well adjusted to this pattern, or they may be wretchedly unhappy about it, but they are no more capable of damming up their sexual drive than are strongly sexed heterosexual men.

This analysis of homosexual types furnishes a frame within which some of the absurdities of the laws about homosexual acts become clear. It is stupid to punish the casual or temporary homosexuals for acts which are only marginal to their lives and which hurt no one. It is barbarously cruel to hold the shadow of punishment over men who have formed more or less stable sexual partnerships with other men, and who live quietly and trouble no one.

At the other extreme are the exploitative and predatory homosexuals, who may corrupt adolescents or who may engage in blackmail; and the compulsive ones who solicit in public places; and the more extreme sex offenders who prey upon children. It is with these latter groups that the law is rightly concerned. But even with them it has proved confused in its definitions, too wide in the net it seeks to cast, crude in its workings.

One reason for this is that our laws go back in their legal traditions to the early English common law, and for their moral sanctions to the Old Testament. The English judges, in Lord Coke's day, called homosexuality "a detestable and abominable sin among Christians not to be named," and this precedent for not naming it has carried over to our own day, so in many states the charge will be broadly for "sodomy" or for a "crime against nature" but will not describe specifically the offense that is alleged. Ex-Magistrate Morris Ploscowe, author of *Sex and the Law* (Prentice Hall), notes that when the court attendant reads the complaint in a case involving homosexual acts his voice is likely to drop—as if the world had to be protected from even the sound of the offense.

The prophets and lawgivers of the Old Testament were so impressed with the enormity of sex deviants that they decreed death for the sodomite and the homosexual. We no longer make it a capital crime. Yet in Georgia and in Nevada a "crime against nature" may be punished by life imprisonment, while in Connecticut there is a maximum penalty of thirty years, and in North Carolina of sixty years.

Other states are less severe. New York, for example, has the sense to set a one-year maximum where the partner is over eighteen and there is consent. Yet what makes the punitive provisions of most states barbarous is the fact that terms like "sodomy," "lewdness," "carnal indecency" and "crime against nature" include most of the acts that a majority of Americans practice in private, and that the variant forms of sex behavior which are thus punished are as old as human history and as contemporary as the material in the Kinsey surveys.

January 24, 1954

One of the striking facts, considering how widespread homosexuality has become, is how few arrests and convictions there are for homosexual offenses. For the most part, the police and the courts deal only with what they consider "overt" behavior.

If the statutes were enforced, the jails would be full. It has been estimated in a report by a Committee on Forensic Psychiatry that for every twenty convictions there are six million homosexual acts committed. Thus the law is cynically ignored, mainly because it would be absurd to try to enforce it.

Yet unless a compulsive homosexual has some continuing and sustained relation with a partner, or can move easily from one to another, he must have recourse to what can only be called soliciting. He may meet a man at a bar or in one of the restaurants that are known to be haunts of homosexuals; he may talk to a man on the street, or sitting on a park bench, or in a public toilet. If he judges rightly, the situation is very similar to a heterosexual "pickup" and remains a private matter for the two people involved. But if he misjudges and turns out to have accosted a plain-clothes member of the Vice Squad, he gets into trouble. He may be able to get off with a bribe; but usually he is arrested.

The problem of blackmail in homosexual cases has recently been given a good deal of public attention. The ironic fact is that the drive against homosexuals in the government, by its sensationalism, may have created blackmail situations instead of removing them. The social penalty of exposure has become far more drastic than ever. Sometimes a member of the police force acts as a blackmailer; sometimes a homosexual "hustler" works with accomplices who pose as plainclothes men.

The most dangerous part of the ordeal of the compulsive homosexual is the role played by these "hustlers," or homosexual prostitutes. A study entitled *Boy Prostitutes in a Metropolis,* by W. M. Butts, showed that most of them were not homosexuals in their psychic make-up but simply boys who were willing to sell themselves for money. As a high New York police official put it, "A male hustler is usually a tough, husky young man who allows himself to be solicited for money. His attitude is no different than the female prostitute. He is no homo himself. But it pays him to make himself attractive to the homo."

The police have had many cases where the hustler is taken to the homosexual's apartment or hotel room and leaves with his victim's wallet or valuables after the sexual act. If the victim objects, he may be beaten up, and the police learn of it only when the apartment superintendent or the hotel detective informs them—since the victim himself fears to make a complaint.

These are all elements of the tragedy of those who, in their own vocabulary, are called the "gay." They are caught between the powerful sexual impulses which society forbids and the hazards of predatory men who exploit their vulnerable situation. And they are helpless in trying to change the laws which hang over them, since to speak out openly would be to expose themselves to social penalties far worse than the legal ones.

January 25, 1954

Under the pressures of a hostile and contemptuous world, the homosexuals tend to become a combination of a fraternal order, a secret society, an underground resistance movement, a defense association, a literary and artistic clique, and a minority group lamenting its state and asking for its civil liberties. By necessity, since they know they will be rejected by the outside world, they cluster together, go to parties and dances and bars of their own, look up their own kind on their travels. They form a subculture of their own, or rather a set of interconnecting circles depending on their economic standards and their intellectual and artistic interests.

They have organized a semisecret order, called the Mattachine Society. They now have a little monthly magazine called *One,* published in Los Angeles and devoted to stories, poems and articles about homosexuality.

As Donald Webster Cory has put it in his sensitive and comprehensive book *The Homosexual in America,* they form a "submerged world" whose members communicate with each other by subterranean symbols. They live constantly with the sense that they are an inner group, cut off from the outer world. There are times when they return the hostility of this outer world by a hostility of their own. But part of their tragedy is that they absorb and carry over the values of the majority world, so that they see themselves in the mirror held up for them by the heterosexual majority, and they are plunged in self-doubt and self-hate.

One of the most striking features of the homosexual way of life is the special vocabulary, or argot, that the homosexuals have developed, especially in talking about themselves. They dislike the words "homo," "fairy," "fag," "nance," "fruit," "pansy," "queer," and others by which a hostile world expresses its contempt. They call themselves "gay," using the word both as noun and as adjective. They call heterosexuals "straight." They call the homosexual ball a "drag," and night prowling for a partner becomes "cruising," while an effeminate homosexual is a "camp" and his opposite is a "trade." I take these terms from the very informative chapter on homosexual vocabulary in Cory's book.

I don't mean to overstress this separateness of the homosexual. Actually the slang of the criminal underworld or of the be-bop devotees is more highly developed and more sharply set apart from the majority world than is the slang of the homosexuals. And the life of "gay bars" and "drag" masquerades, of homosexual haunts and dives and parties, is one that does not cover all homosexuals, many of whom live their lives in private or discreetly merged with the lives of the outer world.

It is a mistake to think that homosexuals are all effeminate-looking, with women's gestures and marceled hair and mincing gait. A good estimate would be that not more than 15 or 20 per cent fall into the effeminate group, and probably much fewer. In the literature that homosexuals write about themselves, there is even a tendency to look down at this group as somehow casting discredit upon the rest.

Most homosexuals are not easily recognizable as such to the world outside. They may be quite masculine-looking, athletic in build, muscular, with a virile walk and a hearty handshake. In a recent issue of *One,* Cory has written a brilliant essay under the title "Can Homosexuals Be Recognized?" Setting aside the effeminate minority, he concludes that they could "function in a hostile society, pretending successfully to be like any other employer or fellow employee, if this be necessary." Many of them do make this effort, very similar to the well-known "passing" of very light-skinned Negroes who want to merge themselves completely in a white society, or the extreme assimilationism of Jews who hate their Jewishness and want to shed it. The difference is that homosexuals are not in reality—although some of them would like to think so—a minority group like Negroes or Jews.

It is true that homosexuals can recognize each other by a number of subtle yet revealing traits—a way of dressing, the type of haircut, a clipped quality of speech, a noticeably masculine and therefore telltale walk, a lingering handshake, a male-to-male stare, and the "homosexual reflex" of automatically turning to notice an attractive man passing by.

Yet it is also true that most homosexuals are compelled, by our hostility toward them, to lead a double life—an open one and a secret one. Their problem is the difficult one of coming to terms with a world that despises them while they maintain in their own hearts the flame of fellow feeling which makes life tolerable.

January 26, 1954

The key to the emotional life of the homosexual is his pervading sense of loneliness, his feeling of being cut off from the main stream of the life of his time. Hence the restless search for companionship and the night "cruising."

Life even for heterosexuals is at best a lonely experience, but love and marriage give it a sense of completion and the focus of a home. The homosexual's love can never have the sense of completion that comes from children, and only rarely does it have an openly shared home with another homosexual. In some cases the homosexual even marries a woman who has children by him while he maintains his central emotional relationship with another man. Yet even this means a fatal and permanent emotional split in the personality. What is tragic about the homosexual is that he cannot avoid the split, just as he cannot achieve anything but a momentary sense of completion. Thus, homosexual love can scarcely avoid being fitful, febrile and frustrated —quite apart from the fact that it must also be secret, carried on in the face of a hostile world, against the very base of the world's mores.

This may shed some light on the creative role of homosexuals in literature and the arts. When the homosexual asks himself whether there is anything productive about his kind of love, his answer must be in the negative—until he hits on the answer that some of the most creative people in the world have been homosexuals. Could the emotional life of these men, he asks, have been barren if it has resulted in the philosophy of Plato and Socrates, the plays of Shakespeare and Marlowe, the many-sided artistic work of Leonardo da Vinci and Michelangelo, the music of Tschaikovsky, the dancing of Nijinsky, the novels of Proust and Gide, and the poetry of Walt Whitman?

The parade of these names, and hundreds of others still alive, by homosexuals represents a defense of the nature of their love. It may be called a defense-through-talent. There can be little question that the homosexuals' contribution to the world's great artistic achievement has been far out of proportion to their number. One reason, we may guess, is that the stream of emotional energy which is dammed up in one direction may be released in another. There is a sense in which all writing and art are forms of neurotic expression: A man must be obsessive to withdraw so long from life itself in order to create symbols that portray life. It is not surprising that men who have a curious compulsion of their own at the center of their emotional being should be able to fuse this with the curious compulsion that moves an artist.

I do not want to leave the impression that all homosexuals are hopelessly frustrated. They carry an additional psychic burden, on top of the other burdens of life. But if they have a measure of emotional maturity, they learn—as the rest of us have to learn—to transcend their limitations and even to use them creatively. The life force is strong in human beings. When it is blocked in one channel, it breaks through in others. There can be joy and generosity, devotion to work, integrity of mind and art, resourcefulness, loyalty among these men as among the rest of us.

5. The Forbidden Burden of André Gide

February 21, 1951

THE DEATH of André Gide has posed some difficult problems for the obit writers. What can you decently say in a family newspaper about the greatest French writer of our century, through whose life and works there runs the scarlet thread of homosexuality? If you divide the great writing into the literature of power and the literature of conscience, Gide belonged with the latter. About many of the torments of conscience in Gide's books most Americans are not concerned.

The French are a highly civilized people, if we may use "civilized" to mean a breadth of taste and a tolerance for varied ways of life. Only among the French perhaps could a writer like Gide, who so publicly agonized over the conflict between his Puritan upbringing and his homosexual impulses, have reached the heights of influence and acceptance that he did. Recently the Americans, too, have begun to take him seriously. I don't mean that we accept his values, but that we are beginning to be concerned about his concerns.

In his long writing career, extending over sixty years, these concerns shifted in an often bewildering way. But always, through his novels, plays, travel books, autobiographies, criticism, there was the continuing theme of the conflict between conscience and experience, the dialogue of his soul as he pursued his search for some fixed points of belief. He had the integrity of his senses, in that he cultivated every sensitivity to experience. He had a thinker's integrity, in that he did not flinch from the logical consequences of that experience. And he had an artist's integrity, in that he refused to fake the conclusions he had, or understate the terrifying complexity of both life and art.

Both of them required courage. One has only to read the passages of his autobiography, *If It Die,* about his sojourn on the edge of the African desert, and how the abandon of life there thawed out his Calvinist training just as the African sun thawed out his body, to see how much courage it took to set it all down. His portrait of Oscar Wilde and of the role that Wilde played in his life shocked the moralists in Paris as it still shocks the American reader today. But no one can deny the fierce honesty of the man.

There was a similar honesty in his adventures with Communism. He came to it in the late 1920s, roused by what he saw of colonial exploitation in Africa. He became one of the artist-showpieces of the Communists, very much as Picasso is today in Paris. He went to the Soviet Union, visited the factories, made speeches and issued statements. But in the end his honesty saved him. For despite the reception the Russians were careful to give him, he asked the right questions of them: "Now that your revolution is triumphant, have you not become enslaved by the tyranny of orthodoxy?" And when they refused to answer his question, or even to let him ask it, he himself gave the disillusioned answer which helped to set free so many other intellectual Communists.

February 15, 1954

I was delighted when Richard Watts, in closing his skeptical review of the Gide play *The Immoralist,* wrote: "Perhaps it should have been covered by Max Lerner." It gives me an excuse to write again about Gide, whose novel of a half century ago was a landmark in the open literary discussion of a forbidden theme.

I rarely take to "message" plays. I feel about them a little like the dowager who was going to an opening night and said, "If it's a play with a message, we won't dress." But Gide's novel—and the skillful Goetz adaptation of it—have nothing of "message" about them. Gide wrote his novel after his own discovery of his true sexual impulses in North Africa. Like Michel in the play, he took his young bride, Madeleine, on a wedding trip to the desert. He tried to tell in his book about his fumbling efforts not to hurt the wife he loved, about the conflict between guilt and a defiant inverted sensuality.

In one respect Gide's story is dated. Its underlying assumption is that the homosexual tendency is inborn, asserting itself more strongly in some men than in the rest. Gide wrote his book before Freud published any of his studies on sexuality in the child or developed the importance of the Oedipus conflict. The view of modern psychiatry is that homosexuality arises out of the life history, especially out of the emotional relation between parents and child.

The curious reader who wants to study Gide's views on this theme will turn to *The Fruits of the Earth* (Knopf, 1949), which celebrates in lyrical prose the joys of responding to the impulses of nature; and especially to *Corydon* (Farrar, Straus, 1950), a book of Socratic dialogues in which Gide develops a theory of the nature of the homosexual drive. He denies that it is "unnatural" or biologically "abnormal," pointing to the animal realm and the whole course of human history. He ascribes it to the male's possession of a stronger sexual drive than the female (obviously a pre-Kinsey view), so that he must seek other males for satisfaction. It is a bizarre sort of book, but not without learning and power.

But while Gide fumbled and blundered when he tried to give a scientific basis to his sexual preferences, he did know the human heart. He did not spare his hero in the novel, the young archaeologist Michel. He made him take his wife cruelly on the journey that led to her death.

The Goetzes have changed the ending of their play; yet, while the present ending is not good drama, it is closer to the way Gide actually lived his own life. He didn't drive his wife to death, and he didn't walk out of her life. He remained married to her and continued to love her as his one great love. Yet he felt he could not change his own inner nature, and most of his time was spent away from her while she lived out her own life on her estate, occupied with her sister's children and with religion.

There is a moving little book on this relationship that could not be published until after Gide's death. It is *Madeleine* (Knopf, 1952), a soliloquy which Gide wrote in his notebooks after his wife died, trying to explain and justify how he had felt toward a woman whom he had married but never approached sexually, yet whom he loved.

It is a book written by a genius, but it is also a sick book—there was a sickly quality about Gide's whole world. The reason why the Goetzes had difficulty finding an ending to their play taken from Gide is that there is no solution to the homosexual problem in life itself. Gide tried in his writings to assert that he had found the solution, and he tried to convince others also to "liberate" themselves. Yet he was haunted by a sense of guilt, and he had to pay a heavy price for his vaunted "freedom." The price was the burden of the forbidden, which is a heavy burden even for those who live according to their own laws.

6. The Twisted Current

November 11, 1953

THE TRAGIC ARREST of John Gielgud, for public importuning, has thrown the English intellectual world into a minor turmoil. The *New Statesman and Nation* has run some valuable articles and letters on the theme of "Society and the Homosexual." The first thing that strikes me about them is that the operation of the British laws relating to homosexuals is as cruel and barbaric as anything in America. The methods of provocation by detectives that Lieutenant Blick of the Washington Vice Squad once described to me were similar to those the London police use. The Anglo-Saxon legal and moral tradition seems to have left the same sort of deposit in both cultures.

"One is overwhelmed by disgust and pity," writes the great English novelist and critic E. M. Forster. "It is terrifying to think of thousands of people going into the streets for a purpose which they know to be criminal, risking detection and punishment, endangering reputations and incomes and jobs. What on earth do they do it for?" And he answers, "They are impelled by something illogical, by an unusual but existent element in the human make-up."

Another letter writer challenges the assumption that homosexuality is a social sickness. To him it is only a social problem. Yet most of the other comments do accept the view that the growing number of homosexuals in Britain is a sign of unhealth. As one of the homosexuals himself puts it, "To live in this world without affection is insupportable. If we suppress our emotional life we wither. . . . I do not like promiscuity; I do not like soliciting; but perhaps those who condemn these actions have not imagined the desolation which has preceded them."

There seems to be melancholy agreement among the psychiatrists that no way has yet been found of effecting a cure. There have been many instances where young men who were active homosexuals, but also heterosexual, have succeeded in giving up their homosexual phase. What is extremely rare is the case of the exclusive homosexual who is able to change his whole sexual conditioning. The homosexual cannot yet get outside the skin of his sexual history. He is what he has been made, either by his nature or by the accidents of biology and by the impact of family, school and the rest of society on his personality. He can try to understand himself, and here psychiatry can help. He may succeed in "adjusting" himself—that is to say, in accepting himself and mapping out a tolerable scheme of life.

No one I know of, including the English writers, seeks to defend the homosexual who preys on boys. The seduction and emotional enslavement here are crimes against the young people, whom society must protect. The real question is about mature males who seek out other mature males. It is against them that the brutality of the law is directed. As E. M. Forster puts it, speaking of the periodic "cleanup campaigns" against them, "Where are these people to be cleaned to? Difficulties always arise when we regard human beings as dirt."

The nub of the matter lies in the social attitudes toward homosexuals who seek to live their lives quietly, doing no one any harm. My guess is that Americans are making progress in these attitudes. In Robert Anderson's *Tea and Sympathy*, it is exactly the belligerently "normal" man who is cruelest toward the victim of the homosexual rumor, since his belligerence expresses his own inner struggle against the homosexual impulse within himself. Our task is to humanize our outworn sex laws and at the same time humanize ourselves. Within this frame the homosexual may become rarer and his fate less tragic.

November 15, 1957

Many of those who criticize the Wolfenden Committee's proposal for liberalizing British law on homosexuals do so because of their fear that softness on society's part will lead to a homosexual blatancy in the culture. The specter that frightens them is that of a vulnerable young man growing up in such an atmosphere who will yield more easily to a deviant or perverse sexual impulse.

There is little question that in most Western countries the homosexuals tend to develop little cliques and coteries. The "homosexual way" may be linked with aesthetic sensibility and with a waspish but attractive wit. In literary and artistic circles it may even become "fashionable and epidemic," as one writer has put it. But it does not follow that the way to counteract it is by harshness in the law or terrorism in public opinion against homosexuals.

There is, however, more to the problem than can be resolved by a leave-it-alone liberalism. The liberal who believes that intelligent neglect of the problem is the best course will have to explain those epochs and cultures in history when, as John Addington Symonds put it, "the habit has become established and endemic in whole nations."

A number of the classic essays on homosexuality in history are gathered in Donald Webster Cory's anthology *Homosexuality: A Cross-Cultural Approach* (Julian Press). Some ascribe endemic homosexuality to the nature of particular races, some to the mode of living of equestrian and nomadic peoples, some to overcivilization.

Richard Burton, in his famous "Terminal Essay" to *The Book of a Thousand and One Nights*, fixes on climate as the principal factor. He speaks of a "Sotadic Zone" that embraces parts of the Latin and Greek peoples in the Mediterranean area, the Moslem peoples from Morocco to Egypt, the Arabs of Asia Minor, the Afghans, the Chinese, the Japanese. Modern students don't take either climate or race as the explanation. Instead they look at the history and institutions of each of the cultures for the clue.

Since we are dealing with sexual relations, the best clue is to ask about the social position of each of the sexes, especially the women. It is generally true that where the gap between the sexes has been greatest—where there has been the greatest social inequality—there has also been a culturally rooted homosexuality that has often become the rule rather than the exception. This was true of the Greeks, of the Arabs, of the Chinese, of the Japanese. Obviously it has not been true of the democratic world of the West, especially in the Scandinavian countries and in France and England and America.

The best insurance against the epidemic spread of homosexuality is a society which refuses to harass it with drastic laws, but which also refuses to set any particular value on it.

To a far greater extent than most of us realize, the sexual direction of a young man is set by the prevailing tone of his culture. If it is one in which men despise women, give them only the menial tasks, demand obedience from them, regard them as nitwits and believe only man-to-man relationships to be interesting, then the sensitive youth will turn toward men. If it is one in which the woman-man relation is regarded as a romantic one between people who are roughly equals, he will be drawn toward it.

Women in America today are tending to lament that men are not really manly any more, and men are lamenting that women are not really womanly any more. These laments are a symptom of something going wrong in the society. Yet it is better that each sex should want the other to be more completely itself than that it shouldn't really care.

What has played havoc with men's masculinity is not the American woman as a person in her own right, but the possessive, overloving mother. Woman as lover has given vigor to heterosexual love, but woman as doting mother—despising her husband, concentrating on her son, seeking fulfillment in him—has spread a path for the increase of homosexuality.

In his famous "Calamus" poems, Walt Whitman looked back to the Greek tradition of a fellowship in arms that went beyond arms. He saw "manly love," with distinctly homosexual overtones, as something likely to become a virtue of democratic nations. But he mistook the nature of a democratic society. It is not one in which the equal relationship is only within one sex, but where it spreads throughout society, including relations between the sexes.

If there are some British moralizers today who are worried about the laws against homosexuals being too mild, I would suggest to them that they stop worrying about the laws and worry more about the schools. For many generations the British "public school," where young boys live in a one-sex barracks society during the whole of their formative period, has been one of the great breeding grounds of homosexuality. It has been the only source of sexual education for them—and a pretty bad one.

There is a passage in Burton's essay which gives a lead on this question of sexual education. He notes that some of the Negro tribes of South Africa have very little homosexuality and suggests that it may be due to their custom of sexual education and sexual initiation into the tribe at puberty. He suggests that this is something for modern Western societies to think about. I would agree. Even more dangerous than the protective mother is the terrible blanket of silence and guilt about sex just at the age when the sexual energies are awakening.

January 14, 1957

In his *Sex and Repression in Savage Society* (Meridian Books), Bronislaw Malinowski noted that the Trobriand Islanders do not interfere with the sexual development of their children and have no problems of homosexuality—except where the white man and his morality introduced them. Certainly many of our problems of the distortion of the sexual drive arise out of the persistence of Puritan repressions. They arise also out of the anxiety of the parents and the community to fit children into a cultural mold of what is supposed to be "male" or "female."

But some parents, having now learned not to put too many cultural pressures on the child, may fall into the opposite error of leaving the sexual education and development of the child severely alone. I call it an error because it abdicates one of the functions of the parent—that of caring about how the child develops and, wherever it can be done without damage, helping him toward a healthy development.

We must remember that our American society is not like that of the Trobriand Islanders. It is bigger, more complex, more bewildering. In a simple society the child is rarely out of sight of home and village; with us he is hardly ever in the home and is subject to every influence from the outside. In a simple society the standards of the group don't have to be preached to him, they get built into him as he grows up and takes part in every activity.

That is why the parent today cannot abdicate the role of parent. But what should the role be? It is to accept each child for himself, to accept a wide range of diversity of character and temperament, to see to it that the child learns about sex and love and learns it without a sense of shock or anxiety or shame. But even more, since children learn by imitating the parents' roles more than by precept, it is to set an example of genuine affection between parents, and of manliness in the man and womanliness in the woman. The rest must be left to nature, luck—and prayer.

As I look back at the controversies on sexual behavior in recent years, I find myself disagreeing most with three very diverse groups: First, the people who tell you to stop writing and talking about the whole theme and think that silence and a strict code of behavior are the only remedy. Second, the people who have followed Kinsey too far and seem to think that any form of sexual expression is as good as any other form, individually and socially, just so long as it is expressive; they treat sexual behavior as if it were like cigarette smoking. Third, the people who are attacking homosexuals as diseased and depraved creatures. Among them is Dr. Edmund Bergler, who has just published *Homosexuality: Disease or Way of Life?* (Hill and Wang). Bergler's book has great value if you read it as an antidote to those of Kinsey, who failed to distinguish between the homosexual component which is present in all sexual development and homosexuals as such. He argued from the fact of the first to the conclusion that there is nothing abnormal about the second. He was wrong on this score, although right on so many others.

Bergler seems to link me with Kinsey, and in a rather lurid passage he attacks me for having views I simply do not have. I have written several times in these columns that homosexuals are sick people, since so strong a current of instinctual vitality takes a twisted and tormented form in them. I agree with Bergler that their "way of life" has been given an undeserved glamour by some of their writers. Where I disagree sharply with him is in his belief that by scolding, condemning and attacking them we shall get very far with the problem. He has insights of value into their mental processes, and the book is worth reading for these insights. But the problem itself will yield as little to these blitz tactics as to laissez-faire and silence. It is a tortured problem, and it needs insight, wisdom in guidance—and (God help us) compassion.

THE TRAGIC TABOOS

1. Death and Abortion

April 9, 1954

THE CAST of characters includes a girl, an unlicensed doctor with a record of criminal abortions, a behind-the-scenes licensed doctor with a large legal practice, a surgical supplies dealer, a practical nurse with a convenient house, her son, and a mysterious detective. The girl is dead. The detective has been suspended. The others have been arrested and are charged with conspiracy to perform a criminal abortion.

Periodically this kind of story hits the news, and the papers play it big. We read all about it, express our shock, and get titillated by the scandal. Then we go on to the next sensation and forget about girls and doctors who are caught in a degradation we do nothing to prevent.

Here are a few facts and figures on abortions: It is estimated that between 1,000,000 and 1,300,000 take place in America every year. Many are spontaneous—that is, either accidental or the result of disease. At least a third are induced. These induced abortions in turn fall into two categories. One is the "therapeutic abortion," carried out legally and under a medical certificate. The other is the "criminal abortion," done under cover and punishable when discovered.

Of the total number of abortions, between 1 and 5 per cent are therapeutic. About 30 per cent are criminal. The rest, or about two thirds, are spontaneous. In more explicit figures, one estimate puts the therapeutic abortions in the U.S. at 18,000 a year. A conservative estimate of the illegal abortions places them at about 330,000 a year —or between 900 and 1,000 a day. Which suggests how many doctors, nurses, respectable "fronts" and corrupt police could be prosecuted. Actually very few are caught and punished—less than 1,000 convictions a year in the U.S.

In the 1920s there were about 8,000 deaths a year from criminal abortions. Since most of them were due to septicemia, or infections from unhygienic conditions, and since antibiotics have cut the death rate, the present estimate is between 5,000 and 6,000 deaths a year. Which means that more than 100 women and girls die every week because of the cruel cloak of darkness and furtiveness with which we surround their plight. I say this because the figures show that when therapeutic abortions are done in hospitals, the death rate is extremely low.

I take these facts and figures from an important new symposium, *Therapeutic Abortion,* edited by Dr. Harold Rosen (Julian Press). I first learned something about the problem years ago, in my early teaching days, when I found how many young college students went through tortures of despair, how many took the dangerous gamble of a furtive abortion, what scars it left on the minds of those who lived.

But the case that hit me hardest was the Ward case, back in 1948, where not only did the girl die but one of the doctors killed himself out of shame and his mother died of grief. In a column I wrote at the time* I said that "when a girl is in a jam, she has to choose between disgrace and criminality." That was the choice the girl in the current case had to make. She is dead now, and those who sought to sell her what she was agonized enough to buy are reaping their harvest of trouble.

The Rosen book deals mainly with the therapeutic abortion and with its medical, legal, religious and psychiatric aspects. No one advocates that all abortions be legalized. The real advance (in addition to birth control) lies in liberalizing the definition of "therapeutic." In the old days doctors were reluctant to certify for abortion any cases except the serious medical ones, as in the case of heart disease, hypertension, t.b. Now the emphasis is shifting. In some hospitals there are "abortion boards" that make the decisions; on them sit experts for every phase of the patient, including the psychiatric. We need to go much further. Doctors have their codes, but whether they interpret them mechanically or with humanity depends on how deeply the whole community feels.

2. The Girl in the Basket

January 16, 1956

THIS ISN'T a pretty column today, because it's about an unpretty subject again—our abortion laws and our abortion attitudes. Maybe it would be better not to write about it, raking up a theme which is taboo in most of our press except when it results in death, raking up an issue about which everyone seems to feel helpless because no legislative assembly would ever dare do anything about it. But my

* "The Shadow World of Abortion," in the New York *Star,* November 23, 1948.

anger about the story of Jacqueline Smith is stronger than my caution
or good taste.

She was a girl from Lebanon, Pennsylvania, blond and pretty, just
two years out of high school, with one of those minor talents for
drawing and designing. She was restless in the small-town atmosphere
and was drawn to New York and its promise of a career, and the
dream perhaps of meeting interesting young men.

Many girls get to New York, have their fling at a career, meet
their young men, fall in love and get married. Which is to say that
I am not writing this as the story of the innocent small-town girl
and the wicked big city and its tall, handsome, villainous betrayers.
The jungle in which Jacqueline Smith was betrayed was not the city
jungle but the man-made jungle of our own laws and attitudes.

So Jacqueline came to New York, took some courses in a design
and fashion school, and got a job of sorts, designing color paintings
for handkerchiefs. She moved into an apartment with two other girls,
but she soon moved most of her things out and went to live with Tom
Daniel.

I am writing this from the clips, and from what has thus far come
out of the D.A.'s office. Tom seems to have been a good-looking,
well-mannered boy with some minor talents. He didn't like his origins,
so he invented new ones and shaped a picture of himself that suited him
better. He said he had been born in Athens and had traveled, and it
was true he had an apartment with books and pictures, where he
cooked special dishes for his friends. But the fact was that he was a
stock clerk in a harness store and came from Warren, Ohio, where his
father had committed suicide and his mother was a dishwasher.

But that isn't really my story either, because Toms have met
Jacquelines before this and have pretended to be what they are not,
and then things have got straightened out. This particular Tom was a
kind of Clyde Griffiths. Jacqueline got pregnant, and one can imagine
how scared she was. Her parents had met Tom and had liked him,
and she wanted Tom to marry her, but like the other Clyde he had
different ideas of what marriage would be like. They waited four
months, and then he persuaded Jacqueline to have an abortion.

This is where the story gets blind and stupid. She might have gone
home to her parents, who seem decent and understanding people, but
she didn't. She might have gone to a welfare agency and asked for
guidance, but she didn't. Tom had met a little man called Pijuan, a
hospital orderly who had mentioned his being available for anyone in
trouble. During the Christmas holidays the crude job was done on a
portable operating table, and everything went wrong, and Jacqueline
died.

Now the two men were really scared. They called in a doctor, who pronounced the girl dead and said it was now a case for the police. But the men had other plans. They cut the body up into some fifty pieces and wrapped them in paper—some of them in Christmas gift paper—and put them in a basket, and distributed them in trash cans and litter baskets along the West Side. None of the pieces has yet been found. Presumably they went the way of all waste in the big incinerators which dispose of the residues of city life.

One wonders how the men could possibly have thought they could get away with it. But remember, they were scared men. Remember that under our laws we doom girls like Jacqueline to the dark underworld of men like the hospital orderly. They are ready to make a quick buck, but an abortion death—with headlines and a long prison term—holds terror for them. So they get desperate in a jam.

There is little more to the story itself. Tom and the orderly have been arrested, and no doubt they will go to prison. Jacqueline's parents have nothing left in life. What was once Jacqueline Smith is no more—not anything, not even a corpse. The newspapers and their headlines, which flare up when there is an abortion tragedy but leave the subject severely alone in between the flare-ups, will soon be yellowed with the age of a few days, and Jacqueline Smith's story will be dug up again only when another abortion death happens.

But I am sad and angry at the whole business—not only at the incredible brutality of the men, but at us, at all of us. Here is another life that could have been lived out, another death that must be placed on the conscience of those who keep our abortion laws rigid and who will not listen to the humanizing ideas of doctors and psychiatrists and social workers.

As long as every abortion is considered criminal, the abortion business will be in the hands of furtive, scared men. I shall keep coming back to this until we figure out some way of handling the hardship cases, broadening our conception of what comes under the heading of therapeutic abortion, and saving other Jacqueline Smiths who walk about in terror throughout our land.

3. Sexual Drive and Social Stigma

March 3, 1958

THOSE WHO THOUGHT we were through with Kinsey and his influence when he died in 1956 must be rubbing their eyes in disbelief as they read the first magazine report, in *McCall's,* on the new Kinsey Institute book *Pregnancy, Birth and Abortion.* It is a sign of how far the women's magazines have moved in the current sexual revolution that the "magazine of togetherness" should risk telling its female readers some of the harsher facts of life—which most of them had probably suspected.

The magazine editors stress how "shocking" the figures in the new volume will seem to their readers. Yet anyone who has studied the first two Kinsey volumes will scarcely find them so. Based on the same sample of 8,000 women interviewed—a sample which comes down to 5,293 after the necessary subtractions—the new figures are consistent with the general American sexual-behavior pattern that has become so familiar by now.

The over-all premarital pregnancy rate among American girls and women is 10 per cent, while the over-all abortion rate is 8 per cent. That is to say, at some point during their lives one out of ten American women will get pregnant before marriage. Of those who get pregnant, 89 per cent will have an abortion. Putting it in round figures, it means that of the present female population, about 8,200,000 have been or will be pregnant before marriage at some time in their lives, and 7,300,000 have had or will have at least one abortion.

These are the over-all rates and figures. Some aspects of their breakdown are even more interesting. The readers of the earlier Kinsey volumes will recall that the striking fact about the male volume was that sexual behavior differed with class differences, while the striking fact about the female volume was that sexual behavior differed with differences between the generations of birth. In the new study, too, the striking differences are those of the generations of birth. For women born in the 1890s, the premarriage pregnancy rate by the age of thirty-five is 7 per cent; for the 1900-1910 generation it is 11 per cent; for the 1910-1920 generation it is 18 per cent.

What these mounting figures mean is that each successive generation of American women has freed itself increasingly from the sexual taboos of the past and has dared to break some of the strong moral conventions in which their mothers and grandmothers were caught. Actually the 18 per cent premarriage pregnancy rate is a more important figure than the over-all 10 per cent rate. It expresses the emerging trend. Whether or not the sexual revolution of women has gone forward in the generation since the Kinsey interviews were held, it has certainly not gone backward.

That is why the authors of the Kinsey study make a guess—and a pretty good one—that the pregnancy rate of the contemporary and future generations is likely to be much closer to an over-all 20 per cent than an over-all 10 per cent. If the 10 per cent figure is "shocking," the double figure is likely to be doubly shocking.

The same is true of the abortion rate. The over-all Kinsey figure of 8 per cent for induced abortions of the total female population is on the careful and conservative side. Here again the figure is rising with each generation. Consider the contrast between 5 per cent for the 1890-1900 generation, 9 per cent for the 1900-1910, and 15 per cent for the 1910-1920. The contemporary and future abortion figures are thus likely to be almost double the 8 per cent figure taken from the total Kinsey sample.

Aside from the pregnancy rate and the abortion rate, there is the question of the relation between the two. Put differently, why do so few of the premarriage pregnancies end in birth, and so many in abortion? The answer has to do with the relative secrecy and stigma of pregnancy, birth and abortion. Underlying the whole problem of premarital relations is the basic conflict between the strength of the sexual drive and the strength of the social taboos against it. The Kinsey authors point out that for a girl to keep herself and her suitor "at a high pitch of emotional and sexual excitement for five to ten years from the beginning of dating to marriage" is difficult without yielding to the sexual drive.

Hence the high pregnancy rate, despite the increased knowledge and use of contraceptives. The pregnancy itself can be kept, at least for a time, relatively a private affair. But the social ban against having an illegitimate child is still a severe one. Thus, in nine cases out of ten, the resort is to abortion—which can also be kept a relatively private affair, even though it involves terrible fear and anguish.

March 5, 1958

All forty-eight states make induced abortions illegal and impose heavy penalties, with only slight loopholes for emergency cases. I suppose the theory behind it is that outlawry will make the expectant unwed mother decide to have the child. But the figures cut the ground from under this theory. Where a "shotgun marriage" is arranged after pregnancy, the girl does bear the child in three out of four cases. But of the unmarried only 6 per cent (one out of seventeen) actually have the child. In nine cases out of ten (89 per cent) there is an abortion.

What this means is that, however terrifying the abortion ordeal, the stigma of having an illegitimate child is even more terrifying.

That is the tragedy enacted in the dark. It would be hard to argue that the youngsters have no inkling of what they are letting themselves in for. The furtive search for a doctor, whether genuine or spurious; the grapevine reports about who is reliable and who is not; the sordid bargaining over the fee; the underground atmosphere of suspicion and fear; the faceless men who run the "abortion mills"—some out of greed, some out of cynicism, some with an admixture of defiance and compassion; the emotional numbness as the business of life and death is carried on with secrecy and anonymity, as on an assembly line—surely these terrors thrust their shadow before, and in this shadow the young people move like sleepwalkers.

Yet they do walk on. The counterterror of illegitimacy, relatively mild in other cultures, is strong with us. All the laws of all the forty-eight states have not availed against it. All they have succeeded in doing is to thrust abortion into the dark underground, where it leaves the kind of scar on the memory and the unconscious which no man can convey and which no Kinsey team could possibly calculate in statistical tables. That is the price we pay for letting a veto group continue to dominate our legislative pattern on the question of abortion.

One striking conclusion of the new Kinsey Institute study is that while the premarriage pregnancy rate varies with social and educational factors, the abortion rate does not. It is pretty steady—that is to say, it has the rigidity that comes from the fear of breaking the illegitimacy taboo.

The question of religion is an interesting one. The religiously devout, especially the Catholics, have insisted hardest on not relaxing the laws. They will perhaps be consoled by the Kinsey study, which indicates that devout girls "get into trouble" a good deal less than the others. The Kinsey statistical sample is largely Protestant, with a few Catholics and Jews represented. By using the Protestants as a base, the study indicates that fewer of the devout girls have premarital sexual relations, fewer become pregnant (only 5 per cent as compared with the over-all figure of 10 per cent for American women) and fewer have abortions (3 per cent as compared with an over-all figure of 8 per cent).

Presumably these conclusions would apply to devout Catholics and Jews as well. Yet even here one notes that, despite the severe religious ban on abortions, three out of five of the devout girls who "get into trouble" go on into the abortion mill. One may infer from all this that religious devoutness does have an effect on the sexual behavior of American women. This being so, it may be an argument for further efforts at religious teaching, although these efforts are not always successful. It is certainly not an argument for imposing this religious view on the large majority of Americans who don't share it. Nor is it an argument for the continued severity of state laws whose only consequence is to thrust the whole tragic abortion story further into the darkness.

There remains the questions of the experience of other countries which have relaxed the legislative ban. The survey deals with the experience of Denmark, Russia, Iceland, Sweden, Finland and Japan. Of these the Danish method of handling the problem seems the one from which we can learn most. The Danes allow applications for legal abortion which are made before a board composed of a psychiatrist, a physician and a social worker. Five per cent of all pregnancies end in legal abortions, although illegal abortions have still not been wholly wiped out. The system is far from perfect, but it is worth serious study and open discussion.

April 7, 1958

I pointed in my earlier pieces to the tragedy of the unmarried mother, who stumbles about in darkness between the social disgrace of illegitimacy and the unnamed terror of the abortion mills. I wel-· come the new Kinsey Institute material which sheds light on the prac- tices not only of unmarried girls, but of women who have been or are married.

They too get pregnant without wanting to, and they too resort to abortions in substantial numbers. Three out of four (75 per cent) of the women who have been married (and are either separated, di- vorced or widowed) continue to have sexual relations. One out of seven of these women (14 per cent) becomes pregnant, and four out of five of these pregnancies end in abortions.

What explains this behavior? The two chief authors of the new Kin- sey study, Wardell Pomeroy and Paul Gebhard, guess that for- merly married women go on with sex relations because the habit pattern has been established. Their frequency is greater than in the case of the unmarried girls, probably because the original inhibitions have been largely removed.

One would add the guess that most men—married and unmarried —find a special sense of sexual adventure attached to a woman who has already been married, and are more direct in their advances. The women, in turn, are likely to be lonely and therefore more vulnerable. The study finds, however, that it is mostly the divorcees, and not the widows, who become pregnant; and their record tends to show that they had been "careless" during their marriage as well, and that they had been sexually experimental even before marriage.

I have said that four out of five pregnancies of the formerly married women, chiefly the divorcees, end in abortions. Although the stigma of bearing an illegitimate child cannot be so great for them as for the unmarried girls, it is still a strong one; but it may be that the abor- tionist holds fewer terrors for them.

But surely for the married woman who gets pregnant there should be little drive toward abortion, because there is no stigma of illegiti- macy, as there is for those without benefit of clergy. Yet 17 per cent of all pregnancies within marriage result in abortion. As the authors of the study put it: "The most frequent patron of the abortionist is—the American wife."

How account for the abortions of married women, when the ur- gency of social disgrace is not present? This is a baffling question until you remember that disgrace is not the only penalty involved in an unwanted birth. For married women the burden of having an unwanted child may be the decisive factor.

We had better accept the fact that the American wife—and her husband—have generally come to regard the planning of their families as both a freedom and a necessity. True, the revolution in contraceptives has placed at their command a means for family spacing and planning not so easily available to former generations. But when for any reason it fails or is not used, abortion has become an added resort. Call it selfish, if you will. Say that it is purchased at a high psychic as well as physical cost. Add perhaps that it blunts some of the sensitivity to human life. But all of these have to be weighed against the dominant fact that American adults have a certain image of what they want their lives to be, and they do not accept the fact of pregnancy as final if it interferes with that image.

That, I take it, is the meaning of some of the figures I have cited from the new study. I should add, however, that there is also a difference between the generations. The highest abortion rate was among the wives who came to childbearing during the Great Depression of the 1930s, and the lowest among the youngest generation of wives (only 10 per cent), whose record seems even lower than that of their grandmothers. The upswing in births came when the depression was conquered and Americans recaptured a faith in their future. The young people these days who are having bigger families are also having fewer abortions.

4. Birth Control and Sin

September 19, 1958

ALL THE NOSEGAYS and brickbats are now in, and it is clear that the decision of the New York Board of Hospitals on the birth control problem is a smash hit—except for the Catholics.

It was unfortunate that the decision had to come after months of bitter public controversy between the great faiths, especially between the Protestant Council and the Roman Catholic Archdiocese, but not all controversy is bad. It would be absurd if in a "three-religion America" the pursuit of good public relations between the faiths were to mean that no great conflicts in community living could be argued out on grounds of principle.

If the Catholic Archdiocese had contented itself with laying down a canon of belief for Catholics, I should not be moved to comment. But it assails the board's action as rejecting "traditional morality, the teaching of all Christian and Jewish belief, until recent times," and claims that "these truths are not the exclusive possession of any church, but the law obliging all men." This is pretty sweeping and includes you and me.

It is true that the widespread use of contraception is relatively recent. The first real crusade for it was launched in England, by a learned and militant labor leader called Francis Place, in a book published in 1822. Place had nineteen children of his own, and five had died in childbirth. He wrote and distributed his book in order to help ease a bit the burden of poverty, starvation and wretchedness which uncontrolled births had placed on English working-class families. In America, too, in the 1830s, there were some pamphlets on birth control that raised the roof for a time.

The turning point in England came in the trial of Annie Besant and Charles Bradlaugh in 1877 for selling one of the American pamphlets. The trial awoke England. And in America, Margaret Sanger went to jail in 1916 for opening a contraceptive clinic in Brooklyn. It is true that we have moved a long way from these barbarities. All that happens now to the members of the Board of Hospitals is that they are accused of "introducing an immoral practice in our hospitals that perverts the nature and dignity of man."

But does it really? How much dignity of man—or woman—could one find among the English poor who practiced infanticide in the eighteenth century as their only way of keeping another child from becoming another burden? When John Stuart Mill walked through St. James's Park on his way to work at India House in the 1820s, he saw a bundle under a tree. It was an abandoned baby, "blue, new-born, and strangled, wrapped up in grimy rags." It was so shaking an experience that young Mill started to distribute birth control tracts, and he spent a few nights in jail.

You can dig out any number of these episodes from history. I mention them only because we tend to forget that contraception is not a matter of "personal whim or caprice," as the statement of the Archdiocese describes it. We shall miss the whole point of it unless we remember that it is a response to the bitter, tragic experience of generations of broken and sick mothers and neglected children.

True, I agree with the Archdiocese that morality is not based on "the power of a majority vote." But surely the experience of history, ever since primitive times, sheds some light on human needs and on what can be done to make the human condition less frustrated, pathetic and brutal.

To speak of the lifting of the birth control ban in New York hospitals as against "natural law" has little meaning for non-Catholics. In a remarkable recent book called *The Sanctity of Life,* which has a chapter on the control of conception, Glanville Williams points out that the epithet "unnatural" has been variously applied to "vaccination, anesthesia, male gynecologists, the emancipation of women, and the use of steam engines."

It would be unrewarding at this late date to argue about the meaning of the Scriptural texts (including mainly the story of Onan in Genesis 38) on which the "unnatural" character of contraception is supposed to be based. The historian of ideas is likely to point out that the Catholic doctrine was mainly evolved by Augustine in the early centuries of Christianity, and by Aquinas in the Middle Ages, and it ought not to be decisive about the fate of a worried, harassed and perhaps sick woman in the New York hospitals today.

The Archdiocese statement recommends that "when a mother's health is in jeopardy," she and her husband practice "abstinence from the exercise of the natural faculty." This is described as a form of "heroism." There can be no quarrel with those who believe in this kind of heroism. But we have learned enough about the highly complex human mind, as well as the human body, to know the frustration and warping and bleakness it carries with it.

Actually the Archdiocese statement refers obliquely to the permitted Catholic practice of the "rhythm method," which is in principle a form of family limitation. I am afraid that the Church, since the 1930 Encyclical of Pius XI, has conceded the principle of family planning: what it is still arguing is the methods. But in arguing the methods it brings in the whole armory of the castigation of sin that it has used historically in fighting against the principle.

5. The Strange World of the Adolescent

October 13, 1958

IF I INTERPRET rightly the remarkable set of interviews with teen-agers by Edward Kosner and Marie Grebenc which ran in the *Post* last week, American adolescents are not as hot on the trail to hell as some of our moralizers have feared.

Here is the portrait I get of New York adolescents, and how they behave and what they think on dating and sexual expression.

The teen-agers are not content with accepting at face value the injunctions of their elders to wait until they are married before they explore the mysteries of sex. They are not sure about what is right or wrong for them and are still groping and experimenting, but they are pretty sure that the moral taboos of the adult culture do not represent eternal verities. Whatever else they may be doubtful about, they are certain that sex and sin are not synonyms.

As I see them, they are caught between two strong drives. On the one hand, there are all sorts of hungers in them, including awakening desire, and a strong curiosity about the other sex, and a hunger for life and for not being left out of things or passed by. On the other hand they are in the grip of fears—the fear of what people will think and say, the fear of being awkward and inadequate on their dates, the fear of hurting their parents, the fear of being bruised themselves in a sexual adventure that could mean disaster.

This explains many of the contradictions in the interviews, as the adolescent swings between exploration and conformity, between an intense curiosity and hunger for adventure and an equally intense desire for security. This is not the "beat" generation but a generation caught in a limbo between a hell of taboos in which they have ceased to believe and a heaven of fulfillment for which they scarcely dare hope.

Some years back I wrote a *Post* series called "Morals on the Campus," in which I used some college interviews to portray the troubled spirit of American youth at that time. The new interviews are with teen-agers below seventeen; even the college freshmen included in the sample of 50 boys and 50 girls were interviewed just at the start of their college year. It is a high-school and vocational-school population we are talking about.

Some parents and observers may be troubled by the fact that 30 of the 50 boys and 10 of the 50 girls have already had sexual intercourse. Given the Kinsey figures, and what we know about the nature and pressures of big-city life, these seem to me to be moderate rather than alarming figures. What would be more important, but what we do not and cannot know short of depth interviews, is the residue these experiences have left on the mind.

If parents and moralists would start not with their moral codes and taboos but with some conception of what a healthy personality is, they would still be troubled about their youngsters, but they would be asking different questions about them. They would ask what self-image the youngster has, what signs he gives of growing and of fulfilling himself, what chance he has of achieving a sense of his own identity rather than of copying what others are doing, how real a picture he has of the world, what wholeness of personality he is developing.

For these are the real badges of mental health, and not the black-and-white statistical questions of whether the adolescent parks in a car or doesn't, pets or doesn't, comes home late or doesn't, gets into bed with someone or doesn't.

On one important phase the interviews trouble me—that of precocity. Of the 50 girls, 32 began to date between the ages of twelve and fourteen. As for the boys, some start at twelve, most of them between thirteen and fifteen. I don't think this is healthy, mainly because at twelve or thirteen the drives are quite unlikely to be those of either sexual desire or of the exploration of personality. The precocity is, I fear, due more to the conformity of both the children and their parents—the child's fear of being left behind by other adolescents, the parents' fear that their children may not prove "popular" unless they start as early as others.

Everything happens fast in our culture. Boys and girls shoot up fast in their physical growth, they learn to drive cars early, they watch TV early, see movies and plays early. They learn social dancing early, and the girls have their hair waved early and wear nylons early. Note that most of this is with the approval—and even the prodding—of parents. Is it any wonder that some of them take the cue, and move ahead faster than the parents want them to? Or that the whole relationship with the other sex becomes mechanical, surfacy, emotionally thin? Or that the same fear of being left behind, the same insecurity which makes them start dating so young, also makes them hurry into marriages which prove disastrous?

It is the insecurity which stands out most strikingly from all the interviews. One gets the feeling that dating and sex are not determined, as they should be, by personal needs and personal feelings for one another, but by social standards. In many cases they date early because they think it is expected of them, they pet not necessarily because they like it but because the other girls and boys do it, and (especially in the case of the boys) they try to "make out" with the girl in order to confirm their manliness, while the girl may yield either because other girls do or because she fears she will no longer be "popular" and will stop getting dates with the popular boys.

Similarly "steady dating" (happily the figures show that it is beginning to lose its hold) seems to be an insecurity pact between two adolescents, not out of commitment but out of a poverty of the imagination.

Finally, I am struck by the pathos of the contrasts in the interviews. Not all our youngsters are precocious or sophisticated. Some are lonely and desolate. There are boys who, at sixteen, have never had a date because they were too shy or too unconfident to ask, or feared they would be rejected. There are girls in the sample who at seventeen have never dated at all, whose parents forbid them to go out or to bring anyone home. There is frustration and heartbreak, or maybe only a kind of numbness, in them.

How many mistakes we adults could avoid with our children if we tried to look at them through the mind and the world of an adolescent.

October 14, 1958

It is hard to remember when you see a seventeen-year-old boy out with a girl on a date that the Kinsey figures show this boy at this age as being at the threshold of his strongest sexual powers. It is hard to remember—but it may prod us into understanding why boys at sixteen and seventeen talk and think of sex constantly. With the girls, we are told, it is love, love, love all the time. With both of them the dating, past and to come, and the petting that is almost inseparable from dates, form the temperature and climate of youth and hope and despair.

If parents and teachers read some anthropology they might see that American adolescents have a harder time with sex than do adolescents in most of the other cultures. To be sure, in some cultures sex (like the rest of life) is full of perils for male and female alike; and Frazer's *Golden Bough* tells of cases of terrible cruelty to girls who broke the code. But Margaret Mead has told us of the sexual permissiveness accorded to youngsters in the growing-up years in cultures she has studied. Among Malinowski's Trobriand Islanders, the sex play of children is not only allowed but encouraged; and the teen-agers there are allowed to pair off and sleep together, although they must not eat together in public. There is nothing secret or tortured about sex with them because, unlike American adolescents, they have never been taught that sex is sinful.

The giveaway on American attitudes toward adolescent sex may be found in the books by the scholars who discuss it under the heading of the "socialization" of the growing child, along with food habits, manners, discipline, height, weight and "interpersonal relations." One almost expects to see it treated along with elimination; and indeed nocturnal sex dreams are mentioned with the same discreet gentility as elimination—both being inescapable functions, but best left undiscussed.

These genteel whispers about what occupies the center of the stage in the adolescent's mind constantly are a mark of the Puritanism which still hangs over our attitudes toward adolescent sex, even when the big media and the novels are blatantly concerned with adult sex. The young people see this contradiction; it is one of the things that builds a wall between them and the adults.

Whoever is responsible for building it, the wall is there. The world of the adolescent is a strange world into which the parent and the teacher are rarely able to enter.

Young people at this age are supremely capturable by all sorts of dreams and hopes, and they are captured by the mystery and wonder and the dark trembling of the veil that still separates them from what life holds in store. Despite the bluster that boys may enact toward each other, or the knowing looks that girls may exchange, the real mind of the adolescent belies both the bluster and the sophistication. There are unsureness and self-doubts and a fear of being inadequate, along with the sense of the mysteriousness of it all. There is shyness, and sudden flushing, and a quickened heartbeat. There is the privacy of the cherished adolescent diary. There are the long letters exchanged, so often full of reflections about life and not just about sex.

Parents rarely know about this strange world—about the aching desire not necessarily for sex but just to have someone to share with and to explore, and about the minor defeats that seem so major and so often account for the sullenness and dejection into which the youngsters are plunged.

Yet this is, I am convinced, the heart of the matter. Young people at this age want to explore sex, but they also want to explore other personalities, and themselves and the mystery and magic of life.

There is another end of the spectrum—that of the young gang members whom Harrison Salisbury has studied with perceptiveness in his just published book, *The Shook-Up Generation* (Harper). Here you move into a very different world, that of "debs" who are as hard as their male gang toughs, of the "fish" dance, the group prostitutes, the "line-up" of the gang for a single girl, and the "club babies" whose paternity it is impossible to guess. This is the area where sex is almost wholly desensitized and nearly always accompanied by violence and sadism.

About these youngsters we must ask what kind of monsters our society is creating out of its inner agonies. But they form only a tiny part of the margin of our young people—only a fraction of 1 per cent. The rest are not monsters. They are mostly sensitive youngsters, trying to find out who they are, trying to test themselves and their dates, asking perpetually, "How far can I, should I, go?"—and rarely finding the answer with any certainty.

Rebels? Alas, no. Mostly pattern followers; only the patterns they follow are not the codes the adults try to preach to them but the operative codes among their fellows. I wish there were more rebellion among them—the meaningful kind of rebellion which leads to growth and individuality, not the shallow kind that looks for "fun" and "kicks."

October 16, 1958

The sexual act itself looms less large in the adolescent imagination than it does in the minds of adults, for whom it may become in one way or another obsessive. The boys who were interviewed tended to be pretty matter-of-fact about the whole subject. They didn't get lyrical about it nor did they surround it with a haze of sentiment. "You get a chance to do it—and that's all," said one. And another: "What do you care who it is, as long as you get your pleasure?"

Even the phrasing used tells a good deal about the American social context of adolescent sex. The most constant expression among boys is "making out"—or perhaps just the verb "get," as in "Are you getting much?" One thinks of how apt was R. H. Tawney's phrase, "the acquisitive society," and how the atmosphere of "getting" carries over from the business ethos into the erotic one.

If the remarks I have quoted are at all characteristic, what troubles me about them is the evidence of our young people becoming desensitized. When boys start with a wholly mechanical feeling about sex ("as long as you get your pleasure"), it won't be long before they feel that everything else in life is a matter of indifferently replaceable parts. The ultimate immorality is to use people as if they were objects, and the final annihilation is that in the process you become a non-valuing cipher and cease to exist as a person.

This comes close to saying, as I am more and more convinced, that the central problem is one of identity. The boys I have quoted deny the identity of the girls they use, basically (I suspect) because they feel no identity in themselves.

I fear that something of the same thing is true of many of the girls who were interviewed, although they used very different language. The shadow of the sexual act hovers over them all the time. "Where is the line?" asked one. "It goes a bit farther each time." Only 10 of the 50 girls admitted to having had sexual intercourse, and 15 more thought it was likely they would before marriage. Yet there were few signs that they took much pleasure in the thought. If teen-age girls are preoccupied with anything, it is not with sex itself but with dating— not with a biological and psychological drive, but with a social one.

"Some things just happen," one girl remarked. And another: "They more or less expect it as a price." And still another: "Everyone else does. You're expected to." And lastly the remark of the girl who was explaining why she succumbed: "I wanted him to like me."

The heart of these comments is that a teen-age girl wants, more than anything else, to date—whether it is casual dating or "steady dating" or "going steady" or "dating steadily." Not to date is to be left out and to appear left out—to be "not popular," which is the ultimate scar to bear.

Along with dating, however, goes petting—an ingenious social invention, where the thus-far-and-no-farther line is likely to be set by the girl, receding steadily as the dating becomes steady. The function of this social invention is to square desire with conscience and allow the boy and girl to experience each other without letting the experience become destructive. As an institutional contrivance I regard it as an American contribution to world culture.

The *Post* interviews indicate that 36 of the 50 girls take part in petting—say four out of five. Whether they do it as an act of their own volition is, however, another question. One girl's comment rang pretty true: "They're afraid they won't be able to hold on to a boy if they don't." This may apply to petting, and it may at times apply to "going all the way."

Again, if these remarks are descriptive of how our teen-agers really feel, the pathos of it lies in the absence of identity. Parents often tell their teen-agers that, whatever their decisions about sex, it should always be accompanied by love. But surely at fifteen or sixteen they can know little about love, despite Juliet and Beatrice and Annabel Lee. It is a difficult and complex emotion, and the capacity to love and to be loved is likely to be purchased at the cost of considerable grief. I should be content if the teen-agers did not aim at quite so romantic a height. I should be content if they aimed at treating each other and themselves like persons, instead of like objects to be used.

If a girl pets because she can't keep the boy without petting, and because she can't date if she loses the boy, all the high-flown talk of love doesn't make a person out of her. If a boy pets because he wants to "make out," he will chase the shadow of "making out" into business or power all the days of his life.

I am less interested in the usual stereotyped worries about the "morality" of our teen-agers than I am in whether they discover who they are. There are some who seem to have an underground river of identity flowing through their being, from which they nourish their strength and zest for life. Such people will never run empty. The problem is to discover the river, and the sources from which it rises, and the sea to which it flows.

THE FLEDGLINGS

1. Conversation between the Generations

June 17, 1952

I SAID GOODBYE yesterday to a class of a hundred students at Brandeis University with whom I have worked for the past three years. When a college is still young, and when the edge of excitement in building everything fresh has not begun to wear off, Commencement can be a moving thing.

In a small college you get to know your students. And alas, they get to know you, with the fierce thoroughness with which a zoologist knows the bug he has been observing through the microscope. After they have had a professor around a while, the students come to accept him as they do the leaky plumbing.

And the teachers get a sneaking fondness for their students too. You watch them come in with freshman eagerness, and you agonize through all their phases—rebellious, sophisticated, aesthetic, religious, cynical, defeatist and all-knowing. You watch them go from phase to phase in dizzying succession, like a car you are supposed to be steering but that gets out of hand and careens down the road steering you.

The speech of the class president was keyed to the prevailing student mood. He said he and his fellows didn't expect much of life, that they had no illusions any of them would set the world on fire, that it was a pretty bleak world anyway. It was the Generation without Illusions talking. It left us with a feeling of being cornered in a narrow corridor, with the exits blocked.

Then Eleanor Roosevelt rose to talk to the graduating class. She spoke of how the university was founded much as the whole country had been settled. "One of the things that made this country great," she said, "was that we were ready to adventure, to try new things of the mind and the spirit . . . You came into a world that is not an easy world to live in. You will find many things that are not what you hoped they would be.

"It does no good," she went on, "to try to place the blame, or to feel badly about this—unless you are determined that you are yourselves going to do better than what has been done before. You say you will not set the world on fire. Perhaps not. But how does any one of you know that it may not be exactly he who does set at least your corner of the world on fire? For nobody knows who it may turn out to be who effects the change that counts.

"Have the courage to be free," she ended. "Believe me, it takes courage. It is often easier to accept the offer of security than to adventure . . . People who achieve things are rarely the secure. Adventure is always more interesting."

This was a conversation between the generations. Curiously, it was the older one that was pleading for courage, and scorning security. I think what has happened to the college students of today is that they have seen so many dreams collapsing and so many wounds inflicted on the sensitive, that they have drawn a protective sheath around themselves.

Who can blame them for a kind of animal wisdom that this shows? But they will learn in time that while people who try to light fires often get burned, they also with their blaze dispel some of the darkness—perhaps in themselves too.

2. Be My Unsteady Date

March 22, 1957

UP TO NOW the campaign of the Catholic Church against too early steady dating, especially in parochial high schools, has been mainly a local matter. But it became a matter of national policy when Msgr. Irving De Blanc, who heads the family division of the National Catholic Welfare Conference, gave an authoritative statement of the Catholic viewpoint at Milwaukee to Catholic laymen and clergy from every part of the nation.

This doesn't mean that the Church is ready to legislate yet on "going steady" by making it a mortal sin, as predicted by a writer in a Paulist magazine. But one gathers that the tentative stage is past, and that the decision has been taken to try persuasion and pressures—pulpit warnings, school assembly talks, school expulsions if necessary.

Readers will recall a constant succession of episodes during the past half year. Last October there was a ban on steady dating at St. Mary's High School at Lynn, near Boston; in November there was a similar ban at Sacred Heart Academy in Buffalo; in December these schools were followed by St. Francis College at Loretto, Pennsylvania; last month the climax was reached when four students of St. Anthony High School at Bristol, Connecticut, were formally expelled because they and their parents refused to go along with a similar ban.

While Catholic circles are most openly stirred by it, the problem is one for all of us, and it needs a candid and searching discussion not limited to the doctrines of Catholicism.

My own feeling is that steady dating of kids of high-school age, before they have achieved any kind of intellectual insight or emotional maturity, is a pretty silly business. I feel the same even about college students, who seem everywhere to be settling down to a dismal boredom-by-the-couple. But my reason for viewing it with a jaundiced eye is rather different from the view that it leads to immorality and sin. It is hard to think of these youngsters as sinners. I tend to see rather the shrinking of their lives into a narrow compass just when everything should be beginning to blossom for them.

Only a decade ago the sociologists were still complaining that American girls were obsessed with getting a different date every time they went out, and that they were rated in their group for their popularity as dates. This was the now classic "dating-rating pattern." But the new pattern is for youngsters to start dating at the precocious age of fourteen, and by the time they are in college (or even seniors in high school) they are behaving like old married couples.

I suppose the definition of "going steady" is that each of the pair, forsaking all other dates, gets into the habit of going everywhere with the other, to dances, socials, to the movies, to the ice-cream parlor or jukebox hangout. Sometimes this premature and precocious fidelity leads to sexual intimacy, sometimes only to petting. In too many cases, especially when early sexual education is frowned upon by church and family, it leads to the tragedy of children out of wedlock or to forced marriages. But most often it leads only to boredom and stagnation.

Why do they do it? They are scared of getting left behind, alone and unwanted. "Without a steady," said one of the Lynn teen-agers, "you are not even in line for a dance at the school record hop."

You don't solve this kind of emotional insecurity by cracking down on it, as the Catholic Church seems intent on doing. All that will happen is that you impose an added burden of guilt on the shoulders of the already anxiety-ridden boy and girl. They will start dating in secret, and the secret steady dater—like the secret steady drinker—can be an object of pity. What little fun is left in it dribbles away, yet the relationship persists.

The best attack is to attack the conditions that breed the insecurity of our young people. A lot of the blame rests with parents who are too competitive and anxious about whether their darlings will have dates, and who pass their anxiety on to them. A lot of it rests on the shoulders of mothers who are worried about whether their daughters will be married at nineteen or twenty, and who are then surprised when they find the daughters digging in for the siege at fifteen. And a lot of it rests with a society where fears are rampant and get communicated very early in life.

But I don't mean to absolve the young people wholly. They ought to have more fun than they are having, not less—they ought to travel more widely, expose themselves to more diverse situations, explore a range of personalities.

Instead of which they seem to be running for the kennels fast, oh, so fast. Worried about their immorality? Maybe they are immoral, but if they are it is because they are too conformist about it. This is not flaming youth that we have; it is the generation of unflaming youth.

3. The Limbo Generation

October 15, 1958

TWO LETTERS in the *Post* yesterday interested me. One was from a high-school senior who wrote, "My parents trust and respect my decisions and I would never do anything to lead them to believe that their faith was ill-placed." Lucky girl. Lucky parents. The other said, "Parents and most adults know what's going on." I wonder.

I start with the matter of sexual education. There are few cultures which leave the sexual instruction of young people so completely to chance. A study by G. V. Ramsey in 1943 found that 95 per cent of a sample of 300 boys knew about sex at fourteen, and that most of them even knew about the use of contraceptives. But in 90 per cent of the cases the information had come not from parents or from school but from other boys. That is still true today. It is true of the girls too; as one girl told the *Post* reporter, "Sex is something you learn by osmosis."

Curiously we complain of the tyranny of the peer group over teenagers, yet we leave to the same peer group the crucial function of explaining the mystery and mastery of sex. One wonders how much an adolescent would know about sex if he knew only what he learned from home, church and school.

The gap between the generations is a real one, not only in recent immigrant families or broken or impoverished families, but also in those that are ready to give the youngsters everything but understanding and love—mainly because the parents don't have understanding and love for each other. They are not at ease with themselves.

The strange thing is that there is no revolt in the present young generation, but only a kind of wariness and discontent, especially on sexual matters. This is not a "beat" generation, nor even a "shook-up" one, but a limbo generation. To be in limbo is to be uncertain of where you are going or how you mean to get there, and to make temporariness and unsureness a permanent way of life.

I have spoken of the need for sex knowledge at this age. There is also a need for shared life experience, and for growth. Who can have forgotten the case of sixteen-year-old Diana Humphries, of Houston, who killed her brother with a rifle? She was blond and attractive and bright, but she had no boy friends, and life at home was empty. "We were always getting up, going to work and school, coming home, eating, cooking meals, washing dishes and going to bed and getting up again . . . It was too much for all of us and we were always tired. So I lay there in bed and planned how I was going to kill us all."

How many times we have heard some teen-ager cry, "Nothing ever happens"—by which, of course, they mean, "Nothing ever happens *to me.*" These are years of growth, and life must not stand still—it must yield a sense of growth. That is why the teen-agers who are shut out of experience—including sexual experience, however mild and tentative it may be—are storing up repressed explosives which may bring them to grief.

Along with the need for experience, there is the need for enough freedom so that the teen-ager can make the experience part of himself. Only thus can he grow into adulthood.

But I don't stop there, as parents a decade ago tended to do. Freedom for teen-agers to make their own decisions on sexual matters can become destructive unless it is contained within a frame of guidance and order. This is where the dilemma comes in. Since the teen-agers have no experience, it is hard for them to make decisions and choices. But unless they can start making choices, they can accumulate no experience to guide them.

Faced with this dilemma the parents often abdicate the whole problem and either bear down hard on their children with a rigid and impossible code or else give up helplessly and let them do as they desire. Both courses of action are disastrous. The teen-ager needs a glimpse of the possible enchantment of life, and its griefs too, in order to shape and confirm his image of himself. But he also needs a sense of limits, because too much freedom—without a firm and consistent set of limits —can only leave him (or her) bewildered and scared.

I have spoken of the teen-ager's need for sex knowledge, the need for experience and growth, the need for responsibilities and choices of his own within a frame of guidance. There remains the most difficult of all—the need for a clear role he can play, which he must get not only by watching other teen-agers but also from adults.

I fear that the models which our adolescents have before them are not often the best. When they turn from the slick stories and the Big Media dreams they must get a terrible sense of unreality as they compare them with some of the adults they see all around them—the brittle women and the tough-talking, cynical men, or perhaps just the empty men and women who have lost their love for each other and their hope for life.

The most important thing that parents can do for the teen-agers is to give them the example of an adult relationship which has not become desensitized. I mean one in which sexual attraction and the life of the senses still remain as part of the shared experience of two interlinked lives.

4. The Beatniks: A Long View

November 12, 1958

WE WERE TALKING about the generations last evening, and someone asked, "How long is a generation?" Thirty years, said one. Twenty, said another. Only fifteen, said a third.

My own feeling was that a generation is not measured out by units of time but is bounded by two dramatic events that enclose it. Thus there was a generation between the Spanish-American War and the First World War, another between the end of the war and the stock market crash of 1929, still another between Roosevelt's first election and the dropping of the first A-bomb in 1945. I shouldn't be surprised if there were to be some great event around 1960 which would round out the generation that began with the "good news of damnation" at Hiroshima.

Note that these four generations stretch out over the first sixty years of our century, with an average span of fifteen years.

The first was the "progressive" generation, whose heroes were the reformers and muckrakers; the second was the "lost" one or the "Jazz Age," whose symbols were F. Scott Fitzgerald's parties and Hemingway's exiles; the third was the "social consciousness" generation, which manned the picket lines and fought in Spain and wept for Czechoslovakia and dreamt of a new world; and the current one is the "beat" generation, which seems to weep (or at least whimper) over itself, and rejects causes, and dreams of discovering some mystic truth on a mountaintop.

Its latest manifesto is Jack Kerouac's novel *The Dharma Bums* (Viking), which one may now add to his *On the Road* (Signet) and *The Subterraneans* (Evergreen). There has been a mellowing in Kerouac—that "nonviolent revolutionary"—which shows less of the revolutionary and more of the nonviolence. The drinking and the sex and the purposeless journeys on freight cars are still there, but the Zen doctrine is now foremost, and I almost expect the next novel to be laid on a peak in Tibet.

It is a curious fact that the most publicized partisans of "beatness" show little despair or directed anger. If it is despair that our young people want they can get it in Genet's plays; if it is anger, they can get it in John Osborne or Kingsley Amis; if it is rebellion, with any vision of another social order toward which they may be rebelling, there are no visible spokesmen for it. At times one concludes that they are out for kicks, and the more desensitized of them may in fact be out exactly for that. Kerouac now says they are out for Truth and Beatitude—which is exactly where he gets (for me) fuzzy and dreary.

But there is one thing about his novels that is deeply characteristic of the continental sweep of America. De Tocqueville pointed out in 1835 that Americans carry their geographical restlessness to the point of a frenzy of movement. It is truer now than ever.

Genet's play *Deathwatch* shows three men pacing a prison cell. Beckett's characters either squat on a bit of desert patch or sit and die in ashcans and are covered up. But Kerouac's are always on the move. And even the quest for the peace of Zen has no Oriental calm in it, but American dynamism.

There is a new book from which I have learned more about the drama of the generations than from any of the touted and advertised novels. It is José Ortega y Gasset's *Man and Crisis* (Norton), another posthumous book of the Spanish philosopher's lectures. These are on the theme of the repetitive beat of crises in history.

For Ortega y Gasset each man's life is divided into five ages or roughly fifteen years each—childhood, youth, initiation, dominance and old age. Men enter history in the two mature ages—initiation (thirty to forty-five) and dominance (forty-five to sixty). The first is the zone of years in which gestation and creation take place; the second contains the years of dominance and command. And for me the crucial point he makes is that in every period of history these two generations do not come in succession but are at work at much the same time, so you have the gestators and creators in conflict with the dominators and commanders.

If I could add to this my own emphasis, that a historic generation presents these two age groups struggling and thinking and feeling within a dramatic frame set by two symbolic world events, I should suggest that this is a working approach to the problem of the conflict of the generations.

That may account, at least partly, for the failure of communication between the generations today. More important in some ways than class or regional or ethnic conflicts are the conflicts between the generations. The older regards the younger as wild, desensitized, demoralized, delinquent, out only for sex and kicks. The younger regards the older as smug, superficial, mawkish, out of touch with reality and truth, hypocritical.

Both are, of course, quite right—each from its angle of vision. And from my own angle of vision I must confess that it is hard for me to accept the truth of either. I find lacking in both of them the kind of outlook that our era (I call it era, not generation, because it includes both the active generations) will need in the days ahead.

This outlook will have to include both a militant humanism and a tragic stoicism—a willingness to fight for human survival in a society that makes more sense, but also (since with all our striving we can never escape tragedy) the embracing of the human fate with fortitude and without whimpering.

5. The Cult of Toughness

March 18, 1959

WE ARE being enveloped these days with speeches, declamations, editorials, sermons and manifestoes on how soft we are in America, especially on our young, and how tough we had better become if we want to save civilization. Every other word you hear is "discipline," or "rugged," or "hard." We are being deluged by rivers of hardness, we are wallowing in seas of ruggedness.

I have been reading the *Wall Street Journal* for my sins, and not a day passes when the editorial and column page doesn't include an attack on the profligate government spenders or the pusillanimous progressive educators, or both. In fact, there seems to be a standing motto on the editor's desk, written in letters of lead, that "soft money makes soft minds"—and vice versa. Up in Massachusetts a high-school principal, confronted by a group of sassy students, simply thwacked them good and hard on the seat of their pants, not bothering to persuade them intellectually or argue with them; his logic, I gather, was *a posteriori*. And in New York State the legislators passed a bill empowering teachers to use "reasonable" physical punishment of students. As the *Post* editorial put it, the theory was to cure the Beat Generation by turning it into the Beat-Up Generation.

If only life were as simple as all these agitated rod worshipers make it. If the trouble lay in softness of heart, then the cure would quite simply be hardness of heart. If this were our problem, all we should have to do to solve it would be to bring up our young people either in military academies or in reformatories. In that case the ideal teacher would be the drill sergeant, the beloved community would be the Marine Corps, which would break the softness of the young American by breaking his will and sense of identity, and the ideal state for America to achieve would be a technocratic Sparta.

The only trouble with this is that it was tried—actually, in Sparta itself. Alas for the theory, it didn't work. In the pride of their military virtues, the men segregated themselves into all-male societies and were corrupted as all-male prisons are corrupted. The women took over power and became viragos. Sparta grew rigid and fell.

My suggestion is that many commentators today are failing to distinguish between toughness and tough-mindedness.

I am all for more stress on tough-mindedness—that is to say, a feeling for the discipline of experience, a willingness to face the harsh facts without flinching, a courage in changing our thinking and policies when conditions change, a refusal to whimper when the going gets difficult, an absence of self-pity, a commitment to the ardors and heroisms of work, a capacity to master whatever skills may be required for the particular job in hand, an insistence on unsparing reasoning and critical intelligence, a sense of your own identity and of the need for striking out on new creative paths and reaching your own solutions in your own way.

In our early history, Americans have been lucky in having had the immigrant experience and the frontier experience, both of which helped make our best people tough-minded. Since then we have had nothing comparable. In many ways we have grown smug and blind: but the worst form of blind smugness is to think that a resort to physical toughness and harshness at home and in the school, will itself restore our greatness.

Certainly we need to be firm in purpose, sure in intent, setting limits within which the young can best grow and reach their own moral and intellectual stature. But our aim should be to develop not a legion of toughs but a democratic elite of the creative who are also tough-minded.

6. The Man on the Roof

January 29, 1958

I CAN'T GET HIM out of my mind—the man on the roof of his Brooklyn apartment house, with his hat and his overcoat, his umbrella and his glasses, plunging over to the courtyard below. He left his umbrella behind. His broken glasses were found near him.

The verdict was suicide, but in reality he was a victim of the tug of war between the guardians of our public safety about how to guard it best. The terror that infests the city's streets has spread to schoolyard and school corridor and has led to a fight about whether cops should be stationed in the tougher schools, with a judge, a school superintendent and a police commissioner engaged in the fight. George Goldfarb, the principal of a junior high school, was a small man compared to these big ones. But he was the man caught in the middle, too weak to take the pressures, and so he became the victim.

A few days earlier he had testified before the grand jury and had a hard time. That morning he was supposed to go back. He never did. Instead he went home, and up the stairs to the roof, as if he were trying to mount as high as he could above the confusions and cross-purposes of which he had been part. And then he plunged.

I think of him standing there on the edge for a moment. He must have thought of the thirty years during which he had served the school system—years of hard, faithful work, and badly underpaid. Of the long pull before he reached the post of principal, less than four years ago. Of the faces of the pupils who had passed through his classroom over the years. Of the new faces, with a new hardness and sullenness on them.

Perhaps he thought of the bewildering changes that had come over the neighborhood in which his school—the John Marshall Junior High —was located, and the constantly shifting mixture of ethnic and economic groups among the parents. He must have been overwhelmed again by the memory of the headlines that had burst around his school —of the rape of a young girl inside the school, and violence to a policeman outside. He must have felt that these left him a marked man, that they were a stigma on him and not just on the school, that they somehow represented his failure as well as the failure of the whole community.

Maybe these thoughts were pounding on his brain as he surged forward.

If we needed any proof of it, his death is proof of how deeply the teachers do care about the impossible task we have committed to them. Teaching has become one of the dangerous professions of our time. But the teacher feels helpless. The old-fashioned injunction to resort to the birch to get discipline won't do any longer; it would take a tough and brave teacher to tackle some of the youngsters, and all he would get for his pains would be a new anxiety about his own safety on his way home.

This, I take it, is largely the reasoning that led to the Judge Leibowitz proposal—or his grand jury's—that we put cops in the schools, or at least start with one in each of the more violent ones and see what happens.

I am sure that the suggestion is well and sincerely meant, and that it comes from the prevalent feeling (I hear it constantly from my oracles, the taxi drivers, storekeepers, deliverymen) that we pamper the kids now and that there is more wisdom at the end of a policeman's club than in all the drivel of the reformers.

Yes, the school has failed to cure the ills of young boys and girls in problem neighborhoods where there is violence in the air. But remember that the family has also failed, and the church, and the cops, and the courts, and the community. If you put a cop in the school, why not in the home? And if you put him in the school corridor, why stop there? The teacher already suffers from a derisive lack of respect on the part of his students. Bring in the cops, and the contempt for the teacher will increase and what is left of the respect will vanish. The cop in the corridor won't be enough; he will be needed soon in the classroom.

There is no easy formula. If parents want to do something, they can get together in every troubled community and try to deal with the problems of racial hate and conflict out of which the school episodes come. School violence isn't something in a vacuum. It is part of the larger neighborhood violence. Parents can deal with the violence inside the schools by getting at some of the roots of the violence outside.

Meanwhile, if we are to put someone extra into the schools, let it not be cops but psychologists and psychiatrists, and more and better teachers too, and give them more of our respect and belief. Then maybe the unquiet spirit of the man who jumped from the roof may have some peace.

January 31, 1958

The late Robert M. Lindner, who had a flair for phrase as well as an insight into troubled young minds, put into currency two phrases; one was "rebels without a cause," the other "the mutiny of the young." Both of them shed light on the present controversy about crime in the schools, which has flared up since the Goldfarb suicide. We are never going to reach a solution of it as long as we use the processes we are using.

Consider what these processes are. A Brooklyn judge calls on a grand jury to summon witnesses in secret session and presumably to recommend action. What a helluva way to run an educational system!

The grand jury may be a perfectly proper instrument—and is certainly the traditional instrument—for getting indictments on charges which are then to be tried by a judge and a petty jury. Its methods are secrecy, summary questioning of often reluctant and fearful witnesses, and the sifting of evidence leading to criminal charges. The members of the grand jury are laymen who may have enough shrewdness to tell when someone is lying, and to appraise a criminal when they see him. But they are scarcely the kind of people who have special knowledge or training for appraising the ills of our school system or the deeper roots of the mutiny of the young. The procedures which we use for indicting criminals are not the procedures of reflective analysis, expert knowledge and incisive judgment which we need to tackle the problem of our kids and our schools.

I have been struck by the statement of Samuel Hochberg of the High School Teachers Association, which described the ill-fated Goldfarb as a "pawn" caught between the grand jury and the Board of Education, fearful of saying something that could displease the board, equally fearful of remaining silent and risking censure or indictment by the grand jury. A stronger man might have ridden it out, a less sensitive man might have dismissed it from his anxieties. Goldfarb, as Hochberg puts it, "was so afraid and felt himself so completely alone" —and was crushed between the two feuding machines.

Instead of grand juries and judges, instead of district attorneys, the mutiny of the young can best be understood if we get at some of the elements of our contemporary urban life. One is the desensitizing of our young people, which is part of the desensitizing of our culture and indeed of our world. Another element is the craving to be recognized as somebody, even as a rapist, a feuding gangster, a killer. The fact that these boys inquire about the headlines shows that their basic drive is to point violently to their own identity. "Look," they are saying to society, "I am here. I am I. Must I kill before you recognize it?"

A third element is ethnic change and ethnic conflict. Many, although not all, of the cases of violence in the schools occur in areas where the shifts of population in a neighborhood produce hatreds and conflict. The children of the minorities often carry about with them a sullen, smoldering resentment which finds expression in acts of violence and rebellion.

I speak of rebellion. Actually, as Lindner demonstrated, these youngsters are not fighting for something meaningful to them. They are striking out against authority, against the community and its symbols, against the world they resent. But they are "rebels without a cause." Catch their imagination, find something useful for them to do, channel their resentments and rebellion into productive channels, and you might get some good human material put to use instead of to waste and destruction.

Obviously this involves something other than a grand-jury investigation or the stationing of cops to patrol the school corridors. It means more full-time Youth Board field workers with the youth gangs, more schools to deal with the troubled youngsters and more psychiatrists in the school system. It also means doing some thinking about education. Here is the city excitedly discussing cops or no cops in the schools, and whether a city official is or isn't a liar, instead of how and what to teach our youngsters, and what to expose them to, and how to infect their imagination with something to which they can attach their energies.

ALL OUR YOUNG KILLERS

1. Guys and Debs

July 3, 1955

I THINK I have learned more from reading the series of autobiographies by gang kids in the *Post* than from all the recent treatises on juvenile delinquency. There is an air of bravado about the narratives, a precocious, sinister quality that can't quite blank out my feeling that these amoral young hoodlums and chippies would burst into tears on the first sympathetic shoulder they trusted.

If I had to pick three crucial insights that the series has offered, I should tag them by abbreviation as sex, vacuum and identity.

"The girls go for fellows with a reputation," one of them starts, "so I joined the Turbans just to get a rep. When you have a rep nobody messes with you and the girls stay loyal." And again, "the only way you can get true love is in a gang. Nobody else will mess with her."

This note is struck repeatedly in the other personal histories. "One of them, they got fresh with one of girls. We went up there and we fight." Again and again the indignity done to one of the gang's girls starts a gang war, as Paris' abduction of Helen started the Trojan War. Before they went into battle, in one of the narratives, they kissed their girls goodbye. And listen to a 15-year-old girl: "All the gangs I've belonged to had debs. Lots of them were pretty wild, tougher than some of the guys. A lot of them got pregnant. They've got to accept it as part of the danger of belonging to a gang. None of the guys ever marry them."

The picture seems clear enough. Gang violence comes at adolescence, and the same pulls that make a boy a gang guy are likely to make a girl on the same block a gang deb. It is the time of sexual stirrings in both sexes, of ripening maturity for the girls and clamorous sexual insistence for the boys. They have few ways of showing off to each other except through gang activities. This is how boys get a "rep" and gain the favors of the girls. The tragedy is that the path to getting a "rep" is the path of violence, and tenderness is scoffed at, and "true love" must find its place in the feudal order of the gang.

The histories thus far have been those of Negro and Puerto Rican boys and girls. Look at their slum housing and congestion, and you will see why they have so much pent up in them, and why something has to burst. Look at the sense of grievance they have because the cops seem to ride them harder than they ride others, and because the people filled with color hatred sling contemptuous names at them.

It is in these groups that a kid's hunger for social acceptance is hungriest, and the distance between the world of the slum street and the world of glamour, importance and sensuality outside seems infinitely far. It is in these groups, therefore, that the kids turn to the only thing that will fill the vacuum of their lives—the gang "rumbles" that have sex, prestige, excitement and the sense of belonging mixed together in a memorable formula.

One of the things that strike you in every gang documentary is the emphasis on totemic gang names and jackets. The Big Barons, the Spanish Counts, the Earls, the Unicorns, the Dukes, the Kings, the Champs, the Turbans, the Enchanters, the Marauders, the Imperials, the Mighty Romans—these are all names that express the yearning of the slum kids who feel themselves outsiders and want to take on the insignia of the royal, the aristocratic, the powerful and the distinguished. And their jackets. "A jacket," says one of them, "is like wearing a flag. If anybody messes with one guy wearing the jacket, he's got to deal with the whole gang."

Here you get, along with the totemic importance of the gang names, the fierce loyalties that attach to the uniform as totem. Only kids with a deep hunger for identity would find themselves nourished thus by a high-sounding gang name and a jacket.

The distance between the generations—between them and their parents—is like an uncrossable gulf. In many cases the father does not live with them or they may never even have seen him. They have no one whom they can pattern themselves after, or who can invest with love the idea of discipline or the sense of limits. They don't know who they are, so they break all the restraints around them, in the wild hope that they may discover themselves.

2. Salvation by Toughness

May 9, 1955

THE WHOLE WAY on the plane to Tulsa I couldn't get Frank Santana out of my mind. I looked out of the window at this spacious, boisterous Southwest area and remembered that in an earlier America there was as much violence in the Western badlands as there is in today's giant cities. For a century, however, the moving frontier served as an outlet

for the too crowded energies of the cities. Today those energies can
only condense, collide and explode.

In one sense the Bronx neighborhood in which Frank Santana
killed Bill Blankenship is also part of a moving frontier. It is an area
of rapidly shifting ethnic populations, where new groups keep pushing
in and crowding out earlier ones, and where at any moment several of
them live side by side in uneasy hostility. It is the kind of area that
Frederick Thrasher, who has written the classic study of the gangs in
American cities, has mapped out intensively block for block, tenement
for tenement, as ripe for delinquency. It has proved ripe for heartbreak, with Bill Blankenship senselessly shot at fifteen, with Frank
Santana at seventeen indicted as a gang slayer and facing the electric
chair, with two families forever wounded beyond recovery.*

Robert Ruark, who has written a novel squeezing the last drop of
sadism out of the agony of the Mau Mau in Kenya, says we must send
all these young gang toughs to the electric chair. It seems that we can
hope for salvation only through electrocution. This will doubtless appeal to many people who are little different from Santana himself, being starved for excitement. People perhaps like the civil-defense
woman aide who watched the atomic explosion down at Yucca Flat
and was left throbbing and titillated, calling it the greatest "thrill" in
her life.

I say to her, "That was no thrill, madam. That was the valley of
the shadow of death." Equally I say to Ruark and all like him, "You
may love to hunt animals, but this quarry you have tracked down is
a sick, scared Puerto Rican kid." We have no permanent vendetta
with him and his kind. Our tragedy is being unable to absorb them
into the healthy stream of American life, as we have already absorbed millions drawn to us from every corner of the world. Suppose
we fry him or even disembowel him? What will it achieve except perhaps to furnish a Mau Mau holiday in the Bronx?

This boy was weak, not fierce. We have the wrong picture of most
killers. It is not the tough who kill. It is more often the weak who
kill, out of fear—yearning to be tough, afraid to face the dismal fact

* The episode took place as part of a feud between two Bronx street gangs, the
Navajos and the Golden Guineas. For a thorough and moving discussion of the
whole case, see Dr. Frederic Wertham's book *The Circle of Guilt* (Rinehart,
1956). Wertham's book is based on an extended study of Santana and provides
material never presented to the court. Originally it was reported that Blankenship
was a "model boy" who had nothing to do with gang warfare. Wertham contends
that he was a member of a gang which had made a practice of beating up Puerto
Rican youngsters. In following all the clues he sees the "circle of guilt" enlarging
to include killer, victim and the culture. A plea of second-degree murder was
accepted in the Santana case.

of their weakness, panicking when the moment of test comes. The strong are confident and can live and let others live. They don't have to prove anything.

Thorough patrolling of the streets is a must, but it scarcely ends the problem. If it is the weak who are the potential killers, then the job is to help them build up their inner defenses. We might also ease up on some of the pressures from the outside that push against what defenses they have.

· In an era when adults glorify the "tough policy" in business, politics, war, shall we be surprised if the glorification seeps through to the young? The point about Frank Santana was not that he shut himself off from our whole social climate but that he was so vulnerably open to it, so anxious to be a Tarzan and champion without having any filter for separating the unhealthy from the healthy.

Every person grows up with a "glory image" of himself. Frank's was the image of a boxer, just as his mother's was the image of bringing up her boys in a "nice place." Neither of them quite managed it, and Frank turned out a failure at everything he undertook. But he went on living in a dream world—a puny boy who ran with the gang, a weakling who saw himself as a dedicated, gleaming boxer with golden gloves and who bought a gun to keep his knuckles inviolate for his glory image.

Knowing in his heart that his dream was a lie, he used the gun to give himself a quick glory with his gang. He hoped that the noise of the shot would drown out the inner voice telling him he was without strength or standing, just a craven little punk.

We can fry them all if we want to—all our young killers. We can say to each other, "Don't chicken out," as Frank said it; and we can pull the electric switch as he pulled the trigger. We can shut them up behind damp stone walls and count them every day as if they were our treasure, letting them fester in helpless rage, adding corruption and hate to weakness.

If what we want is to punish, then it is perfectly in order to kill this young killer legally or immure him forever where we won't have to think about him. But if we have any notion that this helps to prevent other sick minds from killing, or to heal their sickness, then we are self-deluded fools.

3. Cancer of the Mind

October 11, 1954

THE CASE of Kenneth Chapin, the Springfield eighteen-year-old high-school boy who has confessed to stabbing to death a baby-sitter and her charge with a bayonet, raises again the question of just how much we know about our adolescents. There is still a whole dark continent that lies in shadow.

One thing we do know is that the adolescent lives largely in a fantasy world hidden from parents and teachers. From puberty until eighteen this secret existence is probably more highly developed than at any other time in life. We know that the drive toward aggression— toward asserting one's personality at the expense of others, if necessary by destruction—is very strong in these probing, frustrated years. We also know that the aggressions are closely linked with the fantasy world, and that both aggressions and fantasy are in turn closely linked with sexual yearnings and sexual unsureness and restlessness.

The Chief of Police is sure "there is no question of sex" in the Chapin case. What he probably means is that there are no signs of any attempts at sexual violation. But this seems a limited way of approaching the problem. Quite possibly the boy made no advances to his baby-sitter friend—but he may have made them in his own fantasy world, which is what counts. And in his fantasy world also he may have been rejected and have built up resentments.

If, as Kenneth says, he took the bayonet along with him and stabbed the girl as soon as she answered the bell, the stabbing was clearly the end product of a long process and not the beginning. And the repeated hackings with the bayonet—the sign of pent-up aggressions within himself that the boy was unable to control—suggest that under the spell of the terror of his act he became an automaton. Blacking out, he no longer possessed the emotions that surged through him but was possessed by them.

When I read about Kenneth I remembered a book written several years ago by a New York high-school teacher. It is a short novel called *Rickey,* by Charles Calitri (Scribner, 1952), and it is about a high-school boy called Rickey Talbot, someone not too different from Kenneth Chapin. What Calitri does is reconstruct the growing-up years of this quiet, well-mannered, likable but emotionally starved high-school boy and show how he happened to do what he did.

To the parents and the community the whole episode involving Kenneth is inconceivable. It has to be, or else all their values would be turned topsy-turvy. What everyone believes is that crimes like this must be committed by "maniacs," wild-looking and degenerate. It is part of their creed that the nice-looking boy who controls his manners must have inside of him a tidy emotional world where equally he is in control of his impulses.

It is hard for them to understand that even the best-behaved adolescent who has been taught to sit on his impulses may therefore be sitting on an emotional volcano which at some point may burst open and cover everything around with its hot lava. Sometimes I think that the adolescents who need most watching are not the wild ones. Maybe it is the quiet ones—the too quiet ones—who should fill us with foreboding.

I am not excusing Kenneth's monstrous act. I am only suggesting how little we know about the train of circumstances in his young life that led to the act, and how futile it would be either to electrocute him or to send him to prison for life to become there a hardened criminal. Obviously he is a sick boy. Curing so sick a boy is hard. The real task is to prevent such boys from becoming so sick.

Love and emotional expressiveness inside the family, honest relations between parents and child, a less repressive attitude about adolescent sex, more channels for harmless aggression, more open points of contact between the fantasy world and the actual world—these are the ways that need trying.

November 30, 1956

An important chapter in the history of law and psychiatry was written in Boston when the members of the Governor's Council changed their earlier stand and voted 6 to 3 to commute the death sentence of Kenneth Chapin to life imprisonment. Ever since Chapin was sentenced to execution, controversy has raged around the case. Now his life has been saved, not much more than twenty-four hours before his scheduled death.

Usually in a capital case, when efforts are made for a new trial or a commutation, it is the lawyers who make the plea. They may try to prove there is new evidence, or use any one of a number of weapons in the lawyer's armory. The psychiatrist plays his role at the trial itself, and his testimony as expert stands or falls with the jury's verdict. But here, long after the verdict, it was the psychiatrist and not the lawyers who played the leading role and swung the final decision. Dr. Frederic Wertham's testimony in a long Wednesday night session swayed three members of the Council who had previously voted against commutation.

Wertham never attended the trial itself. He talked with Chapin for six hours and studied the trial transcript—that was all. Yet he felt sure of his ground and communicated his certainty to others. He swept aside the testimony of eight state psychiatrists who had examined Chapin and found him sane, and equally of the defense experts who had described Chapin as a case of psychomotor epilepsy. His role may set a precedent by bringing in well-known psychiatrists in the future, not in adversary proceedings in court but as advisers to troubled men facing tortured decisions.

The great old trial lawyers like Clarence Darrow seem to have left no heirs. Darrow argued that the real culprit was society. Wertham in this case did not indict society, but he argued that Chapin had no comprehension of what he was doing, thereby meeting the legal test of insanity. Chapin, as Wertham interprets him, was not a human being moved by reason or passion to kill for any purpose. He, too, was under the spell of a strange compulsion, a kind of emotionless automaton who was the victim of a disease.

The disease was schizophrenia. It is a dread psychosis, far more widespread than most Americans like to admit. Wertham hit on two vivid phrases for it, which seemed to get across to the Council members. One was the image of a glass wall—"I had a feeling in talking to Chapin that I was talking to him through a glass wall. He had no emotion whatsoever." The other was the cancer image—"a malignant disease—the cancer of the mind."

Wertham had to make it relatively simple, yet the whole moral problem involved in the Council's decision was a complex and agonizing one. What is the duty of society and the citizen in a case like Chapin's? To kill him, answer the parents of Chapin's two victims, the baby and the baby-sitter. They are understandably bitter that he should escape the chair. When your child has been slain you feel that his unquiet spirit will not be appeased while the slayer still lives.

But what good will it do to kill him? Wertham says he believes in capital punishment and thinks it may act as a deterrent against other crimes. But when a madman with a mind deadened by cancer has slain someone, how can you justify killing him in turn? The theory of punishment as a deterrent presumes that a man had some idea or purpose about the killing, and that other men with a purpose will think twice before giving way.

Chapin himself is a pretty poor example of a person. His life has not been saved for his sake, but simply because it is a human life, on the principle that society has no right to take the life of a madman in cold blood—or (for those who oppose capital punishment) any life, mad or sane.

But there is a more disquieting question. A school therapist examined Chapin when he was seven and saw then that he was a disturbed child. For over a decade, society did nothing to try to help and cure him, while the cancer spread—not through the body, but through the personality. In this sense the "circle of guilt" includes us, too, in this America that talks constantly about its children but lets so many of them rot.

4. "Do You Recognize Me?"

March 7, 1950

A NINETEEN-YEAR-OLD BOY goes berserk on the Brooklyn streets, stabs four men to death, wounds three others, is captured and overpowered and placed in a strait jacket. He hits the headlines, black and red alike, and is photographed tied to a chair in police headquarters with burly cops holding him down. People pick up the papers, read the gruesome details, cluck their tongues and shake their heads in disbelief, shiver a bit with that just-think-it-might-have-been-I shiver, look about them warily the next day or two on the streets to make sure a man with a maniac face isn't following them. Then they forget.

Look at William Jones's life history. He is a Negro boy in a white world. For fifteen years he has been part of a broken home, with no father to serve as a pattern for growth or as a symbol of authority. He gets arrested for purse snatching and at the age of sixteen he is sent away to a reformatory. At Elmira he gets tuberculosis and at the same time shows himself truculent. He is sent to the prison hospital at one of the toughest state prisons, Dannemora, where desperate men are sent. The prison odyssey goes on, and he is transferred to another prison-reformatory. His plea for parole is denied, and he goes on a hunger strike. They send him to Matteawan, the hospital for the criminal insane, where they examine him a bit, pronounce him fit and release him.

What a life history this is for an American of nineteen. Compare it with that of the children of the possessors of our earth, or with that of your children or mine. Can we say with pride that we gave William Jones a chance at a good start in life, or handled him well when he had made a bad start?

I don't say that the kind of psychotic breakdown the boy suffered has only social and environmental causes. Obviously it has roots in the individual personality and springs from emotional blockages which reach back perhaps to infancy. But we do know that our social stupidities make it harder for the youngsters to grow out of their emotional blockages. We know that Negroes do not get the same channels as whites for showing their abilities. We know that our "reformatories" don't do a real job of "re-forming"—that is, re-building—a mind, and that our prisons harden all the old mistakes. We know that our asylums are understaffed and overcrowded. We can guess that William Jones got only desultory psychiatric study at Matteawan, whose director now says that he seemed to be "a pleasant, good-looking boy"—as if you could tell from a boy's surface the things that are going on inside his mind.

"He was a quiet sort of guy," said a friend (and also a victim) of his who had known him three years ago, "before they sent him away. He never had much to say." But things were happening under the quietness. When William Jones approached his first victim, a stranger, he asked, "Do you know me? Do you recognize me?"

Say I am nineteen, belong to an outcast minority, have never known my father, have gathered festering resentments in reformatories and prisons, have tried to call attention to my existence by a hunger strike. Say I have felt within myself the stirrings of manhood and ego, but have had to cage them up beyond possibility of expression. I cry out to the world that I am not a nobody, not a cipher. People don't listen, and I find myself wishing I had the lethal power to kill, which would make them listen. In this world where violence counts I too can count. "Do you know me? Do you recognize me?"

The search for recognition is part of every one of us. The tragedy comes when the only way to get it is to go berserk.

5. The Thrill-Killers

December 1, 1954

EVERY PRESS STORY about the Brooklyn boys talks about them as "thrill-killers." According to their confessions, they horsewhipped girls, beat up vagrants, applied lighted cigarettes to the soles of one drunk on a park bench, beat him and threw him into the river. Presumably they did all this because it gave them a "thrill." In the words of one of them, the "biggest kick" he had was when they tossed Willy Menter into the East River. What kind of thrill was it that he and the others got?

Let me put the question in another way. The thing that gives most of us a great concern about the case is not that these boys committed violence, nor even that they killed men in their violence. There has been gang violence before and there have been gang killings. What jolts us is the sustained torture they used, and the witless and apparently unmotivated quality of it all. There are also hints that these acts were a species of sex offense, and that they were tied up with sadistic pleasure.

First of all, neither their families nor the neighborhood considered these boys to be "bad" boys. They seemed on the surface to be boys like many others in the neighborhood. In fact, most of the comments about at least three of the four involved are that they were "nice" boys, gentle, well-behaved, well-mannered. One of them is eighteen, two are seventeen, the fourth (whose case was severed from the others') is fifteen. Their families are ordinary Brooklyn middle-class folk—hard-working, well-meaning. "What did we do that was wrong?" was the heartbreaking cry of the parents of each of them.

I think the answer is that the parents overprotected them, denied them nothing, set no bounds for them, furnished them no models for their normal emotional development.

You have to start with the fact of aggression in every child. It is true of some children especially that from early infancy their aggressions are given no healthy channeling. In most cases the aggressions are transformed, as the children grow up, into meaningful work and play, or are directed into heterosexual channels. In some cases they stay on the level of sexual infantilism, or are caught in a fateful homosexuality. We don't know the sexual and psychological history of each of these boys. But Koslow's family physician has reported that "normal sex did not interest him," and this gives us a clue to the relationship of the whole group of boys.

But I doubt strongly whether this story can be told merely in homosexual terms. The real clue must be sought more indirectly. The unchanneled aggressions must have led to a pent-up anger that raged in them, unknown to their parents and neighbors. When anger rages thus it is always on the edge of violence. Even when the boys concerned are gentle and soft-spoken the violence clamors for release. And suddenly there comes a combination of the time, the place, the victim and the collaborators—and the violence spills over the edge and becomes murder and torture.

It is clear that these were weak boys. To be sure, Koslow talked toughly about Hitler and professed a hatred of vagrants and weaklings, but he was at heart himself a weakling. So were the others. These were weak boys with fires of rage burning in them, wanting to express their aggressions somehow, either in doing something violent or in watching something violent done. Thus and only thus, in the show of violence, could they overcome their pervading sense of weakness and feel themselves to be effective human beings.

But the trouble was that each by himself was fearful. Together, however, they could overcome every obstacle. By merging their common fears they could achieve, in a curious transformation, a sense of collective strength. This was the nature of their "thrill." Another way of putting it is in terms of sadism—the pleasure that comes from inflicting pain, especially when the pleasure is tied in with sexual gratification whose normal channels are dammed up.

Meanwhile the true pathos lies in the trust—and the ignorance—of the parents about what was going on inside the twisted minds and hearts of their children. "We never denied him anything," said one parent. "We never laid a hand on that kid," said another. They did not know how charged with violent tensions their sons were, how ready for that collective venture in torture which would give them the "thrill" of momentary fulfillment.

December 3, 1954

Sitting in the courtroom, you let the scene arrange itself in your mind: Judge Barshay conducting the trial with an easy authority; the all-male jury taken largely from white-collar jobs; the D.A.'s staff and the lawyers for the defense; the press, taking voluminous notes, filling the benches opposite the jury box. Then the audience, drawn by whatever pull of motive to this unlikely vigil; and the parents of the boys, with strained and anxious faces, almost filling a spectators' bench; and finally the three young defendants side by side at a table, each with a cop sitting behind him as a symbol of state vigilance applied, alas, too late.

I found my attention straying time after time from the witnesses and the lawyers to the defendants and their parents. Although they are the silent actors in the drama, they easily hold the center of the stage. The boys look like an insignificant trio, contrasting strangely with the buildup they got in the press when they were arrested in August. All their former bravado has leaked out of them, leaving them white-faced and (except for Koslow) almost expressionless. They are as curiously assorted as any other trio of kids you will meet straggling down a waterfront street.

I have seen kids like Jerome Lieberman everywhere—slight of build, with a flair for dress and a quickness in playing the angles. They wear a flickering look about the lips, half ironic smile, half a resigned acceptance of the curious ways of the world. Usually they stay on the margin of trouble, just this side of involvement. Jerome didn't.

Melvin Mittman is the boy you will find on every block, in every neighborhood—husky, not overbright, eager to throw his weight around where brawn is needed, but constantly bewildered and therefore sullen. I tried to recall where I had seen Mel Mittman before, and suddenly I remembered that he was Lenny in John Steinbeck's novel *Of Mice and Men*.

The Lennies are the big, slow fellows who always need a directing brain, and Mittman—as well as Lieberman—found it in Koslow. He struck me as being the really sick boy of the three. His sharp-featured face has a deathly pallor that sets off his reddish hair and his restless, fishy eyes. He clasps and unclasps his hands, squirms in his chair. When the detective who questioned him denies ever having hit him, Koslow smiles grimly, whispers something to his lawyer. There is an inner violence in him that never leaves him alone. His mind is always figuring, his imagination always racing ahead, vaulting into impossible realms of adventure where in his own mind he can play hero and superman.

The front wall, behind the judge's bench, is covered with blown-up photographs of the dolorous streets along which the boys led Willy Menter to the pier where the macabre last act took place. When one of the detectives stood in front of the pictures with pointer, showing the spot where the fatal scuffle took place, I wondered what tricks their minds were playing, these two stolid boys with deadpan faces and the furtive sick boy whose climactic role as sadist king had so ignominiously collapsed.

The detectives repeated the phrases the boys are supposed to have used: "I have an abstract hatred for tramps and vagrants." . . . "This was the supreme adventure of them all." . . . "It makes me feel big and strong." . . . "We wanted a quiet place to beat him up." . . . "Oh, my God, the river." . . . "I couldn't sleep all night." . . . "Now we're murderers."

To give reality to the phrases your mind had to whisk the three schoolboys away from that placid table and set them in murderous motion. You wondered what a nightmare unreality the whole sequence of events must have for them, from the time they spied Willy Menter on a park bench until this moment in a courtroom, with people staring and reporters scribbling and the buzzing, booming confusion of motions, objections, rulings, exceptions. Someday, they must be thinking, the whole dream would dissolve and they would awake. But to what?

And the parents? It is they who add the clinching lines of heartbreak to the whole tragic enactment. They have wept so much and so long that the well of tears has dried up. One of the fathers collapses and is helped out of the courtroom. But the rest sit on silently, asking themselves bitter questions, pushing away the threatening fears. What else can they do?

December 5, 1954

Behind the pervasive concern that parents all over America are feeling about the trial of the Brooklyn boys is an unexpressed fear. We wouldn't mind so much if we were certain that these were unique psychopathic cases which are a law to themselves and don't really touch us in our own homes. But there is a disquieting suspicion that the story may be closer to us than we think. The question that hits us is: Are these Brooklyn boys like all our young? Is there a disease rampant and epidemic in America today among the young generation?

Dr. Robert Lindner of Baltimore has suggested a gloomy answer to this haunting question. In a series of five Hacker Foundation lectures delivered in Los Angeles, he tells us that we are in the throes of a widespread mutiny of the whole new generation—the Mutiny of the Young. It is Lindner's conviction that "a profound and terrifying change has overtaken the character of that time of life we call adolescence." This change embodies "symptoms of a psychiatric condition, world-wide in scope." And, he adds, "the youth of the world today is touched with madness, literally sick with an aberrant condition of mind formerly confined to a few distressed souls but now epidemic over the earth."

If this seems to you like merely flowery and figurative language, Lindner intends it literally. He believes that episodes like those involving the Brooklyn boys are symptoms of a collective psychopathic condition. This marks our young people, he says, because it results from the new social and political trends toward Mass Man and the totalitarian climate he lives in. Thus it is part of the larger sickness of our time. "The sands of our civilization's time are running out," writes Lindner with a gloom deeper than Spengler's. "The plague of psychopathic behavior that sickens us is the chief symptom of our society's expiring agony."

I cannot go along with Lindner in believing, first, that this is a vast collective psychopathy, and second, that it spells the expiring agonies of our civilization. Both his contentions seem to me more literary than actual.

A better way would be to say that there are in our social climate new dangers to which our children get exposed, and that more of them succumb to those dangers than in the past. Lindner sums these new influences up as the "abandonment of privacy" and the emergence of Mass Man. He points out that young people were caught in an inner turmoil in every century of our history, but that our own young people *act out* this turmoil with a complete absence of inhibitions much as a psychopath does.

In one of his lectures, Lindner gives, as an illustration of the new psychopathy of the young, the trend of homosexuality among them. He points not so much to the growing homosexuality in our time as to its growing acceptance. What interests him is the fact that while young homosexuals once fought against their impulses, they are now taught that they need only "adjust" to them.

I go along with his attack on the cult of "adjustment." But I cannot take even the new aspects of homosexuality as a sign of our total decay.

December 6, 1954

Is the sickness of these boys that of young people in revolt against authority, or are they just following the current drift toward dehumanized weaklings? To put it differently, are they rebels or robots? Lindner's answer is that youthful crime today is a response to the forces of Mass Man, not of rebellion. He is worried because the necessary and healthy "instinct of rebellion" which every young generation has expressed has been replaced by a mass mutiny of youth that has become the disease of our time. "In the place of man," writes Lindner, there is "a goose-stepping automaton driven by animal lusts."

At first sight there seems to be a contradiction in this mode of thinking. Lindner seems to be saying two things that don't jibe with each other. One is that our young people are in mutiny, the other that they are too conformist. Quite naturally one asks, How can both of these be true? He gets out of this dilemma by saying that they are "rebels within the confines of conformity." That is to say, they do not protest against injustice or against society itself, but only against the bruises they themselves have received.

Lindner feels that the events of an era moving toward totalitarianism have done great damage to the ego, producing a generation with a larger number of young people whose emotional development is arrested on an infantile level. When the primitive impulses on that level are frustrated they break out into mutiny in the form of violence, sadism and senseless crimes. But they are the crimes of weakness rather than rebellion.

This contains some insights. It is the part of Dr. Lindner's lectures that seems far stronger to me than his gloomy remarks about collective madness in which our young are plunged and which spells the doom of our world.

Let me put it in my own terms rather than his. We may as well face the fact that there always has been and always will be a cleavage between the generations, with the younger one voicing bitter protest and the older one feeling the youngsters are rushing to perdition the fastest way. There is nothing wrong with this cleavage, although it often results in tragic by-products. One can even say that every society must expect a certain amount of delinquency among its young. Up to now I have not been any more troubled about the boisterous violence of boys' gangs or the sexual delinquencies of wayward girls than I have been about adult delinquency.

The new turn of events is the change in pattern from pilfering, violence and waywardness to the senseless crime. It was the sheer senselessness of the beatings, tortures and killings in the Brooklyn episodes that gave us a sense of dismay.

The point about a senseless crime is not that it is without motive (every crime has a motive, however wrapped in layers of mystery and the unconscious) but that the motive seems to bear no relation to human feelings of any but the most perverse sort. That is why we are troubled by recent trends in youthful criminality. They seem the acts of desensitized and dehumanized beings, and we wonder what has made them thus—whether it is the accidents of personality that affect only a few or whether (as Dr. Lindner seems to feel) it is a collective madness that to greater or lesser degree affects the whole generation.

In my own view the danger is not so much of a collective psychosis, but of the cutting away of identity. These youngsters have seen much cruelty among their elders, the wiping out of populations, the image of atomic death. They are caught up in mass emotions that are more sweeping than ever before. And many of them—more than we like to think—are never discovering who they are as persons.

We don't mind if they rebel against us; we rather wish they would. Let their rebellion be against parents, against morals, against society even—but not against humanity itself. The road of the rebels is the road that leads to maturity. The road of the robots leads only to death and nothingness.

December 8, 1954

We are trying these boys in the wrong place—a courtroom. We are trying them by the wrong procedures—the ordeal of legal battle. We are using the talents of the wrong people—judge, district attorneys, defense lawyers. We are searching for the wrong things— namely, who was actually in on the death, instead of what went on in the minds and the personalities of the boys. We are doing it at the wrong time—now when it is so late, instead of long ago when the twig could still be bent.

The wrong place, the wrong procedures, the wrong talents, the wrong search, the wrong time. Wrong, wrong, wrong.

The root trouble was that the whole business was being done in a courtroom at all. In a courtroom you have to concentrate on the crime and not on the personality. The appeals attorney on the D.A.'s staff argued ably that you had to know about the whole pattern of the boys' activities. But he wanted that pattern laid bare only for legal purposes, in order the better to convict all three boys. The real reason for laying it bare is for psychiatric purposes, to study the boys through all their actions.

The whole apparatus is wrong. Instead of a panel of judges from whom a trial judge is drawn, this kind of case required a panel of referees trained in psychiatry and the juvenile mind as well as in law. Instead of two batteries of lawyers sitting like those Renaissance Swiss mercenaries who hired out for any cause, this kind of case required a battery of psychiatrists on whose expertness both sides would agree, with all the best medical and psychological resources of our society at their disposal.

Without being legally insane, it should be clear enough that at least two of these boys are emotionally disturbed, with serious character disorders. Yet the irony of the trial is that no one has mentioned their emotional disturbance, no one has breathed anything about their character disorders. The state won't do it because it might open the door for escaping the penalty. The defense lawyers fear to do it because they know how hard it is to prove legal insanity. No doubt there are psychiatrists waiting in the wings on both sides, yet right now it is doubtful whether any of them will be called.

The fact is that these boys have been in jail since last August. Instead of waiting to do battle by legal ordeal, with motions and objections and exceptions, we should have used that time to have them studied by an impartial staff of clinical psychologists and psychiatrists. The reports should have been ready now.

We study rock formations for oil and minerals, we study consumers' markets for guidance in sales, we study the terrain of other countries for strategy in possible wars, we study the atom for destructive possibilities—but we don't study a group of boys who are clearly sick in order to understand how their acts came out of their sickness and how it can be healed.

December 15, 1954

The two Brooklyn boys have been found guilty, with a recommendation for a life sentence. Thus an episode that began in blind and purposeless aggression ends in tragedy. I suppose the jury would have found it hard to render any other verdict. But I cannot help feeling that in this case, as so often happens, our society is handing out a punishment that can neither prevent other crime nor heal these criminals.

We have an inner drive to use savage punishments for savage crimes. The impulse from which this drive springs is either to get revenge or else to stifle the uneasy pangs of our own conscience, since we know so little about what causes such crimes among our young people or how to deal with them. And so in our blindness we strike out angrily, to give ourselves the sense of doing something.

There was something corny about Clarence Darrow, but I miss him sorely in a time of diminished men. I am certain that material like the crime of these boys would have been exactly the grist for his method of approach. For he would have put some disquieting questions to the jury and the judge. He would have said, "Gentlemen, you may reach a verdict of murder in the first degree. But while it is easy enough to arrive at the verdict, can you in all honesty say where the guilt lies?"

And he would have added, "Can you be sure, gentlemen, that these boys were not as much the victims of dark forces within our organized living as the dead man was the victim of these boys?"

I wouldn't go all the way with this. I don't say the social environment must always bear the burden of guilt. If it did, there would be no individual guilt and no individual punishment. I don't go in for the notion that the blame must fall everywhere except on the criminal himself. Nor do I accept the one-factor explanations of juvenile delinquency which crowd our sermons and our service club speeches.

Thus Police Commissioner Adams said earnestly yesterday that the foremost problem behind juvenile crime is the broken home. The Police Commissioner should know that writers on American society used to hold this view strongly a generation ago, but very few do now. The recent studies show that broken homes create juvenile crime only when they go along with poverty, slum crowding, alcoholism and neglect. Far more important in the recent studies is the whole emotional tone of the home, whether it is broken or not.

We shall be in the dark about these crimes until we come to understand that they are the product of both the outer world and the inner world of the adolescent. Often in the same impoverished and broken family you will have two boys, one of whom turns out well, the other badly. One succumbs to the destructive influences of the outer world, the other has an inner will and emotional strength and drive to resist them. Sheldon and Eleanor Glueck, who have done the best work in this area, say that every person has a "breaking point" at which he could commit a crime—perhaps a savage one. The problem is to find out why this breaking point occurs where it does in the case of boys like Jack Koslow and Mel Mittman.

I am unshaken in my conviction that we have done everything wrong in these cases. Nothing said at the trial gave any inkling of either the outer or the inner worlds of the defendants. Nothing was said about the terrible emotional bleakness of their existence. Nothing was said about how their minds were shaped or disturbed.

As long as we use the ordeal by legal battle as our approach, we shall remain many light-years away from understanding or healing the sources of this young savagery.

6. The Model Boys

April 3, 1953

A YOUTH of eighteen whom the neighbors at Valley Stream regarded as a "model boy" and the "politest boy in town" shoots down five people in cold blood. Why?

The beginning of wisdom in this kind of case is to look beyond what the neighbors say. They rarely know. They see only the outward signs, they value the quiet youngsters and the ones who help at neighborhood chores and picnics. They have no way of knowing what goes on in the inner life of the kids, through whom turbulent storms may be sweeping.

The reporters all had an easier clue in the case of Diane Weggeland. Diane came out of a household of divorced parents and was brought up in a series of foster homes. That's always sure-fire stuff for the social workers and sob sisters who try to explain delinquency. "Broken home" and "lack of love" make a good formula approach.

This is easy enough, but maybe the case of the boy was even worse. I know households where everyone is a Boy Scout or a Camp Fire Girl, or works for the Red Cross or the cerebral palsy drive; where the father has a respectable job and is a community pillar; where the boys shovel snow and mow lawns for the neighbors, and where the girls never stay out late at night. Yet I also know that life for the children in some of these households is a bleak experience.

I don't say there is no love in these families, but it is usually a kind of refrigerator love, where the parents are rigid and frigid. They can't communicate with their children because their own emotions have never been defrosted.

The boy-girl story here has a pathetic, shabby quality. Neither the boy nor the girl had found any particular meaning in life up to the time they met. The girl says she had been "picked on" since she was knee-high. The boy felt restless and unused. He enlisted in the Marines, but instead of being sent to Korea he found himself at a desk job, with the glory dream of some kind of valor and action gone. Finally, they found in each other the meaning neither had found in the world of their elders. They eloped. Then came the series of nightmare holdups and murders, but also the nights together in cheap hotels in Rochester and Minneapolis. Somewhere in the movies they had seen was the model they followed—two young people against the world, clinging to each other, moving toward a horizon where they could start again.

There is a harsh, inhuman quality about Fred. He professes no pangs of conscience about the killings. It was something that happened to people he didn't know—people who might be across the street or miles away. It was "too bad"—but that was that. One recognizes this as the desensitized quality which is becoming characteristic of our age. But in Fred's case it was easier because he equated the people he killed with the "outside world" which had never given any meaning to his loneliness and his life.

It is a heartbreaking story at best. But it is what happens when we put the emphasis on outward manners and codes only. They are fine, where there is also love. Otherwise, love somehow manages to break through, as it did with Fred and Diane. And where it cannot ally itself with life, it strikes a pact with death.

April 23, 1956

I wonder what the thrash-his-hide-off-him school of moralizers on our delinquent young will say about the newest feat of a twisted child's mind. I refer to the eleven-year-old Connecticut farm boy who calmly shot and killed his whole family because of a grudge he had been nursing against them. It would be hard to say that his parents should have spanked young Robert Curgenven and thus prevented him from becoming a killer. The fact is that spank him is exactly what they did, so he brooded about the injustice of it and worked out a plan to get his revenge. I am sure there was more to his act than the spur of spanking, but the point is that in this case corporal punishment proved to be no preventive.

According to the first news reports, the police officer who questioned Robert said that he seemed to be an "average boy" and "not emotionally upset." I assume the policeman judged this from Robert's calm and passivity. Evidently, his picture of an "emotionally upset" boy is of one who is nervous or excited. If he knew more about the mind he would regard the calmness and passivity in this instance as the really deadly symptom of emotional disturbance.

An "absence of affect" is what the professionals call this kind of calm after an act that should carry remorse with it. In other words, where there would normally be some sign of deep emotion, there is only a vacuum. In nontechnical language, we might just say that this is a cold-blooded, emotionless, murderous boy.

Whatever language one uses, it amounts to the same thing. But when a child of eleven wipes out his whole family—father, mother, brother—and when he covers their bodies with blankets and goes to bed and then shows no emotion afterward, you can be pretty sure that there was a perfect tempest of emotional disturbance that led him to do it in the first place.

Child murderers are rare, so many of us harbor a notion that children can't be cruel. This naïve idea should have been shattered long ago. There is a killer deep in all of us, which is why not only murders take place but also wars. The killer in us takes up residence pretty early. Parents and moralists may not like to face it, but the fact is that a four- or five-year-old child can get into a murderous rage against its parents, with the only thing preventing murder being the lack of means.

There is a section on the drive toward aggression in Freud's *Civilization and Its Discontents,* in which he points out that "Love thy neighbor as thyself" fails to take account of this strain of destructiveness all through our lives. Because parents find their love of their children a natural one, they conclude that the child's love of the parents is also natural. It doesn't follow. The child can't love until it has a self to love with. Its self, or ego, doesn't develop automatically. The mother is the first influence to help it develop. The continuous interplay between mother and infant is what gives identity to the ego. All the seemingly aimless hours the mother spends cooing over the baby and handling it are what gives the self shape. Without it, as René Spitz's dramatic studies have shown, the infant grows listless, languishes and even dies.

The story Robert tells is that he was spanked by his father and mother and "pushed around" by his brother, hence his "revenge." "They picked on me," he said. He had, in other words, the sense of a paranoid—that his whole family and environment were against him.

Actually the hostility may have been not *toward* him but *within* him. A child may feel hostile to his mother or father and project his hostility outward, and thus form the image of the ".bad mother" or "bad father." Sometimes, of course, he may in fact be a rejected or even a hated child and strike back against the hate. But often he is only a child whose self has never developed, so he has little sense of what the outer world of reality is like and gets the grossest distortions of it.

That, I suspect, is what happened with Robert. In an older person his loss of a sense of reality would be schizophrenia. In a child it may be only the emotional vacuum and apathy that come with the failure of the self to develop.

It is a chilling, terrifying story, this story of Robert. One is tempted to set him down as a monster, and then let it go at that. But what he did is what children may often dream of doing. How often has it happened to all of us as children, that in our rage and frustration we imagine the parent dead and even wish him dead. We have the dream of omnipotence—that we can lick or kill our elders, and serve them right.

The difference is that the healthy child gets rid of his rages by imagining the death, but the killer child finds no hitch between the image and the act—because he has no sense of reality. Hence the vacuum of remorse, and the policeman's curious picture of an "average" boy.

May 24, 1957

"He was the nicest boy on the block," said a neighbor about Andrew Casey. "He'd do anything you asked him. He was a fine, normal boy." And another neighbor assures us that he belonged to a "happy family—the nicest folks in the world." Yet Andrew, aged fourteen, the nice normal boy who never griped and would do anything you asked him, killed his mother and sister with a rifle. And he would have finished the job of shooting up the rest of the family if they had not fled.

When are we going to discard the naïve notion that the exterior reveals everything worth knowing about the child beneath the skin? And when will we discover something about the strange world of torment and turmoil that churns away under the seeming innocence of the child?

This sort of event stretches you to the farther shore of heartbreak. The tragedies of our culture don't lie so much with the psychopaths and the weirdies and the psychotics. They lie with the "nicest folks in the world," who try so hard to be a happy family, only to find their universe in ashes because normality was pulled too tight and an unaccountable gun blew the careful image of felicity to bits.

After it's over, and the past is unbearable pain and the future nothingness, the survivors are dazed and ask what could have gone wrong. They put their finger on this and that. Andrew (said his father) was a "wonderful kid," but he "did resent authority to some extent, although he did what he was told." The phrases themselves —"resent authority," "did what he was told"—betray the mistake many parents make in believing that the problem is how tight or loose are the reins of discipline.

Beyond the question of discipline or freedom is the question of the inner life of the child. A parent's whole duty is to know as much as he can about that inner life and try to guess what he cannot know. This will give him some notion of how much it needs the enrichment of love, how much it needs fortifying and trust, how much it needs the sense of clear limits which are not to be casually broken.

But the love isn't enough unless the child also learns the capacity for loving. The trust is a thin reed unless the child learns confidence in the parent as well. And the circle of limits around the child's behavior must be drawn with some knowledge of his inner turmoil; otherwise the parent runs the danger of pushing the child too hard, of packing down the dynamite until somewhere in the strange recesses of a child's mind a fuse is lit and the whole thing explodes.

The sign hung on the door of the boy's room said "Dangerous," as so many signs do on the doors of so many adolescent boys. Nine tenths of it is usually boastful and vaunting, but the other tenth may be an effort to warn the world against trampling on his identity.

I am only guessing in the dark. But my guess is that, like many children who have killed others or themselves, Andrew Casey was crying out for someone to recognize who he was—and even in the "happy family" the recognition didn't come.

Think back to your own childhood, and recall what strange things you hid away in your inner life, from teachers and other grownups, things that seemed somehow tied up with shame and disgrace.

A child is a growing something, a being and a becoming. The most important fact about his growth is the dimension of emotional depth. We can't begin to know anything about the Andrew Caseys of our world—the model killers—until we know what form this dimension of emotional depth took, or whether there was any in this case.

We can guess that small things took monstrously large shapes in his mind, that he "got depressed like," that he harbored resentments over the months. The urge to kill is the other side of the urge to create in the fantasy life of every child. He peoples his world with creatures of his own, and he also depeoples his world—rids it (in his fantasy) of people who have hurt him. We all wish certain people dead, but in the child's mind the inhibiting line between wishing them dead and making them dead has not yet been strongly formed. Thus the trigger —fanciful or real—gets pulled.

May 27, 1957

The terrible tragedy of the rape and murder of a fifteen-year-old girl is now joined by the linked tragedy of the eighteen-year-old boy who confesses to having killed her. Again, this New Jersey boy comes from a respectable middle-class suburban family. He is clean-cut, attractive and religious—a choirboy at church and a member of a regular Bible class.

There are many people who, searching for something that will stabilize the unpredictable young generation, have eagerly clutched at religion as the answer. They will be shocked by the case of Ronald Marrone, who was so regular and devoted in his behavior that he might have been taken for a perfect example of how effective religion can be in keeping a boy on the straight and narrow path. Yet this was the boy who confessed to having taken Ruth Starr Zeitler to a parking spot, having strangled her when she resisted him, hidden her body and belongings in a wooded area nearby, and then prayed for the girl with a friend.

The striking thing about Ronald's case is the way he managed to use religion as a way of relieving his sense of guilt. He took a Bible with him to the D.A.'s office. After he was arrested he told a guard at the county jail, "God will forgive me for my sins." And after admitting that he had been involved in several molestation cases with small girls several years ago, Ronald is reported to have said, "I talked with God and made my peace with God, and those things are wiped out."

This is the most disquieting aspect of Ronald's whole mental make-up—this assurance about God's role of ready forgiveness. It is almost a caricature of the message in all the peace-of-mind and power-of-positive-thinking and give-yourself-to-God books.

It turns topsy-turvy everything we tend to think about the role of religion in young people's lives. Ronald used religion not as a way of fortifying his healthy impulses and codes, but as a way of avoiding the necessity of facing himself and his deeds. Instead of its role as a "cure of souls," religion seems to have become for Ronald a needed form of privileged communication, a private system for warding off the sense of personal guilt and responsibility for what he had done. Too agonized to recognize what he had done, too weak to take it upon his young shoulders, he found it easier to place his burdens upon God.

Perhaps Ronald's parents, who seem to be sensitive and religious people, felt more secure about their son when they saw him so wrapped up in the church and prayer and the Bible. But often the denial of the instinctual life does not prevent it from bursting through the bonds of repression; and when this in turn is followed by a deep sense of guilt, and the boy seeks to relieve the guilt in turn by even greater religious intensity, the cycle may prove dangerous.

The most moving figure in the case, for me, is the boy's father. The pictures of his sagging, slumping body will not easily be forgotten. The father may be the symbol for all parents—for society itself, and the blundering way it has of dealing with the growing-up years of the children.

One is tempted to go back to the bitter pessimism of Ecclesiastes: "Wherefore I praise the dead that are already dead more than the living that are yet alive; but better than they both is he that hath not yet been, who hath not seen the evil that is done under the sun."

February 28, 1958

Here in San Francisco the big news is a murder on the campus of Stanford University. A nineteen-year-old college sophomore named Thomas Wallace Cordry III walked into a police station at Palo Alto on Tuesday night and told the cops that he had killed a girl and that her body was in the car.

For eight or ten months he had felt these "urges" and had fought them. "This is the first time I've been unable to control them. The urge was to go out and shoot a girl and then rape her, and then run and hide." So, after trying vainly to pick a girl up, he asked Deena Bonn, a pretty seventeen-year-old high-school student across the street, to drive him to the railroad station in his convertible. He shot her and was about to drive to a prearranged hideaway in the hills but he changed his mind and gave himself up.

On the face of it we seem to have again the American tragedy of the "model boy" who kills, suddenly and brutally, and in the act of killing opens up a frightening gulf from which we recoil because we see in it the depths of human possibility.

What disturbs me about this case is the agreement on what constitutes a "normal" and even a "model" boy. Thomas Wallace Cordry III was a "nice guy." He had a crew cut, he was a "big brother" to the younger kids in his Palo Alto neighborhood. He was the Ivy League type and wore the uniform—"slim gray flannel slacks, a soft-shouldered sport jacket, a button-down shirt and white buckskin shoes," as Hale Champion describes him in a excellent piece in the *Chronicle*. And he adds, "He looks and dresses as the magazines show a clean-cut American undergraduate might dress if his family could afford it."

That's it. The magazine version of the clean-cut American boy. "There's nothing in his personality to set him aside from any other kids his age," said his college fraternity president. And the cops all comment on how "mannerly, considerate and uncommunicative" he was when he gave himself up.

That's it again. If there was ever a better picture of a boy who sinks into his background, a boy who has no identity of his own, I don't know of it. We seem to believe that a killer will give himself away by looking like a monster—a long-haired, excitable, individualistic boy who has fashioned a forbidding personality for himself.

How blind can parents, teachers and neighbors get? Here was this "normal," "model," crew-cut American boy. Yet all the time there was turmoil boiling within. "I never had a girl," he later told the detectives. "For a long time I wanted to be intimate with a girl. I guess this is really a sexual problem. I just felt like shooting some girl, then raping her. Now I'm just sick about it."

The parents spent the week usually in their San Francisco apartment. The boy was left alone in the Palo Alto home—left without family, schoolmates, girl friends. The mother said she had instilled into him "a sense of morality, of sexual morality. I brought him up to believe that women were to be protected and idealized. Maybe that was too rigid," she added. Yes, it was.

The boy was a withdrawn boy. He changed his courses from engineering to international relations (his mother had insisted on his studying engineering because it was "good mental discipline"). He withdrew from his fraternity. He never had much to do with girls. He had a car of his own, an empty house of his own—and the terrible "urges" that came to him, night after night. "There was never anything at the school to indicate anything like this," said Stanford's dean of men. "He never gave us any clues that he had an urge to kill," says the boy's mother.

I should like to ask the mother, the father and the dean what kind of clues and indications they were looking for. Here was a boy whose whole stance toward life was negative. It had been instilled in him that sex was something to be idealized, something apart from his normal urges. So when he still found the urges strong in him, he concluded that they could only be linked with something dirty, something to be hidden, not with life but with the negation of life, with death.

His parents had meant well. But what he made of their teaching was that sexual expression was not a phase of living but was tied to killing and fleeing and hiding.

Parents are perforce watchers. We have to keep a vigil over our children. But we can help our children best not by hiding them from experience but by exposing them to it at the right time, not by giving them an impossible and unattainable ideal of purity but by giving them the conviction that sexual energies are part of life, not of death.

Tom Cordry's parents gave him everything—a house, a car, an education and indoctrination about the purity of womanhood. What they failed to give him was the feeling of identity, and of the naturalness of manhood.

If we in America continue to link sex with negation and death, and not with creativeness and life, we shall have a monstrous reckoning to settle when we confront our children.

7. Clyde and the Trap

September 26, 1951

I HAVE BEEN TO SEE George Stevens' picture, *A Place in the Sun,* based on Theodore Dreiser's novel *An American Tragedy.*

Dreiser was obsessed, when he wrote his novel, with the theme of the good-looking but weak American boy who gets enmeshed with a poor girl, finds her blocking his way to a rich and attractive marriage, and removes the block. He found cases of this sort always turning up in the papers. He studied fifteen such episodes, Mrs. Dreiser says in her memoirs of him, before he finally settled on the murder case of Chester Gillette and Grace Brown. The result was the story of how a boy was torn between a poor, plain girl from whom he could not extricate himself and a beautiful, rich girl whom he would not give up.

One might say that for Dreiser the tragedy of Clyde Griffiths was a fated one, given his early poverty-stricken environment and the religious bigotry of his parents, who ran a sidewalk mission. The movie does little except to suggest that early life in swift, skillful strokes, but I am inclined to think Stevens was right to shift the emphasis. For there is a deeper tragedy than that of a boy badly prepared for life by his early poverty.

It is the tragedy of the American "success system," and it would apply even if the boy came from the middle classes. Success for the boy did not mean just making money or making good in business, although that was part of it. It was rather not losing out on life. It was pretty young girls, and being part of the group that swam and rode horses, and driving around in fast cars, and dressing well, and dancing. These are what Sondra represented for the boy, as opposed to Roberta.* It was to hold on to this that he entered on the train of events which led to his death.

My real regret about the change made by the movie treatment is in the personality of the two girls. In the novel the poor girl has

---

* In this article, the author has used, to eliminate confusion, the names of the characters in Dreiser's novel, which names were changed in the motion picture.

some attractiveness, and Clyde feels at least a residue of love for her; and the rich girl is vain and shallow, along with her beauty—she wants chiefly to annex Clyde as a possession. In the movie the poor girl is wholly unattractive, while the rich girl is everything desirable, emotionally deep as well as beautiful, and genuinely in love. Dreiser made almost a caricature of his baby-talk rich girl and her set; Hollywood knows how to do much better the job of suggesting the graciousness and gaiety of life made possible by money.

The result is that one feels in the movie that the boy had to choose as he did; the cards are all stacked in the direction of beauty and love. How much more harrowing it would have been if Stevens had decided to follow the novel and had shown the expenditure of two lives for only the hollowest of values.

Yet the basic theme is kept. Life on the social heights of America, in the American sun, can be infinitely tempting. Yet when you try to reach for it and are forced to reach outside the conventional boundaries, it slaps you down and makes you pay the heaviest of moral costs.

Many reach for it nevertheless, whatever the cost. In a hundred different ways, millions of times, Americans give away pieces of themselves for a better place in the sun. Nor is it only the money that matters. It is rather the anxiety to feel that you too count; that you are not left out of the swim; that you don't have to stand with your nose pressed against the shop window.

September 25, 1953

While I was reading the story of Roy Schinagle, the Ohio Wesleyan sophomore who has confessed to the killing of his sweetheart, I found myself calling him Clyde instead of Roy. My mind was back in the Gillette case of 1906, which Dreiser re-created in *An American Tragedy* and its story of Clyde Griffiths and Roberta Alden.

The pathetic outlines of the story have been in all the papers this week—how Roy dated a freshman girl from White Plains last year, how she came back to visit him at college, how he met her in a shed near the athletic field, how a quarrel developed and he strangled her, how he drove thirty-five miles with her body and dumped it on a lonely road, smashing her features first to avoid identification, and how she was traced by a pair of red slippers which she had worn that night in the shed and which he left on her. When she was found, she was discovered to be pregnant.

Maybe Roy bears little resemblance to Clyde, and Cynthia to Roberta. Yet the parallel elements are there—the young lovers, the furtive meetings, the pathetic finery the girl brought along, the despair that both seem clearly to have felt, the fact of pregnancy, the confusion in the boy's mind, the tracking down of their relation.

One important parallel seems to be missing, however. The big point Dreiser made revolved around the fact that Clyde had fallen in love with an heiress, and Roberta stood in the way of his making a success of his life. Again and again Dreiser underscored this point—that Clyde was weak, colorless, conformist, and that he was simply behaving as his society had taught him to behave in putting his career and success ahead of everything else.

The reason Dreiser called the tragedy of Clyde an "American" one was because he felt that the real structure of our society was the culprit. Clyde simply imitated its operative credo and got entangled in tragedy.

There is a measure of truth in this, but I think it is time to challenge the mechanical way we now tend to put all the weight of blame on our society. The parents, too, both of the boy and of the girl, seem to feel the burden of guilt heavy, and keep asking themselves where they erred in bringing their children up.

I feel that the core of these cases lies not in the aping of the culture's weaknesses, but in the sense of being trapped. Roy says he flew into a rage over something minor. Roy's rage might have been spontaneous, yet the real point is that when he felt himself trapped with a girl whom he had made pregnant, even a minor incident could have set off his rage. And the fact that he beat her face so savagely may also be seen as symbolic: It is as if he were trying not only to hide her identity but to wipe out the symbol of his entrapment—not by her, but by life and the trick of fate.

Much of the fault, of course, does lie with our taboos—as Dreiser saw when he described the scene where the doctor turned Roberta away, when she turned to him for help. Not all young people have the inner strength to face their crises. But all of them need to be told that no step is forever, that life is not a trap from which there can be only the desperate exit of violence, that parents do not sit in judgment, and that the way to unravel even the worst problem is to bring it into the clear.

PART IV

Democracy as Arena

CONTENTS

PREFACE

AMERICA *in its origins and history has been involved with the working out of the idea of freedom. America in the afternoon of its development is saturated with the idea of power. The problems of a massive democracy like the American are mainly concerned with the reconciliation of freedom and power. That is the theme of the articles collected in this section.*

I have gathered together here some columns bearing on what is usually called the "domestic front"—on politics, economics, and enough of American history to serve as a background for both; on the wielders of power in a democracy, including not only a gallery of Presidents and other political leaders, but also several who represent the business, labor and military elites; on the crucial tests of the American commitment to freedom, in the case of the hunters for "dangerous thoughts" and the hated men who were the quarry; on the bigotries and hatreds stirred up in a pluralistic society where the ethnic and religious minorities must fight for the first-class citizenship which in democratic theory is theirs; on the idea battles involved in the struggles over civil liberties and civil rights; on Constitutional guarantees, and on the bench and the bar and the judicial procedures meant to protect them; on the "democratic class struggle" between the corporations and the trade-unions; on the processes for choosing the political rulers in a democracy; and on the political style of America—for if anything should be clear about politics it is that there is an appropriate and characteristic political style in every civilization.

This theme of the American political style, and of the leaders and the followers who express it, runs through many of these columns. I think of it as a dialogue, sometimes great, sometimes mean and petty and bedraggled, between the people and those who are chosen to wrestle with their collective problems, to protect their individual rights and to hew out directions for the future. I find my material in labor and business (Lewis, Reuther, Hoffa, Wilson), in the Federal bureaucracy (Adams), in the armed services (MacArthur, Rickover), in the judicial process (Holmes, Hughes, Vinson and the members of the Warren court), among the demagogues (Huey Long, Joseph McCarthy, Orval Faubus), and among some of the Presidents and the Presidential hope-

fuls (Washington, Lincoln, Hoover, Franklin Roosevelt, Truman, Robert Taft, Eisenhower). Necessarily, in an era of the treason hunt and the security syndrome, I have also written about the men involved in the causes célèbres *of the past decade—Hiss, Lattimore, Remington, the Rosenbergs, and (with a backward glance at an earlier time of troubles) Sacco and Vanzetti. It would be difficult to find a decade in American history comparable to the 1950s for the profusion of the symbols around which controversy has swirled.*

The temptation is always to divide these men—whether leaders, demagogues, hunters or hunted—into the children of light and the children of darkness. I fear that in the urgencies of battle I have not always resisted it. I can only say that I have at least been aware of the danger. In the spirit of the great German social theorist Max Weber, I have tried to take account of the relation between consciousness and society, and to bring the element of the unconscious bias as far as possible into consciousness.

Yet I have not written with the detachment of the dead, even about the dead, and certainly not about the living. In the case of the dead I have been aware that each generation sees its history and its heroes from its characteristic angle of vision, using both its heroes and its villains as symbols, and seeking to transcend them in the very process of celebrating or damning them. In the case of the living, I have not been loath to break some lances against whomever and whatever I have regarded as the adversary on that particular day, in that particular encounter. Where there was a bully dominating the day, as with McCarthy and his movement, I never had any doubt about where I stood in the fight against the tyrannies of hysterical feeling. Where there was a question of hated and hunted men, as with Hiss, Lattimore, Remington, the Rosenbergs, or the Communist leaders in the Smith Act cases, my first concern was that their rights to fair treatment should be safeguarded, not for their sake as individuals but for our own sake as a society and a culture. On the question of their guilt or innocence, however, I tried not to let myself be swayed either for or against them by the intensities of opinion around me, but to make my independent appraisal where I could and suspend judgment where the available facts did not yet warrant a judgment.

A columnist, by the very fact of his being, is always up to his neck in controversy, and I must confess that I find it hard to stay away from a good polemical brawl. I have called this section Democracy as Arena, *because there is a sense in which the whole democratic process exists by virtue of a conflict of interests, viewpoints, claims and stakes. A democratic society may be viewed as a vast arena on which various influence groups, pressure groups, ethnic groups, idea systems, parties, classes fight it out by means short of war and death for their competing versions of freedom, justice and the good society—all within the frame of a basic ethos of human decency, and constitutional safeguards of fair procedure.*

It is crucial, in such a setting, that the controversy be about meaningful issues and conducted with some regard for facts, history, logic and the life of reason. It is by some such standard that I hope the pieces in this section will be read and judged.

Something interesting has happened in the controversies over our American democracy: The area of controversy has moved steadily away from economic issues to those of ethnic equality (civil rights), foreign policy, national survival and the presumed threats to it (hence the controversies about treason and traitors, and the problems of judicial safeguards they raise). The days of bitter dispute over free silver, collective bargaining, the farm problem, social legislation, deficit spending and the New Deal are largely over. This does not mean that commentators and editorialists have stopped writing about them, but that (as Galbraith shrewdly suggests in his Economics and the Art of Controversy) *the sounds of battle continue even after both sides have largely agreed on the stakes of conflict.*

Perhaps a better way to see it is through the lag between the traditional controversies and the emerging issues. Most men go on arguing over catchwords ("creeping socialism," "welfare state," "farm parity," "Wall Street," "right-to-work laws," and "socialized medicine"). They argue about them long after the reality has gone out of the struggle, but all the time new issues are coming up (desegregation, delinquency, educational standards, radiation and the weapons race) which need defining and confronting, while some of the older ones take on new forms (inflation, trade-union responsibility, the ethics of administrative commissions, judicial supremacy over the claims of regional prejudices and states' rights) which bear directly on the felt needs of the day.

It is part of the task of a commentator to be wary of the empty issues, which retain only the sound and fury, signifying little, and to redefine the old issues and define the new ones that have substance. At every point he must try to see through the hollow verbalisms of past battles and "strike through the mask" (to use Melville's phrase) to get at the heart of the issue.

The prime questions that tie together the areas of economics, politics, law and ideas with which I deal here are the questions of freedom, organization and power. I find as I review my writings here that I have been too little concerned with the theme of organization and management, whether of the government, the corporation or the trade-union. Most of us commentators are not drawn to this theme unless there is some brouhaha—a case of political scandal or administrative corruption or "influence peddling." But these concern only the pathology of the managerial function. In the case of business—whose dirty linen is now rarely washed in public, except when there are inner struggles for corporate control—the principles of organization are usually discussed only in business periodicals.

On the theme of power I take the view that while power is often a corrupting force, we must nevertheless make what we can out of it as an instrument. I do not agree with the neo-Machiavellians who see power as its own validator and vindicator. I see political and business and trade-union power—as I see also the technological power inherent in science—as a two-edged sword, with both creative and destructive possibilities. It is only the negative thinkers and the sad-sack liberals who fear power as such, just as it is the totalitarians of both left and right who celebrate it as such. Liberal realists will seek to use it for ends that power in itself cannot furnish, and will seek to limit and disperse it whenever and as far as possible. While the process of power concentration is a never ending one in American society, there is also a pervasiveness of power throughout the society and a habituation to its use which is not limited to a small power elite, and which therefore makes power hunger a less ominous force in American civilization than it has been in others.

The greater problem today is less that of power than that of freedom and morality. The section I have called On Being a Negro in America *may be read as a case history of the greatest moral problem of our time—the question of whether we are willing to overcome repugnances bred of past history, or whether we will continue to deny to children of the wrong color that equal access to life chances and life choices which is the heart of the American experience.*

THE WIELDERS OF POWER

1. Washington and the Revolution

February 22, 1959

SINCE FRANKLIN ROOSEVELT, a new trend has made itself felt in American politics—the turning of the well-born to the service of government. Washington was the most gleaming instance in our history of one of the well-born and well-bred who did not hesitate to join a revolutionary movement and command a "rabble in arms." I shall confess right off (for, like six-year-old George with the cherry tree hatchet, I cannot tell a lie, Father) that I have never warmed to Washington as one of my culture heroes. Partly the fault lay with the Parson Weems stories and the impossible mask of virtue and rectitude that the historians pulled over his face. Partly also, I suppose, Washington's very moderation and sanity make him less exciting than the more intense and unbalanced personalities.

But in the last few years the popular interest in the Revolution has grown. Take, for instance, the splendidly designed and illustrated *The American Heritage Book of the Revolution* (Simon and Schuster), with its muscular narrative and its lavish pictures and maps. Or take, even better, the two-volume work by Henry S. Commager and Richard B. Morris, *The Spirit of Seventy-Six* (Bobbs-Merrill), which brings together in a brilliant and revealing mosaic the "story of the American Revolution as told by participants."

The fact is that the War for Independence was a dirty, bloody, drawn-out, agonized affair, with enough horrors in it to satisfy the reader who may yearn for dark enactments. There were plunder and pillaging and atrocities in it, there were rape and rapacity, there were scurvy and smallpox and unbelievable filth in the camps, there were starvation and mutiny and the brazenest treason, there were profiteering and perfidy. And we had better not forget that for almost eight years the colonials and their leaders skated on the thin edge of disaster and came fearfully close to losing the war and getting hanged for their pains.

What then, if anything, does the story lack when it is compared with the Civil War story, which has our obsessive interest as readers?

If not darkness nor tragedy, I suggest that what it lacks is a mystique such as Lincoln and the Civil War had.

The story of how we got our liberties is a kind of success story, for all its rough edges of temporary failures and disasters. Washington's role in it is that of a great, well-balanced, tenacious leader who knew the arts of delay and retreat, who never lost courage or hope, and who by sheer will held his ragged soldiers together. But in a curious sense the great theme of American unity is seen best not at the time when the nation first emerged, but when it was savagely rent asunder in the bloody struggle of brother against brother. America has, I think, gone through three great testing periods—the Revolution, the Civil War and the Great Depression; of the three it was in the Civil War that we glimpsed best the mystical idea of a people whose nationhood lay both in its unity and in its freedom.

Washington was not so wise as Franklin, so intellectual as Jefferson, so bold and brash and constructive as Hamilton, so learned as John Adams, so brilliant as Tom Paine. Yet in an age of great leaders, he stood out for the one special quality he had—the quality of command. He had little book learning, was slow of mind and speech, and does not even seem to have been a particularly good military strategist, losing battle after battle as the war dragged on. But always, as in the fateful campaigns on Long Island and at Trenton and Princeton, he managed to keep his army alive and intact. Always he dominated his circumstances and the men around him, because he had trained himself to lead.

How he did it is one of those riddles that defies analysis. All the biographers and historians say it was his "character," but "character" is only a word that restates the puzzle without solving it. There is little in his life that gives us a clue: a boy born into the Virginia planter aristocracy, who fights in the Indian wars, marries a rich wife, buys up land on the Ohio, raises tobacco, rides a horse well, dances well and is quite a fellow with the ladies. Then the Revolution comes, and at forty-three—because he is a Virginian and rich and an aristocrat and a conservative, with some war experience—he is chosen to command the rebel army in a war which shatters absolutism in England and produces the first nation in modern times to throw off its colonial bonds.

All his life, I think, this man had been preparing himself for some great test like this. He knew how to command others because he had learned to be in command of his own often turbulent impulses: he could master any situation because he had learned mastery of himself. He was not a complex man, but he knew who and what he was, and never for a moment could anyone with him forget it. He lived by a set of Calvinist copybook maxims, which it would be easy to ridicule; but when you see how he knitted them into his inner being, the ridicule freezes. He was a man who, whatever his qualities, was all of a piece. And because he knew himself, he had the strength at the end of the war and the end of his Presidency to lay down power, just as he had the strength originally to assume power.

He had emotions, as his officers and men did—it was the Age of Sentiment as well as the Age of Reason. When he bade his officers farewell at Fraunces Tavern, he wept and they wept and there were rivers of tears. But there was also granite within him, and this combination of feeling and granite was what the nation needed—and still needs.

2. Lincoln as Wrestler

February 9, 1959

THE GENERATION that followed Lincoln's death saw him as the Great Emancipator and the Great Martyr. For later generations of Americans he became the crucial folk hero, a legendary figure through whom we were able to express our hunger for a homespun symbol of giant stature—at once tough and tender, rowdy and wry; full of jokes, yet always on the margin of heartbreak; terribly human in his gawky, fumbling ways, yet also the one abiding figure in American history with the authentic stamp of immortality.

Every era fashions its own image of Lincoln, out of the material that the historians furnish, but also out of its own drives and needs. What is our image?

The Lincoln I see, as I have been browsing through a pile of several years of new Lincoln books, is a lonely man, deeply split, who spent most of his life finding out who he was. But once he found out—in the early years of the Civil War—he showed passion and tenacity, and a sure sense of what he wanted and where he was going and how to get there.

We call this kind of search, in the jargon of our own day, the "quest for identity." Lincoln would have rejected the high-flown term, but not the fact. His law partner, William Herndon, said Lincoln had told him his mother was illegitimate. There must have been other racking doubts he had about himself, and sometimes I have felt that the "house divided against itself" was inside Lincoln himself. Yet when the crisis broke all around him, something happened within him to steel his will and make him all of a piece.

Lincoln's lowly origins are part of the homespun-folk-hero figure. But what is not underscored enough is that out of this common stuff came one of the chosen of the earth, perhaps the greatest leader the American nation has had. Our social thinkers have often enough pointed out that there must be a "circulation of the elite" in every

society. If a nation cannot draw constantly upon the vigor and passion of the young men who come from humble stock, and raise them
to the seats of the mighty, it will die.

We need to remember today, in the midst of our own debates
about the schooling of our young people, that we can as readily find
the material for leadership somewhere on a lonely farm or in a city
slum as among the sons of the cultured. But how the unlikely raw
material of Lincoln came to be developed and trained, how it was
shaped by time and circumstance and his own inner fires into the
Lincoln who played his brief but transcending role on the stage of
history—that can never be told with certainty. If we could read this
story aright—the story of a great education, almost without the benefit
of schools and teachers (he did have a teacher—Mentor Graham)
we might know what to do with our young talent today.

The Lincoln I see was an earthy figure, who showed that a leader
can be shrewd, hard and realistic without hardening into one of those
"practical men" who always bring their country and cause to disaster.
One has only to read about how Lincoln managed to get the Presidential nomination in 1860, how he used patronage, how he kept
changing generals until he had the men he wanted, how he kept from
drowning in the swirl of strong undercurrents of politics during the
Civil War, how he got himself re-elected, how he resisted pressures
from the "radicals" yet adopted many of their ideas—one has only to
read about these phases of Lincoln to see that he knew how to get
what he wanted.

But I do not see Lincoln as simply one of the regular run of
politicians. The political strain in him is remarkable mainly in contrast with the twin strains of tragedy and compassion—strains that
are as important for American leadership in a missile age as they
were during the Civil War. The only difference is that Lincoln had
these qualities and none of our leaders today do.

The Lincoln I am describing left his impact on sensitive and
powerful minds, and on the minds of millions of people, right across
the face of the earth. We make a good deal today about the need of
fighting an "ideological" struggle with the Communists, and the need
for finding the right phrases, symbols and techniques to wage it.
Lincoln had an eye for the world impact of his actions, and he had
a good way with his words, which he didn't coin as he ran but which
he polished in solitude hour after hour. Yet what made him the great
world symbol of democracy was his own figure—Lincoln as a person in thought and action.

The Lincoln I see was an intellectual, with a wonderful sense of
the complexity of life and thought. Yet the complexities were in his
own mind. In what he uttered, after wrestling with the demons, there
was a piercing simplicity of approach—to law and labor, to slavery

and freedom, to the self-government of people, to the agonies of fratricidal conflict, to life and death.

His capacity to put these insights into words that ordinary men could understand was met almost mystically by a similar response from the people. There are few of our historic leaders about whom we can say to so great an extent that their careers embodied a great dialogue between the people and themselves. At a time when this dialogue is so strangely silent as now, it is good to think back to a man and a time that expressed it.

February 11, 1959

I went to hear Lincoln debate Douglas last night, and Lincoln had the better of the argument, although Douglas had more fire in his talk and was played by an actor with a touch of wildness in him. Norman Corwin's re-creation of the Lincoln-Douglas debates in *The Rivalry* doesn't have the brooding quality of Sherwood's *Abe Lincoln in Illinois,* nor is it steeped in poetry, as it might have been if MacLeish had done it. Nonetheless it does bring the past to life.

Lincoln was lucky to have Douglas as his antagonist in the Illinois contest for the Senate, and he was luckier still when Douglas accepted his challenge to debate. In the play, Nancy Kelly, who acts Douglas' wife with a quiet charm, warns Douglas against the debates because he has everything to lose from them, Lincoln everything to gain. But Douglas knew this all along. He had his eye on the Presidency, and, confident about winning the Senate contest anyway, he welcomed the national platform that the dramatic debates gave him.

The real inner drama of Lincoln's role was, I fear, something that Corwin couldn't get into his play, since it does not have a narrator who could have known the inside of Lincoln's mind. There was a lost period in Lincoln's life, the decade between 1848 and 1858, between the end of his single term in Congress and his try for the Senate. Thinking himself a failure in Congress, Lincoln came home to Springfield, practiced law, rode the circuit, tinkered around as an amateur inventor, tried for a job as a Land Office commissioner, read algebra, told stories, watched the political scene.

But something was happening inside him. He learned one of the great lessons of life, which can be learned only from failure and defeat—that of withdrawing in silence to touch bottom in your mind, of renewing your strength, and of coming forward again as a new man to seize a new occasion. The Lincoln who stepped onto the platform at Ottawa, at the first of the seven debates, and thus onto the national political stage, had made his own Journey into the Interior. When he spoke with such gravity and sharpness and wit about the one paramount institution of the day, it was because he had been dwelling on it in his mind for years.

We make a good deal of how right he was on the moral issue of slavery, and he was. Corwin has made his selections from the speeches in a way to light up their bearing on the moral issue of our own day—Negro segregation, especially in the school. But Lincoln was a cautious and wily politician. He was no radical and no Abolitionist. He was against the spread of slavery, and for the freedom of the Negro, but he refused to assert that the Negro was his equal.

In a passage of his Charleston speech Lincoln disclaimed any equal-rights position: "I am not . . . in favor of bringing about in any way the social and political equality of the white and black races; . . . there is a physical difference . . . which I believe will forever forbid the two races living together on terms of social and political equality . . . I am as much as any other man in favor of having the superior position assigned to the white race."

This passage, and others like it, are now being cited by the Southern segregationists to bolster their position. I quote it, and I wish Corwin had, because it is better to have the whole Lincoln than only part of him. For his own day the whole Lincoln was pretty good. He kept his eye on a single question, that of slavery and freedom, and refused to be drawn into the problem of intermarriage. He rejected the inference of Douglas that "because I do not want a black woman for a slave I must necessarily want her for a wife. I need not have her for either . . . But in her natural right to eat the bread she earns with her own hands . . . she is my equal and the equal of all others."

Today the fight has moved forward, and the Negro has his freedom, but there are still many who would deny him the access to equal opportunity in school, in housing, on the job, in the voting booth, by which he can use that freedom for his own life purposes. No liberal today would use Lincoln's words about the gap between the races—history has moved too far and fast for that, thanks largely to Lincoln's life and death. But like him we must not let ourselves be deflected from the great moral issue of *our* time, segregation, as slavery was the great moral issue of *his* time.

Lincoln was the rail splitter, who knew just where to drive his ax into the crack in his opponent's logic and break it clean through. Lincoln was the wrestler, flexible, wily, even shifty in eluding the holds of Douglas, yet tenacious when he could get his own grip on him.

The frontier had been a good conditioner of this man, who wore a claw-hammer coat but had also a claw-hammer mind, who (as Shelby Foote puts it in his stirring new book, *The Civil War: A Narrative*) used words and phrases "still with the bark on them," who knew all the falls of the wrestler, with whom anything went, who had a brooding melancholy in him and yet knew most of the arts of showmanship.

So he moved, from the debates to the Republican convention, then to that silent and sinister railroad station at Baltimore on his way to Washington, and finally to the White House. Again he was to be the wrestler, caught in the agony of the antagonism of brother against brother on the moral issue which the debates had not settled.

3. Hughes: A Man without Labels

May 6, 1952

I WAS HAPPY to note among the Pulitzer prizes the biography award to Merlo J. Pusey for his life of Charles Evans Hughes. In spite of the portentous beard, the formal coat and the stovepipe hat of his pictures, Hughes had to face some of the intellectual and moral problems we face today. The reason he seems to belong wholly to another era is that he met his problems in a spirit which even in his own day was beginning to seem old-fashioned. It wasn't that he was "glacial"; the iceberg myth about Hughes has been on its way out for some time, and Pusey gives it a decent final burial. But he was a man to whom duty, freedom, and principle were not words to tailor slickly to one's needs, but fixed points in the conduct of life.

As a boy Hughes had to fight a double fight for liberation: one against the religious rigidity of his father, who was a cast-iron Baptist preacher and tried to regulate every detail of his son's conduct, the other against his own unsureness about himself. It was a struggle which could destroy a man. Hughes survived it and was toughened by it. What remained in him from his heritage was what Justice Holmes described once as "the wall of a Noncomformist conscience." What he achieved for himself was what Holmes also described as "the doubts that open vistas through the wall." Together the wall and the doubts combined to fashion a man who was at once a conservative and a liberal, a man for whom the usual labels simply don't work.

He started poor, practiced law, married the boss's daughter with a disciplined romantic rapture, broke the utility ring and the insurance company gang in New York, was twice elected a reforming Governor, became a Supreme Court Justice, almost beat Wilson for the Presidency in 1916, was Secretary of State, and served brilliantly as Chief Justice of the United States in the time of the court's troubles before and during the New Deal.

Yet it is wide of the mark to talk of this life as a success story. Success was something Hughes scorned, and failure something he never feared. I go along with Pusey's evidence that Hughes accepted the Presidential nomination in 1916 only out of a sense of duty; that he was furious at

Wilson's offer to make him Chief Justice if he would stay on the court; that because of grief for his daughter (he once said he had "a genius for privacy") he refused the nomination again in 1920 when it meant certain election. Hughes is a perfect illustration of what David Riesman means when he speaks in *The Lonely Crowd* of the "inner-directed person" as an American character type of the past, in contrast with the "other-directed person" of today. We have lost much in losing that kind of man.

I wish the know-nothings of today could be induced to read this book and get some of the courage and principle of Hughes. He was a Republican who never feared to face and fight the doughface politicians inside his own party. He was a corporation lawyer who never worshiped business power. Most of all, he was a conservative who stood up for the civil liberties of men far removed from his own principles. He appeared dramatically before the New York Legislature in 1920 to protest the exclusion of the five Socialist Assemblymen. He fought on the Supreme Court against Southern peonage practices, antilabor statutes, Jim Crow laws.

He was a man strong enough to ride the currents of his time. What has become of the conservatives of our day with the courage to do his kind of job? Think how Hughes would behave today in the era of the McCarthy terror. I'd rather take the old Nonconformist, beard, whiskers and all, than a carload of the smooth-shaven boys of today.

4. Hoover: The Elite That Failed

April 29, 1957

THE SHARPEST POLITICAL GAP between the generations today is between those who remember the Great Depression and those for whom it is only a catch phrase. Arthur M. Schlesinger, Jr.'s, book *The Crisis of the Old Order* (Houghton, Mifflin) gives memorably the chronicle of a man called Hoover and a man called Roosevelt. This is history written in the grand style by a scholar still on the threshold of forty, who has already spent a decade mapping out the panels of his projected *Age of Roosevelt*.

The book has a bold, clear over-all structure, an eye for colorful detail assembled in unforgettable vignettes, a feel for the characters who swarm over the stage, a good narrative pace, a skill in intellectual history, and a style which is neither too bare nor (with a few exceptions) too flowery but is a craftsman's style, adapted to its purpose. It has also the passion of a man who believes that the era was at once of tragic and heroic stature, and that its principal figure was a man with plenty of faults but a man for the ages.

A hostile review in *Time* (it would be better if their reviews were signed) says that Schlesinger "lays down a line" that "business during the early years of the 20th Century pretty much ran the U.S." and that "businessmen plundered and ruined" the economy. Yet this does scant justice to a book that weaves together from hundreds of sources ("pasted together," says *Time*) the story not of a business group that "plundered" the nation but of an elite of self-chosen men that was too greedy to know its self-interest, too cocky to believe that the "New Era" of prosperity would ever end, and (when the crisis came) too blind and blundering to save itself or the nation.

Who were these "tycoons" and "titans"? What was the true nature of the "Old Order" that collapsed in days when the stock market broke, and men starved, and farmers held a debt "holiday," and the "Bonus Army" camped hopelessly on Anacostia Flats, and the President sat white-faced and anxious in Washington eating his heart out but too bemused to act and too much a prisoner of old dogmas to venture on new experiments? And what was the nature of the "New Order" represented by the jaunty man with upthrust chin, who had been considered a shallow "feather duster" but gave people somehow a quickening sense of a new national will in action?

These questions are more deceptive than they may seem. Yet a historian must get clear what it was that died in those bleak years of the era of Hoover and what it was that was born in the Roosevelt era.

From another part of the forest, far removed from that of the *Time* reviewer, comes a *Nation* reviewer to deliver a very different attack. Schlesinger, says William Appelman Williams, is talking of the "right crisis" but the "wrong order." The "banker's capitalism," it would seem, really bled to death in the crisis of the 1890s. To be sure, there was a banking panic under Hoover, too, but instead of being the last gasp of the older order, it was "the last adolescent paroxysm of the new order as it lurched into the maturity of full-blown corporation finance."

It is an arresting idea, for if true it would mean that nothing decisive died or was born in those fateful years. It would mean that the whole thing was only an adolescent episode, a case of growing pains in the forward movement of corporate capitalism.

My own feeling is that this was more than an episode. An old order was indeed in crisis between 1919 and 1933, both in the fevers of postwar prosperity and in the chills of depression. But even at that time it was not just a "banker's capitalism" but was all scrambled up with elements of the new corporate economy—which, however, has not died but is very much alive.

The elite that failed under Hoover was a "power elite" of bankers, speculators, corporate executives, and do-nothing government officials, all caught in a futile and fateful mixture. A corporate revolution was in process all through the 1920s. But Hoover and his lieutenants were unaware of what this change meant. They were frightened men, following a blind and frightened leader, like a tribe that had lost its head but still observed all its paralyzing taboos. If they were indeed titans (as their glorifiers called them), then they were wooden titans, mowed down in a row by the thundrous sword of history's wrath. Hoover is not so much a tragic figure as a pathetic one. Like a frozen virgin who had been taught to repulse men and couldn't give herself even on her bridal night, Hoover was too deeply caught in the fear of all state power to use any at the moment of supreme crisis.

So he fell, and had to give way to a man who had been tempered by his own life's tragedy to steel. Roosevelt was a man for whom power was what you made of it—in itself a neutral instrument, taking on the aspect of the purpose for which it was used and the safeguards that offset it.

The later Schlesinger volumes will have to explore how the New Deal had to build a new elite of government officials, yet could never challenge the corporate base of economic power itself. By giving American capitalism a new lease on life, the New Deal prepared for the next stage in technology, which was to bring the soldiers and the scientists to join with the corporate managers. It brought in an Eisenhower, who had learned something from the Roosevelt heritage yet could not shed a good deal of the Hoover respect for the wooden titans.

5. F.D.R.: The Idea in Action

April 29, 1959

I HAVE BEEN a long time getting around to Arthur M. Schlesinger, Jr.'s, *The Coming of the New Deal* (Houghton, Mifflin), but now is as melancholy a time to read it as any. I call it a melancholy experience because the joyousness with which Franklin Roosevelt and his crew of New Dealers went at the crisis problems of their day sets off in sharper contrast than anything else could do the dreary, spiritless immobilism of the Eisenhower Administration.

Malcolm Muggeridge writes in the current issue of the *New Statesman* that there simply is no American government today. If you despair of our ever getting one again, or if you have come to think that the tasks of big government in a crisis era are beyond the reach and the imagination of American leadership, then read Schlesinger's crowded but brilliantly evocative account of how Franklin Roosevelt took over from another Eisenhower called Herbert Hoover, and how in two brief years he helped the American people to restore and reform their economy, revitalize their government and find themselves again as a cohesive nation.

It will restore your hope and belief in the possibility of a great dialogue between leaders and people in a democracy.

During the "Hundred Days" of the great decisions and actions at the start of the New Deal, Roosevelt showed a joyous confidence in the task he had set himself, as if he had been preparing himself for it from the beginning of his life. There was, as Schlesinger puts it, "a combination of power and delight" which was new to the White House. At a time when democracies walked in the shadow of the Nazi *Führerprinzip,* and when liberals were afraid of the exercise of leadership power, Roosevelt knew that power is whatever you make it, and that its quality flows from the frame within which it is used. The Hundred Days after March 4, 1933, saw fifteen major laws hammered out in all-night sessions by the brain trust and sent to a Congress whose leadership was largely Southern but which passed them, basically because they made sense in a time of chaos and gave some hope in a desperate era.

What Roosevelt accomplished, as no President before him had done, was the organization of the collective emotion, confidence and will.

Since the author is describing the laying down of the main lines of the New Deal in its first two years, the book is not only a clearly illuminated portrait of the President in action but also a legislative and administrative history. Triple A, the NRA, the international trade and money policies, the relief agencies, the Civilian Conservation Corps, the PWA, the TVA, the land resettlement agencies, the labor act, the SEC—all are brought before the reader gravely, solidly, but also dramatically.

This is history come to life, its events just old enough to be almost dead for readers under forty, yet recent enough to be extremely bothersome if you try to get some perspective on it. The actors of the drama who have died have left memoirs, yet the younger ones are still alive, and the author has interviewed most of them. Quite understandably he is less sharp in his delineation of the quick than of the dead. Yet usually Schlesinger lets the story tell itself, with shrewd historical appraisals, but without the sharp historical judgments of which he is capable.

The details are abundant, sometimes even cluttering, but are kept within a frame of economy of language. The style leans too heavily upon contemporary quotations, some of which may light up a whole situation or attitude, but too often the method is to get the effect by repetition. Yet the sentences flow warmly, limpidly, clearly, even where they deal with difficult economic theory or administrative techniques. Schlesinger shows a mastery of the expository style such as few historians have today. The mood is quiet and mellow, the portraits of the actors are done with deft, clean strokes, and the emotion —even in the passages where it breaks through—is restrained. This is not the style of a Gibbon, a Parkman or a Churchill. In terms of painting it belongs not with Goya or El Greco but with the Flemish masters.

As one might expect from Schlesinger's own interest in politics, he is at his best when he is dealing with Roosevelt's genius as a political strategist, with the constant tactical warfare inside the New Deal agencies and between them, and with the "resurgence on the Right" which came toward the end of the two-year period, mainly in the struggle over the airmail contracts, the bitter fight over the control of the stock markets, and the activities of the Liberty League.

Where I am most disappointed by the book is in its failure to deal adequately with the idea sources of the New Deal, although some of this was done in Schlesinger's first volume. While Roosevelt was no intellectual and not even a reader, he did have ideas, and the men he gathered around him had even more. Unless we know where they came from, and how they started, we miss part of the drama of how they got transformed by the new needs of the day and the urgencies of action. We do get a discussion of the role that the ideas of Keynes played, and a glimpse (but not much more) of the role of Brandeis, Patten and Van Hise, but almost nothing of William James or Thorstein Veblen.

Since the New Deal was an idea in action, we need to know about the idea as well as the action.

May 17, 1959

In my earlier column on Arthur Schlesinger's *Coming of the New Deal,* I spoke of the New Deal as a liberal revolution with ideas behind it. But a revolution needs a leader to inspire and command it, and a general staff to direct its carrying out. Franklin Roosevelt, as leader, gathered around him as an administrative general staff a remarkable group of men—among them Hopkins, Tugwell, Ickes, Rosenman, Frankfurter, Moley, Richberg, Hugh Johnson, Henry Wallace, M. L. Wilson, Corcoran, Morgenthau, Lilienthal and Jerome Frank.

No stranger human collection has ever before been gathered under a single administrative roof. In my view there can be no great governmental actions that do not flow from the meeting of three facts: a sharp and deep social crisis, a commanding leader, and a creative elite.

What kind of leader and what kind of elite did the New Deal have?

Each of the three great Western democracies has had its characteristic crisis of survival and its characteristic response. America led the way with Roosevelt's New Deal. Britain followed with Winston Churchill as war leader in England's darkest and most heroic hour. De Gaulle fol-

lowed as the creator of the Free French at a moment of betrayal, and—
a generation later—as the creator of the Fifth Republic. All three made
an enemy symbol out of the old order, which they replaced with a new
one. All three were men of dictatorial bent, with a belief in their star. All
had a grand stage for their leadership, and a grand conception of it.

Yet of the three it was Roosevelt alone who gathered together so
bizarre an elite of idea-men, innovators and administrators, and who
came away with so many new strategies for restoring and reforming the
elements of the social order that had decayed.

For me the essence of Roosevelt's leadership lay in a double relationship: the one he had with his Brain Trust, setting in motion an administrative revolution, and the one he had with the American people, for
whom he was a symbol of hope and the educator of new perspectives.

In a minor way I caught a glimpse of both these roles. For a brief spell
in 1934 I found myself in a strange job with the Consumers Advisory
Board, working with Mary Rumsey. I felt like a non-functioning champion of a non-existent "consumer." Yet the excitement was there, as it
was everywhere in Washington.

Schlesinger goes against the prevailing tide of opinion which has held
that Roosevelt was a bad administrator. In any conventional sense, of
course, he was. But he had to handle a melange of social planners, Key-
nesians and followers of Justice Brandeis' anti-bigness school. He had to
gather idealists, power-hunger operators, liberal Southerners, administrative career men, and more than a handful who didn't belong anywhere near the New Deal. He had to keep them working together ("I
want a happy ship"), while he also played them off against each other.
He wooed them, threatened them, cajoled them, lied to them, charmed
them. He had to cope with chronic resigners and prima donnas, as well
as with chronic yes-men. Like few other Presidents he entered into the
middle-level operations as well as the upper ones. The amazing fact was
not that the administrative machinery creaked but that it worked at all.

Roosevelt was a brilliant political tactician, adept at the twin arts of
"high" and "low" politics. I found him sensitive about possible rival
claimants to leadership and about both his reactionary opposition and
such maverick opponents as Huey Long, John L. Lewis and Phil La-
Follette.

In several conversations with him I questioned him at length about
these men and their followers. He was frank and shrewd in assessing
their danger. But in the end he had great confidence in being able to
reach the people with the counteracting truth. When I talked with him
about his role as educator, and how he proposed to reach the people
when the single-party press blocked his access to them, his answer was
classic: "They have the propaganda of the word," he said. "We have
the propaganda of the deed." Schlesinger's detailed chapters on the
TVA, on relief and public works, and on the efforts to save the land,

show how solidly Roosevelt based his strategy on the deeds themselves.

Schlesinger speaks of the "elusive, pluralistic" leadership that Roosevelt represented and contrasts it with the "four-square, monolithic" leadership of Churchill. This is only half the picture. The other half runs in terms of the distance which the leader maintains between himself and his elite and also between himself and the people. On this score the better contrast is not with Churchill but with De Gaulle. Roosevelt used the tactics of closeness and familiarity, although I agree with Schlesinger that he never quite stripped off his public mask. De Gaulle, on the other hand, uses the tactic of distance, and his autobiography shows how consciously he uses it. One type of leader has to carry the burdens of intimacy, the other carries the burdens of isolation.

6. The Huey Long Story

November 14, 1949

OF ALL the American political figures of our era, the only one who has proved rich material for the novelists and mythmakers has been a redneck from the Louisiana north country called Huey Long. Dos Passos and Hamilton Basso have had a try at him. There was also a novel called *Lion in the Streets*. But the man who made great literature out of Huey is Robert Penn Warren, with his novel *All the King's Men*.

It is a complex and tortured novel, written on several levels, terraced like much of the land one sees cultivated on the Italian slopes. But it has the three qualities that are needed for a theme like Huey's: a brooding sense of the tragic waste of great gifts, and pity for the man who could be himself so pitiless, and the excitement of moral and intellectual debate.

Warren wrote *All the King's Men* in its first draft as a play, published it first as a novel, then rewrote the play version. I saw it produced by the New School playhouse group under Piscator's direction. It didn't quite come off as a play, and much of the debate was muddled, but it had a crude power without losing the sense of pity.

Now it has been made by Robert Rossen into a movie. It is a first-rate one, and if it omits the sensitiveness, the poetry, the tortured awareness of moral dilemmas in the novel, it has far more of Huey Long himself. For it has action and gusto and violence and the wonderful crowd scenes that are frightening because they show the material that an American fascism can work with if it ever comes.

The Huey Long—or Willy Stark—story is the story of the boy from the back country with a fire burning in him, who feels himself shut in by the high walls of an old aristocratic social class and a tight and corrupt political gang, and who has to smash the doors and windows in order to feel his power. Since he has his roots in the people and knows their sorrow and emptiness of life, and since his march to power leads at first through their suffrage, he builds things for them—roads, schoolhouses, universities, hospitals—to make their lives less pitiful. But Willy Stark's story is a deterioration story, and his feeling for the people which starts as a passionate strategic measure ends as a cynical joke.

Huey was a clown because, with a fierce belief in himself and his star, he found himself in a society where to take these things seriously is to be set down as a fool. He preferred to clown it, because with all his pose of being a rebel and an idol smasher, he was deeply conventional. His aims were the same as those of the aristocratic and machine gangs against whom he built up his own fascist gang. They were boodle and power. And his outlook on life was the same: the belief, in a moneyed society, that every man can be bought; the belief, in a violent society, that every man can be terrorized; and, in a depersonalized society, the supreme contempt for people.

"Jack," Willy Stark says, "there's something of dirt on everybody. Man is conceived in sin and born of corruption." What is most terrifying about the Huey Long story is that, as a premise for political action in America, it almost proved true. He built up in Louisiana, which has the size and economy of a Latin-American republic, a Latin-American personal dictatorship—a good deal like Peron's regime in Argentina. But he was after something much bigger. He got to the Senate. He promised the American people to share the nation's wealth among them and make each of them a king. It would be stupid to think that they didn't listen. F.D.R. was plenty worried. He had reason to be, for Huey appealed to the empty lives of Americans, he had made alliances with some of the big corporations, and he planned to get to power by exploiting two of the qualities of our culture—corruption and fear.

He died from the bullet of a young doctor whose father-in-law, a judge, Huey had slandered. Warren adapts this story in the characters of Judge Stanton and young Adam Stanton. In Louisiana there are other stories told of the death, including the version that Huey's own gang killed him. I prefer the doctor story. There is more irony in having a cynical and corrupt fascist killed by a man moved by the sense of honor which the know-nothings have squeezed out of the universe of their calculation.

7. The Education of Harry Truman

(New York *Star*)
November 7, 1948

THE WARMTH is coming back to American life. I have never seen so much confessional breast-beating and sackcloth-wearing on the part of usually cocky commentators as after this 1948 Presidential election. I say this with a wry penitence; if there weren't so many sinners stamping down the sawdust trail to testify to their unworthiness and shout contrite hallelujahs, I would myself join them in confessing that I was not very bright in my election forecast.

By this time the reasons for the upset have been spelled out clearly enough—Dewey's outsmarting himself, Truman's courage and canniness, labor's labors in defeating Taft-Hartley men, the farmers' clinging to the price support program, the Roosevelt tradition and the strength it still has.

Why is everyone so happy about the election, including many who voted for Wallace or Thomas or even Dewey? To answer by calling it the biggest political upset in America's history isn't enough. The emotional force with which the whole thing hit us was due not only to surprise at the result, but to the explosion and release of pent-up resentment. Dewey went around the country delivering not campaign speeches but acceptance speeches. He treated Truman throughout the campaign as an insignificant item in a meaningless dream, as the little man who wasn't there. But the dream developed into nightmare and the nightmare into reality. Harry Truman turned out to be the little man who *was* there. And when we discovered it, we all cheered.

But our resentment is not entirely directed at Dewey, or even at the hapless Roper-Gallup-Crosley trio of pollsters. What links Dewey and this trio in our minds is that they are symbols of the same thing—the effort to supplant human life by the slide rule, to run the political animal as if he were part not of a biological universe but of a mechanical one.

Our emotion comes from a rebellion against the machine principle. Dewey had everything figured out, and we were simply parts of his blueprint of power. Roper and Gallup also had everything figured out, and for them we were parts of a calculating machine which unfortunately counted only heads but couldn't tally the psychic intensity inside them. Hence our emotional explosion. But Dewey is now a dazed failure, and the pollsters have become scapegoats for every smart aleck to slaughter with his tired witticisms. The truth is that in attacking them we deflect our fury from ourselves for having been taken in by the machine principle.

Truman believed in himself and his methods of campaigning, but up to the last minute he was not sure he could infect enough of the people with that belief of his. The same thing applies to the people who voted for him and (mainly) against Dewey. They were silent people, because in most sections of the country the whole weight of the respectable was thrown in Dewey's direction. They kept their thoughts to themselves, kept them even from the poll takers. Each of them waited until he was in the polling booth. And each, in his own mind, thought of himself as part of the minority, voting against the nation's grain.

Each lit a feeble little match in the night's darkness, thinking he was alone. And when he looked around him, behold there was a forest of matches, and in their spluttering of combined illumination the American people saw themselves and their strength and democracy's greatness.

(New York *Star*)
January 9, 1949

A President is best judged by the enemies he makes when he has really hit his stride, and Truman's are now good enemies. Hearst accuses him of "squandermania," John O'Donnell says he is forcing a "galloping communism" on the country, Arthur Krock is alarmed at the idea of the government going into steel and calls the program "state socialism." These are only the first pipings of what will soon swell into a chorus of shocked outrage.

It was inevitable also that talk of a brain trust should come back into the picture, as in the golden days of the Roosevelt hatred. John O'Donnell has already begun, with a double-barreled attack on Leon Keyserling and Harold J. Laski as the dark instigators of the Truman treason. The reference to Laski is particularly wild, explainable only by the abysmal ignorance of some who call themselves newspaper craftsmen.

The attitudes of the ruling economic press elite toward Harry Truman have now run almost the whole gamut of political emotions. When he first became President they softly wooed him. Then they derided him when he showed some impulse to follow the Roosevelt policies. When he cracked down on labor they idolized him, when he got tough with Russia they puffed him up as a statesman, when he lost his hold on the country they dismissed him contemptuously, when he showed himself a smart campaigner they condescended to him. When he turned the tables in the election they gawked at him in an unbelieving stupor and fawned on him with a wretched self-abandonment. Now, when he shows signs of meaning what he said, they are growing hot and angry at him.

There remains only one emotion still to be played: the sheer, outright and unremitting hate they directed toward Roosevelt.

All of which ought to be a good education for Harry Truman, as for any man. If a President learns how to bear up under the shifting impact of the attitudes toward him on the part of the potentates and mandarins of our society, without being shattered, his will should emerge as a sharper and more tempered blade in the political struggle. Truman has gone a long way in learning these things in the past year. I doubt whether a single year's experience in the Presidency has transformed any man as much, since Lincoln's Civil War trials.

Truman was a small-town man, from the lower middle class, who had never done anything with distinction until his wartime investigating-committee chairmanship. He was a drugstore clerk, a newspaper flunky, a bank teller, a dirt farmer, a piano player, a soldier, a haberdasher, a hanger-on of Pendergast in a road job and a judgeship. Up to middle age he was largely a failure in almost everything he undertook.

He was largely a failure as President, too. Yet he had one quality that Lincoln had, which is not a common one in American life—the capacity to face failure without being pulverized by it. He has come out of his election victory a stronger man, with a core of self-confidence which he will need badly in the years ahead. He has learned the hardest thing a man can learn about a great predecessor—not to live in his shadow, yet not to react violently against it. He has learned how to adopt Roosevelt's basic New Deal program, but also to go beyond it toward a program of his own.

The American Presidency is the most exacting office in the world. It can be a mantle of quiet personal strength or it can be a burning Nessus' shirt. No man fills the office without being changed. Some are destroyed by it, others educated. It looks as if Harry Truman were moving over from the first category to the second.

March 18, 1952

I like Harry Truman's book, *Mr. President,* whose titular author and cherishing editor is Bill Hillman. I like it because it is exactly what it says it is—raw material, not a finished product. It gives valuable scraps and chunky pieces and juicy tidbits about a man, but the man happens to be the man in the White House.

Harry Truman has pinned his heart on his sleeve for political daws to peck at. They'll try to tear him to pieces, but I don't think they will succeed. Harry Truman is like the fellow who finds himself cornered by his enemies, his creditors, his discarded girls and the sheriff: He throws them an engaging smile and says, "Look, let's sit down and talk this over. I'll tell you about the kind of fellow I am." And they do. And he does.

A good deal has already been written about the courage required to put the book out at this time. But consider whom he principally offends in the book. He offends Jimmy Byrnes, but Byrnes was of-

fended long ago and has for months been bent on thrashing Truman
with a Dixiecrat leather-belt-on-a-pickhandle. He offends Bernard
Baruch, but that idyll was punctured almost four years ago. He offends Henry Wallace, who ran against him in the last campaign as the
enemy symbol of warmongering. He offends some reactionary Senators, who would knife him anyway. He offends Congress in the abstract, but the Congressional fangs have been dripping in anticipation
of his political demise for years.

The men he offends, then, are men he has already had to write off
as political losses. Look at the other side of the ledger, however.
Harry Truman is in many ways a simple man, but he is not so
simple as to be in ignorance of the sources of his popular appeal. He
knows that his credit with the people thrives (1) on the idea of his
having enemies who are his enemies because he is the people's tribune; (2) on the idea of his carrying on Roosevelt's major trend,
yet being clearly someone other than Roosevelt—being a pretty ordinary man much like themselves; (3) on the idea of his having sized
up the challenge of the Russians, yet having a passion for peace.

This is the picture of himself that Harry Truman tries—with a
subtle artfulness that almost conceals his art—to get across. If he
succeeds even 70 per cent, it will be a big political coup. It isn't, I
confess, quite the picture of Harry Truman that emerges for me. I
get not a contrary one but a different one.

I see a man who is in the most genuine sense an American primitive. He is what Grandma Moses would paint if she were to paint an
American President or stitch him into a quilt. He has all the Puritan
virtues, and he believes in them unstintedly. He believes in thrift and
self-reliance and self-discipline, in getting up early and working hard
and going to bed early at night and sleeping the dreamless peace of
the just. He believes in Mom and "my sweetheart and my baby." He
believes in understanding the motives of his enemies, and in sticking
by his friends ("to the last drop of mercy"). He defends his daughter
against criticism as a father should. He believes in utter personal
honesty, and above all in courage to do what he thinks right. He
practices the homely maxims of the copybook and the sampler. He
thinks the Supreme Court should stick to its judicial last, and that all
should be right and orderly in a right and orderly universe.

It is in many ways an appealing portrait. But it is almost wholly a
two-dimensional one, with a flatness as in one of Grant Wood's
paintings. Even his loneliness (and what a lonely man a President
can be) is a flat kind—that of a man who misses his wife and daughter, rather than the tragic loneliness of a Lincoln. He has something
of Andrew Jackson in him, but more of the tailor from Tennessee,
Andrew Johnson.

What the book doesn't tell is what perhaps no man can tell: how the Missouri farm and small-town boy turned into the man on whose shoulders an empire fell, and how those shoulders proved somehow strong enough to carry it without crumbling its power or destroying its freedom. And how a man rooted in all the virtues of order was able to survive in a chaotic world. That is not only Truman's story, but in the deepest sense the story of a democracy.

8. Douglas MacArthur: Eagle of Destiny

August 30, 1950

WE DON'T GO MUCH for Men of Destiny. If you assess shrewdly the clatter in the primitivist papers about the "gag" thrust on General MacArthur, you will find that it is nine parts wind and the tenth venom. For it goes against the grain of two deeply rooted American traditional principles.

The first is the tradition that the American people are military but not militarist. The second is that our government, especially on foreign policy, is a Presidential government. The President is both Commander in Chief of our armed forces, whether in peace or war, and the "sole organ of the nation in its external relations," as John Marshall put it 150 years ago.

I suspect that President Truman had this principle firmly in mind yesterday when he sent his important message to General MacArthur. One part of the message commended him for his conduct of the Korean war; that was the Commander in Chief talking. The other part of the message gravely informed him what the policy of the American people and government is on Formosa; that was "the sole organ of external relations" talking to a man who has tended to stray off his military reservation.

There will, I know, be for a while more clatter than ever from the Yahoos. But it will be short-lived, a thing of sound and fury, signifying nothing but their emptiness of knowledge and their bitterness of spirit.

I fear that MacArthur's conditioning may have a good deal to do with his shenanigans. When a man has been a deputy son of the Sun-God for five years, and his word has been law not only for his own yes men but for the whole of an occupied country, it is hard to break himself of the habit of divinity, reinforced by a brooding conviction of his own destiny. But in America we recognize no political gods but the voice of the people, and no political destiny except what we shape by taking thought together.

January 31, 1951

America, having grown (or leaped) into empire, has produced its full-fledged proconsul in Douglas MacArthur. He is our first combination of military leader and provincial administrator. A few days ago MacArthur turned seventy-one and John Gunther's new book on him, *The Riddle of MacArthur* (Harper), is a kind of birthday present to him, gaily wrapped up in Gunther's jauntiest, chattiest and most buoyant style. It points out his blunders and his egotism, but it is generous in portraying his talents.

The striking thing about MacArthur is that not only has he become a legend, but the legend has gripped people as diverse as Hearst (and his most reactionary readers) and a tough-minded liberal like Gunther. But, given MacArthur's many paradoxes, is it true that this product of the Wisconsin frontier has, as Gunther puts it, "an instinct for understanding Orientals"? To be sure, he landed in Japan at the war's end with only a corporal's guard, and he got away with his gamble. But in his spell in the Philippines from 1937 to 1941 he underestimated Japanese strength; his complete intelligence failure in Korea last June was, Gunther agrees, a worse blunder than Pearl Harbor; and his rout by the Chinese near Manchuria was one of the needlessly blackest hours in American military history.

The key to the riddle of MacArthur's personality is that he is a compulsive man. He is obsessed with his mission, with his work, with his son, with his daily habits that take on a legendary rigidity. And he is obsessed with his ideas on military and political strategy.

Thus what may seem egotism in others (he regards himself and the Pope as the two great leaders of Christianity) becomes in him the expression of his compulsiveness, turned in on himself as the object of his obsession. And like other obsessive people, the only parts of the real world he sees are those reflected in the mirror of his own image of himself. Of course he is able, penetrating, erudite, dynamic, a brilliant conversationalist—all the adjectives Gunther applies to him. If he were not all these things, then—given his compulsions— he would be a ludicrous or mad figure, like someone in an asylum who fancies himself Napoleon. His abilities enable him to get away with his obsessions.

His mind works from within outward, not from without inward. He immures himself from the world and spins his own world out of his innards. He goes through history a little like a sleepwalker, which is a different thing from saying that he is asleep. He is entranced by his own dream, and since he is brilliant his intuitions often come close to the world's realities.

Although he is a lonely man, he has a flair for publicity. When his intuitions fail him, he has to restore his self-confidence by manufacturing history. Thus his escape from Bataan was only a "transfer of headquarters." And his rout by the Chinese in North Korea was, as he tells it now, only a way of forestalling the big Chinese push and throwing it off balance.

A brilliant, obsessive man will usually have successes because the world is made of putty, and we want the impress of a strong, self-confident personality. (Hitler said that the masses are a woman, wanting to be mastered.) But what happens when the sleepwalker encounters a new tough ruling group, like the Chinese Communists, who won't recognize his legend because they have one of their own?

April 11, 1951

It took courage for President Truman to do what he did. When a general hurls a direct challenge at the whole civilian authority of the American government and refuses to conduct his command except on the terms of his own political high policy, his challenge cannot be met by appeasement or double talk or cowardly acquiescence. There is only one way to meet it, and that is by the resolution and courage which the President has shown in his crackdown on General MacArthur.

This MacArthur crisis is the first major internal crisis of the military caste that America has had to meet during this era of world wars. To find anything like its equal one must look to the political adventures of the Reichswehr generals or of the military dictatorships of Latin America. Since the days of Cromwell the British, with their common sense and their discipline, have managed to steer clear of such crises. America has had the good fortune to have military heroes like Eisenhower and Marshall, Bradley and Nimitz, who have had a basic concern for civilian democratic practices. Even the Billy Mitchell affair and the recent battle of the Pentagon over the admirals have been minor compared with the MacArthur crisis.

America itself was caught in a conflict of loyalties, between loyalty to democratic government and loyalty to a flaming military symbol who had become a hero and a myth to many, an anti-Administration messiah who could never do wrong. Such a conflict of loyalties between a military hero and a democratic society is bound to end in disaster unless it is decisively resolved.

But it would be folly to believe that the MacArthur crisis is now over. In one sense the rough part of it has just begun. Don't underestimate MacArthur's flair for the dramatic, or the sense of destiny at whose service his dramatic sense functions. Will he accept his dismissal from his high posts and come home as a private citizen determined to do nothing to split his country further and exploit the split? Or will he lend his name and fame and personality to a movement that can fan all the worst hatreds and the most inflammable emotions in the nation?

John Gunther says there is much of the old-fashioned nineteenth-century political liberal in him. I hope Gunther will be proved right, for a nineteenth-century liberal—or a twentieth-century one, for that matter—would never dream of pushing his fight to the edge of civil strife.

One can guess that on his return to America, MacArthur will be received by press, Congress and people as both a hero and a martyr. I have been traveling currently in the deeply Republican territory of Rochester and Buffalo, and many of the people with whom I have discussed MacArthur give him an almost grotesque idolatry and have made him the symbol of all their anxieties and frustrations.

President Truman has known all this, which is what makes his act all the more courageous. Surely never in the history of a democracy has a civilian government acted so patiently, and never has a military man so blatantly goaded it and jibed at it. In the end there was no other answer but to show that the foreign policy of the United States is shaped in the United States, by the people we have elected to shape it, and not at the whim of a supreme commander in Tokyo.

April 17, 1951

It is a good thing for General MacArthur to come home. His service to his country has kept him away so long that he has cut himself off from the warm, direct sources of its feel of earthiness and its sense of humor. One of the penalties a returning warrior pays, as he steps off his plane, is to step into an artificial atmosphere of almost hysterical greeting. If this hysteria cannot be escaped, neither can it be sustained. Even the magic of a five-star uniform is powerless to keep a myth going once it has begun badly to sag and crack. And the cracks in the MacArthur myth have been painfully evident even to his adorers. A few more days must elapse—the acclaim on the rim of the Pacific, the triumphal flight across the continent, the speech to Congress, the parade in New York—before we shall be able to chart the downward swoop of an arc that zoomed up so explosively.

The General will talk and talk, and his beholders and listeners will cheer and cheer. The words will be majestic and sonorous, for the General was always one for the grandiloquent phrase. Yet what is left will be not a great wave of the future, but the poor spindrift of a spent and tattered symbol.

April 18, 1951

There is a little book called *War and Civilization* (Oxford Press), which gathers all the striking Toynbee passages on the theme of militarism in a convenient compass. Toynbee has spent years studying the rise and fall of the great civilizations of history. He tells us that "war has proved to have been the proximate cause of the breakdown of every civilization which is known for certain to have broken down." And in most cases it took the form of the cancerous disease of militarism.

You will find the melancholy roster of the victim civilizations here —Assyria and Babylon and Persia, Sparta and Athens and Rome, and all the rest. You will find the list of the so-called conquerors: Assurbanipal, David, Charlemagne, Tamerlane, Suleiman, Alexander, Caesar, Cromwell, Bonaparte, and the disasters that each prepared for himself and his people. No matter how brightly the glory of MacArthur burns in the pages of Hearst, Howard and McCormick, it pales before these even mightier military names, whose brightness in turn was quenched by the "suicidalness of militarism."

The moral is not simply that he who takes the sword shall perish by the sword. Taking the sword may be at times—and ours is surely such a time—the only way of collective survival against the thrust of aggression, and therefore a necessary evil. Everything depends on how you grasp the sword, whether with swagger and exultation, thinking there is glory in it and salvation, or with a tragic sense of how dangerous it is even when there is no alternative.

The terrible fact about a civilization which glories in the sword, worshiping the so-called military virtues and making gods of its military men, is that the sword which is first used against the outlying enemy is in the end turned inward into the society itself. The result is always a dry rot and hollowness internally, and if the society does not perish from its overwhelming arrogance it perishes from its dry rot. Toynbee has shown this brilliantly in the detailed story of Sparta and of Assyria.

That is why it was imperative to crack down on MacArthur. But once we took the path of militarism, we would have to reshape our America to fit it. What good would it have done us to know that we were armed to the teeth with the latest gadgets of annihilation? In terms of freedom we would have died an inner death, and become, in Toynbee's unforgettable phrase, a "corpse in armor."

May 7, 1951

Last week, for three successive days, General Douglas MacArthur talked. Today is General George Marshall's day. After that will come Generals Omar Bradley, Lawton Collins, Hoyt Vandenberg and the rest. Our fightingest men seem to have turned out the talkingest in the nation.

May I, as a reader of the thousands on thousands of words with which General MacArthur bore witness, confess my sense of how little was left after the rhetoric and the water had been squeezed out in repeated readings? MacArthur proved himself a good tactician. It would be hard to recall when a witness before a Senate committee had ever managed to dominate the proceedings so completely. If you ask how he managed it, the answer must be sought in the arts of the drama rather than those of statesmanship or generalship. What MacArthur possesses to the hilt is the grand manner. No one in public life in our time has possessed it to an equal extent unless it be John L. Lewis in America and Winston Churchill in Britain. A few of the great old actors and actresses have it also. The spell each casts comes from not dissimilar sources—a legend, a flair for timing, a set of favorite phrases that give you the shock of recognition, and an unshakable inner assurance that the ego of the actor is the center not only of his universe but of yours as well.

One trait MacArthur shares only with the greatest showmen, and that is a sense of distance. There are two kinds of political leaders— those who shake hands and cultivate the familiar, and those who cultivate a kind of inaccessibility. MacArthur belongs in the second group. After a half century spent in giving orders, MacArthur has developed a formidable habit of command which even the boldest Senators scarcely dared to challenge. Senator McMahon alone treated him as if he were a mortal, not a god who had deigned to come down to earth and condescended to be questioned. Some of the other Senators offered a sorry spectacle almost Japanese in its abasement.

What shocked me in the MacArthur testimony was the constant reference to the blood of American soldiers and the effort to evoke blood thinking. It is time to understand that the President too cares about the blood of American soldiers. MacArthur has no monopoly on such solicitude. The problem is still what it was—how to keep blood from being spilled in torrents in a war that might spread.

The most disquieting thing about the whole MacArthur episode is that it has pushed the generals onto the center of the stage, as if the civilians no longer counted and it were only a question of matching Administration generals against anti-Administration generals. When only the generals talk, and the rest of us are silent, you have a pretty good definition of militarism.

9. The World of Robert Taft

August 3, 1953

I THINK that Bob Taft, could he read the comments on his death, would feel contempt for the fawning extravagance of some of them. He was an honest man who didn't like hypocrisy. We have proof again that at a man's death we cannot hope to take his true measure in history.

With all his ability and his cross-grained genuineness, Taft will not belong to the great ones of our time. He had a sharp mind and the skills of a good advocate. He was equipped with a command over his material which the lazy or fuzzy lack. He could deflate sawdust-stuffed men when he chose to. He made no cult of consistency.

All these traits he had. Yet they were not enough, for he had also a poverty of vision that narrowed his view of the world and of America's position in it and made him miss greatness. Even when he shifted his view, he walked reluctantly backward into the future. He must be counted one of those men who have great power and influence during their life, but on whom history takes its revenge after their death because they never dared summon the people to its full stature.

The Taft doctrine of military strategy was a curious compound of 20 per cent sense and 80 per cent nonsense. The American people are coming more and more to feel that we must not take on commitments beyond our actual capacity to fulfill with the aid of our allies. To underscore that vigorously, as Taft does, is a healthy thing. But for all his denials, the overtones of his speeches implied that we might as well write off the chance of defending Europe against aggression. He was wrong on this. In the end a free Europe can keep its hope for freedom alive only with American help, including men as well as arms. To deny this help is to abandon the hope itself. That is why Senator Taft's world was an unreal one. It left out those intangibles which are more important than military strategy, whether that strategy is based only on naval and air forces or on land forces as well.

There is a passage in Henry Adams which may be worth quoting here. "Resistance to something," Adams wrote, "was the law of New England's nature. The New Englander, in a long struggle with a stingy or hostile universe, had learned also to love the pleasure of hating; his joys were few."

This may furnish a clue to the bleak but persistent war that Taft waged against labor, the New Deal and the Fair Deal, and against anyone he suspected of being an internationalist. Taft was not a New Englander, but he had the Puritan strain still in him. For the Midwest conservative is simply the New England conservative transplanted to a flatter landscape. Without losing the New England virtues, Taft had picked up some of the Midwest tensions that narrowed them. His hates were many—the New Dealers, the bureaucrats, the spenders, the welfare state, the intellectuals, the Europeans, the Republican liberals. His joys were few.

What might have happened, had he been elected President, is one of those idle ifs of history. The 1952 defeat was a heartbreaking one for him, because Taft knew that he was more in tune with his party than Eisenhower was, and he could not understand why the party should reject him. How would it have been possible to tell him that the people of a democracy hunger for bigness of proportions in their leaders, and while they might use him when he was a useful weapon, they did not associate him with the future?

He showed stoicism and courage as he faced his tragic death. For a time he will leave a gap in Washington. It is a sad commentary on the present state of the Republican Party that this man, so long a symbol of the Republican right wing, should now be celebrated as the man of the center who held the party together. It is also a sad commentary on the present administration that Taft's death should leave it panicky, for loss of "leadership."

Taft remained an archconservative. He championed MacArthur and his Asiatic policies. He had an understanding with Joe McCarthy which at one time amounted to an alliance, although he had to break with him on the Bohlen issue. His last speech had lamented our being tied to the United Nations. If he did much to hold the extreme right-wingers in line under Eisenhower, we must remember also that he had done much to create their mood. "By their fruits ye shall know them," was one of his favorite quotations. There is a sense in which the dismal roster of Republican Senatorial primitives who now plague the Administration and the nation were the fruits of Taft's teachings.

Taft, when he died, was what he had always been—an American primitive, gnarled, cold, cantankerous, largely wrongheaded, and exasperating even when he was right. But he adds a dimension to the great debate that neither Hoover nor Dewey could add. And if his views had their impact it is because the Administration left a vacuum for someone with vigor—even a wrongheaded vigor—to move into.

His strength and his tragedy lay in the fact that he was far better than his disciples and allies. He was a real conservative, where they are reactionaries. He was thin-lipped, sturdy, often wrongheaded, unsentimental. But he cared about America and he cared about civil liberties, and what he believed he believed with intensity. That is why Joe McCarthy's comment that he was "the greatest man I have ever known" is grotesque in its irony. There was a world of things Taft understood that McCarthy will never know. For Taft wanted to preserve American differences, not strangle them.

10. Eisenhower: The Years of the Vacuum

September 23, 1956

NO MATTER how folksy the candidates and their running mates may get, and no matter how hard they may try to behave as if they couldn't be distinguished from the other faces in the crowd, the fact remains that the Presidency is the grandest, most powerful, and most important office in the world. Whoever is in danger of forgetting this can refresh his image of the office. We are lucky in having available what is probably the best book ever to appear on the subject—Clinton Rossiter's recently published *The American Presidency* (Harcourt). It is brief, compact, compassable and warm. The problems are lucidly explained, the analysis is forcefully argued, the verbal portraits of various Presidents are skillfully drawn, the judgments of them are at once shrewd and just, and—most important—the design of the growth and stature of the office itself is projected onto the page and the reader's mind.

If you once get into your mind the great history of the Presidential office and the stature of its leading figures—Washington, Jefferson, Jackson, Lincoln, Theodore Roosevelt, Wilson and Franklin Roosevelt —you will be less likely to be swept away by the extravagance of the Eisenhower personality cult. I want to make it clear that I am not quoting Rossiter, who happens to be much more moderate in his judgments than I am and is the author also of a history of American conservatism. Rossiter devotes a couple of chapters to the powers and limits of the Presidency. I wish he had added something on the *authority* of Presidents. Presidential power has grown ever greater, and there are fuzzy boundaries around it. But the real point is that the power any particular President sways derives less from the Constitutional provisions than from his conception of the office and his own personality and political style.

You couldn't find a better instance of this than the case of Franklin Roosevelt. Again we are lucky in having an important political biography of him—*Roosevelt: The Lion and the Fox,* by James M. Burns (Harcourt), done with sympathy and candor. It is the measure of Roosevelt's greatness that whatever you may have thought of the man, his achievements have transformed our time—and also the Presidential office. From now on it is highly unlikely that either of the major parties will dare run a Presidential candidate who does not—explicitly or tacitly—stand on the New Deal as base. I doubt—and I note that Rossiter too doubts—whether the same kind of judgment will ever be made about Eisenhower.

Burns uses the Machiavelli image, that "a prince must imitate the fox and the lion . . . be a fox to recognize traps, and a lion to frighten wolves." Clearly Roosevelt had both courage and guile, as every other great President has had, including Jefferson and Lincoln. He combined them in a political style which enabled him to carry through his victories because he used not only the powers of his office but also the persuasion of his personality and the moral authority of office and personality combined.

Measuring Eisenhower by these standards, I am led to conclude that he has some traits in common with Roosevelt, but also a very different style of his own. He has far more guile than you would think if you judged him by his words. He pretends to stand above the political battle, yet he is up to his neck in politics and has proved the most useful party instrument the Republicans have had for generations. How much courage he has is by no means clear. He never suggests, as Roosevelt did, the lion who frightens away wolves. He can be obstinate about some things, like the farm issue. But on matters like the handling of Nixon, Stassen and the whole Vice-Presidential fiasco of 1956, he showed softness and timidity rather than courage.

What he lacks even more is the capacity to use the great fund of authority he possesses. That the authority is there is an unquestionable fact. But on the two great issues of our time, the issue of meeting the world-wide penetration of the Russians and the issue of the imperilment of Negroes in the South, Eisenhower failed to use his office as a weapon of moral authority.

March 16, 1958

I should hate to write the history of the present American era and find a name for it. Richard Rovere, in his book of *New Yorker* pieces, called it "the Eisenhower Years." Samuel Lubell called it "the Revolt of the Moderates." I fear that my own term would be "the Years of the Vacuum."

It is a fallacy to believe that you need only to get a "team" together, and the team will somehow generate the knowledge of where to go and what to do. Even men of ability can discover what is within them in a crisis only if there is someone to evoke it by giving the direction and setting the example.

The way the "team" shapes up now—Adams, Nixon, Dulles, Mc-Elroy, Strauss, Teller, Benson, Seaton, Rogers, Mitchell—does not exactly spell out the brightest galaxy we have had in our history. It is a curious fact that Truman's "team" was in some ways worse, yet the over-all effect was sharper and stronger because it had someone on top who kept the total picture in his head. Even Adams doesn't do that, because his job is to execute, not lead. Nor does the current attack on him, justified as it is, serve to make a leader out of a small man.

I think it is wrong to say that the Eisenhower Administration lacks a philosophy. It has one. I don't mean "modern Republicanism," and I don't mean "dynamic conservatism"—or whatever it was in those dim dead years when the President still coined those curious phrases. I mean the President's own personal philosophy, which more and more is shaping up as one of leaving nature alone to work out its laws, and meanwhile trusting to God and Sherman Adams. The most revealing political acts of President Eisenhower in the past year have been not his decisions to do something but his decisions *not* to do something—not to fire Dulles and Benson.

Both men stayed. What saved them? Not the same passion for loyalty to his "cronies" which used to make Harry Truman loath to take action against them. General Eisenhower is capable of turning against a subordinate, as witness what happened to Wilson, Brownell, Stassen. But Benson stands as the symbol of a "natural" system by which the American farmer must learn to care for himself, even in a corporate welfare state; he stands for the farmer in a state of nature. Even Dulles, for all his brinkmanship, stays in touch with the President constantly and depicts for him a world far simpler than the truth—a world in which we must stand firm against Russia, not abandon our principles and positions, and let things take their course toward the natural triumph of peace, justice and the UN.

There is one area of American government today in which one gets the sense of sharpness and vitality. It is the one area where the men involved, once appointed, are wholly independent of the Administration—the Supreme Court. Legal historians will call it the "Warren court," because Chief Justice Earl Warren has added to it the distinctive mark of his vision and courage. How easy it would have been for Warren to let things ride, to keep postponing the core issue of equal opportunity for Negro and white children alike, and the issue of the rights of people before Congressional committees. How easy it would have been to be mealymouthed, chickenhearted and birdbrained. But Warren, with the help of Black and Douglas, of Frankfurter and Brennan, chose the dangerous course of leadership. He refused to turn the Constitutional process into a vacuum.

Those who believe that the hinge of fate is an exceedingly thin one may engage in reflections about where we would be if Warren, not General Eisenhower, had been the Republican nominee for President in 1952, or even in 1956.

But such reflections are futile, even while fascinating. The harsh fact for a harsh age is that our fate is being ground out in these years of the vacuum. In the three great areas of policy—domestic economics, foreign relations and nuclear weapons—the watchword is to stay as we were and react (always too late) to events not willed by our decision makers.

In dealing with the depression, these decision makers behave like an ancient emperor waiting for the auspices to be read and the soothsayer to speak before he can act. In foreign policy, Dulles manages the near-miracle of perpetual mobility and deep rigidity inside a vacuum. In nuclear policy, there are two men—Strauss and Teller—who are doing everything possible to prevent disarmament rather than to give it a chance. The only man in the Administration who has made sense on disarmament—Stassen—is out in the cold.

I feel a bit cold too, in these years of the vacuum.

11. The High and Mighty

April 17, 1957

THE MOST FASCINATING ITEM that has swum into my ken in the past forty-eight hours is the outburst by Brother Edgar against Brother Milton and sundry other nefarious persons for influencing Brother Dwight in too "liberal" a direction. The three brothers are, of course, in a family called Eisenhower. The cleavages inside the group of men who run Washington and the country have rarely been as nakedly exposed as they are now. Clearly the men who hold the economic power in our system have come to distrust the men who hold political power and who cluster around President Eisenhower. Poor Brother Edgar, in his bumbling explosive honesty, reflects the mood of smarter and more powerful men than himself who are bewildered because the indispensable hero, for whose election and re-election they fought and bled and paid good money, is now behaving like a spending do-gooder from the other side of the tracks.

There is trouble in the paradise of the powerful. There is confusion among the men who sit in the seats of the high and mighty.

Which leads me to ask a question: Who are the high and mighty in America? Is there a single dominant class, built around the interests of property, as Robert S. Lynd said in a review in the *Nation* of the recent book by C. Wright Mills, *The Power Elite?* Or are there a number of elites, or upper circles of top men, each circle enclosing and ruling its own domain? Or is there, as Mills himself seems to believe, a combination or coalition of these elites which forms the "power elite" and really runs the show?

These are not idle questions. If we could answer them we would know who makes the decisions that determine what chances we get in life, and what we are allowed to make of these chances.

Who elected Eisenhower, poured out money for him, blackened Stevenson? In my book it was the big corporate executives, the one-party press, and the buildup artists and symbol manipulators of the big agencies.

Who pushed Nixon through for Vice-President in 1956 over the doubts of some of Eisenhower's closest advisers? Again it was the corporate group, along with the Old Guard wing of the Republicans' local party leaders. Who refurbished Nixon with a "new look"? Again, the experts in buildup and symbols.

Who was behind the catastrophic security hearings of Robert Oppenheimer? Again, the Pentagon leaders, the Atomic Energy Commission head and the corporate executives who have big stakes in the uses and exploitation of nuclear energy.

Who was first complacent about McCarthy and then decided that he was expendable? A group of political insiders on Capitol Hill, in the White House, and among the Pentagon civilians.

Who decided to save Nasser's neck from the Suez noose? Eisenhower and Dulles and the Pentagon, all acting under pressures from the big oil interests.

Who will decide whether, when and where nuclear weapons and guided missiles will be "delivered" against an enemy? A small group called the National Security Council, whose chairman is the President.

I have chosen these examples of big decisions from a wide range. They illustrate how hard it is to give a single answer to the question of who are in the seats of the mighty. Clearly, one group is made up of perhaps a few score top political leaders—in the White House, in the State Department, on Capitol Hill. A second group consists of the military leaders, the Pentagon, and the National Security Council and the Atomic Energy Commission. A third group is the cluster of opinion builders for whom we use the trick symbol of "Madison Avenue," and whom Vance Packard in a new book calls "the Hidden Persuaders." A fourth group includes the big corporate managers who wield the economic power which is largely behind the power of the others. I am not talking here of the "top rich" of our economy, or even of the "big income" groups, but of the men who make the business decisions—even though they don't themselves own the property in whose name and for whose interest they speak and act.

Put them all together and they spell Power, a word that means the world to them.

I don't go with Wright Mills in believing that there is any one single or combined "power elite." There are intersecting power clusters— including also writers and intellectuals and church leaders, whom I have not mentioned. But in most cases the four groups I have listed make their weight felt unmistakably.

THE MASKS IN THE HISS CASE

1. I Dreamt That I Was Alger Hiss

(New York *Star*)
December 14, 1948

I DREAMT LAST NIGHT that I was Alger Hiss. It was a heavy, night-marish imagining, full of the wildest irrelevancies. I guess I had been seeing too many Alfred Hitchcock pictures and reading too many im-probable mysteries.

I was in my study (in my dream) reading one of those mysteries when there was a heavy tramping up the steps and a thundrous knock at my door. Without waiting for me to open, in trooped Parnell Thomas, Richard Nixon, Robert E. Stripling, John Rankin, a man who looked like Orson Welles playing William Randolph Hearst, and (I could have sworn) a man with the head of a pumpkin.

"Are you Alger Hiss?" they asked in unison.

"Yes," I answered, for the dream held me in a hypnotic spell.

"Come with us," said Parnell Thomas, and as he spoke the motley group enclosed me storm-trooper fashion and marched me down the steps and into the dense night. We stumbled over rocky fields and were scratched by thickets and once we plunged into water and I had to fight my way forward against a resisting current. Finally we came into a clearing, and suddenly out of the darkness there was a rush of light and a din of sound, and I found myself in the pit of a vast and brightly lit outdoor theater like the kind at which the Romans used to hold their circuses.

Although I was alone in the large pit in which (I fancied) gladia-tors may once have killed and been killed, I felt as constricted and terrified as they must have felt. All around me, rising tier on tier, were the people. I recognized some of the faces as those I had seen at baseball games, prize fights, in night clubs.

I wanted to tell them the truth, but what was the truth about me?

Suddenly something clicked in my mind, and the phantom shapes of the past took on clarity of form, and I knew I had my answer. I turned to the group of judges, who were dressed in black robes like the Supreme Court, but held axes in their hands like the Thomas-Rankin committee.

"Your Honors," I began, "it now comes back to me. I was a Communist once, a long time ago when I was a young man working for my chief. I was even, I suppose, a spy—at least, in outward form." I paused a moment, while a great silence fell upon the whole assemblage.

"You see," I continued, gaining confidence as I spoke, "the chief wanted to know what was going on. He needed a man who would be willing to become a Communist for a spell—a man who would be willing to run the risks of being a counterspy. He chose me to find out because I could talk Marxism, and the Communists would not suspect me."

The judges looked skeptical. One of them spoke: "Can you call on any witnesses who knew about this assignment of yours and can check it?"

"No," I said. "I cannot. I was the chief's personal agent, and neither the State Department nor the FBI knew anything. The chief swore me to secrecy, and he alone knew."

"Well, then," asked the judge, "how about the man you call the chief? Will he back you up? If he can't come to court, we could take a deposition from him."

"You would have to take it," I said with sadness, "at a grave at Hyde Park. The man I called chief was Franklin Roosevelt."

With that I flung out my arms in despair. There was a roar of disbelief and rage from the crowd. The whole scene crumbled away, and I woke to find that my gesture had swept to the floor of my bedroom an alarm clock and a mountain of books. I was glad to know I was neither Hiss nor Chambers, but simply I.*

2. Two Men with Masks

November 22, 1949

YOU GO to the second Hiss trial with an unquenched hope that this time something will happen to pin down the question of guilt and innocence, one way or another.

You sit in the courtroom, and your eye roves from the shiny bald dome and the bony, almost mummylike skull of Judge Goddard, to the jury box with its eight women and four men who look middle-aged, middle-class, middle-toned in dress and demeanor, to the bat-

* For a sequel to this piece, see "I'll Never Dream Again," page 445.

teries of six government lawyers and four defense lawyers, to pudgy, round-faced Whittaker Chambers on the witness stand sitting back and looking up at the ceiling as he tries to recall details he has been over dozens of times, to Alger Hiss sitting next to his wife, wearing a gray suit and a gray drawn look like a man who has already borne a little more than bone and flesh can bear but is still holding together an unquavering poise which in anyone else would long ago have cracked.

The trial itself? Most second performances of any drama, however great, are simply repeats of the first. In the case of the second Hiss trial, there are new elements—not only a new jury, but a new defense counsel who is poles apart from the flashy and dramatic posturings of Lloyd Paul Stryker, and a new emphasis in the prosecution's line of attack, and a new strategy by the defense.

If you are interested in trial techniques, it is absorbing to note how each side has studied the mistakes it made in the first trial and changed its strategy. The prosecution no longer gambles everything on Chambers' credibility alone. It is focusing on the documents, and everyone holds the rolls of films up to the light, and the enlargements are pored over and stamped and entered as exhibits.

But the big question, that will still have to be solved in both the jury's conscience and ours, concerns not the documents but the two men.

The strength of the Chambers case lies in the colorful details he presents. "Talking about pseudonyms," says Mr. Murphy gently, "was there one for Hiss?" "Yes," Chambers answers blandly, "Colonel Bykoff gave Mr. Hiss a pseudonym of 'Der Avokat,'" which is German for "the lawyer." And again, telling about a trip he claims the two men took back in 1934, to Erwinna, Pennsylvania, he says he remembers it particularly because on the drive back "we passed a policeman carrying an Easter lily, and that pleased Hiss."

There are two ways of answering details like these, which are meant to nail down the Chambers story on the premise that no one could invent a whole structure of them. One is to try, as Mr. Stryker did in the first trial, to show Chambers up as a congenital perjurer, blasphemer, immoralist and no-good. The conclusion would be that a man like that would not stop at inventing whole situations. The second is to depict Chambers as a psychotic personality who did know Hiss, but who, for some curious quirk of a complex and tortured but enormously skillful mind, is out to destroy his former friend.

Chambers tried yesterday to build beforehand a defense against the second. He was explaining why he had waited so long to produce the "Pumpkin Papers." "I wanted," he said, "to give my friends time to break with Communism . . . There are, I said to the grand jury, two kinds of men. One believes that God is a God of justice, the other believes that God is a God of mercy. I am so constituted that I will always range myself on the side of mercy."

Is he? If he is, then he is not the self-appointed Avenging Destroyer (as some have pictured him), bent for some private motive on breaking Hiss utterly. But if, on the other hand, he had indeed dedicated himself to this destruction, then a mind capable of the whole plan would be capable also of fashioning a hypocritical mask of mercy for himself.

I felt in the courtroom that I was in the presence of two men with masks. Which will be stripped off first?

3. Psychiatry in the Courtroom

January 11, 1950

THERE WERE four kinds of spectators in the crowded courtroom at the Hiss trial yesterday, when Carl Binger underwent cross-examination. There was the legal crowd, the psychiatric crowd, the newspaper crowd—and the leathernecks. In the corridors during the recesses there was a seething diversity of opinion about Binger, whom the defense has called to give an expert appraisal of the personality pattern of Whittaker Chambers. But no one can doubt that it took courage for Binger to expose himself as he is doing.

It means that one of the leaders of the psychiatric profession has deliberately put himself in the line of fire. He will be called an eager beaver and even harsher names by many of his colleagues. But there have been so many conferences of psychiatrists in recent years which have asked psychiatrists to come out of the ivory tower and take part in the dust and grime of the actual conflict in the world, that it is good to see someone taking the injunction seriously.

For better or worse the admission of expert testimony about the mental condition of a witness in a case is an event we will recall. It has been clear from the start that the case turns on the question of which of two men is telling the truth. The answer cannot be reached on political grounds but on psychological. It lies in the confronting of two personalities, seeing how true or hollow they ring, tracing their basic life pattern.

What the Hiss defense has done in this second trial has been to indict in psychiatric terms the whole life pattern of Chambers. Judge Goddard has admitted this evidence, wisely understanding that this is a case where the credibility of the chief witness goes to the root. Some lawyers feel this opens the way in the future for infinite badgering of witnesses by litigants who can afford to call expert psychiatrists and put long hypothetical questions to them. But all new steps open up dangers. The greater danger is that the law will grow so stiff and encrusted that it won't be able to adapt itself to a world in which mental unbalance is a reality and psychiatry a powerful, if not wholly tested, force.

I have found other worries among people in the psychiatric field. They ask whether it is healthy for psychiatry to have someone, no matter how expert, sitting in a courtroom and giving appraisals about a man whom he has never had a chance to question. Binger kept drawing the distinction between what he would have to know about Chambers to treat him, and what he has to know to describe him. Yet what he had to build on was, especially for Chambers' early years, thin enough to seem rickety at times.

The prosecutor, Thomas F. Murphy, played this hard. Repeatedly he took traits of Chambers out of the total pattern and isolated them. Repeatedly Binger tried to put them back in the pattern. Two experts were fencing, each equipped with the skills and jargon of his craft.

January 12, 1950

In the Hiss courtroom, during the cross-examination of Dr. Carl Binger, it is psychiatry itself that is being put on trial. And the prosecutor is the layman. The U.S. attorney, Thomas F. Murphy, is a shrewd fellow who knows how deeply the ordinary layman resents all psychiatrists. He knows that the members of the jury are ordinary laymen. There is never a question he addresses to the witness without calling him "Doctor," with the word underlined by heavy irony as if it combined Cagliostro with Judas Iscariot.

To the lay mind, indeed, a psychiatrist seems something of a charlatan and something of a traitor. Does he not pretend to know things in the working of your mind that even you do not know? And does he not betray that most worshiped of all our gods—"common sense"?

It is as the champion of the layman that Murphy plays his most effective role. He stumbles over terms like "schizophrenic." He mispronounces names like Bleuler. It warms the hearts of the jury—and most of the spectators too—when they see a man who seems to know as little about this devilish pseudo science as they do. No fol-de-rol for this sturdy six-foot-four representative of honest-to-God true-blue common sense.

Murphy's method is an appeal to common experience or to folk history. How about the lies we tell about Santa Claus, Doctor? How about our income tax returns, Doctor? Was Moses' mother a psychopath, Doctor, when she hid Moses in the bulrushes? Is that any different, Doctor, from hiding papers in a pumpkin? Don't women in Reno throw their wedding rings away in order to get rid of something that reminds them of the past? Is that any different from abandoning a typewriter on a streetcar? Have you ever registered at a hotel under an assumed name, Doctor?

There is something slightly wacky, as we know, about all so-called "normal" behavior. By playing this up, Murphy hasn't found it too hard to punch holes in Dr. Binger's concept of a special "psychopathic personality," which he attributes to Chambers. For the jurors Murphy was playing the role of the hardheaded man who trusts only the evidence of his senses. When Binger talked of the way Chambers had acted out, in assuming the name of Adams, the fantasy of being identified with the famous Adams family in American history, Murphy asked, "Doctor, you can't *see* fantasies, can you?" I have no doubt he meant that question to dispose of the whole cloud-built structures of psychiatry.

Many of the newspapermen, judging from corridor talk and the write-ups I have seen, felt the same way. It was all a hilarious show, part of a game (as one headline writer put it) of "Who's the Psycho Now?" The layman has always thirsted to reduce psychiatry to a farce. Here was the chance for the lay mind to take its revenge. The typical reporter represents the layman's mind at its toughest and most cynical phase.

What has been obscured by all this is that there is in fact a personality type which can be called psychopathic. Some of the traits of behavior of this type of person will be found in the everyday behavior of all of us. The pattern as a whole will not.

It is the pattern that counts. Murphy insisted on breaking the pattern into its fragmentary parts. He asked blandly whether it is not true that the whole is the sum of its parts. Quite aside from the question of Chambers and Hiss, my own answer would be decidedly No. In human life the whole is *not* the sum of its parts. Certainly a personality is not the sum of the fragments and atoms into which it is broken. You cannot take the heart or the mind to pieces and add them up and get the heart or the mind.

The method of the hypothetical question, as used in the Hiss case, is a tragically inadequate method by which to introduce psychiatric testimony into a courtroom. Dr. Binger had to limit himself almost entirely to the assumptions about Chambers in the hypothetical question. Murphy, using (as was his right) a far different set of assumptions about Chambers' behavior, was able time and again to force Binger to give a different set of answers.

It was not a farce I saw in the courtroom. It was psychiatry being forced to play a cramped role, with not enough room in it to give any actor a chance.

4. The Political Whodunit

January 30, 1950

To INTERPRET the Hiss verdict politically is to dwarf its meaning. There are those who will try to use it as proof that New Dealers were spies and perjurers, and the Roosevelt Administration a pact with the devil. The Chambers partisans, who saw their hero as a St. George fighting the Red dragon, should have almost as little cause for comfort as the devoted Hiss partisans who saw their hero as the victim of another Dreyfus frame-up.

A jury has found Hiss legally guilty of perjury. The case has proved one of the most desolating tragedies of our time. It is the tragedy of the destructive waste of talent, the wrecking of lives, the poisoning of human relations at the source.

I accept the jury verdict for what it is—a legal verdict, based on a trial conducted with fairness by Judge Goddard, powerfully prosecuted and ably defended. But there is a difference between the legal verdict of a jury and the moral verdict each of us must render to himself. I should feel clearer in my own mind if the machinery for getting at the legal guilt or innocence of Hiss had functioned under circumstances of greater fairness. It has taken a thousand years of the Anglo-American judicial tradition to fashion that machinery, painfully, at the cost of heroism and martyrdom.

It involves more than a fair-minded judge, and an orderly courtroom, and scrupulous rules for admitting or excluding evidence, and a jury of one's peers. It involves also a prosecution as interested in getting at the truth as in getting a conviction, and a social atmosphere in which men can think with coolness and clarity and without the overhanging shadow of fear. How far we are from that atmosphere, in this era of the cold war, was shown at the end of the first Hiss trial, when both the judge and those few jurors who dared hold out against a conviction were subjected to a scrofulous press campaign. After that happened, it would have taken great courage in the second trial for a juror with genuine doubts about Hiss's guilt to have clung to them and braved a similar ordeal. Few men and women are fashioned of the stuff of heroes.

That is part of the poison the case has generated—the poisoning of the social atmosphere within which the legal processes work. But there is also the poisoning of human relations, the turning of former friends into pursuer and pursued. Whittaker Chambers has been vindicated by law, and Alger Hiss has been sentenced to a five-year prison term. But both men will be forever entangled with each other before their consciences. What mixture of motives it was that led Chambers to the implacable pursuit we cannot know. Those he has given us were given within the framework of that pursuit. It is hard to separate what was due to contrition, what to a newly found patriotism, what to vindictiveness.

As for Hiss, a prison term is now added to the agony he has been through. If he is innocent, he should have the inner strength to endure that agony. If he is indeed guilty, then he will have only the grim satisfaction of having acted out his false masque to the end.

But for each man the final arbiter will be a conscience from which he cannot escape, though he flee it "down the arches of the years, down the labyrinthine ways of his own mind, and in the mist of tears."

September 19, 1950

I was in Europe during the first Hiss trial in the summer of 1949, and I remember the effort I made to get copies of the Manchester *Guardian*. I wanted to read the articles its chief American correspondent, Alistair Cooke, was sending back on the trial. They had style, color, a sense not only of courtroom theater but of the dramatic clash of ideas. I had seen only the picking of the jury in the first trial before I left for Europe. Back in New York I managed to get to only three or four sessions of the second trial. There were a handful of good reporters doing craftsmanlike jobs, but I still hunted up a copy of the *Guardian* whenever I could.

The man who caused me that trouble has now written a book on the whole Hiss-Chambers case, *A Generation on Trial* (Knopf). Manchester-born, Cambridge-educated, an American citizen by choice, a student of the American movies and the American language by fatality, Cooke has written a book that may endure almost as long as the memory of the case. It is not a quick and easy indictment, nor a hoarse, vindictive shout to bring the vultures wheeling around the carrion. It is as close to being the whole story of the two trials, set down honestly and without rancor, as anyone could have made it.

It is hard to think back to the time, presumably within our own memory, when the Hiss case did not exist. What gave it the impact it had on us? The first thing was its quality as a political whodunit that will probably never be wholly resolved. But beyond the element of mystery, there is the fact that the trial was not only of Alger Hiss. It was, as Alistair Cooke sees clearly, the trial of a whole generation. He has therefore prefaced his book with a brilliant chapter on the 1930s which he calls "Remembrance of Things Past." He does not make the mistake some others have made of throwing out the baby with the bath water, and damning all the works of the New Deal along with some of the more tender-minded illusions of the New Deal decade.

Although the book is history and not judgment, the author seems to lean strongly toward the belief that Hiss was guilty.* This does not mean necessarily a complete acceptance of the Chambers version of the story. But the documents themselves and the typewriter on which they were typed and the mass of detailed knowledge of the Hisses, which Whittaker Chambers and his wife could have obtained only by knowing them tolerably well—all these mount up to a degree that gives the diehard pro-Hiss group a lot of explaining to do.

Toward the end Cooke lists the ten popular theories of the Hiss case. He omits one, however, that I heard propounded ingeniously at the time of the trials: that Hiss had in fact been mixed up with a Communist spy ring, that he had moved away from it in later years, that he tried at the beginning to brazen out the original Chambers charges and invoked the many friends he had made in high places; that by the time the typewriter was found and Chambers produced the Pumpkin Papers, it was too late for Hiss to take his mask off, since he had drawn into the case not only his own fate but the political fate of those who believed in him and supported him.

But even more important than the mysteries of the case are the layers of tragedy in it. Alistair Cooke has done well to give his book a dimension which previous accounts of the case have missed—the dimension of tragic depth. He has written a compassionate, unflinching book. I have sometimes said that American life lacks a tragic strain, but it is not wholly true. From Jonathan Edwards to Hawthorne and from Melville to Faulkner the theme of guilt and punishment runs like a dark thread through our national consciousness.

That is what the Hiss-Chambers affair was about. But what is still unresolved is the question of whose guilt and whose punishment.

5. Rashomon—a Parable

February 21, 1952

I WENT TO SEE the Japanese movie *Rashomon* for the unlikeliest of reasons. I had a hunch it might shed some light for me on the Hiss-Chambers case. It did. It is a good movie in its own right, brilliantly conceived, acted out like a ritual dance. But if you apply it to the Hiss-Chambers struggle, it may add another dimension to that tortured story.

The idea of *Rashomon* is simple enough. It is to take an episode out

* Later, however, in a Washington *Post* review of Hiss's book (see section 8, page 443), Cooke leaned toward the view that the whole process by which Hiss had moved toward his conviction had been distorted and unfair, and that the case needed rethinking.

of feudal Japan involving deep passions—the encounter of a husband
and his wife with a bandit in a wood, the seduction of the wife, the
killing of the husband—and tell it in different versions and with different nuances, each time from the perspective of a different member of
the triangle.

The theme is, of course, old. It stresses the world of illusion, the
subjective way in which each of us perceives what affects him deeply.
It is an idea that Pirandello was obsessed with.

As the bandit tells the story, he is one devil of a fellow, prancing
and prankish, irresistible to the wife, gallant to the husband, killing
him at the wife's entreaty and only after a magnificent sword duel.
As the woman tells it, she is grief-stricken because of her seduction,
is repulsed by the cold, steely scorn of her husband, and in a faint
falls on him with her fatal dagger. The dead husband also tells the
story, through a medium: the story of a wife radiant after her seduction, egging the bandit on to kill the husband; of the flight of the
woman, and his own stoical suicide.

Finally a firewood dealer who happened on the scene tells it. It
was actually a wretched affair, of a bestial woman, and two frightened animal-like men flailing at each other on a battlefield without
dignity or meaning—a struggle devoid of honor or courage.

In seeing some parallels in the Hiss-Chambers case, I do not intend to pass judgment on the basic question of guilt. That is a matter
of evidence, probability, proof. The courts will deal with the appeal
for a new trial, for better or worse. As for laymen like ourselves,
the puzzle of the two personalities still persists. Hiss, still the lawyer,
keeps on fighting his legal case even from jail. Chambers, still the
writer and social theorist, is writing his life story with large generalizations and vivid detail.

If Hiss's legal moves fail, he may serve out his term and live out
his life still seeking to the end to prove that he was "framed" by
typewriter forgery. As for Chambers, he has not changed the basic
role he played as a Communist—that of a man trying to "change history" by the sheer force of intelligence and will. No longer a Communist, he is still proud that in his duel with Hiss he was able to
shift the history of our time. Yet despite the unattractiveness of much
of the portrait that emerges, it must be said that he is submitting a
detailed account of his life and personality for us to pass on. I wish
Hiss would do the same, but obviously that is not part of the image
he has of himself.

In each case the man clings to his favored image. Each dresses
himself up in as decorative a role as he can, giving himself good
motives, grasping a segment only of the truth. One is reminded of
the Max Beerbohm story of the man who wore a mask for years,

and when it was finally stripped off the face underneath had become exactly like the mask itself.

There is no woodcutter in the Hiss case, as there was in *Rashomon,* to tell the story from outside the circle. Yet I suspect that if there were, the real story would be as bedraggled and blundering as in *Rashomon,* with neither contestant maintaining any of the nobility with which he still tries to clothe himself.

6. The Hero as Ex-Communist

May 21, 1952

THERE ARE TWO QUESTIONS with which the reader will approach *Witness,* the autobiography of Whittaker Chambers (Random House). One is: How much light does it shed on the Hiss case, and does it make a convincing psychological case for the guilt of Hiss which has been legally ruled upon? The second is: What kind of man is Whittaker Chambers, and by what motives and passions is he ruled?

The best trial balance I can make on each is this: The case against Alger Hiss emerges as a very strong case, not wholly airtight, but damning enough to make the burden of breaking it a terribly hard one. As for Chambers himself, the picture he draws of himself is anything but attractive, and his motives present puzzles which he seems unaware of. But his mind works powerfully, he knows how to handle language, and the book as a whole is likely to stand for some time as one of the great documents of the 1950s.

It is a book of an ex-Communist. As Chambers points out, an ex-Communist in his sense means something very different from just an anti-Communist. He uses the term in the sense made famous by Ignazio Silone, when he told Togliatti that "the final conflict will be between the Communists and the ex-Communists." He means by it, in his own words, "a man who knew clearly why he became a Communist, who served Communism devotedly and knew why he served it, who broke with Communism unconditionally and knew why he broke with it."

There are three principal figures who tread the stage of the book. First, there is History, which gives sharpness and finality to everything and moves by rigid laws. Second, there is Communism, which is evil and is embodied in Alger Hiss as the Adversary. Third, there is Chambers himself, through whom as through some fearsome ventriloquist's dummy first the Adversary and then God works, and who finally becomes the embodiment of a great brooding compassion.

There was once a heretic sect called Manichaeism. which taught that the devil was coeternal with God. There is a Manichaean quality about this book. In fact, although Chambers ranges himself on the side of God, he is convinced he has taken the losing side, and that the devil is bound to win.

Which leads to the inner quality that I call his violence. A fanatic, Virginia Woolf once said, is a man who feels that in order to breathe he must break the windows. Chambers describes his entrance into Communism in terms of a bleak and forlorn family environment (a brilliantly executed section of the book), a brother who was a suicide, and a feeling of compassion for his society. Yet there is a hollowness about the passages in which he talks about God and pity, and an inner tension in his whole posture toward life which Chambers has carried over from one phase to the other. He is like one of the new tribe of Communist iron men, only he clothes himself in the iron of what he calls God. For all the religious language, there is no genuine religious humility in the book. The aim is still to break windows.

Chambers despises the conservatives as cowards and snobs; he is convinced that they all lined up with Hiss out of flabbiness and the Harvard old school tie. He hates the liberals as the blood brothers of the Communists, and the whole New Deal as a movement whose "inner drift" will make it indistinguishable from Communism. This is another phase of either-or thinking, admitting no possibility of genuine democratic radicalism or reform, refusing to think of American history in its native American terms, letting the Communists in effect lay out the field of battle and adopting their battleground.

For myself, I don't believe in his inevitabilities. I don't think Communism is bound to win, unless we throw our New Deals away as Communist. I think that history, like life itself, often turns out to be neither either nor or. The violence of Chambers' political analysis makes me wonder whether he performs similar violence to the facts of his relation to Hiss. But on that score the sheer weight of detail is so great as to leave a deep impression.

7. Frame-up or Wonderland?

June 5, 1952

NEITHER OF THE TWO principal figures in the Hiss-Chambers case was in Judge Goddard's courtroom yesterday at the hearing of the appeal for a third trial. One is now a well-behaved store clerk at the Federal penitentiary. The other is a successful author of a best-selling autobiography, and a practicing oracle on the theme of God, Satan and the New Deal.

Instead, two men called Lane confronted each other. Chester Lane, the Hiss counsel, was an earnest and intense man, who obviously has lived and breathed the case for many months and was bursting with eagerness. Myles Lane, the U.S. attorney, let an ironic smile play around his lips most of the time as he countered the evidence.

The pattern of the new Hiss evidence, while not convincing, is deeply disquieting to anyone who cares more about American justice than he does about either Chambers or Hiss.

There are two parts to the new Hiss approach. One offers to prove that the Chambers maid could not have seen the Hisses when she says she did, that the "Baltimore Documents" could not have been in the same envelope for ten years, and that Chambers had already left the Communist underground before the date of the last document.

All this implies, as Hiss's attorney argued it, that Chambers had somehow forged some of the documents in order to frame Hiss. This leads to the second and more crucial question: How could Chambers have done it? The answer the Hiss lawyer gives is a forged typewriter. The proof he offers is an expert who has been able to build a duplicate of the exhibit UUU, until now accepted by both sides as the Hiss typewriter; and another expert who has found UUU to have been tampered with.

But here is exactly where the new Hiss argument gets weak. Judge Goddard asked a searching question: "Who do you claim it was that made the Hiss machine?" To that there could be no answer but someone mysterious who helped Chambers. But who? And, as Myles Lane pointed out effectively, if Chambers had the original typewriter available, why did he have to forge a duplicate? And if he did not, how did he plant the one he made? Most difficult of all was Judge Goddard's question: If it took the Hiss expert eighteen months to build the fake machine, how could Chambers have had it done in the three months between the time of the libel suit and the time he produced the documents?

These were the questions that plagued many of the reporters who sat symbolically in the jury box. It was part of the wonderland aspect of the whole case. You can't dismiss the new offers of proof, and Myles Lane found some of them very hard to grapple with. But if you are ready to accept them, you find yourself groping in a darkness blacker even than the original one with which the first trial began.

I think that even the Hiss defense was caught up in this mood. The people who have worked on the new case are a devoted little group, obviously believing in Hiss still, anxious to make this last-gasp effort work before their two-year period for a new trial runs out. But one senses in them a kind of despair, as if they thought they had hold of a great truth but no one would listen to it.

It must be true that they have had difficulties in persuading people to work on the case, and to give affidavits. And one doubts whether the government has helped any. When Myles Lane hinted that he would indict one of the new Hiss witnesses for perjury, it was an example of an unnecessary vindictiveness.

Yet the weakness of the Hiss case has nothing to do with the government. It is an inner weakness, in that we cannot reconstruct how the frame-up could have been carried out. The defense is tripped up by the wonderland character of its own evidence. Yet I still feel that an "evidential hearing," at which the defense will have a chance to show how its proof might stand up, would be useful. The canker of doubt left in a case as fateful as this could play havoc with the conscience of America.

November 26, 1954

Alger Hiss will have a chance to find out how long the hatreds of his time will pursue him. He is getting out of prison tomorrow, having served his term and paid the price exacted from him for his perjury.

The price has been a heavy one. He emerges from prison stripped of everything he had built for himself before his trial, shorn of his pension, without the political privileges of a citizen. A man who stands so alone is not a hard target to aim at, nor does it require much courage to continue to hound him.

There is an irrepressible human will to build anew from the bleakest ruins of a shattered life. The least we can do about Alger Hiss is to let him pick up the pieces somehow. Among his hot and pitiless pursuers there must be many who think of themselves as Christian believers. They might recall a sentiment from a book that will outlast both Hiss and their own hot pursuit: "Vengeance is mine, saith the Lord." The state has had its quota of vengeance.

I have only one word to add. I should not like to be Hiss and to have to wrestle with the demons of remembrance within. Perhaps Lord Jowett was right in saying that the case against him had not been wholly proved. But I should feel much more strongly about it if Hiss were able to give a connected account of his life that would make the loose threads meet.

His brother has announced that Hiss will not write his autobiography, and perhaps this makes sense on the ground that it would only fan again the old fires that have already proved destructive enough. But until Hiss tells his whole story—not before another Congressional committee or the FBI, but in his own way, in response to his own impulse—the story Chambers told will have to stand.

8. *The Demons*

May 8, 1957

THERE WERE TWO BOOKS that Alger Hiss might have written. One was a book of complete candor, laying his life and heart bare—an autobiography sparing no one and least of all himself. The second was an extension of his defense at the trial, but more reasoned and connected, with the vulnerable points in his enemy's armor brought into focus and the strong points in his own refortified.

He has chosen to write the second book. It was his to make the choice. In his place, if I felt myself innocent, I should have chosen the first and tried to locate the case in the total stream of my life and thought. That is what Chambers did in *Witness*. But Hiss is a different kind of person—still tight-lipped, restrained, very much on guard and very much a lawyer.

I respect him for continuing his fight, for neither giving nor desiring quarter. His book—*In the Court of Public Opinion* (Knopf)—should be read by everyone who believes that in a controversy which has shaken a generation the real decision cannot yet be foreclosed. The jury's verdict will have to stand legally, but in his own mind and heart each American must carry on his own lonely debate.

The debate will turn on five crucial questions, as they emerge from this book:

1. Was the House Un-American Activities Committee (and especially Richard Nixon) out to get Hiss? He thinks so; I am impressed by his evidence, but less sure. I think the committee was pretty confused at the beginning, but after a while Nixon saw the chance of a political lifetime—and grabbed it.

2. Was the atmosphere during the trials an impossible one for fair play? Hiss thinks so. Again I am shaken by his evidence but I think he goes too far. Judge Kaufman was scrupulously fair. The vendetta against the judge and the jury holdouts after the trial was a blot on American press history. The second trial was therefore held in a questionable context. Judge Goddard was more hostile, Prosecutor Murphy more skillful, and the Hiss defense suffered when Stryker was replaced by Cross as his counsel.

3. Were there holes and contradictions in the government's case? There were, decidedly, and most of the Hiss book is devoted to exploiting them. They interest me, but they are not decisive.

4. Did Hiss provide Chambers with the crucial State Department documents? Mostly Hiss reargues his old case here. But on one score he shakes my conviction. He points out that the government testimony was intended to show that the documents were typed on the Hisses' typewriter, but there was no testimony as to *who* typed it. Murphy, in his windup, when there could be no rebuttal, egged the jury into

believing that the matching of typewriter samples decided the question of who did the typing. This may well have decided the verdict.

5. Was there "forgery by typewriter"? The whole burden of the Hiss appeal brief was that experts had succeeded in building another typewriter that could produce the same typing, and therefore that Chambers could have framed Hiss by forging a typewriter like Hiss's. This didn't persuade me during the appeal hearing and it doesn't persuade me now. Why assume anything so tortured, when Chambers or someone else could have had access to the Hiss typewriter?

This suggests the strangest aspect of the whole case. When Hiss denied ever having known Chambers in more than a casual way, he cut himself off from his best potential defense. Had he admitted knowing him and seeing him frequently and closely, he could have argued that Chambers had turned against him in bitterness, and—having access to the typewriter in the Hiss house—had framed the espionage documentary evidence against him. But once Hiss took the cold, austere view that "Crosley" was a "dead beat" about whom he had almost forgotten, the only way to escape the documents was to assume the typewriter had been faked.

My own view is that Hiss wore—and still wears—a mask, but that he was not the traitor and underground spy in the Chambers portrait. Others in Washington like him—Pressman, Witt, Weyl—belonged to the Communist Party. I assume Hiss did also, that he knew Chambers better than he admits, and that he lied on the question of Communist membership.

As for the contradictions in the evidence, Hiss tries to prove too much. Everyone is portrayed as against him—committee, FBI, grand jury, prosecutor, judge, jury, the appeals court, as well as the malevolence of Chambers. If Chambers was so complete a liar as Hiss makes him out, it is hard to see how he could have manufactured an entire story out of nothing but his dream and spite and hate, and make the story dovetail with evidence from other sources.

That leaves me with the problem of the espionage. Maybe Hiss was a spy as well as a Communist, but it still seems unproven to me, and it may be the kind of imaginative stretching of a factual core of which I think Chambers was capable.

I think both men have worn public masks. Both have been possessed by demons. Chambers' demon has been to change history by his act of bearing witness, as he once hoped to change it through Communism. Hiss's demon has been never to yield an inch, to keep his image intact at any cost.

9. I'll Never Dream Again

December 17, 1954

OURS IS AN ERA when fact so far outstrips fancy that it is dangerous to release your imagination, lest it be seized as your version of gospel truth. I found this out last week when I read Raymond Moley's *Newsweek* piece, "Could F.D.R. Clear Hiss?" Moley quotes a remark reported to have been made by Hiss to a fellow prisoner at Lewisburg: "If F.D.R. had lived, I wouldn't be here." He says that an "early version" of the "hypothesis that Hiss was a secret agent of President Roosevelt" was first put forward in a piece of mine in 1948. He adds that "Lerner dramatized it by saying that the concept came to him in a dream."

Well, I am not certain of Moley's overtones, but I am glad he recalls an article that I thought had been long forgotten, written for the New York *Star*, a paper with one of the briefest life histories. It was a few days after Chambers had turned up with the Pumpkin Papers, and before the grand-jury indictment of Hiss. I had no fixed views on the case and was searching for an off piece, somewhat fresh and not too serious. Every writer will recognize the stage in the writing process when you are worrying an idea around its elusive edges and can't clap your hand down on it. In this formless, receptive phase, you lay yourself open to every random impulse and association, including puns, wild fancies— and even dream images.

As I searched I found myself, for no reason, repeating the beginning of the old song, "I Dreamt I Dwelt in Marble Halls." Then it changed, keeping the same rhythm, to "I dreamt that I was Alger Hiss." I knew I had my first line for my column.

All that was left was to develop the dream—an improbable nightmare affair that led me as Hiss to a kind of Roman amphitheater where I had to defend myself before a vast jury. I told them I had been a Communist, and even a spy, for "my chief." When they asked me to prove it, I said in despair that the only one who could prove it was in "a grave at Hyde Park." For the "chief" was F.D.R.*

I remember thinking at the time that it had not come out badly for a light piece, but I was a little worried about treating so tragic a theme lightly. To be sure, I recognize in myself (as in most other people) an outrageous zest for cloak-and-dagger political intrigue, and I was unconsciously expressing this romantic impulse when I thought up the secret pact between Roosevelt and Hiss. Let us say the piece was 95 per cent play of the imagination and 5 per cent serious.

I wasn't "dramatizing" any "theory." I was having some fun, say-

---

* For this piece, see "I Dreamt That I Was Alger Hiss," page 429 above.

ing in effect that in a world in which the most fantastic things happen, why not apply it to the Hiss case and stretch fantasy as far as it will go?

But I reckoned without the passionate impulse of men to believe in the fantastic. I got letters from readers and calls from friends, and even a formal inquiry from a couple of news magazines. What proof did I have? On what evidence did I base my double-agent theory? Was I perhaps letting myself be used by the Hiss crowd to suggest a favorable explanation of his deceptions, which they could spread without having to prove it?

My answer to all of these was quite simple. The "dream" was not a dramatic form or a dodge. It had been dreamt up.

That should have ended it. But it didn't. When Hiss had been in jail for a while, the story of his remark about Roosevelt to a fellow prisoner was printed. Now that he is out, and the world is waiting for something sensational to emerge from that Manila package of notes he carried out of jail, and nothing much is breaking, the old story has been revived and I find my little fantasy dressed up as an "early version" of a serious "hypothesis."

I find Moley's elaborate refutation of the "hypothesis" quite convincing and am puzzled only about why he took the trouble. Maybe Hiss will yet surprise me and say that what was fantasy for me was indeed serious fact for him. On the other hand, maybe all he meant by saying he wouldn't be in prison if F.D.R. had lived was that F.D.R. could have been strong enough to prevent the hysteria that Hiss holds responsible for his fate.

But this again is guessing and imagining. I am going to keep away from all this fantasy stuff. I have burned my fingers. I'll never dream again.

McCARTHY: THE LIFE AND DEATH OF A NIGHTMARE

1. Origin of a Word

February 3, 1954

IT IS PROBABLY no great shakes in the total frame of world problems, but in the history of our language-in-the-making, I think I can contribute a footnote on the origin of a word. The word is "McCarthyism."

Along with other things, the junior Senator from Wisconsin has fashioned an interesting legend around the origins of the word. This legend cropped up recently in the letter columns of the New York *Times*. In response to a *Times* editorial, following the excellent series by Peter Kihss on the Fort Monmouth cases, an angry reader called Edward McMahon denied that the Senator had "provided the name —McCarthyism." "This name," wrote the reader, "was first provided by the former adviser to the Roosevelt and Truman administrations, Owen Lattimore, in a Senate hearing on May 3, 1950. The next day, May 4, it was spread over the pages of the *Daily Worker*."

Interestingly enough I note that the January issue of the *American Legion Magazine* contains an article by Alfred Kohlberg called "Brainwashing, American Style," in which there is a paragraph on the origin of "McCarthyism" that reads almost word for word like the letter. No doubt the *Times* reader read Kohlberg before he read the *Times*.

I don't know whom Kohlberg read, but the junior Senator from Wisconsin has several times asserted that the word was invented first by the *Daily Worker*. From that nefarious origin presumably it made its way into the New York *Post*, the New York *Times*, the Washington *Post*, the St. Louis *Post-Dispatch* and other papers. This contribution to philology seems up to now to have gone unchallenged. David Lawrence and Rebecca West, among others, have printed it as a fact.

There was a news story in the *Post* recently saying that the G. and C. Merriam Co., which publishes *Webster's New International College Dictionary*, is planning to list "McCarthyism" as a word in the next edition of its dictionary. A *Post* reader thereupon, out of curiosity, wrote to the general editor of G. and C. Merriam, to ask what he had in his files as the earliest use of the word. Mr. Gove, the general editor, replied that the earliest quotation he had was from my column in the

Post dated April 5, 1950. I looked up the column—and sure enough, there was the term.*

Who was it who said that the greatest tragedy in nature was the head-on collision of a beautiful theory with a hard fact? I should like to call the attention of Mr. McMahon, Mr. Kohlberg, Mr. Lawrence, Miss West, the junior Senator from Wisconsin and sundry others, to the nonpolitical fact that April 5, 1950, is almost a month earlier than May 3 or May 4, 1950. If the blame or honor of first using the word—and it is at best a dubious honor—is to be visited on anyone, I fear I must be a candidate.

"Do you happen to recall now, after these intervening years," the above-mentioned *Post* reader asks me, "whether you invented the word or whether you borrowed it?"

The answer is that I certainly did not borrow it, but that there are few times when any writer consciously coins new words. I have had the same thing happen to me on other catch phrases. You write, and if an appropriate phrase comes into your mind you put it down without noting either in your memory or your diary whether you were its Columbus or simply pulled it out of the atmosphere.

When I was writing about McCarthy in April 1950, I felt that we were dealing with a portent of clouds and storms and thunder to come. It seemed the most natural thing in the world, therefore, to write about "McCarthyism." I suspect that in those same early days many other Americans who were concerned about their country's future were beginning to use the term. If anyone else cares to claim his precedence, I shall gladly yield it.†

None of this is of any importance except insofar as it shows up the hollowness of the attempt to link the word with the *Daily Worker* and thus give it a Communist origin and stigma.

For my own part I doubt seriously whether the word will outlast the political power of the man from whom it derives. But meanwhile I am glad to help nail down another of those shabby statements on which political ignorance feeds.

2. McCarthyism: The Smell of Decay

April 5, 1950

I THINK we have been standing too close to the Senator McCarthy fiasco and the case of Owen Lattimore to see their full social and moral

---

* See page 448 below, *McCarthyism: The Smell of Decay*.

† My friend Herbert Block ("Herblock"), the greatest American political caricaturist of our time, wrote me to say that he used the term in a cartoon at almost exactly the same time as my column. Richard Rovere's *Senator Joe McCarthy* (1959) assigns the first use of the term to Herblock's cartoon.

meaning. To be sure, the Battle of the Secret Files has its legal aspects, and the maneuvers of McCarthy, Bridges and Wherry have their political aspects.

And there is, of course, the underlying issue of whether Americans who love their country are to have their lives blasted because a voice has whispered in the night to a politically desperate Senator, saying: "You have nothing to lose but your political obscurity and your fading chances of re-election. You have the nation's headlines to gain."

To call McCarthyism a fascist atmosphere would be descriptive enough, but I am tired to death of the worn-out epithets of "Communist" and "fascist" being bandied about. What is more striking is the smell of moral decay about the whole business. When desperate men get desperate enough, as the totalitarian experience on both the right and the left shows, they give us a glimpse into the cloacal depths of what is mean and destructive in man. The atmosphere surrounding McCarthyism is this atmosphere of decay.

See what elements go into forming it. There is, to start with, the brassy verbal violence that McCarthy, Bridges and Wherry have succumbed to. When McCarthy tells the President to "put up or shut up," those who have grown accustomed to political invective in America have to remind themselves that the Presidential office is still the symbol of our democracy. McCarthy has aimed at dragging into the gutter with himself not only the President but the Presidency.

There has been about many of his statements a kind of verbal hoodlumism that must take any historical student back to the brass-knuckle polemics of the parliamentary struggles in the Weimar Republic, or the hysterical language that Communists love to use.

Then there is the well-known use of the tactic of the Big Lie. One thing McCarthy has shown is that his talents as a student of propaganda are not to be underestimated. True, he has overreached himself and blundered badly on several scores. But he knows the core lesson of recent propaganda history—to make stentorous use of what little material you have and, if necessary, of nothing.

A striking element in the pattern is the unscrupulous shifting of ground. You start with a charge that there are fifty-seven or eighty-one or some other magical number of card-carrying Communists or their equivalent in the State Department. You make public a handful of names, and when you have been blasted into inglorious retreat on each of them, you stake everything on one name, that of Owen Lattimore, as a "Russian master spy."

When that too evaporates, you say that the question of whether or not he is a master spy is unimportant—that your real point is that he has shaped State Department policy in the Far East. When the secret Lattimore report is finally published, it says little that John K. Fairbank or Harold Isaacs or Walter Lippmann or other students of Far Eastern policy would not say—or that I have not said myself.

I am speaking here not only of McCarthy's shifting of premises, his evasiveness, his cowardice in wrapping his moral nakedness in the cloak of Senatorial immunity. What is important is the contempt he shows for the processes of the mind.

There remains to speak of the elements that remind me of the dreary and ever present fanatic fringe in America. I have had to wade through mountains of pamphlets and literature by men like Gerald Smith, Joseph Kamp, Merwin Hart. I find in McCarthy's stuff the same obsession with cloud-cuckooland conspiracies, mysterious spies, nefarious networks. And, most important, I suspect that the avalanche of mail McCarthy is reported to be getting comes from the people whom Smith and Kamp and Hart had stirred up.

There is a hate layer of opinion and emotion in America. There will be other McCarthys to come who will be hailed as its heroes.

3. Two Who Were Wrong

November 7, 1954

THE CRIME of John Paton Davies, for which he has now been dismissed from the American Foreign Service, is that of retroactive error. That is to say, he is now being punished by being branded a "security risk" because the current ideas about foreign policy in Washington run counter to the reports he made ten years ago from China and the positions he took there at that time.

That isn't, of course, the way Secretary Dulles puts it in his letter of dismissal. He speaks of Davies' judgment and reliability as faulty and notes that the unanimous review board thought he behaved badly and was evasive as a witness. He also speaks of Davies' having carried his dissents (from Wedemeyer's policies) "outside privileged boundaries"—meaning he talked to newspapermen.

It is an interesting thought and might perhaps have been a reason for dismissal—ten years ago. It comes ten years late. It is dragged in now to bolster a decision made on other grounds. Davies' sin is that what he did and said in the climate of opinion of 1944 doesn't jibe with what Dulles, the generals and the security officers are thinking in the climate of opinion of 1954.

Rarely has the State Department let the cat out of the bag so openly as in the charges against Davies.

In his letter of November 2 of this year to General Nece, Davies refers to the charge that he was "the leading proponent in the Department of the separability of the Chinese Communists from Moscow." He answers it well by saying that he had believed that this idea of driving a wedge between the Kremlin and Peiping "should be examined" in State Department thinking and planning.

It was his belief all along that there was "an organic decay" going on in Chiang's Nationalist government while he was still in power, and that American policy should deal with this fact and not with the surface forms of diplomatic and military aid to Chiang. This belief furnishes the thread of continuity in Davies' behavior from the time he was General Stilwell's briefing officer to the present time when he still believes that there may be hope in an American splitting tactic.

I don't know Davies, and I don't even think that you have to agree with Davies' thesis about splitting Russia and China. You may disagree strongly with it and yet hold that it is wrong and foolish to try to run a government on the principle of silencing any official who dares consider a point of view not favored by Nixon, Knowland and McCarthy. And not only silencing him but—even worse—branding him as a security risk and thus destroying him.

Destroy him is what they have done. I don't see how you can read Davies' statement on Friday without a sense of embarrassment at what we do to our public servants by these years of hounding them. Davies speaks of the "magnitude of the problems" Dulles faces. He is "determined not to add to them" by making a fight against his ouster. Dulles, he says, "has more important problems on his hands than the reputation and future of one civil servant."

I suppose Davies gives his words the edge of irony born of years of suffering and humiliation. Yet how pitiful to see a man reduced to this frail irony, hopeless about fighting back because he has been through all the inquiries and all the answers and all the clearings and all the new inquiries, and he is tired and defeated.

I felt embarrassed to find Davies boasting of his "1950 recommendations that we seek a preventive showdown with the Soviet Union." What do we do to these hounded men that they must go groveling to find some shreds of evidence which show them more belligerent against Russia than their accusers are?

The "mortal struggle with the Communist enemy," of which Davies speaks, will not be aided by his irony-plus-groveling. Nor is it aided by the men who have beaten him down until they have destroyed his will to fight back. It is a struggle that can be carried on only by an America which does not dishonor its public servants when their former acts become unpopular. Such an America needs the undefeated of heart and the resilient of spirit.

April 5, 1957

Before he jumped from the apartment house roof at Cairo, he left a note to his friend, the Swedish ambassador. "I have no option," it said. "I must kill myself, for I live without hope."

No doubt the members and counsel of the Senate subcommittee will regard Canadian Ambassador Herbert Norman's suicide as further evidence of the validity of their charges of Communism against him. But it is not only the guilty who kill themselves, out of a sense of shame. More often it is the guileless and guiltless who feel so battered that they can no longer fight on against the monstrous injustice of life. The capacity to fight against odds is linked not with innocence, but with a kind of animal vitality. In the last weeks of his life it was a vitality that was lacking in Norman, and he gave up.

Was Norman perhaps a divided mind, torn in a lonely Hamletlike debate about life and death? His note would deny it. In general, a suicide's act is not that of a torn person, but of one who has moved beyond doubt and is convinced that death is the only road and that there is no choice. But before this terrible certainty has been reached there is a point, earlier on the road, when death first enters as a possible way out. As Kafka put it, "From a certain point onward there is no longer any turning back, that is the point that must be reached."

This point must have come for Norman in mid-March, when the Eastland committee and its counsel, Robert Morris, raked up again the old 1951 charges of Communist complicity. Norman had been through that turmoil six years ago; the Canadian government had again checked his security file and cleared him; American diplomats who knew him well had testified for him. Maybe he had thought that the nightmare was over.

But it did return, as nightmares do. There were the old charges, as if to show that men never learn and life never moves onward. This came, moreover, in the midst of tense negotiations over the Suez Canal—an issue on which, again, it seemed as if life was a treadmill that got nowhere but circled endlessly around. There were work and tension. Perhaps there were suspicious looks from those whom you had thought your friends, showing that the seeds of distrust had been sown and that some of the mud had stuck. And so, "I must kill myself, for I live without hope."

Until I discover differently, I shall continue to believe that Norman was unjustly accused. The charges against him, like those against Owen Lattimore, came at the height of the McCarthy-McCarran madness. They came, too, in connection with the campaign against the Institute of Pacific Relations, of which Norman was a member and under which he did some of his important writing on Japanese history and political institutions.

I don't say that a political double-dealer may not at times hide his true face behind the mask of a scholar. I do say that there is no evidence, in Norman's work itself, that he did so. At one point in the past I had occasion to immerse myself in his books, as part of a brief plunge into the literature on Japan, and I came away with respect for the care and massiveness of his scholarship.

It was another scholar and Orientalist, Karl Wittfogel, who seems to have been mainly relied upon for testimony against him. Wittfogel seems to be convinced that Norman was a Communist when they both presumably belonged to a study group in the late 1930s. Wittfogel could be right about his own scholarly work, yet mistaken in his memories or conclusions about Norman. If Norman ever really belonged to a "Cape Cod study group" almost twenty years ago, which he denied, the Republic would not have fallen if we had consulted with our friend and neighbor Canada about our suspicion.

There are ways and ways of killing a man. He can be killed directly, in battle or by open murder or assassination. Or he can be killed by the remoter weapons of blasting his name and career, so that he reaches the point of no return, where he loses every landmark of hope.

4. The Vigilantes and the Chain of Fear

July 6, 1950

I HAVE TURNED BACK to Nehru's *Visit to America* (John Day), the little book of speeches that Nehru delivered on his swing through America and Canada last fall. In one of them he was talking about Gandhi, and how much he had learned from him. "We were a number of people unarmed," he said about the Indian nationalists under Gandhi, "with no wealth or other outward symbol of strength at our command, and we faced a powerful and wealthy empire." What was it Gandhi taught this group?

It was not so much the doctrine of passive resistance, which has been much written about, but the doctrine of no fear. "There was some magic," says Nehru, "about the message he gave . . . His analysis was essentially that we were suffering terribly from fear, especially the masses in India. So he just went about telling us, 'Don't be afraid. Why are you afraid? What can happen to you?' "

Nehru goes on to recount the fears at the time—the "fear that if we did something that the British Government did not like, we'd be punished. We'd be sent to prison. We might be shot . . . The poorest peasant, the lowliest of our people . . . was kicked and cuffed by everybody—by his landlord, by the landlord's agent, by the police, by the moneylender. Now, whether there was something in the atmosphere, or whether it was some magic in Gandhi's voice . . . when he put it that way, 'Don't be afraid,' [it] caught on and we realized with a tremendous lifting of a burden, that there was nothing to fear."

This can be an infectious doctrine. What Nehru is suggesting is the doctrine of a chain reaction of no fear. "Because we felt that we were serving a great cause," Nehru added, going to prison "became not a thing to be afraid of but something to be coveted."

We lack in our day this clear sense of a great cause. Americans had it in their own War of Independence. The Indian nationalists had it, the Jews had it in the war in Israel, the Communists had it in China. But today Communist movements of independence have been corrupted and corroded by Kremlin imperialism, and American power is allied with reactionary movements. Fear has swept the world.

Is it too late to learn the meaning of Gandhi's lesson? It means, within our own country, a quiet but determined refusal to be swept away by the hysteria which threatens to destroy civil liberties.

August 8, 1951

I'm glad that Senator Benton of Connecticut had the courage to call the U.S. Senate's attention to the facts of life about a member named McCarthy. Benton knows that McCarthy won't resign, and he knows also that the Senate will not drum up the necessary two-thirds vote to expel him. But the time has gone for giving McCarthy the silent or the kid-glove treatment. The Benton resolution at least takes the offensive toward a man whose terrorism has always put others on the defensive.

There are signs that even his Republican colleagues are finding McCarthy an albatross who has fastened himself to their necks and is riding them to their doom. He has debased every issue he has touched. He has made chronic and pathological use of the Big Lie. He has taken a serious issue of our era—the question of whether a public servant can be trusted because of his associations with a potential Communist enemy—and caricatured it until it has become too grotesque to use except by paranoiacs and political mobsters.

We shall never know how many decent and intelligent young men have been kept away from public service, simply because they have recoiled from the enormities of politics of which he has become the symbol. He has worn out the language of political abuse, so that each of his attacks forces him into more extravagant language than the last.

Nothing quite like McCarthy has crawled out of the dark and maggoty crevices of America's Cro-Magnon period into public life. How shall we try to explain him? He is the expression of the deep impulses of violence in our time. In Eastern Europe he would have been a Communist commissar, in Germany a gauleiter, in a Latin-American dictatorship he would have been a putsch-making colonel. In our own culture he plays cops and robbers, setting up an elaborate spy network with money furnished by vague and nameless "friends" and surrounding himself with the air of high secrecy and low terror cultivated only in grade B movies.

Above all he has made hate the central theme of politics. I can only repeat about him what Benjamin Rush, the famous Philadelphia doctor of the Revolutionary period, wrote to his sons: "In battle men kill without hating each other; in political contests men hate without killing, but in that hatred they commit murder every hour of their lives."

June 24, 1953

I wonder how many Americans are aware how deep the issue of the McCarthy book burnings goes.* This is a time when great passions are loose in the world. At such a time it was inevitable that some men, even in a democracy, should make an effort to destroy the words they find dangerous. But it was never more important for sane men to resist such a trend.

You don't have to like a book in order to let it stand on the shelves. A book is a sign of the age-old effort to maintain what one generation hands on to another. When you destroy the books, you are breaking that continuity. When you burn books, however wrong and bad they may be, you are doing an indignity to every book, just as a man who tortures even a bad child shows his hate for all children and destroys the continuity of the race.

I learned this truth after I was out of college. Somewhere at a summer conference, I dropped several books casually on the ground and kicked them out of the way. A German student picked up the books, dusted them off gently. He said how he had worked for years to buy a few books. A book was his blood, and he bled when he saw it mishandled.

Norbert Wiener has defined communication as a dialogue against entropy—a dialogue between two who are allied against their common enemy, chaos. The war against books is thus a breaking of the precarious thread of this dialogue. I am not saying that all books help communication. Some are enemies of it, especially totalitarian books written by men who want to reduce all dialogue to a party-line mono-

---

* I referred here to the removal of books from United States Information Service libraries in Europe, under pressure of Senator McCarthy's charges of their having been written by subversives. In at least one case the press reported that a number of the books were put in a heap and burned.

logue. There is a natural impulse to distinguish between good and bad books, and to burn the ones deemed hostile to the ideas we cherish.

But who can set himself up as God and decide which books belong to the children of light and which to the children of darkness? The men we might trust with such a task would recoil from the thought of it. Those who arrogate the job to themselves, like the McCarthys, are by that very fact the least to be trusted. In the end only the reader and no one else can decide what shall live and what shall die.

That, presumably, was what President Eisenhower meant when he said at Dartmouth, "Don't join the book burners . . . Don't be afraid to go to the library and read every book . . . . How shall we defeat Communism, unless we know what it is, and why it has such an appeal for men?"

Alas, these proved too burning words, scorching the delicate tissue of political relations between the President, Dulles and McCarthy. The President has backtracked, spreading a trail of dust over what was once so plainly traced. When he started making distinctions between the books that might well be burned and those that shouldn't, his brave words went down the drain.

This is one area where it is fatal to start making distinctions. The Nazis didn't stop with burning books by Communist authors. They went on to burn books by Jews, by Social Democrats, by liberals, and finally by all who were critical of the regime. The Communists, doing the same, have ended only with a wholly sterile party-line truth which not only destroys some books but does surgery on others by redoctoring and rewriting them.

We are starting on the same road. McCarthy's favorite question is whether you would dare to leave the Communist books unpurged. But look at some of the authors banned by State Department directive: Walter White, Bert Andrews, Vera Dean, Robert S. Lynd, Upton Sinclair, Gunnar Myrdal, Clarence Streit, and even Whittaker Chambers. Behind this silliness and cowardice is the fallacy that somehow, by leaving a book on American shelves abroad, the American government sponsors it. Actually it means only that you believe in the debate between ideas and want to contribute to it.

The crime of book purging is that it involves a rejection of the word. For the word is never absolute truth, but only man's frail and human effort to approach the truth. To reject the word is to reject the human search.

December 14, 1953

The "four fears" that Adlai Stevenson listed in his Philadelphia speech went to the heart of the crisis of American freedom. He discussed at some length the fear of depression. But the other three—the

fear of Communism, the fear of ourselves, the fear of freedom itself—
are even more important and go far to explain the current climate of
fear. Without mentioning McCarthy by name, it hit at the prevailing
mood of fear which has made McCarthy possible.

It is healthy to fear realities that threaten you, and to face them—
to fear the hydrogen bomb and seek control of its use. It is healthy to
fear the world power of the Kremlin, because it is the first step toward
organizing a counterforce. Know-nothings neglect the real power of
the Kremlin on the world stage and concentrate on Communism inside America—which is exactly where Communism lacks power and
prestige. The less the reality of Communist power here, the more the
know-nothings have had to drum up a fear which feeds on itself.

The ultimate fears are the fear of freedom and the fear of ourselves. The method of freedom has been our main reliance throughout American history. Once you start explaining why it can no longer
be used—whether in Congressional investigating committees or in colleges or factories—you confess a fear of the very principle that has
permeated our history.

Most of the people who today sanction the abandonment of the
method of freedom would not be doing so if they were not scared. A
frightened animal becomes dangerous. A frightened man can no
longer think, and when there are mobs of such men they become a
mortal danger to the whole civilization—and to themselves. In fact,
their fright at the specter of Communism at home makes them even
more dangerous to the liberties of their country than the contemptible
and bedraggled little huddle of American Communists themselves.

The fear of freedom is, in the end, a fear of ourselves. Erich
Fromm pointed out that the totalitarian leaders enroll the people
who do not dare face the burdens that freedom imposes. They fear
freedom because they have no reliance on themselves—they fear their
own capacities to deal with either their personal dilemmas or with the
dilemmas of their society. They become the cat's-paws of tyrants and
adventurers because they do not value themselves. And they do not
value themselves because they do not know themselves and have lost
the sense of their own identity. Having lost their identity, they can lose
themselves in the formless mob of faceless men.

One may perhaps ask about these frightened men why, being
frightened, they are proving so aggressive. Any good student of psychiatry will suggest the answer. In most neurotic people, fear and rage
are inverse phases of each other. It is the people who live in a ghost
world of their own fears who are potentially most destructive to others
and to themselves. In the end, as the Nazi experience showed, they
destroy themselves—but not before they have first wreaked their
frustrations and aggressions on others and destroyed them.

Perhaps it is futile to put the question—but what is there for us to be afraid of? We are a rich and powerful country that has shown its capacity to survive crises and has done an unexampled job of carving freedom and plenty out of a continent. It was not fear that brought our fathers and us to these shores, but affirmation. It was not fear but affirmation that shaped our institutions. What a pity it will be if a people grown great on affirmation should die in panic, on ground hallowed by freedom.

5. McCarthy on Wall Street

September 27, 1953

JOE MCCARTHY, internationally known as the dauntless champion of freedom of thought, came to Wall Street on Friday to get the 1953 Bill of Rights Defense Medal. I couldn't be expected to stay away from so bizarre an event. So I turned up at the Treasury Building, at Broad and Wall, just before noon. With me were some striplings from the First Army band, a row of tired policemen, assorted functionaries of the Wall Street Post of the American Legion (which conferred the honor), some people out for their lunch who crowded the street, and a number of females with terrifying faces and heaving bosoms who had come to greet their hero.

The Legion commander who presented McCarthy with the medal was so flustered that he forgot to pin it on him until reminded by whispers from the wings. I don't know whether he believes in the Freudian slip, which is unlikely, since Freud imported an alien ideology into our country. But according to Freud his memory lapse was the method his subconscious used to telephone the grotesqueness of McCarthy as a champion of the free mind.

I felt a bit sorry for the three doughty fellows who preceded McCarthy, and whose task was to tie him up with the Bill of Rights. They swallowed their own hemlock with a cheerless belligerence. As I jotted down the tortured logic of their oratory, it ran roughly thus: "My countrymen, the right of a person not to be compelled to testify against himself, to have a fair trial, to be confronted by his accusers, is a precious American heritage. Here is the man who is fighting to preserve these rights. But you can't expect him to apply the Fifth Amendment of this precious Bill of Rights to conspirators, fellow travelers and eggheads."

As for McCarthy himself, he seemed strangely detached from the proceedings. He didn't get himself involved in the tortured logic I have traced. Although he was getting a Bill of Rights medal, he refrained with magnificent scorn from paying any respects to the Bill of Rights. I have seen cynical performances before, but rarely a cynicism so engaging in its blatant absent-mindedness.

What McCarthy gave the plebeians instead was roughly the same speech he had given a few days earlier at the convention of the Wholesale Plumbers and Heating Suppliers. He had it on a green slip of paper but knew it so well that he didn't have to look. As he stood on the steps looking down at the clerks and the runners who would have to gobble their lunch faster because of this interlude, he seemed for a moment like a balder and more flaccid Mark Antony doing the funeral oration in *Julius Caesar*. Only instead of exploiting Caesar's corpse, he was using the American dead and the unreturned prisoners in Korea.

Quoting Cato's "Carthage must be destroyed," he pounded away so hard at the treachery of our British allies who insist on trading with China, that it was hard to tell whether the Carthage to be destroyed is Russia or Britain. The odds were on the British. Aside from British knife-in-the-back treachery, McCarthy's two themes were that of a war to the finish with Russia, and go-it-alone-if-necessary. He ended with, "So help us God, we'll win all alone if we have to."

The people he was talking to were mainly from the white-collar classes. For the moment he stirred them, for he knows how to handle a crowd with the sure instinct of a powerful speaker. But you wondered, as you watched them with a puzzled compassion, whether they knew that the medicine he was offering them could only lead to fresh graves on new Asiatic battlefields and to pulverized American cities. And that it didn't lead to freedom at home but to tyranny.

6. Security and Conscience

November 16, 1953

IF LEONARD HALL speaks for the Republican Party leaders, as chairman of the National Committee, then the party of Lincoln, Charles Evans Hughes and Wendell Willkie has plunged across the river and into the jungle. The Eisenhower Administration, he said, will go to the people on its record of having fired 1,456 "security risks" from the Federal service.

It is time we took a good look at the ways by which the 1,456 "security risks" were "separated" from the Federal government. There were many things wrong with the old loyalty-security program under the Truman Administration. If any student of the problem wants a careful and detailed study, he will find it in *The Federal Loyalty-Security Program* by Eleanor Bontecou (Cornell University Press, 1953). But compared with the Brownell-Eisenhower program, the one developed under Truman now begins to look good. The Eisenhower law gave the power of summary dismissal to all Federal agencies. The "security officers" and other officials make the decisions, and the head of the agency has the final word. There are hearings, but there is no machinery of reviewing cases as there was in the Loyalty Review Board.

What real evidence have we that the 1,456 employees who have been dismissed were disloyal or were security risks? Some light is shed on this question by the current Fort Monmouth suspensions. McCarthy's buildup of the Fort Monmouth hearings has been subjected to scrutiny by recent series of articles in the New York *Post,* the Washington *Post* and the New York *Times,* all of which show beyond any reasonable doubt that the McCarthy charges of current espionage are fantastic.

It is clear that McCarthy has hit and run, and is now off investigating in another part of the forest. The newspapers that headlined his charges of espionage, made to the press after secret hearings and with not a shred of evidence, should now have very red faces. But it may be argued that men who are neither spies nor disloyal may still be bad "security risks," especially in an Army laboratory concerned with electronics. True. But again, how about the evidence? There were charges that connected a few of the people with organizations like the American Veterans Committee and the Federation of Atomic Scientists, which are not only useful but patriotic groups. There was also someone whose brother was held to be too far left.

I feel rueful at finding that I had myself been the occasion for one of the men's getting into trouble. I once spoke at Red Bank, and a hapless young engineer had heard me speak and evidently expressed some approval—a harmless enough gesture. It now appears as a charge against him that he is sympathetic to my views. And one of the charges against his brother, also suspended, is that he has a brother who thinks well of me. If it were not tragic, it would be downright funny. My most restrained comment is: How crazy can they get?

If the forty Fort Monmouth people have been suspended on charges as flimsy as this, has the same been true of the 1,456 Federal employees whom the Eisenhower Administration has fired as "security risks"? We have no way of telling, because it is fatal to a man to fight back and thus make his case public—running the danger of never getting another job anywhere. But if a substantial number of the 1,456 cases are like the Fort Monmouth forty, then the new Brownell-Hall crusade will march on the shattered lives of helpless men.

August 26, 1955

The incidents of guilt by blood tie pile up. First it was Lieutenant Radulovich and his father, then Midshipman Landy and his mother, then Midshipman Gaston and his mother, then Airman Branzovich and his father, then Private Harmon and his father. Now there is the story of an Army employee, Martin Wishnoff, who was fired from his job not because of his own mother or father but because of charges against his wife's parents.

The remaining path of guilt degrees of consanguinity seems clearly marked out. There is still to be explored the guilt that derives from one's sisters and cousins and aunts—and of course, in a parallel with the Nuremberg Laws, from at least one grandparent.

Clearly it is dangerous in the eyes of the Wooden Sergeants who run our security system for a man to have any relatives at all, if he wants to be cleared as a loyalty and security risk. The ideal way would be to be born without kith and to acquire no kin—to be born, perhaps, by parthenogenesis, and to stay clear of the temptations of marriage.

The perfect men for our armed forces and government services would be those who were totally unrelated to anyone and anything. They would be men stripped of filial feeling, of friends, of associations, of thoughts, of passions and emotions. They would be ciphers, fit to be kings in the land of ciphers.

I have tried to figure out the theory behind the position of the Wooden Sergeants. Are they adherents of heredity, believing that guilt can be carried in the bloodstream and the genes, transmitted from parents to son? Even then it wouldn't explain the firing of Martin Wishnoff because of his in-laws, who transmitted nothing to him—except possibly the apartment he rented close to them. Or maybe the Wooden Sergeants are believers in the power of the environment. By this view a boy is fatally shaped in early life by his family, and if his mother or father held heretical beliefs he was bound to become infected by them.

Alas, any high-school or college teacher who has watched his students going through the phase of intense rebellion against their parents will tell you how shaky this is. Sometimes if a parent is lucky he is able to leave some mark on his son; more often he looks at him in disbelief, wondering where he picked up the brand of his time that he bears. Actually, I don't believe the Wooden Sergeants have any theories to guide them. They are just scared men who bear a burden too great for their wits.

In the study of the Eisenhower security system in Washington that Adam Yarmolinsky did for the Fund for the Republic, there was the case of the woman government clerk who had a suspected brother. Quizzed in a surrealist way by a security board out of Kafka, she was asked what she would do if her brother were about to commit an act of sabotage. Would she warn the authorities? Faced by this fantasy dilemma, the woman answered, "Certainly I would tell them, because he would only be hurting himself." The answer was not enough, and she was fired.

I have imagined myself being quizzed in this way. What would I answer? I think I should say: "Gentlemen, right now I feel as if I should sit down by the waters of Babylon and weep for the stupidity of the human breed."

I thought that even the conservatives in America—especially the conservatives, who talk so much of natural law—believed in the sanctity of family ties. Where are they now that the ties of blood are being torn in the fancied cause of the servile state?

When some people protested because of the appointment at Brandeis University of Felix Browder, a fine and able youngster whose father had been a Communist leader, President A. L. Sachar of Brandeis shut them up quickly and effectively by quoting Ezekiel to them: "If the fathers have eaten sour grapes the teeth of the children shall not be set on edge: The son shall not bear the iniquity of the father with him . . ." I wish our government leaders read Ezekiel.

There is always a gap, often a tragic gap, between the generations. Sometimes it is as if they were living in two separate worlds. Usually it is the younger generation that is the more radical one. Thus it was in Turgenev's charming, puzzled novel about Bazarov, *Fathers and Sons*. But in our time and place it is the other way around. The younger generation has turned out to be the more conservative one.

They have a right to be. But we had better think about what follows when we force them to disown any association with their parents. If they repudiate those who have given them life and nurtured them with love, they must in turn expect to be repudiated by a generation of Bazarovs who will in time confront them with a rude and barren hatred.

January 17, 1954

In many of the recent cases where the Fifth Amendment was invoked, there has been a crucial contradiction in the reasoning of those who have "stood" on the amendment. This has been made apparent by the answers that Professor Wendell Furry of Harvard gave to the one-man McCarthy subcommittee in Boston.

Furry had formerly refused to answer the subcommittee's questions and had become the number one target for McCarthy's drive against the universities.* He has now changed his position, evidently to McCarthy's surprise. He has done so, he says, partly to keep Harvard from being unnecessarily hurt, but also because the invoking of the Fifth Amendment has been widely "misrepresented" and "distorted." "Though its real purpose has always been to shield the innocent," Furry said, "many people have been misled into feeling that the exercise of the privilege is an admission of guilt."

I have sympathy with this interpretation of the historical meaning

* See column of January 13, 1954, immediately following.

of the guarantee contained in the amendment. But it is interesting that Furry has in fact shifted his own position by answering questions where he had formerly refused. It is hard to see why he did not take this position to start with, or what he gained by the delay, the resistance and the reluctant yielding.

It is now clear that Furry was not in fact seeking to shield himself from prosecution when he made his original refusal, nor did he fear to incriminate himself. He now talks freely about his own activities. He still refuses to talk about those who had been Communists along with him, and with whom he has worked on government projects. In thus refusing, he has exposed himself to punitive measures by McCarthy and has shown personal courage, not in order to shield himself but to shield his former associates, whom he regards as carrying no danger to our country.

It is here that the contradiction enters. Whether a man be himself guilty or innocent of a crime, the intent as well as the language of the Fifth Amendment is to insure his not being compelled to testify against himself or incriminate himself. The amendment was not meant as a shield that a man has a right to use primarily to protect others. Furry has had the honesty to change his position and base himself now primarily on the moral ground that, while he will talk about himself, he will not talk about others.

On the moral issue it is extremely hard to pass judgment. Every man must on that score face his own conscience. If, in taking his position, he exposes himself to danger—as Furry has done in inviting a citation for contempt—one must respect his assumption of a calculated risk. The same is true of the position that Corliss Lamont has taken, in basing his refusal to answer questions not on the safe Fifth Amendment but on the precarious First Amendment.

The problem lies in a sentence of Furry's which will be quoted many times in the coming years. "I am not seeking to protect the guilty from prosecution," he said. "I wish merely to secure the innocent from persecution." The trouble is, of course, that this puts Furry—or whoever else adopts this view—in the position of having confidently to decide whether a former Communist colleague is a subject for prosecution or for persecution, whether he is indeed innocent or whether there may not be some guilt he has concealed.

In the end it may be impossible to avoid such a decision, especially if it involves someone whom you have known intimately. Both the decency and the savor of human life depend on building up a tissue of connections—with kin, with friends, with working associates. These connections may at times be betrayed by the unscrupulous. But if we ourselves betray them by doubting everyone and everything because at some point someone might fail us, then nothing is left to us but a moral void.

January 13, 1954

The million-dollar gift to the Harvard Divinity School by John D. Rockefeller is more than a gift—it is a gesture in response to a challenge. "Thy Chase had a Beast in view," wrote Dryden. Harvard is today the quarry of a hunt by a Wisconsin Senator to bring the proud university to its knees, on the issue of Professor Wendell Furry. The Senator has contemptuously advised "subversives" to seek shelter in Cambridge and now talks of a bill that would deny tax exemption to gifts to colleges that do not summarily dismiss teachers invoking the Fifth Amendment.

This kind of baiting is not new to Harvard. Other universities have, of course, not been exempted from the current intellectual hunt, as witness the blanket abuse leveled at C.C.N.Y. by the same toughs who shoot at Harvard. But Harvard, which sent its graduates and Law School men into the New Deal and is today stubbornly set against letting its policy be shaped by political Savonarolas, is bearing the brunt of the attack. I think it will survive its attackers.

They hated President Conant, who was cool, astringent and a scientist. Thus far they have been baffled by his successor, President Nathan Pusey, whose prime interests seem to be the humanities and religion and who has started his tenure by a big drive for the Divinity School. I can see why the hunters must feel frustrated in trying to depict such a man as the keeper of a nest of subversives. Yet make no mistake about it, religion can be pretty dangerous, especially if you distill into it the essence of the dissenting tradition and take it straight.

The question has often been put: What chance is there for the development of democracy in countries like India, Japan, Burma, Pakistan, which do not have a deeply rooted tradition of Judaeo-Christian doctrine, as the Western democracies do? It can be put another way: Can democracy flourish among people whose gods differ from ours? Or still another way: Is the Christian tradition indispensable to democracy?

I suspect that President Pusey's answer to the last question would be a strong Yes, which is why he feels that our crisis stems from a slackening of religion, and why he is seeking new millions to strengthen religion at Harvard. In accepting the Rockefeller gift, John Lord O'Brian—who is the chairman of the drive—took occasion to underline Harvard's effort "to confront the evil ideas current in the East with the ideals that have been fundamental in the growth of Western civilization."

In a paper I read the other day to the American Historical Association, on "Christian Doctrine and Democratic Thought," I gave a less confident and more qualified answer. I don't think the Christian tradition has always helped produce a strong democracy—as witness Russia and Eastern Europe, which were strongly Christian and yet went Communist; as witness also the strength of Communist movements in the Latin countries. A number of Christian societies have been authoritarian. Their obsession with sin and salvation has not kept them from hunting heretics.

The real democratic impulse comes not from the prophetic or missionary spirit in our religions, but from the religious dissenting spirit. It comes from the emphasis on the decision-making individual, who must formulate his own relation to God and is the keeper of his own conscience. If our divinity schools can teach this kind of integrity to the free spirit, they can strengthen our democracy. The real relation is between democracy and the tradition of individual judgment in religion. I think one of the great reasons for the strength of democratic institutions in America has been that the tradition of religious dissent and religious pluralism has been so strong.

The hunters may find that the quarry they have in view is tougher than they think. I suspect that the hatred which spurs their hunt comes from the beast in their own heart, which has little relation either to God or to country.

June 2, 1957

A Federal judge called McLaughlin has ruled that Arthur Miller is guilty of contempt of Congress, and he has written a fifteen-page opinion spelling out his reasons. The legal problem in the case has to do with a man's rights under the First Amendment, not the Fifth, and opens up an area of law that the courts have not yet clearly mapped out. The coming decision in the Watkins case will be crucial.* The problem of self-incrimination does not enter here, since Miller (like Watkins) did not invoke his privilege under the Fifth. He spoke freely about himself but refused to discuss others with whom he was associated in a Communist study group in 1947. He was not protecting Communists, he said, but "my sense of myself . . . I cannot take the responsibility for another human being."

While the ground was moral, Miller's defense in the trial had to be one of law. His counsel, Joseph L. Rauh, Jr., argued that the First Amendment protects freedom of speech, thought and belief; that the committee's questions had no relation to any reasonable legislative intent of Congress; and that a witness who talked freely about himself but remained silent about others in a Communist study group could not be obstructing the valid efforts of Congress to legislate about passports.

Judge McLaughlin's decision seems to this nonlegal commentator farfetched. Granted his reasoning that since Congress can legislate on

---

* As it turned out, the Watkins decision proved to be a blow in favor of freedom of conscience, and the bottom dropped out of the case against Miller.

passports it can investigate them; granted that Communists have mis-used passports. But then the judge takes a big jump; he says that the committee's desire to know who the Communist writers were with whom Miller "forgathered for the discussion of the works of Com-munist writers" was "logically calculated" to help get the facts on which new passport legislation might be based.

This strikes me as pretty tortured stuff. It throws an extremely wide logical net, which would exclude almost nothing. If you accept it, what line of questioning—so long as it has something near or far to do with Communism and Communists—would be outside the committee's scope? And where a man's conscience is deeply involved, does not the committee (and the courts) have the obligation to prove a very close relation between the questions and valid legislative purpose?

I have been reading something else, too—not about Arthur Miller and his legal rights, but by Miller and about his work. It is his new book *Collected Plays* (Viking), gathering together *All My Sons, Death of a Salesman, The Crucible, A Memory of Two Mondays* and *A View from the Bridge*.

Miller has written for the collection a long introductory essay in which he probes into his plays—their writing and meaning—and necessarily also into himself. A writer aiming at reality, he says at one point, must "not only depict why a man does what he does, or why he nearly didn't do it, but why he cannot simply walk away and say to hell with it . . . For I understand the symbolic meaning of a charac-ter and his career to consist of the kind of commitment he makes to life or refuses to make, the kind of challenge he accepts and the kind he can pass by."

Pretty clearly this sheds light on the decision Miller felt he had to make about his own life. A character in a play he did not write but must somehow act out and live out, he has decided that the commit-ment to the idea of freedom to create is one from which he can't walk away.

This is the decision of someone who sees the world around him as material for the creative act and the moral commitment. It doesn't matter whether his decision was right or wrong, but only whether it seemed (and seems) so to him. "For myself," he writes, "the theater is above all an instrument of passion." This quality of passion, which gives the plays their stature, has permeated Miller's life as well.

It has led him at times into blind alleys and wasteland, especially during the years when he was so certain that there was a gulf between fascism and Communism and failed to see the moral corrosion in both. But anyone reading the essay he has written on his dramatic technique will recognize that he is a groper with the characters and the ideas he tries to put into his plays. It was natural for such a man to be a groper also with the ideas and the commitments he tried to act upon in life.

If his groping and his passion were able to conceive and complete *Death of a Salesman* and *A View from the Bridge,* I don't begrudge Miller the mistakes they led him into in politics. If Judge McLaughlin had some insight and passion, he would have looked into the plays for the clue to his decision. For that is the way a writer must be judged—by his work, and the commitments the work shows.

7. The War against the Army

February 24, 1954

ONE PUZZLE in McCarthy's war on the Army is why the Wisconsin Senator has picked the fight. Perhaps he remembers that the Army surrendered when he first moved into Fort Monmouth, and he thinks he can scatter the remaining Army resistance with a whiff of grapeshot. But I have a simpler theory, which is that he is now committed to an all-out offensive against anybody and everybody who stands in his way. He has reached the point where there is no turning back for him—where he must either conquer or let his inflated movement collapse.

In factual terms, McCarthy has the most pathetically trivial case against the Army. Item: One dentist who was allowed to leave the Army by due procedure with an honorable discharge, in spite of refusing to testify about Communist connections. Item: One woman code clerk, who may or may not be a Communist and is still a civilian employee of the Army while it is investigating her.

Does this mean that Secretary Stevens and Chief of Staff Ridgway are nursing a Communist conspiracy, or that they are "dupes" of unnamed pro-Communists high in Army posts? Even to put this question is to show silliness. If a mountainous process of investigation has labored and given birth only to these two squeaking mice in the form of a silent dentist and a dubious female clerk, you would expect a gust of relief and laughter to sweep the nation.

Unfortunately, we seem to have lost the gift of great anger and large laughter. This is what gives the Wisconsin Senator his chance. He is determined to show his followers that he is tough enough to lick the Army. He has to dig up a fresh (if minor) sensation every fifteen minutes, and he has to win every time. Otherwise the image of Grand Inquisitor is tarnished, and he will no longer appear the scourge that he has built himself up to be. One advantage he has is that he has acquired a far more imposing arena in which to disport himself than Hitler ever had in the palmiest days of his mass meetings at the Sportpalast in Berlin. That arena is, of course, the TV show, built into a tense national spectacle by suspense and showmanship. It is a spectacle in which McCarthy makes the rules, picks the actors and hogs the center of the stage.

To understand what McCarthy is driving at in his attack on the Army, the literature on the Nazi movement in Germany is required reading. J. W. Wheeler-Bennett has traced the whole story in his recent book, already an acknowledged masterpiece of narrative, *The Nemesis of Power: The German Army in Politics, 1918-1945* (St. Martin's Press). Before Hitler could capture power, he had first to penetrate the Army and make it pliant to his purposes. Once the Army showed itself willing to play politics on Hitler's terms its strength as a force on the German national scene was lost. It became only a tool.

McCarthy puts his case in the form of a disarming question: whether the Army can hold itself above the Congressional power of investigation. The real question, of course, is whether an Army that is subjected to the terrorism of a single Senator can call itself an Army and maintain the self-respect of its officers and men. If McCarthy can show President Eisenhower to be a weakling in his own military domain, he will have him on the run. The five-star general will thus have been overshadowed by the self-created six-star general who is seeking to oust him as Commander in Chief.

March 12, 1954

This has been a great and eventful week in the history of our awakening to the McCarthy madness. The week began on Saturday night with Adlai Stevenson's speech, which set off a train of explosive events. It was followed by McCarthy's arrogant blunder in again demanding radio and TV time for himself. This blunder made it possible for CBS and NBC to cease being scared rabbits. With a good sense of timing, Senator Flanders went on to make Senate history by being the first Republican openly to take the floor and peel off McCarthy's skin like an onion. That same night Edward Murrow peeled off an even more sensitive layer just by showing to the innocent eye the pictures of McCarthy in action, and adding a few words of his own. The next day, President Eisenhower had to break his silly rule against naming names in his press conference and said what he should long ago have said—that McCarthy does not speak for the Republicans.

Yesterday came the new epoch inside the Senate committee, which may mark the beginning of its redemption as a committee and transform it from a shabby and scabrous instrument of McCarthy's power. The Democratic members present at the grilling of Mrs. Annie Lee Moss decided to take a hand in the proceedings. Senator Symington told her he believed her story—after McCarthy had condemned her in advance. Senator McClellan called her a victim of rumor and innuendo and demanded that she be confronted by her accuser and his evidence. The committee is no longer a one-man inquisition. The power of that man has been challenged inside his own fortress, where hitherto his victims have been helpless because no one held himself responsible to protect their rights.

I spell the events of the week out at this length because we must all learn that in politics as in love the whole is greater than the sum of its parts. Just as fear breeds fear—which is what McCarthy has counted on—so courage breeds courage. There is a contagion in each of them. Men catch fire from each other in victory or they grow panicky together in retreat.

Everyone stretched himself a bit in the process. Stevenson went beyond the usual caution of politicians who are still in the running. Flanders, a conservative New England Republican, found scorching words to express his contempt for a bully. Even McClellan, a conservative Southern Democrat, invoked the great principles of civil rights for accused men. As for Murrow, he broke with the tradition of suavely "detached" and "neutral" commentators. He discovered that there can be no neutrality in the struggle of freedom against evil.

In no small measure McCarthy has been his own dearest enemy. He has been reckless. He has been obsessed with his image of himself as a potentate in his own universe, and he has let his picture of his little universe blot out the image of the actual America. To say as he did that if the FCC law did not give him the right to free radio and TV time, the law would have to be changed—this was to cut himself off from the American reality and open himself to mockery. The superman is becoming a figure of jest.

But even when he is on the defensive, as he is now, McCarthy is dangerous because he has nothing to lose and stops at nothing. His attack last night on Edward Murrow, seeking to link him with Moscow, is his way of warning other commentators as well that he will destroy them in the act of destroying himself. Murrow will not scare easily. With others he has begun the answer of the American people to McCarthyism.

March 14, 1954

McCarthy and McCarthyism are crumbling. The diary of the Schine Affair that has been released by the Army is one of the most deadly documents in our political history. McCarthy's countercharge, accusing the Army of blackmailing him, is wholly characteristic of his method but is the most desperate move of his career. He will not survive it politically. This is the beginning of the end.

Like most events that make a great splash in history, this Schine-Cohn-McCarthy episode comes onto the stage in fantastic costume. It has the serpentine quality of intrigue, and all the sensation of public scandal. But there are also elements of musical comedy in this spectacle of the saviors of America from Communism spending half their energy saving an unimportant young man from the discomforts and indignities of the life of a drafted soldier.

There is even a thread of comedy in the cries of "Smear" raised by one of the greatest smear technicians in the records of the art. Even if McCarthy could show that the Army has distorted the case against Cohn and himself, there would still be a kind of irony in seeing the pursuers pursued, the wolf pack in full retreat before the Army foxes, the hangman caught with his own noose.

What a picture emerges from the Army account of the antics of Joe McCarthy and his friend Cohn. These crusaders are shown as influence seekers on the meanest and most trivial level. Mc-Carthy himself emerges in the thoroughly unattractive role of a double-dealer even to his own closest associate, Cohn: putting pressure on the Army to ease Schine's life as long as Cohn was watching, and when Cohn's back was turned, knifing his great pro-Schine crusade. What a picture is drawn of the defenders of American security taking up hours not only of the committee staff's time but also of the time of the Secretary of War and his staff, phoning, conferring, nagging, higgling, negotiating, threatening, storming, over whether a favorite hanger-on at the Court of McCarthy would be treated with the honors due even to the camp followers of royalty.

These are not just silly and trivial men. They are sick men— stricken with the sickness of the power-mad. Because they had access to dossiers and the power of subpoena and contempt citation, because they controlled the lethal headlines and could destroy a man on TV, they saw themselves as a privileged little elite to whom the laws of the American community meant nothing because they were more powerful than law.

Let them all go, in the name of American decency. McCarthy gambled for total power in a republic that has always rejected total-itarianism, and he has lost his gamble. Let him depart from the stage of our attention and take his little bedraggled band with him.

May 7, 1954

McCarthy's marathon encounter with the Army is proving immensely valuable in laying bare the whole pattern of McCarthyism. The last two days of testimony have revealed two major features of McCarthy's method. One was made clear by the alleged Hoover letter, the other by McCarthy's refusal to name its source. But by McCarthy's own admission, the Army intelligence officer who gave him the alleged letter gave it to him illegally, violating a Presidential directive with the force of law.

This reaches the heart of the issue. McCarthy talks of the sense of higher duty that moved the intelligence officer to betray his trust and violate the Presidential directive. This, of course, is exactly the reasoning of all undercover agents who betray their sworn oath as government officials in order to aid some cause of whose higher validity they set themselves up as sole judges.

Never has it been clearer that McCarthyism is a challenge to the whole structure of loyalty to constitutional government. "It is a daily and nightly occurrence for me to receive information from people in government in regard to Communist infiltration," said McCarthy. Which is another way of saying that he has set up a counter-intelligence squad inside the government and is in effect aiming to build up a rival government.

This involves more than a network of McCarthy stool pigeons that reaches into Army G-2. It involves McCarthy's effort to convince the people that no branch of the government can be trusted except, of course, McCarthy himself and his lieutenants, now under trial. Under such conditions no administration can hope to carry on constitutional government. Just as dangerous to orderly government as the Communist Fifth Column is the McCarthy Sixth Column.

Brownell had no choice except to refuse permission to have the alleged letter read. For him to have blessed with his approval the fruits of a deliberate and conscious violation of the law and breach of trust would have been to put the stamp of approval on a revolutionary movement within the government. McCarthy's attack on Brownell's order as coming from a mere "appointed official" would presumably apply just as strongly to that other appointed official who works under Brownell—J. Edgar Hoover. Thus McCarthy breaks one link after another that has up to now kept him loosely allied with authority and respectability. Fighting for his political life, he has succeeded only in isolating himself and in revealing the revolution he is aiming at and the chaos through which he intends to march to power.

March 17, 1954

Along with many other things that it is, the McCarthy business is also a constitutional crisis. A constitutional crisis goes beyond the demagogy of a particular man to a disruption of government that strains its functioning in a major way and may even endanger its survival.

Thus we had a serious constitutional crisis before the Civil War, when the balance of government was at stake in the matter of adding new states as slave or free. We had another during the New Deal, when the Roosevelt legislation was stymied by the Supreme Court and the President used the threat of court packing as a way of breaking the jam. The present crisis revolves around the relation of the Congressional investigating power to the whole operation of government.

It is unfair to condemn the whole Congressional investigating power—as some do—merely because one man has gone berserk with it. But it is important to see how it enabled him to go berserk. "Give me a place to stand," said Archimedes, "and I will move the world." McCarthy uses the same leverage principle. Standing in his strategic spot on the Subcommittee on Investigations, he uses every means open to an unscrupulous man who knows how to exploit genuine fears of the external enemies and rouse fantasy fears of internal ones. He has a staff of sleuths. He has the power of subpoena, of asking harassing questions, of citing for contempt. He seems to have the FBI files available to him. He has a flare for the newspaper headlines, and —until now—the free run of TV.

This array of ways and means has made him a counterpower to the Presidency and the administrative agencies. The Constitution has not provided for a Senator or a Senatorial committee who will be a counter-President. Nor can the government function thus. McCarthyism is the effort to paralyze the operation of domestic affairs and the conduct of foreign policy by an unending series of sensational diversions, carried on from the strategic position of a roving Grand Inquisitor. It is the creation of a separate center of conspiracy and disaffection within the government, so that every normal governmental move can be checkmated almost at will. It is the raising of so continuous a turmoil over the fake issues of disloyalty that no other issues can be debated and no other government business be transacted.

I submit that this is the nature of the constitutional crisis which has plagued us since the Republican victory of 1952—although its roots reach to 1950. If it is true that one phase of the crisis has been to raise a counterpower to the Presidency, then President Eisenhower's failure to assert the full extent of the Presidential power has been almost fatal. If the President wants to reassert his power, he will find much of the solution in helping Congress to put the investigating power back into bounds.

Too little has been said about the responsibility the Senate itself must bear for the constitutional crisis. The first task is to recapture from the McCarthy subcommittee the fantastic power it claims as a band of roving sleuths and inquisitors. Every other committee has its scope and its field of legitimate interest more or less limited. That is true of the committee on the armed services, on foreign affairs, on the judiciary, but a committee on governmental operations, which is as broad as the entire field of government, has no limits except the boundless arrogance and ambition of its subcommittee chairman on investigations. Whatever validity the Congressional power of investigation may have in the case of the other committees, in this case it can be only an unending nuisance and danger.

The next step will be for the Senate to assert that no committee can act through the one-man rule of its chairman without making the whole Senate a laughingstock. Further, it must assert that no committee can refuse to confront its victims with the sources of the charges against them without involving the whole Senate in the guilt of such a procedure. Finally it must assert that where there are charges of incompetence or failure on the part of a staff member of any executive agency the committee must direct its questions in the end to the responsible head of the agency, who can either answer them satisfactorily or resign.

More is involved here than a new set of ground rules for investigations. What is necessary is for the Senate to discard its notion that each investigating committee is a separate little empire, off on its own imperial adventures but having little to do with the Senate as a whole.

We shall not restore order in American government and society until we get a new concept of the integral dignity and honor of the Senate, in which all are members.

8. Soliloquy of a Boot

May 14, 1954

"If you want a picture of the future, imagine a boot stamping on a human face forever."—The Inquisitor, in *1984,* by George Orwell.

The committee room is filling up with all the yokels and dopes. The TV cameras are grinding. . . . I must manage a smile, to show this business doesn't mean a thing to me. . . . There goes Roy buzzing in my ear again, like a nervous fly. I have told him a thousand times to stop this never ending whispering to me while millions are watching. . . . How did I ever get afflicted with him and his infernal friend Schine? I guess I needed his smartness and I fed on his admiration. And besides, his name was useful. It trips up the lefties in their talk about Hitler. . . .

There goes Adams now, starting his yap-yap. . . . And that blundering comedian, Jenkins, going after him like a clumsy village lawyer playing Daniel Webster. . . .

How did I ever get here, after four years of buildup and glory, and everything going my way? I had the headlines and the columnists, and my stupid puppet Party colleagues on the committee. Every day, in every paper, on every program, at every veterans' meeting, in every smoking car and every bar and every dinner-table conversation, it was "McCarthy this" and "McCarthy that." . . . It was good to hear the crowd roar when I got up to speak. It was the kind of roar

Hitler got, or Lenin—who wasn't a fool either, even if he was a Commie.

And in every town the mayor and the fat boys coming out to spread a carpet for me . . . And the motorcycle police escort burning up the pavements, and the sirens screaming . . . Not so bad for a farm boy from Grand Chute, who kept chickens and ran a country store and had to crowd four years of high school into one.

Whatever was it that happened? . . . Why did I ever let those baby-faced boys get me tangled up with the Army? I should have known I couldn't take on the Army yet. Later, yes. But not yet. . . . If I had waited I could have crushed them all, generals and civilians, Ridgway and Hensel and John Adams, and that nincompoop woolens manufacturer, Stevens. I could have stamped on their faces—if I had just waited a bit. Oh, they would have bawled and crawled and come over to my side, the way the German generals came over to Hitler, once he was sure of power. . . .

To think that this Adams rat would turn out so nasty and treacherous. I thought I had him eating out of my hand. If I could only get him in front of me, the way I ran the hearings in the old days. I would smash his face in. . . . I wonder how it all happened?

Right now the thing to do is to look bored while Adams talks. . . . There were too many points of order. I should have known I was overdoing it. The other day there was laughter when I said something about my veracity being questioned. The yokels will all laugh on the other side of their mouths some day. My star is still there in the sky somewhere, but everything is blurred. . . .

I must look carefree and even bored and disgusted with this circus. . . . I've told the newspaper boys what the line is now, and they're following it. I'm glad I still have a faithful kennel of writers, who take any lead I throw them like a bone thrown to dogs. As for the All-slops and Wechsler and that Herblock and the smarties on the *Times* and the whole lefty bunch, they'll find I still have a killer instinct when this is all over and I can get at them. . . .

I wish they'd get those Army dopes with those uniforms out of the room, away from the camera. You can't fight a uniform bedecked with Army medals day after day. . . .

I wish I could get Roy off my neck. He double-crossed me and he knows I double-crossed him, but there are millions of eyes on us, and we've got to act it out. . . . Those clumsy fools, bungling the picture the way they did . . . But how did I ever stumble with that letter? It looked like a sure thing. That kind of thing always was sure stuff before . . . I wonder how Hoover really feels? . . . As for Baby-Face in the White House, I'll deal with him in time. He may know war, but he doesn't know war the way I fight it. . . . I was sure he was just another setup like Hindenburg. . . .

I'll have to think, think . . . If only Roy would stop whispering.
What is it that is burning up in me? . . . It all seemed in my
grasp. Now they're talking of Skid Row, and the rats are deserting.
. . . I'll still show them, even if I have to bring the whole country
down in ruins around me. I'll stamp on their silly faces.

9. His Shadow Was Terror

May 3, 1957

THE ANGRY MAN from Wisconsin who died yesterday had really died
before. The death at Bethesda Hospital was the end of the man, but
the political end came three years earlier.

Joe McCarthy suffered his fatal political wound at the hands of
a fiercely gentle Boston lawyer called Joseph N. Welch. Desperate
because he was losing the great TV battle of the Army hearings,
swept by a gust of anger at Welch's sharp cross-examining of Roy
Cohn, McCarthy blundered into an assault on the loyalty of young
Fisher, a member of Welch's law firm. Welch's answer is part of the
history of great utterance. The irrelevance and cruelty of McCarthy's
attack laid bare, as nothing else could have done, the essence of the
man. It was a moment of truth, not for Welch alone but for the millions of the still uncommitted who watched.

"What did I do?" McCarthy asked as the crowd in the hearing room
melted away, leaving him isolated. It was the beginning of the end.
From that point he was politically a wounded animal, the stalker
being stalked. The political kill itself came with the Senate censure,
throwing him out of the club, putting him outside the pale. He ceased
to be a serious force, his ism was no more, and the words that had
once set headlines ablaze now made a few sticks of dull type on an
inside page.

When the man himself died he had outlived his political life. Death
came pathetically, almost mercifully, before the looming primary
contest for another Senatorial term whose result would have been certain disaster. When a man has dedicated his life to the single pursuit
of power and lost it, one can understand that he should lose with it
the will to live.

I fought McCarthy in life as hard as I knew how. I have no intent
now to fight him in death. For him as a human being, as for every
human being who goes through an ordeal at the end, I have only
compassion.

But it would be an insult to prettify him, or to say the silly lies
about him that we mistakenly think are owed to the dead. It is not
true, for example, that he was merely a "controversial" figure; to say

so would be to apply to him the meaningless adjective which used to be applied to his victims. Nor is what Richard Nixon said true— that McCarthy fought "Communist infiltration." That was the mask he used in his lifetime. And it is no service to anyone to use it as a death mask as well.

McCarthy was a combatant on the battlefield of history. As such, one must ask what will be his role in history, what good or evil he did, what was the shadow he cast on his time.

He came on the political scene at a moment of history when the American people had been seized with a vague and nameless anxiety about shadowy enemies within the nation who might be in league with the very real enemy without. He had the political instinct to sense this anxiety and exploit it, as any tribal medicine man exploits the jungle fears in order to build his power. He knew how to play on the theme of patriotism while undercutting the most cherished values by which Americans had lived.

If you chose to forget about the blasted lives and careers, there was a certain edge of fascination in his reckless improvisations, and you couldn't help seeing the cynical smile as he watched himself in the performing mirror. But there was nothing amusing about what he was after. The strength he drew upon was fear, the shadow he cast was that of terror.

The ordeal of the nation had little to do, I suspect, with McCarthy himself. It had to do with ourselves—with the fact that in a moment of crisis most men are confused, vulnerable to the terror from without because they are riddled by fears from within.

It seemed an endless ordeal, but it did end when a few courageous men—liberal and conservative alike—faced him, fought him, stripped away the mask. Once they had shown the way, the nation found itself again. Men looked around at each other, a little dazed and shame-faced when they found that the menacing shapes from which they had fled were the lengthened shadows of their own terrors.

Then came the bitter irony for McCarthy himself. Where once he had been a hero for millions, almost overnight he became a pariah. The courtiers shrank away, the true believers turned out to have been only camp followers, looking for glory and booty, and the stream of mass support turned into the merest rivulet and ran into the sand. Even the intellectual radicals of the right, who had once garlanded him with phrases and praises, turned toward other gods.* In the end he was left alone with the bitterness of his thoughts on political failure in a success society.

* One organ of the right that kept its allegiance was the *National Review*. For a comment on this column, see Willy Schlamm's article "Across McCarthy's Grave" in the May 18, 1957, issue of that journal.

In one sense he performed a function for us. Every people, in a time of crisis, needs some symbol that will serve as the Adversary, against which it can test its capacity to survive its fears. We survived, although by a thinner margin than most of us would be willing to admit. Whether we also came through more mature than we were is something we shall have to test in the years ahead without the McCarthy figure.

ON THE ANVIL OF CONSCIENCE, THE FORGING OF FREEDOM

1. Days with the Remingtons

December 28, 1950

I SPENT A DAY yesterday with the Remingtons. They were receiving, not at home but in the Federal Courthouse, where they were washing their dirty household laundry. She was dressed simply in a wine-colored suit, her attractive face framed against dark hair swept to one side in a bob much cultivated by the Bennington girls a decade or so ago. He—blond, grave, bespectacled, with sharply chiseled handsome features—was dressed in a wrecked career and the shadow of a jail sentence for perjury.

He sat in the defendant's chair, she in the witness chair. Between them were not only two long tables filled with lawyers, but even more the bleak unmeasurable distance that comes between two people who have once been close but have now come to regard each other on one side as an object of hate, on the other as an engine of destruction.

I don't know whether William Remington perjured himself or not when he swore that he had never been a Communist. But I do know that behind the tragic political story at this "little Hiss trial" there is a tragic personal story.

She was a Bennington girl, he was a Dartmouth boy. They were both attractive. Both played around in left-liberal circles at college. She says she didn't love him when she married him. He wooed her, like an Othello wooing a Desdemona, with tales of the scars he had received in leftist battles. She admired him. Four years ago they separated, and now they are divorced. "I would like to say," she told the court, "that I am a very reluctant witness. I find it hard to testify against the father of my children, and I want it known that I hold no malice toward him."

Listening to her, as she tried to formulate a definition of being a Communist that would establish him as one, you couldn't help wondering a bit about her reluctance. You wondered what emotional turmoil was behind that flat, casual tone in which she answered questions. What was left in the ashes when the flame had gone out—bitterness? Or just nothingness?

The nub of the perjury problem lies in just what is meant by the charge of being a Communist. Mrs. Remington agreed that the two of them had never signed anything, nor formally committed themselves. Yet, she insisted, they had been Communists. "Being a Communist," she said at one point, "is largely a state of mind" plus working for a Communist program. At no point did she define the program in terms of violence or subversion, but only in terms of pro-unionism, Loyalist Spain and other Popular Front slogans.

There is a kernel of truth in this. It was such a "state of mind" that led many youngsters in the decade of the thirties to work inside the Communist Party and on its margins. But the government's contention ever since the trial of the Communist Party leaders has been that being a Communist is far more dangerous than a state of mind. It is membership in a disciplined and ruthless international conspiracy.

It is hard to see how we can have it both ways. Maybe the evidence will establish that Remington was a Communist in this conspiratorial sense, accepted discipline, carried out assignments. If so his conviction will have to turn on that evidence, not on Mrs. Remington's vaguely recalled incidents of youthful leftish alliance.

Meanwhile we get a picture of a college generation that read the *New Masses,* talked radicalism vaguely, throbbed for Loyalist Spain, was blind enough to swallow (even after the purge trials) the propaganda version of a never-never-land Russia.

I was teaching at Williams the year Mrs. Remington was a senior at Bennington. On the stand she named a girl as the one other member of the Young Communist League at college. I think I remember that girl when she used to come, along with a whole Bennington deputation, to the Williams dances. She was gay, bright, vivacious. I don't know what ever happened to her, but I hope she never has to sit separated from the man she married in the bitterness of a lost world.

January 2, 1951

The thing I like about New Year celebrations is not the public hoopla, whether at hotels or restaurants or on the streets, but the private renewal of friendships and intimacies. Am I wrong in thinking that this year the handclasp has been a bit tighter between friend and friend, the embrace a shade more lingering, and the feeling ever present although unspoken that in the coldness of the world the flame of the direct human relation is something to warm oneself by?

Notice that when novelists like Aldous Huxley and George Orwell set down their nightmare forebodings of the monstrous shapes to come, as in *Brave New World* and *1984,* the world they fear, yet expect, omits wholly the human tie. That is also one of the frightening things about the Remington trial that goes far beyond the dimensions of the case itself. Whatever other witnesses will be called, my mind keeps going back to Mrs. Remington.

The most depressing aspect of the case has been the way in which the meaning of the private relationship seems to have been erased. Mrs. Remington, once she had decided to testify against her former husband, found herself saying things which she probably felt she had in all conscience to say, but one listened to them with a kind of dismay. She had never, she said, loved her husband. She disliked her mother and denounced her as a Communist. She thought her first lawyer, whom she had consulted on whether she should testify, had sought to betray her interest.

I am not passing judgment on her decision to talk rather than remain silent. I suppose it might be argued that since she had never loved him and divorce had broken what bond there had been, there was no reason for treating the father of her children differently from the way she might treat any other defendant.

Yet such reasoning could scarcely apply to what she said about her mother, nor can it dispose of any human tie that has once been close— as Dean Acheson unforgettably showed when he refused to denounce a man called Alger Hiss, who had been his friend.

If a child of mine should ever turn against me and denounce my politics, or announce his dislike of me publicly, my heartbreak would come not from the public disgrace but from the feeling of private emptiness because so close a human bond had been denied.

Perhaps you will say that, painful as these things may be, it is everyone's duty to put the public interest above private ties. But to say that is exactly the dangerous thing, for it prepares human sacrifices for the omnivorous state.

It is time that we grappled in America with the basic ethical problem that has been raised for us in this era of the snoop, the spy and the denouncer. What we bravely vaunt before the world, in contrast with Russian totalitarianism, is the sanctity of the person. This does not refer, of course, only or even mainly to the sanctity of the blood tie. Yet how shall I honor my lesser ties when I negate the closer and greater ones? I recognize no "public interest" which is not the sum of the meanings of all the private bonds and human relations. When they are corroded the "public interest" is corroded.

In both the Soviet and Nazi regimes one common element has been a ruthless indoctrination that has instilled into the children the idea that the claims of the state override the human tie. As a result, children were encouraged even to betray their parents and turn them over to public vengeance. I recall Bertolt Brecht's play *The Private Life of the Master Race,* especially a scene called "The Jewish Wife," and another called "The Informer" about a Hitler Jugend son and his father.

I don't say that anything like this is developing in our midst. Yet in its extreme way it serves to point up the need for holding on for dear life—in a time of public disintegration—to whatever has integrity and meaning in our private relations.

January 24, 1951

As you watch him on the stand, you know that from Remington's standpoint everything now depends on Remington. In the court of one's peers, as in the even greater court of one's conscience, every man in the end must stand solitary and lonely.

He has a lot to explain, and he goes at it in so earnest and thorough-going a way that—guilt or no guilt—one can understand how he impressed his teachers at Dartmouth and Columbia, and his bosses on his jobs in Washington. He has to explain or deny his former wife's testimony about his promising to remain a Communist if she married him, and both her testimony and that of Elizabeth Bentley about paying party dues to Miss Bentley, and the testimony of several people that he attended Communist meetings at the TVA, and other items that the government has been piling up with the hope of showing that where there is so much smoke there must be some fire.

Does he succeed in explaining these things? So far he has gone through the story of his Dartmouth student days, his TVA days, his courtship and marriage, his two years as a Columbia graduate student, his Mexico honeymoon, his early days in Washington.

All through the trial up to now I had had the heavy, oppressive feeling of moving through a swamp-infested jungle to which no sun penetrated. But unless Remington is a consummate actor—which he may be—you have the feeling that there is nothing furtive and creepy about him, that he is fighting hard but is not drenched in hatred. You may feel that he is perhaps a little stuffy and self-important at times, and every now and then he turns too directly to the jury with a smile and explanation. But if some of his explanations sound too pat, it is the government's job—if it can do it—to blast holes in them.

The picture he presents is of a boy of good family who got into deep waters at college, got out somehow (as he tells it) without joining the Communist Party; a boy who wooed a leftist girl by bragging about the scars he received in leftist encounters. The girl, for whom the left had a glamour, feared his ambition and (again as he tells it) made him promise before she married him that he would never get caught in the American success jungle but would continue his fight for a decent society.

That is the story he has to make stick—the story not of a Communist but of one who had an emotional and intellectual flirtation with Communism.

But as you watch Remington, you see that he might indeed have turned out a business success, a young Time-Life executive, a frequenter of the slick midtown lunch places, a mighty hunter before the Lords of the Big Money. He had the talent, looks, drive. What kept him? Was it a secret and traitorous pact with the Communist underworld? Or was it that when he was skirting the thin edge of the thirties and early forties he never lost sight entirely of the vision of a decent world that comes to most men in their youth?

That is the question we shall have in the end to answer about Remington. The reason the case is important to us is that it is being tried in an America where the individual person must stand to be weighed and assessed in daylight and not annihilated in the darkness of the closed mind and the flinty heart.

November 26, 1954

William Remington died as he had lived, in dubious and ambiguous battle. He was a man who teetered on the edge of ideas, never a wholehearted partisan of any cause—a man who had compromised himself enough in his youth to make a jury vote him a perjurer about his political loyalties. His first wife testified against him at his trial, in one of the shabbiest exhibitions of vengefulness I have ever witnessed. He convinced many people that he was deeply anti-Communist and must have convinced himself, too, since he wrote a letter to the FBI offering to inform on Communist sympathizers among his fellow employees.

He lived a life of bewildering mirror images. But while he was not a man to be admired, he did not deserve the vindictive pursuit he suffered, nor the hatreds he engendered among the unthinking and hysterical. Least of all did he deserve the brick in a sock wielded by two thugs who broke his skull as he slept in his prison cell.

It seems a plausible theory that two brutal men, who may have resented his intervention in some prison feud, picked him more readily as a target because their fury was whipped up by the slogans of anti-Communist hatred. Even the most degraded criminal likes to feel superior to someone he regards below him. The two thugs may have regarded a Remington as outside the limits of even prison fair play.

"There are strange people in penitentiaries," said Remington's widow in an interview with Arthur Massolo of the *Post*. And then she added, "and apparently outside, too." It is not hard to understand the muted bitterness of her comment.

For a prison contains all the swirling crosscurrents of emotion one finds in the world outside, only more so. The unnatural tensions and privations make the violent explosion of hatred seem like a welcome release.

2. The Tragedy of the Rosenbergs

April 9, 1951

FORD MADOX FORD once began a novel (I quote from memory) "This is the saddest story I have ever known." I thought I had known many sad stories, but there are few sadder than that of the Rosenbergs, who were sentenced to death last week for espionage.

I have spent the weekend reading a startling book which includes this story. It is a factual book, 222 pages long, made up mostly of courtroom and official testimony. It is called *Soviet Atomic Espionage* (Government Printing Office) and is a report prepared by the staff of the Joint Congressional Committee on Atomic Energy and released today. It is an even more important document than the report on the Canadian atomic spies.

The theme of this book is the tragedy of treason. The report says with pride that there has been no known case of the breach of American espionage security since mid-1946 when the law creating the Joint Committee and the Atomic Energy Commission was enacted. But before that there were a number of cases, including the famous ones of Klaus Fuchs and Allan Nunn May. On the British side there is also an account of the recent flight of Dr. Bruno Pontecorvo, the Italian-born British scientist, to the Iron Curtain countries.

The case that is foremost in our minds now is that of David Greenglass and the Rosenbergs. The testimony in it takes up almost half of the report, pages 50 to 162.

The important question about this case, I think, is not whether the death sentence for the Rosenbergs was justified. Given the enormity of the crime, and the lives that would be destroyed in a Soviet atomic attack, the death of a man and his wife who were conscious and deliberate spies, and the soldiers of treason, seems a minor concern.

The real question is: Why did they do it? And, having done it, why have they persisted to the end in denying it?

One possible answer is that of the poverty and the slum areas of East Side life in New York. I don't think this is an adequate one. For every East Sider who is involved here, there are hundreds of thousands who never succumbed to the bitterness of poverty and deprivation enough to betray their country. You have to invoke something more decisive than the neighborhood environment.

The answer, if I may suggest it, lies in a seemingly crazy paradox. There are some who become spies for money, or out of vanity and megalomania, or out of ambition, or out of a desire for thrills. But the malady of our time is of those who become spies out of idealism.

That, as far as we can judge, was the case of Julius Rosenberg. He came out of the East Side and fought his way through college. His father was religious and a patriot, but the son's rebellion was a rebellion against the father as well as against society. He was bright and he was tough-willed, and at some point he came to identify his life's meaning with the cause of world Communism. In Ethel, he married a girl who, as her mother put it, had "always fought hard for everything." Together they were Communists, and together they spied, and were caught, and now together they face death in another six weeks, evidently with no trace of remorse.

The case of David Greenglass and his wife, Ruth, is different. David was Ethel's young brother, the classical Kid Brother, who liked to putter with chemistry and was never much of a thinker but looked up to Ethel and worshiped Julius with a hero worship. Julius used the Kid Brother ruthlessly. He was usable, he was pliable, and as luck would have it, he was in the Army working as a machinist at Los Alamos. The stuff he gave the Russians, especially the drawings and descriptions of a lens mold for the atom bomb, was second in value only to what they got from Klaus Fuchs.

Who can doubt that in the end he did what he had to do? Yet I shouldn't like to be in the shoes of a man who, in trying to make some amends for the treason he had done his country, has had to send his sister to her death.

Judge Kaufman too did what he had to do. The sentence is drastic, yet it is scarcely possible to challenge its justice, especially after reading the detailed testimony in the Atomic Committee document. My real dissent from Judge Kaufman's speech to the accused is his evident belief that the death penalty will deter others like the Rosenbergs from committing a similar treason. This is to skim the surface of their action and ignore its deep sources.

June 19, 1952

I witnessed something on Tuesday night that stirred me both to anger and to compassion. I went to Flatbush, to the meeting held by the so-called Committee to Secure Justice in the Rosenberg case. The meeting was run and dominated by the Communists, and my anger was at the cynicism with which they exploited the emotions of good people for an evil cause. My compassion was for the people who came to the meeting, almost all of them Jewish residents of Brooklyn, not knowing that the Communist clique who ran the meeting cared no more for the Rosenbergs than they had once cared for the Alters and Ehrlichs who had been murdered by the Russian commissars.

The case of the atom spies Julius and Ethel Rosenberg is one of almost unrelieved ugliness and degradation; during the whole Flatbush meeting one listened in vain for a single hard fact that would cast a serious doubt on their guilt. The speakers stressed that those on whose testimony the Rosenbergs were convicted had betrayed the close ties of blood. It is a true fact, and a shattering one. Yet it is a sword that cuts both ways. David Greenglass could not have sent his sister to her doom unless she had involved him in a real conspiracy to steal atom secrets for the Russians.

Albert Kahn made the collection speech. He read a message from the Rosenbergs and when he got to the payoff sentences his eyes filled with tears and his words stuck in his throat. A heap of five- and ten-dollar bills and hundreds of dollar bills came to the platform, $3,500 worth.

Yet I do not think the primary purpose of the meeting was to milk these people of their greenbacks. The main purpose was to spread the Communist legend that the American government is anti-Semitic.

I am fed up with that legend, and with the efforts of the Communist clique to exploit the fears and sensitivities of American Jews. The note was struck in Rosenberg's letter from prison. "We are as innocent of espionage and treason," he wrote, "as were our six million brothers and sisters who were put to death in the gas chambers of Europe." The same note was repeated in almost every speech. It is time that someone called the lie that it is. What has happened to the Rosenbergs had nothing to do with their being Jewish.

The climax of the evening was a speech by a little orthodox rabbi, Meyer Sharff, of Williamsburg. He wore a skullcap and a long black coat with prayer shawl under it and a magnificent growth of beard. He was the prize catch of the cynical men who ran the meeting. He spoke in Yiddish with long Hebrew quotations from the Holy Books. No one could accuse him, he said, of being a Communist—and the crowd laughed. The reason, he explained, was that the Communists in Russia had killed his sixteen-year-old son as the son of a bourgeois father—and no one laughed a bit. What seemed to weigh in his mind was that Judge Kaufman, who passed the death sentence on the Rosenbergs, was himself a Jew and inclined to lean backward. I agree that the death penalty was unprecedented and harsh. But I wondered how loudly the Communists would shout out even if the judge had not happened to be Jewish.

I looked around the room, and what I saw were vultures and victims. The vultures were the half-pint commissars, exploiting the emotions of unsuspecting Jews. The victims were the group of lower-middle-class men and women, huddled together in anxiety. I keep thinking of the little orthodox rabbi. He seemed to me a genuine person, with a re-ligious passion and a sense of kinship with his people. He knew that the Communists hated and destroyed Jewish communities everywhere inside the Iron Curtain. Why did he let himself be used by them?

I think it was because he had dwelt so long over the memory of the centuries of scars his people had suffered. Even in a free America it is a hard thing to erase the memory of those scars. That is why it is so unforgivable for the Communists to keep spreading the lie about the Rosenberg case. It is an insult to the overwhelming number of American Jews, who hate every form of totalitarianism, and it is a mockery of the millions of Jewish martyrs in Europe.

June 17, 1953

The last-minute appeals of the Rosenbergs to the courts have been dramatic, but there is every sign that they will be futile. The same goes for the clemency appeal to President Eisenhower. There will be no more doors for the Rosenbergs to knock at. This looks more and more like the last mile for them.

I expect to be at Ossining Thursday night, reporting on the execution. I can think of very few tasks I like less. Meanwhile I want to set down here, as honestly as I know how, some thoughts on the eve of the execution.

I don't see how anyone can have strong doubts about the essential guilt of the convicted pair. The Communists in every country have spread the story that there was no evidence against them. That is not true. There was strong evidence of their recruiting David Greenglass for spying, evidence of the recognition signal for the meeting with Harry Gold, evidence of the plan for flight.

The argument that Greenglass lied to save his skin seems weak. He could save his skin better by telling the truth. Moreover, the truth could never backfire at him, while the lies might.

The most powerful criticism of the government's case is that of the atom scientist Harold Urey. He says that Greenglass could not have known enough to submit the plans for the atom bomb to his fellow spies. He had neither the education nor the training for it, nor was he in a position to gather the many complicated threads that formed a picture of the bomb.

This does not mean that Greenglass and the Rosenbergs were not spies. It means that the crime of the Rosenbergs was not as stupendous in its consequences as Judge Kaufman thought and did not merit the unprecedented death sentence. It undercuts the whole base on which Judge Kaufman meted out a death penalty.

As I see it, this is not anything that the Supreme Court can do much about. It would be hard to show that the Rosenbergs have been denied due process of law, or that our judicial system failed to function. There were mistakes in judgment and policy. The greatest mistake in judgment was, I think, Judge Kaufman's. I say this with humility, and with respect for Kaufman's integrity. But the penalty could well have been thirty years rather than death. Given such a penalty, the whole worldwide Communist campaign to blacken America's image would have been futile.

This mistake of judgment was compounded by President Eisenhower's rejection of the first clemency plea. But it is not too late for him to reconsider it.

The President evidently feels that clemency now would be a sign of weakness on our part. I wish he had studied the history of nations and empires more carefully. It is only the weak nation that must put on a show of face-saving! Only a strong nation can afford to be generous. The President also seems to feel that the execution will deter other spies. He has only to study Julius and Ethel Rosenberg, read their letters, watch their behavior, to understand that they are of the type of Communist fanatic whom nothing could ever deter from serving their false cause.

I have been reading the "Death House Letters" which the Rosenberg Committee has published. They have a pathos in them, especially when the father and mother write to their two boys. But they are stilted and mechanical letters that read like *Daily Worker* editorials. And the effort to exploit the boys themselves is another evidence that Communism dehumanizes its soldiers.

I need scarcely repeat here what I have so often written—that only the Soviet cause will benefit from the execution of the Rosenbergs. They are worth far more to the Russians dead than alive. One of the clergymen who visited President Eisenhower put it well when he said that the case has by now become symbolic, and the symbolism of going through with the execution would be the worst kind. What is at stake is the image that world opinion will have of us. Let us not needlessly spoil that image.

I shall go to Sing Sing Thursday night believing that the Rosenbergs are guilty of espionage, despising their behavior for almost three years as Communist marionettes, but also believing that the death penalty for them is unwarranted, and convinced it is stupid. And whatever they did, I shall go with compassion.

Ossining, June 21, 1953

Julius and Ethel Rosenberg died in the electric chair in Sing Sing Prison just before sundown on Friday evening.

Julius went first. The first jolt of the current was given him at 8:04 P.M., and he was pronounced dead at 8:06¾. Ethel followed him, taking a good deal longer to die, from 8:11½ to 8:16.

Since sundown was officially at 8:31, the government had beaten the falling of the Jewish Sabbath by fifteen minutes. Few noted the irony that two people who in their lives had turned their backs on their religious faith should have had their death hour shifted because of that faith.

Both died with the same impassive lack of emotion with which they had spent more than two years in the death house. Neither of them made any statement before death. Neither one knew which was dying first. There was only one break in their impassivity. It came when Ethel Rosenberg shook hands with her prison matron, Mrs. Helen Evans, then suddenly pulled Mrs. Evans closer and kissed her. Otherwise she went through her ordeal with composure, and with a faint smile on her thin, tight lips.

Both husband and wife died without any break in their persistent refusal to talk and make any confession. If the death sentence had been imposed in the hope that the Rosenbergs might shrink from leaving their two little sons orphaned, and might break the story of the atomic espionage ring, that hope was cheated.

Death, as Justice Douglas has put it, is irrevocable. We shall now probably never know the whole story of the spy conspiracy, and there are men in the Kremlin who must be breathing more freely today because Julius and Ethel Rosenberg will now be forever silent.

I was one of the several dozen newspapermen permitted to enter the administration building to be briefed on the actual execution by the three wire service reporters who witnessed it. I think the briefing was a worse experience than watching the deaths could have been. I have watched deaths in war, and there is a reality to it that wipes out words. What we got in the briefing was only the words, carefully chosen by skilled reporters to evoke images, but the reality of death that could have given dignity to the words was not there. Some of the questions the reporters asked, in their passion for precise detail, only helped to make the whole thing more sickening. I remember especially the reporter who wanted to know what was the color of the smoke that rose from Ethel Rosenberg's head after the first of the five electric charges it took to kill her.

Ethel died very hard—much harder than her husband. Perhaps, despite his stiff pedantic preachings in his death house letters and his show of toughness, his wife had a greater will to live than he, and a greater life force in her.

As we got the story, Julius came in first, walking slowly after Rabbi Irving Koslowe, who was reading from the Twenty-third Psalm. As Rosenberg approached the chair, the rabbi intoned the line, "Yea, though I walk through the valley of the shadow of death, I shall fear no evil, for Thou art with me."

The condemned traitor's right trouser leg was pulled up to the knee, where the strap was tied. With the first charge, he rose in his chair, his neck and chest and stomach swelled up, then he fell back. After the third charge, the switchman—Joseph Francel, of Cairo, New York—came out of his alcove. The guard ripped Rosenberg's shirt off his hairy chest, the doctors applied their stethoscopes, and one of them said, "I pronounce this man dead."

The limp body was picked up by two guards, placed on a white surgical table and wheeled out. That was the end of the man who had been such an eager-beaver Communist that he had badgered the highest officials to admit him into espionage work—the man who comforted himself all through his trial and death house stay with the conviction that the plain people of the world would not let him die.

Five minutes after her husband died, Ethel Rosenberg came into the death chamber. With meticulous detail the briefers described her—plumpish, with heavy legs, wearing a loose, dark-green print dress. I don't know why it is that American reporters have to know exactly what fabric a woman is clothed in when she is brought in to die for espionage. At least a half-dozen reporters asked questions about Ethel Rosenberg's dress as if it were a fashion show at Dior's and she were a mannequin showing off the newest creation.

The chaplain read from the Fifteenth and Thirty-first psalms. The helmet was placed over the woman's head, and the electrodes were attached where the hair was cut a bit. A strap was tied just over the top of her breast. When the first charge came, heavy smoke rose from her helmet to the skylight above the electric chair. This, we were told, had not happened with her husband. We were also told that while the sound of the charge in Julius' case had been a hissing sound, the charge that was applied to Ethel emerged as a frying sound. When I heard this, I thought of the placards in Washington that were answering the pro-Rosenberg placards and that had exhorted us to "burn and fry them." One of the sickening things about the last few days has been the collective sadism it has evoked.

The doctors examined Ethel after the first three charges, held a whispered conversation, then one of them said to the switchman, "Want another." She was strapped in again and got two more charges—two more than it took to kill her husband. Then she too was pronounced dead, and her body wheeled out.

That was the end of a woman who had placed her duty as a Communist above her country and, even more, above her two children that she loved so deeply. Her last death house letter was devoted to her worries over her "baby" Robert, 6, who had a bad case of tonsilitis and seemed so frightened by everything that he could scarcely utter a word.

The most dramatic event while the death watch was being maintained outside the prison gates was the arrival of David Rosenberg, brother of Julius. He drove up with his wife and an unidentified woman in a car with a Massachusetts license plate. There was a folded baby carriage in the back seat, and perhaps I was sentimental but I couldn't help thinking of the Rosenberg boys. Only David Rosenberg—a stocky, neatly dressed man—was allowed into the building, since he alone was a member of the immediate family. He arrived at 6:15 and came out again in twenty minutes, at 6:35. He could scarcely have had enough time to get to the death house and back. The report was that he had come too late, since no relatives are admitted within two hours of the time set for an execution. If so, this means that the Rosenbergs died without seeing any of their kin on their last day.

Several days earlier, before Justice Douglas issued his stay, Julius' mother had brought the two boys, Michael and Robert, for a last visit. On the day of execution the boys were in New Jersey with relatives, and their grandmother was in Washington in the protest delegations. None of the Greenglass family, on Ethel Rosenberg's side, had visited the pair for some time. The last visit was by Ethel's mother, several months ago. There has been great bitterness between the two branches of the family, with the Rosenbergs sticking by the pair and the Greenglasses urging them to talk.

I don't think I shall ever forget the half-mile walk from the prison back to town when the long day ended.

The people along the road were out on their porches or on the sidewalk, clustered around their cars, listening to the radio, talking and laughing. I heard one child tell another she wished she could throw the switch. There were geraniums in the window boxes, trellises of roses, hedges adorned with lily paper cups discarded by the press. A pair of lovers walked down the road, laughing and holding hands.

All over the world, millions of people were waiting for the word that many dreaded, others welcomed. Most of them will attack America, forgetting or ignoring the fact that there have been nineteen reviews and appeals in the Rosenberg case, including two clemency appeals to President Eisenhower.

There is no question that there has been due process of law in this case. Nor can there be any question that the Rosenbergs were involved in atomic espionage. The real question is whether the death sentence was either necessary or wise. President Eisenhower, who does care about psychological warfare, had ignored in this case the terrible defeat America has suffered in its psychological-warfare struggle with the Kremlin. The Rosenbergs are dead, but the propaganda battle which exploits their death will go on.

3. Is Freedom a Luxury?

June 6, 1951

THE BEST WAY to tackle the majority opinions in the case of the eleven Communist leaders (*Dennis v. U.S.*) is to read them while standing on your head. I must report that only the two dissents (Black and Douglas) make basic sense to me; that the majority opinion

(Vinson) is one of the dreariest examples of confusion of thought and betrayal of values in the history of the court; and that the two concurring Justices (Frankfurter, Jackson) come out at the wrong end of the tortuous tunnel into which they have burrowed.

If Chief Justice Vinson had been candid, he would have said quite simply that we're as good as at war, that the Communists are getting what's coming to them, and that all the talk of freedom is fiddle-faddle compared with the need for getting tough.

But Vinson has chosen to use the famous "clear and present danger" doctrine of Justices Holmes and Brandeis to confound the purposes and values for which they stood. He explains the doctrine with so much subtlety that he explains it out of existence. Vinson tells us that Holmes meant "clear and present danger" to be not the test for the protection of a real individual and social value, but only a way of interpreting evidence. Thus he makes the great discovery that Holmes and Brandeis never really meant what we always thought they did and what they said they did.

Hypocrisy, the French tell us, is the tribute that vice pays to virtue. Chief Justice Vinson pays heavily.

The Vinson contribution to the theory of free speech is the distinction between "discussion" and "advocacy." Meaning that if you wear a cap and gown and turn around in a swivel chair, you can discuss Marx and Lenin, but if you get serious and go into the market place and hawk your ideas, it's no go.

Vinson knows, of course, that the Communist movement in America is pitifully weak, that its threadbare bankruptcy has been shown up, that it is ingloriously on the run. To argue that Communist teaching may lead to an "attempt" at overthrowing the government is to touch the margin of the ridiculous. And to suppress speech now because someday the conditions of danger may exist is to throw our present concern for freedom out of the window. As for the argument that the Communist movement includes spies and saboteurs, the answer is that the real spies are rarely enrolled Communists, and that laws exist to deal adequately with overt acts of espionage and sedition.

The court majority seems to be saying that freedom is a luxury we cannot afford in these serious times. But to treat freedom as a luxury is to miss the meaning of the democratic experience. To throw freedom overboard when the going gets a bit rough is like throwing love and loyalty overboard when a marriage is put to real tests.

Justice Frankfurter, in his concurring opinion, sees this clearly, and he shows how the hunt for dangerous thoughts is bound to destroy the inner meaning of democracy. The trouble with the Frankfurter essay is that after giving all the reasons why the Vinson reasoning is basically wrong, Frankfurter ends by voting on the same side. Ditto for Justice Jackson.

Behind both these well-intentioned opinions is the premise that Congress may be wrong but it has the power to punish speech that it regards as dangerous. But this is to surrender to Congress a duty that the courts must hold on to. If the courts are indeed the guardians of freedom of speech, they cannot plead that the invasion of freedom by Congress is not unconstitutional. If the courts will not protect our civil liberties, who will?

It is because Justices Black and Douglas see this that their opinions cut through the fog of half-truths and doubts and shadows in which the other opinions are enveloped. Obviously the problem of meeting the Communist propaganda attack in our time is a problem in the balancing of social values. If you don't believe that freedom is a crucial value, especially in a crisis of democracy, you are sunk before you start. Black and Douglas stick to that belief, and no amount of underlining of the obvious ruthlessness and baseness of Communist propaganda can make that belief in freedom meaningless. The values that have stood the Republic in good stead since its beginning do not date even amidst the urgencies of 1951. The distinction between speech that is allowed and an overt act that is forbidden is still the crucial distinction.

It is a sad reflection that this monstrous backward step in the history of American free speech has been taken by a Supreme Court majority largely appointed by a Fair Deal President. Harry Truman assures his visitors these days that he is passionately concerned about the witch-hunt for dangerous thoughts. Yet the four Justices he has himself appointed—Vinson, Burton, Minton and Clark—need conscript only Justice Reed from the Roosevelt court to form an unfailing majority against freedom. It is a Truman majority.

The wildest irony is that in the context of the struggle with world Communism this is the exact kind of decision that will undermine our fighting strength in the battle of ideas. One need only think of how the news of the decision will be read in Paris, London, Brussels, Oslo, Rome and New Delhi. The strongest weapon we have in the competition with the wretched faith of the Communists is the image of a free society. If the peoples of the free world conclude that we are selling our tradition of freedom cheap, at cut-rate prices of a fancied security gained thereby, they will conclude that what you sell cheap you value cheap. And that will be worth more to the Kremlin than the miserable little group of men who are now being sent to prison.

June 7, 1951

I want to turn now to a second and related argument. There are many who feel that a liberal policy on free speech may have made sense in the days of Holmes and Brandeis, during the generation of

World War I, but that this is the eve of World War III and times have changed.

Has the world changed so radically that the guarantees of freedom in the old sense have become musty and archaic? There seems to be a growing, somewhat fashionable view that it is very unchic and unsophisticated to keep your old convictions about freedom, and that freedom is really out of date. Is it?

Obviously the generation of 1950 lives in a world of social power and mass movements that would seem strange to the generation of 1920. Communism is no longer the flaming ideal it seemed to many then. It has become a cynical organization of power, propaganda and conspiracy, centered in the Kremlin.

But the dangers of the Bolshevik revolution were just as vividly felt in the years after 1917 as the dangers of the Kremlin are felt now. In fact, when the Communist idea still seemed the symbol of a dawning new world which would sweep away the ancient injustices, open the career to talents and bring the millennium to the oppressed, it had a stronger appeal to our young people than it has in these days of cynical Communist ruthlessness. The intervening period has stripped many of the masks and illusions from Communism. And it has shown what can be done in our own country through an expanding economy and a New Deal to reaffirm the faith in democracy. That is why Communism has met with so stony a response from Americans.

In talking of the difference between the world of 1920 and that of 1950, many Americans are off on the wrong track. They talk as if the important change is the shift in the Communist technique of internal subversion. But no one except Senator McCarthy takes seriously the prospect of Washington in Communist hands in our lifetime. That is why the whole discussion of the "clear and present danger" doctrine had such an unreal ring in the Dennis case.

The important changes in world Communism since 1920 are two: first, the growth in the Kremlin's power, and the hardening of the police state under Kremlin Communism; second, and more important, the shift of Russian hopes from internal subversion in highly industrialized countries like America and England to colonial revolution in undeveloped areas.

If I am right about this, the Supreme Court opinions were arguments in darkness. Freedom is anything but an old-fashioned idea. It is the most precious value we have to conserve at home, and the most powerful weapon in meeting the new forms of Communist power. The real direction must be not in the piddling negativism of sending a dozen ineffectual and deluded men to jail, but in taking the ideological offensive all over the world against the police-state bleakness of Communism. If the Supreme Court decision had ringingly reaffirmed our belief in the freedom of advocacy of pernicious ideas, it would have strengthened our hand exactly in those areas where it most needs strengthening against Communism.

The new conditions of our generation require not a bedraggled retreat from the open society and the open mind but a more militant assertion of their value.

4. Darrow: American Primitive

May 6, 1957

THEY HAVE BEEN CELEBRATING Clarence Darrow's centenary at a Chicago meeting where Joseph Welch, Paul Muni and Melvyn Douglas spoke about him and read from him. The real memorial to Darrow, however, is not in the speeches, the meetings, the readings. It is in the fact that playwrights and novelists find him good quarrying, and playgoers and readers are absorbed with him. There seems to be a Darrow revival these days, along with a Eugene O'Neill revival. You can still see *Inherit the Wind* on Broadway—and watch Darrow break a lance for science and against fundamentalism in the Scopes "monkey trial," and see him destroy William Jennings Bryan.

My own tribute to Darrow was to spend the weekend with Meyer Levin's novel *Compulsion* (Simon and Schuster), and also with Irving Stone's biography *Clarence Darrow for the Defense* (Doubleday). Much as I was absorbed with Levin's rousing re-creation of the atmosphere of the crime and trial in 1924, I found myself mostly asking what kind of man Darrow was and what goes into the making of a man like that. For this is the time we need one or two, and need them badly.

It is foolish, I know, to talk of getting another Darrow—or any other man about whom the real point was his uniqueness. In whatever fashion such men are made (and Darrow would have denied it was by God), the mold is thrown away. Darrow was full of paradoxes. But for me the sharpest one was the fact that this man whose witty and cynical remarks have been the delight of the intellectuals was himself a small-town, rural, self-made and largely self-educated lawyer.

In the Leopold-Loeb case there was a sullen popular suspicion that he was aligned with the big-city millionaires and the urban centers of vice; in the Scopes case Bryan tried to rouse the Populist passions against Darrow's city-slicker smartness, just as he had once roused the Western farmers against the East. Yet Darrow was in his origins little different from Bryan. He came from towns called Farmdale and Kinsman in Ohio, he practiced law first in Ashtabula and was scared to tackle Youngstown because it was a city of 20,000. When he moved to Chicago, however, he quickly took the measure of big cities and the big world, and with his first big case—the defense of Eugene Debs—the slow, smoldering fire in him burst into flame.

In the history of American courtroom advocacy, Darrow belongs with the few great names—Daniel Webster, Rufus Choate, Louis Brandeis, Martin Littleton. I have found that lawyers' lists of five or six differ when I put this question to them, but all are agreed on one name—that of Darrow.

One reason we remember him is that he had the courage to take the hard cases that no one else dared take—and they became the great cases. Where else will you find a man who could defend a Gene Debs, a John Mitchell, a Big Bill Haywood, the McNamara brothers, the victims of the Palmer raids after World War I? When he fought for them he was also fighting for the railroad workers, the miners, the copper workers, the harassed and harried everywhere.

He brought to their defense not only a quick and well-stocked mind, but a personality so quizzical and satiric, so full of wit and tenderness and savagery, so completely himself, that a jury had to take notice; and when he talked to the jurors he gave them the sense that here finally was someone whom they could understand and who gave them for a brief moment a feeling that they were being asked to do something out of greatness and generosity.

When I think of him I find myself thinking of a whole company of Americans—very diverse, each of them a unique person, yet somehow belonging together. I think of George Norris and Robert La Follette, of Carl Sandburg, of Theodore Dreiser, of Oscar Ameringer, of Harold Ickes. What ties them together in my mind, perhaps, is the fact that each was hewn out of the American earth, each was ornery, each a fighter, and each—to some extent—a primitive.

I am distinguishing them here from the sophisticated tradition which in its own way has also produced great Americans, but a different breed. Darrow was a debunker, a free-thinker, a professional pessimist, a determinist, a cracker-barrel sage. He relished his irreverence and his shock tactics, and had learned almost as well as Bernard Shaw the great secret that if you think a man has talent you will forgive his insults—and remember and retell them.

Darrow liked to think of himself as a lecturer and debater, liked the applause he got, and the contact with the lay mind on a level where he, the self-taught, could be teacher. He had a rough sort of "philosophy," which was a hodgepodge of the agnostic, the Nietzschean, the proletarian, the disillusioned and the iron-cage philosophy of the determinists. Yet it is not his "philosophy" which survives, but (as in the case of Dreiser) the sense of drama, the capacity to reach the elemental in people, the feel for the role of fate in human life.

5. The Decline of the American Lawyer

February 27, 1959

THE LAWYERS OF AMERICA, in convention assembled, have declared their strong suspicion that the U.S. Supreme Court is soft on Communists, and their conviction that the way to keep it from further serious mischief is for Congress to rewrite the laws so that any fool—including the Supreme Court fools—can understand their intent.

Doubtless the committee chairman, Peter Campbell Brown, and the other framers of the American Bar Association resolutions will regard my summary as too crude and brass-knuckled. To be sure, I have not reprinted any of their nice-nellyisms, such as hailing the judges as "the ultimate guardians of the Bill of Rights and the protectors of our freedom." But these silken words are woven into a mask, and our business as thinkers is to strike through the mask.

I have struggled through the "whereases" and the "therefores" and the "be it resolveds"—over a thousand tortured words of them—and I can only report that they add up to a slap in the face for the court.

Chief Justice Warren, who resigned from the Bar Association last fall and has rebuffed all pleas to reconsider, knew the temper and outlook of these lawyers. I care much more for his commentary on them than for their commentary on him. He might have fobbed them off with hypocrisies, but the same forthright quality that he has shown in his great civil-liberties and civil-rights decisions he shows in this particular gesture.

There are some who feel that the resolutions might have been much worse. They cite two scores on which the lawyers pulled their punches —first, in disapproving any proposals to strip the Supreme Court of its jurisdiction over certain cases; second, in striking out a clause about "technicalities" which are "invoked against the protection of our nation." It would have been curious indeed if a profession which has grown rich on technicalities should dismiss the procedural protections of due process and the Bill of Rights as "technicalities" to be swept away in the urgency to punish hated men.

This may have been in Chief Justice Warren's mind when, after the lawyers assigned as counsel for the Communist spy Rudolph Abel had completed their appeal argument based on a procedural "technicality," he thanked them for their public service in undertaking a case "which normally would be offensive" to them. Trust Justice Warren not to miss the revealing gesture.

Obviously not all American lawyers have turned into hunters after dangerous thoughts. There seems to have been a sizable and even surprising minority at the Bar Association meeting that fought the resolutions. But what has come over the rest of our American lawyers? Here is a profession which has played a great and creative role in American history. Almost half the signers of the Declaration of Independence, and more than half the members of the Constitutional convention, were lawyers. Jefferson was a self-trained lawyer, Andrew Jackson served a brief apprenticeship to the law, Abe Lincoln read law and rode circuit, Woodrow Wilson was a lawyer before he became a professor, and Franklin Roosevelt was one before he became a politician.

Even in colonial times—as Daniel Boorstin tells us in his new book, *The Americans: The Colonial Experience* (Random House)—lawyers were effective in the making of the new American society because most laymen knew law and most lawyers had not grown so specialized as to cease to be men. Politics and law were fused; lawyers had a sense of statecraft, and politicians had a feeling for logic and intellectual order.

What has caused the decline of the American lawyer, as witness the spectacle of a conventionful of leaders of their profession who have been playing G man in Chicago?

Partly, I think, the lawyers have identified themselves with the corporate managers from whom their lushest business and their biggest fees come. Partly also, and more recently, many lawyers have identified themselves with the prosecution phase of the law and have come to see themselves as stern inquisitors who are not to be swerved from the pursuit of politically hated men. It is interesting that Mr. Brown, who headed the committee in Chicago, had served as counsel for one of the inquisitorial groups in Washington. Thus while some lawyers have acquired a Wall Street mind, others have acquired a G-man mind, and some have combined the two. Is it heresy for me to suggest that neither of these mental frames will help the legal profession to fulfill its best role in our society?

I am speaking only about some lawyers, not all. I have no way of telling how representative the group in Chicago was of the profession as a whole, or what the vote would have been if each member had a chance to vote by secret ballot, rather than to "stand up and be counted" in open convention, as one truculent delegate urged. For him, evidently, the vote was not a canvass of conviction but a testing of patriotism.

One thing that has happened to the profession is that a liberal elite —perhaps even a civil-liberties elite—has been separated from the profession as a whole, leaving a big gap between the best lawyers and judges and the general run of them.

Someone at the convention argued for the resolutions on the ground that lawyers must continue to criticize the Supreme Court's decisions. By all means. But such criticism must be hammered out by men who study the law as well as practice it. The law does not grow greater or richer by the taking of a voice vote at a gathering which resembles an American Legion convention more than it does a scholar's study or a judge's chambers.

6. Sacred Cow and Secret Police

November 28, 1950

ONE OF THE DEPRESSING EXPERIENCES of the past week has been the sight of the journalistic wolf pack in full course after its quarry—a man who dared write a searching book about the FBI. The author is Max Lowenthal, and the book is called quite simply *The Federal Bureau of Investigation* (William Sloane).

Like the unadorned title, the book is written in a flat and factual style, and it restricts itself wholly to what is a matter of record. The documentation covers almost a hundred close-packed pages of "Source Notes." The attacks on Lowenthal conjure up someone who sat down and spun out a vicious diatribe, concocting it out of spleen, hatred, un-Americanism, Trumanism, Communism and sheer moonshine. You have to read the book in order to find out that this picture is not the book at all, but some dead mackerel of the critics' own imagining which gives off brilliant and sensational colors as it sparkles in the moonlight, but has no possible relation of substance or form to the Lowenthal product.

While the author has aimed at telling nothing but the truth as he sees it, the book is not (as what book could be?) the whole truth. It omits much of the historic context of the new problems of security that have been thrust up by the world struggle with Communist power. It fails to stress that in the more than forty years of the FBI's existence as a Federal police agency, we have not yet succumbed to the dangers of the police state, although we have several times teetered perilously on its brink. It is in this sense a somewhat static book, but that does not keep it from being in its own terms a documented book and a courageous one. It is a long and sustained lawyer's brief, important because no one up to now has dared to dissect the FBI's record against its initial purposes, its pretensions, and the values of democratic freedom. Lowenthal cares—and dares.

Did you know, for example, that the FBI was created in 1908 in the teeth of Congressional fears that it would develop into a political police agency? Did you know that the first Attorney General had to promise to read the daily summaries of what every FBI agent was doing? Did you know that its first draft-slacker raids in 1918 were a fiasco, with mass arrests that yielded only a tiny percentage of evaders?

There are other items with freshness: that during World War I the

FBI went after the thinkers of dangerous thoughts, including William Randolph Hearst; that it tried with dismal lack of success to solve the great "Bomb Plot" of 1919; that J. Edgar Hoover, although not at that time head of the FBI, was involved in the now despised Palmer raids upon alien radicals in 1919; that the lawyers of that day protested vigorously against FBI methods on searches and seizures, confessions, bail and the doctrine of guilt by association.

One of the best chapters is headed "The Bureau Deals with Its Critics." Louis F. Post, Assistant Secretary of Labor in the 1919 days, dared question the methods of the FBI. A House committee investigated him on the charge that he favored the Bolsheviks and the anarchists of the day. It is worth adding that when it became known that Lowenthal was writing an unfavorable book on the FBI, a Congressman called Dondero delivered a violent speech attacking him, and the House Un-American Activities Committee quizzed him on his possible relation to Communists and spies. Alas for them, they found nothing with any substance.

If Lowenthal is to be answered, let him be answered—as he has himself written—with material from the record itself. If his facts are wrong, if there are glaring omissions of history or mistakes of judgment, let them be stated. But there is nothing in the nature of our government which should set one agency off from the others and make it a sacred cow, immune from even the shadow of criticism.

If the FBI is that sacred, then the whole burden of Lowenthal's indictment—the danger that a political police, with over 100 million fingerprints and millions of dossiers, will overshadow the democracy it is meant to protect—is given a frightening confirmation.

December 20, 1953

No one can question that there must be a Federal police of some kind to deal with interstate offenses not covered by any of the other government agencies. But how about the increasing role of the FBI in the "clearance" of government officials, and the surveillance of an untold number of officials and of private American citizens.

We ought to know well enough, in negative terms, what the role of a Federal police should not be. If we have forgotten, then I recommend a reading of the chapter on "Secret Police" in Hannah Arendt's *The Origins of Totalitarianism* (Harcourt, Brace). She shows that under despotisms like the Russian Czarist regime the secret police was a state within a state, wielding great power, subject to its own rules. It used the "double agent" and the "agent provocateur." Sometimes the police spies provoked political assassinations, as in the case of Azev, the police terrorist who rose high in the Russian revolutionary movement. In the case of Malinovsky, a police agent rose to be a Bolshevik deputy in the Russian Duma and one of the top party leaders. Miss

Arendt points out that often these double agents spurred on the very activities they were supposed to destroy. Thus the great spurt in Russian revolutionary activity came after 1880, when the Czarist secret police, the Okhrana, was formed.

Bad as the secret police was under despotisms, it proved far worse under the totalitarian systems of the Nazis and the Russian Communists. Not only did it destroy the opponents of the regime; it also turned to the "potential enemy" and the "carrier of tendencies." It even punished the "possible crime." It became the most important arm of the totalitarian state, carrying out its vengeance and its purges, conducting its constant surveillance of every person, rounding up the population for the Nazi human furnaces and death factories and for the Communist forced-labor camps which are a living death. One of Miss Arendt's notable conclusions is that the secret police played a very similar role under both the Communist and Nazi forms of totalitarianism. Director J. Edgar Hoover would probably be the first to agree to the truth of this fact, since he has always emphasized the basic similarity of fascism and Red fascism.

Obviously the role of a secret police in a democracy must be as far as possible removed from this. It must stay clear of becoming a state within a state. Yet there is danger of this in the role of the FBI—perhaps a role forced upon it—of "clearing" every political appointment in the Federal government. For a time there was a log jam of diplomatic appointments by the Eisenhower Administration because the FBI was falling behind under its impossible load of investigations. Secretary of State Dulles himself asked for FBI clearance before he assumed office—which implied and sanctioned a veto by the secret police over even the highest Presidential appointments. By the same logic even the President of the United States would have to be first "cleared" before he could assume office. It hasn't happened yet—but it has happened retroactively, in the attack by Attorney General Brownell, with Director Hoover's help, upon President Truman's behavior in the "spy cases."

There are few words more important in our democracy than the word "neighbor." It implies friendliness, good feeling, mutual trust. One of the worst things that happened in both Germany and Russia was that the feeling of trust was corroded, and every neighbor became every neighbor's potential enemy. Can it be doubted that this process is beginning in America, too? One of the standard techniques in security investigations is to ask a man's neighbors what they know about him. What they know may be the merest rumor or even malicious, but it is duly put down in the file.

From one's neighbors, it is a step to one's family and relations. The present tendency is to assume that blood relation involves blood guilt —that if you have a sister or an uncle who is politically suspect, you too are suspect and cannot be "cleared." There may be a possible way of clearing yourself, which is to denounce your relatives. But the problem does not stop with relatives. You may be implicated because you once knew a convicted spy or suspect socially, or once went to the same college as he did and were in the same class.

With the best of intentions Director Hoover and his aides may be caught within a system whose expansion they can no longer control. They deal with a zealous Congress whose members are anxious to establish their own superpatriotism in the press by offering the FBI even more than it asks. They have become the folk heroes of an American people who regard the G man as the supreme achievement of detective efficiency.

7. Big Brother and the Wire-tap

November 27, 1953

THE OTHER DAY the fifty millionth telephone was installed, and to mark the occasion it was installed on the desk of President Eisenhower, with appropriate speeches and all that. It took place in the same week that Attorney General Brownell and FBI Director Hoover launched a campaign to make wire-tapping legal and evidence obtained by it admissible in the Federal courts, thus removing the safeguards of privacy from American telephones.

Most Americans may not remember that this represents a renewal of a long-standing campaign by the FBI to remove the restrictions of Congress and the Federal courts on the wire-tap. The 1934 Federal Communications Act made wire-tapping a Federal crime, punishable by fine and imprisonment. In the two famous Nardone decisions, in 1938 and 1939, the U.S. Supreme Court made it very clear that this prohibition was meant to apply to Federal officials, and that wire-tapping evidence or any evidence obtained by wire-tapping leads would be thrown out of the Federal courts. Yet the FBI chose to interpret the act as prohibiting not the gathering of wire-tap information but only its "divulgence." Presumably the FBI is not "divulging" any such information when it compiles dossiers for Congressional committees.

Congress has until now repeatedly refused to grant the pleas of the Department of Justice to legalize wire-tapping. These pleas are based on the contention that spies, saboteurs and kidnapers could not be tracked down and caught without tapping their phones. However you dress it up, this is, of course, the argument that the worthy end justifies the means, however dangerous and destructive of liberty.

In the first trial of Judith Coplon, before Judge Reeves in Washington, the government counsel denied that any of the evidence had been obtained through wire-taps. In the second trial in New York, before Judge Sylvester Ryan, the judge directed the government to produce the FBI records. It was revealed that at least thirty FBI agents had tapped the defendant's wires, and that this had extended even into the trial period, enabling them to overhear the defendant's conversations with her lawyers and learn the defense strategy. It was also revealed that the tap reports had been destroyed and records burned— in short, that the Congressional laws had been violated by law-enforcing officials.

Before World War II, J. Edgar Hoover had himself said that wire-tapping was "unethical," and that its effect on the operatives who took part in it might be to make "crooks" of them. Later he reinterpreted his remarks, and his position now is that wire-tapping is necessary to track down subversives and security risks, and that it can be "limited" in its operation and still safeguard the freedom of the individual.

In any actual Federal trial, as in the Coplon case, the FBI is likely to be caught in a bad dilemma. Before the trial it claims that wire-tapping is necessary in order to catch the subversives. During the trial itself, as in the Coplon case, it argues that the wire-taps were not essential in getting the evidence, which was obtained without them. Thus how the FBI has to argue depends on whether it is making the plea to Congress for more power or to a Federal court for conviction.

Part of the issue is what the wire-tap does to individual privacy. Justice Louis D. Brandeis handed down some historic opinions in which he traced the history of the Constitutional right to privacy. He argued that the Founding Fathers had tried to provide against illegal searches of the private home, but that since the invention of the telephone the wire-tap has supplanted the technique of breaking into the home without a warrant.

This is today truer than ever before. There are some who argue that peeping through a keyhole or taking pictures through it may produce the same evidence as wire-tap. The answer is that tapping a phone is much more far-reaching in its effect. Conversations are overheard that go far beyond the subject of investigation. Innocent people may have their right to privacy broken. There is a boundless opportunity for blackmailers.

But the final argument is the ethical one. Justice Holmes put it best when he spoke of the "dirty business" of wire-tapping and said it was "a less evil that some criminals should escape than that the government should play an ignoble part." This is as true today as when Holmes wrote. In fact, it is more dangerous today to surrender to the wire-tap than it ever was. The totalitarian state has been proved a reality, in both Germany and Russia. The essence of it is that the rulers of the state must know the inmost secrets of the lives of the people. Under the guise of tracking down opponents, nothing is immune from the state's eyes and ears.

George Orwell described this kind of nightmare society in *1984*. The dictator whom he called "Big Brother" was always watching every citizen. "There was no way," he wrote, "of knowing whether you were being watched at any given moment. . . . It was even conceivable that they watched everybody all the time."

Has the wire-tap ever been better described? Yet this is the Big Brother to whom we are asked to surrender in the name of "security."

May 5, 1957

I must enter a lonely dissenting vote against the way in which the state of New York has acted in the case of "Socks" Lanza. I'll grant you that Lanza is everything you will say he is. Let's say that he is a small-time racketeer and punk, a fixer, a consorter with shady characters, a parole violator, a high-liver on funds unaccounted for, as slippery a customer as you wish. But let me add that nothing Lanza has done is as dangerous to our freedoms and self-respect as the thing we did to Lanza.

We place him in a Westchester prison, pending the disposal of the parole violation case. We say to him and the other prisoners that there is a visitors' room where they can receive those close to them. His brother comes to visit him, and his wife, and his lawyer. And secretly we wire the room for sound.

I don't know what you call this, but I call it mean and treacherous. Whatever Lanza did, first and last, doesn't justify our doing what we have done. The crookedness of law and authority is worse than the crookedness of criminals because it is more corrupting to everyone.

I'm talking of the legalities, partly, but I'm also talking of morality.

On the legal side the state courts admit wire-tapped evidence, although the Federal courts don't because wire-tapping is a "dirty business." But every jurisdiction will hold that what passes between a client and his lawyer is a privileged area of privacy. I take my hat off to Judge Stevens, who had the courage to say that to put an electronic device in a prisoner's counsel room is to make a mockery of the privacy and the privilege attaching to conversations between client and lawyer. You can't "use any and all methods for the acquisition of information," Stevens told the "watchdog" committee. This whole thing is "a subterfuge unworthy of the sovereign state."

Legally this applies to the question of using the taps of Lanza's conversation with his lawyer. Morally it applies to the whole episode, including the conversations with his brother and wife, too.

Not that the Lanzas were overly bright about it. As you read the excerpts of the dialogue, you feel it is stuff for the gods to laugh over.

Here were two brothers who thought themselves big shots, wise to the world, versed in the wickedness of its ways. They were spending money, pulling strings, putting on the squeeze wherever they could. They knew the price tag attached to everyone. They were the ultimate cynics, trusting no one. Even in the visitors' room, clearly empty, they peered furtively around every corner to make sure that no one overheard them.

The one thing they forgot was the bugs. It never occurred to them that in this wicked world the prison and parole officials and the prosecutors might be wicked too. There was no sign hanging there, saying: "Beware. This room is wired for sound." So they trusted the absence of a sign. They forgot that the state has no ethics, that it can connive just as much as any underworld punk, that it can deceive and cheat and lie in wait. They knew that the state tapped wires, but the enormity of a room wired for sound never occurred to them.

Even in the empty room they were not at ease. They felt menace around them, spoke half in Italian, half in English—in scared, disconnected sentences, using initials and cryptic designations for the men they talked about. They were at once trusting and mistrustful, cunning —and basically stupid.

But their stupidity does not excuse the treachery of the state. As the two brothers sat there, there was a third brother in the wired room with them. He was Big Brother, who listens to all, hears all, refuses to recognize that there is any area of the human personality from which he can be excluded.

The warning has been sounded. From now on every visitors' room and counsel room in every New York prison will be regarded as a pesthouse, to be shunned by a careful criminal. The criminals will be the first Americans to learn what every person behind the Iron Curtain already knows in his bones—that if you want to talk, you must get away from rooms and walls and ceilings, and walk and whisper in the open air.

8. Sacco and Vanzetti: Can These Bones Stir?

April 6, 1959

FOR THOSE who like their world tidy and want things that are past to be closed forever, a young Massachusetts legislator named Alexander Cella showed himself unpleasantly tenacious last week, by raking up the dead-and-buried case of Sacco and Vanzetti. Why can't history be left alone, ask the men who want things tidy? Why do the dead bones have to stir?

The answer is, I suppose, that time plays strange tricks with us, let-

ting some of the clangorous names of the past die beyond hope of
reveille, while two humble men who were murdered by law and order
refuse to lie quiet. You can bury a hope and a dream, and sometimes
even an idea if you are lucky and ruthless enough, but the hardest
thing to bury is an injustice.

The phrase that Vanzetti used about Sacco and himself, "a good
shoemaker and a poor fish peddler," has become worn with much use,
but the fact is that both men were men of the book, self-taught Italian
anarchists who had strong ideas about poor and rich in the class war,
and about the senselessness of the state. They were true believers in a
creed that had once been dangerous in Europe, but they were not men
with pent-up violence in them like Hyacinth in Henry James's *Princess
Cassamissima*.

It is hard for us, almost forty years after their arrest and trial, to
recapture either the faith that kept them fiercely gentle or the fear of
their doctrine which made the wielders of power in Massachusetts determined on their death. But Justice Frankfurter, then a law professor
at Harvard, summed it up by saying that they scorned the three things
sacred to those who sat in judgment upon them—God, country and private property.

Sacco and Vanzetti were executed, at least formally, for a payroll
holdup and murder that they did not and could not have committed.
A member of the Morelli gang, waiting in the death house for execution on another charge, actually confessed to this one. But it was
1921, when radicals were feared and aliens were hated, and they
were tried by a judge who had sworn to get "those anarchistic bas-
tards."

The next six years, while they waited for death, were a time of
bloody strikes, of labor spies, of the rise of the American Legion as a
hunter of dangerous thoughts, of the Gitlow case and the Anita Whit-
ney case, of the hardening of mold in the newly formed FBI. It was not
a good time, once the machinery of justice had closed in on two helpless and heterodox aliens, to get the wielders of power to admit that a
ghastly injustice had been committed.

So the two men died, on that August midnight in 1927, while outside an unparalleled death watch was taking place, with thousands
milling about the streets, their hearts edged with frustration and ache.
The liberal Supreme Court judges—Holmes, Stone, even Brandeis—
had refused to stay the execution, each doubtless for reasons that
seemed good to him, but which will do scant credit to his memory.

The day of the locusts had come—of Thayer, the hate-obsessed trial
judge, and Fuller, the frightened and conformist Governor, and President Lowell of Harvard, who headed a review commission that riv-
eted down the death of the two men. And so the electrodes reached
their targets, and the death watch finally broke up.

"America our nation," John Dos Passos was to write (the Dos Passos of the 1930s, not the present one) "has been beaten by strangers who have turned our language inside out who have taken the clean words our fathers spoke and made them slimy and foul."

Thus a shameful chapter closed in the history not only of Massachusetts, but of the nation. Or did it?

Representative Cella, with more faith in his fellow state legislators than I can muster, insisted on presenting them with a bill to ask the Governor to pardon the two men, and the Judiciary Committee held a stormy session for a full day. The legal technicians put a worried Constitutional question: a governor can pardon men who are still alive, but can he pardon two dead men?

But the question is put wrong, because it is not Sacco and Vanzetti who need pardon for a crime they never committed. It is the state and the nation who require absolution—the men who killed out of hate because they thought they loved their country and their God and their property, the petty fearful who were afraid that the admission of error would be the crack that opened the floodgates of revolution.

Why bother now? Not because of Sacco and Vanzetti. "That last moment," the latter wrote to his comrade, "belongs to us—that agony is our triumph." But Massachusetts will somehow have to bother sometimes to set the moral record straight on America. If ever the assumption of class justice was proved right by events, the Sacco-Vanzetti case did it.

The question is whether the America of today and tomorrow has learned from the scars of yesterday, whether history is rigid and ended or whether we know how to burn the shame away with letters of expiatory fire in an unfinished country.

9. A Lance for Laski

March 27, 1950

I FIRST GOT a glimpse of Harold Laski in 1919, when he was walking across the Yale campus arm in arm with Henry Luce. A Yale political club had invited the stormy young British scholar to speak. Laski was under attack at Harvard for daring to back up the Boston police strikers. The very funny young men who put out the Harvard *Lampoon* devoted a whole cruel and stupid issue to him, and frantic alumni showered President Lowell with demands for his dismissal.

What these humorous young men were perhaps too ignorant to know was that this scholar, scarcely twenty-five, had already founded a new school of political theory. These interwoven threads of the creative scholar and the storm center of political action were to run through the whole of Laski's life.

It was in the middle 1920s that I got another glimpse of him, at the Brookings Graduate School, in Washington. He had written his massive *Grammar of Politics,* which was a halfway house for the British Labor Party in its march to power, and he had thrown himself (largely under the influence of Sidney and Beatrice Webb) into the day-to-day tasks of local government.

His most dramatic friendship was with Justice Oliver Wendell Holmes of our own Supreme Court. Felix Frankfurter had introduced them, and the old New England aristocrat-lawyer-philosopher, already in his eighties, was fascinated by the intense young British scholar who had read everything, remembered everything, could quote anyone, and could match story for story even with Holmes. For years they exchanged letters, and those that Holmes sent to his young British friend will soon be published in a volume that should rival the Holmes-Pollock letters.*

He was generous to young scholars, sought them out, encouraged and scolded them. He had a fierce loyalty to his friends, even when their intellectual paths diverged from his. Like the primitives, he could also shrink the skulls of his enemies, but he did it with his withering words.

Many stupid comments have been written about his influence on the New Deal, especially by the know-nothings who wanted to scare fools into thinking that Roosevelt was under the thumb of this foreign radical Svengali. It is true that Laski admired F.D.R., and his book *The American Presidency* was more than half of it a tribute to him. But Laski's real roots were in the great tradition of the French Revolution.

For Europeans he expressed the thinking of the whole generation between the Russian Revolution and Hitler's conquest of power. When Laski became clearly a Marxist, some twenty years ago, he gave voice to the European conviction that capitalism was a dying if not a dead duck, and that the real choice lay between a socialism with democratic freedoms and one armed with totalitarian power. For Britain and Western Europe, Laski never hesitated in championing the socialism with democratic freedoms. But he understood Russia and Eastern Europe well enough to know that their choice could not be the same. What shocked many of his former followers in America was his refusal to join wholeheartedly in the cold war.

Toward the end he found himself out of sympathy with some of

* These appeared as *The Holmes-Laski Letters,* edited by Mark Howe (Harvard). See my comment that follows below.

the cold-war policies of the Attlee Cabinet, especially the Bevan policy toward Palestine. He never hesitated to tell the rulers of Britain just what he thought, and he had a right to tell them. For he sat on the party executive year after year, worked in every campaign, had made speeches to workingmen in almost every town in England, and half the young administrators and civil servants of the Labor Government had cut their intellectual eye teeth on his books. He was the chairman of the party in the successful 1945 election year, when Churchill committed the blunder of a personal attack on him as the leader of a future Labor Government Gestapo.

He was supposed to lecture again in America this spring, but the doctor finally forbade it. He nevertheless took part in the last British election campaign, to a degree far beyond his strength. He died in harness. But also he was sick at heart about a world over which fear had cast a pall. He believed deeply that courage is the price of freedom. It is something worth remembering.

March 30, 1953

Whether or not the evil that men do lives after them, certainly their enemies do. This has been impressed on me again as I have been reading the reviews of *The Holmes-Laski Letters* (2 vols., Harvard). The bitterness toward Laski in such reviews as those by Adolf Berle in the *Times* and Fred Rodell in the *Saturday Review* may have been wholly objective, evoked by a low estimate of his intellectual gifts, letter-writing talents and morals. But whether it is true of those reviewers or not, the fact is that many who didn't like Laski alive are not averse to flaying him dead.

If I may suggest a prayer for political writers it would be: "Please, God, grant me that I outlive my enemies and that I review their posthumous works instead of their reviewing mine."

I don't come to Laski's defense. He lived by the intellectual sword, and he knew that when he died he would be attacked by it. I want only to break a lance for his memory.

I met him a few times fleetingly in my student days. But our friendship didn't begin until 1933, when he read some articles of mine in the law journals and invited me to tea. He was on one of his American trips, and it was characteristic of him to seek out a young and unknown person, barely started on the career of scholarship and writing. After that we saw each other whenever he was in America or I in England. I must add that while he gave his intellectual fealty generously to his friends, he never demanded theirs in return. Our differences, especially in the last five years of his life, were many and not slight. But he always listened gravely to my dissents.

Some of the reviewers have suggested that Laski was a climber, wooing Holmes to boast of his friendship. I can only say that while

I knew the two men had been close, the degree of closeness as revealed in the letters came as something of a surprise. The only time he talked at length about Holmes to me was during the war, early in 1945, in a London still conscious of the V bombs. He opened two drawers piled high with letters from Holmes and told me that as soon as he could safely ship them to America he wanted me to edit the correspondence. After the war, quite rightly, the plan was changed. Mark Howe, of Harvard Law School, who did the first-rate editing job on the Holmes-Pollock letters, has done the more difficult job of the Holmes-Laski letters just as well.

You can pick holes in the Holmes-Laski letters. You can point out that Laski speaks of discovering a book and then, several years later, discovers it again. You can doubt whether he had all the conversations with the great that he reports. But the fact was that he left an impact on the British Labor Party that no other intellectual ever did, and that several generations of students all over the world have carried his teaching into their work and life.

To understand and appreciate Laski you have to care about the life of learning. You have to delight in someone whose reading ranges over law, politics, history and biography, the classics and mystery stories. You have to care about the capacity to annihilate an author with a phrase and impale a book on an epigram.

The letters show several things. They show how possible it is for the son of a Brahmin intellectual autocrat, himself the most distinguished mind in public life in our century, to find common intellectual ground with the son of a Russian Jewish immigrant who had come to Manchester. They show also that you cannot predict lasting friendships any more than you can predict love affairs. For friendships, like love, defy all the sideline critics who stand by and can't figure out how the two people ever got together.

Finally it shows that a doughty New England conservative (which is what Holmes was in his economic views) can find delight in a Fabian Socialist—that political beliefs are less important than personality patterns. The thing that finally tied these two men together was that each of them cared about a life that was, in Holmes's phrase, "tipped with flame."

10. Holmes and the Pygmies

January 17, 1951

A GUTTER TOUGHIE called Pegler, who finds easy pickings by mugging dead men and currently outcast men in dark alleys, has cut out a bigger job for himself than he and his gang can ever carry off. He has set out to destroy Justice Holmes, who, he says, "had no more morals than a pig."

"It will be very hard to bring Holmes down," Pegler admits with a kind of assassin's despair when he has a rubbing-out job that will take some doing. And why "bring Holmes down" at all? Because Pegler is shrewd enough to know that in order to destroy the democratic idea you have to destroy democracy's dead heroes even more than its living champions.

Emmet Lavery did a play about Holmes a few years ago, *The Magnificent Yankee,* and now he has made a movie out of it. Go see it, if you can stand the scorn of Pegler who writes that the people who accept Holmes "as a magnificent Something are the millions of dolts with dull eyes and loose, wet lips."

I suppose Pegler likes such sentences because they give him the feeling of being sculptured of so much finer and firmer a clay than the rest of us, which is pretty ironic when he sets himself against someone like Holmes. Part of Holmes's New England tradition was the belief in a man's worth as a man. Holmes fought for Louis D. Brandeis when all the anti-Semites in America tried to keep him off the Court.

This is the man whom Pegler has the gall to call "totalitarian." He seems to have read, at least in part, an article by a lawyer repeating the now old and weary refrain of one group of Holmes's critics—that Holmes did not hold to the "natural law" philosophy. May I tell Pegler that better men than he have grappled with the problem of "natural law" and come to the conclusion that it is sounder to base law on the historic experience of people wrestling with real problems over the centuries, rather than on the say-so of any moralists or any power group.

"The life of the law has not been logic, it has been experience." These words of Holmes still stand. The usual sentences that are quoted against Holmes are the words of a man who was skeptical of all hundred-percenters, who didn't like to play God himself and despised anyone else who had the presumption to play God. What a pity he didn't live to be amused by the spectacle of a Pegler strutting his ignorance and hurling his pygmy darts.

Pegler purports to quote Raymond Moley as writing (I quote Pegler) that "some of the defections, a euphemism for treason, in our Government during the ascendancy of the Harvard cell are traceable to the influence of Holmes, who had no more morals than a pig," etc. I assume the "pig" phrase was Peg's, not Moley's. Certainly Moley denies ever having written it or anything like it.

But how about the "defections" and "treason" sentence? Moley writes me that Pegler might conceivably have referred to a passage about Frankfurter in an early book of his, but the passage there has no mention of Holmes at all. In his recent book, *Twenty-seven Masters of Politics,* Moley has an essay on Frankfurter which I have read as part of my Pegler research. Along with some very high praise of Holmes, Moley has some critical things about his "philosophic quips," which he believes did "affect the point of view and attitude toward politics and government" of the Frankfurter group.

But nowhere anything about "defections" or "treason." If Pegler knows something Moley wrote that Moley doesn't know himself, and that can't be found in his books, let him come out with it. Or was he just daydreaming, until the word "affect" became "defections," which he then translated as "treason"?

It wouldn't be important, except that when you set up as a moralist, and assign to someone like Holmes the "morals of a pig," you owe your readers at least the common honesty of an ordinary writer who doesn't invent his sources and quotes. Or was his phrase a typo, and did he mean "the morals of a Peg"?

11. Tolerance and Communism

May 8, 1955

"THE BIG-BROW political commentators and my own academic colleagues aren't gonna believe a lot of this stuff." This is how the *Post*'s Helen Dudar quoted Professor Samuel Stouffer of Harvard in an interview about his new book, *Communism, Conformity and Civil Liberties* (Doubleday). Since I am haplessly in both his categories I should be among those who "aren't gonna believe" his "stuff." At the risk of letting him down I hereby swear that I "believe" his figures, in the sense that I trust their accuracy.

My doubts are of a different sort. They are about the interpretive picture he draws of a cross section of American thinking on Communism and civil liberties today—on the whole a far more optimistic picture than I should draw from his own figures.

Two polling agencies independently had 537 people interviewing almost 5,000 "cross-section" Americans and another 1,500 local community leaders. The Fund for the Republic spent a chunk of Ford Foundation money to sponsor it, thereby infuriating some birdbrains on a future Reece Committee. Stouffer, who is one of our best public-opinion students, has worked hard and shrewdly to pull the figures together and present their meaning. My quarrel is less with him than with the blunt uncutting edge of the tools that most of these "attitude studies" use.

Stouffer reassures us on the score of anxiety. In a chapter headed, "Is There a National Anxiety Neurosis?" he spells out the answer No. Hardly anyone in America (less than 1 per cent) is seriously worried about either the threat of Communism or the threat of the cold-war patrioteers to civil liberties. Only 8 per cent are worried about what is happening in the world outside, even about atomic war. The things people really worry about are their private concerns —health, money, jobs, family matters.

As my teen-age daughter always puts it, is this good or bad? Stouffer thinks it is pretty good, since it shows there is no Red-under-the-bed jitters. On that score I go along, especially when we find that 30 per cent of the sample couldn't furnish a single name of a Communist-chasing Senator or Congressman—not even the press-hallowed name of McCarthy. The picture we get is thus not one of politically conscious hysteria.

But alas, it is a picture of a disquieting national political ignorance and apathy. I know there is a theory that America is safe so long as no one really gives a hoot about anything except whether Don Newcombe was treated shabbily or well in his ball game. But we can scarcely feel a confidence in our freedom that is built upon ignorance and apathy—especially when less than 1 per cent of the sample are really anxious about our civil liberties.

At this point Professor Stouffer introduces his community leaders and the concepts of toleration and conformity. The 1,500 local group leaders tend to be more tolerant of the nonconformists (Communists or those suspected as such, Socialists, atheists) than the cross section does. This obviously gives him a feeling of hope, since it means that the more educated and politically conscious Americans rise above the tendencies of the large mass. There are other hopeful items—that the younger people are more tolerant than the older ones, that city people are more tolerant than rural, and that those who have actually at some point known a live Communist (only 3 per cent) are more tolerant than those who had to read about them in the headlines.

Stouffer puts together a good case for his belief that America is moving toward tolerance. A lot of young people are getting to high school and even college, there is a less authoritarian atmosphere in the classroom, American marriage is more permissive than it used to be, there is more freedom inside the family, and the restless mobility of Americans is moving them out of the rural pockets into the daylight of the cities.

I feel like raising at least two cheers for this—until I stop to think about what Stouffer's concepts are like and what his figures really mean.

What does it mean when we say that someone "tolerates" the views of a nonconformist? The *Saturday Evening Post* editorial writer, in a fit of misunderstanding, wrote that if more education means greater toleration of Communists, then there's something wrong with our educational system. Obviously this gets Stouffer all wrong. To tolerate someone doesn't mean to embrace him or agree with him or be complacent about him. It means only that you think he has a right to his views, however wrong they may be.

But being "tolerant" may have varying degrees of conviction about the other person's right to his views. It may mean you don't care enough to worry about his views, or it may mean you are ready to take risks to defend his right to be wrong. Which of these meanings is involved in Stouffer's concept and his figures?

Here is where I continue to be anxious about American public opinion, despite Stouffer's reassurances. His concept of "toleration" is as fuzzy as his "anxiety." The man who cares so little about politics (because he is worried about private and personal matters, not about public matters) that he doesn't worry about the other fellow's views may be equally unworried when the other fellow is hounded by the idea hunters.

There is something curious about the concept of anxiety when less than 1 per cent worry about Communists, yet more than 50 per cent are ready to see them thrown out of their jobs or believe they have forfeited their right to be citizens, or when the large majority think it is all right to tap private phones to get evidence against them and are ready to report neighbors or acquaintances to the FBI on suspicion of being Communists.

12. The Shortest Way with Subversives

(New York *Star*)
December 23, 1948

ALMOST 250 years ago Daniel Defoe, the founder of modern journalism, wrote a pamphlet which he called *The Shortest Way with Dissenters*. He was put in the pillory for it, and afterward in prison. It was an ungrateful way to treat him, for he was only trying to make a helpful proposal. Himself a nonconformist in religion, he was advising the High Church party how to deal with the dissenters. He said: A pox on moderation, on fines and trivial punishment: burn the heretics; wipe them out, and make an end of it. The High Church people thought Defoe was making fun of them and imprisoned him.

I hope I shall not be accused of a similar levity when I say that Defoe's suggestion still ought to appeal to the movers and shakers of our nation. I am talking, of course, of how to deal with the nonconformists of our own time—the political rather than the religious dissenters, the "subversives." The shortest way with them is the way that involves the greatest economy of effort.

Look at the balance sheet. The Dies-Rankin-Wood-Thomas-Mundt committee has been running for a decade, spending public funds, chasing all over the map for witnesses. Add the more efficient, but still costly, work of the FBI. Add the numberless departmental loyalty boards throughout the Federal government. Add the Loyalty Review Board at the top of the pyramid. Add the whole bundle of state un-American activities committees. Add the Federal grand juries. Add the separate investigations being made into the loyalty of scientists working on university and government projects. Add the investigations of college faculties and students. Add the private and public investigations into trade-unions and industrial employees. And —as not the least item—the mountains of headlines and newsprint devoted to the pursuit.

Obviously there is a more efficient way. The shortest way with the subversives is to go through the index of everyone accused by anyone in the Federal and state un-American committee hearings and the various loyalty boards, make a master index, go right down the list, round up the suspects by swift raids at night, take them out into the New Mexico desert or to a Pacific islet, and drop an atom bomb on them.

If you have to throw a tub to the whale of public opinion, then follow the method of Representative Mundt in releasing the record of someone's account of someone else's accusation against Laurence Duggan after he was dead. An official spokesman can salve the public conscience by making these accusations public after the bomb has been dropped. Dead men can't answer back.

You may say this is unjust, but people suspected of being subversive can never again be trusted, and to let them remain free means a costly apparatus of shadowing them. You may say it is undemocratic, but subversives by definition want to overthrow democracy and therefore should not get the benefits of it. You may say it is cruel, but I answer in Defoe's words: "They are to be rooted out of this nation, if ever we will live in peace. I leave it to those hands who have a right to execute God's justice on the nation's enemies."

ON BEING A NEGRO IN AMERICA

1. The Case of the Wolf Whistle

September 9, 1955

HE WAS a fourteen-year-old Chicago boy, and his name was Emmett Louis Till. His father had been killed in World War II, and he was his mother's only child. A photograph of them shows him as an eager, happy boy, who had not yet been bruised badly enough in a white world to rub his radiance away. He went down to Mississippi to spend part of his vacation with his uncle, who had a cotton patch in Leflore County.

One day in late August he and some friends went to a store at Money, Mississippi, run by people called Bryant. Emmett was in high spirits, and Mrs. Bryant was a strikingly pretty young woman, and after they left the store Emmett broke into a wolf whistle.

That night, in the middle of the night, a car stopped at the cabin of the boy's uncle. Two white men came in, pulled Emmett out of bed, and brought him over to the car where a waiting woman said Yes, that was the one. They took him away into the night. Three days later he was found in the Tallahatchie River, his body weighted down with a ninety-pound cotton winch and tied with wire, his face smashed in, and a bullet hole in his head.

What will happen to the case of Emmett Till? Under pressure from all over the nation, a grand jury in Tallahatchie County has indicted Roy Bryant and his half brother, J. W. Milam, on a murder charge. But the custom of the country, in Mississippi, is that white men don't die for killing Negroes, whatever the statute books may say. In a funeral home on Chicago's South Side the battered body of Emmett Till lay for four days and was viewed by tens of thousands of people. Even the editorial writers of newspapers throughout Mississippi have agreed that if these two men are eased off with nominal punishment Mississippi might as well throw away its law books.

There is one aspect of the killing of Emmett Till that goes unmentioned. Why should he have been killed for what he did—the involuntary whistle of sexual admiration that has become almost a teen-age habit in cities or on the Main Streets of small towns? Everyone shies away from mentioning this aspect—the wolf whistle itself, with its sexual note. Yet I don't see how you can avoid it, since it goes to the heart of the white psychosis about the Negro in the South.

You have to start where the psychoanalysts start, by asking why the obsession of the white-supremacists with the sanctity of "white womanhood" is so fiercely obsessive as it is. John Dollard's pioneer study *Class and Caste in a Southern Town* enraged the Southerners by suggesting that the Southern whites were not only repelled but also deeply attracted by the Negroes. It is a theme that has been broached in a dozen novels about the South. The Negro has become a sexual symbol in Southern folksay and in the Southern imagination.

Thus a certain type of Southern woman will point an accusing finger at a Negro youth not because of any guilt of his act but because of a guilt of thought which is in her own mind, and which she projects onto him. She may warm herself thus with a heightened sense of herself through seeing some luckless Negro shot or drowned or burned for daring to look or whistle at her. As for the men, Dollard suggests, their fury in a lynching may at least in part express their sense of guilt about Negro women, and their efforts to square their conscience by acting as protectors of their womanhood.

I don't say this is more than part of the lynching story. What happened to Emmett Till was the end product of the hysteria in Mississippi ever since the White Citizens Councils were set up to put the Negro in his place and prevent school desegregation. They are sick people who behave thus over an issue of public policy. There are complex emotional factors behind this collective sickness. At the bottom of the bitter hatreds aroused by the struggle for school integration is the sick obsession that if boys and girls of both colors sit under the same school roof within the same school walls, it will lead to a sexual pollution of the white by the black.

Emmett Till was an unwitting victim of a hate that took him as a target because, like many hatreds enlisted in a dying cause, it clings to false ideals of manhood and chivalry that only cast their mantle over sickness.

September 25, 1955

Justice was color-blind in that Mississippi courtroom when the all-white jury brought in a verdict of innocence for two white men in the murder of the Negro boy. I suppose there was never a chance for any other verdict from the start. Yet this outrage will leave a stain on the American honor that will take a long time to expunge.

I suspect that the rejoicing white citizens of Mississippi's delta and hill regions don't hold it too badly against the prosecutors and the judge that they tried for justice. After all, the jury was always there to serve as a backstop, to keep anything from happening to a couple of white Southerners who had put a black boy from Chicago in his place—the place being at the bottom of the Tallahatchie River, weighted down with a heavy cotton-gin wheel.

To understand why the two men came away untouched one must understand that a jury is no assurance of justice if there is no justice in the hearts of the people. A jury is only as good or bad as the atmosphere surrounding it, within which it operates.

Suppose you had a jury of twelve men in Strijdom's South Africa, sitting in judgment on two of their kind who had killed a Negro boy. They wouldn't be very likely to convict, would they? Mississippi is not South Africa, but on the sanctity of white womanhood a Mississippi jury is only a vehicle for expressing the mass fear and hatred of the Negro.

The remarkable fact is that on the first jury poll there were three who were undecided. They were seized with pangs of decency, if only for a moment. But they couldn't stand up against the massive force of the others and the people outside. They and their families might have to live as outcasts forever. So they faltered, and on the next ballot there were only two, and then there were none.

I think they will have a harder time with their conscience than they would have had with their neighbors. As for the other jurors and the two men, and the wife who was the cause of it all, what can we say except that when evil acts in the world it always manages to find instruments who believe that what they do is not evil but honorable. The capacity for self-delusion is a built-in part of the psychosis.

The poison of racism has eaten so deeply into the Milams and the Bryants, and the lawyers, and the people who cheered the verdict, that it has made them immune to a sense of truth or even of reality. How else explain the jury foreman's remark that the verdict turned on the failure of the prosecution to prove that the body dragged up out of the Tallahatchie was Emmett Till's? How else explain—in the face of the boy's mother's own positive identification—the cynical defense theory that "outsiders" conspired with the mother to throw another body into the river and put the boy's ring on one of its fingers?

I suppose our mistake is in treating all this cynicism and falsehood on a rational level. Milam and Bryant and their lawyers made little effort on this level. The two men didn't dare take the stand, where they might have had to give an account of their time. The lawyers showed their contempt for reason by offering their farfetched case with a straight face.

And how about the jury, especially the nine who never showed the shadow of a doubt? They were not deceived by Milam and Bryant. They voted for them because they admire their kind of arrogance and brutality, and their cynical slickness. It makes them feel big to feel that these men can get away with it. It makes them feel that the South will resist the advance of the Negro just as Mrs. Bryant (whom for the occasion they mystically identify with the South) kept herself inviolate against a Negro boy's whistle.

The South, even Mississippi, will not always act thus. Someday it will be as ashamed of what happened to Emmett Till as William Faulkner was when he said that America's survival is being tested. Meanwhile the progress of the Negro is so frightening to those who cling to a dying cause that it turns them first into killers, and then into whitewashers of the killing.

2. How Old Is Jim Crow?

February 17, 1956

WHEN ADLAI STEVENSON SAYS, about the problem of desegregation, that "we must proceed gradually, not upsetting habits or traditions that are older than the Republic," his statement is not unique. It, or something like it, has been made repeatedly by Southern "moderates" and "gradualists." You cannot, they say, change the "habits and traditions," the "folkways and the mores," of the South overnight. You can't do it by Federal force, by "troops or bayonets," they say. You can't do it by laws. You are dealing with something very old, very settled, very traditional. It is so ancient, and has been there so long, that you have got to expect to take a longish time changing it.

I won't argue about the troops and the bayonets and force. They are a bad method in any situation. But I certainly will argue about the antiquity of the "habits and traditions" that constitute Jim Crow segregation. They are not old, but relatively recent in the long history of the South and the nation. That is why I ask Stevenson to read a brief jewel of a book which undercuts his whole argument.

It is *The Strange Career of Jim Crow,* by C. Vann Woodward (Oxford Press). Woodward was born in Arkansas, has lived and worked in the South, has written almost wholly on Southern themes. He knows Southern history with so easy a mastery that he can write about it with economy. He gave his book as a series of lectures first at the University of Virginia, and I call it a jewel because its style is clear, unpedantic and brilliant.

The fact is that Jim Crow—that is, the body of segregation laws, practices, attitudes and habits—isn't old at all. So far from being "older than the Republic," Jim Crow is roughly five or six decades old, dating back to the turn of the century.

Southern history, says Woodward, is full of breaks. First there was the Old South, based on slavery, and obviously slavery excluded segregation. Then there was the Civil War South, with its successive phases of secession, independence, defeat and the Federal emancipation of the slaves. Then there was the brief period (1865-1877) of Reconstruction with Northern force and Federal troops as an army of occupation. Then there was the period of Redemption, when the troops were withdrawn and the South was allowed to fashion its own new system.

The crucially new light that Woodward sheds is on this period. There were a few beginnings of Jim Crow practices in the Reconstruction period, but very few. There were more in the Redemption period. But Woodward brings historical witness after witness to testify that during the 1870s and the 1880s—even into the 1890s— both races in the South mixed and mingled in public places and even in social intercourse. Moreover, the Negroes voted, and the competition for their votes was part of the political picture of the time.

This doesn't mean the Negroes were well treated in that period. There was conflict between the races, and the Negroes were exploited, and the whites felt toward them as inferiors. But the important fact is that they were not segregated.

Woodward has a chapter on the "Forgotten Alternatives." From the 1870s, for a quarter century, there were three philosophies of how to treat the Negroes, and three groups of whites based on them: the "liberal," the "conservative" and the "radical." The first never came to power, the second held power through most of the South, and the third (Southern Populism) made a bid for power. But they all held out against Jim Crow, until the 1890s and the first decade of the new century.

That was when the Jim Crow laws and codes grew up like weeds and choked out what might have grown healthy in the South. Right through the 1920s (with only a brief interruption in World War I) they changed the social landscape of the South. The Negroes were first disfranchised, then they were segregated and isolated and reduced to a system of caste.

Every detail of life was Jim Crowed, down to toilets and phone booths. And it happened mainly, says Woodward, because a deeply frustrated South, which could find no other solution for its internal conflicts, turned to attack the Negro as a scapegoat. The frustrations led to aggressions. The aggressions gave the South a sense of unity in white supremacy, and for a time (in the 1920s) it looked as if it might spread over the nation.

The important historical fact to remember is that Southern "racism" —that is, Jim Crowism as a complete system of society—was not part of the Southern traditions. It was grafted onto the South relatively late in its history—at the time of the Supreme Court decisions of the 1890s, and the disenfranchisement dodges, and the turn-of-the-century imperialist adventures in our foreign policy. It came because the three decent Southern philosophies crumbled and because the resistance of the Negro in the South and the liberals in the North was weak.

But whatever its sources, it came as a new thing, not an old. It replaced another and less vicious system of society, and it is itself being replaced now by still another—the "New Reconstruction." It was ushered onto the stage of history, and it can be ushered off.

February 19, 1956

Back in 1907 William Graham Sumner, the Yale sociologist, wrote that "legislation cannot make mores" and that "stateways cannot change folkways." The Southern apologists for racism embraced this creed as a defense of the spreading Jim Crow laws. "Leave us alone," they said to the rest of the nation. "It is a fundamental principle of society that laws cannot change our accustomed ways." The South cherished this *mystique,* this vague mysterious belief in a "Southern way," old and deeply rooted, with which it would be folly to deal through legislation.

Just as Vann Woodward's *The Strange Career of Jim Crow* shows that Jim Crow is not old and traditional but recent and with only shallow roots in Southern culture, so it also undercuts the view that laws are futile where "folkways" are involved.

Those who say that you cannot change habits of action by laws forget that segregation itself rests on law—on a body of statutes and ordinances—and that these laws were passed to change the earlier habits of action, when Negroes and whites could vote together, ride together, mingle together. Evidently not all laws are futile, but just the laws that the racists don't like.

We are in danger of forgetting that it was legislation that changed the habits of the South of the Redemption period (from the middle 1870s to the late 1890s and early 1900s) into those of the South of the Segregation period. Also the Supreme Court decisions in the 1880s and 1890s helped establish segregation, since they gave a green light to the Jim Crow laws and practices.

We are in a new period now, and have been since the 1930s—the period of advance toward Negro freedom and equal rights. Again the Supreme Court opinions, especially the school decision, are playing an important role, this time in undoing segregation. Again laws are proposed, but this time they are Federal laws.

The point about laws is not that they can operate in a social vacuum. Obviously they cannot. But, where more silent and deep-reaching social forces have been at work affecting changes in a society, the laws and the court decisions can register those changes, and they can help to further them. The outcry against the laws is raised not because Southerners regard them as futile but because they regard them as dangerously effective.

A change has come over our American society, both South and North, and the silent forces of change—economic, political, educational, literary, religious—are still at work.

Most of what has been achieved has come since the New Deal in the 1930s, and particularly in the last decade, since the end of World War II. The amazing fact is that the South has acquiesced in most of these changes, and most Southern states (as Adlai Stevenson points out) are acquiescing in the school decision as well. But the new crop of Southern demagogues are determined that the advance achieved should be rolled back.

I wonder how much it helps to retreat from their brutal and direct challenge by stressing gradualism. How slow must change be to be gradual? It is easy to talk of "evolution" as against "revolution." But the Supreme Court itself has allowed ample room for gradualism and delay in compliance with its school decision. The proof it needs is only proof of the intent to carry it out rather than to roll it back. Those who talk of even greater gradualism and more delaying delays might be reminded that the moral issue of giving Negroes a decent place in American society can't slow down to the pace of cosmic evolution.

There is an important lesson to be drawn from the history of segregation: It was adopted in the South exactly when the resistance to it crumbled. It came not because men fought too hard against Jim Crow (as we are now being told), but because they didn't fight nearly hard enough.

Take the Southern Populists, for example. At first they marched side by side with the Negroes against the Southern owning and feudal classes that exploited poor white and poor Negro alike. Then, when the corrupt conservatives manipulated the Negro vote by fraud, they turned against the Negroes instead of turning against the corrupt whites. Leaders like Tom Watson of Georgia found that they could use racist hatreds to get control of the Southern Democratic machines. It was only when they (and the Northern liberals as well) stopped fighting for Negro rights that segregation was established.

I hope that Northern liberals will not again, as they did in the 1890s and at the turn of the century, become part of the Great Acquiescence and capitulate to Southern racism. Some may do it out of absence of courage, some may do it because of their belief that we ought not to meddle with "old and established" Southern institutions, some may do it out of a conviction that laws never change habits of thought and action. But the retreat will be the same.

There are some who are moved mainly by a fear of breaking the unity of the Democratic Party. But they forget that the meaningful unity of the Democrats came with the New Deal, when a coalition was formed that included the urban Negroes in the North. It was in the 1930s that they shifted to the Democrats. To break this coalition is neither a way of maintaining party unity nor a way of getting a Democratic victory. You can never march to victory with bugles that call delay and retreat.

3. Negro Roads and Dead Ends

February 24, 1956

THINGS ARE TOPSY-TURVY in the South. In the old days when a Negro was arrested in connection with a bus it was usually because he was riding the bus without having the fare. Now, in Montgomery, Alabama, they are arresting and arraigning 115 Negroes for not riding the buses, although they clearly do have the fare. While there is no law requiring anyone to ride a bus, there are state laws saying that if you get together with anyone and agree not to patronize some outfit you are conspiring to hinder a business. You get fined for that nefarious activity and may get thrown into jail for up to six months.

There are laws in Montgomery that punish a Negro if he does ride a bus and refuses to move to the Jim Crow section. That's what happened to a seamstress called Mrs. Rosa Parks, and she was fined fourteen dollars or fourteen days in jail. Then there are also laws that punish a Negro if he doesn't ride a bus. That's what's happening to the 115 who met after the arrest of Mrs. Parks, agreed to stay off the buses and organized car pools. Laws are wonderful things—you're jailed if you do, and you're jailed if you don't. You can make a law do your bidding, as was done with words in Alice's Wonderland.

I have a secret to tell the Mayor and the judges and the other leaders of Montgomery: They can't win. They can keep Negroes out of white schools and universities, at least for a while. They can keep many of them from voting. But they cannot compel them to spend their money where they don't want to, or to buy any goods and services they refuse to buy.

The Negroes are finally hitting Jim Crow where it hurts most—in his pocketbook nerve. They are learning the effective use of the economic weapon of their purchasing power and of withholding their purchasing power.

They are also learning how to use the legal weapon. There is a young Negro lawyer in Montgomery called Fred Gray who filed a test suit to overturn the local bus segregation laws, and who now finds himself indicted for malpractice and also reclassified in the draft. Again I have a secret to tell the Mayor and the judges and the citizens. Punitive measures won't work. Mass arrests won't work. You can arrest the 115, and fingerprint them, and fine them, and send them to jail. They will go to jail with the same massive patience with which they have been walking to work and back home. But that won't succeed in putting them back riding the buses.

I think I know what is troubling the Mayor and the judges and the worthy citizens of Montgomery. It is not only that the Negroes of the city have become nonriders, it is that they refuse to be the ridden.

Men live by images, as they live by symbols. Up until recently there has been the image of the "good" Southern Negro—the kind who did what he was told and stayed put wherever he was placed and didn't get uppity and didn't use the law as a weapon for equality of treatment. It was the image of the Negro who was ridden, carrying on his back the whole burden of white supremacy. That image of the ridden Negro has now been replaced by the image of the nonriders of Montgomery, and the contrast is too bitter for the comfort of some whites.

When people are fighting for their worth as human beings they will take a lot of punishment without losing heart. The British had to learn this in India, and they finally did. In fact, there is a curious resemblance between the refusal of the Montgomery Negroes to ride the buses and the passive resistance of Gandhi in India. When Gandhi's followers sat down in the streets the British arrested them and crowded the jails with them. But it didn't do any good. Each day more of them showed up to be arrested.

In the process the Negroes of Montgomery are gaining some valuable experience in political action. A seamstress who sparked the bus revolt, a young lawyer, a pastor who is chairman of the Negro negotiating committee, a Pullman porter who heads the Negro political organization and a teacher who heads the Women's Council—these are all people who have been thrown into the political waters to sink or swim, and who will swim.

March 28, 1956

Our period is a great testing time for Negroes and whites alike, when new ideas are in ferment and new techniques of social struggle are being tried out.

Outwardly it would seem that there isn't much new left for the Negroes to try. Haven't they tried everything? Didn't they once try nationalism (Garveyism), and didn't they have their Communist temptation (one or two of their leaders are still stuck with it), and didn't they try to get some kind of release through jazz and the arts and the "dark laughter" of Bohemianism? And didn't they try the New Deal and its alliances? And haven't they been using the weapon of law and the courts?

The answer to all these is Yes, they have. If you look at surfaces you would say that since Walter White's death no unifying leader has come on the scene. You would note that the N.A.A.C.P. is being battered by storms, and that its enemies are trying to make a dirty word out of it.

But you would be wrong, after all, if you saw only this and failed to see something else. There is a feel of Negro greatness in the air, and it comes from Negro churches and campuses and committees and plain Negro people in towns like Montgomery. It comes, in short, from the battlefields of the new phase of the struggle for Negro rights. When I read the speech in Brooklyn by the Reverend Martin Luther King, a young Baptist preacher from Montgomery, I got the feeling that new shoots of grass are springing up out of the soil in the South, different from anything we have had thus far.

What is the difference? I think it lies in the method of Gandhi, which has stretched all the way over to our shores and has mingled with native American elements to form a mixture never before known. There is a new book called *The Gandhi Reader* edited by Homer A. Jack (Indiana University). It contains two selections especially appropriate for Americans today. One is an account of a talk that Channing Tobias and Benjamin Mays had with Gandhi when they visited him in 1937, and the other tells of a similar visit by Howard Thurman.

Gandhi had some interesting ideas about how the American Negroes might use his method of nonviolent resistance. In the twenty years since these visits took place they seemed to be like seeds buried in the cold ground, but now they are pushing through.

It is a tragic fact about Gandhi that in his own Asian world none of the colonial liberation movements (except the Indian) used his method. The world has paid its lip service to him and said how great a man and a saint he was. But from Indonesia and Malaya and Indochina to Egypt and Morocco and Algeria, the nationalist movements have turned away from Gandhi's "truth force" to the method of terror.

It is only in America—"materialist," prosperous, sensual America, which Gandhi mistrusted so deeply—that his approach is being developed. There is a group of American pacifists, many of them Quakers, who are thinking of how it applies to war and peace in the H-bomb age. And now there is a group of Negroes trying to apply it to things like bus segregation in Montgomery.

There are several possible explanations. One is that the struggle for Negro rights is being carried on by a minority group sure of its legal ground, and for which, therefore, the method of violence would be insane. "How is a minority to act against an overwhelming majority?" asked Dr. Mays, the president of Morehouse College. "A minority," Gandhi answered, "can do much more in the way of nonviolence than a majority . . . I had less difficulty in handling my minority in South Africa than I had here in handling a majority."

But there is also a deeper reason. It is the nature of the Negro religious experience in America, with its roots in the stoical suffering of the slaves, and its closeness to the primitive era of Christianity. Bidding farewell to his visitors, Gandhi said that "it may be through the Negroes that the unadulterated messages of nonviolence will be delivered to the world."

It will be hard to carry the method through. But in alliance with the court struggle, and the great power of the economic boycott used by fifteen million people with rising purchasing capacity, and the balance-of-power vote, and the religious sense of the plain people—who knows? It might work.

March 11, 1957

A historian of the struggle for Negro rights will have to record, as one of the high points of his story, the encounter of Richard Nixon and the Reverend Martin Luther King at Accra. The Vice-President had come to the Ghana celebration to build a record of Republican friend-ship to Negroes for the 1960 Presidential campaign. But when he got to Accra he found that a young American Negro leader, Reverend King, was telling a press conference how much it would have meant to the Negroes of Montgomery if President Eisenhower had come there to offer his moral support.

King is clearly one of the coming national leaders of the movement for Negro equality. He stands for a new approach to the movement, through a Gandhilike appeal to nonviolent resistance and the re-ligious conscience of the nation.

On the other hand, there is the confusing episode at the all-Negro Alcorn A & M College in Mississippi, where almost the whole student body of 750 boycotted their classes in order to force out a Negro in-structor who had written some newspaper pieces critical of the N.A.A.C.P. The teacher is out, the college has a new president, and the students are returning. But the question of what are the best roads to Negro freedom needs to be clarified.

Historically there have been four proposed roads in the course of the American Negro movements. The first was that of the acceptance of an inferior status, with hard work and education to overcome it in time; this was the road of Booker Washington. The second was that of Negro emigration to Africa, out of which came the present republic of Liberia and also the philosophy of Garveyism. The third was the Communist road, which ran for a time in the fantastic direction of a separate Negro republic in the South. The fourth was that of Negro political and legal action, through the N.A.A.C.P.—the road of James Weldon Johnson, Walter White, Thurgood Marshall and Roy Wilkins.

Of these it is the fourth alone that has offered real hope for the Negro people and the whites as well. The others proved dead ends. Every great movement runs the danger of getting into a groove and losing its original fire and flexibility. That is why the Montgomery movement through the churches for a Negro bus boycott had far more than a local importance. It reached beyond the educated and middle-class Negroes to the low-income and even illiterate groups. It stirred their imagination, gave them an active and continuing, if humble, role to play in the struggle day after day, and put their fight not on the dry level of Supreme Court argument but on the ground the saints had trod.

That may be why I heard a local Northern N.A.A.C.P. official say about King: "If we don't watch out, that fellow will walk away with our movement."

But this is clearly unfair at once to the N.A.A.C.P. and to King. Neither has opposed the other. The N.A.A.C.P. uses the methods of balance-of-power voting, legislative lobbying, court procedures under constitutional law, economic bargaining power, public education. These are the chief methods available to the Negroes as a minority, and they have been strikingly successful for at least a quarter century. In fact, King's press conference at Accra, with its needling of President Eisenhower, was an example of balance-of-power pressures on the Administration.

King's method is in one sense an American version of Gandhi's *Satyagraha*. Yet it cannot be used in America as it was used in India, where Gandhi's followers were the massive majority of the population. It can be used only locally, and mainly to supplement the methods of the N.A.A.C.P. The religious passion in the new movement—almost a mystical belief in a God-guided victory—has now converged with the older political, legal and economic techniques. The struggle of the American Negroes is richer and more vital, now that the two roads have converged.

The White Citizens Councils of the South, and their Northern racist fellow travelers like John Kasper, are spoiling for some outbreaks of violence in the South. The method of Kasper and the W.C.C.s is that of the closed mind and the hating heart. When an elderly Quaker, Ashton Jones, asked for five minutes in which to answer Kasper at a segregationist meeting in Miami, Kasper shut him up as an "imbecile."

This is why I was disturbed at the Alcorn College episode, when the Negro student body went on strike to force the dismissal of Clennon King, a history teacher who had criticized the N.A.A.C.P. No doubt the history teacher must have seemed to the students a craven and a traitor. But in the case of Negroes the principle of free expression must be all the more precious because they have been the victims of its denial.

It is natural that oppressed groups, in the bitterness of their struggle, should strike out at those outside their race or faith or at dissenters within their own ranks. It is natural—but also fatal. I don't like the slogans of exclusiveness when used by these groups, whether it is Africa-for-the-Africans-alone or Israel-for-the-Jews-alone or Spain-for-the-Catholics-alone. If my enemy tries to shut me out I prevail not by shutting him out but by including him.

4. The Chivalry

February 8, 1956

ROCKS FELL on Alabama during the graceless struggle of a mob to chase a lone woman from her university campus. Rocks also fell on the tradition of chivalry on which the South has prided itself since its early plantation days.

"The Chivalry" was what the ruling class in the South used to call itself, in a phrase it took from the novels of Sir Walter Scott that were the stock reading of Southern beaux and belles. When a gentleman of the old school died in the South his obituary writer could have no higher praise than to say that he had belonged to "the Chivalry." It meant he was a Southern gentleman and expressed the aristocratic flowering of the Southern way of life, and was dedicated to keeping Southern womanhood pure. In a curious way, the cult of Southern chivalry had an image of the Southern woman as a "more than mortal creature," almost a vestal virgin, as W. J. Cash put it in his *The Mind of the South* (Anchor).

Alas, the Southern gentleman has fallen on evil ways and days, and the girls around whom he built his cult have been shown to be very mortal indeed—no vestal virgins, they. The Age of Chivalry is burnt out. You can see its fag-end residues in the way a couple of thousand Southern males swilled and milled about, howled, chanted and panted for the blood of a college student called Autherine Lucy. Like all true believers, they would listen to no reasoning, would have no compromise. They had the glazed barbaric insistence you will find in thugs, desperadoes, religious fanatics—and Southern gentlemen.

They won their victory. The University of Alabama authorities and trustees surrendered to them. The president of the university said some pious words—but he surrendered. So did the chairman of the trustees. The remnants of "the Chivalry" were left in total possession of the field of battle. They have kept a girl, who stood wholly alone, from attending any more classes. They have kept the university unpolluted by Autherine Lucy.

Don't feel sorry for Miss Lucy. It isn't often that a girl has a chance to sum up, in a few brief days as she has done, the courage and tenacity of a group fighting for its humanity, and the bankruptcy of those fighting to deny it. As the first Negro coed at Alabama, coming just at the height of the Great Year in the wake of the school cases, she was placed at a strategic point in the campaign of history.

The people to feel sorry for are the scared rabble of students and townfolk and factory workers who could find no better crusade than to chase a lone woman off a college campus with rocks and rotten fruit. You can tell when a cause has gone hollow by noting the victims it picks as its targets. The current state of the white-supremacy crusade is well symbolized when you remember that once it hunted grown men, and now it kills a young boy like Emmett Till and chases away a coed woman.

Why do these people do it? I don't think this was just a college prank of high-spirited youngsters, like the "panty" riots that hit our campuses now and then. This was not a good-natured rioting throng. It was a mob, capable of killing. Some of them were students, although it seems clear that the student leaders didn't get mixed up with them but have behaved well. Some of them came of "respectable" families, which have a standing in their community. Some were factory workers with a chip-on-the-shoulder resentment against the world.

What they have in common is their common fear that something is being taken from them, and something is being put over on them. They don't know what is being taken from them; certainly this rabble is not "the Chivalry" that used to rule the South, nor is it even the ruling class of today with whom they try to identify. Nor do they know what is being "put over" on them, except for their feeling that what the Negro gets must somehow be at the expense of the whites and therefore diminish them.

Every mob, in its ignorance and blindness and bewilderment, is a League of Frightened Men that seeks reassurance in collective action. This rabble tried to reassure itself by enacting the ritual of white supremacy. They were both pursuers and fearers. They wanted to be part of something beyond themselves, even if it is built on destruction and cemented by hate.

Ben Tillman, the Negro-hating demagogue from South Carolina, made a Senate speech in 1907 about how Southerners feel when they must protect the purity of their women. "Civilization peels off us," he said, "and we revert to the original savage type . . ." It was true of the Tuscaloosa rabble too; civilization peeled off them, only it was not in protecting a woman but in hounding her.

The tragedy is that no one really stood up to them. The university officials took the easier way, and ran. What they forgot is that a university is a more sacred trust than an army. When it surrenders to a rabble it can no longer teach its students. For students learn not from what the teachers say but from how they act.

5. The Constitution Is Color-Blind

December 13, 1953

"An age of storm and tragedy" is what Winston Churchill called our present era in his Nobel Prize acceptance speech. He was talking of atomic weapons, but storm and tragedy were also present in the Supreme Court reargument last week of the school segregation cases. John W. Davis, speaking for the South Carolina diehard position, ended with an emotional plea for states' rights that made his voice falter and choke. Thurgood Marshall, speaking for the N.A.A.C.P., told movingly what it meant to be a Negro growing up under segregation.

The fact is that in the last generation American race relations have been going through a social revolution without violence. For more than half a century the Negro, who had been made by Constitutional amendment a free man and a legal equal of the white man, has had the gate leading to equal opportunity barred and padlocked against him. Now the gates are being broken open. On housing covenants, on university education, on train service, on restaurant facilities, on admission to movie houses, on access to jobs and public office, on equality in the armed services, our generation has witnessed a historic series of legal, political and social victories, which have been won with relatively little violence.

The struggle over the segregation of the public schools is the toughest of the battles thus far, but it is also likely to prove the last important one. If this rampart of the caste system is breached, the rest will follow.

I cannot believe that the perplexities of the Justices are primarily those of technical Constitutional law. The giveaway on this came when several of the counsel for the Southern states asked the court, if it decided to outlaw Jim Crow in the schools, to allow for a slow transition and leave it to the local courts to determine the pace of transformation. In other words, Jim Crow is in his last agony, but he is trying to win time. And the Supreme Court Justices are searching their consciences to decide whether they will kill him "forthwith" or do it by a "gradual adjustment"—that is, let him take an unconscionably long time in dying.

I don't mean to brush aside the technical legal arguments wholly, especially since I have had occasion in the past to study the art of quoting from dead law cases in order to shape the future or prevent its coming into being. John W. Davis, who has put his great ability in the service of an unworthy cause, made a strong legal case for "separate but equal" Negro schools as fulfilling the meaning of the "equal protection of the laws" guaranteed to white and black alike by the Fourteenth Amendment. He points out with some force that it is hard to know what the exact "intent" of the Congressional framers of the Fourteenth Amendment was on the question of Negro children in public schools. His strongest argument is that if you look not at what Congress intended, but at what it did, you find that it went on to establish segregated schools in the District of Columbia as late as the 1880s.

But this does not clinch the matter. The broad intent of the amendment was to give Negroes the same first-class citizenship that whites have, with the same legal protection and the same standing before the law. The Supreme Court has itself recognized this in a series of cases in the last decade. As Thurgood Marshall put it, the issue is whether the Southern states and the school districts shall be allowed to substitute their own mores for the rights that the Negroes have under the Constitution.

The Justices know that the mixing of white and Negro children seems to many Southerners a defilement of the "purity" of the white children, and the clincher in giving the Negroes "social equality." They also know that the court has the legal power to put an end to Jim Crow in the schools. But they have a right to ask why Congress has not itself acted to carry through the revolution that has been in process, why it does not even give a sign of its present intent, why the burden of crucial decision must rest on nine men who are not even elected.

The answer is that neither the Democrats nor the Republicans—both of whom are wooing the Southern Tories—have the political courage today to push a bill through Congress which would express how the overwhelming majority of Americans feel about school equality for Negroes. The answer is also that throughout the whole silent revolution of our time on Negro rights, the courts have had to lead the way, and even Southern public opinion has followed. The highest judges of the land will be unable to face their own consciences if they falter now at the last and crucial step.

Justice Jackson fears this will mean a "generation of litigation." Even if this proved true, it would be preferable to another generation of injustice—of scars on the hearts of the Negroes and on the conscience of the whites. Southern governors speak of evading the Constitution by making the public schools "private," but they will not get away with it because the courts would rule it unconstitutional.

The real question is not who will win. It is whether the South will accept the future with grace.

May 19, 1954

THE REBEL SOUTHERNERS, making a last-ditch stand against racial equality in education, are calling the Supreme Court school decision in *Brown v. Board of Education* a "political" decision because it overrules the precedents. It is true that the court has now explicitly wiped out the "separate but equal" doctrine of *Plessy v. Ferguson.* But that doctrine was never a Constitutional principle. Anyone who has studied its history knows that it was one of those dodges and devices a democracy often uses to tide itself over a time of troubles.

By the time of the Plessy case, in 1896, the South had passed through forty years of bitterness over its defeat in the Civil War. On the one hand there was the Fourteenth Amendment, with its guarantee to the Negroes of "equal protection of the laws." On the other hand there were state segregation laws and the whole institution of "white supremacy," based on the memory of those forty years. And so the court evolved the "doctrine" of "separate but equal" facilities for both races. In practice they were separate and unequal. The doctrine was intended as a mask to hide the ugliness of the inequality.

This tricky political stratagem—always opportunist, never honest —has long outlived any decent usefulness. In a world of hydrogen energy, in a military setup where black and white alike share in a democracy of death, in a culture where access to schooling has become the portal to a full life, the Plessy doctrine had become a shabby hypocrisy and a misfit. It was time the Supreme Court swept it away.

The real Constitutional principle at stake has always been the "equal protection of the laws." In supporting that principle the judges have overruled a political stratagem which masqueraded as judicial precedent, and they have reasserted that the Constitution comes first.

That is why *Brown v. Board of Education* is a historic decision. It was read by Chief Justice Warren for a unanimous court. It is brief, almost stark in its simplicity, with scarcely a memorable or flashing phrase, as if the court recognized that this moment of sober justice is no occasion for verbal adornments.

For some years the court has been stalking down the doctrine of "separate but equal" facilities. Now it has finally destroyed it, vindicating the great dissent of Justice Harlan in the Plessy case, when he wrote that "our Constitution is color-blind, and neither knows nor tolerates classes among citizens." Lincoln once said that "nothing is ever settled until it is settled right." The court has now settled the issue right.

I want to note how great an influence the social-science studies in our universities had on the final decision. The work of many students of American civilization, in the field that is now called "personality and culture," has helped shape currents of opinion that scarcely existed a generation ago. Very much as Justice Louis D. Brandeis used to lean heavily on researches in economics and labor statistics, so the judges here have used studies by psychologists and psychiatrists showing that the segregation has taken a heavy psychic toll from the Negro children.

The mark it has left on the children is the mark of the outsider. Children need to feel that they are wanted and accepted. They like to wear the badges of belonging. Instead of that they have been made to feel unwanted, unequal and unused. Feeling inferior and unworthy, they have turned often in frustration against the whites and in self-hatred against themselves. By denying them equal schooling we have denied them the life chances that ought to be open to all. By putting on them the mark of Cain's victim we have committed the ultimate crime in any democracy, which is the crime against children.

That is why I cannot take too seriously the Wailing Wall at which the Southern racists are now uttering lamentations and shouting threats. There will be a difficult period of change-over for the schools, but a decade from now it will read like ancient history. Using the triple weapons of law, economics and the conscience of the people, Negro and white leaders together are moving toward inevitable victory. A wind is rising and the waters flow, and as they flow they erase the old landmarks of oppression for the Negro and shame for the white.

May 6, 1956

A psychiatrist from Charlottesville, Virginia, Dr. David C. Wilson, said the other day that the Southern Negro is paying a heavy toll in mental illness both for the way he is segregated and for his fight against it. Compared with the 1914 figures, Negro mental cases in Virginia are coming into the hospitals twice as fast, while the white increase is one third. His explanation is that during these forty years the Negro has been improving his living standards and winning legal gains but that Virginia has kept a tighter hold on him through segregation.

The result is that the Negro feels lost, caught between an earlier security he no longer has and a middle-class freedom like that of the whites toward which he is moving but which is still outside his reach. And being lost he feels bewildered—and disturbed.

The explanation makes a good deal of sense. For one thing, Dr. Wilson confirms the historical picture of Southern segregation that C. Vann Woodward draws in *The Strange Career of Jim Crow*. The real segregation of the Negro has taken place within the last half century. But the transformation of the Negro's living standards and outlook, and the awakening of new life claims in his mind and heart, are even more recent—mainly a matter of a quarter century.

It isn't exactly news that this double strain—of being segregated at the same time that new hopes have been awakened in him—has taken a toll on the Negro. After all, that was the point of the Supreme Court school decision. It was not new legal facts that were presented to the justices but the new psychological fact that segregated schools have left a scar on the minds of Negro children.

We often forget how heavy is the psychic burden that the Negroes of both South and North have had to bear, not only in living under inequality but in fighting against it. The American Negro is subject to most of the same tensions of American life that the white is subject to, and adds some extra ones of his own. Much of his everyday energy is spent in a constant anxiety, a constant need to make choices, a constant uncertainty as to what to expect from the people and the situations he must encounter all the days of his years. This is the portrait that Kardiner and Ovesey drew in their striking book of psychiatric interviews with Negroes, which they called *The Mark of Oppression*.

It is a curious fact, but one we must recognize, that the process of liberation involves a heavy psychic cost. Someday when the struggle for Negro civil rights is over, a new generation of Negroes will have achieved the inner security for which the present generation is fighting. I wonder whether it will know how much was spent in that fight in sheer agony of spirit.

There are compensations in the struggle. Some of the reports from Montgomery have suggested that there is a serenity of spirit among the Negroes involved in the bus struggle, especially since it comes out of religious conviction.

One thing that Dr. Wilson, in his Virginia psychiatric report, seems to forget is that the Southern whites are paying an equally heavy price in mental health. Theirs is the insecurity of a master class that feels it is losing its mastery and has become panicky as a consequence. The mental ills involved here are those of fear and hatred and a paranoid sense of being surrounded by heavy menacing shadows. It is not healthy to try to keep nine million Negroes in poverty and ignorance so that they will not get ideas which will make them unruly. Nor is it healthy to live day after day driven by an obsession and riddled by feelings of guilt.

I should add that the big moral difference between the two scars is the fact that those of the Negroes are incurred in the struggle for freedom and security, while the scars of the whites are incurred in a struggle to keep a subject people in subjection.

Dr. Wilson seems to derive a different sort of moral from his figures. He is quoted as attributing "major disturbances of mental health" to "culture changes which are forced on a people against their will, by fiat or by authority from outside or above." This sounds like the familiar argument against desegregation as being "synthetic" rather than local and "organic."

I am not impressed by this reasoning. What produces the scars is the rankling sense of injustice and uncertainty on one side, and the rage and aggression on the other. There are no ways of getting a people free from subjection except by fighting for their freedom— and the struggle produces the marks of conflict.

I am quite sure that there could be a "normality" in the South if there were no struggle—the "normality" of a master-class society in which the Negro kept his place on the terms of white supremacy.

6. Faubus and Little Rock: Scars Are for the Young

September 5, 1956

THE THING that bothers me about the integration riots in the Southern schools is the question of what goes on behind those grave eyes set in the dark-skinned head? What goes on in the minds of the children themselves—the Negro children in the schools of Tennessee and Texas and the other states, around whom the tides of race battle are surging? Have you seen their faces in those pictures the papers have been running? There is the one showing a little group of Negro boys about to enter the high school at Clinton, passing a line of jeering white boys. And there is an unforgettable one of a Negro girl in the classroom, with empty seats around her, conveying somehow the desolate sense a little girl must have when she feels herself rejected and hated, a target of a battle not of her making.

Writing in *Ebony* about what he would do if he were an American Negro, William Faulkner said he would join with his fellow Negroes in picking a child—clean, neatly dressed, well-behaved—and have him present himself each day at the "white" school.

Well, twelve Negro children presented themselves on the opening day of school at the Clinton High School—and an avalanche of terror broke loose. Faulkner was counseling a patient persistence, and he was right. But it takes a lot of stamina for the children who have to carry the ball. You can teach children something about the meaning of what they are going to do, but martyrdom has to be made of an older and tougher fabric.

What makes it all the more deadly is the fact that, however the fight may turn out in the end, what happens inside the minds of the children can never be undone. They will carry the scar of memory forever. And, for that matter, so will the white teen-agers in the riot crowds, except that their scar is that of the haters, not the hated.

What can we say about the riot crowds, except that they are what happens when a match is touched to inflammable material. The match is not, as many Southerners seem to think, the Supreme Court decision. That is the propaganda inference that the segregationists want the nation to draw, but it is not the true one. The actual match is always incitement from without—by an aspiring young Goebbels from New Jersey, by the head of the Alabama White Citizens Councils, by whoever may be looking for a thrill, a following, a racket. To be sure there was inflammable material in the Tennessee and Texas small towns, and the Supreme Court decision was part of it. But there is inflammable material in every culture, and in every human heart—if you know how to light it.

These particular mobs had hate stored in them, ready to explode. The troublemakers knew the right catchwords to set off the explosions.

Yet the thing to remember is that neither they nor the rioters can claim to speak for the South. The sheriff of Clinton, the Mayor, the volunteers who organized themselves into a protective group until the state forces could arrive, the judge who issued the integration order, the Governor who sent the National Guard, the Senators who backed up the move, the U.S. Supreme Court Justice from Alabama who denied a plea to set the integration order aside—these too are Southerners, and we in the North should not forget it when we are tempted to despair of social peace and human decency ever coming to the South.

I should have added, as another Southerner, the Reverend D. W. Clark, the young Episcopalian minister who had the courage to cry Shame at the crowd in Mansfield, Texas. When he spoke of loving thy neighbor, someone shouted, "This ain't a love-thy-neighbor crowd." The voice was right: The principle that has taken over these little towns is the hate-thy-neighbor principle. When the minister spoke of the effigy of a Negro hanging from the school flagpole, and reminded the rioters that man was created in the image of God, they mocked him.

What the young clergyman said remains true. The segregationists have set themselves against the God these little communities pretend to worship, as well as against the law and the conscience of the nation.

There need be no bloodshed, provided two things happen. One is that we must keep the moral issue clear—a moral issue that I have tried to describe when I have talked of the scar inside the consciousness of the Negro students. The second is that our leaders should exert the force of leadership. Where there is no leadership on an issue as morally clear as this one, the heart of a child perishes.

Venice, September 12, 1957

Every nation has its deep corrosive problem. For the French today it is Algeria; for Italy it is the cancerous poverty and backwardness of the whole southern region; for Spain it is the closed society and the fear of challenging a dictator; for Russia it is the dark night of tyranny over the Hungarian people. For us in America it can be put quite simply as the effort in a segment of the South to block the growth of the Negro child.

It is a futile, doomed effort. But meanwhile the Little Rock story shows what a fearful human cost it involves. When some hate-drunk

Alabama Klansmen pick a Negro at random on a Birmingham street, and use a razor blade unspeakably to emasculate him, they are the bestial survival of an old dying method in racial hatred—that of physical violence. But when an Arkansas Governor, who is too educated to use a razor barbarously on a man, calls out troops to throw a ring of untouchability around a Negro child, he is as surely doing violence to life.

Governor Faubus has learned somewhere how to turn words upside down, to make them mean the opposite of what they normally mean. He speaks of guarding Little Rock from "violence" where no violence existed until his act of calling out the troops set the stage for it. He applies the term "force" to the painfully slow operation of the law in carrying out the Supreme Court decision in the school case. He accuses the Federal courts of lawlessness and plants a martyr's crown on his own head.

His whole course has been a mixture of craft and stupidity—craft in seizing for a brief moment the role of leader of an embattled Southern resistance movement, stupidity because in the end he can't win. For the final word will have to be said by the same Federal-court system which he has tried to turn into an enemy symbol.

He is, moreover, tangling with the Presidential office as well as with the courts. He ought to know that if it comes to a showdown, a President who failed to back up the courts with his executive power would as surely be a laughingstock as a court system which backed away from applying the settled law of the nation.

No one denies the reality of the rights that states retain under federalism, nor the powers that state governors have. But there are sharp limits to both the rights and the powers. The grand Constitutional principle is that on economic and administrative matters the states have a "police power" to act for the health, safety and welfare of their people; but on questions that touch the freedom of the person and his equal rights with others, a state governor cannot behave like a princeling with absolute power in his little domain.

Unfortunately President Eisenhower was slow and clumsy in his first response to Faubus' gesture of defiance in calling out the troops. It seems incredible that he should have chosen just such a moment to point out that the Southerners fear the "mongrelization" of their stock, and that you can't legislate a change of heart. Two days later he swung into a clearer and stronger groove, but Faubus had already entrenched himself in his position by then. This was a time when the nation would have benefited from an Andrew Jackson who knew how to confront a nullification attempt by a state, or of a Harry Truman who would have used the right salty, crisp and decisive language.

In this matter of equal schooling opportunities, the function of the local authorities—primarily the school boards—is to apply the court formula of "all deliberate speed" to their local situation. It is not to countermand the court orders or nullify the court decision. The function of the Federal courts and the President, on the other hand, is to express the policy and the conscience of the people on a matter that concerns the whole nation and not just a state or even a section.

How many Negro children will be admitted each year to the school system, and how fast the change-over will take place, are matters that can be argued locally. But whether a Negro child shall be isolated from the fullness of intellectual and cultural experience which should be available to every American child—that is now beyond argument. It has been settled, and it cannot be unsettled by Faubus or anyone else.

Nine Negro children are involved this year in the high school at Little Rock, as representatives for others who will follow them. To shut the school gates to these nine is like throwing a rope around the neck of each of them, and strangling his chance of developing the strength and talent in him.

Governor Faubus may think that he can stop the course of history and roll back what the nation has so painfully achieved over the years. He will find it a bigger job than he—or any other man—can swing.

Paris, September 23, 1957

I have been reading the debates on the power of a governor in the face of the Federal power—about how to interpret what Justice Holmes said once in the case of *Moyer v. Peabody* as against what Justice Hughes said later in the case of *Sterling v. Constantin,* and while there is usually enough of the old fire horse in me to respond to these alarms I am not really agitated. The final source of constitutional law is what takes place in the mind of a youngster growing up in America. The true test of our governments, state and Federal, is what their acts do to our young people, white and black alike.

How absurd the nullifiers are today is best shown when you look at the picture—republished in every European newspaper and weekly—of Dorothy Counts walking in a Charlotte street with a little rabble of jeering, screaming, spitting children around her. The apparatus of government, civil and military alike, is reduced to a monstrous evil when it is used to strike terror into Dorothy Counts and leave a scar on her heart. Government exists, as society exists, to protect children, not to wound them.

I hope we won't pass judgment too easily on Dorothy Count's parents for giving up the fight and pulling her out of school. She walked straight in that picture, and her pride seemed to sit on her firmly poised head with a quiet grace. But what the picture didn't show was the ravaged heart within, which was too young to build a wall of immunity against the jeers and insults. .

It takes a deal of courage, for parents and child alike, to be in the front ranks of the struggle for equal rights in Southern schools. The weeding-out process is a tough one, and only the sturdy can hope to survive. There are white children to throw sticks at you, to spit at you, to chant insulting choruses. There are grownups from the White Citizens Councils to spur the tormenters to further ardors if their zeal and hate lag. It is hard for a child, at fifteen, not to feel her heart tighten at this.

There is cruelty of a sort, of course, in every school. The thoughts of youth are not always tender thoughts, nor are its songs always the songs of innocence. But whatever petty persecutions your child may suffer—and inflict—in the relatively secure harbor of his school, try to imagine what it would be like to send him off every morning to be battered by the waves of certain and organized hatred. In the South today the constitutional arguments and the political maneuvering are being carried on by men who are old with the corruption of the ages, but the scars are for the young.

Yet scars can hasten the process of growing up. It is a fearful price for the young to pay, but the fact is that the hate-ridden school of yesterday—fighting off every effort toward the beginnings of equality—becomes the integrated school of today. "Say not the struggle naught availeth."

With all our emphasis on concord we make a mistake sometimes in thinking that conflict is wholly destructive. It isn't. For those whom it doesn't destroy it can be a creative experience. The night before Elizabeth Eckford went to school, at Little Rock, she read the lines in the Psalms, "The Lord is my light and my salvation; whom shall I fear? The Lord is the strength of my life; of whom shall I fear?" Despite her lonely long walk back from the line of the Faubus militia who kept her out of the "white" school, Elizabeth says quietly that she is not going back to the Jim Crow school.

Elizabeth plans to study law. Another of the Little Rock girls will be a schoolteacher, still another a social worker. If the Faubus militia putsch has no other results, it is likely to strengthen these girls in their resolve to go through with their careers.

Something does come out of this struggle then, as something has always come out of every struggle for freedom. There are people who will tell you that the South has gone beyond the point of no return, that it can never accept the mandate of justice and rejoin a Union where children have an equal fighting chance at what life offers. Such people can learn from the quiet confidence of Elizabeth Eckford, who will never waver in her purpose, no matter what hurts she must suffer.

This is an education in itself—perhaps a better education than the schoolbooks will ever be able to give. The turning point in the process of growing up is when you discover the core of strength within you that survives all hurt. Am I wrong in thinking that a whole young generation of American Negroes is coming up which is being hardened in this baptism of fire, and which will furnish a new and great leadership in the days ahead?

They might perhaps, at another time, have grown up to be just mediocre people. But history has placed them *there,* at the right spot and the right time to give their lives a meaning beyond anything they might otherwise have had. Even a Faubus has his uses.

I do not mean to pass over the young white children in the South. They too pay a high price for the struggle—the price of hate. But there are a few who sit down by the young Negro newcomers in the classroom, and eat with them in the lunchroom, and walk home with them. It takes courage for them, but it is a courage that redeems the soul of the South.

Paris, September 26, 1957

"Now the crucifixion begins," Governor Faubus cried at the start of last week's injunction hearing in Little Rock. This simulated martyr cry echoes other cries of martyrdom that have been heard from the white-supremacists, their champions and their apologists ever since the Supreme Court school decision. "They are taking away our local rights to deal with schools." "They want to mongrelize our children." "We stand at Armageddon to battle for the Lord against a Supreme Court which has violated the Constitution."

These have been the elements of a crucifixion complex which by now is familiar throughout the South. But even in the North there are commentators who are so worried about the liberal trend on the Supreme Court that they find constitutional arguments on which Faubian-ism can rest its battered and bloody head.

I consider first the case of Arthur Krock. "The root of the problem," he writes, "is the Supreme Court finding . . . that the Constitution forbade the racial school segregation which the Court for many years had found permissive in the same Constitution." Which is like saying, in 1865, that the root of the slavery problem lay in Lincoln's Emancipation Proclamation.

I should have thought that the root of the problem at Little Rock was the Governor's attempt to use the National Guard not to protect the community against violence but to prevent the carrying out of the community's decisions about integration.

"There are plenty of precedents," says Krock, to establish the "Governor's power to take action," as well as "the Federal judicial power to pass on the validity" of the action, and he adds that it is a matter of "policy" and not of law. But what is law, in the end, but the distillation of long experience with protecting rights and powers within a broad frame of community wisdom?

Krock invokes the name of Justice Holmes, so persuasive with liberal opinion, and cites his opinion in the case of *Moyer v. Peabody,* which involved the Governor's power to call out the militia in an extremely violent labor dispute. I happen to have spent some time in the past grappling with the elusive outlines of Holmes's judicial and social thinking. Holmes believed, as a Darwinian, in the right of the community to survive. When he wrote that ordinary individual rights must yield he was speaking of "a decision by the head of a state involving its life." It would be little short of fantasy to say that the opening of a high school to nine Negro students, three years after the Supreme Court decision, involved the very life of the state of Arkansas.

It will not do to invoke the name of Holmes to give support, however unintended, to a course of action which has no foundation either in policy or in law. The only "life" that was imperiled here was not the life of the state but the political life of the Governor.

But Krock has legal learning, and he is a monument of reason compared with his contemporary in another paper, David Lawrence, who has been writing a series of tirades against the Supreme Court as the villain of the situation.

We have already had Lawrence's delightful suggestion that Congress investigate who really writes the Supreme Court opinions that the pliant Justices sign their names to. Now, avowing that he himself went to an "integrated" school in Buffalo and would do so again, Lawrence comes up with the idea that the Supreme Court has broken into a field where it doesn't belong. It has tried, he says, to compel Negro and white students "to alter their mental attitudes toward one another." This, he says, is an effort "to legislate in the fields of psychology and sociology," and quite unconstitutional.

Every journalist has, of course, the inalienable right to be his own amateur constitutional expert. I have played at it a bit myself. But no journalist or scholar has the right to ignore the nature of the judicial process which is open for anyone to study.

One may disagree with the decision of the Supreme Court on the school case without pretending that it is the first time the court has overruled precedent and struck out on a new course. Often the judges try to obscure the fact of overruling a case by "distinguishing" the new decision from the old ones. Chief Justice Warren was too honest for such a subterfuge and the case was too important to play games with. Surely, the fact that Warren spoke for a unanimous court should make anyone pause and gulp hard before he plunges into battle against the constitutionality of the decision.

As for this business of the court's trying to coerce the "attitudes" of white children, I can only call it poppycock. If you say I can't keep a man out of a public bus—or park, or hospital, or school—it doesn't mean I must like him. The distinction between public rights and private attitudes has been too clearly established to be muddled now, whether by a judge, a governor or a journalist.

Athens, October 4, 1957

Governor Faubus' latest outburst against Federal intervention in Little Rock, with its sickening allusions to the Nazi occupation of Paris and the Russian drowning of the Budapest revolution in blood, continues his crucifixion complex but extends it from himself to the South as a whole. McCarthy, at least, exploited a fear that was nationwide, and since he associated it with the power of the nationalist emotions it might have spread out and deepened. The fear and hatred that Faubus exploits are local and sectional and have no potential, although they are intense enough among those who possess them—or, rather, who are possessed by them.

This group is not a majority of the people of the South. It is a minority of a minority. It may well be that a majority of the Southerners believe that the Supreme Court school decision was unwise and are against desegregated schools. But once the highest courts and the conscience of the nation have spoken the issue is whether Southern communities will carry their dissent to the point of hysterical obstruction. On that issue the Faubians are only a ragged band of fanatics.

The words shrieked by a hysterical girl in the crowd at the Little Rock high school—"A damn nigger sat right in my English class. Black as she can be. Just sat right down there"—have had parallels in other parts of the world. A Nazi girl shrieked them about Jews in Berlin, a Utashi girl shrieked them about Greek Orthodox Serbs in Croatia, a Chinese Communist girl shrieked them about unreconstructed "enemies of the people" in Canton.

In every society, at a time of inner spiritual crisis, the surface of civilized behavior and feeling is easily scratched away and what shows beneath it is the mark of the beast. Millions have died all through history as victims of a ferocity in their brothers and sisters which has inscribed on its shield the slogans of church and God, of nation and patriotism, of states' rights and the invasion of freedom.

Today Communism and racism are the twin scourges of the world. Both of them take naked hatred and give it a mystical intensity and a feeling of absolute rightness. Some of the nationalist movements, old and new, also have this quality, but they are barbaric only when they embody elements of racist hates. But if we have some perspective we shall see that the racists at Little Rock (unlike those in Algeria or Syria, and unlike the Communists) have no organized power behind their hate. That is why Little Rock, too, like Clinton and Baltimore at the opening of past school years, will take its place as part of the price our people are paying for coming to maturity. In time it will be a dim memory of past pain.

The Faubus stuff about the parallel with the Civil War seems terribly farfetched. To make a Fort Sumter out of Little Rock is to dignify a huddle of fanatics, fighting an inglorious rear-guard action, and make them into a historical movement. The Civil War was a clash of two systems of property, two theories of government, two ways of life. That is now over. The reason the rabble on the Little Rock sidewalks is so frantic is that they know that the law, economics and conscience of the nation have all moved the other way.

I don't underestimate the pain and strife still to come, in this town or that, this year or the next or the next. But did we ever expect that a major struggle, to give actual everyday equality to fifteen million of our people, could be accomplished without pain and tears? We Americans have a curious feeling that tragedy cannot be part of our lives, and we are surprised when it breaks in. We seem to believe that, outside the economic market place, we can get things without paying for them. We can't.

But it is worth the price. I am writing this in Athens, where the idea of freedom was first given shape. Despite centuries of tragic world history it is one of the great ideas that has survived in the world—that and the idea of the Jewish and Christian religions that all men are equal before their God. It will take more than the screams of the Little Rock crowd to drown out the validity of these ideas.

August 29, 1958

The one man who wasn't there—in that drafty and impossible Supreme Court chamber where the voices of counsel and judges are hopelessly lost, but where something majestic manages nonetheless to come through—was Governor Orval Faubus.

He should have been there. It was like trying to play *Othello* without Iago, or *Richard II* without Richard. For Orval Faubus is the symbol of the barbaric forces of counterrevolution that have been unleashed in the South in response to the great constitutional revolution on Negro education. He is also the symbol of the unleashers—a small group of cynical Southern whites who see their chance for power and attention in exploiting the crude frustrations and hates of a sick regional mentality.

Yet even if Faubus had been in court at Washington he would have cut a far less glorious figure than at Little Rock, where he deploys the state legislature like an army commander, convening and recessing it, presenting it with bills to sign, moving the schools and laws and politicians of the state around like a hillbilly Napoleon sticking pins into a field map.

In the Supreme Court, when his name was mentioned by the lawyer for the Little Rock School Board, Faubus was a more squalid figure. He was only an adult delinquent, whom the board's lawyer was sadly using to bolster his argument that the minds of the Arkansans were confused when they compared the Supreme Court decisions with the Faubus pronouncements. "I have never heard such an argument made in a court of justice before," said Chief Justice Warren. That disposed of that.

For three and a half hours, in the Supreme Court, two counsel and the Solicitor General talked gravely before the nine judges, trying to use logic and stay within the frame of reason. The nub of the school board's position, as presented by attorney Richard C. Butler, was that the board must get a stay of two and a half years because it cannot carry on the education of white and Negro children together without incurring violence. And, Butler added, if you have violence you don't have education.

It is the best argument that can be made today for the program of delay as a way of adjusting to the law. It was, incidentally, strengthened from a strange source at President Eisenhower's press conference, when the President reneged on his earlier position that he could take no stand on desegregation, and finally gave his own view that integration ought to go slower.

But Butler's isn't a good enough argument. The Justices riddled it with their questions. If the courts now choose to retreat before the threat of violence in Little Rock, they will invite a similar tactic of violence in every Southern city and state. And if the school board argues—through Butler—that education in a frame of violence is not education, one must ask: What kind of education is it for Southern children, white and Negro alike, when they are shown that a mob of juvenile and adult delinquents can defeat the conscience and the will of the American nation as expressed through law?

If we can break away from these formal, legal and rational arguments, and take a long view of what has been happening in the past five years, it takes on the form of a vast battle for the direction of American policy on the shaping of our children's minds.

On one side there has been no less than a revolution by law, in which the weak and temporary doctrine of *Plessy v. Ferguson* has been wholly supplanted by the clear and firm doctrine of the great school decision. On the other side there has been a revolution—or, better, a counterrevolution—of terror and destructiveness, engaging the worst energies of the South, pushing the Faubusards to the fore, isolating the liberals, making the position even of the moderates one that requires a measure of courage today.

I want to be very explicit about the nature of this second revolution, or counterrevolution. It is as surely sabotage as the blowing up of gasoline storage tanks by Algerian saboteurs in France. But it is a worse form of sabotage, because the raw material being set aflame is not gasoline—which is expendable and can be replaced—but the minds and hearts of Southern children, which can never be replaced but when once scarred are scarred forever, black and white alike.

Suppose Faubus does act to shut the high schools of Little Rock, or of the whole state; how long can the South endure if it continues to sabotage its children? And how long will it be before the decent Southerners express—in the great words William Pitt once used—their "eternal abhorrence of such preposterous and enormous principles," and find some way "to save us from this pollution"?

September 14, 1958

The Supreme Court decided, as everyone expected, that constitutional law cannot retreat before the show of violence, and that constitutional rights cannot be postponed because a demagogue Governor incites the people to rebellion against them.

There is a defect in the American political system when considered as a system of federalism. The Supreme Court has the power of final decision as between individual rights and the government, and as between the states and the Federal government. But where something like the desegregation of schools is concerned, it must get someone to administer the process of opening the schools ("with all deliberate speed") to the Negro children.

The judicial agents whom the Supreme Court chose to make the decisions about the speed or slowness of desegregation in each community were the Federal district judges. The administrative agents had to be the local school boards, because they control the educational system.

That is where the defect comes in. The local school board like the one in Little Rock has two masters. One is the Supreme Court, whose decisions it must apply, but the other is the state government, which has administrative and legislative power over the schools of the entire state. Caught between the two the Little Rock School Board tried to maneuver between them. But when Governor Faubus made a ruthless battleground of Little Rock the board lost whatever fighting spirit it may have had, threw up its hands and begged the Federal courts for a two-and-a-half-year delay.

It failed to get it. But the question remains: What will other school boards do, in other states whose governors take the Faubus way of organizing violence against Negro children? Shall the whole constitutional revolution in education, which promised finally to fulfill the dream of equal access for children of all races, collapse because it is built on the frail local school boards, whose members are especially vulnerable to whipped-up local feeling?

Where did things go wrong? There are a number of men, including some law professors and a majority of state supreme-court judges, who believe that the Supreme Court should never have ruled as it did in the first place in *Brown v. Board of Education.*

I don't hold with them. The issue had to be resolved strongly or not at all. Those who speak darkly of the Dred Scott case show their ignorance of one crucial difference: The Dred Scott decision was fragmented into nine pieces, with each judge writing a separate opinion. The school case was decided by a unanimous court, speaking with one voice, one conscience, one judgment.

In one sense the court made a miscalculation. It did not foresee the full extent of the counterrevolution that would develop in the Deep South. Nor did it foresee the miserable failure of the Administration in Washington to back up the decision by moral authority and by the necessary enforcement machinery. In other words, the court did not calculate on the gravity of two important political developments—one in the form of organized state violence, the other in the form of the abdication of national leadership.

There are actually two groups in the South with which both the court and the President must now deal. One is the Faubians, the other the Fabians.

The Fabians are people like the members and the counsel of the Little Rock School Board. They are men of good will, moderate, decent in their willingness to go along with a decision they don't like. They have been scared by the violence but have no philosophy and no plan of action. All they know is that they need time and want delay. That is why I call them the Fabians, after the Roman leader— "Fabius the delayer"—who tried to trade time for survival.

While the Fabians want to go slow, terribly slow, the Faubians don't want to go at all. They don't really care about gaining time, although a delay in enforcement would play into their hands and help them to consolidate their victory. What they want is the same thing that the Mosleyites of the recent anti-Jamaican riots want in England, and the same thing the apartheid leaders want in South Africa. They want to put the Negroes "in their places" and perpetuate a system of higher and lower status.

If their reactionary strategy works, it will spread over the world by a chain process. Thus the coming struggle is more than a struggle for power, or justice, or even the rule of law. It is a struggle between two views of whether human beings can live together, be it in Little Rock, Brooklyn, London or Johannesburg.

October 1, 1958

The most delicious item in an otherwise grim school situation was the posting of signs on the Little Rock high schools announcing "This

School Closed by Order of the Federal Government"—and misspelling it "Goverment." It raises some reflections on the high resolve of Governor Faubus and his clan that government of illiterates, by illiterates and for illiterates shall not perish from the South. And it opens up a forbidding prospect of how the signs of the future will look and spell if the schools should be closed for years in order to guarantee the racial purity of the children of the South.

It is a consoling reflection that the same America which produced Orval Faubus also produced Earl Warren. Faubus said, in response to the whiplash of the Supreme Court's most recent opinion, that he has not surrendered, does not surrender and will not surrender. That is good unreconstructed Confederate talk. But the fact is that Faubus, for all his gesturing and posturing of defiance, has met not only his match but his master. Chief Justice Warren may not be as great a legal scholar as some of his colleagues, nor does he possess the spare, limpid style of a Holmes; yet he does possess courage and tenacity and— above all—the resourcefulness which has enabled him thus far to out- maneuver Faubus as well as outargue him.

There can be little question that the latest Supreme Court opinion contained strategic elements, as indeed most of the historic Supreme Court decisions have done. The court was careful to stress its unanimity, putting the ruling in the form of an "opinion of the court," with every member participating in it, and reminding any doubters that the three newest Justices, appointed since the school case was first decided, join their brethren both in the original decision and in the newest one.

On another score, too, the court went beyond its ordinary function. Not only did it strike down the petition for a delay in integration; it also warned Faubus, Almond and Co. that it will tolerate no evasion of the law. The "massive resisters" of the South have not been quite as ingenious in their maneuverings as they had advertised themselves to be. They are caught in an impossible situation. No one denies that they can—as administrators of the state's schools—close the schools and presumably keep them closed. They can close them, all right, but they can't reopen them on their own terms. They cannot get the teachers to come in defiance of the Supreme Court ruling.

Thus it would look as if the governors and the Supreme Court had fought each other to a standstill, neither of them being yet able to re- open the schools in the way it wants. Yet the smell of long-run victory is on the side of the court. Faubus can't win because the voice of the law and of conscience, and the logic of American economic and cultural change, are aligned against him.

Surely the governors must see that they have allowed the fight about schools-or-no-schools to occupy the center of the stage, which once was occupied by the plea of the Southerners that they have a constitutional right to their "peculiar institution" of segregation.

Nor have they reckoned with the strength of the American belief in education of some sort. When the high schools are shut, a good many things happen. Colleges get worried about whether they will accept the high-school graduates who have had their education shrunk in this fashion. Parents get worried about what will happen to their children in their plans for a higher education. Teachers get worried about how valid their teaching contracts are. School boards get worried about opening themselves to contempt of court. Investors get worried about putting their money into local school bonds.

A demagogic governor may be smart, but there is little he can do to offset the impact of such forces. And when, in addition, parents start getting tired of having the kids lolling around the house or clustered on street corners or around jukeboxes, the segregationists may have second thoughts about their no-compromise position.

If the ultimate issue is going to be fought out between integrated schools and no schools, I have no doubt that the integrated schools will win.

Williamsburg, Va., October 6, 1958

The *Virginian-Pilot* of Norfolk and Portsmouth reports interviews with four members of the six-member Norfolk School Board. While they are for segregated schools, all four of them say clearly that they would, in the words of their leader, "much rather have a minimum amount of integration" than no schools at all. The fact that the four have spoken out means that other school board members in the South may repair to the standard they have raised. Then what will happen to the Almonds and Faubuses when their ramparts crumble?

The close-the-schools strategy of Governors Faubus and Almond may thus prove a fatal one for them. As long as they are damning and defying the Federal government, in the spirit of "unreconstructed" Confederate rebels, they could pose and strut as leaders of a resistance movement. Even when Faubus was inciting white students to violence in the integrated high schools, he held the offensive. But once the governors decided to close the schools rather than allow equal justice before the law, they had to move to the defensive. For by closing the schools they are using the children of the South, white and Negro alike, as pawns in their political struggle against the Supreme Court. The people of the South are now beginning to ask themselves how high a price they are willing to pay in following Faubus and Almond, and whether it is worth the cost in their children's lives and futures.

What has happened is that the cult of states' rights and white supremacy has crashed headlong into the cult of the child. It was this belief in the child, and in the conditions essential to his mental health, which made the Supreme Court judges decide as they did in the great school case. Now we are confronted by the narrower but even more tenacious belief that American children must have open and not closed schools, whatever their nature.

This may prove to be a turning point in the resistance movement. It is something that the Almonds and Faubuses cannot blame on the N.A.A.C.P. or on the Northern liberals or on the Supreme Court. It comes from their own local people. And it comes not out of any political theory or social doctrine, but quite simply out of the conviction that children must have schools, and that public schools of some sort must be kept open for them.

The governors, in their efforts to turn the school clock backward, have forced a choice on their people. They are getting a surprise. They are now discovering that if the choice is between integrated schools and no schools at all, the local school boards may choose integrated schools, no matter how distasteful the pill may be.

I have been using my Virginia visit as the occasion for reading an earlier spokesman of the liberal South and a more recent one. The greatest of the early liberals was George W. Cable, a novelist, who brought into currency the phrase "the Silent South." There is an excellent new anthology of his writings, *The Negro Question,* edited by Arlin Turner (Doubleday). The other is a courageous book, *The Southern Heritage* (Knopf), by J. M. Dabbs, a white Southerner who is the head of the Southern Regional Council.

Cable, who endangered his career as a popular novelist by his outspokenness on the Negro question, ended in failure. He wrote and talked his heart out trying to get his fellow Southerners to see that the Negro wanted civil rights, not social kinship or intermarriage, and that the denial of these rights hurt the whites as badly as it did the Negroes. He finally had to leave New Orleans and move North.

As for Dabbs, I fear that the Dabbses have grown fewer in these recent years. A former Southern liberal called Virginius Dabney wrote a recent piece for *Life* which was an apologia for the segregationists. He took a column of mine about the school delinquents in New York and ripped it out of its context in an effort to show that when you mix the races in the schools you get violence.

I never said this or meant it. Dabney failed to understand what I have been trying to say in all my school columns—that legal justice for children in schools, white and black alike, will not solve all the problems of bringing up our youngsters, but it will at least do something to heal the scar left by inequality and injustice. We can take care of the rest.

So the Dabneys have fallen away and other summer soldiers and sunshine liberals have grown shivery with cold in their exposed position. Yet now the Norfolk School Board members seem to show that there is still a Silent South for whom the Faubuses and the Almonds do not speak.

They may yet make themselves heard. I do not minimize the insight and the courage it will take. The South had a great tragedy cutting across its history in the Civil War and the Reconstruction. One might have thought that the tragedy would purify it of its white-supremacy attitude. But it does not always follow. Sometimes tragedy deepens and purges a person, sometimes it only desensitizes and destroys him. The Southern tragedy desensitized too many of the Southern spokesmen and people.

The silent ones must regain the capacity for feeling before they learn how to speak out.

7. Judges and Principles

April 27, 1959

SINCE DAVID LAWRENCE in the *U.S. News* has seized upon a passage in a Harvard Law School lecture by Professor Herbert Wechsler for purposes which I suspect were not the purposes of the lecturer, I must step in and give my own view of the issue raised. I shall be far more critical of Wechsler's reasoning and conclusions than Lawrence is likely to be, for Lawrence eagerly embraces anyone who dissents from the Supreme Court school decision in the Brown case. But I find myself in basic sympathy with Wechsler's desire to get "principled" decisions in the law, as I do with most of his social values.

Wechsler's paper was read as the Oliver Wendell Holmes lecture, and I share with him his admiration for Holmes, who is one of my culture heroes, and who in his judicial opinions tried to practice an austerity of mind that would disregard his own social or economic views and stick to principle. But from there on I must dissent from Wechsler, who in turn is dissenting from most of the current liberal thinking about the school case.

Wechsler's is a long, forty-page paper of which the last ten pages are on the Supreme Court cases involving anti-Negro discrimination and only the last four on the school case. He pays one kind of tribute to the major recent liberal decisions involving the "white primary," the restrictive housing covenant and the school segregation cases, saying that "they have the best chance of making an enduring contribution to the quality of our society of any that I know in recent years." But he goes on to ask "how far they rest on neutral principles," for it is the burden of his paper that judges must be neutral.

I gather that Wechsler agrees with the social principles of the Warren court in the school case but he does not believe that the legal principle on which the decision rests is neutral enough to stand up as good law.

I want first to examine what objections he has to the law of the case, and then I want to go back to the broader question of Wechsler's version of Auden's "double man"—the schizoid judge who is split right down the center between being a man and being a judge.

As is well known, the unanimous opinion in the Brown case held that the *Plessy v. Ferguson* idea of "separate but equal" facilities can have no place in public education, because the very fact of segregating children in the schools makes them inherently unequal and harms them and their growth by leaving on them the scar of inferiority. To bolster this view the Supreme Court had the evidence of the whole trend of psychological thinking. What is wrong with this? For Wechsler what is wrong is that this is not good principle—legal, or even psychological. He points out that white children are also hurt by segregated schools—which is true, but only makes the case against such schools stronger. He says that some Negroes may prefer segregation, if it means peace in the community.

Alas, it is always true in a minority's struggle for its rights that there are some who can't take it or who prefer the ghetto, but their timidity should not chain those whose passion for equality is strong enough to endure the battle. But when I find Wechsler quoting from *Plessy v. Ferguson* the passage saying that if "enforced segregation stamps the colored race with a badge of inferiority" it is because the Negroes choose "to put that construction on it," I rub my eyes. When the Nazis compelled the Jews to wear the Star of David on their arms as a "badge of inferiority," they were not ashamed of the Star of David, but it nonetheless left a scar on them because it singled them out for a denial of the rights of human beings.

Wechsler's own solution of the problem of the school case is that, at bottom, it is "freedom of association" that is involved. And using that test, he points out that while the Negro children are denied the freedom to associate with whites, it is equally bad to force upon the white children the compulsion of associating with the Negroes. Here he finds himself stymied by the opposing claims and confesses his inability to write his own opinion between them. Thus his own "neutral" principle turns out to be frustrated and not very useful.

In my own mind it is no more "neutral" than the one the court used—the principle of what harm is inherently done to children of both races. The court's position has the advantage of being based on a great principle of the American experience—the principle of equal access to equal opportunities.

The Negroes are not asking for the right to associate, in the sense of social equality; they want only equality before the law. The whites

can refuse to invite them or their children into their homes, refuse to
eat with them, court them, marry them. They can refuse whatever is
in the province of a private person to refuse, but they cannot deny
them the public rights due them as citizens of the community. For
without this equal access to equal opportunity, no child can develop
his potentials or have a chance to grow and fulfill himself as a person.

That is my own principle, both legal and social. I don't split them
from each other. I try to apply to law the insights from every area—
whether economics, politics or psychology. If I were a judge I should
ask, as Holmes did, whether my philosophy holds together and flows
from the whole American social experience, or whether it is part of a
prejudice or preference I must overcome.

8. A Dream Deferred

April 8, 1959

ALTHOUGH my own vote, if I had the suffrage, would have been cast
for *JB*, I'm glad that *A Raisin in the Sun* squeezed through to get the
Critics Award for the best American play, and that the prize went
for the first time to a Negro playwright. Lorraine Hansberry, dealing
here with a theme as homely and craggy as the life of a Negro working-class family in the Chicago South Side, has shown a quality of fire
which uses a basically realistic method but fuses it with a streak of humor and imaginativeness that falls just short of poetry.

Outwardly *Raisin* tells the story of what happens in the Younger
family when the compensation check of $10,000 for the death of Mr.
Younger arrives, and what happens to the son—Walter Younger—
when he tries to use it in a business scheme that will get him out of his
chauffeur rut and make the family rich.

But on an inner arc the play is about a dream. You get a clear clue to
this from the title, which is taken from a poem of Langston Hughes':

> *What happens to a dream deferred?*
> *Does it dry up*
> *Like a raisin in the sun?* . . .
> *Or does it explode?*

The Hughes lines are part of a long poem of Harlem today, with
varied meter and beat, called *Montage of a Dream Deferred,* and
you will find it handily in an anthology, *The Langston Hughes Reader*
(George Braziller). As you read further, you will find Hughes singing,
"There's a certain amount of nothing in a dream deferred," and a certain amount also of "impotence," and of "confusion." In fact:

There's liable to be confusion
When a dream gets kicked around.

Raisin is a striking confirmation of these leads from Hughes. It is
in many ways a deceptive play. It reminded me at first of Clifford
Odets—a kind of *Awake and Sing* or *Golden Boy* in sepia, with a
tradition-directed mother, an explosive dreamer of a boy, the struggle
of the generations, the sense of tragedy in which an ethnic minority
is enveloped.

But when I thought harder, I saw that Miss Hansberry had not
copied from anyone, whether Odets or Langston Hughes, but had
succeeded in one of the hardest tasks a playwright could confront:
She has portrayed Negro life in America, with all its pressures, pulls
and heartbreak, yet she has done it without hysteria, with a quiet yet
unrelenting strength; and she has made persons out of her characters,
not categories.

I must confess that my own preference is for plays that are freer
in method, less literal, less rooted in realism, more daring in the exploration of the wilder phases of the imagination. There was one scene
in *Raisin*—in which Walter and his college girl sister, Beneatha, do an
African jungle dance—which lifted me for a moment out of the circle
of description and reflection. But like a respectable girl who shows
for a moment the streak of Jezebel in her, the author quickly resumed
her proper poise, and the trembling of the veil was over.

The dream deferred is Walter's. Examine it—the dream of getting
away from his despised job, of setting up a business with a liquor license, of building it up big, of having pearls to hang around the neck
of his wife, of enabling his young son to drive to school in a taxi—
and you will see that it isn't particularly Walter's dream as a Negro, nor
yet an intensely private one.

It is a dream that comes out of the larger culture of the whites in
which Walter has been caught up, just as George, one of Beneatha's
suitors, has been caught up in it. (The other suitor, a young Nigerian
intellectual, is captivatingly portrayed, yet the whole theme of the
African heritage and possible future of the Negro is marginal to the
main theme of the play.) Walter's dream is a middle-class dream,
and it reminded me of a memorable sentence from E. Franklin Fra-
zier's *Black Bourgeoisie:* "The black bourgeoisie suffers from nothingness because when Negroes attain middle-class status, their lives generally lose both content and significance."

Thus one goes back to the Langston Hughes jingle, "There's a certain amount of nothing in a dream deferred."

Walter struggles through the "nothingness," yes, and the impotence
and the confusion, too. His dream gets kicked around. His mother
has a dream, too, of a house in a better neighborhood. The dreams

clash, and out of the conflict and the resolution of the clashing dreams Walter finds himself.

But just as the dream was never really his, but the dream of the white culture, so it may be a weakness of the play that he finds himself not through himself but through his mother. He is, in effect, shamed into maturing by his mother, when she dares him to humiliate himself in the presence of his own son. The theme Helen Lynd has stressed, that in a moment of shame one may confront and discover one's true self, is illustrated in the magnificent closing scene.

One almost forgets—so deceptively simple and human is Miss Hansberry's writing—that the story is not only about the Younger family but in a sense about the whole Negro people in America, about its heritage, and its trials and confusions, and its dream of equality deferred.

THE JEWS: ORDEAL AND FREEDOM

1. The Furnaces at Dachau

Munich, June 29, 1949

To GO to Germany without visiting Dachau would be a sin worse than ignorance and moral callousness—a sin of willful blindness.

I saw Dachau on a flawless sunlit afternoon. You enter it now as you enter any American military post—driving past white-helmeted military guards. Gleaming in the sun from a distance, the pink-stuccoed buildings that used to house the Nazi camp commanders look now like a cluster of Italian villas. You catch your breath and ask, "Can those be the houses where tortures were conceived and death was planned on a massive scale?"

As you drive along—it seems endlessly—you feel yourself surrounded by a forest of the dead. The air, they tell me, is still pestilential; and even the doctors, with all their science, are half inclined to believe that the essences of death which once came out of the smokestack and filled the air are not easily extirpated.

Here is a "hanging tree," and farther away another. Here are the gallows, and by them a memorial sign in four languages. Nearby is the pistol range, where marksmanship could be practiced on living targets.

Suddenly you look up and you see a high, well-made brick chimney piercing the sky. It is the only bold architectural feature of the whole landscape, and you know you have come to the thing itself—the crematorium. Near it is a sign with a simple and classic inscription: "This Area Is Being Retained as a Shrine to the 238,000 Individuals Who Were Cremated Here."

I stood a while and studied it. I found it hard to keep the sentence in my mind. When a single human life—one that you know and have nurtured—is an infinity, how much are 238,000 human lives? Are they 238,000 infinities?

You walk in. It is a large furnace room. There are four brick furnaces in it, two in the center, one on each side. Each furnace is big enough to hold two bodies at once. There are carriers, shaped like hospital stretchers, still standing in each opening. They will creak when you push them on their iron rollers.

Next to the furnace room is a shower room. This is where the naked ones were driven to have their pores opened by the hot steam, so that the gas would take quicker effect and would not be wasted. Next to the shower room is the big low-ceilinged gas chamber, with the jets still in the ceiling and the ventilators still in the walls. The sequence is clear enough: shower room, gas chamber, furnaces. Outside is a shed where the ashes were shoveled out and heaped up.

There is not much to say. The thousands of penciled scrawls on the wall, made by those who had loved the dead and had come later to visit their death chamber—scrawls with names in every language, Polish, Czech, French, Yiddish, Russian—these are words enough.

But one sentence will stand out in my mind. It is on the wall of the crematorium itself, in German, addressed by the commanders of the camp to their employees. Here is what it says:

REINLICH IST HIER PLICHT
DESHALB
HANDE WASCHEN NICHT VERGESSEN

(*Cleanliness Is a Duty Here. Therefore Do Not Forget to Wash Your Hands.*)

As we drove away I turned to my German driver and could not help glancing at his hands. Then, an American, I looked hard at my own.

2. Life and Death of a Young Girl

June 24, 1952

ANNE FRANK was thirteen when she began to keep her diary. She was fifteen when she died in a Nazi concentration camp. Her crime, for which she died, was to have been born of Jewish parents. Her talent, which blossomed amidst the squalor of the back rooms of the house in Amsterdam where eight people hid for two years from the Nazis, was to bring to life with her pen whatever situation and character she touched.

Her *Diary of a Young Girl* (Doubleday) is part of the tragic underground literature of the martyred Jewish millions of Europe. Anne was too young to know much about either Jews or tragedy, but what will make the book a little classic is the portrait it gives of the heart's awakening of a teen-ager. It is an artless yet almost perfect self-portrait of an adolescent bursting into flower in the sunless quarters of a hideout, surrounded by fear and hate, and in daily danger of death.

In this unlikely setting Anne Frank falls in love with Peter, who is two years older than herself, sits with him in the evening on a packing box propped against pillows, notes her first kiss, talks incessantly with Peter ("I explained everything about girls to him and didn't hesitate to discuss the most intimate things"), exchanges curious letters with her sister Margot to console her about being "the odd one out" whom Peter has not chosen, writes (again inside the prison-household) to her father to assert her independence, cries in shame when he chides her, agonizes over the morality of petting ("what would my girl friends say about it if they knew that I lay in Peter's arms, my heart against his chest, my head on his shoulders and with his head against mine"). And always, always, she puts everything down in her "Dear Kitty" communiqués to her Diary.

Anne's parents came of wealthy Jewish stock, but they lost everything and finally, to escape being sent to the death camps, they hid in a set of back rooms behind a camouflaged doorway next to the offices of Mr. Frank's firm. Another family and an elderly dentist hide with them. Amidst the doubts, agonies and ecstasies of her sexual awakening, Anne is also aware of the human comedy of eight ill-assorted people thrown together in close quarters, grating on each other, sometimes hating each other, the women quarreling about how to bring up children, the men holding forth on the progress of the war outside, the constant richly human counterpoint of ugliness and tenderness.

She has given us a thumbnail portrait gallery of the little ménage: Mrs. van Daan, vain and foolish, quarreling with her husband, picking the best food for herself, longing for sweets, flirting with the dentist; Mr. van Daan, always talking like an oracle about the war; Dr. Dussel ("His Lordship"), the "pedantic doctor," "trousers wrapping his chest, red coat, black bedroom slippers, and horn-rimmed spectacles," taking implacable possession of the common toilet at his regular "sitting times," five or six times a day; Mrs. Frank, whom Anne has no warmth for; Mr. Frank, whom she adores, withdrawing into a corner with his beloved Dickens; Margot, once pretty, who wilts and fades in the dark quarters; and finally Anne herself, "a little bundle of contradictions"—Anne the chatterbox, the sassy little girl who talks back, but hungry for love and school and the sight of the sun and the unfolding of life.

Her great quality is her devouring eye, which sees the telltale trait, the revealing situation. "My greatest wish is to become a journalist some day," she tells her diary, "and later on a famous writer." She knew—how could she not know?—what her literary gift was. "I want to go on living after my death. And therefore I am grateful to God for giving me this gift."

But the Nazis willed otherwise and broke into the hideout and sent all its occupants to the death camps. Only Mr. Frank got back. Anne herself died at Bergen-Belsen. With all her startlingly mature insights, she was still a little girl who, when the air raids came, used to run in her nightgown and bury herself in her father's bed.

The Germans snuffed out her talent, along with her life. What they were not able to kill was the life force that her diary reveals.

3. The Animated Fossil

November 19, 1956

IT ISN'T OFTEN that a book review is written by a whole people in action, but that is what has happened to Arnold Toynbee's massive ten-volume work, *A Study of History*. Toynbee, as everyone knows by now, treated the history of the Jews as that of a "fossil civilization" —inert, petrified, dead. Recent events in the Middle East would suggest that if Israel is any test at all the Jews are a very animated fossil indeed.

At a time of great actions it is important to set those actions in perspective. Israel has had a "bad press" in the past few weeks— largely, I think, because we have seen its action of marching into the Sinai desert in the too narrow frame of the breaking of the armistice lines. If we enlarged the frame to take in the whole experience of the Israelis at the hands of Egypt and the Arabs, and then enlarged it again to take in the whole experience of the Jews in history, we would not be so swift to criticize and so narrow in judgment as the press has been. Maurice Samuel's eloquent answer to Toynbee on the Jews, *The Professor and the Fossil* (Knopf), was written and published before these events. But it gives us the frame we need, exactly because it takes the subtlest argument that has ever been woven against the Jews and Israel, and in the process of refuting that argument it roams all over Jewish history and culture.

It is Toynbee's belief that the Jews started well but then went off the track and got cooped up on a siding of history. They started with a great insight into the religion of One God and had a burst of creativity at the time of the prophets. But then they rejected Christianity, and by that rejection they were doomed to sterility. Since then (so Toynbee's case runs) they have survived as a people largely as a response to the challenge of the cruelties and discriminations practiced against them. Toynbee deplores those cruelties, especially the Nazi crematoria. Yet he believes that, even in the act of surviving, Jewish civilization has been a fossil.

It has, he says, adopted the ways of violence used by its enemies, and its treatment of the Arab refugees has been no different from the Nazi treatment of the Jews. It has lost the arts of gentleness and of acceptance, and in the Zionist movement it has adopted the nationalism of the West, thus losing its role as a "peculiar people" and becoming assimilated to all the others.

It is, as I have said, a subtle argument, and Toynbee's show of erudition and his great authority have carried considerable weight with those who have read him or half read him. Before Maurice Samuel gets through with Toynbee's case there is pitifully little left standing of the whole elaborate structure, and the ground is strewn with what Samuel calls Toynbee's "confusions, prejudices, and intellectual distortions."

I have read other criticisms of Toynbee. In fact, there is a valuable recent symposium, *Toynbee and History,* edited by M. F. Ashley Montagu (Porter Sargent), which gathers together some thirty essays in criticism, with almost every author rejecting Toynbee's work in the special field that *he* knows best. But none leaves the field as completely a shambles as Samuel does, with his swordplay of logic and history, learning, wit, irony and passionate anger.

I will leave to the reader to discover what Samuel does with the texts he quotes from Toynbee, and the pitiless way he grinds them to pieces. Yet the real answer to Toynbee cannot lie in the textual analysis alone, effective as that is. It cannot lie in the logic and learning that any one man uses and what he says in composing a book about a book.

The real answer lies rather in what the Jews *are* and *have been,* in what they have done and the culture they have built. That is why the most moving and persuasive parts of Samuel's book are not the polemical parts but those in which he weaves back and forth over the whole sweep of Jewish history, giving vignettes of the prophets and the Pharisees, of the kings and their hosts in battle, of Alexandria and Spain, of Maimonides and the great rabbi-teachers, of the wrestling with God and the fashioning of a language, of the great Chassidic revival and the Jewish communities of Russia and Poland, of the creative tension involved in remaining alert to God and their experience as a people and retaining their awareness-in-history.

If the reader does not feel this he may still be intellectually convinced by Samuel's argument, but it will be all in the head. I suppose the trouble with answering any anti-Jewish case, whether Toynbee's or the cruder ones, is that you must feel yourself part of the answer.

Ben-Gurion and the Israelis have given the answer, by facing death and opening themselves to life. In a sense their whole recent adventure reads like the Old Testament in action. But it is a mistake to see it— as the Toynbeeans do—as simply another example of nationalism gone rampant. It is far more. It is the whole of Jewish experience and the Jewish ethos expressing itself at a moment of history, rejecting the role of eternal victim, rejecting passive acquiescence in the indignities visited on Jews, asserting not just the will to survive (which can be barren if it is only physical) but the will to fulfill the meaning of history.

Khrushchev said yesterday that "Israel carries no weight in the world"—which may be only a Russian commissar's way of saying it is a fossil. But I suspect that this fossil will still be alive when the Kremlin and its tyranny are dust.

4. The Web of Hatred and the Web of Freedom

June 5, 1950

IT SAYS HERE in this pamphlet spread in front of me that everyone in the know about F.D.R.'s death knows that he committed suicide. In fact, we are asked to believe that there were even eye witnesses. "I know a man who saw Roosevelt blow his brains out," said a man to the author of the pamphlet, who relays it at third remove to us. The only problem that still bothers the pamphleteer is the motive for the suicide. There are, he says, two schools of thought. One says F.D.R. was so conscience-stricken by his own crimes that he "could bear it no longer and ended it all." The second says that he was a conscienceless gangster who knew the game was up and "took the coward's out."

The pamphlet I am quoting from is called *Suicide,* with a subtitle, "An Index to Blood Scandal in Washington, D. C." It was given me by a well-known Federal judge who picked it off his desk and held it between thumb and index finger for the slimy stuff it was. With a burst of courage, the man who wrote it signs himself "Mr. X." It is put out by the "Christian Nationalist Crusade," which is the name of Gerald L. K. Smith's mail-order anti-Semitic racket, with its headquarters in St. Louis.

The legends about F.D.R.'s death will survive the factual narratives about him. Not only are there stories that he killed himself; there is even a persistent legend that he never died at all, but is shut up even now in an insane asylum. The "proof" offered in this pamphlet is the fact that Roosevelt's body did not lie in state.

Here are some other fantasies from the pamphlet, which will never find their way into the histories for the very good reason that they are spun out of hate and delusion:

Did you know about James Forrestal—that he did not jump out of that Walter Reed Hospital window, but was pushed? So the pamphlet says. Who pushed him? The Jews, of course.

Did you know about John Winant—that his suicide was also due to the Jews? The mysterious author of the pamphlet says that after the war Winant wanted to tell the truth about what had happened, but he didn't dare, so he blew his brains out.

Did you know about Huey Long—that he was assassinated by the Jews, and that the assassination was plotted in the White House?

Did you know that Gerald Smith himself was "poisoned with arsenic" in 1947, presumably by the Jews? "Miraculously" he recovered, but "confidential police records" in a half-dozen cities reveal other plots to kill him, which would succeed if there were not hovering over him the special protection of God.

Did you know that General Patton did not die "accidentally" in that auto smash? He made the mistake of revealing that he had "a little black book" which would blow everything wide open when he got back to America. Hence he was murdered.

Did you know that "Westbrook Pegler might be murdered any night?"

So the pamphlet says, at any rate. Like the other spawn of its breed, it is part paranoia and part cunning. There are some people whose insanity takes the form of paranoid delusions—the constant belief that plots are being hatched against them and that they are always in danger of death. But I doubt whether many of the Gerald Smith and Joseph Kamp crowd belong among the genuine paranoiacs. Theirs is rather an open-eyed and deliberate attempt to exploit the plot psychosis from which too many Americans are already suffering.

May 1, 1951

New York, we are told with wearisome repetition, is not America but the archenemy of America—a veritable City of Treason.

That, I take it, is the main thesis of a rather violent letter from a Frank J. Merkt which the *Post* ran last week. It is drenched in hate for New York and its people.

Obviously this hostility to New York is not new. Anyone who has traveled in the United States over the years has run into it. Partly it is a resentment against New York's role as the intellectual center from which there fan out all over the nation the ideas, books, shows, magazines, radio and television programs, advertising, managerial patterns, intellectual movements that become the symbols of power and therefore the targets of rebellion. It is because of this power, real or fancied, that New Yorkers are so deeply suspected by other Americans—suspected, feared and not a little hated. The attacks on New York are one of the great national pastimes, especially in the South and Midwest, where it is sometimes a cloak for a defensive feeling of cultural backwardness and sometimes only a thin mask for the ugliest racist passions.

There used to be a fascist demagogue called Joe McWilliams who had great fun (and his audiences, too) by referring to the Jews as the "Eskimos." He would gloat with obvious hilarity on the time when all the "Eskimos" would be cleaned out of America, and his followers would howl with glee not only at the sentiment but also at the artistry with which his meaning was so cunningly concealed as well as revealed.

Am I wrong in sensing the same device in the letter I am discussing? The writer doesn't say "Eskimos," but there is a festering hatred behind his words which any student of racism at once recognizes.

He writes throughout on a warning note. "I tell you," he says (who is the "you"?), "that your days of influence are rapidly coming to a complete close, because the American people . . . are at last awake . . . are wise to you . . . America is awakened, and that means just one thing, or several. You and your friends in New York, Washington, and a few other points are finished, washed up, done—you're on the run at last . . . I've taken the time out to tell you this because I think it will make you a little frightened to know that there are people, little people like me, who are your enemies and who will not forget."

It sounds a little like "wave-of-the-future" stuff, like the Nazi warnings of the coming of *Der Tag,* or the Communist warnings of the impending revolutionary victory when every lamppost would have a capitalist or a liberal intellectual hanging from it.

May I add that I doubt whether New Yorkers will be particularly frightened by these menacing words of the Armageddon to come. For any reading of American history will show that none but the lonely hate-filled hearts will dare exclude any section of the nation from the continuing struggle for decent human relations, or arrogate to any section the monopoly claim to Americanism.

December 28, 1949

How does it come about that a people which has been able to produce an Einstein has had millions of its members massacred by hatred? This is one of the haunting questions that has baffled social thinkers over the centuries. Is there something about the fact that the Jews have numbered in their ranks creative intellects from Moses to Freud and Einstein—is there something about that fact that attracts to them the hatred of the haters? Or turn the question the other way around. Is there something about being the hunted and the hated which has caused the Jews to recoil on themselves, and out of that recoil to find the resources and the strength to turn into creators?

The latter theme was argued by the American social thinker Thorstein Veblen in a classic essay called "The Intellectual Pre-eminence of the Jews in Modern Europe." * Veblen contended that exactly because the Jews have been ghettoized and ringed around by the indict-

* For this essay, see *The Portable Veblen* (Viking), edited by myself.

ment of being aliens, they have been forced into an attitude of detachment and skepticism; and these qualities have enabled them as outsiders to question many things which the insiders have taken for granted. Hence their ability to make new discoveries that others have ignored because they have not asked the right questions.

It is just as hard to answer the other question—not why the Jews produce Einsteins, but why they are hated with such a persistent and murderous hatred. The answers have tended to be of two broad kinds. One is the economic answer, the other the psychological.

The economic—or sociological—theory is that anti-Semitism breaks out most virulently as a disease whenever and wherever you get the collapse of the normal economic structure. It tends to equate anti-Semitism with depressions and unemployment. It has held the field for some time, chiefly under the influence of the Marxist thinkers, who have seen in the decay of capitalism other forms of social decay as well. In its sharpest form it used to hold that anti-Semitism, as a weapon of fascist finance capital, was simply the last defense of a dying capitalism.

The psychological theory emphasizes what happens not so much in the economic and social system but inside the mind of the individual. It has developed as a theory chiefly under the influence of Sigmund Freud and the later psychoanalytical writers. It starts with people who, for whatever reason, think of themselves as failures and come to hate themselves for their inadequacy and frustration. Then comes what the Freudians call "projection." No mentally sick person can bear facing the fact of his inadequacies. He sets up "defense mechanisms" to protect himself against this fact. One of them is to project what he hates in himself onto others. The Jews have for centuries been the targets of this projection. The haters are the sick and inadequate people.

It is time we liberated ourselves from the exclusive emphasis on the economic. True, there are more mentally sick people when the economic struggle is severe. But the crucial enactments take place on the warped stage inside the shell of the human mind.

March 19, 1958

The hatred-warped hysteric who planted the bomb in the Nashville Jewish Center must have reckoned that this method of terrorism would scare the Jews out of supporting the struggle for Negro civil rights. He reckoned badly. The Jews as a people have had considerable experience with terrorist campaigns against them. They have lost many victims. In the process they have learned that the hate movements which use death and the threat of death cannot be appeased, and that the only way to keep from being destroyed by them is to stand up to them and fight.

"Everyone is guilty," an overexcited lady once shouted at a public hearing on subversives. The true hater would add that everyone is part of a conspiracy. Doubtless those who planted the bomb saw the Jews of Nashville as involved in some sort of conspiracy against the Southern way of white supremacy—and Christian too. There are two kinds of hatred involved in this act. One is racial hatred, directed against the Negroes. The other is religious and social hatred, directed against the Jews. It is one of the curious facts about them that one can be transformed into the other.

In fact, there is a whole pattern of connected hatreds in American life. The authors of *The Authoritarian Personality* discovered, in their interviews, that when you scratch an anti-Semite you are also likely to find the kind of person who hates Negroes, inveighs against labor, despises liberalism and is ready to sweep away the whole laborious structure of civil liberties in his drive for destruction.

Thus there is a web of hatreds. But similarly there is a web of freedom. One of the hardest things to learn, especially in a democracy where the appearance of evil is so deceptive, is that no minority group can offer another as a burnt sacrifice and thereby save its own skin. If you break the web of freedom at any important point, you leave it nakedly vulnerable at every other point. I think most Jews in the South are learning the lesson that their own freedoms will not survive the destruction of Negro rights. It is a lesson that needs to be learned, running the other way, by Negroes as well.

The terrible Jewish experiences of the cremation camps has made Jews everywhere more sensitive to the smell of totalitarianism. The Jewish Center in Nashville will be rebuilt. But if any Nashville Jew in a position of public trust had lost courage and betrayed his deepest impulses about the struggle for schools in which all children can get an equal chance to grow, he would have betrayed something that could never have been rebuilt.

The shocked reaction of the Nashville community as a whole to the bombing is a pretty healthy sign that the terrorism was the work of a few warped minds. It will prove a net gain if the jolt is drastic enough to make them see that the extremists are often merely those who carry all the way the logic of what their fellows talk about. When we have an intense campaign which makes the simple enforcement of our constitutional law a crime against the community, can we be truly surprised when it generates the extremism of the fanatic who vows to destroy "every nigger-loving place and nigger-loving person in Nashville"?

That is, for me, the meaning of the Nashville story. In the South there has historically been very little anti-Jewish feeling, partly because there have been few Jews, and a number of the Jewish families belong to the earlier rather than the later immigration and were integrated early into the local communities.

It may appear, at least to some Jews, very unwise to endanger this relatively privileged position by taking a stand on so touchy a subject as school desegregation. But such cautions have never worked in the history of the Jews, and they will not work now. Every person in the South, whether Protestant, Jewish or Catholic, has to decide where he stands as a person on the greatest issue of our time. He can find no refuge from decision by any anxiety about his group as a whole.

It is well to view even these dynamitings, moreover, as part of a nation that is breaking up the old caste system and is on the march toward a new equality. The bombings are a protest by the most backward and barbaric elements in the South against the fact of this progress. The great integrative force of American life is more powerful than the few paltry sticks of dynamite that a twisted mind placed in that community center.

THE DEMOCRATIC CLASS STRUGGLE: LABOR AND BUSINESS

1. The Devil and John L. Lewis

December 1, 1949

FOR ALMOST TWO HOURS last night I talked with John L. Lewis. What gave the talk something of a dramatic frame was that it ended just half an hour before the witching hour of midnight, at which the three-week resumption of work by the bituminous miners expired, and close to 400,000 miners went out on strike again.

Lewis has been described by some of the commentators as a man with frayed nerves and a harassed countenance, who has come to the end of his rope. If this is true, he gave no inkling of it to me. He spoke with confidence, and with that vivid flow of metaphor for which he is famous. He spoke in the mellow and reflective tones of a labor leader who has been in many fights before this and won most of them.

We have known each other for some years, and Lewis knows that I have not always been in sympathy with him. I have opposed his vendetta with Franklin Roosevelt, his isolationism during the Great Debate which preceded World War II, his backing of Republican Presidential candidates, his wartime strikes and the iron hand with which he used to maintain his power in his union. He knows these things about my views.

Throughout the conversation he kept using the metaphors of military strategy. He considers the present struggle over the welfare fund and wages only one battle in a larger campaign to reach the union's objectives. He is utterly a realist in assessing the strength and weakness of the coal operators, as well as those of the union. "I am not unmindful of the human equation," he told me with a wry smile.

I questioned him, quite naturally, about what tactics he would use to get out of this dilemma. "For every practical problem that presents itself," he said, "there's always an answer, if—" and here he smiled— "you can think of it." He added slowly and with emphasis, "We can't be beaten."

I taxed Lewis with some of the criticisms which students of the coal industry and the miners' union have made of him, and the power he has in the union. He defended himself against the charges of dictatorship, of egomania, of lust for power, of suppressing opposition within the union. The miners, he said, "are not afraid of anyone, least of all of me." Whatever one may think of this, the fact is that Lewis' position with the mineworkers is strong. They don't follow his advice about how to vote in Presidential elections. But they feel that this man is a doughty fighter for their interests, and that their position now is infinitely better than at the time when he began the fight.

Some commentators have suggested that Lewis knows his next tactical move, but not much beyond that. They may be right. "I am not one of those fellows," he told me, "who knows beyond peradventure what he will do next week and next month and next year. It would be foolish to be that rigid. There are always a number of alternative things to do, and which of them you will choose depends on the facts at that particular time." Which means that, like his old opponent Franklin Roosevelt, whom he hated with a lusty hatred, Lewis still plays by ear. And he has always played by ear.

But in long-run terms, he is certain that "labor can't sit still and rest on its laurels. It always has to be fighting to participate in the returns from the increased industrial efficiency to which it contributes." The failure to carry on that kind of aggressive and continuing fight, he thinks, was one of the things that was wrong with British labor in the last few decades. The result was that the efficiency of the whole coal-mining industry was reduced, and the owners withdrew their royalties without any fight being made to have some of it plowed back into better mining machinery. In this sense the interests of miners are bound up with the interests of the whole coal industry and the whole economy.

I felt at the end that I had been talking with the last of the Romans. Whatever one may think of his politics and tactics, Lewis is a labor leader who still carries over some of the vigor and imagination that made the America of the nineteenth century what it was. When he leaves the scene, American labor and the whole stage of American public life will never again be the same.

December 6, 1949

Today being the day when John L. Lewis meets the hard-coal operators, I want to ask a question of my fellow newspapermen, columnists and commentators, especially the liberals among them.

Why is it that men and women who care about trade-unions and the labor movement, and who will fight hard in support of legitimate strikes based on legitimate grievances, always make an exception in the case of Lewis and the coal miners? Why are they so obsessed with their resentments against Lewis himself that in effect they join the enemies not only of Lewis but also of the miners, and make a half-million men and their families the victims of their obsession?

Whatever you may think of Lewis—of his paternalism, his cockiness, his vendetta with F.D.R., the running feud with the Truman Administration, the isolationist streak in him, his iron control over his union—is there any doubt that the miners' cause is a just cause?

These men work in a savage industry, where industrial accidents come with barbarous frequency. If a union health-and-welfare fund has any meaning in any industry, it has its greatest meaning in this one. These men work in an industry of chaotic cutthroat competition, especially in the bituminous fields. They work also in an industry which in many ways is a dying one. The new sources of fuel and power have come in to undercut the coal industry. There are not enough markets to keep all the mines working, and not enough work to keep all the miners working.

These are the objective facts about a savage, chaotic, dying industry. When some of the numerous anti-Lewis crowd among the newspapermen and radio commentators let fly their slings and arrows against John L. Lewis, it must make them feel like heap big Injuns. I ask them to remember that when they do this they make life harder for a half-million men and their families—men who are devoted to Lewis exactly because they feel isolated, and because he has been their champion.

Lewis is a Carlylean figure, one of the few left in the labor movement. I could write academic essays about him as such. But the miners couldn't eat those essays, and they couldn't pay their grocery bills with them and couldn't educate their children with them. What they need is help here and now. The fact that their goal is also Lewis' is a tribute to him and ought not to be a penalty on them. To treat Lewis as an untouchable is to cut yourself off from a labor battle which is part of the campaign of history in our time.

February 21, 1950

The devil has got into the weather and is helping John L. with his coal strike, and I have got myself caught in between the devil and John L.

By some perverse mischance the week I had fondly chosen to hole in at the old farmhouse at North Sea (a hundred miles out on Long Island), to get some writing done, is exactly the week the elements have chosen for a cold war against humanity all along the East Coast. When I roused myself at six on Monday, to drive my family to the early train for the city and school, I looked out at North Sea Harbor, to find its edges frozen. Moreover, the hot water was frozen, and the tanks of cooking gas which are thoughtfully stored outside were frozen. Only the miracle of my having lovingly piled a heap of blankets and old rugs on the radiator of my 1937 car the night before enabled me to get it started after fifteen minutes.

The sudden onslaught of cold increases the pressure for a settlement all round. It strengthens Lewis' position. How can the operators hope to bargain with the diggers when the devil himself joins them in the form of the wind and the frost? And how can the Administration ever conquer the mighty John L. when it has to face the belated artillery of winter, before whose raking fire the dwindling coal reserves seem like soldiers carved in butter?

I remember a conversation with Lewis some weeks back, in which he told me proudly, "We're not licked." He was not a beaten man then, nor do I think he is now. Even with all the injunctions and restraining orders that have been slapped down on him, he retains a great measure of flexibility of movement and strength. The strength is not so much in his own stubbornness as in the stubbornness of certain facts which the operators and the government have wished to forget.

It is a fact that while you may be able to tie the hands of a labor leader, you can't lick a labor movement.

It is a fact that the coal diggers are solidly behind John L. Lewis even when they openly flout his repeated public instructions for them to go back into the pits. The best way to understand the minds of the strikers is to think of the psychology of a resistance movement, when one of its leaders is compelled to say and do things under compulsion by the occupation forces. The followers go on interpreting what their leader says in the way to which their bitter struggle has accustomed them.

It is a fact that the whole effort to regulate labor relations by the method of the court injunction and the leadership strait jacket is baffling, wasteful, trivializing and in the end stupid.

If you were a miner, would you not prefer starving with a leader to knuckling under to a court writ? Even the defeats he has suffered have strengthened Lewis' hold on the miners. For they remember each defeat with bitterness, but they attribute it not to him but to the ruthlessness of the occupation forces, which means the courts and the operators.

There is no getting away from it: The devil is in the man. Daniel Webster once wrestled with the devil and outmaneuvered him by legal argument. But who is there now among operators or judges with the greatness of Webster?

2. Charlie Wilson and the Bird Dogs

October 13, 1954

THE ADMINISTRATION'S CHAMPION carrier of the foot-in-mouth disease has again gone and done it. Defense Secretary Wilson's burst of canine imagery in talking of the unemployed today ("I've always liked bird dogs better than kennel-fed dogs") is one for the history books. President Eisenhower says that Wilson couldn't have meant what he said because he's a kindhearted man who cares about human suffering. Wilson himself says not that he was misquoted but that his meaning was distorted (the warped woof, so to speak). But the anxiety of Republican candidates throughout the country to put a safe distance between themselves and Wilson shows that his meaning has been all too clearly understood, and not only by Democrats.

Yet it would be a mistake to treat it only as a personal boner. Wilson is the best Republican documentary. What others try discreetly to conceal, he always manages to expose with unconscious candor. No doubt this particular witticism about the unemployed as bird dogs and kennel dogs is one he has used many times, saying it privately perhaps over coffee and brandy and cigars in the great houses of Washington. No doubt it always got a good hand from the General Motors contingent, who may feel that the unemployed are sadly lacking in the good old American spirit of enterprise, and that what is good for roaming bird dogs is good for America.

You can see Wilson sitting there in one of the after-dinner huddles, with the other fat cats, with the possessors of the earth and the holders of power and the receivers of government contracts, all of them glowing with self-satisfaction. Wilson's crime now, in their eyes, is not that he thought what he did, since they all believe it, too. It is that he said it publicly.

There is a streamlined arrogance in Wilson's whole discussion of the unemployed (including the comment on those who "can go back south when it gets a little cold") which expresses the outlook of the small group that rules both the American economy and the American government today. It reminds me strongly of the attitude of the same governing class in the 1870s, after the Civil War, just as the whole Eisenhower Administration is strongly reminiscent of that of another victorious General called Grant who sat bewildered in the White House and who admired the masters of finance more than any other of God's creatures.

The gist of economic thinking in those untrammeled days was that all of life was a kind of Darwinian jungle governed by the law of tooth and fang and claw, and that the animals who survived were obviously the superior ones. In this dog-eat-dog universe the bottom dogs were expected to cling to the virtues of humility. "Teach the working men to live more economically and practice self-restraint," wrote a Republican economist in 1877; adding that one should "show them that if their wages descend slowly and steadily it will avoid a crash of business and . . . do them good rather than harm in the end."

Wilson phrases it differently. He wants the unemployed worker to "get out and hunt for food, rather than sit on his fanny and yell." Yet the Darwinian universe is the same. It is a bit frightening to note that, with all the changes in American life, this kind of Republican thinking hasn't changed in essentials in the past seventy years.

The thing that strikes me finally about Wilson's remark is the outlook of a man who, when talking of economic problems, uses the language and imagery of the landed gentry who are the masters of the hounds. It has become fashionable among our social thinkers in recent years to deride Thorstein Veblen as having drawn a caricature rather than a portrait of the American possessing groups in his *Theory of the Leisure Class*. You will remember that Veblen's point was that the economic masters in modern society still carried over the basic attitudes of the predatory gentry who rode to hounds. If Veblen were alive today Wilson's press conference would form one of those long hilarious footnotes in his book.

October 15, 1954

Secretary Wilson has pleaded guilty to being "inept" in his comments on dogs and other matters, and the whole Republican press has labored mightily to convince us that he is actually a lovable old character who lacks only the skills of the politicians. Wilson has shown that spontaneous candor leads to catastrophe.

The confusion in Republican headquarters was like the chaos in a broadcasting studio when the announcer, after his paid spiel about the breakfast food, gives his candid opinion about the juvenile audience under the impression that the mike has been shut off. After a hurried huddle the sponsors may put the offending unfortunate back on the air and compel him to make public confession of his "ineptness" and his bluff lack of the broadcasting graces. He may recount the long record of his fondness for kiddies and with a choking voice recall that he was once a kid himself. He may even grow virtuously irate over "the way my remarks were distorted by our left-wing opponents" of the rival breakfast food company, without troubling to add that they gave apoplexy to half the executives of his own company, who agreed with his views on the blasted kiddies but thought he was a fool not to wait until the cocktail hour when he could express them privately.

The deadliest effect of the Wilson episode has been to call attention to the existence of the unemployed as a national problem. It was the strategy of the Republican campaign chiefs to pretend that the problem is not there, and by attacking the Democrats as "prophets of doom and gloom" they have tried to lull the country into an opium dream of well-being. With his few ill-chosen words Wilson has been able to dispel the dream.

He dramatized for troubled and inarticulate Americans just what it is about the Administration record that dissatisfies them most deeply. Like all great historical parables, the parable of the bird dogs and the kennel dogs went in its meaning far beyond the intent of the artist. It got its effect not just because Walter Reuther sent a telegram but because without intending it in the least Wilson had touched a deep chord in many people.

If the Wilson episode compels us to look hard at the unemployment figures, it will have done the country a service. In the few exchanges that have taken place about the problem, the Administration has contended that the people are enjoying their second-best year of prosperity, while the Democrats have answered that unemployment is more serious than the President's speech writers seem to think.

Curiously both have hold of a truth by the tail. The clue is to be found in the profound industrial revolution through which the country is passing, which means that employment cannot keep up with the increases in the labor market. And that fewer men working fewer hours are producing the same national product and the same volume of business profits as before. That is one of the explanations for the curious fact that while so many communities are in the economic doldrums the stock market has been steadily rising.

In other words, what we are now discovering is that under the conditions of the present machine revolution it is possible for serious unemployment to coexist with a measure of what we call "prosperity."

3. The Seventeen Million

November 25, 1955

FRED CRAWFORD, who used to head up the N.A.M. and now heads an outfit called "Citizens for Eisenhower," made a bad gaff the other day in a speech exhorting the Eisenhower battalions to fight, fight, fight. He spoke feelingly of how a fascist minority had come to power in Germany while the rest of the nation was not looking, and then with heavy emphasis he pointed out that at the same time labor was coming to the fore in America.

There is no doubt that the gentleman said it, but he now insists that he didn't mean to draw any parallel between the Nazis in Hitler

Germany and the trade-unions in New Deal America. Mindful of Charlie Wilson's history of foot-in-mouth disease, Crawford insists that he will not be made into another Wilson. In all innocence I want to ask: if the gentleman didn't mean to draw a parallel between the Nazis and American labor, then what did he mean? And what was the reference to labor doing there?

This is not the only sign of a renewed Republican attack upon American labor. Senator Barry Goldwater, of Arizona, has been holding forth in and out of the Senate on what he calls a labor conspiracy to capture the governmental machinery of the United States. He talks darkly of vast union funds gathered for this purpose.

The Gompers tradition, which has kept the trade-unions from separate political action and from forming a labor party, is as strong today as ever. But this does not mean that the trade-unions intend to be ciphers in the political struggles. I can remember when labor was the most important single partner in the "great coalition" of unions, farmers, minority groups, city machines and the new professional middle classes, all of which together elected Roosevelt and kept the Democrats in power for twenty years. Those were the days of the war, the new organizing drives in autos and textiles and steel, the sit-down strikes, the Wagner Act and the Political Action Committee. They were the days when the unions grew from less than 3,000,000 members in 1933 to almost 10,500,000 in 1941, and 15,-500,000 in 1947. They were a mighty political force, to be reckoned with even by those who hated them.

In the last decade the union growth has slowed up drastically. The Bureau of Labor Statistics has just put out its report showing a total union membership of 17,000,000, with an added 1,000,000 in Canadian locals of American internationals. These 17,000,000, however, are not the political force they once were. It is true that 15,500,000 are now in the newly merged A.F.L.-C.I.O., under the leadership of George Meany and Walter Reuther. But the workers have been caught up in the general current of changes in America, and increasingly they have become more independent as voters. That is why they are a big question mark in the next election.

Many reasons for this have been advanced. I think the crucial one is that the worker—like any other American—is not a man of a single class loyalty, but of multiple loyalties. Take an automobile worker or a clerical worker or a member of a carpenters' union. He is not only a trade-unionist. He may also be a homeowner, a stock investor, a Democrat or Republican, a Mason or Elk, a Presbyterian or Methodist, a suburbanite, a golf or sailing addict, a TV fan, a father of sons about to reach draft age.

In appealing to him, both parties will have to recognize that he is a bundle of multiple loyalties and will have to meet the demands of those loyalties. But they will also have to remember what Lincoln once said: "If any man tells you he loves America, yet he hates labor, he is a liar. If a man tells you he trusts America, yet fears labor, he is a fool."

4. Walter Reuther and the Auto Giants

June 8, 1955

THE POINT about the Ford agreement that makes it "historic" is that it recognizes the corporation's stake in what happens to the worker when the job fails. Walter Reuther and John Bugas, the two top people in the negotiating teams, both talked carefully of "stabilizing" industrial employment, and they are no doubt right. Reuther had the added aim of trying to induce the automobile industry, which has special seasonal habits of peak overemployment and short-week underemployment, to iron out the hills and valleys.

But the plan can be applied in other industries, too, including many with special features of their own. The new fact about it, common to all, is that management undertakes to look beyond the payroll it gives the worker when he is working, or the pension fund it provides for his retirement. It rounds out his annual income so that, even when there is no work for him, he gets a good income chunk consisting of his state unemployment insurance plus a payment from a special management pool. This is a big stride toward the security of the worker's life and the assumption of management responsibility for what happens to him.

In the joint press conference after the settlement Reuther was asked whether he had talked to any state governors about integrating the state and management contributions. "No," he answered, "we had better see what kind of an animal we have before we proceed. It's a very lovely animal." It must look like a highly desirable one to other union leaders and a pretty formidable one to the managers of other industries. They had better take a good appraising look at it, because it is an animal that will soon be at home in their bestiary.

To use the adjective "revolutionary" about this agreement does not imply a class victory of "labor" over "capital" or a transfer of power from management to the union. The old class struggle clichés have ceased to have much meaning in this situation. The negotiation was carried on by groups of skilled technicians, each acting under a strategy command anxious to keep in harmony with public opinion. Reuther did his job with skill, and the Ford people showed how far they have come from the social primitivism of their founder.

Without smugness, we Americans can feel that we have learned to do these things with the minimum of conflict, tears and waste.

The N.A.M. feels far more alarmed than Ford about this new step, and it has declared verbal war in the public prints against what seems to it a highly unlovely animal. The ads say that there are no guaranteed profits or sales or anything else in industry, so why should there be a guaranteed annual wage for workers?

There is force in this argument, but logically it would mean no place for pension and welfare funds and even for trade-unionism itself, which is supposed to cushion the risks and insecurities for the worker.

The trade-union was once a volcanic idea, but it is a volcano that no longer erupts. Our American labor movement, as Daniel Bell points out, has reached a membership plateau. Its leaders are much the same type as management leaders, only a bit younger. Their job is largely concerned with bargaining, grievances and welfare funds. If the N.A.M. can find anything very socialistic or revolutionary about them, it is misreading all the signs.

In one sense, however, a great change is taking place, and men like Reuther and Henry Ford II are its harbingers. It is this: Most of the claims and questions about work and the job that in other societies are finally settled by the government are getting settled in America by the trade-union and the corporation. The Great Depression did much to bring in the welfare state. But the new industrial revolution is bringing new burdens and duties to the welfare corporation and the welfare trade-union.

In the best sense we may say that the Ford Company has agreed no longer to view labor as merely an hourly commodity on the market, but to see it as something attached to a human being who plans his life in years and decades, not in hours and weeks. If this is the animal that was born in the hotel conference room, it is a lovely animal in-deed.

5. The New Industrial Empires

November 9, 1955

THE SALE of Ford stock to the public does not mark the "end of an empire," as the *Wall Street Journal* would have it. Rather does it mark the replacement of the family empire by the impersonal corporate empire. The tie-in between the rich family and big enterprise goes back all the way to the merchant princes at the time of the breakup of the Middle Ages in Europe. You will still find it in force on the Continent, and the defeat of Japan did not wipe out the big Japanese industrial families (*zaibatsu*).

In America the Fords held on after most of the other tycoon families had allowed their closed family control of their industrial empires to be broken. The only way they could do it up to now was through the Ford Foundation, whose trustees have now wisely recognized the facts of life. It is not only that they must diversify their portfolio. It is also that the concentration of voting power in a family foundation over a family enterprise means too much linked power.

What is happening, of course, is that personal power is giving way to impersonal power. This seems to be the law of American life in every area. I have been reading sentimental laments about the passing of the era of Old Henry the First and his co-buccaneers, and I have also been reading jubilant self-congratulatory comments about how progressive our corporate enterprise is becoming, as witness this event. I can share neither the lament nor the jubilation.

If Old Henry the First was a colorful and bold industrial Titan, he was also erratic, cranky and bigoted. One area of his mind was always a child's mind, and toward the end he became a paranoid child. I cannot lament the passing of that kind of industrial monarch.

On the other hand, however much I admire the progressive policies of the present Ford family and managers, the billionaire empires we have today are too impersonal for the development of individuality and too vast for our national health.

If this is true of the Ford empire, how much truer it is of General Motors, the biggest industrial colossus of history. In an Administration in which General Motors executives hold high positions of governmental power, it may seem a kind of sacrilege for the Democratic Senate majority to start an investigation into its size and power. Yet that is what the O'Mahoney subcommittee is now doing.

The initial testimony by a former General Electric official, T. K. Quinn, makes pretty lively reading. But if you are interested you will find even livelier Quinn's book *Giant Business: Threat to Democracy* (Exposition Press), subtitled "The Autobiography of an Insider." Quinn is not very subtle, nor does he have the patter of professional economists and of copywriters, but he has the merit of having lived through what he is talking about. If you want to balance Quinn's book and testimony by arguments on the side of the giant corporation, you can do no better than to read David E. Lilienthal's book *Big Business: A New Era* (Harper). Lilienthal, whose liberalism on basic issues cannot be doubted, has come to the conclusion that the opponents of bigness—from Jefferson to Brandeis—were wrong, and that the efficiency and creativeness tend to go with business size.

Here then is one of the commanding debates of our day. But alas, no one seems to debate it any more, and most people have come fatalistically to accept bigness everywhere—in the corporation, the trade-union and the government.

There were fifty-eight billion-dollar corporations in the U.S. a few years ago, and there are more by now. They do crowd out competitors, and the "new competition" between them is rarely a price competition. They reach into areas far beyond the products they directly produce. They have power over advertising and publicity. Their employment and investment policies can change the whole economic picture. They get most of the government contracts. To be a small businessman and try to survive alongside them, and not in their shadow, is a hard thing.

These are the facts. One may argue that they are inevitable, and one may also argue (as Adolf Berle does in *The 20th Century Capitalist Revolution*) that they are getting a public conscience and a soul. But the facts are the facts. Judging from the Ford stock episode, I have sad news for Senator O'Mahoney and his committee counsel, Joseph Burns: Most Americans don't worry about the giant corporations. What they want is to be cut in—on even a small slice of them.

The brokers and the bankers in every city have already been flooded by requests for the Ford stock at almost any price. Considering the almost obscene bitterness with which Old Henry the First hated Wall Street and the stock market, this is pretty ironic. But the big fact is that we are reacting to the opening of the Ford stock issue much as the Americans of an earlier day reacted to the opening of new land. A kind of land rush is taking place, only it is a stock rush.

The American of today seems to think that the right to be in on the rich stock profits of the boom era is a natural right, part of the "pursuit of happiness" guaranteed by the Founding Fathers.

6. Hoffa, Beck and the Image of Labor

March 17, 1957

IF AMERICAN LABOR has many other friends like John S. Coleman, president of the U.S. Chamber of Commerce, it won't need any enemies. Coleman is practically prostrate with sympathy for the unions in their present ordeal of the rackets probes. For years, he says, industry has suffered the tyrannies of American union monopolies and boycotts, but no one seemed to understand or care. But now, he says, "everyone understands the language of pinball racketeering, callhouse arrangements, and dickers between public officials and labor chieftains." And he adds, "My hope is that labor will reach for its own broom."

Mistrust a man who weeps for the crimes of your erring blacksheep brother, while he seeks to pin the fraternal relation on you before all the world. The great danger of the McClellan committee's researches into the darker phases of union behavior has always been the danger that they will be used as a stick with which to beat the union dog. Coleman has made the beginning.

I have to tell Coleman and the others who weep for the sins of labor that the unions in which racketeering flourishes are almost always those which are least socially conscious in their philosophy and least militant. If Coleman really cares about honest unions that stay clear of corner cutting and collusion with criminal officials, he should run up a flag for the kind of militant unionism—that of Reuther, Dubinsky and others of their brand—which most chambers of commerce regard as leftish or at least pinkish.

The sad fact is that every union which has thus far had any ties to racketeering exposed has been a union whose officials cared for nothing—no cause, no program of social reform, no ideology, no vision of social justice—nothing but the almighty and extremely seductive dollar. In short, the point at which unionism spills over into racketeering is the point at which it is drunk with power in its pursuit of swag. In this respect it is very similar to business.

The dramatic arrest of Jimmy Hoffa has put the spotlight on the rotten phases of trade-unionism. Understanding Hoffa and his personality is only part of the story. American labor, especially since the days of the early New Deal, has done extremely well. It has won most of its basic fights, its bitter drawn-out strikes seem a thing of the past, its place in the councils of the nation is recognized. The time when labor leaders led their men in a crusade to storm the ramparts of corporate power is over. The European philosophy of the class struggle never took much hold in American labor anyway, and what there was of it is gone. And the excitement of the era when the trade-unions joined the New Deal in fighting the "economic royalists" is also gone.

The result is something of a vacuum. Into this vacuum it is possible for men like Jimmy Hoffa to move—men who are not labor leaders but mercenaries, like the Italian *condottieri* of the fifteenth century, ready to move wherever the swag is.

Let me put a question to Mr. Coleman and to others like him who are ready now to pounce on the Hoffa episode in order to topple labor's strength. What is it that holds a great organization like an international union together? Is it profits, as in the case of the big business corporation? A trade-union doesn't operate on the profit principle. Is it class militancy and revolutionary fervor? No, that may have been true in the left-wing unions once, but it has died down in our day. Is it power and prestige, as in the case of the government and its leaders? Only partly.

I think the answer is that the best unions are held together by the feeling that without them the individual workers will be victimized. They are held together, then, by the notion of what men can achieve when they strive together, and what the combined union power can do for liberal programs in the nation as a whole. This is the same principle that holds the business corporation together, except that the labor managers tend to get less salary than the corporate ones and get no profits or stock bonuses.

There are some unions, however, where social consciousness never meant much to start with, but only a kind of organizing toughness. These are also the unions into which leaders have come who are primarily business-minded men like Beck and Hoffa. What happens, naturally and almost inevitably, is that such unions lose sight of what it was that brought them into being. The money-mindedness turns to complacency and greed.

There is a kind of twilight world where crooked labor, crooked business, crooked gamblers and other adventurers, and crooked law enforcement officers all converge. In that dim area it is hard to say that this man is a labor official, that one a government official, that one a racketeer, that one a businessman. At the points where their common greeds converge they lose their identity, and they become faceless men.

About someone like Hoffa there is an added edge of tragedy because he has the fire of self-assertion and a fierce contempt for what others may think. But when such a man as Hoffa talks of how he has "had to fight labor's battles on the picket lines and in the courts," and the classic language of labor militancy is mouthed by a man who needs a shield against his fear, the tragedy becomes merely pathos, and you try to think of something less painful.

March 31, 1957

Dave Beck is down for the count of ten. His view of the world, seen from the floor through bloodied eyes, must be a bitter one. As he sees it, everyone has turned against him—his own workers in the locals that he thought impregnable to outer attack, the press that used to be so favorable to him, the news magazines that gave him glowing cover stories about his power and glory, the business tycoons who liked to do business with him because he had none of those devilish ideas borrowed from foreign socialists, the Senators who once courted him and who now glare at him as if he came from another world. Yes, even the Republican Administration has turned against him—the Ike whom he liked and supported in both elections, paying out to his managers some of the good money which is now being handled and smelled and passed around for the taint of corruption. (Oh, place not your trust in princes.)

And now—unkindest cut of all—his own labor peers have turned against him: they have suspended him as an officer of the A.F.L.-

C.I.O., and will soon inevitably judge him and convict him as an enemy of labor. Thereby they cut from him the last pillar of defense —that he did what he did for his union and for labor.

The truth is that Beck has never in any meaningful sense been a labor leader—as were and are, for example, men of such diverse political and industrial faiths as Gompers and John Mitchell, Green and Lewis, Bill Haywood and Dubinsky, Bridges and Murray and Hillman and Reuther.

The only thing he has shared with them, as indeed with Marx and Lenin, was the feel for power and a subinstinctual knack for turning toward it. I am certain that, as he stands Samsonlike with the building bricks and columns falling around him, he has not even a glimmer of conscience about the fact that some of labor's structure of influence is coming down along with the rubble of his own career.

He was only a fellow traveler of the unions, for his temporary convenience. Those to whom he turned, with the strongest tropisms of his being, were those other men of power—the businessmen. The trade-union model after whom he shaped himself was Bill Hutcheson, the tough boss of the Carpenters, who wouldn't stand for any foolishness about democracy or voting or workers' education.

If Beck wants revenge against the A.F.L.-C.I.O. leaders whom he hates, the irony of it is that he may get it. An antilabor mood is building up in the nation, among people who have never been taught to distinguish between the men who work the dark and wild side of the labor street and the men who care about making an accounting of their work to their culture and their conscience.

There is an ugly tide rising against labor, and those who have always wanted to shrink the legal standing and political influence of the unions are riding gleefully with it. If I were a union official I would happily join in the effort to let the sun and air in on the work of all unions, as they are already in on the work of the best. But I would be anxious about the crippling laws, and I would think how we could all best fight them.

It is, at bottom, a question of labor's image. What kind of image is it that the American worker has of himself? What kind of image does he present to the rest of the American people—the white-collar men, the engineers and technicians, the farmers, the business executives, the editors and politicians and teachers and preachers?

The past image of the worker, both to himself and to the world, has been that of the underdog—fighting hard to get out from under, snarling perhaps, but determined not to be frightened away from what is rightfully his.

More recently this has changed. The new image has been that of workers as not different from others—good conformists all—and of union leaders as little different from business executives, as men who are merely doing the managerial job on the other side of the bargaining table.

I suspect that this image has come to the end of its usefulness. People have learned that a labor "manager," like Beck, can be as much without a basic sense of values as the iciest corporate executive that ever stepped out of his executive suite. We must get back to the notion that the worker and his leaders are fighting for something.

But for what? From where I sit it is for three things. First, for a welfare unionism that enables him to find dignity in his work and give content to his leisure. Second, for an America that cuts across union and business lines and keeps its society open, its ethics honest and its world peaceful and free. Third, for a chance to develop himself as a human being, with his own stamp and uniqueness but with a special quality because he is a worker and therefore close to productiveness.

7. Say Yes to Growth

March 1, 1959

THERE WAS A TIME—so long, so long ago—when the line that divided camp from camp in the great debate on American policy was the line between internationalists and isolationists. That is now ancient history. The division today is between the static and the dynamic, between those who want to "hold the line" both at home and abroad and those who want a positive policy, between (I use W. H. Auden's terms) the "fearers" and the "farers," between those who want to rest on past growth and those who say Yes to growth today and tomorrow.

Am I speaking here of foreign policy or domestic? I'm speaking of both. More strikingly than at any time since the end of the war the two areas have converged, and what we are debating in both is much the same question—that of capacity and willingness for growth.

Consider the current American stand on the Berlin issue, and on the seemingly very far removed issue of inflation at home—that the sum of wisdom is to hold the line, to dig in, not to yield an inch, and that nothing more is required of us than rigidity.

Khrushchev and Mikoyan have flung a challenge at America which in the long run may prove more important for us than even the very dangerous immediate challenge on Berlin. I mean their threat to overtake the national income and living standards of our economy. The rate of Russian economic growth is estimated at something like 7 per cent a year. Khrushchev talks of a 60 per cent increase in the next seven years—or a rate of over 8½ per cent. Those who know something about the Russian economy tell us that this is no empty boast.

How do our own leaders respond to this challenge? The President and his whole Administration "team" have flung themselves into an effort to slow down wage rises, to make "spending" a dirty word in all respectable circles, to go back as soon as possible to budget balancing, and to convince the nation that the central problem we face is that of inflation.

If they are wrong, as I think they are, then they are fighting the wrong enemy at the wrong time, in the wrong way, with the wrong weapons. Inflation, as Representative Chester Bowles said in a fine speech the other day, is a problem but by no means our major problem. Prices have been rising pretty steadily at an annual rate of somewhere between 1½ and 2 per cent, but this is a creeping rise and not a runaway one. We can absorb it and have absorbed it. Wages have been rising, but the rise in the productivity of labor has kept pace with the wage increases.

These are indexes not of disaster but of movement and growth. The concentrated effort to focus our attention on inflation as the great enemy can become one of those paralyzing abstractions whose danger is even greater to our thinking than the economic doom it depicts.

The key to our economic future is not the negative one of warding off inflation, but the positive one of economic growth. If our man-hour productivity and our national product keep growing, at a more rapid pace than they have done, then the economy will be able to take the problems of price and wage rises in its stride, and the obsession with balanced budgets will be shown up for what it is. But if our rate of economic growth slows down, then wage and unemployment troubles will become mountainous, and the contraction of the economy and therefore of the tax base will threaten even the dream of a balanced budget.

I don't say that the problem of economic growth—that is, the problem of getting richer as a nation—will resolve everything. As John K. Galbraith points out, one of our problems is the shoddy and contrived wants on which we spend our increased income, and the sacrifice of the public sector of the economy to the private one.

But I regard this as a two-front war: We need not stop our efforts for increasing the national output while we step up our efforts to fashion better national tastes and a surer confidence in the wants that are not created by the arts of persuasion for profit.

ELECTING A PRESIDENT

1. On a Campaign Train to the Crusades (1952)

September 24, 1952

IT WAS the most extraordinary climax to the most dramatic political story in the history of Presidential campaigns. What other campaign meeting, assembled to hear a Presidential candidate, had ever before begun with a piped-in broadcast in which the candidate's running mate defended his political honesty by giving a national audience the story of his life and love? And in what other campaign meeting had the Presidential candidate afterward thrown away his prepared script on a national issue like inflation and spent his time lauding the courage of his running mate, making clear his admiration for him, and then promising to bring in his judgment in the next act?

The dramatic skill of Nixon's television performance threatens to overshadow a more important drama that has been played out on Eisenhower's campaign train during the past six days, ever since the Nixon story broke. I mean the drama of General Eisenhower's struggle with his conscience.

It is General Eisenhower who—in spite of the fact that for the moment Dick Nixon stole the show—has been and remains the central figure in the whole drama. It was Eisenhower's campaign for virginally honest government which was thrown into confusion by the disclosures about Nixon. It was Eisenhower's own moral sense that seemed at first to have been outraged. It was on Eisenhower's campaign staff that the plans for the Nixon show were laid, although they were announced from California. It was to Eisenhower, as well as to the national audience, that Nixon addressed his most tremulous final plea for justification.

Let me describe the setting in Cleveland last night. The press watched the Nixon television show in a room on the second floor of the Cleveland auditorium. Eisenhower and his party watched in another room. When the curtain-raiser was over the real show began. George Bender, Republican Congressman from Ohio, who was the cheerleader of the Taft forces at the Chicago convention, introduced the notables, including Senators Taft, Bricker, Knowland and Mundt.

Then the General appeared. I have heard him speak more than a score of times during this past week. He has rarely been effective, but last night he was. Dramatically he threw away his prepared inflation script—which was a good thing for the country as well as for him. He was a different Eisenhower—keyed up, responsive to the audience, and with an obviously deep emotional involvement in what had been happening.

With nostalgia General Eisenhower recalled the episode of General George Patton, and the famous slapping scene. "He committed an error. He made amends for his error." And it was clear that Eisenhower was putting Nixon into Patton's place. "I happen to be one of those people," he added, "who, when I get in a fight, would rather have a courageous and honest man by my side than a whole boxcar full of pussyfooters."

General Eisenhower seems to have shifted his ground. When he now speaks of Nixon committing "an error," he is speaking in technical terms—in terms of the morally indifferent question of whether a Senator is technically wrong or right in letting his friends help him carry his expenses in fighting Communism. And when General Eisenhower now says—as he said last night—that his final criterion in judging Nixon will be "Do I myself believe that this man is the kind of man that Americans would like for their Vice-President?" he is opening himself to the test of the stream of telegrams and letters that is bound to come in after the effective Nixon performance.

It is hard to escape the conclusion that this is not a new script or an accidental one. It is part of the political game and there can be no valid objection to the Republican professionals using their best skill on it. But when General Eisenhower lets the high moral purpose with which he started be shifted and twisted until he ends up exactly where the most cynical and manipulative of the professionals do, it is hard to escape the feeling that one has watched the crumbling of that moral purpose.

On the level of political soap opera, there can be no question of the effectiveness of the Nixon performance. No hero as handsome as Nixon, as clean-cut in looks, as tremulous and pulsating in his delivery, has hit the political circuit for a long time. The pretty and adoring wife, the mortgages on the houses, the saga of a poor boy who became Senator—these were sure-fire stuff. They mark a new era in campaigning.

But it isn't enough to say, as Nixon did, that the fund was not secretly given or handled. If it had all been aboveboard from the start, how explain the outcry Nixon raised when the disclosure was made? How explain his insistence that it was an Alger Hiss plot? There could be no plot or smear in revealing what had all along been an open transaction.

It isn't enough to say that he got no funds for himself. Where there is a double compensation, there is bound to be a personal advantage for anyone in political life.

It isn't enough to say that only the rich can afford to stay clear of such subsidies. Other Senators on the level of Nixon's own means have been able to get along without either corruption or subsidy. It means a real burden, but they are bearing it.

It isn't enough to say that he saved the government money by not sending out his speeches with the government frank, and by getting rich men to pay for them. By this same logic, why not let the same group of rich men pay the salaries of the Senators as well as their postage and office expenses?

It isn't enough to say that he gave the rich men nothing in return for their subsidy. In the original interview Dana Smith had made it clear that Nixon was chosen for the subsidy exactly because the rich men knew that he voted right from their viewpoint. One of the fatal defects in the speech was Nixon's failure to talk about his voting record on housing, on price control, on tidelands oil.

Nor is it, finally, enough to say that he was using the money to fight the Communists. The fight against Communism is not something separate from Nixon's other duties as Senator. It was part of his public image and his public function.

September 25, 1952

With all the synthetic Nixon telegrams flooding the Republican National Committee, I propose a cheaper crusade. It is the drop-a-postcard-to-yourself campaign. All it requires is two cents plus the courage to ask yourself whether you are fool enough to fall for one of the slickest and sleaziest fake emotion routines that ever gulled a sentimental people. If the answer is Yes, then look at your mirror and consider how easily you can be had.

The Republican press gloatingly assures us all that the Nixon case is not what it used to be. I agree that a new layer of meaning has been added to it. In its earlier phase it pointed up the hypocrisy of public officials who preach morality and practice the double take. But the lesson of the Nixon case now is how a cynical group of men, using money and the new communication arts and the tried and true techniques of the propaganda masters, can stand an issue of morality on its head and make the faker appear the martyr.

A few months back I went to see a revival of the political musical satire *Of Thee I Sing.* We all roared at the grotesque slapstick version of how a gang of political professionals, who had nothing else to sell the people in a Presidential election, sold them a barefaced version of the boy-meets-girl romance and got the heart-throb vote. When we left the theater we dismissed it as a funny but fanciful flight by a couple of song-and-dance writers.

I hereby eat my laughter. The Nixon show the other night was a blending of the *Of Thee I Sing* theme with the theme of Orwell's *1984*. Instead of love, the story line was the mortgaged home, the little woman, the clean-cut crusader against Communism, the bared breast. As in *1984*, everything got stood on its head: The Senator with easy morals became the stern Cato, hypocrisy became shining sincerity, and the unexplained slush fund became a monument to the public good.

I shall never again doubt that life imitates art.

I recall a little scene from the Cleveland meeting the other night. After the Nixon broadcast, and before Eisenhower came on to speak, we watched one of the most curious performances in recent campaign history. George Bender, the chairman, decided then and there to hold a kind of plebiscite of the audience on whether Nixon should be kept or dropped.

The resulting vote was never seriously in doubt. Bender called for those who would support this great, courageous man, and there was an animal roar from the hysterical crowd. Then Bender called on any so-and-sos who might dare to oppose him, and there were only a few faint voices. How these dastards and Democrats kept from getting lynched will always remain a mystery. Then, not content, Bender went through the entire ritual again and then announced the results, leading the cheering himself.

It was like a "stab-in-the-back" rally at the Berlin Sportpalast, or the fine justice of the People's Court in one of those East European countries.

To those who may say this is Nixon or Bender but not General Eisenhower, I should like to say a few sobering words. I think the time has come to stop thinking of Eisenhower as the Great Innocent surrounded by wicked people but himself inviolate.

Eisenhower started as a man furiously angry at Nixon's betrayal of his office and his loyalty. Yesterday in his whistle stops he talked of the "smear" against Nixon, and later they embraced in Wheeling. Not a single new fact about Nixon has appeared in the intervening time. Eisenhower is more graceful than Bender was the other night, but the technique is the same. First you stir up the mob with a fake tear jerker, and when they are howling the loudest you then pass a quiet judgment on the moral issue in the solitude of your heart.

I think back to the beginning of the campaign, and I find this latest Eisenhower turn all of a piece with the rest. There has not been a single case where an issue of principle was presented to him when Eisenhower didn't in the end surrender. He usually gags at the bitter potion for a few appropriate moments, but then he swallows and grins.

There was another general once who pretended to be better than the politicians. He was Ulysses S. Grant. When Grant finally embraced them, one of them gave the word, "Now we will let him into the church." I feel sure that Ike has earned his admission. But he will learn that man does not live on soap operas alone, nor will the Republic be held together with wires.

October 8, 1952

That fortress of Luce opinions, *Time,* has tucked me under a wing of the house that Pegler lives in. Commenting on a less-than-kind column of mine on the Nixon soap opera blitz, my unknown *Time* admirer says that I "write like a left-wing Pegler"—that is, when my "theories are crossed." This is probably as much of a surprise to Pegler's readers as to mine.

To add to the confusion, in another part of the *Time* forest—and also in *Life*—I find myself linked with Walter Lippmann as well as with Pegler. Three weirder sisters are unlikely to be spotted anywhere outside the pages of *Macbeth.* What ties us together like Siamese triplets is evidently our common skepticism of Richard Nixon's television performance. I didn't, as it happens, catch Pegler's act, but I did catch Lippmann's. One way of saying that I feel in better company with him than with Pegler is to say that I found Lippmann's column on the Nixon broadcast one of the sharpest and wisest utterances of a great writing career. It will survive the badly wilted enthusiasm Lippmann once had for Nixon's running mate, General Eisenhower.

I am still skeptical about Nixon, his speech and his subsequent silence. As the weeks pass, distance does not lend enchantment to his role. I am less inclined than ever to rank the speech, in either its political theory or its immortal phrasing, with the Gettysburg Address.

I can understand the great sense of relief *Time*'s editors had when their Republican cause was, as by a miracle, fished out of the Slough of Despond. Ever since Ike's own halo got frayed, they have been seeking a hero—and they found one. Let them continue to carry a love-struck torch for their hero. But I shall continue my own job, which is to analyze and criticize, jab and prod, but most of all to expose the shoddy and impale the hypocritical.

I am happy for this chance to say again that Nixon's performance has been both hypocritical and shoddy. The subject for discussion is not my political views, which are unimportant, but Nixon's record. I wonder why so great a silence has fallen over the Republicans and their one-party press on the Nixon episode. If it was so great a triumph, wowing the fans and evoking an unrehearsed wave of enthusiasm, why has the door been so abruptly closed? Why don't the Republicans capitalize on Nixon, push him forward, let him wow the still unwowed, let him pursue further the theme of his poverty, purity and patriotism?

The suspicion persists that the Republicans would rather have the issue a closed and silent one than an open and fighting one. Perhaps they fear that the American people will discover, once the closet is unlocked again, that most of the skeletons are still there in the form of unanswered questions.

The importance of the Nixon episode lies in what it has revealed about the view the Republicans take of the minds of the American people. When in my earlier column I described the way George Bender handled the Cleveland meeting, my sharp language was not directed at the audience but at the cynicism with which it was handled. I found the same cynicism in the speeches written for Ike when I was on the campaign train. The most recent example of it is in the Republican plans for a final-week TV spot barrage which will try to sell the General much as soap powder or a deodorant is sold.

Senator Fulbright laid bare the nerve center of this cynical approach when he said that the countries in which leaders have exploited the hatreds and emotions of the people are the countries that have become dictatorships. The dismaying thing about the Republican strategy, with its slogans and the Big Money behind it, is that it is based on the principle that the people can be panicked and gulled.

2. Sickness and Health of a Candidate (1955–56)

December 30, 1955

THE CURRENT *Reader's Digest* has a lead-off article that fell to a luckless fellow called William Hard to write. It is called "Run Again, Ike." Its burden is that the widespread appraisal of the American Presidency as a "man-killing" job is sheer myth, that a coronary thrombosis is highly overrated in its effects and may actually leave a man more chastened about excess and therefore better equipped to live a long life, and that Ike alone ("Who but he?") can save America and the world and therefore must run again.

Isn't Mr. Hard overdoing it by insisting so cheerfully on the almost therapeutic effects of a thrombosis? No one will deny that heart attack victims may live long and reasonably vigorous lives—but also, they may not. Generally a doctor's advice afterward is to slow up, to limit your activities, to cut out the harder phases of your work and above all to avoid worry and tension. This seems scarcely an accurate description of the world's most powerful—and most exacting—public office.

You can quote Scripture to any purpose, as is well known. You can rewrite history to suit whatever political ends you have, as the Communists have shown. But it seems to have remained for the Run-Again-Ike school of political doctors and medical politicos to rewrite accepted medical history and knowledge.

Similarly it is fascinating to see how the outlines of the Presidential job are changing under the ministering hands and the magical touch of Republican writers. Only a short time ago it was generally described as a "killing job" and "the toughest job in the world." I have before me an objective article from the New York *Times* Magazine, dated last October, with the title "The Crushing Burden of the Presidency," and asking whether the job is not too big for any one man, whatever his physical endurance.

But now we are being told that this was just a brouhaha promulgated by unthinking and irresponsible men. We are being fed the veriest pap that any people was ever suckled on, by sentimentalists who seem able to believe whatever they wish, or by cynics who are sure they can get others to believe anything.

Thus Mr. Hard, who may be a little of both, tells us that the administrative chores of the Presidency are disposed of before they ever get to Ike by an administrative machine the like of which has never before been constructed in human history. He also tells us that even the ceremonial duties can be cut (Did Ike have to make all those speeches?), and that the big policy decisions don't really take very much out of a man.

In fact, after reading Mr. Hard's article the *Reader's Digest* reader may feel tempted to dream of the Presidency for his old age as a kind of rest cure for the semiretired.

The facts, alas, are not with the new Republican theory as promulgated by Mr. Hard. He points out triumphantly that Lincoln didn't die from his work and emotional stress, that Wilson didn't die until after his second term, and that Roosevelt lived into a fourth. But any Lincoln scholar—and any study of the portraits—will testify that the four years of the Presidency changed Lincoln from a vigorous man of middle age to an old and worn man. Any Wilson scholar will tell you that it was the strain of fighting for the League of Nations against the Senate that killed Wilson off effectively, although he lingered for a while as a broken man. Any Roosevelt scholar will acknowledge that his iron will and frame (the upper part of it was strong enough) were exhausted by the strain of the war decisions.

Who is trying to fool whom in this curious game of twisting history to the purpose of politics?

The history of the Presidential office in America is a great one. While it would be stupid to exaggerate its lethal effects, and old-fogeyish to refuse to adopt administrative improvements wherever possible, the fact is that the Presidency cannot be made into a part-time job to be performed by a semiretired man within the frame of measured exertions.

Mr. Hard ends his piece by calling on Eddie Cantor to testify that the solution for the problems of a man who has had a heart attack is prayer. "The prayers of the people will be as important as the doctors. Through prayers the President will be hearing from the Great Physician."

It is a moving idea. In addition to their matchless administrative team that distills away all the hard work of the Presidency, the Republicans seem now to have conscripted God in their campaign. If you are going to make political use of the Deity, I should have thought that He would fall into the category of the Independent Voter who will not take the party line on the question of whether Ike should run.

March 4, 1956

Those shouts of exultation, from the Potomac and the Pentagon to Wall Street and across the country in every locker room, board room and executive suite, proclaim that God's in his Republican heaven, all's right with the corporate world, and victory is in the bag.

Not only has the indispensable candidate of the Republicans agreed to run, but the word is around that with his standard leading them against the Democratic foe the possessors of the earth—who have also possessed the White House the past four years—can't be beaten.

I detect some long faces in the Democratic ranks who seem to agree that the campaign will be a hollow formality, that all is over except the shouting and counting, and that the only burning question is how big will the Eisenhower landslide be.

The men who are running the Republican campaign are planning for the heavy use of the big mass media on which they will project the hero image of their candidate. They will have plenty of money in a campaign that may cost them at least fifty million dollars.

Actually they have at their disposal a double hero image. In 1952 Eisenhower was the man who had come back from the wars where he had risked his life for his country. In 1956 this will carry over somewhat, but another image will be added—the Eisenhower who is endangering his life in peace by becoming a candidate and taking the risks and strains of Presidential office. Certainly the hucksters will have a potent product to sell.

The thing that is most frightening is the sense one gets of a monolithic acceptance of whatever Eisenhower and his group do. Almost the entire press throws itself at the hero's feet. The broadcasting and TV chains join the press by taking the incredible position that when a man comes out to announce himself as a political candidate it is not a political speech and therefore requires no equal time for the other party. No one challenges anything. No one protests against anything.

If democracy is, in its innermost nature, a system where things get settled in the struggles of the political arena, one begins to wonder what has happened to the arena and what has happened to the critical, fighting energies we once had.

July 9, 1956

There is little question now that President Eisenhower will decide again to run again. This is the second decision he will have made to run for a second term after a major illness. Even if there were to be a third occurrence of some physical affliction, I do not doubt that the decision would be the same. It may not be good for him and it may not be good for the Presidency and it may not be good for the country. But it is good for the Republicans, and what is good for the Republicans is what counts in business and communications circles.

There is a people's saying which is sweeping the country: "They'll run Ike if they have to prop him up to do it." Like many folk sayings it has a deep core of truth. But it is not only "they"—the corporate and party leaders—who want Eisenhower to run at any cost. Eisenhower also wants Eisenhower to run. The stress on the men behind him has played into their hands by making him appear a reluctant hero on whose head an eager people presses a garland of leadership. Power and fame are heady things, and holding the center of the stage can become so enduring a habit that it is an indispensable drug against boredom. For a man who has commanded captains and walked with kings, length of years is not the ruling aim. What else would Eisenhower find to do with the years that remain if he were not in the White House?

So I'll go out on a not-too-risky limb and say that Eisenhower wants to run, that he will be nominated in August, and that (except for a possible act of God) he will make the campaign with Nixon.

I'll go out on a more-risky limb, too, about the Democrats. I assume that Kefauver is out of the running, and I am pretty certain that Harriman is not the man who will give Stevenson his major fight. Out on my limb I see Stevenson as the choice.

The race will be close. If the election were held tomorrow Eisenhower would win.

Having been in darkest Africa when the President had his intestinal attack, I have on my return had to read the piled-up medical bulletins, the polemics on the nature and course of ileitis, and the cheery postoperational medical-political reports.

I have, in short, traversed the whole odyssey of the President's ileum. This is not because of any morbid interest of mine in internal medicine, but because Sherman Adams, Jim Hagerty and their doctor assistants have, Rembrandtwise, been conducting a national anatomy lesson.

Never in history have so many millions hung so intently on a subdivision of the small intestine, and never have so many billions in stock sales fluctuated with its health or unhealth.

Since the Republican leaders have boldly made the President's bodily condition their major strategy field, we have the right to speak frankly about it. Despite the prevailing belief that God is a registered Republican, I cannot help feeling that fate has dealt unkindly with the Grand Old Party. It could have postponed the President's heart attack, and his ileitis, and whatever else, until after the elections.

Yet, given their cross to bear, the Republican leaders have made the best of it in the worst of all possible campaign situations. They have done what every artist has to do—worked with the material at hand, to give it the twist of their artistry. They have turned a frail, convalescent President into a symbol of swelling strength. They have marshaled doctors to prove that the President's life chances are better now, after his intestinal attack and operation, than they were before.

After so dazzling an exhibition of public-relations brilliance by his managers, what can we all do except cheer—and what can Eisenhower do except run? If nothing else, like the girl in the clever stocking ads, he owes it to his audience.

3. Daddy Cometh, Little David Dieth, the Pygmies Inherit (1956)

San Francisco, August 22, 1956

I STOOD on tired arches from four o'clock until seven at the airport under the vigilant eye of police brass, sheriffs, and secret-service men, watching for the Presidential candidate of the Republican Party to descend from the heavens and walk the Republican earth at San Francisco.

While we waited for the Republican Godot one of the apostles appeared, in the person of Leonard Hall, and was immediately surrounded by a huddle of admiring reporters. Cut off from his words by the greater height of my colleagues, I lost the story but I caught the glint of the setting sun on the back of his bald head.

After a while there was a commotion, and the Fallen Archangel in the person of Harold Stassen appeared, and immediately the circle around Hall was dissolved and re-formed around Stassen. Again I pressed forward hopefully, only to be pushed back by the sturdier shoulders of my colleagues of the open notebooks, and again all I saw was the sun's glint on Stassen's thinning hair. Someone jibed Hall about losing his audience, and Hall retorted, "All you have to do to attract a crowd is to become a controversial figure."

All this excitement and repartee helped to pass the time, but it did no good to my arches. The pity of it was that I couldn't find anything to sit down on, or even to lean against, since the cars that had brought the celebrities or were waiting for the Eisenhower party were shiny new Cadillacs and Lincolns, and I felt it would be a sacrilege to risk scratching their polish.

Finally there was a flurry of excitement, and the sun which had once illumined the heads of Len Hall and Harold Stassen was now all shimmering silver on the *Columbine*. The lines tightened and surged forward, the apostles and their wives and the Fallen Archangel lined up in front of the landing ramp, the door opened, the President came down the steps to a line of eagerly outstretched hands. He bestowed his handshake on Richard Nixon and Harold Stassen impartially.

The Republican worries were over. Daddy had come again out of the sky to take charge of his children. He would quiet their fears and lift their spirits. All was for the best in the best of all possible personality cults.

I was quite certain that Eisenhower could walk on the waters, but can he bring life to the corpse of the Republican convention? This is, up to the present writing, the flattest and phoniest excuse for a national political convention that I have ever had the unhappiness of living through. Maybe it will take on a spark of genuineness if Harold Stassen can persuade the delegates to let him make a speech before they vote on the Vice-Presidency. But except for the battered-but-unbowed figure of Stassen, there isn't a politician here with a milligram of guts or a millimeter of backbone.

How has it happened that this assemblage has been stampeded into clamoring for Nixon? Not because Eisenhower has asked them to nominate Nixon, or even wants them to. In fact, there is more than a suspicion that he would have welcomed a Herter boom if it could ever have got off the ground.

One reason for it is that, despite the desperate need the Republicans have for Eisenhower as their candidate and ikon, there is a counterstrain here as well. The old Taft men and the McCarthy men have not died; they have only gone underground and are living in the catacombs of their own repressed minds. The right-wingers have not suddenly sprouted wings of angelic moderation.

They don't dare show their true feelings toward Eisenhower himself because the general mood is now one of uniting behind him. But, whether on a conscious or unconscious level, their feelings are still there. And the threat to dump Nixon has evoked their anger all the more massively. It gives them their only chance to express how they feel about the Top Man who is their only hope but to whom they are not wholly reconciled.

As for the rest of the convention delegates, who belong genuinely to the Eisenhower wing of the party, they go along with the Nixon boom because of the Great Taboo—the issue of the President's health. They have grown so sensitive to any mention of it that they dare not confront it even in their own minds. After saying so many times that the President is sturdier than ever, they have convinced themselves that he can run up Nob Hill at double-quick and not miss a heartbeat.

San Francisco, August 23, 1956

The last fragmentary hope of even a tiny spear of dissenting courage to pierce the darkness and dreary uniformity of this convention was snuffed out last night when Harold Stassen crawled up the speakers' ramp, lay down before all the delegates and ate dirt. I wrote yesterday that he was the only man left here with even a millimeter of backbone. I was wrong in my measurement by the whole millimeter.

His crusade to save his party and his country from the incubus of Nixon had been dictated (he said) by conscience. But when he rose to second Nixon's nomination his conscience was a bedraggled wraith of a dog scurrying around the corner with his tail between his legs, and all that was left was an oily voice begging to be taken back into the councils of those who hated him as a party traitor. His high resolve to fight and fight turned out to be a work of sculpture enduringly carved in butter.

When I heard President Eisenhower say at his shotgun press conference that Stassen was folding, I thought of the delightful stanza of "It Ain't Necessarily So":

> *Little David was small, but oh my,*
> *Little David was small, but oh my.*
> *He took on Goliath*
> *Who lay down and dieth—*
> *Little David was small, but oh my.*

The Little David from Pennsylvania, in taking on the Nixon Old Guard and the Eisenhower High Command, had taken on a Goliath. But in the end it was Little David—and not Goliath—who lay down and dieth.

Stassen's collapse had at least one merit—it came out of human weakness. The rest of the convention was the child of automation, governed by a passion of neither heart nor brain.

Everything ran as if it had been first fed into an electronic machine and then returned to us by feedback. Charley Halleck, the aging boy wonder from Indiana, made an idiot nominating speech with a climax couched in the second person in the form of a prayer to the deity whose name was being put up. At any moment I expected him to burst into a new version of the Twenty-third Psalm. While the speech was still winding its tortured way along, banners and gadgets for a spontaneous demonstration were being distributed through the hall.

The seconders had been picked by one of those card-punching machines that sorts out your sex, color, occupation, residence, race and religious faith. A young mother of six children from Texas gave a little talk as for a TV testimonial to soap powder. She was followed by an ex-Notre Dame football coach, who was followed by a young Southerner testifying as a reformed Democrat, then a farmer, a Rhode Island steelworker who started out by flashing his union card, a Boston woman active in Jewish organizations, and finally Theodore Roosevelt McKeldin of Maryland, who brought along his best elocutionary manner and sounded his final syllables with a manic perfection.

When the delegates got their chance for a demonstration, after Halleck's speech, it was a bedlam of sound and fury signifying little except that it had been carefully prepared. In fact, they had overprepared the event and the result was an anticlimax.

The drama of the Nixon nomination lay not in the lifeless nominating speech of Chris Herter, who performed the miracle of presenting Nixon as a liberal and "an Eisenhower man all the way down," but in Harold Stassen's achievement in turning defeat into dishonor.

Despite the bitterness that Stassen had attracted for three weeks, he drew no boos when he got up to speak; the managers had spread word to all the delegations that he was to be accorded the honors of an enemy in complete surrender. There was nothing Stassen said last night that he might not have better left unsaid, while all the things he had previously said about Nixon as a burden to the ticket were clamorous in the memory because they were now carefully left to silence.

Not content with hauling down his own colors, Stassen high-mindedly pleaded with his remaining battalions to haul down theirs, and to follow the Eisenhower-Nixon standard all the way. As he wound to a climax he got drunk with his own imaginative flight. Having to find a reason for his surrender, he looked into the future and saw Eisenhower (and Nixon too?) leading the nation and party "for another ten years or more," which would mean a third and fourth term. He even saw Eisenhower returning to bless a convention, like Herbert Hoover, at eighty-two.

To swallow Nixon, Harold Stassen had finally managed to convince himself that there was no danger in him because Eisenhower is immortal.

Let it be said for the record that Harold Stassen was not more craven than dozens of his fellow Republicans in the high councils of the party and the nation. He just took longer to surrender and did it more conspicuously. History will say of him that as the Nixon shadow passed over his conscience he had at least the honesty to utter a brief agonizing cry in the night. That cannot be said of the rest of the Eisenhower command, who had surrendered to the Nixon forces months ago, and who threw all their energy at the last into the near-lynching of Stassen.

Stassen's three-week ordeal is chiefly notable because it illustrates the "tyranny of opinion" which De Tocqueville noted on the American scene even a century ago. It has never been illustrated better than in the cruel mood of hate that surrounded Stassen during the whole week here. It needed a man made of sterner stuff than Stassen to stand up under it and keep taking it.

November 4, 1956

One of the strangest campaigns in American election history is drawing to a close. None of the great issues of the life and death of the nation, which Stevenson has raised, have been met or answered.

Warnings have been met with ridicule, arguments with slogans. In the area of Middle East policy the irrelevance of the Republican response reached a kind of climax. If there were some relation between performance and responsibility, Dulles would be forced to resign, Eisenhower would wear sackcloth, and the architects of our disastrous Middle East policy would be buried in the ruins of their own making. Yet the pollmakers tell us that the Middle East fiasco may have strengthened, not weakened, the Republican chances.

Perhaps this is less strange than it seems. On the level of double talk the slogan makers cannot be beaten. If you are searching for a father symbol you don't examine too closely what Daddy says. In the realm of chaos it is fitting that Topsy-Turvy should be king. Where great issues are dwarfed to the dimensions of a personality cult, it is natural that the pygmies will inherit the earth.

We stand on the edge of some of the greatest events of our era. Yet in this time of the crumbling of empires and the testing of nations we seem about to entrust our destinies to a bewildered and uncreative soldier whose days may be numbered, and to a cynical young man with a gray flannel heart.

4. The Triumph of Conformity (1956)

November 7, 1956

WHEN YOU MEASURE the massiveness of Eisenhower's victory you glimpse the full outlines of the American urge to cling to normalcy in a time of world disorder, and to worship at the shrine of an immaculate Daddy figure in a time when little children are afraid.

It isn't just the morning-after mood that brings to my mind a sentence from a letter of Tom Wolfe's, the last letter he wrote—"I've made a long journey and been to a strange country, and I've seen the dark man very close." It has been a long campaign for all of us. In a real sense the campaign began with General Eisenhower's first illness, when he had to decide whether he would run and the country started to decide whether it wanted him. We have seen many strange things in the course of this long journey. And we have glimpsed, much too closely, the particular "dark man" I have in mind—the figure of an American electorate that shuts its mind to logic and reason and the evidence of events and makes a cult of one man's personality because it has been shrewdly fashioned and shrewdly sold.

The victory belongs not to Eisenhower but to the traits in the American people that have made him the dominant figure on the political horizon. The victory belongs to what is popular and fashionable, to what is familiar and comfortable because it is mediocre, to the "adjusting man" who adjusts to what everyone is doing. It is the triumph of conformity.

It is too easy for us to talk of the Republican "slogans" as the key to the landslide. If slogans alone could win, then Madison Avenue would become the permanent ruling group of the nation. The real point is that this time the slogans "took" because of the elements in the contemporary situation and contemporary character that prepared people's minds for them.

Despite the anguished mood of those for whom the election results are dismal, the Republic will, of course, survive even four more years under the Republicans. American industry will continue to boom, not because of the wisdom of those who own and run the country but because of the magnificent technological plants and skills we have. Money will continue to flow. Violence will continue to erupt all around the rim of disintegrating empires, and Daddy will continue to issue reassuring bulletins.

It should be clear from this that the Republican victory leaves me unconvinced and unreconstructed. I accept the verdict of the jury in the sense in which we all accept wrongheaded verdicts that seem to go against all the evidence and are the product of a mental fixation the jury had even before the trial began.

But the fact that Eisenhower's popularity has been vindicated doesn't make a peerless leader out of a confused man struggling with hackneyed thoughts. Readers of *War and Peace* will remember Tolstoy's description of General Kutuzov, who felt that a general can do little more than watch the battle and smile reassuringly while he pretends to know what is happening and why.

General Eisenhower is our General Kutuzov. He continues to be a powerful symbol because he meets the needs of those who want to believe in something, and who fix on a man because they are too shallow and scared to think for themselves. Nietzsche wrote that "it is only the great thought that gives greatness to an action." There is no greatness of thought in Eisenhower, just as there is no real passion of belief in those who voted for him. Their victory seems a curiously joyless affair, as if they had a bad conscience and retained a lingering doubt about the verdict they rendered.

Some very good men went down under this Eisenhower wave, and some evil men have been floated on the wave into positions of power in Congress. The election has proved a triumph not only of conformity but also of coattails.

It is as if those little levers, all in a row, were lined up like good little soldiers. Once you pulled the first it took a giant intellectual effort not to pull down all the rest. "We do not ride on the railroad," said Thoreau. "It rides on us." One might say that the people didn't run the election; the election ran the people, by the same principle of mechanism that made them respond to the slogans and the smile and the arms held high as a sign that all will forever be well.

But just as Eisenhower's victory doesn't make him a great man, so Stevenson's defeat doesn't make him into a small one. Whatever his mistakes of strategy (and it is always the loser who turns out to have made all the mistakes), he fought hard, he stuck to his ideas, he went down with integrity as well as with grace. He would have made a President of the first rank. Even in defeat he may have contributed more to the processes of democracy by the nature of his campaign than Eisenhower contributed even in victory. For while Stevenson's proved a lost cause, Eisenhower has proved the lost leader. It is a tragic waste of great human material to send a man like Stevenson into political obscurity.

But it is idle to shed tears over political might-have-beens. The causes for which Stevenson and Kefauver fought still remain to be fought for in the years ahead. Two years from now and four years from now the factor of the personality cult will no longer be present in the elections. The Democratic Party is still a strong party, and it contains fresher energies and younger and more committed men and women than it has contained for some time.

Meanwhile there is the reality of an ailing President who, with all his faults, is a man of good will; and behind him the reality of an heir apparent whom all the synthetic perfumes of his recent campaigning have not washed clean.

THE POLITICAL STYLE IN AMERICA

1. Family Album

February 8, 1951

IN AN ESSAY on Hitler's childhood, in his book *Childhood and Society,* Erik Erickson says that psychologists "overdo the father attributes in Hitler's historical image." Hitler was, he says, "the adolescent who refused to become a father by any connotation . . . He was the Führer, a glorified older brother." So, of course, is Stalin. And there is always Big Brother in George Orwell's *1984*. This gives rise to some reflections on our political leaders in terms of the relations of a family.

F.D.R. was father in a democratic family where authority is not tyrannical, but he was none the less father. No one has replaced him in that role. The more his memory is pecked at by the monstrous carrion birds, the clearer it is that he left a void no one has filled. I don't mean someone to tremble before, or to imitate adoringly, or to hold our hand in the dark. I mean the feeling that on these uncharted seas it would be good to have someone with strength and wisdom at the helm.

Now that we must learn to lead a life without Father, I have amused myself playing a little game called Family Album.

Take Eisenhower. Ever since the end of the war, many of us hankered for Ike to take Father's place, but he didn't quite make the grade. He is the Trusted Family Friend, who is called in every time there is a crisis in the family. And his earthy face is good to look at even when you are not sure how much he really understands.

Then there is Dewey, who is the Pushing Suitor nobody likes. Taft is the tight and crotchety Uncle, whom we respect although it's hard to warm up to him. Hoover is the Other Uncle, who went broke during the Crash and has been living ever since in a world of illusions; we humor him but prefer not to talk about him.

Stassen is the Young Cousin from the dubious side of the family, who is always turning up with unpredictable schemes that cancel each other out. McCarthy is the Bully Boy from next door who likes to frighten little girls in dark corners, and skins dead cats. MacArthur is the Great-Uncle with delusions of grandeur who went off years ago to seek his fortune in Asia and has been sending back rich gifts and tall stories, but he is too busy playing Son of the Sun-God to the Japanese to be a father to anyone else.

Thus far the Republican side of the family. On the Democratic side, Barkley is Grandpa, who is younger and spryer than his years and kisses all the girls. Byrnes is the Distant Relative from the South, who was taken into the family business, made a flop of it, and quarreled with everyone. Chief Justice Vinson is the Southern Relative We All Like, who has a warm Kentucky way with him and settles family quarrels with a drink of bourbon and a folksy story. Acheson is the Brother Who Turned Schoolteacher, who lectures us every day on our duties and has strict ideas about what neighbors we can play with.

But how about President Truman? He isn't Father, and he isn't Big Brother, but still he is the Head of the Family, so who is he? He is Mother's Old Suitor from her home town, who was always too shy and never thought he had a chance. But he happened to come to visit us just as Father had his accident, and to everyone's surprise including his own he got accepted, and now he makes an uneasy Stepfather. We would all like to help, but Father's portrait still hangs on the living-room wall smack as you come in, and that's enough to undermine any-one.

I rather like his refusal to give up writing letters about Margaret. It is a welcome reassertion of the private outlook in public affairs. Or maybe it's his way of saying that since we don't accept him as a political father, he'll be damned if he'll stop being a real one.

2. The Presidency Eats Men

(New York *Star*)
January 20, 1949

ON THIS DAY of President Truman's inauguration, one may ask, What is it that impels a man to move heaven and earth to get into the world's toughest job?

There is no question about how punishing a job the Presidency is. It eats men. It left John Adams and his son, John Quincy Adams, embittered men. It made Jefferson and Jackson the targets of the most extreme abuse. It quite literally killed Lincoln and Garfield and McKinley and Franklin Roosevelt. It broke Woodrow Wilson's heart and, in a somewhat different way, Hoover's.

It is not so much an office as an obstacle race and a Gehenna combined. You have to deal with a Congress which remains only briefly in a honeymoon mood. You have to listen to every pressure group and seem to give in to none. You have to handle the press and trust you will be the bird on the front page every day, but mainly for the brilliance of your plumage and not to be roasted, boiled, fried, carved up or flayed alive. You have to seem knowing about an administrative structure so vast that no dozen men could know its details. You have to run a foreign policy that girdles the globe, yet be aware of what opinion is sprouting up from the grass roots of every hamlet in your own country.

You have to keep yourself from being run by the generals and admirals who run the biggest military show on earth, and also to hold at arm's length the corporation bigwigs who run the biggest economic show on earth. You have to be statesmanlike in language, yet present an image of boldness and decisiveness. You have to be a nonpartisan national leader without ceasing to be a very partisan party leader. You have to attract talent, yet see to it that plenty of gravy gets to the patronage boys. You have to have your wrist broken shaking hands and your memory tortured remembering faces. You have to be remote and dignified, as the world symbol of the greatest democracy in history; and at the same time warm and earthy, so that no one will regard you as glacial and high-hat.

You have to remember to smile even when your temper is at the boiling point and your digestion is gutted—for a frown might send the stock market tumbling and the chancelleries of the world into hysteria. You have to forget you were ever a private man with a private life. You have to get used to seeing the members of your family roasted for things over which they have no control. You have to learn how to take it, but be restrained in dishing it out. You have to assume that your mistakes will be magnified and trumpeted from the market place, and your achievements either ignored or credited to some kingmaker in your inner circle. You have to wake up every morning and go to bed every night in the midst of a fresh crisis. You have to learn how to ride the whirlwind and command the storm, with only your own limited mortal capacities to aid you.

What makes men hunger for a chance at such a martyrdom? The immediate answer, of course, is the power and the glory. The American Presidency is today the most powerful office in the democratic world, and in some ways more powerful even than Stalin's. For while the head of the American state does not have the arbitrary power that the Russian leader does, the consequences of his power are more far-reaching. A decision he makes will change the destinies of people in Paris or Tel-Aviv, and on the steppes of Asia and on the banks of the Congo. Such power is a heady stimulant, and a man would be scarcely a man to be immune to it.

Another answer lies in the dreams the young men dream in our American culture. They are the dreams not of the contemplative life, or the philosopher's wisdom, or the saint's saintliness, but of always being midstream in the current of action and excitement. The style of American culture is the style of continuous dynamic movement, and the dream of the Presidency is the ultimate dream in American life because it is a dervish dance of activity, the succession of your pictures in the papers and your name on every lip. This is at once the strength and the weakness of America.

Finally, there is no other culture in which the head of state has so direct a relation with the people. Martin Van Buren, writing in his autobiography about Andrew Jackson, pointed out that Jackson got his strength from contact with the people. "They were his blood relations—the only blood relations he had." In a symbolic sense this must be true of every President. It is the old fable of Antaeus and how he kissed the earth his mother and renewed his strength thereby.

3. The Steel Case: The Nine and One

May 12, 1952

WE ALL HUNGER for theater, and when old John W. Davis gets up in a crowded Supreme Court this afternoon to argue the steel company's case against the Presidential seizure, it will be great and historic theater. It is almost like the old times of the New Deal cases, when almost any day the nine judges of the court would be listening to fervent invocations of Magna Charta and King Charles I, and when every expensive lawyer preparing for a big corporation would end his plea with a dark prediction of certain doom for the Republic under the Presidential dictatorship.

I notice that everyone is pinning his hopes or fears on the court's decision: those who expect it to save the Republic from Hitlerism or Stalinism, those who expect it to solve all strike problems in crucial industries, those who expect it to bring certainty and order into a troubled world. Even the more intelligent commentators are saying, in effect, "Now we will know just how much power the President has or doesn't have."

Would it were that easy, but alas, it isn't. Presidential power is a shifting thing. It isn't marked out beyond peradventure, like the path of the constellations or the freshly painted traffic lanes. The reason is that American government is not parliamentary government, as the British is, but Presidential government. The main axis of power lies with the President, because it is he who more and more has had to give direction to what might otherwise become chaos or deadlock. That is the effective criticism of Judge Pine's decision against the government in the steel case: you cannot really talk of strictly limited Presidential power in a government where the crucial leadership has to come from the White House. The Presidency is more than an enumeration of powers. It is a set of functions. The real question about a particular Presidential act in any crisis is whether he could have performed his function in that crisis without it.

Every President has had different notions about where his power extended. The "strong" Presidents, like Jackson and Lincoln, T.R., Wilson and F.D.R., have stretched it as far as they could. The "weak" Presidents have preferred to let Congress give direction to the government. Yet even a President like Jefferson, who believed in principle that Congress should overshadow the executive, acted in a crisis to stretch the President's powers—as witness the Barbary War and the Louisiana Purchase. In the case of Lincoln, you get the example of a President who was not a dictator at heart but who went very far in meeting the war emergency—in his treatment of the war governors, in raising a Federal Army, in the habeas corpus cases, in the Emancipation Proclamation—knowing all the time that his true judge was to be history.

This will be, of course, new law that the Supreme Court will be shaping. You can't decide what power the President has over the steel crisis by quoting what someone said about Andrew Johnson almost a century ago, or what Theodore Roosevelt wrote about the "stewardship theory" in his autobiography. Neither can you decide it by talking of the tyranny of the Stuart kings.

I don't envy the judges their job. The man who is the President has one of the hardest jobs in the world. But the nine who sit on the Supreme Court have a hard job too: They must find good arguments to back up a hunch that each of them may have about how a good democracy ought to operate. Just as each President has behaved differently about his powers, so each Supreme Court justice brings to the case his whole life experience—and then looks around for precedents.

One fact is clear: It is the court that will decide, and the President who will listen, because (as Harry Truman has said) he is a constitutional President. This running the gantlet of judicial review has not always been happy in our history. But in the present phase of the world it is a triumph to know that the President's powers—however great—are subject to the law of the land.

May 13, 1952

You can never figure how the Supreme Court will vote on a case by studying the questions they throw at the lawyers, but it is at least a clue. Sometimes the judges indulge in a bit of intellectual fun at the expense of the poor, sweating counsel (like Solicitor General Perlman yesterday), and sometimes at the expense of each other. Sometimes, no matter how clever you think your guesses about them are, they cross you up on decision day.

If the court decides the Constitutional issue of the President's power to seize an industry like steel, it looks now as if the decision will turn on three questions. First, what test is there to show it is an emergency? Second, has the President exhausted other methods than seizure? Third, what is there to determine where the President will stop? There were questions thrown at the Solicitor General yesterday on each of these issues.

The most critical judges seem to be the liberals, including four of the five Roosevelt appointees—Justices Black, Douglas, Frankfurter and Jackson.

Black, who belongs to the Populist tradition of the South, has been the most consistent liberal on both economic and civil liberties issues. If he thought the emergency were real, he would not hesitate to uphold a broad conception of executive power. But he is skeptical of the President, and, given his brilliant experience as Senator, his first impulse is to see most issues of the division of powers through the eyes of a legislator.

Douglas, like Black, is suspicious of the President and the group around him. He has spoken out against the fear that has been engulfing the country in the name of emergency, and that has endangered civil liberties. He is likely to keep asking, as he did yesterday, where the President's power will end in the name of emergency.

Justice Frankfurter used to be a law professor at Harvard, and he still likes to act the professor in the courtroom, peppering the attorneys with a steady stream of caustic, witty, and sometimes involved questions. He helped give the Solicitor General a bad time yesterday. Expert on procedural matters, he likes to avoid deciding broad constitutional issues, holding that the nation is better off if the judges refrain from too many sweeping decisions.

As for Justice Jackson, he is the Peck's Bad Boy of the court and seems to relish the role, taunting his colleagues and pointing out that their opinions make them dolts, nincompoops and worse. He remarked, for example, of the Douglas opinion in the released-time case that it would be more useful to future students of psychiatry than to those of constitutional law. He is a stylist with gaiety and abandon, but he can also be bitter. I think he will cast an acid anti-Truman vote.

Given these four Nos, Justice Burton can be counted on for the fifth that makes a majority. A gentle, insignificant Republican, he kept hammering yesterday at the President's failure to use the Taft-Hartley law. As for Justice Reed, who is schoolteacherish and unimaginative, the absence of a clear statute on which to base seizure will probably sway this "swing Judge" in the same direction.

Which leaves three judges for the minority—the last three Truman appointees. The leader of the trio, Chief Justice Vinson, is good-natured and politically shrewd and may yet figure a strategic way of saving the President from a bad drubbing. The other two are dreary wheelhorses, whose opinions have been utterly without distinction. They will probably go with Vinson.

June 3, 1952

Six judges of the Supreme Court have written separate opinions to give six good reasons for slapping down President Truman's steel seizure. I assume this is not just the feverish literary impulse of the prolific brethren, but their recognition of how historic the decision is. They use different routes, but they arrive at the common view that Harry Truman has blunderingly (though innocently) tried to take hold of a dangerous extension of Presidential power.

The anti-Truman and pro-steel company press would do well not to celebrate too hastily. The majority has not denied that the government can seize an industry, or even that the President might seize it where Congress has failed to provide for other action. But where Congress has spoken, the court tells us, even the Commander in Chief has no power except as Congress has directed. The court has thus grappled directly with the massive issue of the division of constitutional powers in a crisis state. Here was no occasion for technical legal coyness, but a frontal attack on the problem. Future Presidents will not be grateful to Harry Truman for having raised this great issue of the scope of Presidential power through a case riddled by irrelevant matters, and one which rested on so shaky a foundation.

Writing several weeks ago, I was brash enough to hazard that it would turn out to be a six-to-three opinion against the President. I was luckier than usual for an amateur. I had no pipelines, but the records and opinions of the nine men were available, to be interpreted in the light of their personalities.

The legislative emphasis of Justices Black and Burton found expression yesterday in their opinions. So too did Justice Douglas' fear that the power used in this case against the corporations might be used tomorrow against the unions. Justice Frankfurter, always aware of how complex the task of government is, was swayed by the evidence that Congress had consciously withheld the power of seizure. Justice Jackson, the most pungent of the judges in style and attack, hit at the jugular when he showed what the power claimed by the President could mean if he used it to back up his already immense power over foreign policy.

Where I went sadly wrong was on Justice Clark. I thought that he, and not (as it turned out) Justice Reed, would be the third dissenter along with Justices Vinson and Minton.

Chief Justice Vinson's dissent, upholding the President, was neither fainthearted nor apologetic. It dealt its blows lustily at his colleagues.

They had behind them Jefferson's tradition of the fear of swollen executive power. The Chief Justice, in turn, had behind him the tradition of effective crisis action, reaching back to the great authors of the Federalist Papers. By painting the President as only a temporary trustee for the power of Congress, to keep its legislative intent from being destroyed, Vinson showed strategic skill. But where he was most telling was in his contemptuous rejection of the "messenger-boy concept of the Presidency," which sees him as running to Congress with a message whenever action is needed.

Charles Curtis once called the Supreme Court Justices "lions before the throne." The lions have roared, defending the throne of liberty. They have put a bad crimp into the expansion of Presidential power, which has been going on at least since T.R., and even since Lincoln. They have elevated Congress to a position of supremacy in the scheme of government that it has not had for a long time. Congress is the new and glittering Golden Boy, for whom the whole creation moves.

4. Portrait of the Warren Court

September 30, 1953

GOVERNOR EARL WARREN'S APPOINTMENT as Chief Justice of the United States is surely one of the two or three most important that President Eisenhower will have made. Here is a man upon whom will descend the mantle of Marshall and Taney, Chase and Hughes. Is he big enough to wear it well?

My answer, obviously still a guess, is Yes. I will not say confidently what Cardozo said when the appointment of Charles Evans Hughes was announced in 1930, that it is "a great choice of a great man for a great office." Warren's stature, despite his long years of public office, has never fully been measured. But his record as Governor suggests that he will not close his mind to the demands of the great office.

Some will lament the fact that Warren is a political rather than a judicial figure. I pointed out, in my comment after Vinson's death, that politicians in judicial robes are not the medicine the doctor ordered. Yet this is not a decisive reason against Warren. The thing to lament is never the appointment of a strong and able political figure, even to the Supreme Court, but the choice of a weak party hack, such as Clark or Minton. Only one of the three great Chief Justices we have had—Hughes—was primarily a jurist. The other two—Marshall and Taney—were picked because their political views were so close to the views of John Adams and Andrew Jackson.

Along with many others, I should have liked to see Associate Justice Robert H. Jackson raised to the Chief Justiceship, but he was once a New Dealer, and his chance for the top job was thrown away in his dramatic attack on Justice Black. If there were another Federal judge somewhere like Learned Hand—whom both Roosevelt and Truman foolishly passed over—he would be the inevitable choice. Thus, failing and forsaking all others, the Warren appointment is a logical one.

Warren's abilities for the post are considerable. A Chief Justice must be a good administrator, and he has shown himself one. He must have the capacity to make people work together, especially since four of the seven Democrats left on the court—Black, Frankfurter, Douglas and Jackson—are men of tough and independent mind. Taft once wrote that the job of a Chief Justice was that of "massing the court," by which he meant holding it in line with some degree of agreement. No one could do it with this court, but Warren's skill in California in winning in both party primaries shows that he should be able at least to tangle with the much harder problem of conciliation on the court.

But all this does not reach to the heart of the matter. The real point is that the Supreme Court, in the coming years, will be tested mainly in the area of civil liberties, which needs a generous spirit and a devotion to the principles of the open society.

Warren has shown his liberalism as a Republican. But, more important, he has shown his belief in civil liberties, in the valiant record he made in the University of California oath case, where he fought both Hearst's regent, Marshall Neylan, and his own reactionary Lieutenant Governor Knight. If he can maintain this doughtiness, he will deserve to rank with the great ones of the judicial tradition.

June 5, 1957

If you ask how the tide of thought and feeling is running in America today, the most hopeful and exciting place to look is the United States Supreme Court. If you are searching for people in the seats of the mighty in whom the fires of democratic belief have by no means burned out, but glow with light and heat, look for them—at least four of them, perhaps more—on the court.

I have been wanting to write this for some months, but have held back because I feared that the evidence for it was still not strong enough. But now I may as well go out on a limb, even if I land in limbo. This week the Supreme Court handed down two decisions of major importance. I refer to the Du Pont antitrust case and the case involving FBI informers. Add to this last week's decision on the Fifth Amendment and the assumption of a feeling of guilt, and you have the clues to my strange euphoria.

Of these cases it is the Du Pont decision that got the most excited press. I notice in the editorial of one of our contemporaries that "the whole American corporate structure is shaken by it."

But when I look into the court's majority opinion itself, to see what rulings it contains so monstrous as to shake "the whole American corporate structure," what do I find? The doctrine that when one big corporation has come to dominate another big corporation by the extent of its stock ownership, when they are "vertically" linked (that is, one supplies the raw material for the other to manufacture), and when the dominant corporation (Du Pont) uses the other (General Motors) as a market outlet for its own products (GM bought from Du Pont two thirds of its paints, almost half its textile fibers), competition is crippled, the antitrust laws have been violated, and the two companies had better do something about it.

Is this the kind of treasonable doctrine to shake the foundations of our corporate economy? If so, it must be because those foundations rest through and through on monopoly. And if that is so, how can these same editorial writers become lyrical—as they so frequently do on other less mournful occasions—about "free enterprise" in America?

The Du Pont decision shows that there are still Americans who remain unimpressed by the magic of two of the world's biggest, most successful and most powerful corporations. The four majority judges have dared to challenge a symbol.

By the same token the decision in the Jencks case, calling for the opening of FBI files to the defense when they contain reports from an informant who is a government witness, is an even more important one than the Du Pont decision. For here seven of the Justices dared confront the symbol of the FBI and its director, J. Edgar Hoover. The lone dissenter, Justice Tom Clark—who had been Attorney General once and spoke feelingly of his experience in pursuing political offenders—invoked Hoover's name and prestige as his shield and buckler.

The same press contemporary sees the Jencks decision as "crippling the FBI in its effective watch." No doubt it will be harder for the FBI to get convictions in political cases (that of Jencks involved the charge of perjury about a non-Communist labor affidavit) if it must give the wretched accused man the elementary right of testing the veracity of his accusers by studying the original file material and comparing it with the court testimony.

But when was it a rule in constitutional law that the comfort and convenience of a government agency must override the constitutional rights of an accused man? Surely, in order to keep itself informed about dangers to its security the nation is under no imperative to give the informer a specially enshrined place denied to all others.

One of the striking facts about these decisions is that both were written by Justice William J. Brennan, Jr., and that he has shown in his voting so far a tendency to stand with Justices Black and Douglas on issues of civil liberties and corporate power. It is also interesting that Chief Justice Earl Warren often joins with them.

Little was known about the judicial views of either Warren or Brennan before President Eisenhower appointed them to the court. Few would have guessed that these appointees of a Republican Administration would show up as so much more militantly liberal than the rather sorry lot of Truman appointees. Yet this is what has happened.

If there is a moral, it is that the quality of a Justice goes beyond his politics or that of the President who appointed him. It is a matter of his realism, intellectual sharpness, courage—and the image he has of himself. Warren and Brennan, like Black and.Douglas, are beyond political reward or reprisal. They have cut out for themselves a great task in a great age—the task of conserving and extending the freedom of an open society.

September 17, 1958

No matter how much the Confederate twins—Governors Faubus and Almond—may twist and turn and squirm in their evasive tactics, they will in the end come up against a Supreme Court which has given a sign to the nation and the world. The sign was that the court will not equivocate and will not yield.

All the tricks of shutting the schools, holding plebiscites, reopening them as "private" schools with state "donations," "assignments" on a Jim Crow pattern—all will be of no avail. It is clear that the court as constituted today is sophisticated enough to strip away the mask of hypocrisy that covers the true intent of the white-supremacists, and courageous enough to confront and defy the ugly visage of racial hatred. If there were any doubt of this hitherto, a reading of the questions which the Justices put to the counsel for the Little Rock School Board at last week's hearing should dispel it.*

One got from this particular session both a total portrait of the Supreme Court and a set of individual profiles as each of the Justices asked his questions or was silent.

I start with Justice Frankfurter because he is easily the most controversial and dramatic member of the court, as well as the oldest. A number of the bright young men who have written recently about the court have had fun with Frankfurter's way of treating the lawyers as if they were back in his old Harvard Law School class as students. Statistically, Frankfurter is ahead of all his colleagues in the number of questions and comments he throws at the lawyers—so much so that former Chief Justice Vanderbilt of New Jersey used to advise young lawyers about what to do with the "Felix problem." Yet no one can deny that it was Frankfurter, last week, who kept firing questions showing up the role of Faubus in the whole Little Rock mess. He re-

* For the broader discussion of the issue of school desegregation, see page 515ff.

stated the argument of Richard Butler, the Little Rock School Board's lawyer, with the utmost clarity to show that the board had been doing pretty well until the Governor stepped in with his militia.

Justice Hugo Black had relatively few questions—almost deliberately few, as if he were trying to contrast his restraint with Frankfurter's loquacity. But when he did talk, as he did several times, it was to say something sharp and stern, as in his questioning about Faubus' "sovereignty law" and Butler's attitude toward it.

The remaining Roosevelt appointee, Justice William O. Douglas, asked no questions at all, thereby living up to his habitual chariness in making comments in court. But there are no lawyers who are ignorant of where Douglas stands on almost every issue before the court or who have any doubt that he will express his views in his written opinions with the same breezy and drastic forthrightness that marks his whole public personality. Douglas is a walker, a mountaineer, a world traveler, a prolific writer of nonlegal books—a man who lives with gusto and wants others to have a chance to fulfill themselves in their own way.

The two Truman appointees still on the court, Justices Harold Burton and Tom Clark, were not silent in the questioning. One of the achievements of Chief Justice Warren is to have managed to keep them both in team harness along with Black and Douglas on issues where in the past they might have aired their disagreements. They are both marginal men on the court. Neither of them is brilliant, yet both keep the lawyers guessing on how they will vote.

There remain the four Eisenhower appointees. Justice Harlan was active in the questioning, as befits a man whose grandfather had been the lone dissenter in the original "separate but equal" case of *Plessy v. Ferguson*. The younger Harlan is not the firebrand that his grandfather was and is unlikely to burn his name into constitutional history as the older man did. But he will be remembered for his recent opinion setting aside the conviction of Communists under the Smith Act.

As for Justices Brennan and Whittaker, the youngest members of the court, who had not been involved in the original school decision, little was heard from them the other day. But judging from Brennan's courageous decision on the FBI files, and the opinion by Whittaker on denaturalization proceedings, they will make themselves heard in the long run.

I have left Earl Warren to the end, partly because he is the Chief Justice, partly because his role in the whole integration controversy demands that he be discussed separately.

In his few years on the court, Warren has already shown himself one of the best Chief Justices in the court's history because of his shrewd and firm way of holding his colleagues together. But his friendly manner is deceptive, since it conceals a vein of iron. The iron showed pretty clearly when poor Richard Butler talked of the post-poning of integration as involving only "personal and intangible rights" for the Negro children, and Warren drove over the fleeting un-fortunate phrase like a tank. It showed also when he wondered out loud whether the Negro youngsters' school days would be over before the postponement was.

Warren is today the center of swirling and intense currents of con-troversy. He will need all his coolness and resourcefulness and courage to ride out the storms still ahead, and so will his colleagues. I think they will hold together, even the prima donnas among them. It is a great Supreme Court we have today, and it is not less great because it has had to move into the vacuum of leadership which the Administra-tion has left.

5. All-American Nine

November 26, 1958

YOU MUST HAVE SEEN their new group portrait in the papers yester-day. Each time a Supreme Court Justice dies or resigns, and a new one is tagged (this time Justice Potter Stewart of Ohio) they call in the photographer and pose stiffly for posterity in their new order of seniority. In the reshuffling, as with a game of musical chairs, every-one junior to the departed member moves up a chair, leaving the bleakest spot (farthest right, rear) to the cub.

I am glad the Supreme Court sticks to this ritual, for—aside from the foolish black robes of the Justices, and the quill pen on counsel's desk as he argues—not much else remains unchanged. The court's burdens have been multiplied, as have its enemies. The calendar is more crowded, the cases more complex than they were, yet they have to move faster. Almost every condition under which the judges of the past lived, worked, thought, conferred, wrote their decisions, has been changed. The court, moreover, has always been mixed up in the politi-cal embroilments of its time, but it is living as dangerously in our day as it ever lived.

If you like the human and dramatic, there is a book to your taste about the court—John P. Frank's *Marble Palace* (Knopf). The au-thor clerked for Justice Black, taught at a couple of law schools and is now a working lawyer—which ought to explain the interesting mix-ture in the book of the academic and the human.

He tries to do too much—to give too compressed a survey of the court's development, describe its inner workings, pass on the literary frailties as well as on the philosophical and technical skills of the judges. In the end it is a bit of a hodgepodge, but what of it? It isn't great scholarship or deep theory or even bitter polemics. But it is part of the humanizing of knowledge which makes the Tuesday accounts of the Monday decisions add up to more sense.

I like the article that Fred Rodell has written on some of the court greats, in "A Gallery of Justices," for the *Saturday Review*. He has put together an All-American Nine, or what he calls "One Man's Dream Court." It's a fascinating game. If you like to choose the Ten Best Plays, or Ten Best Movies, or Ten Greatest Scientists, why not a benchful of the great justices?

Of the ninety-three men who have served on the court since its beginnings here are Rodell's nine. He takes John Marshall and William Johnson from the Marshall court. Then he jumps and takes Samuel Miller and John Harlan from the courts that sat between the Civil War and the turn of the century, the latter being the *Plessy v. Ferguson* dissenter. Then another jump, and he takes the great trio of giants— Holmes, Hughes and Brandeis—from the court of the early twentieth century. He ends with his two favorite judges from the present bench —Black and Douglas.

Note that, except for Marshall, Rodell has packed his bench with liberals; and, except for Marshall and Hughes, it is also a bench of rebels and dissenters, on both economic and civil liberties issues. Even on a tribunal so massively based on precedent, it is the nonconformists who have done the most creative work.

I don't quarrel overmuch with this bias. But there are really only two judges whom everyone would choose—Marshall and Holmes. After that it is pretty much a grab bag, if you are willing to defend what you grab.

I have two dissents from Rodell's list. I cannot accept a list of Supreme Court greats which omits Roger Taney. Marshall and Taney, between them, not only dominated the court for an interminable stretch but also laid the foundations of our constitutional law. To include Taney, I omit William Johnson—an interesting man, but a relatively slight figure. Similarly I find it hard to omit the craggy figure of Chief Justice Stone, especially after Mason's biography. To make room for him, I should have to drop Douglas.

Thus my own list reads Marshall, Taney, Miller, Harlan, Holmes, Hughes, Brandeis, Stone and Black. Not a novel list, but in such matters novelty is not the deepest consideration.

One of the harshest compulsives in making such a list is to limit yourself to only one member of the present court. Despite the attacks on it, mostly by know-nothings, it is a court that contains some extraordinary men. In an age of rubber-stamped political personalities, our justices have managed to be themselves.

Actually there are four men on the court—Black, Frankfurter, Douglas and Warren—who could sit on an all-time bench without diminishing its stature. Black is hewn out of the Alabama soil, with a powerful mind that has remained steadfastly militant. Frankfurter is scholar and tactician, unfailingly and infernally articulate, the "concurringest" judge who has ever sat on the bench, ever searching an agonized conscience. Douglas has a good deal of the same outspokenness as Black and—like him—courage and a fierce passion for freedom. And Warren, while he has been on the court too briefly to show the whole profile of his future development, has already displayed the qualities of a great Chief Justice.

6. The Fall of Adams

June 13, 1958

ONE COULD PREACH a moral sermon on it, or write one of those elegant eighteenth-century poetic discourses on the Vanity of Human Wishes.

Here is Sherman Adams sitting pretty, like a feudal baron of the crags, commanding every passage to the fortress of power at the top. Here he is, in effect exercising the daily power of the Presidency, hurling his brief but searing thunderbolts as he snaps sharp orders or initials little memoranda that can move mountains. And suddenly, because of some hotel bills and a few Washington calls, a minor deity is toppled.

There are some almost comic aspects about the Adams case, using "comedy" in the large sense of social irony in which Balzac used it. I never trusted the legend of Adams as a crusty, ascetic Yankee who had strayed from Walden Pond, where he had lived on beans, as Thoreau did, for twenty-seven cents a day. But certainly there is nothing Byzantine about the Adams standard of living. He has been held up as a model of all the Puritan virtues. In fact, only the other day he gave a commencement talk in which he exhorted the youth of America to go back to the simple imperatives of the Bible.

To have such a man fall from grace for a couple of measly thousand dollars of hotel tabs gives you the same kind of jolt as the discovery that a practicing prison psychiatrist has himself been in and out of twenty-three mental hospitals. What makes it worse is the nature of Adams' job—a job that Franklin Roosevelt used to describe as one requiring a "passion for anonymity." I am afraid that Adams is going to be the most publicized anonymous man since the Unknown Soldier.

I am sure Adams feels sincerely the note of injured innocence which his letter to Oren Harris strikes—that his relationship with Bernard Goldfine was a private one, and that it was none of the committee's business. But a man with as much power as Sherman Adams cannot argue that he is insulated against the kind of facts which would damn any lesser official.

Two of his arguments in defense crumble right away. One is the plea that he thought he was staying in Goldfine's "personal apartment" at the Sheraton-Plaza—in effect in his home; but given the variety of suites he bedded down in, the Goldfine hotel home was amazingly mobile, even for our era of frenetic change. The other is that he never interceded for Goldfine but only passed on his inquiry to the appropriate government agency. This is too clever to pass as Spartan simplicity. If he was only a kind of common carrier, or conduit, why would Goldfine bother to appeal to him? Surely Goldfine could send a three-cent letter himself to the FTC. Or would he have thought, like the rest of us, that even a phone call of inquiry from Adams was worth a thousand letters?

The basic Adams defense is that the whole thing concerned only "the entertaining of myself and my family by an old friend." When Jim Hagerty was asked how the Adams case differed from the famous minks of the Truman Administration, he answered lamely that he didn't know enough about the Truman cases. How ancient can contemporary history get?

But Goldfine's counsel, a nimble fellow called Robb, was not so coy. "It's quite different," he said. "These are old friends of long standing. The people who got mink coats were not friends of long standing." The moral is clear. Friendship conquers all. The cash nexus—or rather, the hotel tab nexus—withers away (like the state) under the spell of time and brotherhood. Minks can die and be skinned for auld lang syne but not for acquaintanceships that pass in the night.

The Adams case seems to be a family affair in still another sense. It involves not just Sherman Adams but the whole White House family. I suppose Eisenhower can convince himself that Adams is a martyr, tell the House committee and the newspapers to go chase themselves, affirm again (as with Nixon in the dim past) that Adams is clean as a hound's et cetera, and sit tight with Adams under the White House shelter while tempests rage outside.

It is a terrifying thing to ask what would happen if Adams decides that his usefulness is past and that he must go. Who will take his place as President—I mean, as the executive officer of the Executive? Who will ride herd, who will say No and sometimes Yes, who will sweat from morn to night and take work home, who will know the President so well that he can anticipate what the President will think before the President thinks it? Who will run the wheel within a wheel that keeps the whole vast machine of the Presidency moving?

Yet in the end, I think Adams will have to go. For a quite simple reason: If he stays, the whole moral authority of the President in cases of this kind will melt away. If in the future there arises another case like that of Air Force Secretary Talbott or FCC Commissioner Richard Mack, how will a President who defended and kept Adams be able to ask for the resignation of any man who is not Adams?

That is why I go out on a Cassandra limb and say the luckless Adams is through, and we shall have to find another President.

June 15, 1958

If the case of Sherman Adams is a symbol, then the disease of our time is the moral slackness which can see nothing wrong in taking gifts from a man who stands to gain or lose considerably from the governmental power the gift receiver can wield.

The character witnesses for Adams say that his ethical standards are conspicuously high. Their testimony needs to be weighed against the known facts about the gifts. But if Adams is to be counted as a Puritan in Babylon, then we can only say sadly that Babylon must be a crumbling city and we are all lost in it.

Despite Hagerty's effort to say that the gifts are irrelevant, the known facts are stubbornly before us, and Adams has admitted them. Whether he also got a rug and a vicuña coat as gifts, he did let Goldfine pick up his hotel bills, and he did make inquiries of two government agencies. These are not disputed. What the White House trio (Eisenhower, Adams, Hagerty) disputes is the motive for accepting the gifts and the interpretation to be placed on Adams' intervention for Goldfine.

Motive is a hard thing to be sure about. If you want to do a little fancy psychologizing you might wonder whether Adams is one of those people who are so sure of their purity that they feel the ordinary rules of ethical behavior don't apply to them.

The trio's basic contention is that Adams didn't intervene at all for Goldfine—that he just passed on his queries to the appropriate agencies. A nation that will believe this will believe anything. Goldfine was no innocent who didn't know the Washington ropes and didn't know the address and phone number of the Federal Trade Commission. Nor was Adams a hard-working Congressman trying to keep a bewildered constituent happy, and passing his letter on to the appropriate office.

Adams was in effect the acting head of the United States government, performing the practical daily functions of the number two man in Washington, and known all through the government for the immense power he wields. As such he was performing an act, if not of outward intervention then of symbolic interest, for a friend who had done him favors.

If an agency official knew the Washington ropes he would know how to behave. Maybe he would write an austere memo for the record, and maybe even rule against the friend of Adams on the particular pending matter. But he would be careful in the future to give very special attention to anything that involved him.

Morality is an individual matter, but the setting which shapes it is a social one. It is hard for all except unusual men to rise above the prevailing ethic of their age and society, and Adams clearly is not an unusual man.

I do not argue from this that our whole society is going to pot. I am more interested in what the Adams case shows about the frame of mind of the Eisenhower Administration. What is crucial here is not so much the extent of intervention in behalf of a particular rich man, but the extent of identification with the whole community of rich men.

June 20, 1958

The President read his words bravely from the big cards with the big type. Next to an Edward-Wally tragedy ("All for Love; or The World Well Lost"), the hottest political drama you can put on the boards is "Hypocrisy Exposed; or The Marksman Pinned to His Own Target." The reporters were there for only one theme. The prevailing note at the press conference was of a leaden hopelessness. The hopelessness lay in the fact that something had happened which could never unhappen, and that all the President's horses and all the President's men could never put this particular Humpty Dumpty together again.

What the conference really came up with, after all the talk, was the President's cry from the heart about Adams—"I need him."

There is not much you can say in answer. Evidently the two Presidential campaigns of 1952 and 1956 were quite right in the Republican slogan about the "indispensable man." But they had the man's name wrong. It was not Eisenhower, but Adams. The President's "I need him" was meant to cut through all the arguments about the meaning of what Adams had done. Whatever he had done, the President was saying, and whoever he was, the Presidential job simply could not be accomplished without him.

This was what I was driving at when I wrote in an earlier column that the Adams case was more than a case of political ethics, it was in effect a constitutional crisis. Unlikely as it may seem, we have a new gimmick in the American Presidency—a built-in feature whereby a President who cannot or will not himself transact the daily business of office can stipulate a kind of tenure at will for the man he picks to run the nation. Try to knock the props out from under that man, and you suddenly find yourself faced by the possibility that you may knock them out from under the office of President itself.

If anything was needed to underscore how thin the base of talent is on which the Administration is built, this episode does it. In a nation of 175 million people, the President cannot find one other man whom he can use (as he himself puts it) to prepare the material on which he will himself make the decisions. Where has all the talent gone to? Where is the new blood that the Republican orators told us about, which was going to be pumped into Washington?

And how will he ever find the talent with which to cope with the Russians in every area of policy if we cannot find a replacement for a man who laid an egg ethically and must now go?

Or am I wrong in my "must"? I don't think I am. I do not base this, as so many are now doing, on the argument of political expediency for the Republicans in their coming campaigns. I suppose it is true that the Republicans will suffer politically, but they will suffer whether Adams goes or stays. Besides, it strikes me as a curious piece of reasoning, to raise a howl about a man's conduct in office, on the ground of principle, and then to call for his removal from office on the ground of expediency. Adams might then turn a cold eye on the whole array of Republican state chairmen and Republican Congressional candidates, and ask in what way they are holier than he is.

My belief that Adams cannot stay, but must go, has to do not with political expediency but with moral authority. His job consists mainly in telling people, in the President's name, what they can and cannot, must and must not, do. His strength has always consisted of three elements of belief—the belief in his own granite quality, the belief in the President's stern standards, and the belief that the President will unquestioningly back him up. Now all three have been undercut. Adams is not what he was. The President is not what he was, and the President's trust in Adams' judgment is no longer unquestioning.

Like the Presidency itself, the job of the President's stand-in depends less on explicit laws or bounded powers than on the intangibles of moral authority. That authority is now eroded for Adams.

Hanover, New Hampshire, September 24, 1958

The news of the Adams resignation happened to come while I was at Dartmouth, opening the "Great Issues" course. Adams cherished his old college, as did another famous alumnus, Daniel Webster. But where Webster (as Stephen Benét tells the myth) grappled with the devil here in New Hampshire and won, Adams never grappled with any devils at all but took the straight path of power—and lost.

Much of theology revolves around the trials of the Virtuous Man as he faces the Adversary. But there was a flaw in Adams' virtue, and despite his stock talk about the "campaign of vilification" against him, the Adversary had not taken up diabolical quarters in either a Republican or Democratic conspiracy against him. If the Adversary was anywhere, it was in him.

For all his stoniness of will, which brought him almost to the peak of the great pyramid of power, what toppled him was a fatal slackness which had led him into the Goldfine mess—a slackness which seemed the worse because of the contrast with the stoniness, and which all the explaining could never explain away.

Leafing through some old columns I find one at the time the Goldfine case first broke, in which I went out on some sort of limb and wrote that "the luckless Adams is through, and we shall have to find another President." It wasn't hard to see from the start that the resignation was inevitable, for Adams had lost all the moral authority that his power required if he was to hold on to it.

The urgencies of the coming election merely added their own inevitability. Adams might perhaps have been saved for a while by a Republican victory in Maine, but the reverse of it came and so he had to go—with whatever shabby attendant graces he could muster in his TV farewell in order to qualify the basic disgrace.

The fall of Adams is a sad story, as the fall of any man is when he had played for high stakes in power and the day comes when the power stops dead. But Adams had few tears to shed for others, and there will be few to shed tears for him.

Here in New Hampshire, where they know Adams pretty well, I get two explanations of how it all happened. One is that when Adams was running for Congress in 1944, and later for Governor, he was glad to get what help he could as a politician, and once made, the relationship with Goldfine, carried over even into the period when Adams was supposed to be an Untouchable. The second is that Adams is a Yankee, with the thrifty cast of a Yankee's mind.

These explanations will have to do for a while. But who can explain any man adequately, especially so complex a man as Adams? The quest for motives will pass, and what will remain will be the tragedy of the whole story.

There are a few Republican commentators who will try to draw him in the martyr's role, but that too will pass. Adams is not the stuff that martyrs are made of. "An innocent man went to the gallows . . . tonight," says David Lawrence. How naïve can a man get? Adams is not dying for a cause, just as he never lived for a cause—unless you count his own retention of power a cause. Our American society is pervaded with power, and inevitably there are some for whom power is a good and a goal in itself—now power *for* something, but just power. Not to eat, not for love, but only ruling, ruling . . .

The most subtle apologia for the fall of Adams was left to Richard Nixon to make: "Because to do his job well he had to say No more often than Yes, he had his share of critics." What a slick and slippery way of gliding over the question of guilt, and making Adams' only fault the admirable one of saying No at times. Unfortunately for Nixon, he left Adams and himself wide open with his statement.

The trouble with Adams was that he didn't say No often enough: there was *one* time, surely, when he should have said it and he left it unsaid.

Anyway, a good deal depends on whom and what a man says No to. And also on whether he has it in him to say Yes to the surging waves of human aspiration. Adams' tenure of power, during his six years in the White House office, was not a distinguished one and not a liberal one. The nation will lose little.

If anyone thinks that the political passing of Adams will mean some kind of New Order in Washington, he is letting his hopes play him false. The most depressing fact about the whole episode is the failure of the President or anyone high in the Administration to say a single word condemning what Adams did.

Adams liked the legends which depicted him as the Great Stone Face. There was one bit of truth in them: Adams was part of a little group around the President who have lent a fatal rigidity to American policy, both at home and abroad. There was one thing that Adams and Dulles shared: Each derived his power from the vacuum left by President Eisenhower. Each man achieved his power by the sheer will which enabled him to move into the vacuum and do the daily chores and make the daily decisions for a grateful Chief Executive.

*

7. Rickover: Armed with Madness

August 13, 1958

THE REASON that Navy Secretary Gates now gives for the snub in forgetting to ask Rickover to the *Nautilus* ceremony is interesting. It was due, says Gates, to "our preoccupation with the operational significance" of the cruise of the *Nautilus*. Which means, in words of less than five syllables, that the Navy was so busy crowing about the boat getting there that it plumb forgot the man who had turned the boat from dream into fact.

Look at that phrase "operational significance." Maybe that's where the real trouble lies. At a moment of triumph our military bureaucracy wears blinkers so narrow that it can look only at the operation itself, and it can't look either backward or forward. If the Navy bureaucrats had spared a moment to think of the "historical significance" of the feat, they would have given Rickover a bit of the symbolic spotlight.

As for Rickover himself, he was "too busy to worry about snubs," but was already thinking of the submarines still to be contrived. "When we get missile subs like the *Polaris*," he said—and away his mind raced into a not impossible future.

An institution, Emerson said, is but the lengthened shadow of a man. The nuclear-powered submarine is more than a technical feat. It is a symbol of a way of thinking, dreaming, willing the dream into actuality. Here, almost alone in our military establishment, was a segment of it where the scientific imagination worked the way we used to boast it works in America.

That segment was the lengthened shadow of a man named Rickover. Against the opposition of most of the top Navy brass, he *bulled through* the atomic sub. He had to fight and feint, wheedle and argue and storm. He had to use courage and cunning and take long risks with his whole career, for if anything went wrong he had a legion of colleagues waiting to pounce on him and crush him for his gall. The Old Guard thought he was mad. He might have answered, with that wonderful line from the Greek Anthology, "I am armed with madness for a long voyage."

Every age is known in history by the kind of men who are its rebels. In our military age our rebels are men like Admiral Hyman Rickover and General James Gavin—men who, for better or worse, have to cope not only with the intricate technical and strategic problems of their craft but with the Old Guard as well.

The problem of the rebel in the military services today is that of getting them to think imaginatively and dare greatly. Bertrand Russell was sent to jail in England in the first World War because, in a pacifist tract, he had written: "I do not say that these thoughts are in the mind of the government. All the evidence tends to show that there are no thoughts whatever in their minds." The military rebel today must make sure that there are some thoughts in the minds of the top service bureaucrats.

In this task men outside the services, like Senator Anderson, play a big role. Anderson's speech in the Senate was a brilliant indictment of the disease of creeping caution that is paralyzing the bureaucrats. Anderson sees that Rickover's achievement involved "a pitfall of risks," and he is pushing for his promotion as a sign to young men that risks are worth taking. And Senator Jackson in the same vein, asks whether "there is a place for the egghead in uniform."

It is good to see some of the Senate Democrats awakening to the real cancer of the Administration, which is not short on good intentions but quite simply on brains. Its bureaucracy is all dead, aimless weight, as Kafka saw so brilliantly in his novels. It overlooks easily, forgets easily, gets "preoccupied" with "operational significance." The thing it sticks to with tenacity is an old way of doing things—and a grudge against those who would disturb it. It operates through rigid, repetitive ritual. It needs more men inside who will bull a program through, and more men outside who will support them.

It is because Rickover sees these things that he has become something more than just a military man. He has jumped into the educational debate with fervor and wants a revamping of our school system to get at the youngsters with talent for scientific research and ideas.

Rickover himself operates, as a military man, within a frame of assumptions that I cannot accept. Even if we get missile submarines and are able to blast the Russians from under the North Pole ice, we shall not have solved the problem of how we—and the Russians, too —are to survive in an idiot arms race.

But a nation shows its essential quality in the way it pursues war just as much as in the way it seeks to control it. A people that surrenders to the Old Guard in its military services will show the same cautionary deadness in its diplomacy, too. What counts is the quality of mind and imagination that informs our whole national effort.

That is why the men who forgot Rickover are a portent to make us tremble about peace as well as about war.

August 27, 1958

It is hard to associate Rear Admiral Hyman Rickover with a triumphant ticker tape parade. In his *Post* series on Rickover, Stan Opotowsky calls him a "sandpaper" personality. There are many things an abrasive can do, but winning affection is not one of them. The popular welcome in this case is not an outpouring of warmth but an offering of respect for a man who fits the mood of an urgent time because he does not suffer fools gladly and will not pass the time of day with a stuffed shirt.

Since Rickover is assigned to both the Atomic Energy Commission and the Bureau of Ships, a reporter asked him how it felt to shift from one hat to another. "The easiest way," Rickover answered, "is not to wear any hat at all."

The question would have fitted an organization man, for in organizations the hat you wear is like a telltale heart that ticks out the truth about you. It tells where you belong in the hierarchy and what job you have.

The happy thing about Rickover, for me, is that he is so acidly and so joyously an antiorganization man. I don't mean it in the vapid sense of the sort of man who finds an easy brand of comfort and withdrawal by mocking at organizations while he lives off them. Rickover recognizes that we cannot get along without them. But he works and fights inside them, daring them to match what he can do with his methods by what the others can do with theirs. Now that the old puritanism is dead, there is no real puritanism left in American life except this harsh inner rigor of exasperatingly high standards of achievement.

A man who can fight organizations as Rickover has fought the Navy, from within, and still get a ticker tape welcome from Fifth Avenue and Wall Street, is a bundle of a man.

We live in a time when it is hopeless for an isolated individual to triumph over the massive forces of his society. The best he can hope for, if he wants to leave his mark on life, is to find the small group with which he can work best; and if he is a leader of sorts, he can set the group in motion, and keep finding new combinations for each phase of his productive life.

Working in the service of his country, Rickover has had to face this problem in acute form. As a people we are competing with a system of commissars who get things done in war technology by a medley of lures, pressures and threats. But what they have, above all, is total control which can be tightened or relaxed as the need arises.

In peacetime we have no psychological fuel that will drive men to their limit, unless we happen on individuals who are all fuel. Then they break through the locked doors, past the empty, insipid faces, and sweep away the obstructions and inanities that come built-in with any organization.

This is, I should guess, Rickover's quality. Would that we had a small legion of such men.

As far as I can figure them, their rules of action are simple. Decide what you want to do; rove as widely as you must, to find the men who can do it; educate a supply of new men behind them, so that the reservoir of talent won't run dry; forget rank, seniority, whatever is alien to the job in hand; put on top the men who belong there, and give them the goal and the tools, drive them harder than they can bear, defend them fiercely against blundering interferers, and manage somehow to contaminate them with your own sense that nothing in life can match in excitement what they are doing. Do that, and you can consign the commissars (to use their own favorite expression) to "the scrap-heap of history."

I don't know the right word for this acid disregard of everything about a man except his worth in the operative group. It is a kind of human functionalism, if that word had not been badly overused. It despises what used to be called "station." It is contemptuous of rank, color, religion, age, wealth, dignities and indignities. It strips away all the pomposities and gets down to a man's worth.

To say, as has sometimes been said, that Rickover has made enemies because he is a Jew in the Navy is to see only the superficial. Actually, being a Jew may have helped him to develop that special crispness and biting quality of mind that a man on the margin of his culture so often has. Rickover's enemies were against him because he was a continuing threat to all the cluttering debris of pretension to which they had to cling—or drown. Any man who wears no hats is a danger to these men. If he survives and prospers, then by that fact he will strip them of their hats—that is to say, their masks. Hence their hate and fear of him.

But their real hate and fear are not of him but of their own weakness and bewilderment in the face of new forces they cannot understand and dare not confront. Rickover is of the breed of men in our time who dare confront them. Whatever else you may think of this breed, you cannot mistake the stress and passion within them.

I hope you will not mistake me, and think that what I have been describing is the art of "trouble shooting" or "brainstorming" or any of the other fancy new arts to which we give fancy new names. Nor is it the art of management. It is, if I may contrive a barbarous phrase, the art of coremanship—of getting to the heart of any problem. The best thinkers, writers, artists, soldiers, businessmen, labor leaders, politicians have it. Admirals too should not be without it.

PART V

The Underground River

CONTENTS

PREFACE

I END with first and last things—with the eternal recurrence of death and birth, with failure and despair and the secret places of the heart, with love and the pain of loss and the plunge into nonbeing, with time and the sense of identity, with the dialogue between the artist and his vision. I end with the enduring stuff beneath the skin which reveals spurting blood wherever you prick the surface of life, with the Journey into the Interior which every man must make to know who he is, with God and man and their curious relation to each other. I end with the Underground River, which runs deep and silent beneath our consciousness, filling our waking lives with a dark meaning.

The transient and contingent elements of existence keep changing, like particles of water in a stream; but the stream itself keeps flowing. The reason why it has the appeal of endless fascination for us—in the novel, the drama, philosophy, theology, even in journalism—is that it is the river of life, which outlasts the trivia of polemics and the dryness of dogma.

The reader may be surprised to find so many of these pieces filled with images of chaos, death and annihilation. Yet given the time we live in, those of us who aim to function, in effect, as cryptographers of our time can scarcely avoid such imagery. The enactments of human beings on this continent take place not only on an American stage but on the larger human stage, a little like the setting of MacLeish's J.B., where peanut vendors and circus roustabouts go through their paces against the backdrop of the cosmos.

It may be my interest in this human-cosmic stage which accounts for my preoccupation with the theater, where it is harder to fake than in the novel or philosophy, and where a writer reveals skeletally his view of the human plight. This may be also why I am drawn to the themes of failure in life, and suicide, and to the people in the "mean places" where life hangs by a thin thread. They cut against the grain of the American cultural beliefs, as death itself does. Americans lack a tragic vocation. Tough-minded in many other respects, they are tender-minded and evasive about confronting death and failure. I have tried to avoid the easy and ready-made answers to the tangled riddles of human destiny.

*There are a number of such answers that I reject. There is the slick
and slack answer of the soap operas and middle-class morals and the
corporate man. There is the too compassionate answer of love as a
kind of universal solvent. There is the hopeless answer, as in O'Neill,
who saw man balefully trapped by heredity and the malevolence of
fate, and fell back for solace only on illusion. There is the answer of
some design in the universe, unknown and unknowable to us, but
there because to doubt its being there is to court nothingness. And
there is the answer of Beckett and Ionesco who do precisely that and
embrace nothingness.*

*Obviously each of these angles of vision attracted me enough to
draw me to write on it. But my own approaches to the human drama
lie elsewhere: that life is a protracted struggle against the Adversary,
who is in man himself; that there is no design in the disposition of man's
fate, even though there is order in the physical universe; that if the
answer is to be found in man—and where else shall it be found?—we
must seek its clues in the dark continent of the human mind (this is
what led me to the sequence on Freud and his followers); that man
cannot rest upon the arrogance of his mechanical triumphs over nature,
for even the machine which embodies these triumphs is bound to fail
him; that he must know himself, stretch himself, and believe in his own
daimon; that only as he stretches himself, becoming thus in the deepest
sense an artist, can he win a victory over chaos and carry on that centuries-old dialogue, at once time-spanning and humanity-binding, which
is the essence of the life of the mind.*

*In short, in dealing with the underground river which runs beneath
the dark continent of the mind, I am seeking to deal with the sources
of human creativeness. These sources lie not only in the intellect but
beyond it; man must live the life of reason, and human goals must
remain the measure of his achievement, yet his deepest fulfillment
cannot arise from reason alone nor be explained by the rational. This
is not meant as a celebration of unreason in its destructive aspects, nor
of death as such. For unreason does not release man, nor does death
fulfill him. It is meant only to suggest that there is far more in the
mainsprings of life than can be summed up in logic or calculation. Man
must transcend both logic and destructiveness in the interests of life
and more life—life that stretches him to the utmost of his aloneness
and joins him with others in the human connection.*

BENEATH THE SKIN

1. To the Failures

December 29, 1957

SOMEWHERE toward the year's end there is always an avalanche of writing in the press about the Most Outstanding This and That of the Year. I don't intend to join them. Allow me to drink my toast rather to the forgotten, the failures.

We newspapermen usually turn our sticks of space into celebrating someone or something—the newest theater hit, the latest idol of the screen, the sensation of the mass market. We run after significance, however ephemeral it may be.

I want, even if briefly, to drink to the eternal thread that runs through our lives—to the lonely ones, the frustrated. Not to the Man of the Year, but to those for whom the year and the years have been empty.

Yes, to the rejected. To those who have hoped for love during this past year and have been jilted. To those who have not even found anyone to turn their love down. To the solitary ones who have tossed on their beds, loveless.

To the married ones, too, who are not truly mated, who have lain awake during the unending hours waiting for sleep that never comes.

To the disappointed ones. To those who have made plans that have misfired. To all who have tried to build something of their own—a small business, a project, a family, a career—only to have the faulty and unfinished structure go to pieces around them.

To the misfits. To the unconfident, whose life is lived tremblingly in the mirror of others. To the eccentrics, the square pegs, the men living on the margin of their society. To all the people who will never "amount" to anything, never be men of distinction or women of glamour, never crop up in the calendars of celebrities.

To the desperate ones. To those who have borne—as it seems to them—more than the mortal fiber can bear. To those who feel themselves teetering on the thin line that sometimes separates the still lucid world from the world of complete confusion.

To those who awake suddenly in the clutch of a nightmare terror.

Yes, and to those for whom day and night together are nightmare, and who think fitfully of extinguishing the light altogether, in the frantic illusory hope of finding peace.

Again, to the lonely ones. To the women—poor and rich alike—having dinner alone. To the childless. To those with children who have watched them grow up, only to find them strangers.

To the men and women who stand somewhere, night after night, watching TV because they have no one to go home to. To the haunted, driven men, wandering from bar to bar in search of what may make them forget something, until sometimes they end up bloody, in the gutter.

To the women who sell themselves over and over. Yes, and to those who sell themselves only once, and feel caught forever.

I drink also to the outwardly successful, who are in truth failures and know it in their hearts. To those who have risen high on the shoulders of other men, and are scared to make a move of their own, lest they fall to their doom. To those who have made a funeral pyre of their early dreams and thrown themselves into it, to burn brightly and make a big show of it.

To the men with money who have spent themselves in getting it and are unable to enjoy it. To the men with power, who have busied themselves so completely in amassing it that they have forgotten why it was that they started. To the "big shots" who have cut themselves off from their fellows and are more terribly alone than the lowliest human beings who have learned how to cling together.

And—I almost forgot—to the children. To all the unsure ones, stumbling and floundering as they try to make some sense out of a world not of their making. To the blundering ones, and to the angry ones, who look for human connection and find only scared and censorious elders. And to the timid ones.

To all these I say: Despite the myth that it is the meek and the childlike who will inherit the earth, I don't think you will. I think it is the ruthless, the single-minded, the unimaginative who will inherit.

But I must add that I am not sure, when the earth has been in the keeping of the successful, whether there will be much of it left to inherit.

2. The Unwanted

March 19, 1952

GEORGE TABORI's *Flight into Egypt* is a disturbing play, cutting against the pattern of the open-your-gates plea. In fact, this play turns the moral around and tells the refugee heading for America that even if he is admitted he will find no solution here for his problems of personal failure, and that he cannot run away from the memories of home and the tasks still to be done there.

I suppose the modern psychiatrist would approve of this theme and call it a mark of the mature man. But what will stay in your mind long after you have seen the play is not the argument—largely carried by an intense and too wordy socialist turned cotton buyer—but the sheer spectacle of human beings in agony. They are rootless human beings, and they camp in fly-by-night refugee hotels, living at the will of the police who extort money from them, sustained only by the hope of someday getting to the Promised Land.

This is the human material of the play, which furnishes its power and provides that reading of the human heart which is the proper business of any work of art. A refugee story is a story of human beings under extraordinary tension, stretched to the depths of the most degrading experience, yet keeping their resilience because they keep their dream. The dream is to reach America. Maybe Tabori is right in saying that foolish dreams don't heal anything, but there they are. And America is the lodestone that draws them.

It always has, from the beginning. And it has never been easy for the D.P.s and refugees who settled America, and for all the men for whom the road had come to an end without a turning.

In the century between 1820 and the First World War, 35 million immigrants came to America. They were peasants eaten by land hunger, or they were driven by bigots, or they thought the streets were paved with gold in the American El Dorado, or they dreamt great dreams for their children. Oscar Handlin, in *The Uprooted,* tells what they suffered in the holds of the ships, how they set themselves to the most menial and backbreaking tasks, how they lived in ghettos, how they clung to their gods and rituals because nothing else that was firm was left for them. He tells of how alien they felt and were made to feel in the new country, and how even their children broke away from them and rifts came between the generations.

I mention the American story because Engel, in the play, carried it around in his mind like a burning city, and as he died he could read by its flames. I mention it also for the benefit of a man called McCarran, if he should ever read this. Himself a descendant of immigrants and aliens, he has set himself to be their scourge. His McCarran Security Act keeps out as unwelcome visitors some of the best antitotalitarian minds of Europe. And now the Judiciary Committee, of which he is chairman, has reported out a bill intended to freeze the racist thinking behind the immigration acts of the 1920s, although millions of people are now dead as witnesses to the inhumanity of such thinking.

The gates of America were once open; they are now all but closed. The attitude of Americans toward aliens was once generous. It is now hard and niggling. Maybe it would be healthy for us (as Tabori hints) if the refugees decided we are not worth the effort.

3. Mean Places

June 12, 1951

I WAS REMINDED the other day, with the confession in the Staten Island murder, how much of the life of a city remains unknown to us. I am thinking of the world of cheap midtown "transient" hotels, of side-street bars in which men and women pick each other up casually, of disorganized lives whose darkness is lit up only when a sordid murder breaks in the papers.

The woman's name in this case was Dorothy Sarasky, and the papers called her "shapely," which might have harked back to a former time when she had been a burlesque show girl. She was working as a waitress and lived in a cheap hotel with a subway worker.

One day in a bar she met August Jagusch. He had been arrested ten times, convicted five, been in jail, and had a half-dozen aliases. When he asked her one day to go on a "treasure hunt" party she went off with him to Staten Island. A love-making scene followed on lonely Todt Hill. His story is that she bit him, that both of them kicked each other in the groin, that he killed her in anger and dumped her body in the woods. He was caught through his estranged wife. He re-enacted the crime for detectives.

I pick this case at random. There have been others. There was the woman who had once been a Ziegfeld show girl and a beauty queen sought after by wealthy men, who had slipped down the ladder of prestige, had become a drunk, and lived in a cheap hotel with a taxi driver. One New Year's night she went on a drinking spree with a visiting lumberjack and ended up dead. And there was the man who killed his woman, stowed her torso and limbs in a couple of large suit-cases and checked them in a Long Island Station locker. While he was on the run from the police, he moved about from one furnished room to another without anyone's noticing him.

I suppose you could call these the human driftwood of a big city, not so much living as lived, moved about at will under the pulsing of half-spent passions and the random currents of a city life, inert, purposeless, anonymous. Our imagination was caught by the desolateness of the site in Staten Island where Dorothy Sarasky's body was found. But what we missed was the parallel desolateness of the lives these people lived.

They live in mean, graceless places. This is different from saying slums, although often people come out of the slums to live in this twilight world. More often they come from a Southern or Midwestern farm or small town, find their hopes dimmed, are unwilling to go back or have nowhere to go back to, and drift along on the margins of prostitution or petty racketeering or in some transitory white-collar or service job, their unstable relations punctuated by bar pickups and one-night adventures.

One of the classics of American sociology, Harvey Zorbaugh's 1929 Chicago study called *The Gold Coast and the Slum,* had a chapter that touches on these shadowy people and mean places. He studied the "Rooms to Rent" district of the Near North Side in Chicago, with its rows of rooming houses. Out of 23,000 people he found 52 per cent single men, 10 per cent single women, and 38 per cent couples living together as married people. Though they were in the productive age of life, they were childless, and thus without either the human ties or the social roots that children help provide.

In New York two decades later the world of furnished rooms has been supplemented by the world of cheap hotels, where you pay in advance when you sign the register.

The slums have their novelists and so does the world of wealth and beauty and talent, but after Dreiser it is hard to think of the novelist of this twilight world of the marginal men and women. For many of the marginal people there are no human ties. There are no children and therefore no neighbors (for, as Zorbaugh shrewdly puts it, "children are the real neighbors"). There is no family, school, business, shop, church, lodge or any other agency that can provide a cement for the atomized incidents of life.

There is only the anonymous, the rootless—the restless desire that ends in the degrading experience, and the violence which is the last hope for expression but becomes itself strangely meaningless, like the violence of two lonely people in the twilight of a May evening on a desolate Staten Island hill.

4. An Element of Blank

December 11, 1952

THE CONVERSATION at dinner the other evening turned to the theme of pain. No one has yet been able to probe the diverse strands of biological destiny that seem to doom some of us to ordeals of pain that others escape. What family is free of the succession of encounters with bleak hospital corridors and men in white, with the surgeon's knife that cuts and the blessed draughts that bring anesthesia? Each time it has happened to someone close to me, I have left a little chunk of my life on deposit with the fates.

There are ways and ways of approaching pain. One is truculence. Do you recall Clarence Day's father, who believed in fighting pain as one fights the adversary, and who refused to show his weakness? Another way is to seek pain and court it, as something that cleanses sin and burns away weakness. I am skeptical of both.

My own experience has not been heroic. There is an old remark that there was never a philosopher who could stand a toothache, and I am not even a philosopher. I remember once, as a child, fainting with some pain or other, and the wise remark of my parents that it was the warning signal the body gives you of the limits of its tolerance. This is, I suppose, the confession of a weakling; but Spartanism has never seemed to me the highest virtue. You accept the bodily organization you have, and you discipline it according to what is seemly in your culture, but you don't make a fetish of a cast-iron nervous system. When I went about recently with something pulled or strained in a ligament, I didn't mind admitting that it hurt. I am a living disproof of the theory of the survival of the fit.

I find it hard to watch pain in others, since there is no way of releasing your tension by crying out about it. One of my worst memories is a hospital behind the lines in Belgium during World War II, with amputations being done on a large scale.

I suppose one way of measuring progress in mankind's march is the steady mastery over pain that medical science has made possible. Yet it would be a mistake to make the painless life the test of the good life. The desire of so many women to bear their children without anesthetics is another way of saying that it is worth risking some pain in order to stay sensitive to a life experience you value.

In fact, one could argue strongly that the capacity to feel pain is deeply connected with the capacity to respond to levels of sensation in life. When the exposed nerve of your tooth stops aching, it is either because it is desensitized or because it is dead. In this sense, pain is a sign of life; and some of the great religions have therefore associated the agony of suffering with the depth of fellow feeling. "Pain has an element of blank," Emily Dickinson wrote; and there are times when pain reaches a degree of intensity where you find yourself dissociated from it, watching yourself experiencing it almost as if it were someone else.

In this sense one can say that the effort to develop "hard" people who are immune to pain is an effort to develop desensitized people. The lack of fellow feeling, which is one of the more disturbing signs of our time, flows from the lack of self-feeling. To deaden yourself against any hurt is to deaden yourself also against the hurt of others.

The Nazis used to employ torture to make their victims break down. But the Kremlin inquisitors recognize that there is a point at which torture fails. In his account of his Soviet prison experiences, *The Accused,* Alexander Weissberg writes that "with flogging a man could grit his teeth, knowing that it must end, or lapse into unconsciousness if the pain got too bad."

The more effective method used in extorting "confessions" is the ceaseless questioning that wears down a man's will and makes him a cipher. If he felt pain, he would know he was still a man.

5. The Ledge-Sitters

August 28, 1953

THEY STILL KILL THEMSELVES in all the classic ways. Some turn on the gas jets, some slash savagely at their wrists or throats, some take barbiturates, some throw themselves in front of autos or subway trains, some shoot themselves, some tie loops around their necks and hang themselves.

There is a relatively new kind of suicide attempt worth noting in our Big City civilization. It is that of the hesitant jumper, who perches on the ledge of a high building and debates the yeas and nays of leaping or living. I think of the case of Sidney Herman, the young veteran with ulcers who sat on a ledge outside the fourteenth floor of a hospital for more than thirteen hours.

A distinction must be drawn between the ledge-sitter and the ordinary jumper. A man intent on killing himself may simply open his window—often in those early morning hours when despair is deepest and the voice of inner resistance dimmest—and jump out. But your true ledge-jumper must first get someone's attention.

There was a man who sat on the roof waiting for a cop to snap his picture before he jumped. There was another who smoked cigarettes while the cops tossed matches to him; when a cop pinned him down at an unwary moment, he said, "I knew you'd get me sooner or later." There was the amateur pilot who took a plane up and radioed his intent to crash. Some call a newspaper. In one Cincinnati case the whole scene was caught by TV.

It will be clear that there is a share of exhibitionism which makes the ledge-sitter want to be watched—and perhaps to be coaxed out of his decision. The pattern has become classic. There is always a quick-witted policeman who gets to the location and keeps the sitter engaged in a philosophical dialogue on life, death and the vagaries of fate. The mother—or wife, or husband—is brought. Almost always there is a priest or rabbi who pleads with him, while the victim bitterly denies the existence of a God. There are firemen who spread a net below him, while a High Command huddles over strategy. And there is, of course, the Crowd—snapping pictures, making bets on whether the poor devil will jump, shouting taunts.

The whole pattern forms a harrowing mixture of misery, pathos and drama. The ledge-sitter is almost always an unbalanced person who has become obsessed with the futility of his life, but in whom there remains the still, small voice of doubt. His mind is an arena in which two gladiators are locked in deadly embrace—the will to die and the desire to talk. Being consciously aware only of the desire to die, he is genuine when he warns against anyone coming closer. Yet unconsciously he wants to be argued out of his intent. He is a lonely man who wears his bitterness as a mask to conceal his hunger for human warmth.

The taunters in the crowd sense his indecision. Too many are sadists who take courage from another man's ebbing of courage, and whose life is renewed by another man's death. But most who stand on the sidewalk below are more than curiosity seekers. We pray against the jump, because every suicide raises doubts of the worth of life. We knock ourselves out to keep a man from dying, when a hundredth of the same effort would have kept his hope fresh in the first place and kept him from ever getting to the ledge.

The fourteenth-story ledge of a veterans' psychiatric hospital seems a fit symbol for the not-so-lonely debate of the hesitant jumper. In a sense, our H-bomb civilization is also perched perilously on a ledge, while we debate whether to jump or not to jump. As long as we keep talking, there is hope. The dilemma of the civilized is betrayed in our debate. When the debate ends, then we shall know that the dark blood-urge to cultural death has triumphed.

6. They Kill Their Brood

May 11, 1953

THERE IS A TERRIFYING CRUELTY in the frequent cases of mothers who kill all their brood. In recent months there was one case where the mother drowned her two children; another poisoned three, still another slashed the throats of three. Monstrous as is the current case of Mrs. Carol MacDonald, the New Jersey mother who asphyxiated her four children, it is by no means unique.

Why do they do it? One can understand the classic historical instances of infanticide when a whole community killed a number of its children, either through some religious taboo or because of a lack of food supply. But in the cases of the murdering mothers, where the acts go against the deepest instincts of the culture, what source could they have except in the wild illogic of deranged minds? It is true, of course, that the mother who kills her brood is deranged when she does it. But the striking number of cases makes us ask why the derangement takes this form.

To start with, it is clear that in the act of killing her children the mother commits a form of suicide. I agree with Helena Deutsch, that a woman is crucially a woman through bearing children and fulfilling herself in them. Thus there are few women of whom it could not be said that in the death of any one child a piece of her dies, and in the death of all her children all of her dies.

True, one might say the same of many fathers. But a father has to make up in other ways for the organic relation that a mother has to the children who have grown in her body and come out of it. The murder of her brood is thus in the deepest sense self-murder, since it means the wiping out of her identity as a woman.

This leads to the question of why the mother is moved to annihilate her identity. The common element is a feeling of her worthlessness and failure as a woman. Every suicide is an act of anger and aggression against the world that turns inward on oneself. In many of the cases, as in the New Jersey case, the anger is directed against the husband. Perhaps he has been faithless, or has sued for divorce, or has abandoned the woman. She turns her grievance over and over in her mind, until it takes the form of a thirst for revenge.

The classic instance of such a revenge motive is the Greek myth of Medea. She has sacrificed much to run off with Jason. But later Jason turns ambitious and decides to marry a king's daughter, and to get back at him Medea butchers her children. There are many modern instances of the Medea story. The woman feels that to kill only herself will not hurt the husband—may possibly relieve him of a burden. But to kill his children means to leave a gaping hole in his life.

In some cases, instead of rage against the husband, there is only despair and a sense of worthlessness. Where there is no hope and no feeling of one's own value, the world is an empty, intolerable place. The mother reasons, in blankness, that to leave her children in such a place would be an indignity to them. She wouldn't want them, she says, to repeat in their lives what she has had to go through. In any event, the wish to punish—whether her husband or herself—becomes stronger than the wish to love.

Note also how frequently the mother stops short in her effort at suicide after the children are dead. Most of the women seem to try to kill themselves; few seem to succeed. They want to wipe out their identity and yet retain it, for how can they taste their vengeance against the faithless man unless they live to witness his desolate loss?

This seems heartless, yes. Yet there is also an element of pathos in the love the mother feels for the children in the very act of killing them. She dresses them neatly before she takes them into the auto to asphyxiate them, or she combs their hair carefully before she strangles them. It is part of the ambivalence by which so often each man kills the thing he loves.

7. The Secret Places

September 21, 1958

IT ISN'T JUST MOVIE STARS and crooners whose private lives harbor skeletons that get revealed in public. The troubles that writers get into are sometimes more disreputable than the ones they write about.

"His sins were scarlet," wrote Hilaire Belloc in an immortal doggerel, "but his books were read." There are two writers currently on the front pages not because of their best-seller books but because of their newly unveiled old sins. They are John McPartland, who wrote a novel called *No Down Payment* about suburban families in California, with its central female an attractive and haughty young wife who gets raped by a hillbilly neighbor and finds that she loved it; and Harry Golden, who put together some tangy columns of his from a one-man magazine into a volume called *Only in America,* and found that a big audience loved it.

There is little these two men had in common except sudden literary success and the fact that their hidden skeletons came clattering out roughly at the same time. McPartland, who died the other day, had a wedded wife and a child he did not acknowledge to the world; while the woman whom he acknowledged as his wife, who had borne him five children, was one to whom he was not married. As for Golden, the white light of a best seller has compelled him to lay bare a secret which he wore like a flaming Nessus' shirt for years— the fact that he was once convicted and served three and a half years for mail fraud.

I expect a certain malaise among my writing colleagues as they speculate on whose turn it will be to get packed off in the tumbrel next.

Yet I wonder why all this should strike us as a rarity. Writers are like any other mortals—if anything a bit more complicated in their make-up, with inner agonies out of which (if they are lucky) they can spin ideas or invent fictions that seem to apply to the whole human situation.

Literary history is full of writers whose secrets were well or badly kept. One thinks offhand of Wordsworth's illegitimate French child, of the sexual legends that have clustered around Byron's name (with incest less disputed than some other strains), of Poe's Lolitas, of the

ménages maintained by a number of French writers, of the double
lives of even such eminent Victorians as Dickens and Thackeray and
Mill. Only recently have we learned that the brilliant geologist
Clarence King, the intimate of John Hay and Theodore Roosevelt,
the man whom Henry Adams called "the most remarkable man of
our time," lived an underground life with a beautiful Negro woman,
Ada Todd, who bore him five children.

The remarkable fact about McPartland and Golden was not that
they had secrets to keep, but that the secrets remained so long
hidden. Here was Golden, with the tragic prison episode in his life,
going into the most exposed of all trades next to politics, personal
journalism, and putting out issue after issue of his *Carolina Israel-
ite* without being spotted. Here was McPartland, with his two ménages only 150 miles apart, letting his common-law wife in Monterey
get herself chosen as "Monterey Mother of the Year."

We keep chattering incessantly about how small the world has become. But no matter how much it shrinks, there are secret places that
every man carries around with him in his heart—and gets away with.
The Orwell fantasy about Big Brother who searched out everything
in your life and mind was terrifying exactly because it is in these
secret places that a man most truly knows himself.

No, the danger is not that our secrets will be discovered; it is all too
easy to get most people to take you at your current face value. The
real danger comes at the point when the secret gets too clamant
within us and cries to be spoken. When you have something that eats
you from within, and that you dare not tell the world about, you start
by being afraid that it will be revealed and you end by finding it
intolerable to live with, and feeling the need to share it.

This tension between the fear and the desire of discovery is one
that every anguished man knows. Cops know about this impulse,
and D.A.s; it is one of their most potent weapons, since what they
offer their suspect is the relief of ripping the burning shirt from his
skin.

Well, McPartland is dead, and there is only the wrangling over
his estate between his multiple broods. As for Golden, who is very
much alive, he asked the reporters to tell him whether he was a dead
man.

This is what terrifies any writer—the fear that he may not be
able to function. The drive to function is the greatest force in any
man's life, underlying the drive to survive and to create. For a quarter
century since he left prison, Golden hugged his secret to himself
because he wanted to function for what he was, not what he had
been. When he became too well known to keep the secret any
longer, he had to take the risk of spreading it across the papers, in a
gamble that once more he would be allowed to function.

I am all for it. Who dares sit in judgment on a man like this, whose energies have been spent in joyous attack on so many hypocrisies in American life, perhaps because his own split life was yearning to be whole?

There is no question here of repentance, expiation, redemption. You don't become a new man at some point of high resolve. Every day, every moment of his life, a man is renewed because he is washing away the past in the stream of the present. Whatever Harry Golden once was, he is no fake now. He does not have to prove he is a new man.

SUICIDE AND ANIMAL FAITH

1. The Image of the World's Evil

April 4, 1950

THIS WAS THE NOTE: "I have been depressed by conditions throughout the world for many months. I am a Christian and I also am a Socialist. I believe firmly in international peace."

When I read it in the Sunday papers, my mind went back to my Class of 1923 at Yale. Among my classmates there was Francis Otto Matthiessen ("Matty," as we used to call him), who became a Harvard professor and a distinguished literary historian and critic.

Last Friday night Matty spent the evening talking with a friend about the McCarthy crusade and the Harry Bridges prosecutions. Then he rented a room on the twelfth floor of a dingy Boston hotel and, leaving behind the suicide note I have quoted, plunged to his death.

This is not a piece about Matty, who needs no dry garlands of eulogy from me. He was a creative and deeply loved teacher, and there are too few good teachers to spare even one. He was a sensitive critic, as his work on T. S. Eliot and especially on Henry James shows. He wrote one of the great books of American literary and cultural history, *The American Renaissance*.

This is rather a piece about all of us in this era of the hydrogen wasteland, especially those in whose personal anguish the world's anguish is reflected. There can be little doubt that for sensitive people a haunting, corrosive anxiety has become the prevailing mood of our time.

Matty was distressed by what has been happening on both sides of the cold war. He spent some time in Europe a few years ago and wrote a book about it, *From the Heart of Europe,* chiefly about the Czechoslovakia he loved. It was in many respects a politically naïve book, especially in a long apologetic footnote added after the Communist coup. But it had one overwhelming merit: It was a plea by a Western intellectual for an effort to keep open the channels of communication between the West and the East. You can imagine what happened to the book. The nasty boys got after it—those who win cheap victories in the review columns by gunning for every thought that is not murderous enough on the subject of Russia. Matty was crushed.

But I suspect he was even more crushed by what has happened since then in the world. On our side there has been the hunt for dangerous thoughts, the big armament race, the hydrogen bomb issue. On the Russian side there is what the Russians have done to people like the Czechs, cynically squeezing every non-Communist to the wall.

The image of the world's evil is one that many today carry around with them like an albatross. The horrors of our time are repeated so often in the press and in conversation that for most people they become worn-out banalities which no longer have the power to move them to anguish. But for the more sensitive they are still realities.

Some fall back on a personal stoicism as a way out, some become cynics and nihilists, some turn to religion and mysticism. But most of us, I think, live on two levels. One is the level of cultural anxiety. The other is the level of what George Santayana used to call "animal faith" —the inner vitality that springs from sources beyond our comprehension but holds on to life and life's purposes.

2. The Thin Thread

April 16, 1952

THE MOST STARTLING INCIDENT revealed in the Whittaker Chambers memoirs* is the story Chambers tells of his attempt at suicide, just before the grand jury indicted Hiss. The low point in Chambers' mood (as he tells it) came after he had brought out of hiding the microfilm which became known as the "Pumpkin Papers." The Eastman Kodak experts at first said that the rolls of film had been made in 1945, whereas Chambers had insisted he got them in 1938. Even though a second report came quickly, saying the company had also made them in the 1930s, Chambers found himself plunged in gloom. "An error so burlesque," he writes, "a comedy so gross in the midst of such catastrophe, was a degradation of the spirit."

He went to a seed store, bought an insecticide containing cyanide powder. One night, when he felt lowest, he went to his room, spent several hours writing letters to his family and friends, put the chemical in a contraption of carton and towels, and went to sleep with it next to his head. The towel fell off during the night, and he found himself sick instead of dead.

* For a discussion of these memoirs (*Witness*) see page 439. For a group of articles on Hiss and Chambers, see "The Masks in the Hiss Case," page 429.

Soon after that the grand jury indicted Hiss.

I have tried to retell the episode briefly but with fairness. The motives that Chambers makes explicit—his despair at the difficulty of making a dent in public opinion, and his desire "to spare those I had been forced to implicate in the conspiracy," don't ring very true to me. Hiss must have felt far drearier than Chambers at the state of public opinion. And as for sparing Hiss, while (as he puts it) "my witness against the conspiracy would remain, in the form of the documents and microfilm," the logic seems leaky. Chambers must have known that had he killed himself, the world would have interpreted the suicide as final proof that the documents too were false.

Yet I am not writing this to argue the motives of Chambers. When a man finds himself sunk in despair, there isn't much use in our debating its sources, except for the purposes of healing it—and the events that followed seem to have healed Chambers of his despair.

What strikes me most in the story is the terribly thin thread which ties us to life, even the strongest and most determined of us. Here was Chambers, a man who had devoted himself to the single-minded pursuit of Hiss. Yet at one point he was willing to smash everything, even the pursuit itself, because of his sense of futility.

I recall a conversation about the Hiss case with a friend of mine several years ago. He was a shrewd lawyer, who had some knowledge of people. It was in the middle of the second trial. Even after a victory, my friend said, it would not surprise him if in the end Chambers committed suicide. I had no inkling at the time, nor did he, of how close he had come home to the inner structure of Chambers' personality, as now revealed by his own strange story of the earlier suicide episode.

Each of us, however stable we may seem as personalities, at some point in his life feels that he has come to the end of the road. We touch bottom. For a few, who feel there is no exit from their problems, death may seem the answer. For the overwhelming number of us, there is somewhere in us a life force so strong that it holds on to life even by the thinnest thread. We survive our ordeal, and we look back at it as something strange we passed through, something also a bit awesome.

If any man said to me, toward the end of his life, that the thought of suicide had never occurred to him, I should ask him to search his memory again. And especially to dig into the buried part of his mind, below the threshold of ready memory. He will find there some episode, perhaps hidden away, when he touched bottom. And when he found it to be rock, he could again begin his ascent.

3. Codes and Anomie

November 17, 1952

THE STORY of a man's plunge to death gets musty in a few days and is crowded out of the papers by bigger things. What is one man's death to the hundreds of thousands the H-bomb can kill? Very little. But for each man, his life is all. An Abe Feller's suicide lights up a moral scar across the face of our era.

The human side of it has by now been told: the weeks of work strain, the gathering melancholia at the McCarran attacks on his cherished UN, the snapping of the link that held him to a sense of life purpose, the talk of suicide, the effort of his wife to reason with him, the terrifying picture of how he ran through room after room while she tried to cling to him, the plunge to the courtyard, a woman standing at an open window screaming . . .

Before Feller jumped to his death, he said several times to his wife, "It's no use, it's no use." Every man carries on within himself a lonely debate, usually drowned out, even from his own inner ear, by the sounds of the world's turmoil and his own busyness. What arguments Feller had invoked within his own mind on the side of living we shall never know. Evidently they did not balance the heavy weight of nothingness on the other side, and so he put an end to the debate for good.

The students of human behavior say that suicide is a sensitive barometer of the changes in our society. Most of us don't pause to think how much of a killer it is, ranking tenth among all the causes of death in America, and ranking second (after auto casualties but before homicide) among violent deaths. With the world tumbling around our heads, one might expect that suicides would have increased in our generation. Actually they have decreased somewhat since 1930. But when suicide claims a victim like Feller, who was a brilliant and successful man, with great resourcefulness and with a seemingly quenchless flow of energy, one asks what fatal flaw he glimpsed in his vision of a cracking world that caused his own will to crumple up.

The most famous study of the causes of suicide is Émile Durkheim's *Le Suicide,* published in 1897. In it he discusses the major sources of suicide, but the most important one for our time he links with what he calls *anomie*. There is no good way to translate it, but let us call it the "normless" type. More and more we have lost our inner codes of conduct, the strong norms by which we guided ourselves. With wars and revolutions and the uprooting of the old ways, people are left normless and codeless, and the result is often a sense of despair.

In Feller's case I think we must correct this in an important way. The world is becoming codeless, but Feller tried to cling to his code, which was world law, and to his ideal, which was the UN. He was a perfectionist, said his wife. The McCarran attacks and the forcing out of Trygve Lie must have seemed so grotesque an answer to his dreams that he saw only the blankness of his own failure.

In a letter to the *Times,* Telford Taylor suggests that what hit Feller hardest was not just the attacks on the UN by the McCarran know-nothings, but even more the failure of any American officials to answer them. It is a good insight. Feller himself was never under suspicion. But he saw that to treat American members of the UN staff only in terms of their being American nationals would destroy any chance of building a truly international civil service.

It is not an easy time for sensitive men. It takes tough people to survive the barbarians of the Kremlin and our own home-grown vigilantes. In every era there are sensitive men who succumb so that the life force may flow more strongly in the rest of us. Abe Feller was one of them.

4. *Less Self-Pity, More Fight*

March 9, 1953

LOATH as I am to preach a sermon over a suicide's corpse, I want to add a somewhat skeptical footnote to the comment on the death of Raymond Kaplan. He was the Voice of America engineer who jumped in front of a truck in Cambridge, preferring death to the agony of a McCarthy inquisition for himself and his family. It is natural for liberals to see Kaplan as another martyr victim of McCarthyism, but I don't think this goes very deep.

Without knowing anything about Kaplan other than what has been published, I think his response to McCarthy's tactics was that of a sick man. In the case of suicides like those of Stefan Zweig, Ernst Toller, Klaus Mann, a sensitive writer who saw humanity moving irresistibly toward the bottomless pit was moved to protest by plunging into nothingness. But Kaplan went to his death, not out of a generalized despair, but because he recoiled from a concrete ordeal. In such a case the only possible protest is not death but life, defying at once the inquisitor and the ordeal.

There is a new kind of self-pity which threatens to engulf many liberals as they watch the march of McCarthyism and the cowardice of administration, Congress and press in the face of it. This self-pity is the liberal sickness of our age, as a paranoid hunt for dangerous thoughts is the reactionary sickness, and a hands-off panic is the sickness of the nonpolitical multitude.

Feeling himself hunted, the liberal of faint heart cries, "We are the innocent quarries of the hunt. They are making life a crucifixion for us. Were ever harmless men so beset?" As Kaplan put it in his suicide note, he feared he would be "harried and harassed for everything I do on the job." "I am the patsy for any mistakes made," he said. "Once the dogs are set upon you, everything you have done since the beginning of time is suspect."

This self-pity has been implicit in the liberal tradition. The compassion for others can become a compassion for oneself. What we need in this ice age is less self-pity and more fight.

I don't know what Kaplan may or may not have done that made him dread the ordeal of investigation. In the life of almost every one of us there are indiscretions, subterfuges and mistakes that may not look pretty when exposed to daylight. There is a wry story about a man who had a realistic view of his fellow men. He picked ten names at random out of a phone book, and sent each of them the same wire, "All is discovered—you must flee." Each of the ten packed his bag and took the first train out of town.

This is the weapon McCarthy uses in an age where the sense of guilt is so widespread that the unprincipled inquisitor, firing his shots wildly, has an immense power of blackmail.

Is the moral one of caution—that life should be lived with a chary, grudging, ungenerous calculation of potential risks? Only the niggardly and timid of heart will reach such a conclusion. If the aim of life is to be free of risk and blame, then the mawkish hollow men will inherit the earth, and what they will inherit might as well be a desert of bleached bones.

Is not the aim rather to drink deeply of life, to taste the richness of experience, to take risks and develop the inner strength of those whose mastery over themselves has meaning because they have wrestled with demons?

The real ordeal is not that of confronting a Congressional committee. It is confronting oneself: facing the sum of what you have thought and done and been—and what you have left unthought, undone, uncreated. Most of us come to terms with our past selves only piecemeal and thus keep a sense of continuity. When you have to confront yourself all at once, and do it publicly, there is a sense of panic. Some obviate it, and exonerate themselves in advance, by an elaborate public confession. Others use a constant attack on what they once believed. Still others shut up tight. A few, overwhelmed by self-pity, kill themselves.

My own hat is off to the men who are willing to face themselves and the world, who frankly admit where they were wrong while still holding to the core of their life view; who spare self-pity and fight those who set themselves up as inquisitors. When such a man speaks up, he speaks for us all, and he sets millions of hearts beating with exultation.

5. The Lonely Decision

May 12, 1957

THE CASE of the Detroit psychiatrist who tried to hire a gunman to kill him, and who got cold feet at the last moment, will feed the widespread popular conviction that psychiatrists ought to have their heads examined. Most people, of course, miss the point that every analyst *has* had his head examined first, before he can analyze others.

The field of psychiatry does attract people who have been through emotional turmoil. Some of them, like the late Harry Stack Sullivan, are for that reason all the more sensitive to the emotional turmoil of others. Dr. C. L. R. Pearman—the psychiatrist who wanted to get himself killed because he was depressed—was a man who lost his perspective at a crucial moment of emotional imbalance, but then found it again.

There has been some talk that Pearman will be charged with "attempted conspiracy to commit murder." It seems curious that in a few jurisdictions the law still steps in, when a man has tried to kill himself and failed, and punishes him for attempted murder. It would be more sensible to bolster his ego with generous treatment, rather than batter it further.

The Pearman case started me reading *The Sanctity of Life and the Criminal Law* (Knopf) by Glanville Williams, an English lawyer, which deals with the problem of controlling life and death at every stage from conception and abortion to suicide and euthanasia. The chapter "The Prohibition of Suicide" is full of sense and courage, and beautifully reasoned.

I assume that, like myself, you are drawn to these themes. To be absorbed with death is the other facet of being absorbed with life. The Elizabethans, who lived in a gusty and lusty age, did some of the greatest writing on death. It wasn't because they held life cheap, but because those who live with directness are not fearful of facing the fact of death with directness. Those who find roundabout ways of talking of it (like that horrible phrase "he passed away" instead of "he died")—those who turn away from the face of death—are the ones who are insecure about life and feel they must ward off the evil eye.

The point about Pearman was that, from the start, he went at his death without directness. The whole plan was too ingenious, too roundabout; clearly he never meant it. In a study of a group of two hundred university students under thirty, four out of five said that at some point they had wished for death. Most of us don't commit suicide, however, because the life impulse is stronger, and the moment of doubt or despair passes. But some do. The American figures for the 1940s show more than 18,000 suicides a year, and another 100,-000 unsuccessful efforts. For every attempt that succeeds, there may be six or seven, even ten, that don't. We can't know the figures, because so many tries never get reported.

The attempts that fail are likely to be gestures, conscious or unconscious, to reach someone you love, to warn him or frighten him, to make contact with an unfeeling world. In Dr. Pearman's case, according to a dramatic story in the Detroit *Times,* he was hopelessly in love with an attractive young married woman. He felt that life was empty, yet the very act of pretending to prepare his death was a "you'll be sorry" gesture—an act of warning, and therefore of wooing.

We have abandoned the idea, which used to be common, that suicide is a disease of civilization: you find it in primitive groups too, and even a dog may refuse food and die if he is cast out of a household. We are also abandoning the idea that suicides are always insane. In many cases they are thoroughly rational; it is their angle of vision that has become warped.

The nub of suicide seems to me despair or isolation or both. Where intolerable pain is involved, and the decay of bodily functions, a man may decide that it is more dignified to die while he is still in possession of himself as a man. But mostly suicide comes among the lonely people—those who live in the mean streets and rooming houses, those who have lost a life partner or a lover and feel a sense of utter emptiness, even those whose life seems outwardly a going concern but who in their innermost selves feel forlorn.

It is always a desolate impulse that moves such people, or a lonely decision that they make. They have lost their sense of connection with life, and therefore their sense of identity, and where there is only nothingness it seems logical to make it nothingness forever. It is the zero becoming eternal.

I write thus myself in an effort at understanding, but against the grain in myself. Every cell in me is tenacious of life, perhaps absurdly so—but the life impulse goes beyond both the absurd and the rational. It is simply an affirmation of the unreasoning aliveness of life, not to be despised, not to be discarded.

THE DARK CONTINENT OF THE MIND

1. The Tempests in Freud

October 12, 1953

IN THE LIFE of a trivial man, even the shaking events become trivial; in the life of a great man, even the trivial details take on importance. Sigmund Freud was one of the great—not the impossible wooden statue that some of his idolaters make him out, nor the target of fun and of cartoon jokes about the psychoanalytic couch. He was a massive figure of earth and salt and granite in whose shadow our time still lives, and who was none the less a great man for being a very human one. That is why the first volume of what will be a three-volume *Life and Work of Sigmund Freud* (Basic Books), by the English psychoanalyst and associate of Freud, Ernest Jones, is an important event.

One fact that emerges from it is that the man who boldly, almost singlehandedly, created the new science of psychoanalysis was himself in many ways a vain, touchy creature, and even prudish and stuffy. He shared many of the middle-class conventions of Vienna in the 1880s and 1890s. He refused to let his fiancée see a friend of hers who, as it happened, had "married before her wedding." He reprimanded her because, on a walk they had taken, she stopped frequently to pull up her stockings. He wouldn't give her permission to go skating, because it would involve her putting her arm through that of a man; finally, after consulting a colleague, he let her skate—on condition that she skate alone.

These are all trivial details, yet Freud has taught us to see how just such details illumine a personality. They are part of the dour life struggle he waged, in which he drove himself hard. Freud was a Jew, but there was a strong Puritan streak in him. He had the Puritan's passion for work as a sign of God's grace, the stern sense of duty, the driving urge to achievement, the sense of the Adversary and therefore the capacity to hate as well as to love.

One instance may be found in his courtship. When he quarreled with the family of his betrothed, Martha Bernays, he was furious with her because she did not stand up to her mother and break with her brother; their love required, he felt, that she should side with him in every matter and hate where he hated. Similarly he broke with Josef Breuer and Wilhelm Fliess, on whom he had leaned almost abnormally. Freud's intensity did not allow generous scope for differences which a man who took life more easily would find possible.

He showed the same intensity in his love relations. At sixteen Freud saw a girl who bemused him; yet he scarcely spoke a word with her, and it was clear that it was an image of his own psychic hunger for love to which he was responding. For ten years after that there was no grand passion in his life, and—as Ernest Jones assures us— very little sex. He was working too hard as a medical student and in the hospital, repressing and sublimating his sexual urges.

When he met Martha Bernays, who was visiting his sisters, he threw himself into wooing her with a lyrical intensity that is a joy to read about. He showed gallantry, devotion, whimsy and a wild imaginativeness—but he also wanted to make the lady over in his own image. Freud had scarcely a gulden to his name, and they had to wait over three years until they could scrape together money enough to marry and set up house. They were years of separation, of constant letter writing (Freud and his fiancée also kept a *"Geheime Chronik,"* or "secret record" of the chills and fevers of their love); they were years of hope and of torture.

His great enemy was poverty. For more than a decade, while he was at the university and in the hospital, he was never free of anxiety about money. He was always pinching, scraping, denying himself things he needed, constantly borrowing from his friends, increasingly in debt.

Thus Freud had to wrestle with his demons. And out of that wrestling, one can surmise, came a measure of his strength and final assurance.

October 13, 1953

"Do you really think I produce a sympathetic impression?" Freud wrote to his fiancée. "I really doubt it. I believe people notice something strange in me, and that comes ultimately from my not having been young in my youth, and now, when maturity begins, I cannot grow older."

But this leaden mood was rare. More often he wrote of his restlessness. "I still have something wild in me," he wrote her, "which as yet has not found any proper expression." And again, "I am violent and passionate, with all sorts of devils pent up that cannot emerge." These "all sorts of devils" were to give him a tormenting time before they emerged. Until Jones's book we have had the impression of Freud as he seemed in the latter years of world fame—mellow, mature, ironically serene. Jones has traced a very different sort of picture of the Freud of the "formative years," up to 1900.

Throughout the 1890s, for a solid decade, Freud "suffered from a very considerable psychoneurosis"—another way of saying that he came close to having a breakdown. A minor phase of it was a travel phobia which made him arrive at the station long before the train was to leave. More important was a constant sense of depression, a writing paralysis which made him despair, a bad case of heart trouble whose causes the doctors could not diagnose although they felt it was related to his excessive cigar smoking, but which turned out finally to be mainly psychic. When Freud's psychoneurosis ended, his heart attacks also ended. Along with Freud's other neurotic symptoms there were attacks of *Todesangst,* or fear of death, and even the wish to die.

Freud had a superb courage and stoicism. Jones tells that, in his latest years when he was suffering from the agonies of cancer of the mouth, the only comment he heard from him about it was *"Hochst überflüssig"*—highly superfluous. In the case of his own neurosis, while he sought the help of his intimate friend Wilhelm Fliess, he mainly relied on himself.

What he did was to launch on a self-analysis, starting in 1897, which Jones calls the first successful self-analysis in history. It was a painful process and required daring and a massive persistence that would not be turned back. A number of threads were tied together in it—the death of Freud's father, to whom he had been deeply attached; the breakup with Fliess, which came through a quarrel over the latter's views on bisexuality; the effort to achieve independence; the fact that he was writing his book *The Interpretation of Dreams* and exploring the nature of the sexual life of children.

Freud relied chiefly on a searching examination of his own dreams and the memories they evoked from his childhood. He made several discoveries in the process. One was that his overt affection for his father had concealed a covert hostility to him. The second was his key discovery that his patients, many of whom told him seduction stories of incestuous sexual approaches by their parents, were expressing their own childhood fantasies.

Going back into his own childhood, Freud found fantasies of his own which embodied incest wishes. There flashed on him, from this personal experience, something of the meaning of the Oedipus myth and the Hamlet story for the universal experience. And he came to understand from it the fact of the sexuality of children, even at an early age. He came to understand his love-and-hate feeling for his own father, and how he had searched for a father substitute among a succession of his medical friends, including the notable cases of Josef Breuer and Wilhelm Fliess.

Freud not only resolved his own psychoneurotic torments, and reached some of the serenity he was later to show, but in the process he converted his own problems creatively into the great theories of his work.

One of the problems about Freud is why and how he chose his life work. It is clear that he didn't really care about medicine and had a positive dislike for its practice. He had no confidence in himself as a general practitioner. The story of how he studied under Charcot, in Paris, and later under Breuer, and how he found his way from medicine into psychopathology, has often been told. But the real reason why Freud shifted his life work was that he was not a technician or practitioner, but an explorer who wanted to uncover some great truths about human beings. He had some vanity, and he wanted recognition—but mainly he wanted to strip away layer after layer of what had been hidden from view.

One guesses that this impulse of his came from his awareness of his own "wildness" and the "tempests" within him. He sensed the hidden life of his own that he had to uncover; from this, by a leap of the will and imagination, he has helped many others to uncover theirs.

October 14, 1953

The lives of all the towering figures—Carlyle called them "heroes," we call them "great men,"—are the stories of men who made their way to greatness by a path they did not find ready-made but had to hack out. Freud had a constant sense of being possessed by strong forces which somehow gave him the strength to drive toward his unknown goal. "Do you know," he wrote Martha, "what Breuer said to me one evening? That he had discovered what an infinitely bold and fearless person I concealed behind my mask of shyness. I have always believed that of myself, but never dared to say it to anyone. I have often felt as if I had inherited all the passion of our ancestors when they defended their Temple, as if I could joyfully cast away my life in a great cause."

Freud found his "great cause," although he didn't have to cast away his life in it. It is interesting that, in this flash of insight, he should use symbols from the Jewish tradition. Freud was far from being stridently self-conscious about his Jewishness. In fact, if anything he leaned overfar in the other direction. He had a rationalist's horror at the religious rituals of the Jews. He and his bride were married in a Jewish ceremony, but his biographer guesses that he found it an ordeal. He was a European man, the inheritor of the humanist traditions of Europe, and one who in turn enriched and deepened them. Yet he speaks of "the passions of our ancestors when they defended their Temple." Obviously when Freud thought of his career—its hopes and obstacles—he saw with clarity the burdens his being Jewish imposed on him, but also the strength it gave him.

His dislike of Vienna was intense; it was "physically repulsive" to him, and again, "I hate Vienna almost personally." The reasons are not murky. The notorious Karl Lueger, whom Hitler was later to admire for his anti-Semitism, was mayor of Vienna. Anti-Jewish discrimination was the rule in the government, the professions, the university. When Freud competed for the traveling fellowship to go to Paris and study under Charcot, he feared he stood little chance, partly because of this prejudice. When he was appointed professor, it was long overdue. He felt throughout—and not without cause—that the professional resistance to his theories was the more intense because anti-Semitism was interwoven with the blindness of the men brought up in the old doctrines.

Yet one should add that Freud had a feeling for Austria and refused to leave Vienna on one occasion after another that offered itself. At length, when Hitler entered Vienna in 1939 and Freud's life was in danger, Jones argued that Austria had ceased to exist and persuaded Freud to go to England.

But it is hard to measure Freud by his attitude toward being Jewish, or Viennese, or by his other loyalties or hates. It is even wrong to measure him by the complex web of his friendships and quarrels with his colleagues. Whatever may have seemed narrow or provincial about Freud was less important than the strong universals in him: his passionate search for truth wherever it might take him, his belief in his ideas and his willingness to fight for them, his respect for what Jones calls the stubborn "single fact" that failed to fit into any of the accepted theories and haunted him until he had explained it, his brooding over some train of thought until there came to him the flashing insight into its inner meaning.

Freud was open—generously and expansively open—to impressions from every source. Jones chides Thomas Mann for saying that Freud might have spared himself a lot of trouble if he had known literature. The fact is that Freud was soaked in both classical and modern literature and got many leads and illustrations from it. But it was not only the intellect he cherished, or the intellectual classes. In a remarkable letter to Martha, Freud contrasts the "refined" life of the Viennese of the upper middle class with the common people. He saw the latter as closer to the instinctual life, more capable of a feeling of community and of the whole life cycle. Here was a man who was great because, in his absorption with a life of science and speculation, he had not cut himself off from the great life sources.

"We economize with our health, our capacity for enjoyment, our forces," he wrote in a letter. "We save up for something, not knowing ourselves for what." I think Freud did know for what. When asked what life offered, he used to answer, *"Lieben und arbeiten"*—to love and to work. Today Freudianism has been turned by many into a search for a "happiness" that is often empty of the kind of vitality which the founder of psychoanalysis embodied in his life and work.

Even today, a century after the birth of Freud, almost twenty years after his death, all discussion of psychiatry is dominated by his name. It doesn't end with him—there are important changes that have taken place since Freud—but it must still begin with him.

In 1953 the first volume of Ernest Jones's *Life and Work of Sigmund Freud* was published; in 1955 came the second volume; last fall the third and last appeared, *Sigmund Freud: The Last Phase, 1919-1939* (Basic Books). Thus for five years those who are interested in modern psychology—and who is not?—have been mulling over the rich and loving detail that Jones gives us about this man.

The measure turns out big. The Freud of the early years and the first volume (1856-1900) had devils inside him, but he was impressively mature at thirty-four when he published *The Interpretation of Dreams*. The Freud of the middle years (1901-1919) continued to search restlessly and to grow as he fought hard for the recognition of his doctrine—fought against enemies outside the "Cause" and defectors within it. The Freud of the last phase shows few signs of failing powers, and continues to think and live on the arc of greatness.

Yet there is a deep sadness in the portrait of these last years. Freud was a success, and his fame and doctrine were established beyond any chance of being overthrown. But the success and fame, once eagerly sought, no longer meant much. The city of Vienna, which he hated and loved, celebrated him. He got the Goethe Prize for literature (which pleased him), people came to see him from every country, and his name had become a symbol for the miracle of uncovering the most hidden recesses of the mind.

It now mattered very little. He was a shrunken and sick old man, constantly in pain with cancer of the jaw, constantly tired yet having to continue to treat patients because he had to support himself. The defection of some of his closest disciples and collaborators—especially of Jung and Ferenczi and Rank—hit him hard. And then, added to sickness and money pressures and these defections, there were the Nazis. It took a strong character to show fortitude, as Freud did, under this rain of blows, and it took a strong mind to continue its creativeness, as his did.

Freud was a good analyst of personality and he even knew some things about culture (as witness the insights in *Civilization and Its Discontents,* written in his seventies), but he was naïve about national psychology and about politics. "It is not certain," he wrote Ferenczi in February 1933, "that the Hitler regime will master Austria, too. That is possible . . . but everybody believes it will not attain the crudeness of brutality here that it has in Germany. There is no personal danger for me . . ."

He was a bad prophet. Five years later, in February 1938, on the eve of the Nazi invasion of Austria, he wrote: "It undeniably looks like the beginning of the end for me." In March his faithful friend Ernest Jones flew to Vienna and found that the storm troopers had invaded Freud's home, forced their way into the dining room, looted his safe of what schillings it had. I leave the rest to Jones's own words: "A frail and gaunt figure appeared in the doorway. It was Freud, aroused by the disturbance. He had a way of frowning with blazing eyes that any Old Testament prophet might have envied"—and, abashed, the Nazis left.

With the help of Freud's pupil and friend, Marie Bonaparte, and of our ambassador in Paris, William C. Bullitt, Jones managed everything, and on May 6, 1938, Freud and his family left for Paris and then settled in London, where he was to live out the few remaining months of his life among civilized people who loved him. One shrinks from speculating about what would have happened if Freud had not left. We do know, however, what happened to his four old sisters— Rosa, Dolfi, Marie and Paula—who could not get exit visas and were left behind. Five years later they were all incinerated. Freud, already dead, was never to know about this final instance of what the irrational in man could do.

Freud had escaped the Nazi enemy. He could not escape sickness and death. In 1923, when he was sixty-seven, he learned about his cancer. In a terrifying episode, Jones tells of his first operation, when he almost bled to death when left alone and neglected in a clinic. During the sixteen years before he died he had thirty-three operations. He wore a prosthesis in his mouth which he hated but took with grace and raillery. The one thing on which he insisted was that no one was to keep from him any part of the truth. Also he would have no opiates, preferring to think clearly even in pain.

This was an expression of his fierce independence, his sense of the autonomy of the human being even in the face of death. Since he could find no consolation in religion (he had called it an "illusion," although in his *Moses* he asserted it had some historical truth) and refused to make a myth of it, he faced it as it was, permitting himself only a wry irony about it all, describing his world as "a little island of pain in a sea of indifference." Thus he died with the stoic detachment and strength with which he had lived. How else could the founder of psychoanalysis, the pioneer of psychological realism, have died?

February 5, 1958

Since Freud spent his life probing into the hidden drives and motives of others, it is a kind of historic justice that we now have the material on which to base a psychoanalytic interpretation of Freud himself. By presenting so fully the details of the life of the first psychoanalyst, Ernest Jones provided in his biography an opening for a hundred new books and articles to come, began a new phase in the history of psychiatry, and gave us the material for taking apart Freud himself.

Freud felt that his new science could shed light even on the life and work of men already dead and therefore beyond the reach of the analyst's help. He did a famous study of Leonardo da Vinci and another of Dostoevski; and, of course, he tried to reconstruct the life and personality of Moses. One of his studies was never published. During a six-month visit to Berlin in 1930 Freud, with Ambassador William C. Bullitt, wrote a psychoanalytic study of Woodrow Wilson. Jones says that it "contains some astonishing revelations."

Freud, of course, analyzed himself: there was no one yet to analyze him. We know about it from the recently published letters that he wrote to Wilhelm Fliess, who was his friend and father symbol, and with whom he broke as his self-analysis gave him new insights. Jones and the other Freudians accept those insights, but as good disciples they stop there. Here, as on other matters, my criticism of Jones's work is that he wrote it all within the frame of Freud's own ideas and did not step outside that frame to get a new and more critical angle of vision on Freud.

Like other men Freud had a hidden, unconscious life that was rooted in his childhood relations and experience. As a child he was very close to his mother. His father was twenty years older than his mother, and Freud felt that he should have been his grandfather—which would have given Freud a chance to think of himself as his mother's mate. Freud discovered in his self-analysis, after his father's death, that his affection for his father was in reality a love-and-hate feeling, and he concluded that the search for a father, along with the rebellion against him and the love for the loving mother, was a universal, found everywhere as the Oedipus relation.

In his *Death and Rebirth of Psychology* (Julian Press), Ira Progoff —who writes largely as a critic of Freud—notes that he lived an ascetic life, despite the "erotic sensitivities" that were awakened at an early age. He concludes that Freud, drawn strongly to his mother, tried to fulfill her hopes that he would be a great man. To prove she was right and to show his love for her, he repressed his desires for a life of erotic pleasure, devoted himself unswervingly to his career. But his repressed erotic desires could not be dammed up; they surged back in the form of highly sexual dreams, which Freud made the basis for his first great book, *The Interpretation of Dreams*. They also surged back in the form of Freud's heavy emphasis on the sexual life, with its repressions but also with its irresistible power.

There was another childhood relationship that left its mark, one with the son of Freud's stepbrother, his nephew yet a year older. "We had loved each other and fought each other," Freud wrote. And he added, "An intimate friend and a hated enemy have always been inseparable in my emotional life; I have always been able to create them anew, and not infrequently . . . friend and enemy have coincided in the same period."

To read Freud's life is to see the truth of this insight, in Freud's passionate friendship for Fliess, for Joseph Breuer (with whom he worked on the hysteria studies), and for C. G. Jung. Progoff describes the friendship with Jung as "certainly the strongest and the one with the greatest libidinal overtones." And he notes that in each case the breakup of the friendship was followed by rancor and resentment on both sides.

When you compare him with several of the other founding fathers he lived a healthy and at least outwardly calm life. After Jung's defection from the psychoanalytic movement, Freud felt closest to Sandor Ferenczi and Otto Rank. The latter, who (as Jones explains) had suffered much in his youth both from "brother hostility" and "father hostility," came under the spell of a "cyclothamia"—a manic-depressive sickness in which a melancholic phase is succeeded by a manic one in a recurring cycle, but which did not prevent Rank from doing creative work and writing as an analyst. Ferenczi, brilliant and attractive, was for a quarter century the closest friend and the favorite of Freud, who used to call him his "son." He suffered from a growing psychosis, complicated by an anemia which attacked his brain, so that he died insane, with wild paranoid delusions. Another disciple, Horace W. Frink, whom Freud called the ablest American he had come across, had a psychotic phase during his analysis, seemed to recover, but spent the last ten years of his life in a mental hospital.

These should not be taken as typical of the movement. Yet they were part of its stormy history and of Freud's life which, outwardly calm, was in reality full of tempests.

2. New Horizons of the Mind

February 3, 1958

AMERICAN PSYCHIATRY is growing surer of itself and is growing up a bit. People are no longer ashamed to have it known that they—or their sons or daughters, husbands or wives—are "in analysis" or getting other kinds of psychiatric treatment. In some circles it is almost fashionable, which is still a form of immaturity about it. The stigma has largely vanished, although parents of children who need psychiatric help still feel that somewhere something has gone wrong.

Along with this acceptance of the fact of psychiatry, I find a continuing and perhaps even a renewed wariness about some of the people in the profession. The figures are vague, but there must be roughly 30,000 people actively engaged in helping other people with mental problems—say about 18,000 psychologists and maybe 12,000 psychiatrists, including the psychoanalysts. Not all of them are good at their work, although some are wonderful and some pretty bad. I should think the ratio might be like that of doctors as a whole, or teachers, painters, novelists, religious leaders. With the new wariness has come a readiness on the part of the patient to shop around until he gets someone to trust.

The profession is taking itself more seriously too. Using legislation, it is tightening the requirements for practicing psychologists and requiring arduous training for the psychiatrist. A crop of young men are going into the medical schools, the hospitals, the clinics, the graduate schools—young men who are probing for new insights that will help them in their day-to-day practice.

It could once have been said that psychiatry was an art all of whose practitioners were foreigners and all of whose patients were Americans. Since Freud first gave his famous lectures at Clark University and went home feeling that Americans were amiable but irritating Philistines, Americans have felt like colonials under the spell of Vienna. The names of Freud's European disciples struck terror into Americans working in the field. But that has largely changed. True, the respect for Freud, even mingled with reverence, is still with us. The Ernest Jones biography of Freud had a greater impact here than in either England or Germany. But American psychiatrists are no longer as cowed as they once were by the European names, and American mothers no longer make themselves sick with worry about the shaping of destiny in the nursery, and about the sibling rivalry, penis envy or castration fears of their youngsters.

The new sense of relaxation shows itself in the current ways of American speech. It is hard to be in any group containing actors, TV people or advertising men without hearing someone talk of the "head shrinkers." The phrase combines a wry skepticism about the methods of psychiatry with an affectionate acceptance of its aims and its place in our society. So also the phrase "sick, sick, sick," which usually brings a laughing recognition of how much we overplay the "sick mind" as an explanation of everything from a child ax murderer to someone who has beaten you out in a business deal. But along with the laughter there is a recognition that many people have sick minds who don't know it, and that the "sick-makers" wreak destruction on every level of our life.

Outwardly, at least, the biggest recent development in American psychiatry has been the chemical one—the almost overnight zooming

up of tranquilizer drugs that have made difficult patients more trac-
table and have shifted many of them out of the mental hospitals,
making room for other cases that need treatment.

But my own feeling is that there has been a subtler and less tangible
development which is more important. I can put it best in Prospero's
words (in *The Tempest*) when he takes responsibility for Caliban:
"This thing of darkness I acknowledge mine." Freud and his fellow
creators of psychiatry dug into layers of darkness and inaccessibility
in the human mind. For some time we feared to acknowledge them.
Then we tried to "adjust" the patient to some idea of the "normal"
mind and life. I think we are now moving beyond both. The word
"normal" has lost what little meaning it ever had. Instead we are
talking and thinking of mental "health," of the fulfillment of the
potentials in each of us, of productive and creative living.

February 6, 1958

There is nothing that is simple and little that is clear about psychology, psychiatry and psychoanalysis. My shelf is sagging under the
number and weight of the recent books that "explain" these subjects
in simple, homely terms to laymen, and while the effort is laudable
the fact is that usually the "layman" books are clearer and simpler
than the truth. With few exceptions they treat the labyrinth of the
human mind as if the students of it were basically agreed but lacked
the literary power to express their common insights.

Actually Freud himself was a great master of style, as his letters as
well as his lectures show, and he could write with economy and
clarity. The trouble is that those who write about the depths of the
human mind are like a band of men crawling about in the subterranean darkness, each holding aloft his little light and crying out with
a sense of discovery as it faintly illumines one corner of the cave. And
as they scurry about they get in each other's way and call each
other minions of darkness and traducers of the light.

Freud wrote about Albert Einstein, after their first meeting in
1926: "The lucky fellow has had a much easier time than I have. He
has had the support of a long series of predecessors from Newton onward, while I have had to hack every step of my way through a
tangled jungle alone." Certainly Einstein had a tradition to break
from, while Freud had to create his tradition, which then made it
possible for others—showing their originality—to break from it.
Freud combined the double role of being both the tradition *and* the
rebel. He had to hold his movement together by sheer force of intellect and will, giving his followers and disciples the heady sense of
having opened a wholly new path, but also keeping them in rein lest
the excitement of pioneering lure them off on new paths of their own.

Is it a wonder that he didn't succeed in preventing psychoanalysis from breaking up into various "schools"? The real wonder is that he could hold it together even as well as he did. He had a "committee" consisting of himself and his six closest associates. They were (after Adler's and Jung's defection) Sandor Ferenczi, Karl Abraham, Otto Rank, Ernest Jones, Max Eitongon, Hanns Sachs. It is fascinating to read how they parceled out the posts—presidencies, secretaryships, editorships—in the empire of their own creating, how they jealously guarded against intruders.

Freud parceled out his affection to them, in conferences, conversation, letters (he was a demon letter writer). There was even a hierarchy of affection; Jones, somewhat naïvely, ranks the committee in terms of how close Freud was to each, and what degree of affection he had for each, like a king and his favorites.

The idyllic little empire had to crumple. The group dispersed and died, and today Jones is its only survivor. But of all of them, the names that are likely to last for a spell, along with Freud's, are those of Jung, Adler and Rank. They were the major rebels, and in his rebellion each of them founded a school. Yet even in their differences they share enough common elements so that we can talk of them as branches of a single tree.

In grouping present-day psychoanalysts and psychiatrists into "schools" there is a valuable scheme in Ruth L. Munroe's *Schools of Psychoanalytic Thought* (Dryden Press). The central school is that of Freud and the Freudians, who are well established in the New York Psychoanalytic Society and in the other urban centers where the seven hundred or more American psychoanalysts cluster—Boston, Baltimore, Washington, Chicago, Los Angeles, San Francisco. Their basic approach is "genetic" and "libidinal"—that is, they stress childhood conflicts and relations, and the role of sexuality.

Adler, who is famous for his theory of "organ inferiority" and the "family constellation," tried to move away from these emphases of Freud to an "individual" psychology. Miss Munroe places alongside him a number of important "revisionists" who have worked in America—Karen Horney, who emphasized the impact of the culture; Erich Fromm, who brings over a Marxian emphasis, along with a stress on character and ethics; and Harry Stack Sullivan, whose "interpersonal relations" was his own way of presenting a picture of interacting individuals. The Sullivan-Fromm group is usually known as the "Washington-Baltimore School," and they are closer to each other than either of them is to Adler or Horney.

Miss Munroe is unfortunately too brief in her discussion of Jung and Rank, whom she puts together although they had sharply different approaches. Jung became famous for his "psychological types" and for his "collective unconscious" and its "archetypal patterns," but his best recent work has been on religion and myths. The Jungian analysts are few in America, but stronger in England and on the Continent.

Rank spent the last part of his life in America and left a strong influence on social caseworkers, especially in Philadelphia. His early work was on the "birth trauma," and on the relation of analyst and patient, but in his later years he became absorbed with the psychology of the artist and with the religious experience.

February 9, 1958

Freud was a giant in his life and is still a giant in his influence on the theory and therapy of the mind. But each age must live by its own needs, and our need today is for new horizons that include Freud's basic ideas but put them into a new setting.

The world of Freud was a great and dark world, one of his observing and describing; also one of his creation, since every great thinker is an artist who creates the world anew as a mirror in which we can behold the image of man. The image he showed us was somber, tragic, deeply pessimistic. He saw that most of our deepest being is hidden away from us in the dark subterranean "id"—a region of instinctual drives which are biologically inherited, sweeping through us with primal forces unknown to us and largely inaccessible, yet also inescapable, since they shape our personality and indeed our destiny.

To be sure, Freud also depicted an "ego" and "superego" in addition to the "id," but they did little to brighten the picture. The ego—the "self"—was in a sense the executive of the id. It was not autonomous, did not legislate for itself, did not make the choices and decisions for a free personality. Rather did it do the bidding of the id and carry through its command decisions. As for the "superego," it was the region of the personality which embodied the ideals and institutions of the culture and expressed its pressures. It was the admission price a man had to pay to live with his fellow men—a structure of artificial values that nevertheless represented the world of reality.

Thus the self was caught between the demands and pressures from both worlds, compelled to do their often contradictory bidding, sometimes crushed between the nether and the upper millstone. The resulting picture of the human situation is one of an arena swept by conflict and frustration, by winds of unfulfilled and repressed emotions—a battlefield "where ignorant armies clash by night."

The ego does what it can, of course, to save itself from destruction. It tries to displace, to repress, to sublimate the pressures it feels from within the id; and it "introjects" the codes and values of the culture. It resorts to every variety of defense mechanism in order to live with itself, its instinctual drives and its culture. It becomes adept at dodges and stratagems, generates almost incredible cunning in learning how to preserve itself, but to a large extent it is caught.

The human personality, as Freud saw it, is basically shaped in the early stages of growth in infancy and childhood. It passes rapidly through the "oral," "anal" and "phallic" stages, then has a "latency period," when it is poised for what comes later. And then in adolescence comes the time of turmoil, when the early history of sexual crisis in the child comes in for a final showdown and the conflicts are either resolved in a genital maturity or else the mind is left warped and distorted.

This is a bleak picture of man, woman and child, and Freud knew it. Look at his world and what do you find? It is a world of trauma, guilt and conflict, of hostility, fear, anxiety and repression, of libidinal sexual energy as the great clamant force, of homosexual and incestuous urges in every human being. For many observers who had a tragic view of the human animal anyway, this pessimistic picture had an attraction of its own. This was particularly true of novelists and dramatists for whom the Freudian approach was a key that unlocked their creativeness.

As for Freud himself, he was a sturdy realist who refused to prettify the truth he felt he had discovered or seek consolation in a religion which was in itself (as he saw it) an illusion. When he did seek to revise his system and go "beyond the pleasure principle," he came up with his later idea of a death instinct—that death is not merely the cessation of living but is part of life throughout, and that there is a kind of built-in will to death as there is a built-in will to life.

Given this Freudian outlook, we can understand better the meaning of recent movements in psychology and psychiatry which are in effect phases of rebellion against Freud. Roughly the rebellion has taken five main forms.

First there is the rebellion against the Freudian emphasis on the sovereignty of the id over the rest of the mind. Adler and Rank were forerunners of it but today many thinkers and therapists have taken it up. It is a movement toward the independence of the ego, the "self-actualizing" individual (as Kurt Goldstein puts it), the problem of identity and its crises, the role of the will and the personality as they reach out to the tensions and resolutions which spell growth.

Second there is the rebellion against the Freudian emphasis on libidinal sex as the surging pervasive motive force in the personality. Adler and Jung both broke from Freud on this score. Harry Stack Sullivan and the "Washington School" followed them. We may call this the movement toward a view of multiple motives, toward seeing the sexual drive as one of a number of deep impulses.

Third there is the rebellion away from the genetic approach and the obsessive emphasis on childhood experience. The new emphasis is on the total life pattern, the continuing life experience and the capacity for change and choice at every stage of life.

Fourth there is the rebellion against a too instinctual emphasis, away from heredity and toward the role of culture and society in the formation of the personality. Here, too, Adler pioneered, followed by the impressive work of Karen Horney and Erich Fromm in the cultural influences that bear on the individual.

Finally there is the rebellion against Freud's pessimistic and deterministic view of man and toward a view which emphasizes man's will and the healthy resources he possesses for a productive life. It tries to see man not as a prisoner of his past but as the subject of his choices.

February 10, 1958

One of the principal counts against psychoanalysis, when it first broke on the world, was that it made sex into the primal drive in life and the mainspring of emotional energy, and that therefore it dragged man—and woman with him—down to the level of the beasts. Was Freud misunderstood from the start? I don't think so. He based his theoretical system on the strength of the instinctual drives. In treating his patients he found deep sexual wishes which they did not act out, and of which they were largely unaware. This led him to formulate his ideas about the realm of the preconscious and the unconscious where these drives operated. Despite his own Victorianism and that of his times, he did not flinch from the fact that the human organism had needs and made demands which could not go unfulfilled. The erogenous zones of the organism, including the genital zones, were thus the arena of tension and of "pleasure"—that is, the reduction of the tension.

Thus there came into history one of the master ideas of the modern world, the Freudian libido, the "pleasure principle" of the sexual drives which shared the life of man with the "reality principle" of the ego drives. The libido was at once physiological and irrational. Modern literature came to be filled with heroes and heroines, mocking and serious, who worried about their sexual unconscious.

The three most important disciples who broke away from Freud—Jung, Adler and Rank—broke largely on the ground of his overemphasis on the sexual drive, although each of them later went far beyond this point of difference and developed important and productive theories of his own. Deeply troubled by the defection of the three, Freud kept re-examining his own ideas. Instead of counting his system completed, he wrote one book after another in his later years which threw the faithful into confusion as they tried to readjust their own thinking to the new Freudian party line.

Much of the difficulty of the jungle of psychiatry is due to the need of tracing each changing stage in Freud's thinking, and also each changing stage in the thinking of each of the defectors.

Freud never repudiated the importance of sex and the libidinal energy, or of the early years of childhood when the groundwork of the conflicts and the repressions is laid. But he did change and broaden his view of the instinctual life. In his later years he came to see the drives in the human being as clustering around two centers. One was Eros, which is broadly the principle of love and tenderness, of sexuality and procreation, and which draws not only upon the id and the unconscious but also upon what he formerly called the "ego drives" of self-preservation. The other was Thanatos, broadly the instinct of death and aggression, which are part of human life from the start.

Thus Freud had to come to terms with the principle of creativeness, largely left out of his earlier thinking but very much a part of the thinking of his defecting disciples. But in doing so he did not forget the principle of the Adversary—of destructiveness and death. He saw love and death together and grasped the fact that life was a continuous interweaving of dying and being born. This has made possible for many Freudians the transition to the emphasis which our own generation puts upon the capacity to love and to receive love. The climate of psychiatry has changed in at least one crucial respect—in the shift from the libido to Eros, from the reduction of sexual tensions as the prime aim, to the achievement (or recovery) of the capacity for loving and being loved. Pick up almost any one of the books written for laymen these days—*The Art of Loving, Love or Perish, Love and Conflict*—and you will find this a dominant theme.

Another change is taking place. For Freud, the sexual drive is an ambivalent one. Jones, in the third volume of the biography, prints a letter that Freud wrote to an American woman who had discovered that her son was a homosexual and who wrote for advice. Freud answered with a moving, compassionate letter, saying that the double sexual urge was present from the start in everyone, and that in her son it had been arrested instead of going on toward sexual maturity. He added that her son was not a sick man—a viewpoint which is being sharply challenged today.

The challenge is partly due to the current emphasis on men being manly and women being womenly. One of the charges made against Americans is that we are becoming a nation of feminine men and masculine women. Perhaps some future Edward Gibbon will sit among the ruins of New York and write about the decline and fall of the American male.

The point I stress here is simply that our culture is making demands on the Freudian Eros. The secondary traits of female sexuality, covering homemaking and mothering the children, have to some extent been pushed upon the male in the society where women work, where domestic servants are hard to get and keep, and where women and men seem to be interchanging their secondary roles. I suspect that this will form a new theme for discussion during the psychoanalytic hour.

February 11, 1958

To read the psychiatric literature on family relations is a depressing experience. A marriage can be wrecked by the early family experiences of husband and wife alike. The children of the marriage, in turn, can be wrecked by being rejected by their parents, or being overprotected and overcoddled, or by an emotional seduction on the part of one of the parents, by inconsistencies in discipline, by too little love and also by too much love.

After soaking myself in this literature of gloom and doom, I look at my baby son Adam, just past the age of fifteen months, and wonder what will happen to him emotionally on the perilous path of passing through his oral, anal, et cetera stages, what terrible burden of psychic travail will be placed on his little shoulders before he can reach maturity, what unconscious conflicts he is already storing up out of our family situation, what emotional scars he will bear, and how he will survive it all.

Then I look at him again, forget much of what I have been reading, watch how his radiant smile expresses the life force in him—and conclude that while the psychic casualties in the battle of growing up are heavy, there are depths of psychic strength as well as of sickness somewhere in the wellsprings of any child.

That is why, in the end, I am far from shattered by all the signs of family neuroses. I have been looking, for example, at a book called *Today's Neurotic Family,* by Dr. Harry F. Tashman (New York University Press). On its cover is a picture of a mother, a father and two children, their faces crisscrossed by wire-netting zebra stripes to enforce the point that they are the prisoners of their shadowy neurotic conflicts. It is a good enough book, informative, lively and intelligent, although a bit overwrought for my taste. As I read it I remembered an earlier book, published some years back, *The Happy Family,* by John Levy and Ruth Munroe, and I wondered whether the difference in title also implied a shift of emphasis in the past decade or two.

Maybe the terms are tricky. If you took the outer lid (or façade) off every family in America, and got a psychoanalytic look inside—or even an honest, unflinching layman's look—you would have to conclude that there are few families in America which are not streaked with the neurotic. The mother, maybe, is trying to do too much, the father is driving himself too hard outside the home and fails to assert his weight inside it, maybe one or both parents have spells of infidelity, one child is too shy and withdrawn, another is compulsive and repetitive in his various energy aggressions.

But my feeling is that many of these families are tolerably good going concerns, with plenty of strains and irritations but also with a give-and-take of affection as well as hostilities, and that in the end they make a go of it.

We ought to do two things with the adjective "neurotic": stop over-using it, and stop being scared of it. The dramatic title of an important recent book, *Neurotic Interaction in Marriage,* by Victor Eisenstein (Basic Books), leads to the thought that marriage itself may be an interlocking (good or bad) of unconscious needs on the part of husband and wife. Actually the principal difference between a bad marriage and a good one is that in a bad marriage these unconscious needs (or wishes, or drives) clash with each other, and in a good marriage they fit in with each other, complementing and supplementing each other. Lucky the man and the woman who find a good partnership of neurotic drives.

I don't mean that the mating process is wholly a fumbling in the dark, the blind clutching the blind. In the effort to find a partner whose deep unconscious drives will match ours, we have certain clues—looks, tastes, attitudes, opinions, family background, education, sexual tempo, psychic temperament. But even with all the clues, and with every effort at being oh-so-rational, the decisive factors are hidden in unconscious and irrational drives within us. Nor do many of us learn much from experience. Again and again we see instances of men and women caught in a compulsive pattern, seeking out the same kind of partner as before, making the same kind of mistake.

What psychiatric help can do before marriage is give each partner some self-knowledge, some courage in making decisions, some inner maturity in evaluating the outer clues. But at best the area of self-knowledge is small compared with the hidden interior life.

Once the marriage takes place, I am afraid that the ensuing "family constellation" is in the cards. The best way to deal with a disturbed set of family relationships is to patch them by preventive action at the point of marriage. If husband or wife is mentally sick—or both of them are—the whole family is likely to get sick. The family can be a germ carrier for mental disturbances.

Of the things that were wrong with Freud's outlook, one of the most striking was his blind spot on the family. His basic approach to the patient was to an individual. He failed to see that the individual was as much a product of the going family pattern as of his early experiences with the "primal scene" (witnessing the sexual act of the parents) or of the Oedipal crisis. Nor did he understand the mother's role in the family, nor the cementing function of love and intimacy.

As a result the psychiatry of the family has had to overcome a false start, which led to individual members being treated separately by different psychiatrists. A much more sensible approach is to see the family as a whole and treat it as a whole.

3. The Ordeal of Therapy

February 12, 1958

FREUD, for all his brilliance as a theorist of therapy, was not masterful in its practice. He was often gullible, and he was too anxious to believe what fitted into his theories, including the tales of sexual seduction in childhood which proved to be not memories but fantasies. It is usually noted that the analyst becomes a father figure, and doubtless he was exactly that in the father-dominated Vienna of Freud's day. Today in our more democratic America, the younger men speak of a "partnership" between analyst and patient, instead of stressing the father authority.

But much of this may be rhetoric. The real question is one of helping a troubled person, caught in the grip of unconscious forces, a prisoner of his life history or of a weak will in which he has lost confidence, a victim of a shattered self-image or of a damaged self-dynamism. If he is a psychotic, wholly withdrawn, cut off from a real world, with a will-to-live ebbing away, how can the analyst make a contact with him and lead him back to life?

To start with, there is the problem of access to the forgotten, repressed experience. This becomes a quarrying or dredging job, a search for "material" which the patient must get at so that he and the analyst can "work" at it. The analyst will have had some clues through the various clinical tests made before the analysis, but he cannot prejudge what he will find in the interviews.

The patient (usually on the couch, but with some therapists now a chair is used) tells of his dreams and of the events of the day, rambles on in "free association" (Harry Stack Sullivan was critical of this and thought that direct communication is better), tries to recapture forgotten trivia and relive buried experience. The title of Proust's great novel, literally "in search of a lost time," prettied up as *Remembrance of Things Past,* expresses the nature of the process as it creaks along through memory, reverie, fantasy, and through a patient-and-doctor dialogue.

It is a painful ordeal, with wide scope for a variety of techniques by the analyst, and with ample chance for the whole thing to get bogged down and stay stuck in the mud for weeks or months. There are differing versions of what the doctor-patient relation should be. How can the analyst best get the patient to "work through" his material, overcome the blocks and resistances, achieve the insights into himself that he needs?

The dilemma of the analyst gets acute when the "transference" of the patient's emotions to the analyst takes place. The analyst must be at once warm and reserved, he must give the patient the feeling that someone cares about him and believes in him, yet he must also be detached and keep the patient at a distance. The problem gets more acute when—as sometimes happens—a "countertransference" takes place, and the analyst gets emotionally caught up in the patient. Readers of Lindner's case history, "The Jet-Propelled Couch" (in his collection called *The Fifty-Minute Hour*), will recall how the analyst who started by getting his patient to recount his fantasy "trips" to interplanetary galaxies ended by almost believing in them even after the patient had come to see they were fantasy.

Sullivan tried to describe the analyst's role as that of the "participant-observer," which is a neat phrase but leaves the working out to the skill, intelligence and integrity of the analyst. The later tendency —with Rank, Horney and Alexander, as well as with Sullivan— has been toward greater frankness in recognizing that the analyst is a participant and that he is not God. This means a degree of direct communication, encouragement, advice about the current life situation of the patient.

February 13, 1958

The stock criticisms of psychiatry have been, first, that it is a fraud and not a science, for it cannot make accurate predictions (what "science" of human behavior can?); and second, that it focuses on sex and degrades the human being (actually the trend is toward the "nonlibidinal" schools, some of which now go too far in downgrading the force of the sexual drive).

The stronger fears today about psychiatry center on the person of the psychiatrist and the claims he is presumed to make. "There is nothing wrong with psychoanalysis," an astute observer has said. "It is the psychoanalysts who are at fault." He put his finger on the strong worry of many people today, who are ready to believe that there is something to psychiatric theory and insights, but also that it takes an extraordinary combination of qualities to apply this instrument to the extremely delicate problem of probing into a mind and reorganizing a personality.

I have read two recent novels which deal in different ways with the psychiatrist who suffers from the delusion of being God. The more lugubrious and intellectually pretentious of the two is Geoffrey Wagner's *The Dispossessed* (Devin-Adair). Its hero—or victim—is a young Englishman who suffers concussion and shock in battle and wakes up to find himself in a mental hospital, wholly in the power of two sadistic psychiatrists who are intent on dispossessing him of his personality, and who even after his release pursue him to his destruction. The hero's conversations with his American wife are little intellectual essays against Freudian intellectualism, and his report of the cocktail party conversation of people "in analysis" is clumsily meant to reduce it to an idiot gibberish.

It isn't much as a novel, but it does embody the nightmare image which pursues many people today—that of being helpless in the clutch of the head shrinkers and the brainwashers. We tend to take this extreme image of the mad charlatan and transpose it to the groping, self-critical, overworked psychiatrists who in many cases are immersed in their work with the troubled and sick.

I don't mean that they are saints and true believers. They have the miseries and grandeurs of human beings. You will find among them the unscrupulous adventurer, the sensualist, the power seeker, the *voyeur* looking through a legalized peephole, the show-off who wants to demonstrate how superior he is to his patients, the insecure spirit who can feel secure only when he plays God to his patients.

The God-playing psychiatrist who succumbs to the erotic charms of his patients is the theme of another novel—*The Horizontal Hour,* by Robert W. Marks (David McKay). With all its weaknesses as a novel it has considerable interest for those who care about the analyst figure in psychiatry. One feels that its central character, Kurt Bucholz, the Viennese who loves music, can talk about painting and books and manipulates the lives of his patients, is not wholly invented. He and his patients seem to be people whom the author is drawing from memory, and in the case of the psychiatrist one guesses that the portrait is an act of mingled justice and revenge.

I am certain that someone roughly like Kurt Bucholz may have sat for this waspish picture. But I am even more certain that he represents a tiny, negligible fraction of the profession. The erotically vulnerable therapist need not concern anyone who is weighing the question of psychiatric treatment.

There are more important problems: the length of the analysis, its expense, its psychic anguish, its success or failure. The chances of a ruthless and unscrupulous person's becoming an analyst are diminished by the severe gantlet that any young man must now run before he is admitted to a didactic analysis. Many apply but few are chosen.

That still leaves open the central question of the psychiatrist's personality. The outlook of the analyst is bound to break through into the world of the patient; every word he uses expresses something about his values. That is why the analyst himself and his personality form a more important factor in the success or failure of the analysis than the theory or school from which he works.

The therapist has need of an infinite patience, a resoluteness of purpose, an empathy with the tortures through which the patient has gone, a flexibility and courage in changing his interpretations as he discovers new insights, and a capacity for the kind of warmth which the patient will experience as love. In most instances the patient needs the sense of being loved but he neither knows how to ask for it nor how to receive it. To feel that he is valued by someone he has come to trust is for him the beginning of his self-acceptance.

But this does not happen for the asking or even the willing. It demands enormous resourcefulness on the part of the analyst, and an investment of psychic energy in the choice of tactics to use from day to day. In our culture nothing quite like this kind of psychic investment has been known, not even in corporate finance and tax law which have hitherto claimed our greatest resourcefulness. The capacity of the analyst to immerse himself in this universe of flexible insight and interpretation does not necessarily go with other admirable traits of character and attractiveness, nor even of maturity and psychic balance. That is why an unimpressive and even unadmirable person may prove effective in therapy beyond anyone's guess.

This is a specialized talent that goes with a special sort of sensitivity. It is a talent for what, in Buber's phrase, might be called "healing through encounter."

May 2, 1956

A neurologist called Dr. Percival Bailey gave a talk yesterday to the American Psychiatric Association which might start a good knockdown fight. He attacked psychosurgery, especially the lobotomies, and also shock therapy, both electrical and insulin. He had just as little use for the new "tranquilizing drugs," even less use for psychoanalysis and its "deep therapy." And his opinion of Sigmund Freud may be gleaned from his asking "how long the hoary errors of Freud will continue to plague psychiatry." I gather that Bailey made a shambles not only of his pet hates but also of his subject, the cure of sick minds. For by the time he got through, there was no crack of light left in the dark vista except possibly through biochemistry and biophysics in the incalculable future.

It is curious that fifty or sixty years after his first great discoveries, Freud should still be the center of a storm of abuse and praise. No one with Freud's stature is to be found in the whole history of the efforts to explore the depths of the mind and cure some of its ills. Those who are snippy and condescending about Freud's historic achievement are poor historians of ideas, however good they may be as therapists. But I should then go on to say that, even with the Freudian revolution, the little bit of terrain we have charted and won from the dark continent of the mind is still terrifyingly little.

Dr. Bailey's attack was centered in the area of the psychoses. Get back into the asylums and laboratories, he told the psychiatrists, and prove that your theories are valid. And he pointed to schizophrenia— where the victim is cut off from the world of reality and loses bearings and direction—as an index of how little we have done.

On this score he is mainly right. Certainly it is true that surgery, shock treatment and drugs have as yet yielded little in the realm of the psychoses, and that the risks and psychic cost have been great. Yet this is scarcely the fault of Freudianism, because these are not the methods of Freudianism. They are desperate short cuts intended for a break-through because "deep therapy" is so slow. Freud recognized that this method was not well fitted for dealing with psychotics, be- cause the task of communicating with a schizophrenic is infinitely hard. "A normal ego with which we can enter into relations is lacking," Freud wrote in 1930. What Bailey seems to forget is that Freud saw a quar- ter century ago a hope for psychotics mainly "in organic chemistry or through endocrinology."

But surely there is far more that challenges us in the realm of the mind than just the problem of the psychotics, severe and difficult as that is.

There is a challenge from the neurotic person who can't live with others because he can't make peace with himself. There is the chal- lenge of self-knowledge and self-fulfillment for millions who may be neither psychotic nor neurotic, but who want to guide their lives pro- ductively and bring up their children not too badly. There is the chal- lenge of preventive effort in the wide field of mental health, among people who live in worlds of personal, national and international ten- sion.

These are great challenges. To meet them we shall need every bit of light we can get. Freud's illumination of the dark places was the most intense and searching of any. We shall do well not to imitate slavishly a man who imitated no one but struck out boldly into the unknown. But one of the things he taught us was that medicine and therapy are only part of the whole task; the larger part is for the explorers of the mind, and for every person who has to light a little candle in the dark- ness inside himself.

February 16, 1958

Psychiatrists have often been guilty of extravagant claims for their profession. It is no cure-all for the mind's ills or the world's problems. But it can take a derailed personality and, under the proper guidance, enable him to function pretty well. If we ask with what sureness of success it does this, the answer is still murky. Recent studies show that roughly two out of three neurotics under psychotherapy report substan- tial improvement as a result. But W. J. Eysenick insists that the same ratio applies to recovery without psychotherapy of any kind. Another study, by David M. Levy, estimates a cure—removal of the specific symptom—in only 20 per cent of the cases.

These figures are good ammunition for the skeptics, yet they leave me unmoved. Therapy is useful even if its results are only partial. It is striking that each of the schools of psychotherapy seems to get results, with pretty much the same ratio of success, probably because there are reserves of psychic strength in every human being, and a trained person with warmth and sympathy is able to get at them.

One of the things that the bruised ego seems to need is a full measure of love, so as to awaken again the capacity to love, which is the capacity to escape from the prison of self and to embrace life. The studies of René Spitz have shown what happens to babies in institutions, even those who get good care, when they are deprived of mothering. Other studies, like those of Anna Freud and Dorothy Burlingame in wartime Britain, note the incredible capacity of children to meet the hardest blows of life, provided they have a sense of connection with their families. The adult has just as insistent a need for this sense of connection with something outside himself. There are few who are not pursued by a constant desolating sense of loneliness. This is what Alfred Adler meant by the "social interest," which was only another way of saying that men need some kind of belief with which to nourish themselves.

Freud had little tolerance for religion in its usual sense, calling it an "illusion," and for a long time the churchmen (especially the Catholics) held psychoanalysis to be a damnable error. More recently the churches have changed their view; Protestant and Jewish leaders have come to use psychiatry in their pastoral counseling, and the Pope has said that there are permissible forms of psychiatry other than Freudianism. The psychiatrists, in turn, especially the Jungians, are coming to recognize the role of religious belief in the personality as a going concern.

Psychiatry has hitherto been practiced by the few for the few. One eminent American psychoanalyst, after some fifteen years of practice, counted fewer than seventy cases that he had treated. This is why Franz Alexander has been crusading for a shortened analysis, and why Karen Horney and Harry Stack Sullivan felt that even a brief, direct effort at helping troubled people was useful. The whole trend today— with the mental-health movement, low-cost psychiatric clinics, group therapy and family counseling—is to make therapy available to an ever larger group of people.

But whatever the number of people reached, there is still the question of the goal at which therapy aims. Otto Rank, who broke with Freud on a number of scores, was not interested in the concept of the "normal" or even the "healthy." He was almost obsessed with the problem of the artist—not as a specialized creative person but in the sense that there is a creative potential in all of us.

Freud too was fascinated by creativeness, but in a different dimension. "Before the problem of the creative artist," he wrote, "analysis must lay down its arms." It was the same expression he used in a letter to Ernest Jones about death. Yet he kept coming back to the theme of how great artists, like Dostoevski and Leonardo, turned their neuroses to the uses of their art. There has been a tendency throughout psychoanalysis to overplay the creativeness of the artist's sickness (I agree here with Lionel Trilling) and to underplay the directive power of the artist's character and personality. The psychoanalysts are at their best in literary criticism when they talk of the great *themes* of art, as when Freud points out that the three greatest literary creations—*Oedipus Rex, Hamlet* and *The Brothers Karamazov*—all deal with father murder; they are less helpful when they talk about the treatment of the theme by a particular artist.

One of the fondest assumptions of psychoanalysis is that mental health consists in taking the unconscious drives to which the individual is blindly tied and bringing them into consciousness, thus liberating him from his bondage. It is good, I agree, to make articulate to yourself whatever it was in your hidden infancy that has tyrannized over you. But my own emphasis would still be on whatever is left in the unconscious, as the life force out of which our individual personality style is drawn and without which we would be drained of the fire and drive of being. To make the irrational rational is not enough; the greatness of life lies in such irrationals as love and fellow feeling and the identity of self.

That, I take it, is why the Soviet leaders continue with their bitter hostility to psychoanalysis. They resent it exactly because it is still deeply oriented toward the unconscious. For the Communist mind, everything must be kept above the threshold of consciousness, where it can be organized, directed—and above all *watched*. Freud knew how frail this conscious censor is and how futile all of cultural indoctrination is in comparison with the storms deep in the human psyche. That is why he left a great legacy to freedom.

TIME AND IDENTITY

1. The Fragmenting of Self

December 19, 1955

THE OTHER DAY, at a party, a friend of mine and his wife came in and I glimpsed them across the crowded room. In ten minutes I saw them finishing their drink and about to leave. I asked why, and my friend said they were due at two other parties before dinner and a show. They asked me how I was, and I scarcely had time to start an answer before they had disappeared.

This isn't an isolated instance of the fragmentizing of our lives. We can all think of numberless others. We read the papers and magazines quickly and throw them away, scarcely bothering to read anything through yet determined not to miss a single item that might mark us a fool if we didn't know of it. We turn the radio and TV dials idly and rapidly, not so much with the intent of finding something to settle upon as out of a nervous fear of missing something and an unsated passion for a variety of impressions. We are, most of us, like the cocktail guest who wouldn't linger. If I had to choose I think I should prefer the man who came to dinner and stayed, or even Coleridge's Ancient Mariner who held the Wedding Guest overlong with his sea tale.

I find something of the same trend in my own craft of journalism. It is always a temptation to do a column of "briefs"—a succession of gleaming items that titillate the mind without ever stopping long enough to strain or test it. I am not attacking this as a journalistic form. Some very good columnists (as well as a number of bad ones) have made it their métier. The point is that it has increasingly become the journalistic form of our time, since it fills the need we all have of visiting briefly with a succession of people and items. There are many lonely people in America, including sometimes the very busy ones, and they enjoy a quick and intimate chat. Sometimes I do such a column of "briefs," brushing lightly over a succession of ideas and events, and I always find it fun—but I can never recall later what I said about what and whom when.

The great journalists whom most of us accept as masters—Broun,

Mencken, Bolitho, Orwell—lived in a more unhurried time and re-sisted more strongly the impulse toward fragmentation.

One finds the effects of it in every phase of our life. Take conver-sation as an instance. I have a friend who listens to the radio, reads most of the columns, watches TV at every chance, goes to all the plays, follows the stock market quotations, subscribes to the foreign journals. His is an interesting as well as omnivorous mind. But to spend an evening or weekend talking with him is a form of purgatory, because any chance phrase or idea makes him abandon whatever is being discussed at the moment, and off he goes on his new chase. He knows everything: who has married whom and is being divorced from whom, who will star in what movie, what went on inside the last French Cabinet, what stock to buy when and why. Drop a name or event, and it starts a chain of free-association comments.

I don't assert that an evening of talk should exhaust a single subject and all the listeners, but it should stay long enough to illumine and explore what it settles upon. Even cocktail talk, hurried as it is, can be good, if you can stay longer than Jesting Pilate did and wait for your answer.

I don't mean to press my point too hard. In some respects the new generation is more adhesive than mine was. I think particularly of the way my generation flitted from date to date in our courting, like a buzzing fly, while our teen-agers date and dance in the same couples, as if they were trying to stick to "the sweet flypaper of life," as Lang-ston Hughes has it. I am not sure I like the change, but change it is.

But for the rest, we seem to illustrate in our fragmented mode of living the statement of the scientists that the universe is discontinuous. Partly, I think, it is because we live amidst the crowd, so each contact we make has to be a dramatic one. But mainly the fault lies with the surplus of stimuli that surround us, creating in us the constant need for new and fresh stimuli. That is why most of us fear being alone more than we fear anything else. For to be alone means to be without outer stimuli, and to have to fall back on inner ones.

At death, too, perhaps, we shall be laid in our graves and rest not in peace but in pieces. And if there is an afterlife the particles of our dust will have to reassemble themselves in a unity they did not possess in life.

2. The Parceling of Time

January 1, 1956

WE AMERICANS are probably the most time-geared people in the world. We are wakened by the alarm, catch a train or bus or subway by the skin of a time schedule, work and eat by the clock, hurry to appointments or the theater harried by the demon of time, turn on the radio or TV to a performance that is timed to the second and dare not spill over or run under. I suspect that many of us even make love by the clock.

In due time we die, but our deaths are the only phase of our lives that isn't regulated by the schedule. You don't hold a stop watch on death. We may not have much time for living, but we have all the time in the world for dying.

Being thus geared to time, we make the mistake of thinking of every unit of it in equal terms. The stop watch beats away with regular precision, and the clocks march on like grenadiers in lock step. We have a democratic feeling about time, as if every minute of it were born free and equal.

But the fact is that time is wildly irregular and every unit of it is incalculably different from every other. Some minutes carry joy and others boredom. Some skip on, vanishing insensibly into the darkness of forgetfulness; but others last forever. Some years follow each other like indistinguishable sheep, but some are great and memorable years in human history.

We have much to learn on this score from the Continental philosophers and writers. Henri Bergson, for example, thought of time as *duration,* in which an hour might have the quality of a month and a century might be a year. And who will forget Thomas Mann's *Magic Mountain,* the novel whose people found themselves in the rarefied atmosphere of the t.b. resort in the Alps where time lost all its conventional dimensions, where the years seemed to hang suspended without motion, while a single month could contain within itself all the intensity of experience of a lifetime.

Call this un-American, if you wish. Our trouble is that we measure time with a prosaic regularity largely because every minute has its value set on it. "Time is money" is what the businessmen say. "Don't waste time" is what the parents and teachers say. The workers punch the time clock. The radio and TV advertisers "sell time" on the air. People hurrying to business dates and to assignations must be "on time." Idlers find ways to "kill time." Even the prisoner, condemned to measure out his life behind the bars, thinks of his punishment as "doing time." Just as life is reduced to these regular beats, so nonlife —the negation of life—is parceled out in the same fashion.

I find a very perceptive understanding of this in a new book by George Soule, which deals chiefly with the current revolution in machinery and is called *Time for Living* (Viking). Soule points out that the classical economists used to reckon with three principal resources —land, labor and capital—but that in our modern economy there is a fourth great resource, namely time. The worker, he points out, doesn't sell his labor, nor does the employer buy it. What one sells and the other buys is the worker's *time*. Labor saving, Soule points out, is time saving. And since our economy is a consumer's economy, the scarce commodity is time in which to consume.

Soule concludes from this, quite rightly, that the present revolution in automation machinery will provide our workers and consumers with much extra time, which he calls "time for living." We go round and round in our discussions, but no matter how round, we are bound to come out with the same conclusion: The new automatic factories and offices will release us as mankind has never been released before—but release us for what?

To say it will give us time *for living* is only another way of saying that we will now be able to put our surplus labor into the occupations involving education and recreation, travel and music and reading and art, plays and play, all the refinements of living that used to be reserved for the elite in other civilizations.

We shall now have leisure for the masses and not just for the classes. But what will the masses do with it? This question applies beyond our own capitalist economy. American industrial experts who have been traveling through Russia report that the Russians have made enormous advances in automation, just as we have. They too will have a leisure which their masses will for the first time be able to afford. But what will they do with it? Khrushchev no more has the answer to this question than does Harlow Curtice, the head of General Motors.

3. The Perfumed Ship

June 2, 1954

I DREAMT LAST NIGHT that I was floating down the Nile in a perfumed funeral ship with the lovely Queen Nefertiti at my side. Slaves unloosed the linen ropes that had tied us to the shore, and their oars dipped in the moonlit river as they rowed us on our celestial voyage. We sat on chairs of sycamore and cedar, and the soundless air carried a smell of incense mingled with the scent of wood as I whispered reassuringly to the Queen, giving her my vows as a journalist that her last river journey would some day be written up on the front page of the New York *Times*. . . .

The perfumed ship is bound to join King Tutankhamen as one of those episodes of scholarship that become part of the folklore of our time. As for the handsome young Kamal el-Malakh—part architect, part archaeologist, with more than a touch of the journalist, and with a talent for detecting scents that have lasted five thousand years—I doubt whether he will be counted with the great Egyptologist company of Sir Arthur Evans and Sir Edward Carter, Maspero and Breasted; yet he has given each of us a chance at one of the persistent dreams of history—that of being for a fleeting moment the Great Pharaoh who, in death as in life, lacks nothing that human hand can make or human will can provide.

Egyptian royalty, in fact the whole Egyptian culture, was obsessed by the idea of death. Maybe it was because life was good but the life span short, what with violence and dynastic rivalries and the dread toll of disease. Or maybe the men who had thought of hieroglyph writing and invented the calendar, who watched their crops grow in the rich alluvial soil under the spell of the changing seasons, were deeply conscious of the Eternal Recurrence.

They must have seen that birth was a kind of dying and death a kind of being born. Even in their life, at the height of power and vigor, they prepared for death. But it was not a tragic notion of death that they had in their minds, nor an agonized one, nor (as with the contemporary Spaniards) even a mystical one. There was a delightful literalness about them, as there is in the imaginings of children. Since there was to be a future life, it was well to take with you all the things you would need—wives and cattle, clothing and jewels, gold and goods.

"None can take his goods with him," was the way one of the Egyptian songs went. Yet evidently the real Egyptian belief was that you *can* take it with you. They were great buriers of worldy possessions—first in crude pit graves, then in deep ones, then in underground apartments and vaults. Then they started making markers for the hide-out—first mounds, then structures divided into rooms, then the Pyramids. But while the markers became great monuments, the thing itself was the sunken establishment meant for the eternal years.

The kings grew neurotic about the whole business. They came to put into these tombs a good portion of their portable wealth and even their retainers. They skimmed off a good deal of Egypt's prosperity in the process, bled the people, and kept large gangs of manpower at work on the things the priests said were necessary for the future life. One of them was the funeral ship of King Cheops, or Khufu, on which the young Egyptian of our time seems to have stumbled.

How curious it must seem to some all-encompassing eye—the Egyptians in their day moving busily about, burying, burying, and we in our day burrowing, burrowing; they digging holes to hide their goods in, we digging holes to find the holes they dug, coming upon their treasures with shrieks of delight, discovering tombs and mummies, thrones, vaults and desert ghost ships, saying "Oh" and "Ah," pleased because some of the patina of the age-old dynasties and their dream world rubs off on our own lives and deaths.

It was a good time to find the perfumed ship. Maybe it hit the front pages because more desperately than anything else we need this sign of continuity, this proof that there are delicate scented things—perilously wrought, perfectly sealed—that can last five thousand years. In our own age of cobalt and the megathon, whose threshold we have just crossed, to look ahead for five decades or even for five years is like looking ahead for five millennia.

You can't help wondering what some diggers of a future era, stumbling across some huge aluminum ghost ship of our own age, complete with wings and propellers and fuselage, with slip-covers and cardboard containers, will make of us and of our symbol of the mechanical bird. Perhaps he will wonder how a people so skilled in the riches and details of life should have plummeted to death.

4. The Impostor

February 15, 1957

THE MEN I like don't run with the crowd, and that is why I give you today the name of Ferdinand Waldo Demara, Jr., of Lawrence, Massachusetts, one of the happiest, most rollicking, most talented and do-goodingest impostors of recent history.

This is a strange and wicked world we live in, and the wickedest thing about it is that a man so often gets frustrated when he tries to do virtuous things for his fellow men under other men's names. Take this fellow Demara. His whole life has been a succession of highly ingenious disguises in order to practice as a college professor, a theologian, a military surgeon, an assistant warden, and now a small-town high-school teacher and Sunday school superintendent. Each time an unfeeling society, in the form of detectives, judges, authorities, has stepped in and stripped Demara of his disguise and doomed his talents to stay unused like a rusty sword in a scabbard.

The latest episode was a delicious one. Demara, in one of his dry seasons, read somewhere that the schools at North Haven—a little island in Penobscot Bay off the coast of Maine—needed teachers badly. He took over the name and teaching credentials of a Martin Godart who had a degree from Wagner College.

He became the Abélard of the lonely little island community—teacher of English, Latin and French, assistant principal of the high school, speech coach, recreation adviser, organizer of a Sea Scout unit and Sunday school leader at the local Baptist church. He lived at a boardinghouse, visited with the principal, watched TV and joined the American Legion. Whatever he did he did well and everybody loved him. He lived the quiet, useful, dedicated kind of life that is celebrated by all the civics books and is the backbone of the American way. He made others happy and he must have been happy himself.

But into this idyllic scene came a teacher from a neighboring town who suspected he was a fake and told the Maine state police about him. Two detectives came, arrested him, took him away on a Coast Guard cutter to the state capital, where he is now standing trial. The man who turned him in says now that his victim "was doing such a lovely job," and he hopes the island people will take Demara back. Not for the first time betrayal comes with a kiss.

Nor is this the only hypocrisy in the case. Demara may be as great an impostor as you wish to call him, but the society that hounds him is made up of hypocrites. What is it we teach our young people? We teach them to use their skill and brains at whatever comes to hand. Well, Demara did that. We teach them to be virtuosos, jacks-of-all-trades. Well, Demara was a king-of-all-trades. We teach them to be useful, helpful citizens. Well, Demara has spent his whole life looking for things to be useful and helpful at.

What he gets for his pains is exposure and arrest. What an irony that the first honest-to-God authentic do-gooder I have seen in the news for years should turn out to be, by our humdrum standards, an impostor.

Let me make clear just what kind of faker he is. He isn't a swindler who uses the confidence game on you and takes you for your roll. He has never made money at his fakery, and once when he was getting surgeon fees for chest operations in Japanese hospitals as "Dr. Cyr" he turned the fees back to charity. He doesn't hunger for kudos or publicity or the easy racket. He is just a terribly competent, honest impostor.

I'd gladly match him against a number of teachers I know—or surgeons or prison officials or Sunday school superintendents or businessmen or politicians—who are careful to use their own names but who are walking lies in everything they do. There are a lot of respectable men who are deeper fakers than Demara ever was.

Take this question of fake identity. The psychologists tell us these days that everyone is searching for his true identity, trying to find out who he really is. Sometimes he may be looking for a father or for a brother or for the perfect woman or the love goddess, or for an embodied saint, but all of them are variants of the final quest of identity.

From this angle I'm not sure on what level to take Demara. He can perform brilliant chest operations after having been only a hospital orderly and taken a bit of Navy training. He can talk several languages, get by as a prison warden or a deputy sheriff, discuss theology, bandy academic small talk with faculty colleagues. Maybe he is searching for the lost ideal of Renaissance man—the many-sided personality who could do everything, before the modern age turned so many of us into specialized flunkies in our corporate cubbyholes.

His father once said he was "on the borderline of genius." Perhaps he is just trying to live up to this paternal advance billing. Perhaps he tries all the disguises because he doesn't have a personality of his own and is like a woman in a dress shop, drunk with the chance to watch herself in the mirror in a succession of fascinating costumes.

But I have a pet theory of my own about him. I think he is tired of the rest of us who are such sticklers for a name. "What's in a name?" he asks. He takes the working definition of identity: not that a man is what he is called, but that he is what he does. If he works as a teacher or a surgeon or a warden or a Bible superintendent, that is what he is.

It's a refreshing base on which to operate—the code of a man who says that whosoever shall lose his identity in the service of his fellows shall find his identity. Instead of putting this impostor into prison let's give him the run of the country and put the real fakers to shame.

5. The Two Clocks

March 7, 1958

I HAVE BEEN LOOKING at the pictures of Dr. Wernher von Braun and General John Medaris at Cape Canaveral, as they assessed the failure of our second moon launching. Both were understandably strained and tense, almost as if they could lift the missile into space by sheer will. I felt like asking, "Why so hot, little men?" It has taken countless centuries for mankind to uncover what we know thus far about the secrets of the earth, the sun, and space and time. Getting this particular little gadget up can wait a few months more.

More important than the immediate weapons race, or the later vistas of space travel, is the steady yielding of the secrets of life by every means that science can open.

Either my science teachers at high school and college were dull, or I was dumb, or both, but the fact is that I am no great shakes on scientific matters. Yet these satellites have set me reading. I came across an interesting item in a ten-year-old biography, *Einstein: His Life and Times,* by Philippe Frank (Knopf). Einstein came to the United States first in 1921 on a visit with Chaim Weizmann. He was at the height of his fame, was greeted by armies of reporters everywhere, and the papers were full of popular summaries of relativity. Representative J. J. Kindred, of New York, asked for permission to insert one of these pieces into the *Congressional Record,* but Representative David Walsh of Massachusetts objected, on the ground that it was incomprehensible.

"Besides," asked Walsh, "what legislation will it bear upon?" It seemed a clinching question, but Kindred was equal to it. "It may bear," he answered, "upon the legislation of the future as to general relations with the cosmos." He proved to be an unsung prophet. Today there is a blue-ribbon Senatorial committee chosen especially to deal with legislation bearing on space.

One aspect of the present rocket era hits my own imagination more than anything else—certainly more than the idea of space travel, which would merely open a new and farther exurbia for more tired commuters. I am talking of what has happened to the idea of time.

A few months ago, in an issue of a technical journal called *Science,* there was another installment of a debate that has been raging for more than a half century, ever since Einstein's early work which argued that time is a fourth dimension of a four-dimensional space-world, and that "a moving clock runs slower than an identical clock that is at rest." From it came the "clock paradox"—the idea that if one clock were in a rocket ship going to Sirius and the other remained on the earth, they would keep different times. Or instead of the two clocks, scientists have talked of twins—one on the ship, one remaining behind, with the result that the space-exploring twin on his return would be younger than the stay-at-home.

I have tried out this two-clock paradox on a number of my friends, only to be met with derision. But now I have found a delightful book, *The Inhabited Universe,* by Kenneth Gatland and Derek Dempster (McKay), which does many things to clear up in simple language the problems of life and space. I am especially grateful to it for two chapters, "The Time Paradox" and "Other Universes," which open up new perspectives for me.

If you are interested in time as a relative idea, there are two other books, both of them rather difficult going. One was first published thirty years ago and excited me when I was teaching my first college classes. It is Wyndham Lewis's *Time and Western Man.* Lewis, a talented eccentric who loved a fight, took his contemporaries to task for being so time obsessed. The other is *Man and Time,* which is Volume 3 of a handsome series called the *Eranos Yearbooks* (Pantheon), with essays by philosophers and psychologists, including Jung. What it does is show that each great culture and era—the Greeks, the Christian Fathers, Islam, Buddhist India, modern industrial society—has had a different conception of the nature of time. For us Americans time runs in a single straight line (not a spiral or a circle) and is severely democratic. But other cultures have been subtler about it.

There is a delightful quotation from Gerald Heard about the three attitudes toward time in the evolution of life: "We see successively the time-unaware animal, the time-haunted man, and the time-understanding mind." Fine, but the rub, of course, is whether any two of us will agree on just what the "time-understanding mind" is.

There are some for whom the new discoveries of the expanding universe confirm the old religious and mystical ideas about "timelessness" and the "universal oversoul." It may be that the combination of our new anxieties and our new sense of awe at what is opening up in galactic space will produce a religious revival.

As for me, what it does is stir the imagination and make me feel pretty ignorant. And one thing more: It makes me reflect how ironic it would be if, just as we stand trembling on the threshold of this new knowledge, we were to be hurtled into nothingness.

6. "A Vast Death-Happening"

December 13, 1950

WILLIAM FAULKNER has a low opinion of the "general and universal physical fear" that has spread over the world in the atomic era. He says the only question we ask in this generation is "When will I be blown up?" And he adds, "The questions of honor or no honor, courage or no courage, virtue or no virtue, don't exist." Which makes us out to be a fine lot of groveling, sniveling weaklings, caring only for our own skins, with nothing deeper to keep us rooted and nothing higher to aspire to. This is a serious indictment. It's not pretty, and it's tart, but is it true?

The Communists also have a low opinion of our courage and honor in capitalist democratic societies. Courage and honor, they think, are only opiates we have swallowed, given us by our masters, and as soon as we are confronted by a vast danger we wake from our drugged sleep and become an anarchic scramble of terrified animals seeking safety. Of course, when the issue concerns a Communist country they feel differently. Thus a Paul Robeson, who has no word of praise for American soldiers, can talk of "the valor of the Korean people and Chinese people."

The fact is, of course, that personal courage is widespread, and it knows no national barriers and no class divisions. The Marines fighting their way back to the coast had it, and so in their own way did the Chinese trying to destroy them, and the mourned and unmourned dead on both sides are a forever silent rebuttal of both Faulkner and Robeson.

It is true that all life comes out of death, but one can carry the theme pretty far. Thus even a Bertrand Russell, who is skeptical of most fancy ideas, falls for the notion that wars somehow spur the vitality of men. I am glad to see that John U. Nef, of the University of Chicago, has just written a book, called *War and Human Progress* (Harvard Press), in which he tramples all over that idea. The only things war spurs are war production, war technology, war controls, war memoirs, war novels, warriors and worriers.

In leafing through Edmund Wilson's delightful anthology *The Shock of Recognition,* I found again a letter of D. H. Lawrence's that I had all but forgotten. It was written to Gilbert Seldes, in 1923. "No, I am not disappointed in America," Lawrence wrote. "But I feel about the U. S. A. as I vaguely felt a long time ago: that there is a vast unreal intermediary thing intervening between the real thing which was Europe and the next real thing, which will probably be America, but which isn't yet, at all. Seems to me a vast death-happening must come first. But probably it is here, in America (I don't say just U. S. A.), that the quick will keep alive and come through."

Lawrence believed that only death could lead to cultural creativeness and the stirrings of new life. But history belies him. World War I was "a vast death-happening," yet it bled Europe white and led only to the establishment of Communism and the murderous agony of fascism. World War II was also a vast death-happening, yet it led only to the expansion of Communism and to our present dilemmas. World War III can lead only to the final victory of some form of totalitarianism—death leading to death.

My own feeling is that it is not just a skin-preserving fear that turns men everywhere against atomic war, but the collective life instinct itself. Honor is not dissolved. A new feeling for honor is emerging—the sense of honor not just of the individual or the nation but of man himself as a whole being whose greatest dishonor is murderousness. America will have to find some other way of keeping the quick alive than by another vast death-happening.

7. Together and Alone

June 15, 1955

I HAVE CONCLUDED that life is a numbers game in which we require no higher mathematics but can limit ourselves to the fingers of one hand—at least, for everything that is elemental.

To start at the beginning, you can be conceived only by two, and no ingenuity or brain power has ever been able to change it to either three or one. I am dealing, of course, with neither gods nor amoebae but only with human beings.

You are born alone, out of a lonely woman who struggles to give birth, so that where there were two flames, one within the other, there are now two separate ones.

You grow up always together, in a small group called the family. If you try to grow up without it you can only grow twisted. There are babies in foundling hospitals who die because they have no mother, nor anyone else to give them the affection of a mother. Nor is any father merely a given one; every boy must search for his father until he finds him, and every father for his son. The family cores come two by two; when the core is there the rest of the family follows.

Outside of it is the peer group. You go to school with dozens of your own age, and find among them two or three who are your best friends; the rest count for little. You eat with a group; a solitary eater, like a solitary drinker, gets to be a morbid one. You run about with a gang, whether it is a street gang, a fraternity gang, a lodge gang, a women's-club gang, a Ku-Klux gang, or a church gang. You work and play and do business with shifting multitudes. You fight in a whole army. But in the end you always have to live alone —with yourself.

I am no Pythagoras, who built a whole philosophy on the meaning of numbers. But I know that there is a gulf between one and two. When you have two you get something that belongs wholly to neither but has been created by the fact of their coming together. There are always two in a friendship, and this applies even more strongly in a courtship. "You and me it's gotta be," was the way a stricken businessman used to plead to the show girl of his dreams.

What applies to courtship applies to sex. As Kinsey's figures abundantly show, you can have sex by yourself, but similarly you can't court yourself in the mirror alone for hours. It isn't true courtship or sex unless there is someone to share. Sex is a social fact.

You need two for a secret; beyond two it is a precarious secret. You need at least two for a conspiracy, although the usual form of cabal or junta is a small handful. You need three before you can have a love entanglement, as witness the term "triangle."

You read alone; I regard reading aloud as a bore, unless it is a dramatic recital by Dickens or Laughton. You often go to the movies alone or watch a TV screen alone, but it is martyrdom to go to the theater alone, since it is a social occasion. You can walk alone, although it is a wholly different experience from walking with another: but when more than two do it, it is no longer walking, but an expedition.

To dress up or to act implies an audience. I suppose this applies also to painting or writing, but they seem to me lonelier arts. I am sure that one writes alone. There may be discussion with others beforehand and criticism by others later. But the act of writing, like almost every other creative act, is a terribly lonesome thing.

Society and solitude—these are the twin poles of our existence, and each of us creates a somewhat different mathematics out of them. We vary in our feelings and habits about the numbers within which we like to do what we do. There are some who run only with the crowd and are lonely even within the crowd, but they dare not face themselves. Others draw too much into themselves, peopling their inner world with multitudes, although that seems to me the lesser failing.

But the imperatives remain. You vote alone in a booth, with your conscience. You worship in congregation with others, but the only worship that counts is the silent one in your heart. You sleep alone, even though you go to bed together—alone with your tensions and memories, although sometimes with a warm and saving sense of the body next to yours. You dream alone, however your dreams may be peopled, and you have nightmares alone.

You may think you face dangers together, and it is easier that way, but (as Stephen Crane saw) in the end you face danger alone. But it is rarely that a man stalks a victim alone: hunting and persecution are far easier when done in a pack.

You die alone, no matter how many people there may be around your bedside. And you lie in your grave alone—alone and forever.

THE DIALOGUES OF ART

1. Malraux: A Victory over Chaos

(New York *Post* book review)
November 22, 1953

ANDRÉ MALRAUX has crowned a lifetime as novelist, archaeologist and student of history by a treatise on world art which is at the same time a discovery of the emergence of a world culture. Those who have followed Malraux know that, even in the days of the 1930s when he was most committed as a political man on the extreme left, he was also rooted in the study of man's expression through art.

I recall a day spent with him in New York during the Spanish Civil War. He had come to America to plead for aid for the Loyalist forces. Yet all through the evening he talked about art and literature; it was his thesis that, more than reflecting life, they gave it its impulsion and meaning, and that we see the reality of the sensory world in a different light because of what the great artistic traditions have done in transforming that reality.

In his new and sweeping survey of art through the ages (*The Voices of Silence: Man and His Art*, translated by Stuart Gilbert) Malraux has carried out this insight. He does not make the mistake of the Marxists in seeing art as merely the expression of social forms. He sees both the social forms and the art forms together as the expression of man's questing and creative spirit. He has therefore ransacked the culture of every region and historic period, studying its art forms and masterpieces as the expression of the daring, the sensibility, the passion, the dream-forging, the God-representing and God-making energies of man.

This is a close and compact book. Just as Malraux describes El Greco purifying his style in the successive versions of "Christ Driving the Traders from the Temple" in a quest for austerity and depth, so Malraux has pared away everything extraneous from his own style and thought. He has reorganized and rewritten the three-volume work which appeared recently both in Paris and in English translation and has made a new work of it in the same sense that El Greco's Toledo version of the "Traders" was a new work.

It is swift, elliptical and allusive. He assumes in the reader a basic knowledge of paintings and periods that few of us have; yet in the process of assuming he also communicates it, so that even the non-expert reader can get much from the book. The arrangement of the hundreds of reproductions, both black-and-white and color, to accompany the running text is one of the great feats of bookmaking.

It is clear that Malraux did not produce this book, after two decades of work, merely as an intellectual or aesthetic exercise. Without laboring his thesis, he has one. He writes as a West European man who for decades has been obsessed with the need to create a European man who will transcend national limits. He has now gone beyond this earlier European vision and writes—much as Lewis Mumford does in America—as a man in quest of a universal cultural heritage which ties men together everywhere.

It is lucky that Europe, in its downward arc, has produced a man capable of such passion, and also with the personal history that Malraux possesses. He is at once a man who has taken part in great historic action, one who has stretched himself in trying to resolve the intellectual puzzles of our time and one who has yearned for faith. He can thus understand aspects of the art of the Euphrates and the Congo, of Greece and Rome, of Renaissance Italy and France in the era of its triumph, of the primitive tribes in Africa and Oceania, which would escape most students.

He understands also the modern spirit in art—the spirit which expresses itself in multiple rather than unified forms, in a consciousness of history, in a sense of fatality, in the fragmentizing and transfiguring of what was once whole.

Yet he does not fall into the current cliché of those who bemoan the evils of "standardization." He points out that it is exactly the arts of reproduction, made possible by our mechanical revolutions, which have broken the limiting bounds of the old-fashioned museum and have placed within the reach of everyone a "museum without walls." When you had to travel to Rome and to Paris to see the great works, you were limited by the vision of the few you could get to. Today it becomes possible to get a total view of man's spirit in all its art expressions—Bantu or Byzantine, Chaldean or Hollywood.

This is a work of synthesis, insight and that restless probing spirit which Malraux finds in modern art. At times he seems to lament the passing of the "absolute" idea which was embodied in the art of the medieval cathedrals and in the great primitive art. Yet mostly he notes its passing as a perceptive observer. He has a capacity to sum up the beginnings, endings and transition points of whole historical eras by symbolic phrases. He sees the history of art as a continuing dialogue between men far removed from each other, in which the voice of the artist pierces the silence of the eternal.

"For a very small number of men, keenly interested in history," he writes, "it is a complex of riddles asking to be solved, whose progressive elucidation is a series of victories over chaos." Not the least of those victories is the one Malraux has now given us.

2. A Visit with Marc Chagall

Vence, August 11, 1954

THE LIFE OF ART has laws and survivals of its own. Marc Chagall, the boy from Vitebsk in Russia, the young painter of Montmartre who was the idol of the Surrealists, the refugee from Nazism who had to flee France in 1940 and spent six years in America, is living now in this sun-soaked little Provençal town and painting as he has never painted before.

We spent several afternoons together talking on the terrace of his villa and walking through the little town up the hilly street that contains six ruined chapels. We had met first in New York over ten years ago when he lived in the shadows of the Nazi terror and his paintings showed his bitterness. In 1949 I saw him again at Orgeval, outside Paris, and last year briefly at the home of his daughter, Ida Chagall-Meyer, on the Île de la Cité. He looks vigorous and almost serene—if the turbulence of spirit that has marked him through the years can ever allow serenity.

We talked in a mélange of French, Yiddish and German, shifting from one to another in the same sentence. "I don't try to understand my paintings," Chagall says as you wander around in his house, where the walls are covered with paintings he has saved from every period of his development over half a century. I quoted the line from Archibald MacLeish, "A poem should not mean, but be," which he received with eager agreement. Yet he has packed a lifetime of meaning into his paintings, if you want to read it there.

He told me of his father, who tried to raise nine children in the Russian town on the few dozen rubles a month he earned in a herring plant, lifting the heavy barrels of herring. "I saw him becoming a clod," says Chagall. "I watched the zest for life ebbing out of him. When I asked him for the two rubles a month I would need for some art instruction, an unimaginable look of disbelief came over his face. He was a good man but too burdened. I couldn't bear to add to his burdens, so I left home."

His almost childlike openness and his dreamy, poetic bearing mask a shrewd understanding of the world's trends. He has none of the illusions about the Russians which blind Picasso and Sartre. He understands what the Communists in Russia have done to the best friends of his youth, and what they would do in France. He remembers what the Nazis did, too, and has not ceased to wonder that a people as cultivated intellectually as the Germans should have sunk to the bestial. Britain he finds too gloomy, not at home with the sensuous life. The British have a great literature and politics, he says, but little in the plastic arts. Their great art is that even when they have been pushed out of one part of the world after another, they retain the friendship of those over whom they have once ruled.

As for America, he remembers that in his hour of despair it showed him generous hospitality. He never learned the language and remained a stranger, and for a few years his work suffered. The symbols of suffering he put on his canvases were not at ease with the fiddle, the cow, the languishing submissive maidens. He finds Americans lusty children, with a child's immaturity but also with an unspoiled creativeness. The French, on the other hand, with their centuries-old wisdom about ways of living, are anything but children. In fact, he adds, they may never have been children: they are born sophisticated.

I spoke of his Paris exhibition that I had seen, and how deeply French it was in theme. And I asked what had happened to Vitebsk and the life of the Jews. "The critics all think Vitebsk is still in me," he said. "But it isn't. It couldn't last. It was destroyed, first by the Nazis, then by the Communists." I asked about Israel, which has several times invited him to make his home there. "There is enough of Israel for me in the Bible," he answered. "I am not in any sense a Jewish nationalist any more. What is inside of me is—humanity. That's what counts."

The striking quality of the paintings in Chagall's new Paris show is their color, which ripples and sparkles and bursts into flame. To be sure, Chagall used these reds, oranges, purples, ultramarines, chrome yellows in his earlier phases, but he uses them now as if they were a discovery and the world of color had just burst on him. When he came back to Paris from America in 1946, the beauty of the city flooded over him again, and he did the sketches for this new painting cycle which he completed in the last two years at Vence.

This, I take it, is what Chagall meant when he told me that he cared now only to paint humanity itself. Chagall's dream world, which many critics have underrated as a kind of playfulness, is—like the mythological explorations of Picasso—a deeper way of getting at reality.

It is natural for him, therefore, to turn now to the great religious themes, which are in a different sense a dream world. He has been asked by the town government of Vence to decorate six old chapels that the town owns and wants to reconstruct. Chagall has in mind scenes from the Old and New Testaments and from the great sacred writings of all religions. Together they will form perhaps fifty or sixty large works, constituting a kind of natural history of the religious experience.*

When I saw him last, he was working on sketches for "Moses Crossing the Red Sea" and planning a series of illustrations for "Daphnis and Chloe" which will take him to Greece.

3. Conrad and His Dream

November 22, 1957

THE FIRM of Doubleday had to pay hard cash for an ad to the memory of Teodor Józef Konrad Korzeniowski on the hundredth anniversary of his birth yesterday, but no one else remembered to remember. Since such occasions come only once a century, and I can't wait until the next time, I offer my own homage to Joseph Conrad.

You don't have to be a sea enthusiast to like Conrad, although it helps, since his sense of the sweep and mystery of the ocean is related to that "oceanic" feeling (in Jung's meaning) that one finds throughout his writing. As for me, I like a few of his dry-land novels even better than his storm-and-voyage celebrations. I am, I fear, an associative reader. I read *Heart of Darkness* right after I had been to the Belgian Congo, and *Nostromo* after coming back from a recent Guatemalan unpleasantness. I forget how I happened to read *The Secret Agent,* but it must have been spurred by some recollections of the London jungle. I am the sort of reader who will probably enter the portals of hell with an asbestos-back edition of Dante's *Inferno* in my pocket.

As you will note, it is partly the political novelist in Conrad that draws me. Not because Conrad knew much about politics; actually he knew almost as little as Henry James. But both men were drawn to the psychology of conspiracy and terror—which is to say, to that phase of politics whose essence is the enemy and the fanatic.

There is a curious new timeliness to such novels of Conrad's as *The Secret Agent* and *Under Western Eyes.* I have just added the latter to the little storehouse of novels I cherish, tearing some time away from the hullabaloo about the real Russians and their purges and their missiles, to swim in the dark sea of Conrad's fictional Russians with their purges of soul and their so tiny bombs compared with what Kapitza's technicians are now producing. But though the old-fashioned anarchist bombs were tiny, aimed only at a minister or

* This project never came through.

some public building, Conrad saw the approaching shadows that darken our own age. The conspirator, the true believer, the Informer, the *agent provocateur*—he had a prevision of the world in which they would become the type figures.

He carried it over, doubtless, from his memories of his father, Apollo Korzeniowski, who was a violent Polish nationalist and who spent his last years as a political exile in a bleak town in northern Russia, where Conrad's mother died of illness and heartbreak. Conrad nursed a bitterness not only against the Russians, but against every form of revolutionary violence. As Irving Howe points out in his highly suggestive essay on him in his recent book *Politics and the Novel* (Meridian), Conrad was proof of the remark that the sons of revolutionaries revolt against revolt. But out of that recoil Conrad fashioned some unforgettable books.

The story line in *Under Western Eyes* is about a Russian student, Razumov, who informs on a fellow student who had committed an assassination and betrays him to the police. Afterward in Geneva, where the exiles have gathered, his fate gets tangled with that of the sister and mother of the man he betrayed, and he tries to explain himself to them and come to terms with his conscience.

It isn't much of a story, but Conrad treats it—as he treats every other theme—in the grand style of a man who took himself and his own art and the complex mind of men with high seriousness. The simplicity of his earlier sea stories—man against nature, courage against the storm, and so on—gives way in these later novels of political psychology to a restless probing of the ironies and contradictions of life.

Not that I agree with Conrad's obsessive view that there was something terribly mysterious in the Russian soul which separated and would always separate Russia from the West by an unbridgeable gulf. I feel that the romantic in Conrad romanticized both Russia and the West, plunging the one into a mystical agony and bathing the other in the golden glow of reason. "The apes of a sinister jungle" is the phrase Conrad uses for several of the exiles in Geneva. It conveys at once Conrad's own intensity about the people whom he both hated and was drawn to, and the dark atmosphere in which he envelops his characters and story and which furnishes their fascination for me.

It is a fair guess that if our world ever gets destroyed in a missile war, it will not be because of the Russian soul—sinister or not to Western eyes—but because of a crazy weapons race which may pass beyond the point of no return. But if you ask in turn from what roots that manic frenzy springs, your answer will have to fix on the dark, irrational component of the human mind which Conrad knew so well how to explore among his fanatics and terrorists.

That is why the novelists are better reading today than most political and social thinkers. They see the "heart of darkness" (in Conrad's phrase about the Congo) and darkness in the heart. They have what Henry James, in one of his letters, called his "imagination of disaster." Conrad as a young man wandered all over the world, and then sat down in England to record his memories. Yet his best books are not written out of recollection. He had to sit there and *dream* his world, as every writer must do in the end, lonely and ravaged by his dream.

The terrifying thought for us today is that the dream may come true, and that the novelist's imagination of disaster may be fulfilled.

4. Blake: Till We Have Built Jerusalem

December 9, 1957

ONE OF THE DELIGHTS of growing up is to learn poems as a boy (when your mind is first on fire and malleable) which you recite all the remaining days of your life. My memory poems were a grab bag, and I don't know whether it was at high school or later that I acquired William Blake, bursting into his deceptively simple lyrics at any inappropriate moment, and making life wretched for whoever was my victim at the time. That is why the bicentenary of his birth, which is being celebrated this year, brings back some old memories which I have tried to renew.

You don't have to underscore the parallels of Blake's time and ours, as J. Bronowski did in the *Nation* in a piece on Blake as "a prophet for our age." Any time is good to read Blake in, provided men feel caught in the forest of the night and wonder about the mystery of creation, and grieve about man's inhumanity and the stupidity of institutions, and contain within themselves the marriage of heaven and hell, and long to find release in the realm of vision rather than in the narrower confines of reason.

I think I should feel a good deal safer about my country and my culture if Eisenhower read Blake instead of Westerns.

But Blake was neglected during his life and ignored for a good while after his death by his own British nation. His was a strange sort of genius, this Londoner whose father was a hosier, who had visions and said he saw a treeful of angels and who had an encounter with Ezekiel at eight, who was apprenticed to an engraver and barely supported himself at that vocation the rest of his life.

I keep thinking of this man who never traveled and never left London, except for a few wretched years in the country, yet could visualize worlds way off our earth map and knew the shape of the prophets and the contours of heaven and hell; this radical in politics, who knew the left-wingers of his day in London and hoped for much from the Bolsheviks of the French Revolution, and was shocked by the popular revulsion against the Revolution, writing his *Songs of Experience* as a counterweight to his *Songs of Innocence*; this heretic in religion, who was more deeply Christian than the churchmen and theologians, and insisted on making up his own Christian myths and peopling his world with his own mythical and allegorical figures about whom he wrote endless epics; this poor, yearning fellow who cried out against the puritanism of the moral codes of his day and dreamt of harems of lovely girls (as most men do), but who wrote his dreams into his poems.

There were many who thought Blake was mad, as indeed he was a little by any standard that would be recognized by the mental-health movement. Who could help getting a bit "touched" and crotchety when he saw with terrible clarity the folly and cruelty and blindness of a world which in turn condemned his dreams as futile and just ignored them? So he spent his years doing his harrowing pictures, and selling his poems—which he lettered and decorated himself, never using the printing press—to the rare buyer who glimpsed his genius.

This outwardly mild little man, who wrote butter-wouldn't-melt letters to mediocre friends and patrons, could also be one of God's angry men. He had an unforgettable fusion of compassion and anger. Sometimes I find his poems about "Mercy, Pity, Peace, and Love" too cloying, and his identification with the suffering of every living thing can become in itself almost insufferable, because in making life all sensitivity it leaves no room for anything else.

But the cutting edge of his savage anger more than restores the balance. Blake had a peculiar theology, all his own, which represented the Accuser (Satan) as having usurped God's place and saw the Jesus Child as the only hope of ousting him. His eternal rebellion against authority expressed itself in his conflict with the God father figure (sometimes he called him Nobodaddy), but he was at the same time drawn to his vigor. Deeply influenced by Milton, he carried over a good deal of the Miltonic fascination with the Accuser, and saw also—what it has taken modern psychology a good while to catch up with—that we carry the Accuser always within us in our "selfhood."

Yet Blake did not make the mistake of flattening out his own personality with a sense of guilt. Actually he valued the uniqueness of his personality. In a passage of one of his great letters, he writes: "Since the French Revolution, Englishmen are all intermeasurable by one another; certainly a happy state of agreement, in which I for one do not agree. God keep you and me from the divinity of yes and no too—the yea, nay, creeping Jesus . . ."

Thus we have back in 1827 one of the most fiery blasts against conformity of mind and the throttling of the imaginative life.

Years earlier in his poem on Milton, he had written some of his most famous lines:

> *I will not cease from Mental Fight,*
> *Nor will my Sword sleep in my hand,*
> *Till we have built Jerusalem,*
> *In England's green and pleasant land.*

Bemused by Biblical images, Blake never got quite clear what his ideal Jerusalem would be. But he knew what we had to fight against —the "dark Satanic mills" of an uncontrolled industrialism, the "mindforged manacles" of intellectual oppression, the poisoning of love by commercialism, the "marriage-hearse," the insanity of war.

5. O'Neill and the Cage

May 27, 1956

I SPENT close to five hours the other night at the O'Neill play, *The Iceman Cometh,* presented with skill and honesty at the Circle in the Square theater. I saw *The Iceman* when it was first done in 1946, and the intervening decade has given more point to it. In our downbeat era of automation, radiation and alienation, we are bound to go in for downbeat literature and theater.

The dozen assorted drunks (including a saloonkeeper and a couple of bartenders) and the three prostitutes who adorn Harry Hope's saloon in *The Iceman* are all refugees from life. Each has found reality too hard to face and has retreated into drunkenness and stupor as into a kind of Nirvana. Each also has spun around himself the cocoon of an illusion, fooling himself with the belief that tomorrow and tomorrow he can shake off the spell of drunkenness and inaction and resume the work he once did and the life he led.

O'Neill wants to show they never can. He does it through a brash, fast-talking hardware salesman called Hickey (magnificently played by Jason Robards, Jr.) who periodically comes to carouse with the derelicts and pay for their drinks. This time he is a changed Hickey, who has come to cure each of them of his pipe dream by mercilessly exposing his illusion and forcing him to face reality. Well, you can guess the rest. Stripped of his illusion, each character collapses, since it is only the illusion that has kept him going. But as Hickey unfolds his own story, the derelicts learn that he has murdered his wife in a fit of insanity. As he is taken off, the little community at

Harry Hope's resumes its illusions and each character returns to the warm womb of his lie.

It is one of O'Neill's weaker plays, building a vast superstructure on the thin foundation of an oversimple and overmechanical idea. What O'Neill says, in the parable of his drunks and whores, is that all life is an illusion, for the sober and virtuous as well as for the derelicts. We are all wrapped in dreams that are lies; once we face them they crumble into dust, but then we have nothing left, not even the dream that is a lie.

This sounds too much like a college bull session. The problem of illusion and reality is more complex than what O'Neill grasped. Instead of saying that all life is illusion, I find it truer to say that there are many bewildering forms of reality in life, and that even the illusions we need for making life tolerable are themselves a kind of reality. The fact that we require the dream, however pitiful it be, is itself a sign of something beyond the dream. The reason our illusion is precious is that it is a token and a garment of reality. That is why the sick mind must be brought back to its identity. The value of the lie is to give perspective to the truth.

But if the play is a failure, it is a grand failure, such as only a playwright of genius, working on a big canvas, could have attempted. O'Neill hated American optimism and revolted against its easy harmonies. He felt that the only relations worth exploring were not between man and man, but between man and God—but if you approach his plays from this angle you find man always the victim. Hence the note of self-pity which so often mars and weakens the tragedy in O'Neill.

Given his family memories and a tragic life, one can see why O'Neill felt before his death that only the illusion remained true. One can understand his bitterness against Hickey, the meddler and interferer, who (like a reformer or a psychiatrist) wants to expose the illusion. And one can understand O'Neill's obsession with the sea, limitless and enveloping, with the oceanic sense of death.

The Iceman, of course, is also Death. Trapped in a murderous era, we are as fascinated with him as O'Neill was, trapped in a sensibility too raw-nerved to endure.

January 7, 1957

A father who was a tyrant and a miser, a mother who was a drug addict, a brother who was a ne'er-do-well and an alcoholic—what a doom-ridden family this was for a consumptive, poetic boy to carry with him in his life and memory. Yet out of this neurotic life came the work of Eugene O'Neill, and out of this haunted yet incandescent memory came what is certain to be reckoned as the

greatest single American play of the first half of the twentieth century
—O'Neill's autobiographical *Long Day's Journey into Night*.

To have seen it as I did the other night—with Fredric March's
crowning performance of his whole crowded career, with an impassioned and flawless playing of the older brother's role by Jason
Robards, Jr., with a blending of torment and tenderness by Florence
Eldridge as the mother and Bradford Dillman as the young O'Neill of
1912—was more than to have seen a play; it was to have been through
an experience which made playgoing a creative living-out of the ordeal
and wonder of life.

I came out of the theater like a sleepwalker, and it will be long
before I can shake off the sense at once of nightmare and of purge.

There is almost no "action" in the play, in the sense of event and
violence which we have come to associate with a play's action; there
is only a succession of confrontations of the characters. Everything
takes place in the course of a single long day into which O'Neill has
miraculously crowded four lifetimes. The opening morning scene
seems sunny and pleasant, yet uneasy. Then with each successive
scene the audience discovers the wounds from which every member
of the family is bleeding, as layer after layer is peeled away and the
rawness of relationship beneath the skin is laid bare.

Not since Strindberg has there been anything in world theater to
match this bitterness and self-revelation on O'Neill's part. Yet where
O'Neill's play is greater is in the fact that he is not content with
savagery in itself. Here, along with hatred and guilt, is a brooding
lyricism, a sense of compassion (including perhaps a bit too much of
self-pity), and a cleansing forgiveness.

In his dedication to his wife, Carlotta, when he presented her with
the play in 1941, O'Neill calls it "this play of old sorrow, written in
tears and blood," and speaks of having written it "with deep pity
and understanding and forgiveness for *all* the four haunted Tyrones."
One can guess that it was harder for him, as is true of all of us, to
forgive himself than to forgive those whom he had loved as well as
hated. He speaks also of having been able "to face my dead at last."
This is, I suspect, what gives the play its core of strength—the
pitiless determination to face the worst in our experience and ourselves, which is what we mean when we face our dead. Before he is
through, O'Neill has walked all around his characters, so that we see
each in full dimension. The overwhelming emotion at the end is a
compassion that overrides the self-pity, makes the tragedy bearable
and gives it depth.

These Tyrones are, in a sense, the primal family—father, mother,
two brothers: Adam, Eve, Cain, Abel. But it is the primal family
ridden by contemporary curses—alcoholism, drugs, whoring, the

vulnerability to money. The confrontation scenes start with accusations and hatred, but before they are through each member of the family has made a revelation of himself.

The father has been through poverty and squalor and has been searching for security; fearing that he will end in the poorhouse, he scrimps on trifles, hoards land as the great tangible, uses quack doctors for his family. He has taken the easy roles as an actor because they have brought him money, and he finds himself at the end with a shriveled talent he never dared develop, with sons who hate him, and a shattered wife.

The mother, with her girlhood convent memories, is a corrupted Eve in a lost Paradise. Her drug addiction, brought on by emotional loneliness as well as by a quack prescription, is used in the play to precipitate the guilt of each of the others in the family. At first each of them blames the others for it. But in the end each must carry and accept his own burden of guilt and see the others with some pity.

The relation of the brothers is in a sense the most terrible. Banded against a tyrant father, cut off from a mother who has shut out everyone, they cling to each other for human warmth. In a climactic, ravaging scene, the older brother reveals to the younger one—O'Neill himself—that he has taught him about drinking and women not just out of brotherly comradeship but in order to corrupt and destroy him and bring his life of promise down to the level of his own life of failure.

The whole play unfolds with a mounting, intolerable tension. In writing it O'Neill discarded his earlier experiments with masks and interior dialogue and the rest. It is as if he felt that no adornments are needed when you face the ultimate truth. He has faced it with a terrifying honestly. There are no solutions in the play, because there are none in life. The characters are trapped within themselves. The only solution is the honesty itself. And no one, after seeing it, can be content again with anything less than the unflinching truth about his work, his world, himself.

October 22, 1958

I went to see a strange and moving play the other night, about a man who lived most when he was sunk in a dream, and who when his dream ended died and didn't rise again; and his wife who reached a kind of greatness because she never sneered at his fantastic dream; and his daughter who fought him every moment, but in her moment of victory wept because her triumph was ashes in her mouth. The play was Eugene O'Neill's *A Touch of the Poet,* the last full-length play of his complete enough to be published and produced. True, it falls short of *A Long Day's Journey into Night,* as what would not? But what play on Broadway today, by a living writer, plunges so abruptly into

a tragic theme and works out so brooding a philosophy of man's entanglement with his image of himself?

It is part of O'Neill's greatness that we argue over not only the
merits but the meaning of his plays. The Playbill I got in the theater
included a little essay by Harold Clurman on the meaning of this
one, and since Clurman is also the director of the production, it was
good to know what angle of vision had guided him. To him it is a
play about America—about the romantic world of the poet which
stands for our preindustrial society, and the world of trade and go-
getterism that followed. It might have been called, says Clurman,
"The Making of an American," and "it voices . . . O'Neill's credo:
that America can only fulfill its promise when its inherited idealism
becomes truly one with its genius for the practical."

Maybe so, but I prefer a view less restricted to the American
scene. Major Con Melody has fought in Spain under Wellington,
and he has come to America in Andy Jackson's time to open an unsuccessful pub and get drunk every day and relive the battles he
once fought. He treats his wife sadistically, he is in a constant state
of war with his daughter, he despises the popular rabble and feuds
with the Yankee upper class. A love affair of his daughter's with a
son of one of the Yankees leads Melody into a fiasco of violence
which ends with his killing his dream image of himself, while his
daughter mourns for the man who is now dead in him, so much more
vital than the more "normal" man who now tries to come to terms
with the world around him.

America is the natural setting for this enactment because its
bustling democratic newness is a good foil for the old aristocratic
values of Europe. But aside from the setting the play reaches to the
universal—to the "touch of the poet" in man himself, anywhere,
any time, which makes him a ridiculous poseur, but which he kills
only at the risk of losing his true identity.

Like any artist dealing with the problem of identity, O'Neill was
obsessed with the questions of dream and reality, with the mask and
the face. In this respect he followed Hawthorne, as he followed him
also in the haunting preoccupation with sin and guilt. In the *American Notebooks,* in which Hawthorne entered jottings for future tales,
there occurs this one: "In a grim, weird story, a figure of a gay,
laughing, handsome youth, or young lady, all at once, in a natural,
unconcerned way, takes off its face like a mask, and shows the grin-
ning bare skeleton face beneath."

O'Neill goes at it differently. There is nothing "natural, unconcerned" about the stripping away of the mask: it is a tortured process. But he shared with Hawthorne the conviction that the mask a
man wears may be so integral a part of him (so deeply does it reach
to his unconscious drives and dreams) that it *becomes* the face, and

when you strip away the mask the face comes away too, and what is left is empty. Whoever has seen Eric Portman playing Con Melody as he comes back from shooting his mare, the utmost symbol of his cherished life style, the thing he loves more than anything in the world, will remember the blankness of face and spirit that he presents.

This is a play to be seen, but it is also one to be read and savored; there is an edition of it, published by the Yale Press. I must also mention the memoir that O'Neill's first wife, Agnes Boulton, wrote about their early years together, *Part of a Long Story* (Doubleday), fragmentary and disjointed yet somehow revealing. "He loved his own tragic conception of life," she writes, "and would not have given it up for the world. . . . He would never permit any knowledge or idea . . . that would interfere with it, to enter his mind." This may be part of the clue to this narrow, unyielding, tenacious man, who clung to his own mask—his tragic conception of life—and would let no one strip it from him. But out of it he fashioned a great many-paneled vision.

In some ways I prefer *A Touch of the Poet* to the longer, more ambitious *The Iceman Cometh,* which showed a saloonful of derelicts, each of them sunk in his illusion, each fleeing back into it for security after he had been given a taste of the "real" world. Con Melody has moved beyond that. However much he may have died when he shattered the mirror, shot the mare, he doesn't come crawling back into his old illusion for comfort. He has the stamina to go on, even with a death-in-life.

Perhaps it is because he is loved. In a curious way, although the play seems to be about masks and poses and dreams, it is also about love. The daughter loves her young Yankee upstairs, the mother loves her husband, the father loves his mare, who stands for the impossible qualities of a traditional society and a lost way of life.

IDEAS ON THE STAGE

1. The Theater of Ideas

December 16, 1955

"I GO OUT to explore the astonishment of life," says the governess in *The Chalk Garden,* and one feels that Enid Bagnold has summed up here not only her own intent in writing the play but the essence of the theater itself. If characters may have to go searching for an author, as Pirandello tells us, it is because they are incomplete as characters unless they are informed with some idea; the idea comes to life in them, and they in turn are given form by the idea.

When Walter F. Kerr wrote a delightfully scathing book called *How Not to Write a Play* (Simon and Schuster), he demolished the idea that a play can be involved with either a thesis or even an idea theme, and there are few, if any, to say him nay. All honor to friend Kerr and his redoubtable artillery. Yet judging from the plays I have seen this season the exciting ones are exactly those that can most meaningfully be called the theater of ideas.

Let me start with *The Diary of Anne Frank,* which Kerr agrees is a "radiant play." But it would be far less radiant than it is if it did not assert an idea—that the gaiety of life shatters and the flowering of life wilts under man's inhumanity to man, but something remains which outlives the inhumanity and triumphs over it. Or take Arthur Miller's *A View from the Bridge.* It too has an idea—that a man may have something within himself which is so possessive that it will destroy others and finally him.

Notice that I don't put any of this in terms of "problems." When someone tells me that a play is about the problem of divorce or the free-speech problem or the problem of drug addiction or illegitimacy or missing fathers or vivisection, I shrink from it because I prefer my sermons in the church or synagogue. Yet I hasten to add that much of Ibsen and Strindberg is still powerful theater, and that the sheer force of Shaw's ideas still fills a theater with storm and thunder and radiance.

I give two other plays as illustrations that character, idea and theater must form an unbroken web. One is Tennessee Williams'

Cat on a Hot Tin Roof, which I read as saying that no one can possess anyone or use anyone, that a husband cannot become a man because his wife needs his virility or his father needs completion in a dynasty; but that in an inscrutable way creation feeds on corruption, and life feeds on disaster, and that out of the futility and turbulence of life (as out of the storm on the plantation) a stillness may be born which is the seed of self-understanding and therefore of life.

The other is *The Chalk Garden,* which, for me, shares with *Tiger at the Gates* the top honors on Broadway this season. You can see *The Chalk Garden* on two levels. On one it is very funny, witty, full of quite insane characters. There are many who will go to see it to be titillated by the bizarre and released by the outrageously trivial. But on another level it is a serious play, as Siobhan McKenna shows it to be in the gravity of her whole demeanor and the weight of every gesture. It is an allegory to which there are many keys—an allegory about nature and nurture, about growing things or people in a limestone garden or a story world, about love and compassion, about freedom of the mind and the dead hand of authoritarianism.

Every good play of ideas should be full of storm signals and stir a storm. Take *A View from the Bridge* again, as an example. If I were a theater critic I should go back to read Budd Schulberg's novel *Waterfront* (Random House), and see the Kazan picture that was made from it. For what we have here is a great conversation, a polemical dialogue, carried on between Schulberg and Kazan on one side and Miller on the other. The "problem," if you will, is how you fight what you regard as evil. Schulberg and Kazan say that when you find corruption (whether on the waterfront or in Communist politics) you fight it even if it means working with the authorities against your former associates, even turning them in. Miller says that if you betray someone you commit the ultimate crime out of some inner flaw of hatred and destructiveness. For Schulberg and Kazan the theme is the strength of sacrifice, and the movie ended on a Christlike figure with a crown of thorns. For Miller the theme is betrayal, and the closing image is that of Judas.

Tiger at the Gates has lasted thirty years and is still alive, because the intellectual passion of the French playwright gives it life—because Helen is beautiful and Paris glowing and Hector curiously moving as a man of arms who has turned against the waste and futility of war. The dialogue between Hector and Ulysses sums up the whole dilemma of the human animal who contains within himself both guile and idealism, and is caught between the two.

The customers storming the box office for all these plays are proof that the theater of ideas is coming to life in America.

2. Sartre: Dirty Hands and Freedom

(New York *Star*)
December 7, 1948

THE PLAY whose opening I saw the other night, *Red Gloves,* was a badly cut, badly adapted version of Jean Paul Sartre's *Les Mains Sales* (Dirty Hands).

Here is the story Sartre tells. In a Central European country that seems like Hungary under Admiral Horthy during the war, a young man, Hugo, is given the mission by a Communist faction to kill the party's leader, Hoederer. Hugo comes of a wealthy family and has joined the party out of an idealist belief in revolution and a desperate desire for direct action to achieve it. But he is really a sensitive, torn intellectual and not a man of action.

Hoederer's crime is that he wants the Communists to join a coalition government along with both the Social Democrats and the fascist aristocracy and business group. Hugo finds himself drawn to Hoederer against his will, and so does Hugo's wife, Jessica, a warm, sensuous, unpolitical girl. After several fumbling impulses to carry out the assassination Hugo gives it up in despair—only to find himself, in the end, killing Hoederer after all in a setting which is ironically that of a *crime passionelle.*

The final twist Sartre gives the story is what counts. Hugo goes to jail, but is released when the Russian armies approach the city. He comes back to his party comrades who had ordered the assassination, only to find that Hoederer is worshiped as a party martyr, and that the comrades have now adopted the very same coalition tactic for which they had ordered Hoederer killed. For Hugo this is the cream of the whole tragic jest. He refuses to be reclaimed as a party comrade and goes to his death crying, "I am not reclaimable."

Is the play primarily an anti-Communist tract? Sartre is kicking up a great fuss, claiming that the American version twists his play into a Red-baiting shocker. In quarrels of this kind I am on the author's side of the fence. I think he has the right of final say on what goes in and comes out.

Yet the play itself, even in its original form, cannot escape being anti-Communist, just as it cannot escape being antiliberal, antisocialist. It is an honest and searching exploration of what happens when you try to achieve social change and are faced by the dilemma of modern political action—the dilemma between the totalitarian and the ineffectual.

Hoederer, the Communist leader, dominates the action and mood of the whole play. Everyone is drawn to him—either to follow him or to destroy him. Whether Sartre intends it or not, he emerges as the heroic figure of the play. He is the ruthless, unsplit, whole man, who rejects purity as the luxury of the hypocrite and the monk. He asserts that to get social change one must plunge one's hands up to the elbows into dung and blood.

Hugo, on the other hand, is the spokesman of the modern man who wants revolutionary change but is unwilling to destroy his soul for it. Hoederer kills and lies, accepts men for what they are, hopes to impose a new system on them. Hugo also is willing to kill, but he is unwilling to tell lies to the people or to himself. With all his Hamlet-like weakness and indecision, there is something he ends with that the others do not have—a belief in the indestructible meaning of the man who lives and dies responsibly for an idea.

That is why Hugo chooses to die as he does. He has never been quite certain why he killed Hoederer—whether it was for his coalition-front idea or because he found his wife in Hoederer's arms. He has clung to the party as his only guiding line. But when he finds that his comrades have lost the meaning of their own acts and want to turn Hoederer as leader and Hugo as assassin into meaningless ciphers, he rebels and in his rebellion becomes a free man.

3. Darkness in the Heart

January 16, 1951

WESTBROOK PEGLER and I went to see a play last night. It was Sidney Kingsley's *Darkness at Noon*. To be sure, we sat a few rows apart and never exchanged a word, which was probably a good thing all around. But I couldn't help thinking what a handicap a political play like *Darkness at Noon* labors under when it has to find an intellectual common denominator that will satisfy someone like Pegler and someone like myself.

One critic has expressed disappointment because the play is not as subtle in character overtones and as rich in implication as the Koestler novel is, and because Kingsley has made a melodrama out of it. I find myself agreeing with the fact, but not with the disappointment. When you go to see a play you go to see theater, not reflective fiction. Part of Kingsley's strength is that he is a sly old hand at melodrama.

But he has turned that melodrama to the illumination of Communism. Where Koestler delighted and stirred his readers by giving them the clues to the long-standing riddle of what makes an old Bolshevik confess to things he never did, Kingsley has shifted the emphasis from inquiry to indictment. The light he sheds on Communism is as harsh and implacable as the spotlight that Gletkin, the robot-minded interrogator, directs at Rubashov while he is breaking him down.

If you ask who Rubashov is, one answer is that he is all the old Bolsheviks whom Stalin's revolution crushed like eggshells—he is Radek and Piatikov, Trotsky and Bukharin and the rest. Such a character composite must have in him something of the contrived. With his usual fidelity Kingsley has put into his mouth snatches of speeches and writings from many authentic figures of the Revolution—including the famous one that Gorki says Lenin used, about wanting to stroke heads when he hears the "Appassionata." In an earlier version (now happily cut out) the public prosecutor blasted Rubashov with authentic sentences from Vishinsky's speeches at the purge trials.

But what we have here is not only the documentary accuracy of a research job. It is the essential moral truth about what Communism does to human beings, or—even better—the natural history of the Communist idea in action. The revolution, said Danton, devours its children. The men who interrogate Rubashov—the sympathetically drawn Ivanoff and even the too sinister Gletkin himself—do not pursue him out of hatred and evil but because they too are caught as Rubashov is, and by doing what they think right they wreak moral havoc.

The most frightening thread in the play is the way in which each successive generation of revolutionaries devours the preceding one. Everything is stripped away except a meaningless logic and an arid power. "I am not your son," says Gletkin. "Oh yes, you are—that's the horror of it," Rubashov answers at the close. "The means have become the end, and darkness has come over the land."

The *New Statesman* ran a lively series of polemical articles about what the British call the "play of ideas," in the sense in which Bernard Shaw is a playwright of ideas. The Kingsley drama, I think, falls in a different category—that of the political play, which does not have fun with ideas, as Shaw used to do, but tackles a basic ideological problem. Unlike Sartre in his *Dirty Gloves,* Kingsley has not set out to be a political thinker on his own. His forte has always been that he is a kind of seismograph to register the convulsions of his era. He has set down here with a deep seriousness the consciousness and conscience of an anti-Communist generation.

In doing so, the danger has been that in concentrating on the darkness of Communist logic he has almost bypassed the darkness of the human heart. I could wish that he had probed deeper into the tragic nature of the human destiny itself, so that I could have left with more feeling of having been purged—not in Stalin's sense but in Aristotle's.

4. Billy Budd

February 28, 1951

YOU WILL OFTEN FIND the good writings on politics between the most unlikely covers. The novelist and the playwright have become the carriers of political ideas mainly because the political problems of our time have become once again the old moral problems.

That is why it is disheartening to see a play like *Billy Budd,* based on Herman Melville's short novel of that name, about to close on Broadway. I can't understand why the audience that throngs to see *Darkness at Noon* doesn't also throng to see *Billy Budd.* Long before Koestler, and better, Melville probed into the problem of evil, and the moral-political questions of human destiny and human choice that cluster around it.

Take any young boy of today. Say he is a good-looking youth (Billy Budd was, says Melville, the perfect type of the "handsome sailor," loved by all on board), and that he has miraculously failed to be corrupted by a corrupt civilization (Billy was a foundling, a kind of "noble savage" who personified purity of motive, courage, directness, innocence). Say that our boy is drafted and goes off to war against the Chinese (Billy was also drafted—"impressed" was the term used—by the British Royal Navy in the days of the French Revolution).

Say further that the boy acquits himself well but runs athwart an officer who is both a fascist and a sadist (like John Claggart, the master-at-arms, or chief cop, of Billy's ship, who was the personification of evil). The boy is framed by the evil one, strikes out from his burning sense of injustice at his oppressor, kills him. Say his commanding officer, who reads books and has ideas and cares about justice but puts military duty ahead of everything else (which is the case of Captain Vere) holds a drumhead court-martial, and condemns the boy to death.

There you have the story. I have translated it into today's situation not because Melville's novel is timely but exactly because it is timeless. Melville makes much of the setting of the contemporary mutinies in the British Navy, and the fear of the revolutionary infection. Captain Vere cares deeply about Billy Budd, but Billy has struck a British officer, and the Captain fears that to acquit him will be a confession of weakness which may revive the fires of mutiny in the rest of the fleet.

And so Billy dies in his goodness, with a "God save Captain Vere" on his lips. And when the Captain dies in battle several years later, "Billy Budd, Billy Budd" are his last words.

It would be easy to fight the case of Billy Budd all over again, to argue the wrongs and rights of the execution as every member of the audience must do on his way home. But I don't think it would serve much purpose, for Melville was not a problem writer but a great novelist of the human allegory. The play, necessarily giving one interpretation of the novel, seems to be saying that Melville uses Captain Vere as spokesman for his own view and thus affirms the inescapable agony of the hard choice the captain must make.

As I read Melville, I find him dumping the problem into the reader's lap. The novel is great because it is not a thesis novel which provides a solution, but because Melville sees all around the problem. He has a mixture of feelings about Billy Budd: annoyance at his perfection, for he sees that perfect good cannot endure in an imperfect world; fascination with the face of evil, in the form of Claggart; acceptance of the iron necessity represented by Captain Vere's choice and Billy's death; and finally, a sharp ironic protest against the nature of things which makes a humane man trample on both goodness and justice in pursuit of duty.

"We are not free to choose," says Captain Vere at one point, "as if we were private citizens." In that sentence we must seek the canker. The separation between private morality and public morality is one that Machiavelli made centuries ago in *The Prince*. It was the task of his age to make it. But it is the task of our own to undo his work and bring public and private morality back into the same unity, which is the human situation.

5. *Saint Joan and Saint Queeg*

December 3, 1956

I HAVE JUST CAUGHT UP with the Phoenix Theatre's version of Shaw's *Saint Joan*. It is a beautiful performance, especially in Siobhan McKenna's peasant girl with the rich brogue coming out of the rich provincial earth.

Being Shaw, the play is part of the theater of ideas. The Irishman makes his characters human all right, yet what we recall about them is not (as in other great playwrights) that they are woven out of earth and air and fire and water, with passions and irrational tempests coursing through them, but that they are wonderful vehicles for Shaw's discourses on ideas. It is his genius that makes the ideas come to life in the shape of human beings, but it is also his weakness that never for a moment do the ideas surrender the center of the stage to the people.

Shaw pushed his own world back into the Middle Ages, which is why his lines crackle with modern instances. But how about the American theatergoer? If he is content only to read Shaw's England in Joan's story, then he is unfaithful to both Shaw and Joan. He must add a third dimension—that of contemporary America.

Shaw's picture of Joan is clear. The reason why she burns at the stake is that she cannot surrender her "voices"—cannot give up her right to interpret the will of God by her own best lights. The bishops, generals and nobles use her for a time beCause the fierce contagion of her belief gives the people a fighting faith against the English. But in the end the mighty of the earth turn against her, since she becomes a menace to the massive Establishments of the time—the Church, the feudal nobility, the Army.

In the epilogue, dramatically an anticlimax but intellectually the cream of the jest, Shaw brings Joan and her friendly enemies back in a dream fantasy. The peasant girl who was burned at the stake at Rouen four hundred years earlier is now canonized by the Church and acclaimed by all. But when she offers to come back to earth in reality, they recoil with horror. We pay lip service, Saint Joan (Shaw) is saying, but we still fear the idea she incarnated.

He was right. Coming home from the Phoenix, the memory of Joan's terrible moral dilemma made me idly look up some contemporary American writers who are tussling with much the same problem. There are some good instances in *Great Moral Dilemmas,* edited by Robert M. MacIver, where each of a number of critics has picked a novel or play, ranging in time from Job and Sophocles to Herman Wouk, and dissected it to see how the author poses and resolves the moral dilemma.

The essay I was looking for, coming closest to the problem of heresy and conformity, was Robert Bierstedt's "The Tergiversation of Herman Wouk." It was about *The Caine Mutiny,* a book and play so dramatically conceived and smoothly brought off that most critics failed to note the shabbiness of its basic theme and the moral somersault that Wouk takes at the moment of choice.

All through the book (Bierstedt reminds us) the reader is carried along by Wouk, sees Captain Queeg as a tyrant and coward with mental aberrations who imperils ship and crew, and sees Maryk—compelled to take over the ship—as its savior. After Maryk is acquitted by the court-martial there is a victory dinner, and Barney Greenwald, the lawyer who has defended Maryk successfully, stumbles in with a few drinks too many and some harsh truths on his tongue. In a dizzying moral switch he tells Maryk and the junior officers that Queeg is a hero, and that except for him and the massiveness of the Navy Greenwald's mother (he is a Jew) would have been boiled down for soap by Hitler. And he dashes a glass of champagne in the face of Lieutenant Keefer.

Thus Wouk gives us a canonizing very different from Shaw's—not Saint Joan but Saint Queeg, not the country maid who paid with life for the right to think in despite of the princes and the Church, but the man in authority who was part of the System.

The final fillip of this theme comes in another critic of Wouk, who deals with Queeg, Maryk and Keefer as symptoms of American culture today—William H. Whyte, Jr., whose *The Organization Man* (Simon and Schuster) traces the character, ethic and mode of living of the new American. For Joan is dead, and Shaw, too, and the Church is no longer the dominant feature of our social landscape. But the defense services and the big corporations are very much with us. It is they and not the Church or monarchy or feudal princes who are now the Establishment—or, as Whyte calls it, the Organization.

Whyte sees that Wouk's *Caine Mutiny* is a novel celebrating the new Organization, underscoring the sin of heresy in doubting its premises and breaking with its authority. Whyte got an ingenious idea. He ran a prize essay contest in a boys' prep school. Its theme was "the moral issue of *The Caine Mutiny*," the boys being asked to state the moral problem, tell how Wouk resolves it and give their own reaction. With only one exception, Whyte reports, the boys upheld Wouk and Queeg and favored the System. All but one said that "a subordinate should not have the power to question authority," or words even stronger. The one holdout wrote that it was a man's "moral duty to act as he thinks best." He alone proved the heir of Joan and Shaw. The rest illustrate the new American imperative (as Whyte puts it) "Love that System."

6. The Banners Fall

March 12, 1958

I SAW Henry Fonda and Anne Bancroft do magic in the theater last night, in *Two for the Seesaw*. It was magic because, with only two people in the cast, they managed to keep the action tense and flowing and produce an illusion of the richness of life. But having said this, and paid my respects to the skill of William Gibson's writing, I must add that this entertaining little play will soon vanish from my memory. I shall probably hold on to a breathless line here and there of Anne Bancroft's, but the rest will sink into the vast sea of our accepted and acceptable thinking about marriage.

What is wrong with *Two for the Seesaw*, as with some other current plays, is that they lavish talent on the writing, production and acting, yet about the steep and craggy places that men must climb in the ascent of life you find that they say only smooth and shiny things, soon forgotten.

Even with only two actors this is a triangle play, with the third member (the wife) missing from the stage. In Gibson's earlier novel, *The Cobweb* (Knopf), there is a doctor, a wife (bitchy and frigid) and a mistress; in the movie, he goes back to the wife, courtesy of the Hollywood Code.

Here in *Two for the Seesaw* there is a lawyer, his wife (not bitchy and frigid, but too protective, stripping him of his manhood) and the mistress. The movie won't have to change the ending; after seesaw ups and downs with the mistress, he goes back to the wife, having learned how to be a man, and determined to take her from her rich family and live in Lincoln, rather than Omaha. Gittel Mosca, the little Jewish girl who is hungry for life and love, has her crust taken away; Jerry Ryan goes back to the place and the class to which he belongs, where a wife sends letters on scented note paper. J. P. Marquand and Herman Wouk have triumphed.

But not without genuflections to the power of love—heady, violent, releasing love. This is how we do things in our dramatic slicks: love is proclaimed; there is an intense affair, with all the accompaniments of bed and board; there are even a few words of Yiddish thrown in, and, running through the whole play, the quickening warmth of Gittel's Jewish temperament; and then suddenly the banners of love, so defiantly lifted, are lowered.

What reason does the author give? Just that Jerry has found himself, and his jealous wife has come to need him, and besides they have between them the shared experience of marriage. The wife has a taste for bridges, and Jerry can't snatch a view from the bridge without seeing it through her eyes.

Very moving, but the author's time sense is limited. He forgets that the shared experience of the present becomes the shared past experience of the future. You have lived with a woman for eight years and emerge a psychological cripple; then you live with another for a few months one fall, and you find yourself released. So you say "Goodbye, infant, nice to have known you—next to 'love' the word 'help' is sweetest on the mouth"—or something to that effect. Since the wife is never on the stage, Jerry's feeling about her is a thin and fabricated echo not of life but of a thought about life, and never is made persuasive.

But love has been proclaimed, and marriage has been sustained, and everyone cheers, and everyone is happy in the highly moral world of the cultural superego. And you take a taxi home with your wife, loyal and true, both of you clutching your eaten cake, but the passages of the play both of you remember are the heady, exciting ones about how two people can lose themselves in each other, wholly alone and in love in the vast impersonal jungle of New York.

I use this play as an example, only because I have just seen it, and since it is so charming it makes the letdown all the soggier. There have been others I might have used. The "sudden death" system on Broadway makes it desirable to play it safe and have the good-bad boy meet the good-bad girl but do nothing really reckless, and nothing to weaken the marriage institution. We have plenty of new talent writing for the theater. William Gibson is part of its promise. But what happens to it? Why does it seem to exhaust itself?*

The playwright is a fellow who has to put his inner torment and vision into living symbols on the stage. Some care deeply about their social vision (Odets, Hellman), but when the generations change and their form of intense caring is no longer possible or valued, they lose their drive. Others (Saroyan) care all the time, celebrating life with a compulsive euphoria that becomes monotonous because it has no change or growth in it, but only love, love, love. Still others (Tennessee Williams) see the frightening Medusa head that lurks in each of us, full of writhing snakes. What they produce is intense and poetic, but as you watch them (witness, for example, the remarkable psychoanalytic revelations in Mike Wallace's TV conversation with Williams) you wonder when they too will shrink in horror from their own vision of the Medusa head or, gazing, turn to stone.

There remains O'Neill, who never turned away and never turned to stone, and who cared, but who also grew with every phase of his life and retained his almost manic drive. And—who knows?—perhaps William Inge, if he can learn the difference between a neat play and a great one. Or perhaps Arthur Miller, who has the caring and the drive and the grandness of vision, if he can continue to grow. And some still unknown playwright, struggling against Broadway and its gods, a fellow who won't scuttle Gittel and settle for the easy solution.

7. Ionesco: Chairs on a Stage

January 12, 1958

I HAVE JUST BEEN to the Phoenix Theatre, where I saw a crazy play by a crazy Romanian, called Ionesco, who writes in French. And I can report the paradox that while the play deals largely in negations, everything about me is more alive as a result of seeing it.

Of course, I am a hopeless addict of playgoing, which means that I like to see the curtain go up and then I surrender all my senses along with my mind in order to see magic done. And the kind of magic I like is not just the photographic variety (look-the-clock-on-the-mantelpiece-is-just-the-kind-my-grandmother-used-to-have). I like to be stretched, and to have my thoughts and emotions disarranged. I

* Since this was written William Gibson's *Seesaw Log* has appeared, relating his struggle against the Broadway system in getting his play produced.

go to the theater not to get the comfortable feeling of recognizing a drawing-room interior but to get the uncomfortable one of discovering new things about the interior of the human mind.

With one or two exceptions, most of the theatergoing professionals on the New York papers had a lukewarm-to-cold feeling about Ionesco. Of the three I read regularly, Watts saw in the author only "hollow and pretentious fakery," Kerr found his philosophy distressingly "nihilist," and Atkinson—who thought it was fun, and good theater—had first to dismiss any suggestion that he took the play at all seriously.

As a lay and fitful playgoer, I have to dissent. Ionesco doesn't give you any near parables, and I agree that he is a ragged fellow intellectually. You can read your own meaning into his play. But who can deny that it took some imaginative fire in the writing to make an empty stage, with an old man and an old woman and a collection of chairs, come to life and strike a fire in your brain?

What *The Chairs* tried to present—at least for one viewer—was the emptiness of reality and the reality of fantasy. The stage was the world and its pomps and vanities, surrounded by the encompassing oceans as in the beginning of time; the chairs, empty except in the illusion-ridden minds of the old man and woman, are the nameless beings who people our waking and dreaming life; and the whole episode is about the effort of a man to give meaning to his life by giving a "message" to the world.

Bleak? Yes it is, but Beckett's *Godot* was bleak, too. There is something about the French, with their terrible tradition of rationality, which spurs those who write in their intellectual climate to revolt against the tradition, and which makes them go the whole way and deny reason itself, and perhaps life.

But Ionesco isn't orderly enough to be a consistent nihilist. He belies himself at every point, and there are sparks of recognition in us each time that he does. The old man struts about, as most of us do when we try to deny the emptiness and failure of our lives. The old woman, who is at once wife and mother to him, cradles him in her lap, butters his vanity, echoes the sentences in his final harangue, fortifies his ego. She too has her vanities, as when she fancies that she is being seduced, but mainly she is the perfect spouse.

The attempt to burlesque a middle-class evening in entertaining guests doesn't come off. Ionesco may fancy himself a social satirist, but he isn't much good at it. But he has a sense of the ironies of life. There is a wonderful passage where the old man and the old woman tell their guests simultaneous and wholly contrasting life stories, and in which Ionesco catches the terrible subjectivism of a man's life, whose reality is in the mind and not outside it.

But the biting scene comes when the doors start opening, the invisible people crowd in, the whole stage is caught up in a wild rhythm of movement and sound and light, and the old man gets upon a chair to thank everyone (a delicious take-off on a dinner chairman's speech of appreciation). This is all preliminary, however, to the great event, which is to be the reading of the old man's Message to the World. The Orator arrives, but before he can unfold his scroll the two old people have vanished through the windows into the waters below. And when the Orator finally reads the Message, the only syllables he can utter are idiot sounds.

One is reminded of Henry James's story, "The Beast in the Jungle," about the man who has hinted all his life at having a mark of distinction, a special secret; in the end the woman who has loved him suddenly knows that his distinction was to be the man to whom nothing whatever was to happen. In one sense Ionesco is almost a sentimentalist; the old woman, to the very end, believes in her man and in his Message.

I don't see why the American theater should not make a few efforts of its own in this direction, instead of relying on Beckett and Ionesco. American painting, which is probably as good as you will find anywhere right now, profited by the European expressionists who lived here during the war, and today it has a thriving school of artists who work with symbols. Why are the critics afraid of this trend in the theater?

8. Tennessee Williams: Sweet Bird of Eden

April 5, 1959

AT THE END of *Sweet Bird of Youth,* when the hero of the Tennessee Williams play is about to be seized and castrated by the Southern racist storm troopers, the action stops and he turns to the audience, asking not for pity, or even understanding, but the recognition of him in themselves. I fear it was a sign of a measure of failure in the play that I didn't feel the trauma of recognition, or even much of a twinge of it. The note of universality at which Williams aimed he doesn't quite achieve.

I don't want to underestimate the play. There is a brooding, lyrical quality in it, along with a wonderful realism of dialogue. It is all compounded of poetry—the poetry of terror and decay. When he embodies that poetic sense in his two main characters, whose portraits he has drawn with a sure mastery—the aging movie star and the self-hating gigolo who has in him the pent-up violence that is in all dreamers—no one can write as he does. But when he tries to be a philosopher and a social critic, not even all the magic of Kazan's directing nor the almost flawless performances of Geraldine Page and Paul Newman can rescue him.

It is a pretty talky play, for all its violence, and the talk is about success and failure, about time and its ravages, about how men are emasculated not only by women but by their cupidity and their false goals, about how people die and walk about as corpses—and are not reborn. In fact, there are too many clues and too many themes, so that the stage of the mind is cluttered up with them. I found myself having to throw away most of the leads and cling to one or two themes. In the closing scene the loud, steady ticking of a clock is heard, as if time were the real protagonist. For me it is not time, but a kind of virginity corrupted.

I suspect that if we go back to some of the other Williams plays, especially *Streetcar*, we will find the same theme of innocence which has been violated—not by time but by a timeless rot which Williams has never quite been able to define, because he has never quite been able to decide whether to locate its source in man himself or in his society.

The image of virginity, which runs through the play, lies in some past golden age, some state of nature and innocence in which human beings once found themselves, but which they have lost, lost, lost. Williams is a contemporary Rousseau of a sort—the Rousseau who cried out that man is born free, yet he is everywhere in chains. While Williams defines this original freedom and innocence largely in sexual terms, it is striking that there is no genuine sexuality portrayed on the stage, but only the bought sex act of a gigolo, the sickly prurience of a father for a daughter, the sadistic and mutilated sexual relation of the politician and his mistress.

The only time that sex takes on the overtones of lyrical sensuality is in the remembered love of Chance Wayne and his girl, Heavenly, in their early days of wooing. "The great difference between people," Williams tells us through his young and luckless hero, "is between those that have pleasure in love and those who watch it with envy . . . between the spectators and the performers." And he adds that "nothing can ever cancel out those many long nights . . . when we gave each other such pleasure in love as few people ever had."

But note that even this notion of love-as-sensuality is never seen in a going relation; it is the remembered Paradise, the sweet bird of Eden. Presumably it is our doom—the doom of all of us—to be expelled from the Garden, and to go wandering all the rest of our lives in shame and forlornless. Instead of enjoying delight our women shrink from the mirror, or are corrupted with a rot that must be cut out of them; and our men are emasculated.

Those who saw *Suddenly Last Summer* will doubtless offer a prayer of thanks that the new play stays away from the theme of cannibalism.

Yet in the other play Williams did give us the terrible but unforgettable image of the slaughter of thousands of baby turtles by murderous birds, and he contrasted it with the cold human murderousness of
Mrs. Venable. In the new play there is no such theme from nature to
contrast with the ferocity of man or woman. We have to take it
straight.

In the form of Boss Finley, and his son, and his henchmen, it is
hard to take. The whole second act, which focuses on them and their
sadism of Southern massive resistance, is too clamant and cluttered to
be persuasive. The portraits in this act cease to be portraits, and they
become political posters. What is even worse is that by bringing in the
theme of Southern terrorism, Williams misses the tragic possibilities of
his hero. For if you seek the tragic flaw in Chance Wayne—the thing
that turned his innocence into corruption—you do not find it in himself, or in destiny, but in the accident of his girl's father who had to
destroy him as he destroyed everything.

Tragedy, Nietzsche wrote, must overcome pessimism. It must be
"the yea-saying to life, even to its strangest and most difficult problems." I find in *Sweet Bird of Youth* no yea-saying, but a stageful of
people who either died inside themselves or never lived.

THE STRETCHING OF MAN

1. The Destructive Element

January 9, 1952

IT IS as if he had stepped right out of the pages of a Joseph Conrad romance, perhaps *Youth* or *Typhoon,* this hardy young captain with his fierce sense of what he had to do. Whatever happens to his battered ship, to which he has stubbornly clung, Captain Carlsen has stirred something in the hearts of men.

It is not only a feat of skill or endurance, like that of a flagpole sitter or a Channel swimmer. Nor is it the heroism of a soldier in battle, performing some shining deed. Henrik Carlsen did something also beyond the call of utility. He may save the ship line that employs him a goodly sum, but it is not this that moves us or him. His fanaticism is not that of a man dedicated to his crew or his company or his country—in fact, to any collective group. It is that of a man standing alone in a crisis, making his lone decision, answerable only to himself. It is a man living by the code of the sea which has taken centuries to build up, but doing it because he—like all of us—has to live with himself.

In one sense, of course, this is the old story of man against the sea. You can view it, if you wish, as a tussle with the fierceness of nature, and read Carlsen's story much as you might read the great adventure stories of the sea or the fabulous tales of shipwreck. But I prefer a somewhat different view of the Carlsen story. I take my clue from Conrad's wonderful sentence about the ocean: "To the destructive element submit, and it will bear you up."

Who can know what went through the captain's mind when he made his fateful decision to stick it out on his ship? My guess is that he did not view the sea as an adversary to be fought, but as the "destructive element" which—once he made his peace with it—would bear him up and his ship as well. Every artist loves and understands the element he works with, and a good captain is a good artist, carving out some design of human fate which only now and then he—or we—can glimpse.

The idols of our group and time are combat, success, money,

power over men. The thing that stirred us about Carlsen's act was that it seemed so unmotivated by any of these spurs. Here was a man who did what he did not for money, nor for utility of any kind, nor for war or glory in killing, nor for sport. He did it because it was part of his craftsmanship and calling, because it was in the nature of a good sea captain to do it, because he loved his ship and the sea as well, because with himself on his ship he could trust it to the "destructive element." He did it, in short, because he had to in order to be himself.

To call him a hero has something of the mawkish about it, because we have come to think of heroism in terms of success and the applauding multitude. Yet if you define heroism as what a man has to do, in going beyond himself in order to be himself, there is a truth in it.

And in that sense I suspect that we underestimate the hero urge and hero capacity in most human beings, even today, and even among that "younger generation" which is taking a terrible drubbing from the oldsters. The trouble is that we do not seem to have given them a code (like Carlsen's code of the sea) to live greatly by, nor a "destructive element" to which they can trust their strength.

2. The Summit

June 3, 1953

"GODDESS MOTHER OF THE WORLD" is what the Tibetans call her, and for a century we have called her Mt. Everest. For decades expeditions have tried to scale her and failed, some repulsed just short of the goal. Now a New Zealand climber and a Nepalese guide, part of a British expedition, have reached her summit. They have stood higher than any living man has ever stood on this earth, have breathed the thinnest air.

Both the crowning of the Queen and the reaching of Everest's summit are important symbolic events. But symbol for symbol, who will say that what the Nepalese and the New Zealander have done was of less moment? In the history of the human spirit the gradients are not those of earthly rank, but those of passion and dedication.

I will even say that the two events may in the end serve the same purpose. The British Empire has cracked, but in its place the Commonwealth is a reality. Nevil Shute has written a novel, *In the Wet* (William Morrow), which is set thirty years in the future and shows the Australians coming to the rescue of Elizabeth II when her own people have grown too socialist for a monarchy. Shute makes his point in a labored and even tortured way, yet it is true that the future of British power is likely in time to shift to Australia, New Zealand and Canada. The symbols of the Coronation, in all their majestic setting, will do much to hold the Commonwealth together when there are few ties of opportunism to do so. And the achievement of reaching Everest's summit, rightly hailed as a British achievement, will serve as a cohesive force for the distant ramparts of British prestige.

I mention these political consequences only in passing. The point about the climbing of Everest is that, in any immediate utilitarian sense, it is pointless. The claim to the North and South poles, and the charting of the area around them, have come in this crazy world to possess military importance. But no one is likely to build an airstrip on the peak of Everest, nor anchor a space station to it. No one can sell concessions on it, nor dig for uranium where men gasp for breath. It is wholly, bleakly, magnificently useless.

I am not arguing that useless things must therefore be great, but only that you cannot judge a human event by the standards of political power or the economic market or the calculus of immediate needs. What makes a human event great is the intensity of the human spirit condensed in it as a symbol. That spirit may manifest itself as courage or resourcefulness or skill, gallantry or endurance, insight or wisdom or suffering. But always the common denominator for these is the passion for excellence. Wherever men stretch themselves in meaningful ways in the quest for excellence, there the human spirit has its undying triumphs.

That is why the age-old question, "Why do men try to climb Everest?" is not as puzzling as it seems. The classic answer to it, "Because it's there," is probably as good as any, if one understands it. Men take the universe as given—its oceans, its deserts, its firmament, its mountains. What is given is a challenge for them to pierce, explore, possess. Whatever continues long to elude this thrust of man's ego takes on redoubled importance as a challenge.

Perhaps the harder question is: Why do the rest of us who are not mountain climbers, the earth-creeping dwellers in cities and stoopers over jobs—why do we applaud the completion of this useless feat?

I may offer myself as instance. I have rarely climbed more than a hill, and I always come down again panting. One summer, almost thirty years ago, a friend and I rashly climbed a minor peak in the Colorado Rockies. We were not prepared, we didn't have the equipment or training, we hit deepish snow in our thin shoes, we were terrified when we slid a bit or sent an eagle screaming out of his nest. Yet when so many other days of my years have faded from my mind, this is one of green memories.

Why? Because we feel stretched. And what we all applaud in the

Nepalese and the New Zealander is that they have stretched human capacity, in which all have a stake.

3. Man's Belief in Himself

January 5, 1958

SIR EDMUND HILLARY and his tractors have reached the South Pole, but my own mind keeps dwelling not on him but on a man named Captain Robert Falcon Scott who died at the end of March 1912 in the dreary wastes that Hillary has now conquered. It's a curious thing, isn't it, that of all the men who have pitted themselves against the Antarctic, it is not the men who achieved their goal—Amundsen, Byrd, Hillary—who seize our imagination, but it is Scott, the man who got to the Pole after Amundsen and then failed to get home, who remains the memorable figure.

Despite the success cult, men are most deeply moved not by the reaching of the goal but by the grandness of effort involved in getting there—or failing to get there.

Clearly Hillary is no ordinary man. In the span of less than five years he reached the top of Mt. Everest and got to the South Pole by an overland route, for the first time in forty-six years. The fact that he could do both suggests an amazing convergence in him of the character traits of the great explorers—daring, resourcefulness, persistence, soaring aspiration, infinite attention to detail, sheer will.

But for a story of how human beings stretched themselves to the limits of endurance and beyond, there is nothing in the history of exploration to equal Scott's. You can read it in a recent reprint, *Scott's Last Expedition: The Journals of Captain R. F. Scott* (Beacon Paperbacks). The journals cover about eighteen months, and Scott knew how to use words. There is a mounting tragedy as he tells of the unexpected blizzards, the loss of the ponies and the dogs, the casualties of man after man, the few men left pulling the sledges with dwindling supplies, the weakness of the survivors as the food gave out, and how they lay down finally to die.

When a search party found the corpses the next year, they found the journal and the letters that Scott had written at the end. They are the letters of a brave and generous man. "We are weak, writing is difficult," he wrote, "but for my own sake I do not regret this journey. . . . We took risks, we knew we took them; things have come out against us, and therefore we have no cause for complaint. . . . Had we lived, I should have had a tale to tell of the hardihood, endurance, and courage of my companions. . . . These rough notes and our dead bodies must tell the tale."

We usually speak of these adventures as "man against nature." Yet I wonder whether this simple opposition of two forces quite tells the story today. It is no longer nature alone that dwarfs man—nature, in this case, in the form of a vast Antarctic Continent, with hundreds of miles of floes, crevasses and ice walls, with temperatures that sometimes reach 80 degrees below zero, and with blizzards of raging strength. There is science also, which can dwarf man as well as aid him.

In the success of the Hillary dash for the Pole, science was a help. It made possible the use of tractors rather than dogs or ponies, and the charting of what was once uncharted waste. Admiral Byrd's "Operation Highjump" succeeded in making the Antarctic accessible from the air and led to the American station only a few miles from the Pole, so Hillary was not faced with Scott's tragedy of having to get back again.

But we have also seen that science, especially in its triumph, can prepare new disasters for man that peril the survival of the race. Thus man is caught in a curious contradiction. He must keep some shreds of humility as he faces nature, even while he triumphs over it. And his pride as he uses the tools of science must be tempered by the fact that this creature of man can in the end dwarf and destroy him.

That is why, reading the story of Hillary in the safety of my own stay-at-home armchair, I rejoice in it. Not only in the face of nature, but even more in the face of science, we need some reassurance that the human being can stretch himself to the utmost limits of human performance. When Hillary decided to make that "hell-bent dash" for the South Pole, he was making a dash for something else too—perhaps for the goal of man's belief in himself.

The real story is not Hillary's alone. It is that of the whole sequence of Antarctic explorers, starting with Cook in the eighteenth century. This is one segment of life in which the tradition as a whole is more important than any particular man who adds to it. Hillary's task was to keep the tradition alive. By doing so, he has made it more endurable for the rest of us to face all the "wonders of science" that lie ahead, like a lurking tiger in the forest of the night, and that threaten human survival long after nature itself has become a domesticated house cat.

GOD AND DESIGN

1. Seekers and Losers

December 23, 1952

I HAVE JUST READ a little maverick volume called *A Personal Jesus,* by Upton Sinclair, which could scarcely have been written anywhere except in America. It has some controversial things in it, and some crotchety things, but mostly it has warmth and shrewdness and a quality of honesty.

He has written about "little Yeshu" as a small Jewish boy from the interior of Palestine, growing up lonely in the desert. I find Sinclair's account, for example, of the boy's visit to Jerusalem and his disputing with the learned men in the Temple as charming as any I have read. Building on Robert Eisler's study of some fragments from Josephus, he makes Jesus the man into a short and unprepossessing figure, very different from the way he appears in the great paintings. But added to his inner spiritual light there was a remarkably acute mind, a magical way with words, and a sense of mission that carried everything before it.

Although Sinclair writes mainly as a rational humanist (which is also the book's weakness), he is ready to accept the supernatural appearances after the death of Jesus, fitting them into what we have been recently learning about thought transference and "mental radio." In the absence of authentic life details, Sinclair has a right to his own reading of personality. As a novelist he reconstructs the fabric of character around the few threads given us by history. One of the strengths of the great story of Jesus is that it offers room for every age to read its own beliefs into it, and for every writer to find in it his own delight.

Yet at the heart of this book, as of every other book about Jesus, there is the picture of a God seeker who was caught up in the religious ferment of his time and by his life and death created what he meant to be a religion of mercy and love.

We often ask why there are not more people in the world who are truly religious. The answer may be that it requires a special view of life. There are some men who are primarily truth seekers, searching for glimpses of insight and philosophy and science that are of this world. There are others who are beauty seekers, whether they are themselves creative in the arts or revel in the creations of others. There are still others who are life seekers, asking for the fullness of experience, and intent mainly on fulfilling their roles in the life cycle. Nor should we forget, especially in our society, those who worship the idols of the market, and who seek only money and power and success.

Thus the God seekers need a special quality that sets them off from these others. Their whole being strains to reach beyond themselves to the cosmos of which they form part, to pierce the veil of experience and achieve a glimpse of salvation and the kingdom of Heaven. The great religious thinkers have told us that this is not easy to do. You can't do it just by belonging to a church, or by the pride of separateness. You can't do it as one of the Princes of the Earth, or by piling up riches. You can't even do it by brilliance and sophistication of mind. Often it is the poor people and the untutored who are able to do what the rich and powerful cannot, and it is out of their striving that the great religions have been formed.

December 25, 1955

If I read Christian history aright, it was for the losers that the Christian doctrine was originally meant, and in their behalf it was preached. The Roman Empire, like the Babylonian Empire before it, had abundance and glitter and high living standards. But the lowly and despised felt like outsiders, and the failures felt that they had doubly failed when so many were successes.

It was to them that the Christian message was brought most effectively, and its greatest impact was on them. It gave dignity to their privation and meaning to their suffering. The Christian doctrine spread like a wild blaze throughout the Roman world, helping to topple the Empire, and in time building a new civilization on it.

If we seek to get at the heart of the Christian doctrine, we must go back thus to its origins and ask what magic there was in it for slaves and gladiators, for landless and homeless. For it is this same appeal which today spreads the Christian doctrine to the rim of strange continents, the farthest reaches of Africa and Asia.

As I have read the various Christmas issues of the magazines, with their efforts to interpret the spirit of Christianity, I find in them far too much about the churches as institutions, and about the recent swelling of church membership. We are back again at the dogma of success, whereas the original appeal was to the losers.

The heart of the Christian story is to be found in the haunting words "He was despised and rejected of men, a man of sorrows and acquainted with grief." Even in the midst of our burnished Babylonian living there are those who are despised and rejected, who know sorrow and are acquainted with grief.

I think of those who live in squalor and cold. I think of the homeless. I think of the alcoholics and the addicts, caught in a cruel trap, driven by their agony into becoming prostitutes and criminals.

I think of the children in bleak institutional quarters, without the sense of being wanted.

I think of those who are politically harassed and despised, however mistaken they may be.

I think of the Negroes who have been shot in Mississippi, and those who still face the threat of shooting and outlawry because their skin is a badge reminding a little group of arrogant white men that their unquestioned domination is coming to an end.

The question is not just one of compassion for the weak and the failures. This was the phase of Christianity that infuriated a thinker like Nietzsche, who felt that it overstressed the element of meekness and pity. The point about those who suffer is not that they are the objects of compassion, but that they are the symbols of the whole human situation. Who is there among us who does not share some sense of failure and insecurity? Who is there that has not felt a sense of bleakness and even of deadness in him?

One way of seeing the Christian story is through the cycle of birth and death and rebirth which is part of the basic human experience. There is glory at birth, and infinite hope, but there is also death inherent in the whole process of life. If we understand the meaning of the Man of Sorrows, it is that only through suffering can one achieve the continual rebirth which productive living requires.

No one can be exempt from this need. Psychiatry won't solve it for you, nor will religion, although both can help. Neither power nor success nor prestige can be a substitute for the thing itself—birth and suffering, death and rebirth.

It is the function of the losers to serve as a reminder of this fact, which we should all like to forget.

Christmas has become largely a national secular holiday. But since it still has a religious base, it is a good occasion on which to raise some questions of religious belief that go beyond Christianity itself to the core of the Judaeo-Christian tradition.

A man would be a fool if, in an age of anxiety and terror, he did not try to believe, and did not seek to explore the ultimate assurance that so many have found in the idea of God. But I add that a man would be too calculating if he turned to God only to save himself and to find peace of mind, only because of anxiety and insecurity, only as a way out of a personal blind alley; or if he turned to church membership, as so many are doing, only out of social convenience or for community standing.

Religion, for those who can achieve belief genuinely, should involve more than this. I have seen church members—including priests, ministers and rabbis—who struck me as lacking any real belief; and conversely I have seen humble people who stayed away from institutional ties, yet in their presence I sensed something that evoked my respect for religious belief. I give this respect only where I find the questing mind along with the believing spirit and the loving heart. And in such a person I am likely to find also a passion for justice, and a fire of devotion to the freedom of others to dissent from his own belief.

Freud wrote that religion was an illusion, although he implied that it might be a necessary one. But one might say equally that the whole life of the mind and spirit, including love and friendship and the sense of place and the recognition of beauty, is also an illusion. It is something we dream up—but it is none the less important. Usually we don't know it because the noise made by our everyday world drowns out the dream. Only when the noise subsides, in the great moments of life, can we hear the dream ticking.

I think it might be said not (with Voltaire) that we invent our gods, but that we carry them with us and inside us. Cutting across the differences in doctrines between the great world religions—of Moses and Jesus, of Lao-tzu and Buddha, of Confucius and Mohammed—there remains the truth that God is what man finds that is divine in himself. God is the best way man can behave in the ordinary occasions of life, and the farthest point to which man can stretch himself.

When he stretches himself to the utmost without reverence—for human life and its meanings—man becomes not a god but a lethal and bestial machine. The Nazis showed this when they got the intoxicating assurance that anything was possible and permissible, including the cremation of unbelieving subman. The Russians showed it when they set up "history" as a god and sacrificed human beings to it.

Thus the godlike in us tells us always to break through the plodding and niggardly, the earth-creeping and mediocre, and stretch ourselves to heroism of the mind and spirit, but never to break through the human itself. It is in this sense that man remains the measure. If, in his arrogance, he attempts the forbidden—which is to say what is antihuman—then he is using his human and religious pretensions as instruments of evil.

2. Religion in a Democracy

December 26, 1954

I HAVE READ with admiration two remarkable essays by Edmund Wilson in the *New Yorker*. The first was on his adventures in learning Hebrew and on the genius of the language and the people—"On First Reading Genesis." The second was a portrait of life today in Israel—"Eretz Yisrael." I mention them here because, while Wilson calls himself "neither a Jew nor a Christian," there is a deep religious feeling in the essays. Wilson derives from the tradition of an early America where the Old Testament spoke directly to Christian believers with tongues of flame. He feels that Europe today is slack in purpose and exhausted in spirit. By contrast he sees in Israel an alertness and vitality that mark a reawakening of the zestful strength he finds in the compressed language of the Book of Genesis.

In my own thinking I have found it hard to decide how much of this strength lies in the religion itself and how much (I think the greater part of it) is due to the historic experience of the people who are its carriers. A fanatic religion does not always go along with a vital people, as the Arab countries are now demonstrating. I talked with a thoughtful Indian the other day who said that the Moslem religion is still relatively new, and that the people of Iraq and Egypt and Pakistan are "not relaxed" with it. They use their religion as a sword, narrowly and fanatically.

The Indians, who are more "relaxed" about their religion, do not allow it to dominate their statecraft. Yet this does not mean that they are indifferent about religion. Note that one of the few recent creative religious figures of the world was Gandhi, who found a way of combining his own traditions with the Christian one, and who evoked great moral energies by fusing holiness with nationalism.

As for Communism, it does not long remain a political religion. In Russia, for example, where it was first seen in action, it has moved in less than forty years from a political religion to a political church which has organized a new kind of materialism even less nourishing to the human spirit than our own.

It is an axiom that belief can always beat nonbelief. But in a conflict between two systems of belief, the question is always: Belief in what? The new political religion of the fanatics on the American right wing is a belief in nothing except power and hate. That is why it will never beat Communism. If we are to win the future it can only be by an effort of the moral imagination which gives us a body of belief in man's possibilities, in the deepening of both his sensitivities and his decency. Religion alone cannot give us that belief, but it can help to give the belief nobility. That belief in man's possibilities may be found both in Christianity and in Judaism. That is what the early

Bible-reading Americans knew, and out of their knowledge of it came the strength of our democracy.

November 6, 1955

Two recent events have converged to mark a new and important trend in American religious life. One happened last week at Brandeis University, when three student chapels were dedicated in a moving ceremony to the three great religious faiths of America. The other is the publication of Will Herberg's book, *Protestant—Catholic—Jew* (Doubleday).

The Brandeis story is an interesting illustration of what is happening to religion, as well as to education, in our country. The university was established in 1948 under the sponsorship of the Jewish community, as a way of repaying its debt to the larger American culture and also of fighting racist and religious discrimination. Faced by the question of organizing student religious services, it found no clear precedent and had to chart a course of its own. Traditionally the university chapel on the American campus has always been a Protestant chapel, and in the Catholic universities a Catholic one. At Yale, in my college days, I went to the regular Protestant chapel. When I taught at Williams the faculty members took turns at reading from the Bible in the college chapel, again Protestant. Brandeis might have followed this pattern and established a Jewish chapel that would welcome students of all faiths. Or it could have ventured upon a revolving chapel, as at M.I.T.

It chose instead to give each of the three religious faiths its own uniqueness, on the theory that they must respect each other but are not interchangeable. In doing this, Brandeis has expressed one of the deep impulses of American cultural development toward a three-religion country. While the American tradition and the large majority of the people are Protestant, the United States is no longer a Protestant country. The Protestants are no longer dominant in the big cities and are moving toward the suburbs, leaving the cities largely Catholic and Jewish. In a city like Boston the vanishing Protestant is, alas, somewhat in a category with the vanishing Indian and the bison. I say "alas" because I regard the Protestant tradition, with its passion for dissent, as a great one.

Instead, America has become what Herberg in his book calls the "Triple Melting Pot." He cites an interesting study of intermarriage in New Haven, done in the 1940s by Ruby Jo Kennedy. She found that between 1870 and 1940 the members of various ethnic groups (Italian, Pole, Irish, German, Scandinavian, British) married less and less within the group itself ("in-marriage"), but that the in-marriage within the three religious communities remained much more constant.

In other words, Americans are breaking through their bounds of national origin, but they are staying within their bounds of religion. On one front the lines of division are dissolving, on another they are remaining somewhat rigid. There are some who even believe that they are hardening.

There is no other country than America that could have moved so far in such a direction. The Founding Fathers of America lived and worked in the atmosphere of eighteenth-century deism—that is to say, in an atmosphere in which men respected each other's religion, feeling that all religions converged upon the worship of the same God. This is what led to Madison's idea of a separation between church and state, so that no established religion could have a monopoly of the state machinery.

Herberg points out rightly that to a large degree religion in America is becoming secularized. It is becoming part of the American creed. "Being a Protestant, a Catholic, or a Jew," he writes, "is understood as the specific way, and increasingly perhaps as the only way, of being an American and locating oneself in American society." Alas, for many people the new religious renascence seems to mean mostly not a way of finding one's relation to God, but a way of finding peace of mind or happiness or standing in one's community. These are the dangers of the new trend toward the three-religion culture. Its strength is that religion is being removed as a barrier toward first-class citizenship, and that each individual feels free to pursue his own worship in his own way without a feeling of inferiority.

The German dramatist, Lessing, long ago expressed this angle of vision in his great play, *Nathan the Wise,* whose hero was a Jew. "Nathan! Nathan!" says the friar to the hero. "You are a Christian! By God, you are a Christian! There was never a better Christian!" To which Nathan calmly answers, "We are of one mind! For that which makes me, in your eyes, a Christian, makes you in my eyes a Jew."

3. A Universe of Chance

March 21, 1958

ONE OF THE HORRORS of the loft fire is the thought of the panic that must have seized the hearts of the trapped victims. What shall we make of a universe in which a horror so pointless can occur? How can we square it with the idea of justice or order in the universe? These are questions as old as the great religions, but despite their antiquity they are still tangled questions, and there is still no clear answer. The core problem is that of chance as against design in life, of chaos as against the orderly functioning of God or fate.

There was a report of the simple dignity with which the relatives of some of the victims received the news of their death. They had few tears. "If they are dead," said one woman who had lost her brother and his wife, "it is God's will."

I don't think we can write these words off as mere routine for the occasion. It is the kind of faith in some principle outside ourselves—the principle of God's will—which enables the poor to bear their tragedies with a quiet resignation. The loss of a job, a serious sickness or accident, the news of a death: instead of wrestling with the question of what justice there is in them, and why they should strike whom they do, these people murmur "It had to be," or "It is the will of God," and their grieving hearts have that much burden less to bear.

The night of the fire an old cab driver gave me his philosophy of it. "Mister," he said, "there's something that brings us here, and something that keeps us going, and something that takes us away whenever it wishes. I may like it or dislike it, but I can't do anything about it. The millionaire can't fight it, or else he could buy off death or pain with his millions. And even the man who has led a good and decent life can't fight it, because it may strike him even worse than those who are no better than they should be."

This was not the "will of God" necessarily, but a principle of the inevitable, a pattern of fate. The cab driver had resigned himself to it as completely as the woman who said, "It is God's will." Maybe both of them got some peace out of their unquestioning acceptance of something outside themselves, something given. Quite clearly the hope for such peace is the deepest root of belief.

Just as clearly there are other ways of looking at this disaster. If there is a God (one might say) why should He act thus to twenty-four girls and men who shared no common guilt, but who merely happened to work in the same shop? If He has knowledge of everything, and therefore, if He had purpose in what happened, one can only say that the purpose is utterly beyond scrutiny—which is scarcely a consoling thought, even if it is a convenient one. If there is design or destiny in the universe, why should it take so senseless a shape as the deaths that came to these innocent, trapped people?

One is tempted to say that it is not an overarching purpose or design that rules life, but some principle of injustice. In his *Bertrand Russell, the Passionate Skeptic* (Simon and Schuster), Alan Wood quotes the doughty old unbeliever as saying that "the secret of happiness is to face the fact that the world is horrible, horrible, *horrible*. You must feel it deeply, and not brush it aside. You must feel it right here—" hitting his breast—"and then you can start being happy again." For Russell "the universe has no principle of justice at work in it." Wood calls this "practical wisdom," since "if you can give up believing in cosmic justice, then nothing can make you have a grievance against the world."

This too, I must confess, strikes me as playing tricks with your mind, just as the believer in a great and unknowable design plays tricks with it. Both are forms of hedging your bets, and manipulating your mind so that you won't feel too much grief or grievance.

I prefer to believe that we live in what the philosopher Peirce called "a universe of chance." It operates with both evil and good, in a mixture hard to find a formula for. It does not carry any built-in principle of justice. And when something happens as senseless as these deaths, and we ask, "Why these particular people?" we fall back on little more than the wild, blind happening of chance.

But I agree with Russell that there is little point in eating our hearts out in anger at this. The things to be angry at are the things that can be mended—the man-made laws or lack of laws, the negligence, the delay in acting. As for the loom of fate or of chance, it is something we must live with, but not with our eyes closed to the reality. We can approach it with compassion for its victims, and a feeling of awe at the mystery of it.

The simple mind, as well as the sophisticated one, knows that protest against the chaos of the universe is futile. Besides, how can we rail against the fact of particular deaths when there remains in the universe the vaster fact of death itself, whose irrational injustice no rational philosophy can ever explain away?

4. God from the Ash Heap

January 7, 1959

ARCHIBALD MACLEISH has written a morality play, in the old sense of bringing to the stage the great issues of justice and injustice, suffering and faith, embodied in traditional characters taken from the great religious writings. In this new play, *J.B.,* he has used the most moving single story in the history of religion—the story of Job and his trials, and the triumph of his faith in God. In doing so he has brought great poetry back to the theater.

MacLeish had a double problem: how to present God and Satan on the stage—always difficult, especially with God—and how to give us the running debate between them. He has used two strolling players attached to a traveling circus, who amuse themselves with putting on the Job story, one of them playing God (Mr. Zuss, or Zeus) and the other the devil (Nickles, or the Old Nick). As they argue about how the play should go, they carry on the great debate as a running commentary on Job's motives and the meaning of his strange fate—a commentary that cements the episodes of the Job story with meaning.

As the Old Testament tells it, Job was a chieftain or emir in the land of Uz, humble and generous, and renowned for leading the life of a just man. As MacLeish has rewritten it, J.B. is an American businessman, slightly on the Babbitt side, whose enterprise has prospered, and who lives with his wife and five blond children, serene in the consciousness that God is on his side.

When the blows fall on him they are the classic blows, but they take a new form. The oldest son is killed in the war, by a post-armistice blunder. Two of the children die in an auto crash. The youngest little girl is the victim of a hideous sex crime. The final blow is a chemical blast which wipes out J.B.'s plant and home, kills his remaining child, and leaves him a sightless and unsightly human mess, shivering in his rage on a heap of ashes, abandoned even by his wife, who has gone off cursing the God of affliction.

What MacLeish has done, of course, has been to present evil and suffering in their modern guises. "There's always someone playing Job," says Mr. Zuss. And Nickles answers, "Job is everywhere we go, his children dead, his work for nothing, counting his losses, scraping his boils, questioning everything—the times, the stars, his own soul, God's Providence." MacLeish has put it in terms of contemporary evil, whether it takes the form of racist persecution ("walking round the world in the wrong skin, the wrong-shaped noses, eyelids") or war and atomic radiation ("sleeping the wrong night, wrong city—London, Dresden, Hiroshima").

The Job issue has been thrashed out for centuries, from the early Jewish commentators and the medieval rabbis up to the Harvard philosopher Josiah Royce, who did a famous essay on it. Royce resolved the problem by saying that when Job suffered God suffered too, because God was in Job and both his suffering and his triumph were part of the great design of the universe.

Ingeniously MacLeish parades Job's three comforters (each generation has its own comforters, he says) in the form of a Marxist, a Freudian and a professional preacher, each resolving the issue by evading it—the Marxist by appealing to history, the Freudian by denying free will and therefore guilt, the preacher by giving the easy answer that all men are guilty.

MacLeish's own answer rests on love. To be sure, there is no mention of love in the Old Testament story. But MacLeish invokes the New Testament to redress the default of the old. He knows, of course, that the answer to the Job problem, as to why a virtuous man must suffer and the guilty go unpunished, is that there is no answer. Instead there is only the great force of love. In short, the resolution of the riddle of life is the life force itself.

This assumes, as Royce does, that there is a grand design in the universe, which puts human suffering and divine injustice into a larger frame. God argues for this design, in the Old Testament story, in words of unparalleled poetry: "Where wast thou when I laid the foundations of the earth . . . Hast thou given the horse strength? Hast thou clothed his neck with thunder?" Thus God's own answer is the mystery and miracle of the universe.

One might argue, as Bertrand Russell does, that there is no design, that injustice is at the root of things and blind accident holds sway. The traditional retort in turn is that it is presumptuous of man to question the ways of God. But in the end Job no longer questions. "Now mine eye seeth," he says, after the terrible and beautiful words of reproof from God. "Wherefore I abhor myself and repent." It is from the ash heap, says MacLeish, that God is always seen best.

I find his lines poetic, his philosophy and reasoning weak. If man must console himself in some way for the ugly contradictions of life, this is probably as good a consolation as there is. The tough-minded, however, will prefer to face the harsh visage of injustice, and while they may make up fables about it they will know that it is fable and not truth that they are making up.

5. Waiting for God

April 25, 1956

THEY ARE a disreputable, aimless, scarecrow couple of burlesque bums, looking as if they were on the boards only until the stripper was ready to start. One is Gogo (Estragon) and the other Didi (Vladimir). They sit around, bellyache, and argue for a whole evening in the theater, alone, except for an episode in each act with an even more gruesome pair—a resplendent Pozzo and a slave called Lucky. The crucial character is never seen. He is Godot—presumably God—with whom Gogo and Didi think they have a rendezvous (although they are never sure) and whom they never glimpse.

Unlikely material for a play, yet it is an exciting one. The seasoned first-nighters were a puzzled group at the single intermission between the two acts of Waiting for Godot. The whole thing seemed like some prolonged business between two burlesque comedians, yet you had to talk about it. But what could you say without sounding foolish?

That it was about man's plight? Too solemn. That it was about God indifferent and man estranged? Too theological. That it was about being lost, lost—about the whole desolate race of men, seeking to find their identity, restlessly waiting to unite themselves again with the primal source of life? Too Freudian or Jungian.

Let's just say it is about all these things and a lot of others you might choose to read into it. Let's say it is of, by, and for those who suffer from schism of the soul—which covers a lot of ground.

But don't think it is only for eggheads, any more than Chaplin is— or Bert Lahr, who happily plays Gogo. Samuel Beckett, who wrote it, is an Irishman who writes in French, who taught at Trinity but bummed all over Europe, who has an avant-garde claque and cult but who can also be understood as well (and as badly) by a truck driver as by the bearded young men of the Left Bank or the Village.

The play is a producer's dream, having only five characters, with rags for costumes, and for scenery only a few rocks and a scraggly tree. Since the issues Beckett explores are the final issues of life, he has written his play by a process of *reduction,* stripping it as bare as the tree. Some plays are rich by all the loving details of time and place that are put in. *Waiting for Godot* is rich for all the things that are deliberately left vague or left out. What is included is infinitely inventive, but the inventions are variations on the cosmic theme of nothingness.

Beckett and his universe are, I suspect, schizoid. His novel *Molloy* is in form two novels about two people who are really split halves of the same person, one the pursuer, the other the pursued, but each becoming the other. In the play also the characters go two by two. There are Gogo and Didi, who are two aspects of man, seeking to be saved. There are Pozzo and Lucky, on whom lies the curse of Cain and Abel, who are beyond being saved. And there are Godot and his unreliable goatherd messenger boy.

Didi (beautifully played by E. G. Marshall) and Gogo are a touching pair, who seem to crop up in world literature from Don Quixote and Sancho Panza to Huck Finn and Jim. They are the ego and the id. Didi's head is full of all sorts of literary and Biblical and philosophical knowledge, and he is given to poetic and imaginative flights. Gogo is vegetable and animal man, eager for food, interested in sex and sleep and the other body functions. They have been together forever and know each other so well that they talk in counterpoint, making a conversational game of interpersonal relations. It is Gogo who is the weaker and more dependent, and Didi who must feed him and reassure him, even while he is himself deathly afraid.

The second pair, Pozzo and Lucky, are the two sides of institutional society. They are, if you will, master and slave, or property and sweat, or the possessors and the possessed. Lucky is the beast of burden and obedience—the horse, the dog; he is driven by a whip and a long rope yoked around his neck; he fetches, dances, thinks at his master's command. When asked to think he utters a discourse on God ("a personal God quaquaquaqua with a white beard") which is a take-off on the academic philosophers, but which assumes such a wild, compulsive intensity that his listeners can end it only by pinning him to the ground. He can't come to life again until he grips the bag and the basket in his hands; the burdens have become the man.

There is more, much more, but you will have to go see it. The style is at once delicate, despairing and savage. There is the wonderful scene when Pozzo and Lucky return, and Pozzo is blind, and the leader has become the led. The two together are caught in the principle of work or performance which fastens itself upon us through the slavery of habit.

Gogo and Didi are wise enough, at least, to escape this form of madness. The only thing that afflicts them is—humanity. They cannot escape the body of this death. Each day they wait for Godot, hoping he will come before the terrifying night falls. They try to sleep, they think up things to while away the time, they even play with the thought of hanging themselves on the tree.

Only Pozzo comes, and the young goatherd. The suspicion crosses their minds that perhaps Pozzo is Godot, or even that the young boy may be. It would be an ironic thing, wouldn't it, if instead of an old man with a white beard who has a hayloft for the afflicted, God should turn out to be a bellowing blind man thrashing about on the ground, or a young boy echoing your questions with a guileful innocence? Or perhaps just no one.

ABOUT THE AUTHOR

MAX LERNER, author, teacher and columnist, received his B.A. at Yale in 1923 and his Ph.D. at the Robert Brookings Graduate School of Economics and Government in 1927. He has taught at Sarah Lawrence College, Harvard University and Williams College. At present he is Professor of American Civilization at Brandeis University and a daily columnist for the New York *Post*. He is married to Edna Albers Lerner, a clinical psychologist, and is the father of six children.

His previous books have included *It Is Later Than You Think* (1938; revised edition 1943), *Ideas Are Weapons* (1939), *Ideas for the Ice Age* (1941), *The Mind and Faith of Justice Holmes* (1943), *Public Journal* (1945), *Actions and Passions* (1949), and *America As a Civilization* (1957). He has published editions of Machiavelli's *The Prince* and the *Discourses*, Adam Smith's *The Wealth of Nations, The Portable Veblen,* Aristotle's *Politics* and Jack London's *Iron Heel.*

Mr. Lerner is currently at work on a book on American education —*Toward a Democratic Elite*. He is spending the academic year of 1959–1960 in India as a Professor of American Studies in the Graduate School of International Studies at the University of Delhi, under a Ford Foundation grant.